D1710629

Notes and Sources for
Folk Songs of the Catskills

Notes and Sources for Folk Songs of the Catskills

Norman Cazden

Herbert Haufrecht

Norman Studer

State University of New York Press

Albany

Published by State University of New York Press, Albany

© 1982 State University of New York

For information, address State University of New York Press, State University Plaza, Albany, N.Y., 12246

Library of Congress Cataloging in Publication Data

Cazden, Norman, 1914–
 Notes and sources for folk songs of the Catskills.

 1. Folk music—New York (State)—Catskill Mountains region—Bibliography.   2. Folk-songs, English—New York (State)—Catskill Mountains region—Bibliography.
I. Haufrecht, Herbert, 1909–   II. Studer, Norman, 1902–1978.
III. Title.   IV. Title: Folksongs of the Catskills.
ML128.F74C4   016.78449'74738   81-14610
ISBN 0-87395-582-X   AACR2

Contents

Notes I

List of Sources   **125**

Notes

These notes are designed to provide succinct reference information in abbreviated form. For the most part, they follow a set pattern of information categories. These categories are shown in **boldface type,** and comprise:

Previously available: the location, whether in accessible printed form, in recorded form or in both, of this particular documentary version, by the original performer, prior to the present publication.

Variants: the location of other renderings by the same performer.

Adaptations: treatments of tunes and texts of the primary version, as learned and performed, notated or recorded, by persons other than the original performer. Such adaptations often include alterations, amendments, and accompanied or otherwise elaborated additions.

Comment, references: discussion and notes appearing elsewhere about the given song or ballad. Notices in standard bibliographies and other literature of the field are included. For the most part, available reference material is not then repeated in the present Notes.

Broadsides, songsters: appearances of the song or ballad, usually of its text alone, in inexpensive and often ephemeral printed form.

Sheet music and comparable publication of the song or ballad in folios or in song collections containing music are noted at this point for some items.

Texts: sources containing the text only, or sources containing that text with a different tune, chiefly as obtained from oral tradition.

Related texts: texts on the same theme, using the same manner, in the same poetic form, on the same model, or with other relationship of interest, as discussed in the headnotes. Subheadings under these related texts may include some of the same categories [shown in boldface type] used for the principal item.

Unrelated texts: texts with similar titles or other points of seeming connection, as discussed in the headnotes.

Text and tune relatives: the core portion of the Notes, citing sources where both a similar text and a similar tune appear.

Tune relatives: citations of similar tunes, with a presumed generic relationship to the tune of the item, set to other texts. Such other texts as show related tune settings

1

often are listed individually, for the most part in alphabetical sequence of their titles, though sometimes also in such groupings as Child Ballads or hymns. Subheadings under these tune relatives may include some of the categories [shown in boldface type] used for the principal item. Text titles for other or miscellaneous related tunes are given, wherever they are deemed of interest. Textless uses of the tune, as for instrumental dance tunes, are most often noted separately.

Unrelated tunes: citations of other tunes discussed in the headnotes, having some connection with this item, but for which no generic tune relationship is judged valid.

Within each of these categories or subheadings, primary citations are given in alphabetical order. However, where it is known or presumed that a commentary or other reference item, whether text, tune or both, is reprinted from another source, the presumed earliest appearance is cited first, in its normal alphabetical placement. Its derivatives are then tagged on, in alphabetical sequence, connected by + signs.

Each citation in the Notes begins with its short title, as that is shown in the bibliographical List of Sources.

That short title may be followed by an identifying year [of publication], by a volume number for a multi-volume book [shown in lower case Roman numerals], by both, or by an item number [#], as required.

Following their abbreviated short titles, volumes of periodicals are given in italicized Arabic numerals. Thus *JAF 72* refers to the *Journal of American Folklore,* Volume 72.

For periodicals that do not have continuous pagination throughout a volume, their short titles are extended with both volume and issue numbers, given in italics. Thus a citation like *SO 5 #3* refers to *Sing Out,* Volume 5, Number 3.

Such italicized numbers are also used for publication series not gathered into volumes. Thus *Delaney #23* serves as short title reference to *Delaney's Song Book,* Number 23.

Short titles, some with these added identifications, are then followed normally by the page number or numbers of the reference.

Where references are identified in their original sources chiefly by item numbers rather than by page numbers, as occurs frequently in hymnals, or in such compilations as the Joyce and the Petrie Collections, the item number is accorded preference. Thus Joyce #13, *The River Roe,* refers to tune number 13, with that title, which appears on page 9 of the Joyce Collection.

For many references, both the page number(s) and the item number are given, in that order.

Certain standard bibliographical references, such as Child Ballad numbers or items in the indices by Malcolm Laws, are given in their common form, for example as Child 283 or as Laws P 14, thus obviating page citations.

Unless it is obvious from the author or editor name for its short title, for example when appearing for writings in periodicals or as editorial commentary to a recording, the name of a commentator is given (in parentheses) following its citation. Similarly, if it is not evident from its short title, citation of an adaptation is followed by the name (in parentheses) of its maker.

Where more than one item, usually a tune, appears on a single page in a reference, it is distinguished by adding to its page number any other identification that appears with it on that page. Thus C. J. Sharp 1932 i 191 H refers to the tune marked H (for *Barbara*

Allen), appearing on page 191 of the first volume of Cecil Sharp's classic *English Folk Songs from the Southern Appalachians*.

Should such a necessary detailed distinction not appear in the original published form, the item is arbitrarily assigned a subscript letter in the citation. Thus 47d would refer to the fourth tune appearing on page 47.

Where items are most conveniently identified by their dates, as in Flanders *SR*, consisting of columns contributed by Helen Hartness Flanders to the *Springfield Republican*, such dates are abbreviated in the sequence day – month – year. Thus 10.3.35 refers to the column published on 10 March 1935.

Archive tape recordings or disc recordings are alike identified by their short title entries, followed by the letter or number designating the side of the tape or disc, and then the specific sequential or band number. Thus AFS 1007A.1 indicates Archive of Folk Song disc 1007, side A, band 1. The reference FO 12.2.3 is to be read as Fowke Collection, tape number 12, side 2, item 3. And FM 4051.1.6 is to be read similarly as disc FM 4051, side 1, band 6. The full name of the performer is added (in parentheses) to most such citations.

Where reference is made to commentary, or to a song text, printed in a folder or booklet that accompanies a recorded disc, it is identified by the disc number (for ease in its location), followed by the letter F and the page number. Thus FM 4051F 8 refers to page 8 of such a folder, accompanying the disc FM 4051. If such a folder is not paginated, or if the reference would otherwise prove imprecise, the side and band number of the designated song item are given in its place.

Where such a commentary or song text is printed on the record jacket that accompanies a disc, similar reference is made by adding the letter J to the disc number. Thus SLP 72J 1.1 refers to a comment, a song text, or both, printed on the jacket for the disc SLP 72, and pertaining to the song on side 1, band 1 of that disc.

For some notes, an asterisk [*] or two may be used to call attention, in abbreviated form, to some special feature of the citation, such as the absence in it of any notation for the expected tune. Such an asterisk normally precedes the page number or other identifying number for its citation, and its meaning is always explained [in square brackets] at the outset of its notes category.

As in the headnotes, all titles of songs, song texts or tunes are printed in *italics*. Such titles are separated from italicized short titles of books or songsters by their placement at the end of any citation.

I.
A Shantyman's Life

Previously available: *JAF 72* 344, Ex. 5 [tune only]; *Neighbors* 1941 6.

Variants: AFS 12309A + EC 329.5; ATL 626.17.

Adaptations: AFS 12312A.1; Cazden 1949b #3; Cazden 1958 i 11 + Cazden 1978 11; Cazden 1963 ii 18; Haufrecht 1943 8-9. Haufrecht 1956 14-20; Haufrecht 1965 i 6-8.

Comment, references: Cazden 1958 i 121 + Cazden 1978 121; Gardner 1939 258-59; W. R. Mackenzie 1928 362-63.

Broadsides, songsters: J. Andrews, List 5 #98 + Gray 55-57 + Wolf Index #2085; De Marsan #93.

Texts [* indicates text with tune strain of #76, *The Foggy Dew*]: Ph. Barry 1939 *60 + Botkin 1947 *877-78; E. C. Beck 1941 26-27 + E. C. Beck 1948 33-34 + Emrich 1974 558-59; E. C. Beck 1956 103-6; Dean 87-88 + Rickaby *45-46 B + FP *19B.1 + *Sam Eskin* i *1-2; Eckstorm 33-38; Gardner 1939 258-59; Gray 53-57; *HFB 1* 82, listing; HTA; Korson 1949 348; McTiernan 59-60; Rickaby *43-44 A + Fowke 1954 *66-67 + A. L. Lloyd 1965 *84 #51 + Silverman 1975 ii *401b + SLP *71.1.4; C. Sandburg 1927 *390 + Carmer 1942a *243-44 + Carmer 1942b *37-38 + Horton *19-21; Shoemaker 261-63 + Downes *280-81 + Siegmeister 1944b *34-35; H. Thompson 1940 256-57.

Related text (*The Dreary, Dreary Life*) [* indicates related tune]: AFS *L28A.7; AFS L28F 12-13; AFS L49A.1 (Alan Lomax); *American Cowboy* *38; *Arkansas Woodchopper* 1932 *44-45; *Big Round Up* *31; K. S. Clark 1932 25; Emrich 1974 559; Felton 36-39; Fife 1969 234-36; Larkin 53-57; J. Lomax 1938 15-17, 233-36 + Lingenfelter 348-49 + A. Lomax 1960 369-70; P. Patterson 42-43; *PTFLS 7* 174; Silverman 1975 i *29b; Thorp i 228-39; Thorp ii 38-39 + *SO 13 #3* 32-33 + Silber 1965 78 + Silber 1967 192-94 + Silverman 1975 i 46a; *Treasure Chest* 1935 *29.

Related text: (*Drumdelgie*),
   Comment, references: *CAY 4* 156-57 (Bartlett); *Miscellanea* ii 191-92.
   Texts: FSS 34.2.8 + FSS 34F 18-19; G. Greig *FSNE* #4; Kemp 52-53; *Miscellanea* i 24-25; *Miscellanea* ii 191-92; Ord 209-11 + N. Buchan 1962 50-51 + *CAY 4* 155-56; Topic 12T159B.10 + Topic 12T159F.

Text and tune relatives: ATL 194.7, 194.10 (Jake Loucks); ATL 626.13 (Charles See-

ley); ATL 626.14 (Frank Edwards); Creighton 1950 274; Doerflinger 211-12; Grover 198-99; Rickaby 47 C; SLP 71A.4 (from Adirondacks).

Tune relatives (*Andro and His Cutty Gun*): *Calliope* 410-11; Chambers 162-64; Collinson 1966 7; G. F. Graham 1891 412 + 124-25; *Howe* 188- 54; MacColl 1956 47-48 + MacColl 1965 7 + Charles Seeger 309 Ex. 10e + *SRIE 1 #1* 154 Ex. 10e; Oswald vi 4b + Charles Seeger 309 Ex. 10b + *SRIE 1 #1* 154 Ex. 10b; Ritson 1794 i 268-70 #36.

Tune relatives (*The Battle of Sherra-Moor* [*Sheriff-Muir*] by Robert Burns, with tune name *The Cameronian Rant*),
   Comment, references: Dick i 462-64 #280; Emmerson 1967 57-59; Kinsley iii 1338 #308; Laing 321-22 #282; Stenhouse 270-75 #282.
   Tunes with this text: *Caledonian* 236-39; Dick i 262; J. Johnson #282; Kinsley ii 534 #308; *Lyric Gems* ii 254-55; Oswald xi 2 (instrumental).

Tune relatives (Blythe, Blythe and Merry Was She): *Charmer* i 267-68; G. F. Graham i 58 + G. F. Graham 1891 124-25; *Howe* 188- 55a.

Tune relatives (*The Boyne Water*),
   Comment, references: Bronson iii 314; R. Ford 1900 135-41; *JFSS 8* 36 (Gilchrist); *JIFSS 27* 52-55.
   Broadsides, songsters: Lowens 93 #290, listing; *Street Literature* (Catnach, Pitts).
   Tunes with this text: Bunting 1809 ii 40b, *Marcaigheacht in Boinne,* + *JIFSS 27* (Bunting Collection, Part 5) 52 + Graves 1914 10-11 #8 + Moffat 1897 128-29 + Zimmerman 126; *JFSS 8* 36; Joyce #377; Murphy 41-43; Roche i #4; *Spirit* 32-33; Charles Seeger 309 Ex. 10c + *SRIE 1 #1* 154 Ex. 10c.
   Tunes identified by this title, for other texts [* not notated],
   (*As Vanquished Erin*, by Thomas Moore): Lampe 1955 8; T. Moore 142-43; Stanford 1895 206-7 + Stanford 1906 125 + Stanford 1958 127; Stevenson 1891 228-29; Wright 635.
   (*The Siege of Plattsburgh*, "air: *Boyne Water*, or *Barbara Allen*"): *Book of Popular Songs* *209-10 + *Every-Day* *131-32 + J. Lomax 1934 510 + Neeser *233b-234.
   (others): Breathnach i 206, 334, 348; Breathnach ii 164; Crawhall 1864 72, "*Boyne Water*—old set, 1829"; Galvin 41, *Native Swords;* G. F. Graham 1891 76-77; *Howe* 1874 123; Korson 1949 48;

Orange Standard *18-19; *Spirit* *33-35, *35-36, *36-37; *UFL 17* *23.

Tunes identified by this title, instrumental: *CEOL 3* 101 #8; Flanders Index *232; Howe 1864a 106a; Karpeles 1951 29b, 54c; *New Preceptor* 11c; O'Neill #260; Riley i 80 #293; *SO 22 #5* 18; *Whittier Perkins* 30c, *The Buoying Water.*

Tune relatives (*By Oughtertyre, or Blythe Was She*, by Robert Burns),
Comment, references: Dick i 361 #30; G. F. Graham 1891 125, 412; Kinsley iii 1249 #179; Stenhouse 174 #180.
Tunes with this text: C. Brown 116-17; Diack ii 25; J. Greig ii 145-47; Hopekirk 16-17; J. Johnson #180 + Dick i 29 + Moffat 1894 28; Kinsley i 362 #179; Lampe 1914 15; *Lyric Gems* ii 66; Maver 107b #214; Pittman 179; R. A. Smith iii 33.
Tunes with this title, instrumental: Howe 1864a 156d; Kerr xii 11i.
Tune relatives (*Melinda*): Carden 40a; Davisson 36a; Hauser 1848 22a; J. B. Jackson 192 + G. P. Jackson 1942 104 #83; Rhinehart 24a.
Tune relatives (*O May, Thy Morn*, by Robert Burns),
Comment, References: Dick i 379 #82.
Tunes with this text: Dick i 79 #82 (with corrected phrase sequence); J. Johnson #464 + Bronson iii 324-25 #35 + M. B. Foster 179.
Tune relatives (*The Rashes*): JFSS 6 115-16 (with Gaelic text); JFSS 6 141-142, 144-45 (with Gaelic titles); MacColl 1963 51; Oswald v 26a + Bronson iii 324 #34.
Tune relatives (*The Wee, Wee German Lairdie*, with tune halves in reverse sequence): Bantock 1930b ii 14-15; N. Buchan 1962 28-29; N. Buchan 1963 33a; I. Campbell 27; Chambers 47; Gleadhill 311; J. Greig iv 82-83; Hogg i 85; Lampe 1914 100; *Lyric Gems* i 81; MacColl 1956 42-43; Maxfield 124; Murphy 69-70; Pittman 129; Peggy Seeger 1960 95; R. A. Smith vi 44a.
Tune relatives (other complete tune forms):
(*Christian Fellowship*): G. P. Jackson 1952 150 #139 (from *Wesleyan Harp* 1834 198).
(*The Days of 'Forty-Nine*): Wilkinson i #314.
(*Happy Friendship*): *Musical Treasury* #494 (*1849*).
(*The Haughs of Cromdale*): Hogg i 3, "air: *Andro and His Cutty Gun.*"
(*The Jolly Anglers*): Crawhall 1864 251, with tune name *Happy Friendship* (from *The Fisher's Garland* for 1855).

(*O'er the Muir amang the Heather*, by Jean Glover),
Comment, references: Dick i 501 #356; Dick ii 57, 109-10; Findlay 69-76; Laing 365 #328; MacFarren 186; Stenhouse 313 #328.
Tunes with this text: G. F. Graham 1891 200; *Howe* 188- 37; Jarman 26n (instrumental); J. Johnson #328 + Dick i 344-45; MacFarren 186; Pittman 125; *Vocal Companion* 256-58.
(*Weeping Mary*, B): G. P. Jackson 1937 78 #47 (from William Walker's *Southern and Western Pocket Harmonist* 1846 102).
(*When the King Comes Over the Water*): G. F. Graham 1891 76; Hogg i 45-46, "air: *Andro and His Cutty Gun*"; Hopekirk 113; Oswald xi 23c (instrumental).
Tune relatives (*Sir Neil and Glengyle*, with complete tune forms): Creighton 1962 94 B; *NEF 7* 73-74.
(*Sir Neil and Glengyle*, with second-half tune forms): Christie i 82 (with tune additions by Christie); Creighton 1962 92 A, 94-95 C; W. R. Mackenzie 1928 395 #20 + Ph. Barry 1929 xxxvi-vii; *Miramichi Ms.* 16.3.
Tune relatives (Child 84, *Barbara Allen:* all second-half tune forms),
Comment, references: Bronson ii 321, Group D; Charles Seeger 273-320 + *SRIE 1 #1* 120-67.
Tunes with this text: AFS L54A.1-.6; Bayard i 110; Bronson ii 321-91 #138-#160, #164, #165, #170-#191; T. Burton i 51; FG 3519.2.4 + Charles Seeger 309 Ex. 10d + *SRIE 1 #1* 154 Ex. 10d (Lucy Stewart); Gainer 1963 #59 + Charles Seeger 311 Ex. 11b + *SRIE 1 #1* 156 Ex. 11b; Gainer 1975 57; Hubbard 20; *JAF 70* 351 #15; M. Johnson 8; LCJ (Braden); Musick 30 #15; Ritchie 1953 53; Ritchie 1965a 79 + Ritchie 1965b 100-101; J. Roberts 95; Schinhan iv 62 #17 G + Charles Seeger 309 Ex. 10g + *SRIE 1 #1* 154 Ex. 10g; Charles Seeger 288 + *SRIE 1 #1* 134, Ex. 1a, 1b, 1c, ix: Charles Seeger 292 Ex. 2 + *SRIE 1 #1* 138 Ex. 2; Charles Seeger 293 Ex. 3 + *SRIE 1 #1* 139 Ex. 3; Charles Seeger 309 + *SRIE 1 #1* 154, Ex. 10f, 10h; Charles Seeger 311 Ex. 11a + *SRIE 1 #1* 156 Ex. 11a; Pete Seeger 1973 213; Spaeth 1948 25-26; E. K. Wells 113.
Tune relatives (second-half tune forms, except where noted, for Child Ballads other than *Barbara Allen*):
(Child 13, *Edward*): Bronson i 241-43 #7-#9,

5

#11-#13; B. Ives 1953 48-49 + B. Ives 1962 44-45; ZDA 73.2.3.

(Child 20, *The Cruel Mother*): ATL 616.11 (Minnie Ward of Pepacton, New York); Bronson i 283-84 #19, #21.

(Child 25, *Willie's Lyke-Wake*): Bronson i 306 #3.

(Child 63, *Child Waters*): Bronson ii 45 #2.

(Child 65, *Lady Maisry*): Bronson ii 56 #13.

(Child 74, *Fair Margaret and Sweet William*): Flanders 1953 84.

(Child 81, *Little Musgrave*): Bronson ii 302 #53, #54.

(Child 99, *Johnny Scott*): Bronson ii 494 #12.

(Child 112, *The Baffled Knight*): D'Urfey v 112 + Bronson ii 549 #3 (with the complete tune form, as noted); Charles Seeger 309 Ex. 10a + *SRIE 1 #1* 154 Ex. 10a (second half only).

(Child 129, *Robin Hood and the Prince of Aragon*): Ph. Barry 1929 233 + Bronson iii 34 (with complete tune form, in major).

(Child 199, *The Bonny House of Airlie*): Bronson iii 197 #15.

(Child 200, *The Gypsy Laddie*): Bronson iii 210-13 #22-#29; Jameson 1967 59; LCJ (from Kentucky).

(Child 209, *Geordie*): Bronson iii 283-84 #39-#42.

(Child 214, *The Braes of Yarrow*): Abrahams 124-26; Ph. Barry 1929 291 + Bronson iii 325 #37 (with note that the singer used the same tune for *Barbara Allen*); Kidson 1891 22 + Bronson iii 324-25 #36 + Duncan 1927 221-22 #276 + Charles Seeger 309 Ex. 10c + *SRIE 1 #1* 154 Ex. 10c.

(Child 217, *The Bonny Broom*): Bronson iii 338-43 #1-#18 (of which #1-#8 show tetrachord transposition of the opening).

(Child 251, *Lang Johnnie More*): RLP 12-626.1.3.

(Child 276, *The Friar in the Well*): RLP 12-618.1.7 + Bronson iv 142 #3 + Charles Seeger 309 Ex. 10e + *SRIE 1 #1* 154 Ex. 10e (complete tune form as reconstituted by Ewan MacColl).

(Child 299, *The Trooper and the Maid*): Bronson iv 430 #14.

Tune relatives (other second-half forms): Arthur 18; ATL 184.2 (George Edwards); ATL 477.3; Ph. Barry 1939 83; Bissell 16-18; Cazden 1951a 55a (this second-half tune form used as opening of a longer tune); Creighton 1962 207 + Fowke1967 170; Creighton 1971 33; Graeme 44-45 + *Clancy* 1971 44-45 (with added refrain); G. P. Jackson 1944 104 #83;

JAF 42 207; Karpeles 1934 ii 10 + Karpeles 1971 182; Karpeles 1971 146; Karpeles 1974 ii 607a, 607b + *JFSS 8* 35a, 35b; Moffat 1894 252-53 (this second-half tune form used as opening of a longer tune); Randolph iv 51 #616; Ritchie 1953 35; Ritchie 1963 43; Ritchie 1965a 87; Ritchie 1966 72-74 (with added refrain); Rosenberg T87 44B.1; *Sam Henry #785, My Darling Blue-Eyed Mary;* Peggy Seeger 1960 64; C. J. Sharp ms. #1757, *Navigation* and #2597, *London Pride* (instrumental), as cited in Charles Seeger 309 Ex. 10c + *SRIE 1 #1* 154 Ex. 10c; Wilkinson i #381, *The Foggy, Foggy Dew;* Wilkinson i #558; Wilkinson ii #164 + *SFQ 6* 7, *The Foggy Dew* (a dance tune without text); WLP 724.2.8.

2.
Cutting Down the Pines

Previously available: *Neighbors* 1943 9-10.

Variants: AFS 7762B; AFS 12309A.7 + EC 329.7; ATL 613.4.

Adaptations: Cazden 1958 i 8-10 + Cazden 1978 8-10; Haufrecht 1953 4-5; Landeck 1944 54 (Charity Bailey).

Comment, references: AFS L55F 17; Cazden 1958 i 111 + Cazden 1978 111; FH 5323F 5 (Edward Ives); Fowke 1970 36, 39; Greenleaf 322-23; J. Lomax 1947 132-33, 382 #46; Peacock 135; Rickaby 207-8, 225.

Broadsides, songsters: Delaney #13 23 + Rickaby 72-75.

Texts: AFS L55F 18-19; E. C. Beck 1941 36-43; E. C. Beck 1948 101-7; E. C. Beck 1956 92-102; E. C. Beck 1960 38-40; Cutting 12-14; Doerflinger 210-211; Eckstorm 25-26; Emrich 1974 534-35; FH 5323F 5; FHE 79; Gardner 1939 260; Gray 150; HTA (2); *NYH 17* 1512 (Gray); Piper; Rickaby 69-71; RLP 12-648.2.8; Shoemaker 93-95 + Korson 1949 350-51.

Related text [and tune] (*Cruise of 'The Bigler'*),
  Comment, references: Laws D 8; J. Lomax 1947 132-33 #46, 382 #46.
  Texts: Dean 19-20; Eckstorm 243 #17; *JAF 28* 10-11; H. Sandburg 51a.

Texts with related tune: AFS 2323B, 3398A, 3398B, 3405A; E. C. Beck 1960 45-48; Colcord 196-98; Creighton 1962 141; Dean 19-20 (with tune in Rickaby 168-72) + Botkin 1944 843-45 + Mursell 53 + Silverman 1975 ii 264-65; FO 8.2.1 + Fowke 1965 142-144; J. Lomax 1941 220-22; J. Lomax 1947 148-50; Luboff 22-23; C. Sandburg 1927 174-75 + Doerflinger 130-31.

Adaptation (*The Sealing Cruise of the 'Lone Flier'*), with related tune: Blondahl 76-77; Doyle 1940 14-15; Greenleaf 246-47.
Related text [and tune] (*The Dogger Bank*), **Comment, references:** FG 3507F 4.
Texts: FG 3507F 6-7.
Texts with related tune: FG 3507.1.1c.
Text and tune relatives: AFS L55B.1 (Emory De Noyer); ATL 191.2 (Tom Kelly); ATL 601.5 (James Edwards); Dibblee 38-39; FH 5323.2.1 (Edward Ives); Flander 1953 141-43; FO 2.1.7 + Fowke 1970 34-35 B; Fowke 1965 142; Fowke 1970 34-36; Greenleaf 321-22 [tune 246] + A. L. Lloyd 1965 42-43 #24; *NA Ives* 1.10 + ATL 2143.1; *NA Ives* 1.22 + ATL 2149.9; *NA Ives* 1.28 + ATL 2154.4; *NA Ives* 1.29 + ATL 2154.6; Peacock 750; Rickaby 72 + Siegmeister 1944b 36-36 + Vornholt 10b.
Tune relatives: AFS 4196B.1 (Warde H. Ford) + Bronson i 375 #26, *Captain Wedderburn's Courtship;* AFS L56B.6, *Johnny Carroll's Camp;* ATL 170.2 #la; ATL 606.9; Clifford 12-13; Creighton 1962 144a; Dallas 1973 98-99, *Musselburgh Fair; JWFSS 2* 188-89 #121, *Mí Fum Yn Caru 'Nghariad* [second half of tune]; Long 149; Manifold 90; Morton 1970 82 + IRL 12B.3; Morton 1973 112 #22; *NA Ives* 1.21 + ATL 2149.4; *NA Ives* 1.23 + ATL 2150.8; *NA Ives* 1.149 + ATL 3156.3; *NA Ives* 1.150 + ATL 3157.4; O'Shaughnessy 1975 41, *The Grimsby Fishermen's Song;* E. Parry 7, *Dafyold Gwinn, the Tinker;* Peacock 132-33, *The Herring Gibber;* Peacock 750; *Sam Eskin* v, *Captain Walker's Courtship; Sam Henry* #501; Weatherly 8-9, *Sally Lee;* Wilkinson i #324.
[See also notes to #146 A, *The Knickerbocker Line*].

3.
The Woodsmen's Alphabet

Previously available: *Neighbors* 1947 26.
Variants: none.
Adaptations: Cazden 1958 i 12-13 + Cazden 1978 12-13; Cazden 1962 39.
Comment, references: AFS L56F 7 (E. C. Beck); Cazden 1958 i 123 + Cazden 1978 123; *FFMA 8 #1* 23-29 (Dorson); Flanders 1939 171; M. Leach 1965 179; Manny 267; H. Thompson 1940 194-95.
Broadsides, songsters: none. Gray 10-11 quotes a text from *Maine Sportsman 11* (1904).
Texts: C. S. Adams 126-28; AFS L56B.2 + AFS L56F 7; ATL 182.4; Ph. Barry 1939 50-

51; E. C. Beck 1948 37-40; E. C. Beck 1956 33-36; E. C. Beck 1960 11-12; H. P. Beck 1957 265-66; Bethke #57; Cass-Beggs 1963 8-9; *CFMJ 3* 28, listing; Creighton 1932 212-13; Doerflinger 207-9; Eckstorm 30-32 + Emrich 1974 530-31; *Elmore Vincent* 44-45; *FFMA 8* 23-29; FHE 408; Flanders 1939 169-71; Flanders 1953 112-13; FM 4052.1.9; FO 2.18.2.1.9; Fowke 1960 168-69; Fowke 1970 25-27; FSA 33F 10, listing; Gardner 1939 255-57; Gray 10-14; Grover 197-98; HL 500.1.4; HTA (Aussicker); *JAF 35* 413-14; Kimball 183, listing; D. D. Lawrence 78; Linscott 235-37 + Botkin 1947 874-75 + *Sam Eskin* ii; Manny 265-67 + FM 4053.1.1 + FM 4053F 2-3; Mursell 50-51; *NA Ives* 1.26 + ATL 2153.2; *NA Ives* 1.33 + ATL 2158.6; *NA Ives* 1.42 + ATL 2166.7; *NA Ives* 1.50 + ATL 2174.4; *NA Ives* 1.54 + ATL 2178.4; *NA Ives* 1.67 + ATL 2186.1; *NA Ives* 1.84 + ATL 2203.1; *NA Ives* 61.1, 68.7.2:14; *NYFQ 14* 209, listing; Piper + Peterson Index 72; Rickaby 35-38; RLP 12-648.1.1; H. Thompson 1940 262-63; J. R. Wilson 75-76, 93-94.
Related text (*The Sailor's Alphabet*), **Comment, references:** AFS L126F 11 (E. C. Beck).
Broadsides, songsters: none. Eckstorm refers to a text in *Sea Stories Magazine*, February 1926.
Texts: AFS L26B.1 + AFS L26F 11-12; Belden 1952 ii 259-60; Cass-Beggs 1975 40-41; Cobb 127-28; Creighton 1932 210-12; Eckstorm 233-34 + Emrich 1974 489-90; Emrich 1973 471-72; Erdei 96 #133; Gundry 52; Harlow 52-54; Hugill 456-58; B. Ives 1956 2-3; *JAF 38* 298; A. C. Morris 57-58; Peacock 885; Rosenberg Index #1235; Schinhan iv 143-44; H. Thompson 1940 194-95.
Related text (others, in matching verse-form), **Comment, references:** Opie 1951 47-52.
Texts: *Central Park Show* 49, *Topical-Politcal Alphabet;* Dearmer 1915 lb, *Archer Alphabet;* Hubbard 459-60, *Religious Alphabet;* Jordan 269-72, *A is for Apple* (facsimile, New York, 184-); M. Leach 1965 178-79, *Air Force Alphabet;* McCaskey iii 159 + McCaskey v 188, *Musical Alphabet;* MacColl 1968 72-73, *Politician's Alphabet;* E. Moore 370-72, *Civil War Alphabet;* Opie 1951 48-49 #2, *Nursery Alphabet;* R. Palmer 1974 270-71, *The People's Comic Alphabet;* Peacock 125, *Fisherman's Alphabet;* Randolph iv 405-6 D, *Average Boy's Alphabet;* Reeves 1960

63, *A is for Apple; SFQ 4* 150 + A. C. Morris 433-34, *Religious Alphabet; Sol Smith Russell* 1876 14, *Alphabet Song; Universal Songster* ii 14, *The Soldier's Alphabet;* Zimmerman 95-96, *Land Leaghe Alphabet.*

Related text (Alphabet song to the tune of *Twinkle, Twinkle, Little Star,* not matching the verse-form of #3),

    Comment, references: Wilkinson *510* 18.

    Texts with this tune: C. B. Adams 24; Bullard 41c; A. T. Davison 1922 I #1; C. Johnson 51a; Leisy 1957 24 #61; McCaskey iii 159b; McCaskey v 170a; McCaskey 1899 249b, 303a; Wier 1918b 135a; Wilkinson *510* 15.

Related text (other Alphabet songs, not matching the verse-form of #3): AFS L12B.2, *Singing Alphabet; Child's Song Book* 5a, 5b, 5c; Dearmer 1915 1a; Diprose 1865 123, *The Odd Fellow's Alphabet,* by R. Brockman; Diprose 1865 171-72, *The Citizen's Comic Alphabet,* by J. A. Hardwick; Diprose 1865 244, *The East-End Alphabet,* by J. A. Hardwick; Garretson 46-50; A. Mills 1949 12 + Dominion 1280A.2; *Musical Bouquet* #4014/5 (ca. 1868), *Lover's Alphabet.*

Text and tune relatives: none.

For examples of the tune strain most common for this song, see: C. S. Adams 126-28; ATL 169.7 #1b (Beck); Ph. Barry 1939 50; Creighton 1932 210; Doerflinger 207; Fowke 1960 168-69; Fowke 1970 25; Linscott 236; Rickaby 37; J. R. Wilson #33, #33a.

For the unusually fine adaptation of the *Down, Derry Down* tune strain to this text, sung by Wilmot MacDonald: Manny 265 + FM 4053.1.1 + J. R. Wilson #21; *Miramichi Ms.* 15.5; *NA Ives* 1.42 + ATL 2166.7; *NA Ives* 1.50 + ATL 2174.4; *NA Ives* 1.54 + ATL 2178.4; *NA Ives* 1.67 + ATL 2186.1; *NA Ives* 61.1.1.

4.
The Jam at Gerry's Rock

Previously available (#4 A): *Neighbors* 1942 10-11.

Variants: none.

Adaptations (#4 A): Cazden 1958 i 8-9 + Cazden 1978 8-9; Haufrecht 1963 16-17.

Comment, references: AFS L56F 3-4 (E. C. Beck); E. C. Beck 1941 133-36; Belden 1952 ii 501; *BFSSNE #10* 18-20 (Barry); *BFSSNE #12* 2-6, 21-23 (Barry); Cazden 1958 i 115 + Cazden 1978 115; Cox 1925 236-38; Doerflinger 341; Dorson 103-5; Eckstorm 176-98, summarized in Laws 1950 63-65; *FFMA 8 #1* 13-18; FHE 246; Flanders 1939 45-46; FM 4001F A.4 (Cowell); FM 4052F 3; Fowke 1954 79; Fowke 1970 98-99; Gray xv-xvi; Edw. Ives 1978 156-60; Korson 1949 345-46; Laws C 1; Linscott 217-20; Rickaby 192-93.

Broadsides, songsters: none. A text from *Maine Sportsman,* 11 January 1904, is quoted in Eckstorm 82-84 + Flanagan 450-41 + M. Leach 1955 771-73. An undated text from the *Toledo Blade* is in the Piper Collection.

Texts: C. S. Adams 121-22; AFS L49.1.5; AFS L56F 4-5; AFS L56A.4; H. P. Beck 1957 260-62; Belden 1952 ii 501-6; CMS 670F.1 + CMS 670F F.1; Combs 1967 209 #53, listing; Emrich 1974 545-46; FHE 243, 245-46, 247, 248-49; Flanders *SR* 23.12.34; FM 4001A.4 + FM 4052F 3-4; FSA 33F 7, listing; Gordon *NYT* 58-60; Greig *FSNE* #132; HTA; Edw. Ives 1978 314-15; *JIFMC 3* 95, listing; Ch. Kennedy 1954 215-17; LCJ (from Malone, New York); LCJ (Thayer); A. L. Lloyd 1945 29; *NA Ives* 1.21 + ATL 2149.5; *NA Ives* 1.33 + ATL 2158.5; *NA Ives* 57.1.9, 64.7.9; *NYFQ 14* 208, listing; *NYH 17* 148-50 (Gray); Piper + Peterson Index 47; RLP 12-648.1.2; *Sam Eskin* ii; Shay 1961 180-82; Shoemaker 86-88; Silber 1973b 101a; Silverman 1975 ii 418-19; Stekert 1969 B 15.

Text and tune relatives (#4 A and #4 B): AFS 3286 A; Bayard 46-47; *BFSSNE #10* 20; *Sam Eskin* ii.

Text and tune relatives (#4 C): AFS 2323B.1; ATL 183.5, 191.3; ATL 194.4 (Charles Hinckley); ATL 602.3 (James Edwards); ATL 602.6, 602.9, 627.14 (Frank Edwards); ATL 621.12 (Reuben Edwards); E. C. Beck 1941 133-36 + E. C. Beck 1948 195; E. C. Beck 1956 126-30; E. C. Beck 1960 20; Bethke #6; *BFSSNE #10* 18; *BFSSNE #12* 3a + Ph. Barry 1939 52-53; *BFSSNE #12* 22-24; *CFMJ 3* 40b-41; Chosky 214 #151; Cox 1939 ii 23; Creighton 1950 267-68 + Fowke 1954 78-79; Dallin 160-61; Doerflinger 238-39, 239-40; Flanders 1939 44-46; FM 4052.1.2; FO 10.2.1 + Fowke 1970 97-99; FO 10.2.2 + Fowke 1970 95-96; FO 14.1.4; FSC 9.1.5; Gardner 1939 270, 272; Grover 181-82; Edw. Ives 197- [367]; M. Leach 1965 256; Linscott 217-20 + Boni 1952 222-23; Manny 115-17; *Miramichi Ms.* 15.19; E. Moore 341-43; A. C. Morris 107-9; *NA Ives* 1.2 + ATL 2137.2; *NA Ives* 1.11 + ATL 2143.4; *NA Ives* 1.30 + ATL 2155.11; *NA*

Ives 1.42 + ATL 2166.8; *NA Ives* 1.151 + ATL 3158.2; *NA Ives* 1.158 + ATL 3165.3; *NA Ives* 61.2, 66.8.1; NW 239.1.8 (Lawrence Older, in *a – b' – a – b'* form); Rickaby 11 A + Botkin 1944 847-49 + Friedman 418-21 + J. Lomax 1947 170-71 + A. Lomax 1964 30 + Silber 1965 70-71; Rickaby 15 B, 18 C, 19 D; Pete Seeger 1964 33 + FP 3B.4.

Tune relatives, #4 C (*Brennan on the Moor*): Farnsworth 6-7 + C. J. Sharp 1916 52-53 + C. J. Sharp *Selection* i 8-9; *NJ 12 #7* 28; C. J. Sharp *FSS* i 52-53 + Karpeles 1974 ii 166-67 A + Karpeles 1975 i 44-45 #42 + Novello #966.

Tune relatives, #4 C (*The Maid of Sweet Gartine*): FO 1.1.10; Manny 272 + *NA Ives* 61.2; *Miramichi Ms.* 16.5; *NA Ives* 1.53 + ATL 2177.6; *NA Ives* 1.78 + ATL 2197.4; O Lochlainn 1939 44; Peacock 375; Petrie #328, #329; *Sam Henry* #594.

Tune relatives, #4 C (others):

Comment, references: *BFSSNE #12* 2-6 (Ph. Barry); C. J. Sharp *FSS* i 70 #26.

Tunes: Ph. Barry 1929 96, 419; Bayard 9; E. C. Beck 1948 219, *Harry Bail;* Belden 1940 129; *BFSSNE #9* 19b; *BFSSNE #10* 14, Pat O'Brien; *BFSSNE #10* 20b + Ph. Barry 1939 56; *BFSSNE #12* 3b, 4a, 4c, 5a, 16; Botkin 1951 776; Broadwood 1893 116, *The Farmer's Daughter;* N. Buchan 1962 118; Colcord 122; Creighton 1962 195, 202; Doerflinger 243-44; Flanders 1931 35 + Botkin 1944 826; FM 4052.2.2; FSC 62.2.3; Gardner 1939 278; *Howe* 1878 275b + *Fireside Library* 63b + *Trifet* 1890 180b, *Willie Reilly;* HTA, *Tebo;* Edw. Ives 1971 225; Edw. Ives 1978 260b; *JEFDSS* 7 243; *JFSS* 2 216; *JFSS* 7 61, 62; *JFSS* 8 129, 222; Joyce #291; Karpeles 1971 169; Kidson 1891 49 (in *a – a – b – a* form); Knox 23; J. Lomax 1941 324, *The Rowan County Crew;* W. R. Mackenzie 1928 408 #56; Manny 220, 241; *Miramichi Ms.* 16.1; A. W. Moore 230-31; *NA Ives* 1.51 + ATL 2175.4; *NA Ives* 1.130 + ATL 3137.1; Nettel 210; Peacock 518, 566, 757, 775; Petrie #185 + *JFSS* 7 63b; Purslow 1965 69; QC 903.2.2; Randolph i 418, 419; C. J. Sharp 1965 93-94; *Sing #4* 50a.

5.
Adieu to Prince Edward's Isle

Previously available: None.
Variants: ATL 190.6.
Comment, references: Ph. Barry 1929 264; *BFSSNE #2* 13-14 (Ph. Barry); Doerflinger

348; Eckstorm 98-103; FH 5323F 7 (Edward Ives); FM 4053F 3; Edw. Ives 1964 xi, 51-52, 59-61, 171; Laws C 27; Laws 1950 159; Manny 160-63.

Broadsides, songsters: none. *BFSSNE #2* 13 quotes copy from the *Boston Sunday Globe*, 22 January 1930; Eckstorm 100-102 B is from *Maine Sportsman*, December 1903.

Texts: E. C. Beck 1948 87-88, Doerflinger 227 + J. R. Wilson #27d; Doerflinger 231-33; Eckstorm 99-100 + Emrich 1974 548-49; FHE 279, 280, 281, 283, 284, 290, 394; Flanders *SR* 22.7.34; FH 5323F 8; FM 4053F 3; FO 2.2.6 + Fowke 1970 127-30; Gray 63-69; Greenleaf 334-35; *NA Ives* 1.33 + ATL 2158.9; *NA Ives* 1.109 + ATL 3116.1; *JAF 48* 347-49; Peterson Index 46; RLP 12-648.2.6; J. R. Wilson 82-83.

Unrelated text (*Prince Edward Isle, Adieu*, by Lawrence Doyle),

Comment, references: Edw. Ives 1964 46-49; Edw. Ives 1971 61-86.

Texts: Edw. Ives 1971 67-70.

Text and tune relatives: ATL 182.6; Bayard 47, 49a, 52b, 53; H. P. Beck 1957 255-57; *BFSSNE #2* 14 A + Ph. Barry 1939 68-69; *BFSSNE #2* 14 B; Creighton 1932 301-3 + Fowke 1954 80-81 + J. R. Wilson #27g; Creighton 1971 231-33; Dibblee 33; Doerflinger 229 + J. R. Wilson #27c; Flanders 1939 115; FH 5323.2.6 (Edward Ives); FSC 9.2.5 (Marie Hare); FW 8744.1.7 (Alan Mills); Linscott 269-72 + J. R. Wilson #27n; Manny 160-62 + FM 4053.1.2 + Fowke 1973 72 + J. R. Wilson #27b; *Miramichi Ms.* 15.1; *NA Ives* 1.4 + ATL 2139.2; *NA Ives* 1.13 + ATL 2144.7; *NA Ives* 1.27 + ATL 2153.4; *NA Ives* 1.28 + ATL 2154.3; *NA Ives* 1.31 + ATL 2156.10; *NA Ives* 1.45 + ATL 2169.4; *NA Ives* 1.48 + ATL 2172.5; *NA Ives* 1.61 + ATL 2181.7; *NA Ives* 1.69 + ATL 2188.6; *NA Ives* 1.105 + ATL 3112.3; *NA Ives* 61.2, 62.2, 62.5, 66.9.3; *NA Ives* 66.11.1 [in *b – b – b – a* form]; *SO 15 #2* 32-33.

Tune relatives (*The Farmer's Son and the Shanty Boy*): ATL 187.7A; ATL 604.13 (Frank Edwards); ATL 623.8 (George Edwards); Belden 1940 443 + A. Lomax 1960 109; FA 2354.2.7; Flanders 1939 166; FO 10.1.1, 10.1.2; FO 10.1.3 + Fowke 1970 183; FO 14.2.8; Rickaby 48 + J. Lomax 1934 446 + J. R. Wilson #27k; Rickaby 51 + J. R. Wilson #27l (from M. C. Dean).

Tune relatives (*The Irish Girl*): Ph. Barry 1939 22; Copper 246-47; Joyce

#382 + Karpeles 1956 68 + J. R. Wilson
#27r + Wright 385; C. J. Sharp 1961 iii 104-6
(Gardiner).

Tune relatives (others):

Ph. Barry 1939 44; Bayard 49-52; E. C. Beck
1941 204, 255; E. C. Beck 1948 212; E. C.
Beck 1956 152; Behan 1965 19; Breathnach i
218, 338; Breathnach ii 202, 204; Breathnach
iii 134, *The Irish Champion;* Breathnach iii
195; N. Buchan 1973 62; W. Chappell 1859 ii
739; Colcord 199 + J. R. Wilson #27q;
Creighton 1932 173, 175; Creighton 1932 326
+ J. R. Wilson #27e; Creighton 1950 198;
Creighton 1962 200; Dibblee 71; Doerflinger
136; Flanders 1939 79 + Dwyer 58, 77 +
Lingenfelter 136; Flanders 1953 148 + Bronson iii 309 #25 + J. R. Wilson #27o;FM
2354.1.3, 2354.2.3, 2354.2.7 (Ellen Stekert);
FM 4001A.4; Gallagher #50; Greenleaf 88 +
J. R. Wilson #27i; Grover 41; Hughes 1903
40, 41; *JFSS 1* 25; Joseph 71; Kidson 1891
121b + R. Palmer 1974 225, *The Plains of
Waterloo;* Korson 1943 403 + Korson 1949
390-91 + *WF 3* 161-63 + J. R. Wilson #27p,
The Avondale Mine Disaster; M. Leach 1965
302; A. L. Lloyd 1955 6-7; Manny 166 +
J. R. Wilson #27e; Meredith 1968 166;
Miramichi Ms. 16.13; Murphy 18-19; *NA
Ives* 1.104 + ATL 2111.2; *NA Ives* 1.136 +
ATL 3143.2; *NA Ives* 61.1, *Samuel Allen;
NA Ives* 62.4, *Samuel Allen; NA Ives*
65.19.3, *Howard Carey;* O Lochlainn 1939
18 + J. R. Wilson #27s; O'Neill #165,
#262, #365, #394; Ord 78, *To Pad the Road
wi' Me;* Peacock 181, 641, 967; Petrie #498
+ J. R. Wilson #27t, *The Maid of Timahoe;*
Petrie #657; Petrie #868 + Zimmerman 194;
Ranson 116; Rickaby 76 + J. R. Wilson
#27m; Rooney 1905 12; *Sam Henry* #711;
*Schools National, Mo Slá Le Dútráct
d'Éirinn;* Silber 1973 104; Stuart 176-77; J. R.
Wilson #27f.

Tune relatives (others, in *a – a – b – a* form):
JIFS 3 26; Long 27; O'Shaughnessy 1975 33.

Tune relatives (others, in *– – b – a* form): H. P.
Beck 1957 204; Creighton 1971 210; FM
4005B.5; Kidson 1927 34-35.

Tune relatives (*The Lincolnshire Poacher:*
similarity in *a* phrase only): Buck 1916 118-
19; W. Chappell 1859 ii 733; Chilton 178-79;
Copper 1973 236 (parody text); *Ernest Newton* 16; E. Haywood 8 #7 (instrumental);
V. Jackson 182-83; Leisy 1966 216; Moffat
1901 118-19; *Singer's Companion* 93 (parody
text); *SO 1* #6 14-15; *Trifet* 1890 157; Scottish Students 224; *University Songbook* 254;
Woodgate 1951 82-83.

Unrelated tune (*Paddies Evermore,* by W. E.
Hudson): Graves 1914 48-49 #33; Graves
1928 174; *Howe* 1864a 99f (instrumental).

6.
The Flat River Raftsman

Previously available (#6 A): *Neighbors* 1943
23-24.

Variants: none.

Adaptations: AFS 12312b.1; Cazden 1958 ii
100-101 + Cazden 1973 100-101.

Comment, references: AFS L56F 6 (E. C.
Beck); E. C. Beck 1941 123-32; E. C. Beck
1960 13; Belden 1952 ii. 610; Cazden 1958 ii
116-17 + Cazden 1973 116-17; Eckstorm
124-26; FM 4025F 8 (Fowke); FSC 10F 29-30
(Fowke); Gardner 1939 267-68; Laws C 25;
Laws 1950 62-63; McTiernan 62-63; *MLN 50*
465-68 (Chickering); Rickaby 191-92; *WF 24*
38-39.

Broadsides, songsters: FHE 425, from an
unidentified newspaper source.

Texts: AFS L56F 5-6; E. C. Beck 1948 140-47;
E. C. Beck 1960 15 B; H. P. Beck 1957 262-
63; Belden 1952 ii 610-11; CMS 670F F.5;
Doerflinger 245 + *WF 24* 106-8; Emrich 1974
539-40; FM 4052F 8-9; FSC 10F 30-31; Gordon *NYT* 61-62 + Friedman 421-23; *JAF 48*
344-45; Ch. Kennedy 1952 218-19; Ch. Kennedy 1954 271-72; *NA Ives* 1.15 + ATL
2145.7; Piper; Ritchie 1965b 118-19;
Shoemaker 218-19; Stekert Listing B 18.

Related texts [* *indicates related tune*],
(*Brakeman on the Railroad*): *NA Ives* *1.28
+ ATL *2154.5.
(*Cowboy parody*): E. C. Beck 1948 149-50;
Botkin 1951 768-69; J. Lomax 1938 268-69;
PTFLS 7 177-78 + K. S. Clark 1934 33-34.
(*Teamster parody*): ATL *629.12 (James Ed-
wards).

Text and tune relatives: AFS 2358A; AFS
L56A.5; ATL 191.4; ATL 601.2-3, 605.7
(James Edwards); ATL 627.11-12 (Frank
Edwards); Ph. Barry 1939 74-75 + Botkin
1947 876-77; E. C. Beck 1948 141 A; E. C.
Beck 1956 182-84; Bethke #55; CMS 670F.5
(Tom Glazer); Doerflinger 245-46 + J. R.
Wilson #20c; FM 4052.2.1; FO 2.1.2; FO
10.1.4; Fowke 1970 187-89 + FSC 10.2.8;
Gardner 1939 267-69; Linscott 214-17; *NA
Ives* 1.5 + ATL 2140.1; *NA Ives* 1.11 +
ATL 2143.5; *NA Ives* 66.10.8; QC 903.1.6;
Rickaby 8-10 C + J. R. Wilson #20m; Rick-
aby 10 D + J. R. Wilson #20l; RLP 12-
648.2.2.

Tune relatives (with fairly direct derivation

from this model; for others, see notes to #38): AFS L55B.3, *The Little Brown Bulls*; ATL 606.10, *The Little Mohee*; Bethke #29, *The Little Mohee*; FO 2.1.1; FO 13.2.2 + Fowke 1970 61 + FM 4052.1.8.

[See also notes to #159, *The Hills of Last Chance*].

7.
Jack Gardner's Crew

Previously available: none.
Variants: ATL 486.10;
Adaptations: none.
Comment, references: Studer IX 00; *NEF 17* 123-24.
Broadsides, songsters: none.
Texts: none.
Related texts (*Camp Thirteen*): E. C. Beck 1948 58-73; E. C. Beck 1956 55-63;
Unrelated text (*The Little Brown Bulls*): See references in notes to #93, *The Rock Island Line*.
Text and tune relatives: ATL 189.10 (Walt Wermouth); ATL 193.1 ("Dick" Edwards);
Tune relatives: See notes to #15, *The 'Cumberland' Crew*.

8.
Paul Jones

Previously available: none.
Variants: ATL 616.3.
Adaptations: Cazden 1958 i 16-17 + Cazden 1978 16-17.
Comment, references: Belden 1952 ii 523; Cazden 1958 i 119 + Cazden 1978 119; Emrich 1974 424-25; *JFSS 3* 212-13 (Grainger, Gilchrist); Laws A 4; W. R. Mackenzie 1928 205; Morison 223-50; Neeser 24-33; Purslow 1972 132-33; *SO 16 #2* 18-20; Winslow 145-55.
Broadsides, songsters: *American Songster* 1845 159-61 + *Marsh's Selection* iii 159-61; *Book of 1000* 511-12, 532-34; *Delaney #30* 34; W. C. Ford #3004, #3005; *Forecastle Songster* 32-34; *Forget-Me-Not* 24-25; *Isaiah Thomas* ii107; *Jack Tar* 100-103; *Lover's Harmony #47* 375-76; Neeser (frontispiece: facsimile); *New Book of 1000* 24-25; *Pearl Songster* 159-61; *Rough & Ready* 84-87; *Street Literature* (Catnach); *Wehman #13* 6; Winslow (frontispiece: facsimile).
Texts: *American War Songs* 24-26; Barrett 56-57; Belden 1952 ii 524 A + Flanagan 439-40; Belden 1952 ii 525 B + Friedman 290-91;

L. Chappell 48-49; CMS 650D.1 + CMS 650F D.1 (Tom Glazer); Creighton 1950 225-26; Downes 66-67; Emrich 1974 425-27; S. B. Gould 1892 220-21 #108 + S. B. Gould 1905 220-221 #108; *JAF 31* 171-73 (Barbeau); W. R. Mackenzie 1919 141; W. R. Mackenzie 1928 205-7; Morison 247-48; Purslow 1972 66; Rosenberg Index #1130; Silber 1973 132-33, *SO 16 #2* 19; F. M. Warner 67.
Related text (*A Memorable Victory*, by Philip Freneau): *Champagne Charley* 1867 44-45; Neeser 29-33.
Related text (*Paul Jones, the Privateer*): Rickaby 154-55 (M. C. Dean).
Text and tune relatives: *JFSS 3* 206-13 + Grainger #112.
Tune relatives: Creighton 1962 161; Peacock 143, 145; *PTFLS 6* 123; *Tocher #5* 146.

9.
The Kingston Volunteers

Previously available: AFS 12309B.26 + EC 700.11.
Variants: none.
Adaptations: none.
Comment, references: Belden 1940 296-97; Burt 183.84; Eddy 267; FA 2163F B.5 (Charles E. Smith); *JAF 35* 379-80 (Tolman), 382-83 (Kittredge); *KFQ 6 #4* 3-13 (McCarthy), 13-17 (Swetnam); Laws A 5; *New Book of 1000* 180; *NYFQ 7* 142-44 (Mary Elizabeth King); H. Thompson 1940 344-48 [citing articles by C. B. Galbraith in *Ohio Archaeological and Historical Quarterly 20* 415-56 and *26* 52-57, and another by A. B. Culver in the *Westfield [N. Y.] Republican* for 29 December 1897]; H. Thompson 1958 124-27.
Broadsides, songsters: *Book of 1000* 393-96; *Book of 1001* iii 225-27; *Delaney #16* 25; *Forecastle Songster* 246-49; *Forget-Me-Not* 97-99 + *Jenny Lind* 97-99 + *New Book of 1000* 97-99; *Nancy Till* 116-19.
Texts: Belden 1952 ii 525-28 + Emrich 1974 438-39; Bonar 99-101; FA 2163F B.5; Flanders Index 247 #11 + Flanders 1953 18-21; FSA 33F 8, listing; Gardner 1939 479, listing (from two ms. sources); Hubbard 287-89; *KFQ 6 #4* 11-13; E. Moore 271-73; *NYFQ 14* 208, listing; Peterson Index 47; Pound 1922 93-97; *Ring Ms. #14, John Bird*; Rosenberg Index #686; Schinhan iv 273; Shoemaker 164-66; H. Thompson 1940 345-47.
Unrelated text (*MacPherson's Lament*): Peggy Seeger 1960 77, 89; *SO 10 #3* 10-11.

Text and tune relatives: Carlisle 68-70; *JAF 35* 380-82 + Eddy 265-67 + FA 2163B.5 + Silber 1973 200-202.
Tune relatives: none.
Unrelated tune (*The Tempest, or Cease, Rude Boreas*),
  Comment, references: W. Chappell 1840 i 35-36 #8; W. Chappell 1859 ii 597-98, 786-87; Duncan 1927 257; FH 5279F 4 #6 (Schrader); S. B. Gould iv p. viii; Grover 124; Huntington 72; *JAF 35* 383 (Kittredge); H. Johnson 120-21; Rabson 94.
  Tunes for this and other texts [* not notated]: *American Musical Miscellany* 1798 52-55; Barron 46-50; *Beeton 1865* 30; *Boosey 1862a* 9 #32 (instrumental); *British Orpheus* 149; *Calliope* 30-32; *Cease, Rude Boreas* [a late eighteenth century broadside, with the tune, at Morrison Library, University of California at Berkeley, M1619.C654]; W. Chappell 1859 ii 598; *Crosby* 1812 25-29; Davidson i 126; Duncan 1927 257; *Edinburgh Musical Miscellany* 1804 177-80; FH 5279.1.6 (in 2/4 time); S. B. Gould viii 72-73; Grover 122; Hatton ii 40; Hogarth ii 169-75; Huntington 68; H. Johnson 121-22; *New Musical* ii 83-86; *Quaver* 1844 *182-84; Rabson 21; Ritson 1813 ii *144-46; *Sky-Lark* 136-39; *Songster's Favourite Companion* 133-37; G. A. Stevens *198-200 #151; *Vocal Magazine* *345 #1278; *Yorkshire* 33-36.
Unrelated tune (*The Tempest*, instrumental): ATL OT 1538.2d; M. M. Cole 24h; *EDS 16* 113 + *Community* iii 3a + P. Kennedy 1951 32 #66 [distinct from others]; Fessenden 127b; Goodwin 1955 i 146a; Gott 31b; *Howe 1851a* 35b; *Howe 1851c* 35b; Howe 1858a 46b; *Howe 1859* 12a; Howe 1864a 41f; *Parlor Companion* 142b; Rollinson 39b; *Violin Made Easy* 26c.

10.
The Drummer Boy of Waterloo

Previously available: *Neighbors* 1942 9.
Variants: none.
Adaptations: none.
Comment, references: *JAF 60* 217; Laws J 1.
Broadsides, songsters [* with indication, "air: *Woodland Mary*"]:
  American Songster 1845 145-46 + *Marsh's Selection* iii 145-46; *Bobbing Around* * 235-36; *Cozans* ii *75; *Delaney #13* 25; *Dilly Burn* 23-24; *Elton* 84; *Forget-Me-Not* 202 + *New Book of 1000* 202; *Humming Bird* 126; *London Melodist* *14; *Nighting-*

ale Melodies 57-58; *Pearl Songster* 82; *Singer's Gem* 126; *Singer's Journal #28* 186; *Wolf Index #530*.
Texts: Belden 1952 ii 357-58; Davis Index 67; Eddy 164 C; Gainer 1975 155-56; Hubbard 284; E. Moore 148-49; *NA Ives* 66.12.1; *Sam Henry #728*; H. Thompson 1958 78-79 (from a New York manuscript of 1841-56); Wilkinson i #233.
Text and tune relatives: none.
Tune relatives: none.
[Unidentified "air: *The Drummer Boy of Waterloo*," for the text *Parting Friends*]: *Pacific Song Book* i 8 + *Pacific Song Book* iii 12-13.
Unrelated tune (*Woodland Mary*),
  Sheet music: M 481.246.
  Broadsides, songsters: M. Raven iii 33 (facsimile); *Street Literature* (T. Birt, London).
  Texts: Grainger #270.

11.
The Kerry Recruit

Previously available: AFS 12309B.25 + EC 700.10.
Variants: none.
Adaptations: none.
Comment, references: Dallas 1973 157; Fowke 1973 213 #78; Laws J 8 (Irish); *SO 8 #4* 4 (Dyer-Bennet).
Broadsides, songsters: O'Conor 95-96; Wehman *617* 123.
Texts: Dallas 1973 154-56; Flanders *SR* 24.3.35 (from Mooer's Falls, New York); Fowke 1973 168-69; Healy 1967 i 105-6; M. E. Henry 1938 402; HTA; Knox 71-72; LCF (from Mooers, New York); J. Lomax 1941 200-201; McTiernan 75-76; O Lochlainn 1939 2-3; Randolph iii 240-41; Ritchie 1965b 58-59; C. J. Sharp 1932 ii 228; Shoemaker 225-27; Silber 1973b 274a; A. Williams 1923 284.
Text and tune relatives: ATL 606.3; Creighton 1962 162-63; Dyer-Bennet 1971 94-96 + J. Edwards 178-79 + RLP 199-34.2.8 + *RSO #6* 8-9 + *SO 8 #4* 4-5 + Silverman 1975 ii 294-95; Healy 1962 77-79; T. Wood 1928 26-27.
Tune relatives: none.

12.
As I Went Down to Port Jervis

Previously available (#12 A): *Neighbors* 1942 11.
Variants: none.

Adaptations: none.

Comment, references: none.

Broadsides, songsters: none.

Texts: A. M. Williams 1895 47.

Related text and tune (*The Crimean War*),

Comment, references: Laws J 9.

Texts: Dean 49; *MF 13* 146, listing (Fowke).

Texts with related tune: Gardner 1939 231-232; *NA Ives* 1.121 + ATL 3128.2.

Text and tune relatives: none.

Tune relatives (*Driving Saw Logs on the Plover*),

Comment, references: Laws C 29; Philo 1022J 2.9 (Bethke).

Tunes with this text: Bethke #3 + Philo 1022.2.9; FO 10.1.6 + Fowke 1970 204; Rickaby 89-91 + Carmer 1942b 173-74 + C. Sandburg 1927 396-97 + J. R. Wilson #11b.

Tune relatives (*John Ladner*),

Comment, references: *NEF 5* 13-14.

Tunes with this text: Manny 122; *NA Ives* 1.3 + ATL 2137.7; *NA Ives* 1.31 + ATL 2156.8; *NA Ives* 1.32 + ATL 2157.6 + *NEF 5* 15; *NA Ives* 1.47 + ATL 2171.2; *NA Ives* 61.2, 62.5, 65.8.1.

Tune relatives (*The River Roe*): Joyce #13 + J. R. Wilson #11d; Roche i #79.

Tune relatives (*The Smashing of the Van*): Galvin 50 + Moyes 23 + *SO 6 #2* 6; O Lochlainn 1939 28 + J. R. Wilson #11e.

Tune relatives (others),

Comment, references: *CAY 1 #2* 7; J. R. Wilson 43 #11.

Tunes: AFS L56A.2, *Michigan-I-O*; ATL 621.14, 621.15 (Reuben Edwards); ATL 626.7 (Charles Seeley); Behan 1967 85; Brand 1961 8; Breathnach i 47; Breathnach iii 220; Bronson iv 223 #28, Child 279, *The Jolly Beggar* (in *a – b – a – a* form); I. Campbell 71; *CAY 1 #2* 7; *Chapbook 3 #2* 9; L. Chappell 63-65 (in second-half – – *b – a* form); L. Chappel 84; Clayre 60; Creighton 1950 78 B + Bronson iii 311 #26; Dallas 1974 236, 240-41; Dibblee 42, 61; Doerflinger 113; Doerflinger 222 + J. R. Wilson #11a; R. G. Edwards 1956 39 + R. G. Edwards 1971 28; R. G. Edwards 1971 24b-25, 155; FM 4051.1.4; FM 4052.2.7; *FMJ 3* 58; FO 1.1.4 + FM 4051.2.9; FO 4.2.1, 16.1.10; Fowke 1965 22; FSE 7.1.1; Gardner 1939 66; Graeme 124-25 + *Clancy* 1971 124-25; Grainger #239; Graves 1914 #97 + Graves 1928 64-65, *The Winding Banks of Erne*; Healy 1969 20-21; Hughes iv 94-96; *JIFS 11* 18; Jolliffe 52, 93; Joyce #771; P. Kennedy

1975 789; Kidson 1915 25; Kidson 1926 52-53; M. Leach 1965 186, 198; A. L. Lloyd 1967 400; MacColl 1954 14; MacColl 1963 42; MacColl 1968 40; Manifold 56, 58; Manny 82 + J. R. Wilson #11; Manny 140; Meredith 1956 22; Meredith 1968 30, 98, 185b; ML 4941.1.10; Morton 1970 72 + IRL 11B.6; Morton 1973 101 #5, 102 #6, 108 #16; *NA Ives* 1.4 + ATL 2138.7; *NA Ives* 1.68 + ATL 2187.1; *NA Ives* 62.2, *Molly and Harry*; *NA Ives* 62.5, *The Dungarvon Whooper*; O Lochlainn 1965 32; R. Palmer 1974b 29; Peacock 620, 942; Randolph ii 32 A, 36 E; Rickaby 164 (from the singing of M. C. Dean) + J. R. Wilson #11c; *Sam Henry #37*, "air: *The River Roe*"; *Sam Henry* #199, #540, #549, #577, #612, #622, #665, #672, #727, #774; Schinhan iv 341; Peggy Seeger 1960 50 #46 + Peggy Seeger 1970 35 #20; *SO 11 #2* 18; *SO 12 #4* 8; *SO 18 #4* 26; *Tocher #11* 94; Topic 12T160B.1; Wright 422.

See also notes to #29, #38, #60, #111, #167.

13.
The Yankee Man-of-War

Previously available: *Neighbors* 1944 27.

Variants: ATL 615.12.

Adaptations: none.

Comment, references: Belden 1940 379.

Broadsides, songsters: *Beau Monde* 53; *Delaney #3* 24 + Kimball 143-44; *Singer's Journal #16* 95; Wehman listing, 1887; Wehman iv 106-7; Wolf Index #2691 (three issues by De Marsan and two by Magnus, #127, #128).

Texts: ATL 490.13, 606.5; Belden 1940 379-80.

Related text (*The Bold Privateer*): *Beadle's Dime #1* 49; Kidson 1891 102-3; C. J. Sharp 1932 ii 175.

Related text (*The British Man-of-War*): Diprose 1865 71; FHE 183; Huntington 108-10; *JFSS 7* 9-10; Karpeles 1974 i 526-28; Kidson 1929 58-59; *MF 13* 153a (Fowke); Peacock 181; Purslow 1968 58; SIF 1001.1449B.2 (Peter Bellamy); *Street Literature* (E. Hodges, London).

Related text (*The Fenian Man-of-War*): Galvin 48-49 + Wright 529.

Related text (*A Yankee Man-of-War*): Wolf Index #2692, #2693.

Unrelated text (*The Yankee Man-of-War*): *Delaney #19* 3; B. Ives 1962 264-65; Neeser 25-26; Rickaby 158-60; A. M. Williams 1895 15-17.

Text and tune relatives: none.
Tune relatives: ATL 621.4, *The Good Ship, 'Cumberland'*; Ph. Barry 1929 96; Creighton 1950 220-222; Fife 1969 261, *Cole Younger;* R. Ford 1904 59, *The Plains of Waterloo;* Fowke 1967 88-89 + Fowke 1970 197-98; HTA, *The Bounty Jumper;* Hubbard 267; B. Ives 1958 90; *JFSS 5* 165 + Clayre 72; *JFSS 8* 14-15 + Karpeles 1974 ii 283 A, *The London Man-of-War;* Karpeles 1971 122, 208; *NEF 7* 49; Ohrlin 142, *Cole Younger;* O Lochlainn 1939 88; Ord 34; Peacock 204 B, 515, 996; Petrie #704, #753; Randolph ii 13; E. K. Wells 304.

14.
The Battle of Gettysburg

Previously available: none.
Variants: ATL 614.9.
Adaptations: none.
Comment, references: Belden 1940 383; Belden 1952 ii 539; Laws A 17; W. R. Mackenzie 1928 298-300; Randolph ii 297.
Broadsides, songsters: none. A copy from the *Boston Globe,* 18 August 1912, is one of four listed by Barry in *JAF 27* 70.
Texts: Belden 1940 383-84 A, 385-87 B; CMS 670F B.6, *Custer's Last Fierce Charge;* Combs 1967 208 #47, listing, *The Battle of Gettysburg;* Dean 14-16; Eddy 301-4 + Friedman 295-96; Emrich 1974 456-57; FHE 405-6; Fife 1970 114; FSA 33F 8, listing; Fuson 94-96; Hubbard 277-79; Koehnline 41-42; *NA Ives* 1.34 + ATL 2160.3; *NA Ives* 66.5.4; Piper + Peterson Index 80; Randolph ii 297-301; Shearin 14; *WF 17* 237a; J. R. Wilson 51-52.
Parody text: *PTFLS 6* 133-34.
Unrelated text (*The Battle of Gettysburg*): Wolf Index #100, #101.
Text and tune relatives: Abrahams 69-72; Bethke #25; N. Buchan 1973 19 [tune in *a – b' – b' – a* form]; CMS 670B.6 (Tom Glazer); Dallas 1973 197-98; Dibblee 86-87; *NA Ives* 1.7 + ATL 2141.6; *NA Ives* 1.118 + ATL 3125.2; *NA Ives* 1.157 + ATL 3164.3; *NA Ives* 62.2; Peacock 1004; Ritchie 1965b 104-5; Schinhan iv 274-75 + J. R. Wilson #3a; *SO 14 #3* 8-9; Wilkinson *128* 6b.
Tune relatives (*The Charcoal Man*): Converse 1863 70; Converse 1865 79-81; Unsworth 1861 [text only].
Tune relatives (others): Bethke #1 + Philo 1022.2.5, *Alan Bain;* Doerflinger 318 + Wright 389, *The Irish Girl's Lament;* Flan-

ders 1939 253; Greenleaf 233; Ritchie 1963 67; Ritchie 1971 105-106 [first part]; Schinhan iv 153-54; Schinhan v 453-54; C. J. Sharp 1932 ii 199; Wilkinson *128*, fiddle tune #5, *Lovely Nancy.*

15.
The "Cumberland" Crew

Previously available: *Neighbors* 1945 28.
Variants: none.
Adaptations: Cazden 1958 i 20-21 + Cazden 1978 20-21.
Comment, references: Cazden 1958 i 110-11 + Cazden 1978 110-11; Doerflinger 332; FA 2188F 18 (Nye); FH 5323F 4 (Edw. Ives); Gray 162, noting especially J. Henry Hayward's *Poetical Pen-Pictures of the [Civil] War,* 3rd ed., New York (1864) 233-34; and other broadside and songster prints; Laws A 18.
Broadsides, songsters: Auner, List 5; *Beau Monde* 62-64; *Book of Songs and Ballads* 188; California Checklist 118, listing of a broadside by Bell, San Francisco; *Callender* 48-49, "as sung by Geo. F. Jarvis"; *Captain Kelly* 30-32; *Daytons* 1881 26-27; *Delaney #2* 23; De Marsan, List 3 #20; *Murray & Murphy* 18-19, "as sung by Geo. F. Jarvis"; *Pat Rooney* 1882a 46-47; *Wehman #47;* Wehman i 13-14; *Wehman's Collection #13* 2.
Texts: AFS L29F 6-7; E. C. Beck 1948 274-75; CMS 660F F.5; Creighton 1932 244; Emrich 1974 442-43 (from Yankee John Galusha, Minerva, New York); FA 2188F 19; FH 5323F 4; Edw. Ives 1978 228; *JIFMC 3* 95, listing; *NYFQ 14* 210, listing; Shoemaker 217-18; Stekert Listing B 112.
Related texts (parody: *The Battleship 'Maine'*): *Delaney #18* 2 + Silverman 1975 ii 292b-93.
(*The 'Cumberland,'* by Herman Melville): Ch. Kennedy 1952 236-37 + Ch. Kennedy 1954 230-31.
(*The Iron 'Merrimac'*): AFS L29A.2 + AFS L29F 4-5.
(*The Men of the 'Cumberland'*): *Touch the Elbow* 58-59.
(*The 'Merrimac'* or *The Good Ship 'Cumberland'*): see notes to #16.
(*The 'Monitor' and the 'Merrimac'*): *Touch the Elbow* 33-35.
(*On Board the 'Cumberland'*): *Soldiers & Sailors* 15-17.
Text and tune relatives: AFS L29A.3 (Captain Pearl R. Nye, with tune in major); ATL 606.8; CMS 660F.5 (Tom Glazer); Doerflin-

ger 134 (second half of tune only); Emrich 1973 426-28; FA 2188A.2 (second half of tune only); FH 5323.1.5 (Edward Ives); Glass 1968 183-85; *NA Ives* 1.2 + ATL 2136.3; *NA Ives* 1.14 + ATL 2145.3; *NA Ives* 1.18 + ATL 2147.9; Rickaby 140, from the singing of Michael C. Dean (complete text in Dean 36-37); *SO 4 #1* 12-13 + *RSO #5* 34-35 + Silber 1963 83 + Silber 1964 24-25 + Silverman 1975 ii 312b-13.

Tune relatives (*The Blantyre Explosion*, tune in *a – a – –* half-tune form): Dallas 1974 204; Fowke 1961 60; A. L. Lloyd 1952 129 + MacColl 1956 59 + MacColl 1965 14-15; Pete Seeger 1972 119; *SO 5 #2* 4-5 + *RSO #2* 58-59 + Silverman 1975 i 376.

(*Canny Cummerlan'*): *JFSS 3* 41.

(*Sussex*, in 4/4 time): Hauser 1948 174 + G. P. Jackson 1952 142 #239.

(others, complete tune form): Bayard i 119.4; Creighton 1971 69; Hickok 80-81, *The American Star*; Joyce #191; Roche i #9, *The Old Shady Bohereen*.

(others, in *a – a – –* form): ATL 182.1; Ranson 106; Rickaby 24 + J. Lomax 1934 445, *The Lost Jimmy Whalen*.

(others, in *– – b – a* form): *JFSS 1* 269-70.

(others, condensed tune treatments): Korson 1949 380-81 + J. R. Wilson #6a; Manny 150, versions ii and iv for *The Miramichi Fire*; Manny 238 + J. R. Wilson #6.

16.
The "Merrimac"

Previously available: none.
Variants: ATL 484.9.
Adaptations: none.
Comment, references: Belden 1952 ii 530-32, including notice of a broadside issued ca. 1862 by Johnson, Philadelphia; FA 2354F.2.2 (Stekert);
Broadsides, songsters (*The Good Ship 'Cumberland'*): Auner; *Delaney #13* 26; Wehman iv 84-85; Wolf Index #787;
Texts: ATL 488.3b, 606.9, 621.4; Belden 1952 531-32; Creighton 1932 282-83 + Emrich 1974 445; Emrich 1974 443-44, from Yankee John Galusha, Minerva, New York; FA 2354F.2.2 + Stekert 1969 B 66; FM 4001B.5 + FM 4001F B.5; Peacock 909-10;
Related texts (*The 'Cumberland' Crew*): see notes to #15.
Text and tune relatives: ATL 601.6 (James Edwards); FA 2354.2.2 (Ezra Barhight).
Tune relatives: see notes to #178.

17.
The Bounty Jumper

Previously available: none.
Variants: ATL 625.10.
Adaptations: none.
Comment, references: none.
Broadsides, songsters: no texts located.
Texts: Dean 101 + Kimball 162-63; HTA + Kimball 162a; Shearin 14.
Related texts (titles, subject matter): *Billy Holmes* 19-20; *California Checklist* 8, listed for *Novelty Songster No. 1*; *California Checklist* 117, noting a broadside by T. C. Boyd, San Francisco; *Hooley's High Daddy* 18-20; *Marching through Georgia* 28, "as sung by Charley Rhoades"; Peterson Index 20; Wolf Index #183, #184, #185.
Related text (*Bold McCarthy*, or *The 'City of Baltimore'*): Creighton 1932 117-19; Doerflinger 128-29; Greenleaf 354; Manny 224-25 + ATL 2177.1 + *NA Ives* 1.52 + J. R. Wilson #5, 53-54; *NA Ives* 66.3.6, 68.4.2.9; O'Conor 54; Peacock 860-61 + Wright 285-86; Ranson 54.
Text and tune relatives: ATL 477.2 (Irving Grant, New Jersey).
Tune relatives: ATL 614.10, *The Foggy, Foggy Dew* (George Edwards); Bronson i 377 #1, *The Riddle Song; Chapbook 4 #2* 7; R. G. Edwards 1971 32, *Ned Kelly Was an Irishman*; S. B. Gould 1892 16-17 + *Folk #1* ii, *The Roving Journeyman*; Levy 1971 85, *The Boy with the Auburn Hair*; O Lochlainn 1939 50, *The Bold Belfast Shoemaker*.

18.
The Bright, Sunny South

Previously available: AFS 12309A.6 + EC 329.6; *Neighbors* 1943 19; *NYFQ 4* 38.
Variants: ATL 484.8.
Adaptations: Cazden 1958 i 18-19 + Cazden 1978 18-19.
Comment, references: Cazden 1958 i 109-10 + Cazden 1978 109-10; Cox 1925 279; Harwell, *passim;* NW 202F 1-2, 6 (Charles Hamm); A. M. Williams 1895 59-70.
Broadsides, songsters: none.
Texts: Cox 1925 280; Creighton 1950 273 B; Davis Index (3); W. R. Mackenzie 1928 139; Piper + Peterson Index 81; Rosenberg Index #1180 (3).
Unrelated text (*The Rebel Soldier*),
 Comment, references: Belden 1940 374-75; Cox 1925 279; *JAF 30* 345 (Kittredge).
 Broadsides, songsters: Allan 80-81.

Texts [* with related tune; ** with related tune showing tetrachord transposition of the ending]: Belden 1940 376 B, C; Cox 1925 279 A; C. J. Sharp 1932 ii **212 A, **213 B, **214 C, **214 D, *214-15 E, **215 F, **215 G; Wilkinson i *#179, #343, *#349, #350.

Unrelated text (*Take Me Home,* or *The Sweet, Sunny South*),

Broadsides, songsters: Allan 119b.

Sheet music: Harwell, listing.

Texts [* with related tune]: Belden 1952 iii 475-76; *Heart Songs* 20-21; Hubbard 220-21; Schinhan v 265; C. J. Sharp 1932 ii *262 A, *263 B.

Text and tune relatives: ATL 602.13 (James Edwards); Creighton 1950 272 A; Gardner 1939 242-43; Grover 195; *NA Ives* 1.12 + ATL 2144.1; *NA Ives* 62.2, 66.8.8; C. J. Sharp 1932 ii 263 C.

Tune relatives (Child 74, *Fair Margaret and Sweet William*): Karpeles 1934 ii 95 + Karpeles 1971 47 A; Karpeles 1971 49 C; C. J. Sharp 1932 i 143-44 L.

(Child 77, *Sweet William's Ghost*): Karpeles 1971 52 B, 54 C, 54 D, 55 E, 55 F, 56 G.

(others, with condensed tune forms): C. J. Sharp 1916 108-9 #48 + *JAMS 3* 132 #21 + Karpeles 1973 22 Ex. 6 + A. L. Lloyd 1967 82a + C. J. Sharp 1920 i 74 + VRS 1001B.4 (Alfred Deller), *Searching for Lambs;* see also notes to #87 in this collection, *The Rolling Stone.*

19.
The Shades of the Palmetto

Previously available: *Neighbors* 1944 29.
Variants: AFS 7757A.2; ATL 613.10.
Adaptations: none.
Comment, references: AFS L28F 13 (Emrich); Laws A 14; Randolph ii 196, 264.
Broadsides, songsters: *Delaney #69* 24, *The Dying Ranger; Joe English* 50-52, *The Dying Soldier Boy.*
Texts: Abrahams 31-33; AFS L28B.1 + AFS L28F 13-14; J. V. Allen 84-87; *American Cowboy* 20-21; Belden 1940 397-98; *Big Round Up* 80-81; K. S. Clark 1932 30; Cox 1939 ii 28; Davis Index 289, *The Texas Rangers;* J. Davis 47; Doerflinger 274-76; Emrich 1973 511-13; FHE 312, 315-16; Finger 170-73; FO 13.1.4; *JAF 45* 164-65; *JAF 46* 27-28; M. Leach 1965 146; Lingenfelter 270-71; J. Lomax 1938 366-68; E. Moore 316-19; A. C. Morris 47-48; *NA Ives* 61.4; Ohrlin 127-28;

Piper + Peterson Index 31; *Powder River* 74-75; Randolph ii 196-99, *The Dying Cowboy;* Randolph ii 264-65, *The Dying Soldier;* Rosenberg Index #344; Shay 1961 137-40; Silverman 1975 ii 367; Siringo 24-26; *Tip Top* 1935 47.
Text and tune relatives: none.
Tune relatives: see notes to #18.

20.
The Texas Rangers

Previously available: none.
Variants (#20 B): ATL 629.11.
Adaptations: none.
Comment, references: AFS L28F 9 (Emrich); Belden 1940 336; Cox 1925 262; Emrich 1973 508; FA 2188F 26 (Nye); Flanders 1939 227-28; Laws A 8; *PTFLS 32* 188-98, "The Texas Rangers" in Aberdeenshire" (Goldstein); Randolph ii 169-70.
Broadsides, songsters: Wehman #748; Wehman ii 40-41; *Wehman's Collection #30* 3; *Wehman's Collection #33* 4.
Texts: Abrahams 14-15; AFS L28A.5 + AFS L28F 9; Allan 38; G. Anderson 177; Belden 1952 ii 544-46; Brewster 316-17; Buford 105-6; T. Burton ii 23; Carmer 1942a 234-35; *CFQ 2* 102; Combs 1967 208 #45, listing; Cox 1925 262; Davis Index 290; Emrich 1973 509-10; FA 2188F 26, *Longstreet's Rangers;* Fife 1970 112-13; Flanders Index 231 (5); FSA 26.2.7 + FSA 26F 25-26; Fuson 191-92; *JAF 25* 14-15; Kimball 136-37; Koehnline 17-18; Lingenfelter 266-67; J. Lomax 1941 245-46 + A. Lomax 1960 331-32 + Veal 22-23 #11; McIntosh 1935 112-13; A. C. Morris 44-45; E. A. Palmer 130-33; Piper (1912) + Peterson Index 77; Rosenberg Index #1379 + Rosenberg T85.20A.2-.3; Schinhan iv 277a; Shay 1961 152-53; Silber 1973b 274b; Silverman 1975 i 45; Siringo 9-11; Stekert 1969 B 54; Stout 106 #84; Thomas 1939 57; Welsch 31-32.
Unrelated texts (*The Alamo, Song of the Texan Ranger,* 1846): Dichter 1956.
(*Buckskin Sam, the Texan Ranger*): Dichter 1956.
(*Song of the Texas Rangers*): Simms 172-74.
Text and tune relatives: ATL 190.3 (Walt Wermouth); ATL 603.2-.3 (James Edwards); Bayard i 93.1; Belden 1940 337-38 E; Botkin 1951 774-75; M. E. Bush i 45-47 (tune in minor); K. S. Clark 1932 59-60; J. Cohen 150-51; FA 2188B.2 (Hermes Nye); Flanders 1937 30-31; Flanders 1937 30 + Flanders

1939 226-27 (first and last phrases of tune);
Hubbard 291-92; INT 25014.2.3; *JAF 35* 417
+ Eddy 291-92 (second half of tune); M.
Leach 1965 264; J. Lomax 1938 361; E.
Moore 312-14; A. C. Morris 29-31 (parody
text); A. C. Morris 44-45; *NA Ives* 1.87 +
ATL 2206.3; *NA Ives* 1.88 + ATL 2207.1;
NA Ives 1.154 + ATL 3161.3; *NA Ives* 62.2,
66.8.5; Ohrlin 130-31; *PTFLS 32* 191, 194-95;
Randolph ii 172-73 C; *Sam Eskin* iv 118; C. J.
Sharp 1932 ii 253.

Tune relatives (*Howard Carey*).

    Comment, references: Edw. Ives 1978 128-30.

    Tunes with this text: Manny 111 + J. R. Wilson #19b; *NA Ives* 1.122 + ATL 3129.7;
NA Ives 1.131 + ATL 3138.1; *NA Ives*
1.145 + ATL 3152.1; *NA Ives* 1.154 +
ATL 3161.2; *NA Ives* 64.6.4, 64.7.5,
64.7.12, 64.8.4, 64.9.2, 65.5.1, 65.5.2,
65.7.2, 65.8.3, 68.3.2.6; *NA Ives* 65.9.8 +
Edw. Ives 197- 0000 [155 #2].

Tune relatives (others): C. S. Adams 123;
BFSSNE #2 8; *CFQ 1* 223; K. S. Clark 1934
48-49; Cox 1939 144; Creighton 1962 150;
Dibblee 17; Doerflinger 318; Doyle 1940 55,
The Roving Newfoundlanders; Flanders
1934 42; FM 4053.1.5; Fowke 1970 123; FSC
9.2.1; Greenleaf 369 + J. R. Wilson #19c;
B. Jackson 47; J. Lomax 1938 81; Manny 52
+ J. R. Wilson #19a; E. Moore 163, 168-69;
NA Ives 1.52 + ATL 2176.4; *NA Ives* 1.79
+ ATL 2198.1; *NA Ives* 65.9.3; *NEF 7* 81;
PTFLS 6 126; *PTFLS 23* 72, 74, 87; Randolph i 233; Randolph ii 67, 160, 162, 275;
Ritchie 1953 55; Sires 30-31; Thomas 1931
108-9, 148-49; Thomas 1964 19-20 + Botkin
1944 891 + J. R. Wilson #19d; Thomas 1964
97-99 + J. R. Wilson #19b; *WF 30* 135, 136;
J. R. Wilson #19.

21.
On the Shores of Havana

Previously available: none.
Variants: none.
Adaptations: none.
Comment, references: none.
Broadsides, songsters: Delaney #18 ; *Rogers
Bros.*
Sheet music: New York: Howley, Haviland &
Co., 1898 + *Collection* ii #31; London:
Chas. Sheard & Co., 1899.
Texts: Shearin 29, listing.
Related text (*On the Banks of the Wabash, Far
Away*),

Comment, references: Boni 1960 30; J. Burton i 228-30; Dresser viii-ix (Dreiser); Fuld
1955 60; D. Gilbert 312-13; Goldberg 252;
R. Lloyd 1969 197; Mattfeld 237; Spaeth
1948 278-79.
Broadsides, songsters: *Delaney #16* 2; *Taggert & Witt.*
Sheet music: New York: Howley, Haviland
& Co., 1897 + Dresser 72-75 + Fremont
230-34 (facsimile).
Texts [* with tune of #21, ** with tune of
refrain only]: Agay *230-31; Arany *98-99;
Boni 1960 *30-32; K. S. Clark 1930 **49
#61; De Vore *6-7; Gamse *128-29; Goodwin 1956 *144; Hansen *148b; C. Johnson
*30-31; R. Lloyd 1969 *197-99; Lynn **24;
Morehead *102; D. Thompson 33-34.
Related texts (others): Belden 1952 ii 547-48;
Carlisle 73-75, *That Old War; Delaney #18* 2
+ Silverman 1975 ii 292b-93, *The Battleship
'Maine';* A. C. Morris 32-33, *Down in the
Harbor of Havana;* Randolph iv 139.
Text and tune relatives [* tune by reference
only, ** tune of refrain only]: Belden 1952 ii
*546-47; Carlisle **71-72; *SFQ 4* *185
(Brewster).
Tune relatives (others): none.

22.
Johnny Riley

Previously available: *Neighbors* 1944 25-26; *NJ
4 #7* 29-31; *PSB 2* #118.
Variants: ATL 618.1.
Adaptations: AFS 12312B.12; AFS 19250.8
(Laura Stein); Cazden 1958 i 32-33 + Cazden 1978 32-33.
Comment, references: *AFSPB 14* 173-74
(Laws); Cazden 1958 i 115-16 + Cazden
1978 115-16; Cox 1925 316; *EDS 32* 104;
Laws N 42; O'Shaughnessy 1968 32; Randolph i 258; *SFQ 23* 215-32 (Rennick), form
1; C. J. Sharp 1932 ii 403 #98.
Broadsides, songsters: as in Laws and others.
Broadsides, songsters (*The Valiant Seaman*
form): *EDS 32* 103a (facsimile); *PMLA 42* 93;
Roxburghe vii 518; Simpson 149; *Vocal Library* 525 #1421.
Texts: Abrahams 186, listing; AFS 104A.1 +
AFS L21B.3 + AFS L21F 104A.1; G. Anderson 69-70; Boette 41; Brocklebank 17;
Buford 44, 45; T. Burton i 80-81; Christie i
264-65; Christie ii 200-201; Combs 1967 214
#106, listing; Creighton 1940 1-5 + Creighton 1950 134-35 A; Creighton 1950 136-37 C,
138-39 E; Creighton 1962 59 + Fowke 1967
28; Creighton 1971 57-58; Davis Index 45-49

(30); Decca 574.24213B; J. Edwards 123;
Emrich 1973 568-69; Emrich 1974 152-53;
FM 4005B.3 + FM 4005F B.3; Fowke 1973
152; Gainer 1975 128-29; Grainger 1907
#121; *JAF 41* 467 (from Bahamas); *JAF 70*
345-46 #18; *JFSS 4* 127-29 + R. V. Williams
1959 104-5; *JFSS 6* 272-73; Karpeles 1974 i
552-55, A-D; Kincaid ii 34; LCJ (Quinn,
Wagner); A. L. Lloyd 1967 223; J. Lomax
1938 168-70 (cowboy variant); W. R. Mackenzie 1919 133-34, 177; McDowell 1947 60-
61; McIntosh 1974 45-47; McMurray 1; *MF
13* 148, listing; E. Moore 187-89 (cowboy
variant); Munch 51-54; Musick 24 #18;
NYFQ 5 80-81; O'Shaughnessy 1968 8 #7;
Peacock 584-89; *PTFLS 8* 155-56; Purslow
1965 29; Reeves 1960 64-65; *Ring Ms.* 41;
Ritchie 1963 210-11; Ritchie 1964 61; Ritchie
1965b 74-75; E. Robinson 25-26; Rosenberg
Index #141 (13); *Sam Eskin* iv 111, 157; *Sam
Henry* #471; Schinhan iv 169-70; Peggy Seeger 1964 64; Pete Seeger 1973 211; *SFQ* 165-
66; Shearin 27; Silber 1973b 149c; Sires 20-21
(cowboy variant); R. Smith 1928 162-63 +
R. Smith 1937 65-66; *SO 13* +*3* 7 + Silverman 1975 i 124a; Solomon 51-53 + VRS
9078.2.1 (Baez); SRL 7624.4.5 (Odetta); Wilkinson i #41, #100, #199, #237, #517,
#551, #585; Wyman 1916 34-37, 90.

Text and tune relatives [* tune distant but related, ** tune in complete *a – a' – b – a'*
form]: ATL 602.7 (James Edwards); ATL
605.6 (James Edwards); ATL 621.6 (Reuben
Edwards); *JFSS 6* *272; O Lochlainn 1939
**4-5.

Tune relatives (in *– – b – a'* form): AFS L21A.7
(Carrie Grover); *All Time* 21; Creighton 1962
130; Creighton 1971 47; FSA 33.2.1 (Sarah
Cleveland); Grover 127-28; Healy 1967a 82
+ Wright 401; Edw. Ives 1964 30-31; Ritchie
1953 15; Rounder 0017.2.6 (Almeda Riddle);
Silverman 1975 i 91b; *Sing 11* #1 25.

23.
The 'Rainbow'

Previously available: *Neighbors* 1942 24; *NJ 4
#8* 38.
Variants: ATL 624.13.
Adaptations: Cazden 1958 i 36-37 + Cazden
1978 36-37; Haufrecht 1943 14-15; Haufrecht
1965 i 1-5.
Comment, references: Belden 1940 155; Cazden
1958 i 120-21 + Cazden 1978 120-21; Cox
1925 328; Laws N 43; *SFQ 23* 215-32 (Rennick), form 9.

Broadsides, songsters: as noted by Cox, Laws.
Texts: R. Chase 1956 179-81; Emrich 1974 154-
55; FHE 427; E. Moore 183-85; *NYFQ 5* 79-
80 + H. Thompson 1958 23; *Sam Henry*
#156.
Text and tune relatives: ATL 194.6 (Jake
Loucks).
Tune relatives [* indicates close resemblance]:
Ph. Barry 1929 *96; Creighton 1932 328; Dib-
blee 47; Doerflinger 270; Doyle 1940 9; Flan-
ders 1939 92; Fowke 1970 117; Gardner 1939
278; Huntington 105-6; Edw. Ives 1971 214;
JFSS 2 155 #9; *NA Ives* 1.22 + ATL 2150.6;
Peacock 763, 765, 860; Schinhan iv 207 #124
B; Topic 12T123.2.5.

24.
Famed Waterloo

Previously available: *Neighbors* 1944 28; *NJ 4
#9* 25-26.
Variants: ATL 615.11.
Adaptations: none.
Comment, references: *AFSPB 14* 176 (Laws);
Greenleaf 177-79; Laws N 38; Manny 285-
86; Randolph i 371; *SFQ 23* 215-32 (Ren-
nick), form 8; Topic 12T123J 2.5 (Lloyd).
Broadsides, songsters: *Delaney's Irish #3* 7; De
Marsan #26; *Howe* 1878 276; *Hyland* 161-62;
That's the Style 59; Wehman *617* 120 +
Kimball 110-11; *Wehman's Irish #2* 24-25;
Wolf Index #1371.
Texts: Bethke #38 + Philo 1022.1.1; Combs
1967 214 #104, listing; Creighton 1971 67-68;
Dallas 1973 81-83; Darley 3 #6; Emrich 1974
155-56; FHE 275; FM 4053.1.5 + FM 4053F
4.5 + *NA Ives* 1.77 + ATL 2196.2; FO
11.2.6, 21.2.11; FSA 33F 8, listing; FSC
9.2.6; Grainger #280; Grover 109-10; Healy
1967 i 284-85; Huntington 122-23 (from an
1859 ms.); Joyce #325; Karpeles 1974 i 565-
68, A - D; LCJ (Golden); M. Leach 1965 312;
Manny 285-86; Meredith 1967 214-15; *NA
Ives* 1.47 + ATL 2171.1; *NA Ives* 1.104 +
ATL 3111.3; *NA Ives* 61.1; *NEF 5* 29-31 +
ATL 2163.2 + *NA Ives* 1.37; O Lochlainn
1939 14-15; Ord 155-56; Peacock 555-57; QC
903.1.7 (Marie Hare); *Sam Henry* #76; Topic 12T123.2.5; J. R. Wilson 78-80.
Unrelated text (*The Plains of Waterloo*), **Comment, references:** Laws N 32; W. R. Mackenzie 1928 182-84, 192-94.
   Texts [sampling]: Gardner 1939 227; Greenleaf 172-73; Kidson 1891 120-23.
Text and tune relatives: ATL 625.11 (Frank Edwards).

Tune relatives: Creighton 1962 111; Joyce #409, MacColl 1956 67 + TLP 1015A.1; O Lochlainn 1939 58.

25.
Glencoe

Previously available: *NJ 4 #10* 31-32;
Variants: ATL 627.6-.7;
Comment, references: Bronson ii 429 #2; *JFSS* 5 100-103 #3 (Kidson); Laws N 39; W. R. Mackenzie 1928 180-81; Randolph i 435; *SFQ 23* 215-32 (Rennick), form 7.
Broadsides, songsters: *Delaney's Scotch #1* 3; De Marsan #263; *Shamrock Shore* 1; *Singer's Journal #15* 85; *Wehman's Irish #2* 21-22; Wolf Index #1354;
Texts: ATL 192.9 (Chauncey Blackmore); Daughters 148; FHE 373; FO 11.2.8; R. Ford 1904 247-48; LCJ; Meredith 1967 52-53; Peacock 579; *Sam Henry #655*; J. R. Wilson 86;
Unrelated text (*Glencoe*): Beethoven Nʳ 260 26-27 #10.
Text and tune relatives: ATL 630.7 (Elizabeth Misner); Creighton 1962 60; Creighton 1971 77-78; FO 11.2.7, 20.1.3; Huntington 113-16; *JFSS 2* 171 + Sharp 1961 105 + Sharp 1965 105b; *JFSS 5* 100 #3c, 103; Karpeles 1971 186-87; Petrie #677; *SO 22 #6* 4.
Tune relatives (Child 93, *Lamkin*): Bronson ii 429-30 #1, #2; *FMJ 3* 15.
Tune relatives (others): Creighton 1932 34; Dallas 1973 81, *The Mantle So Green*; FHE 314 + *BFSSNE #2* 7; FO 3.1.8, 21.1.3; Fowke 1970 132; FSA 33.2.5; *JFSS 5* 102; Joyce #322; Morton 1973 101 #4; Purslow 1965 70; Rickaby 119 + J. R. Wilson #12a; Ritchie 1953 17;

26.
The Maid on the Mountain Brow

Previously available: *YIFMC 3* 71 Ex. 5 (tune only).
Variants: ATL 485.10.
Adaptations: Cazden 1958 ii 68-69 + Cazden 1973 68-69.
Comment, references: Cazden 1958 ii 120 + Cazden 1973 120; Fowke 1965 181 #36; FSC 10F 10 (Fowke); Laws P 7.
Broadsides, songsters: Healy 1967 i 256 (reprint); *Walton's Treasury* 131 + *Walton* ii 117.
Texts: Colum 612; *Dubliners* iii 4-5; FSA 33F 8, listing; FSC 10F 10-11; Graeme 26-27 +

Clancy 1971 26-27; Hayward 85-86; B. Ives 1958 44-45; *JAF 48* 351, listing; LCJ (from New York City); *NA Ives* 1.151 + ATL 3158.7; O'Keefe 112-13; *Sam Henry #688*; J. J. Ward 2; *Well Known Songs* 36-37.
Text and tune relatives: ATL 604.15, 605.1 (Frank and James Edwards); Fowke 1965 90-91; FSC 10.1.5; Greenleaf 153-54; Grover 180-81, M. Leach 1965 128, *NA Ives* 1.23 + ATL 2150.9; *NA Ives* 1.85 + ATL 2204.3; *NA Ives* 1.88 + ATL 2207.3; *NA Ives* 62.2; *NEF 5* 70-72 + ATL 2166.2 + *NA Ives* 1.41.
Tune relatives [* by title reference only]: Bayard 11-12; Bethke #17, #18, #23, #44, #51; *Dublin Comic* *279-80; Fowke 1970 58; FSI 40.1.3 (Gordon Bok); Edw. Ives 1971 65; *JEFDSS 8* 18; W. R. Mackenzie 1928 391 #4; Manny 299.

27.
Wild Americay

Previously available: *JAF 72* 344 #7; *Neighbors* 1941 5; *Sam Eskin* i 173.
Variants: none.
Adaptations: AFS 12312A.11; Cazden 1958 i 44-45 + Cazden 1978 44-45; Haufrecht 1943 4-5; Haufrecht 1945 L 151; Haufrecht 1965.
Comment, references: Cazden 1958 i 123 + Cazden 1978 123; Laws O 19; *NA Ives* 1.27 14-15 + ATL 2153.5 ff.; Wright 1-10, 34-105.
Broadsides, songsters: none located.
Texts: Greenleaf 195-97 + J. Lomax 1947 250-51 + Wright 417-18, *Rich Americay*.
Related texts (*Mullinabrone*): Wright 391; (*My Charming Mary*): Morton 1973 44-45.
Text and tune relatives: none.
Tune relatives: Ph. Barry 1939 32, 78; Creighton 1962 62; R. Edwards 1956 24, 40; FO 19.2.6; Fowke 1973 138; Grover 14; Healy 1962 44; Hughes ii 14-21, 37-44; Edw. Ives 1964 42-43; *JFSS 5* 67, *The American Stranger*, in 3/4 time condensation; Joyce #211; Joyce #374 + Zimmerman 150, *Billy Byrne of Ballymanus*; Joyce #580 + Zimmerman 155; Leach 1965 104; Morton 1970 53; *NA Ives* 65.17.5; O'Keeffe 84; O Lochlainn 1939 34, 40, 82, 94; Peacock 75, 77, 551; Petrie #8, #245; *Sam Henry #558*, #568.

28.
The Hills of Glenshee

Previously available: Neighbors 1947 14.
Variants: AFS 12309A.2 + EC 329.2; ATL 623.9-.10.

Adaptations AFS 12312A.2, 12312A.3; AFS 19251.47 + ATL OT 5141.47 [instrumental] (Pete Seeger); Cazden 1949a 2-22 + CRI 117.2.2; Cazden 1958 i 92-93 + Cazden 1978 92-93; Cazden 1963 ii 8.

Comment, references: Cazden 1958 i 113-14 + Cazden 1978 113-14; FA 2354F 1.2 (Stekert); FM 4051F 5 (Fowke); R. Ford 1904 14-15; *JFSS* 5 104-8 (Broadwood); Laws O 6; Laws 1957 53;M. Leach 1965 99; Ord 75-76; SLP 82J A.2 (Goldstein).

Broadsides, songsters: as in Laws.

Texts: FA 2354.1.2 + FA 2354F 1.2 (Stekert) + Stekert 1969 B 29; Flanders Index 221; Flanders 1931 131-32; FM 4051F 5; R. Ford 1904 12-14; Gardner 1939 202; M. Leach 1965 98; *NYFQ 14* 208, listing; Ord 75-76; *Sam Henry* #590; *WF 20* 248.

Related texts (*The Braes of Strathblane*): R. Ford 1904 77-78; Kidson 1891 90-91; Manny 220-21 + *NA Ives* 62.6; *MF 13* 150, listing: *Miramichi Ms.* 17.16.

Related texts (*The Pretty Girl Milking Her Cow*): see notes to #31.

Text and tune relatives [all end a fourth lower than tune #28; * indicates doubled length]: Creighton 1971 79-80; FO 12.2.3, 12.2.4; FO 15.2.6 + FM 4051F.1.6; *JFSS* 5 106; *JFSS* 5 *107b (instrumental); *JIFS 10* 15; Maver 216a #431; Ord 75-76, tune *152; RLP 12-634.1.8; SLP 82.1.2.

Tune relatives (*The Lost Jimmy Whalen*), **Comment, references:** Laws C 8.

Tunes [all end a fourth lower that #28] with this text: AFS 3287A; *BFSSNE #11* 4 + Barry 1939 12; *BFSSNE#11* 5, 7; Creighton 1950 186; Creighton 1962 114, 115; FO 2.2.4; FO 2.2.5 + Fowke 1970 114 + Fowke 1973 70; Fowke 1967 77; Manny 263; *NA Ives* 1.24 + ATL 2151.7; *NA Ives* 1.30 + ATL 2155.12; *NA Ives* 1.67 + ATL 2186.3; *NA Ives* 1.155 + ATL 3162.1; *NA Ives* 62.4; 62.6; Peacock 385, 387, 388, 389; RLP 12-648.2.5.

Tune relatives (others),

Comment, references: *JFSS* 5 104-8 (Broadwood); P. Kennedy 1975 625 #272.

Tunes [all end a fourth lower than tune #28; * indicates doubled length]: Bayard i 116.2; Creighton 1950 72; Dibblee 74; *JFSS* 5 *104, *Lucy's Flitting*, by William Laidlaw; *JFSS* 5 *107a, *The Crafty Wee Bony*; Fowke 1965 132, *The Road to Dundee*; Joyce *#489; *The Kerryman's Visit to Dublin*; P. Kennedy 1975 604; Korson 1949 44; Leach 1965 210; *NA Ives* 1.41 + ATL 2166.3; *NEF*

5 23; Ord *152, *The Road to Dundee*; Ord 367; Peacock 127, 155; Petrie #602; RLP 12-602.1.3 (in c-b-c-d form); Topic 12T159A.12, *Farewell to Whisky*.

29.
It Was Early One Monday Morning

Previously available: none.

Variants: ATL 194.3.

Adaptations: none.

Comment, references: Belden 1940 177-79; Gardner 1939 169; Laws N 8; W. R. Mackenzie 1928 108-9; Randolph i 215-17; *Sam Henry Index* #561.

Broadsides, songsters: as in Laws.

Texts: G. Anderson 71-72; ATL 604.14 (Frank Edwards); Belden 1940 178-79 + Emrich 1974 166-67; FO 11.1.6; *JFSS 2* + Karpeles 1974 i 535 C; Karpeles 1971 179 B; Karpeles 1974 i 532-34 B; O'Shaughnessy 1968 14-15 #13; *Sam Henry* #561; Stout 47 #32; I. A. Williams 48c.

Relates texts (*The Banks of the Nile*, Laws N 9): Belden 1940 179 A, 179 B; Creighton 1962 147;(*Jack Monroe*, Laws N 7): Belden 1940 173 B, 174 C, 175 D, 176 E;

Text and tune relatives: Karpeles 1971 178-79 A.

Tune relatives: see notes to #12.

30.
The Jolly Stage Driver

Previously available: *JAF 72* 342 #2; *Neighbors 1947* 23; *YIFMC 3* 72 #7b (tune only).

Variants: ATL 625.1-.2.

Adaptations: Cazden 1958 i 100-101 + Cazden 1978 100-101.

Comment, references: Cazden 1958 i 116 + Cazden 1978 116; Doerflinger 298; Laws O 13; M. Leach 1965 103.

Broadsides, songsters: none located.

Texts: Creighton 1962-53; Doerflinger 298-99; Flanders *SR* 5.5.35; Karpeles 1971 224-25; Knox 76-77; LCJ (Crump); Leach 1965 102; Meredith 1968 188-89; E. Moore 198-99; Peacock 582-83; *Sam Henry* #620.

Text and tune relatives: ATL 603.7 (Frank Edwards).

Tune relatives: Flanders 1931 29; Flanders 1939 172; *PTFLS 6* 123.

Tune relatives in 4/4 time [* cadence points do not match #30]: Fowke 1970 136; Galvin

*34; Manny *276 + J. R. Wilson *#28; O'Neill *#169; Peacock *187, *582 A; J. R. Wilson #28a.

Tune relatives, in 6/8 condensation: Peacock 105.

Tune relatives (*The Nightingale*) [similar contour in the *b* phrase, cadence points do not match #30]: Belden 1940 241 D, 242-43 F; C. Sandburg 1927 136; Schinhan v 11-16 F13 - F17; C. J. Sharp 1932 ii 192-94, A - E.

31.
The Green Mossy Banks by the Lea

Previously available: none.
Variants: ATL 618.7-.8.
Adaptations: none.
Comment, references: *AFSPB 14* 176-77 (Laws); Laws O 15; W. R. Mackenzie 1928 135.

Broadsides, songsters: *Delaney's Irish #5* 24; *Hayland* 205; *Lover's Harmony #43* 339-40; M. Raven iii 32 (facsimile); *Shamrock Shore* 3; Wehman #924; *Wehman's Irish #1* 9-10.

Texts: Gill 1917 16-17; Hubbard 86-87; Kimball 141, listing; Purslow 1968 50; I. A. Williams 35-36.

Unrelated text (*The American Stranger*),
  Comment, references: O'Shaughnessy 1975 61 #1.
  Texts: Grainger #142; Greig *FSNE #59*; *JFSS 3* 309; **JFSS 5** 67 + Karpeles 1974 i 576 A; Karpeles 1974 i 577-78 B, C; O Lochlainn 1939 94-95; Ord 127-28; O'Shaughnessy 1975 1-2; RLP 12-656.1.7; Stokoe 170-71; Stubbs 6.

Text and tune relatives [* indicates half-tune]: Creighton 1932 167-69; Giblin 7 #12 (instrumental, 3 × 3/4 phrasing in *a–b–b–a* sequence); *JAF 22* 81; *JFSS 2* *150-51, 210; *JFSS 4* 91; *JFSS 7* 24; Karpeles 1974 i 466 B, 467 C, 468, 469 D (all in 3 × 3/4 phrasing); Leach 1965 *84; W. R. Mackenzie 1928 135-36, tune *397 #47; O Lochlainn 1965 194-95; R. Palmer 1972 38; Peacock *523, *600; C. J. Sharp *FSS* iii 34-38 + Karpeles 1974 i 464-65 A.

Tune relatives (*The Banks of the Little Eau Plaine*),
  Comment, references: FM 4052F 7 (Fowke); Laws C 2; *NEF 5* 48-49, 78; Rickaby xxiv-xxxviii, 196-98.
  Tunes with this text [* indicates half-tune]: E. C. Beck 1948 151; Bethke #22; CMS 670F.2 (Tom Glazer); Creighton 1971 135;

Fowke 1970 100 + FM 4052.1.8; *NA Ives* 1.21 + ATL 2149.3; *NA Ives* 1.61 + ATL 2181.9; *NA Ives* 1.80 + ATL 2199.5; *NA Ives* 1.111 + ATL 3118.8 (in alternating 9/8 and 12/8 phrasings); *NA Ives* 1.123 + ATL 3130.2; *NA Ives* *1.149 + ATL *3156.7; *NEF 5* 48-52 + ATL 2163.4 + *NA Ives* 1.38; Rickaby 30 B + J. R. Wilson #22b (from the singing of M. C. Dean); Rickaby 34.

Tune relatives (*Erin's Green Shores*) [* indicates half-tune]: Boette *158; Creighton 1932 171-72; Creighton 1962 164, 165; Fowke 1965 88 + INT 25014.1.1; FSI 59.1.5; Gainer 1963 *#27; Gainer 1975 *126-27; Greenleaf 248 + J. R. Wilson #22a; Hubbard 134-35; Korson 1949 45-46; E. Moore 194-95; *NA Ives* *65.9.5; Nye; O'Neill #44 (instrumental), #486 (instrumental); Peacock *362 + Wright *356; *SO 25 #4* 2; Thomas 1931 176-78; Zimmerman 180. [See also #73].

Tune relatives (Child 226, *Leezie Lindsay*),
  Comment, references: Bronson iii 365; Dick i 403 #160; G. F. Graham 1891 264-65; G. Greig 1925 164; Stenhouse 382 #434.
  Tunes with this text [all in half-tune form; ** indicates final cadence on relative major]: Bantock 1930b ii **32; Beattie **203; Botsford 1937 **102; Bronson iii 366-67 **#2, **#3, **#4, **#5; Buck 1916 **116; Child v **421 #226 H; W. Cole **178-79; Davison 1924 **136 #119; Ditson 1859 **7b; G. Greig 1925 164 + Bronson iii 367 #7 + Hendren 96; Hitchcock #403; Hopekirk **180-81; J. Johnson **#434 + Bronson iii **366 #1 + Dick i **143 + Eyre-Todd **148 + Kinsley ii **849 #565 + Lampe 1914 **110 + MacCunn **138 + MacLeod **66-68 + Pittman **152 + R. A. Smith ii **100 + Spicker **70-71; Kinley **90; MacFarren **172; *120 Scotch Songs* **97; I. Roberts **#11; *Song Purpose* **107; Stanford 1958 **92.

Tune relatives (*The Pretty Girl Milking Her Cow*),
  Comment, references: Hannegan i 22 #45; *JFSS 6* 176-83; *JIFS 25* (Bunting Collection, Part 3) 28-37; *JWFSS 2* 56; Moffat 1897 210.
  Broadsides, songsters [* includes Gaelic title and refrain]: *Delaney's Irish #1* 12; *Delaney's Irish #3* *12; *Erin-go-Bragh* 95-97; *Hyland* *29, 47-48; *My Father Sould Charcoal* 63; *Nightingale Songster* 41-42; *O'Conor* 58-59; *Rocky Road* 32; *Shamrock* 9-10; *Shamrock Shore* 3; *Singer's Journal*

#27 181; *That's the Style* 46; *Universal Irish Song Book* 45; *Walton's Treasury* *115-16 + Walton ii *109; Wehman #240; *Wehman* 617 59; *Wehman's Irish #1* 68-69; *Wehman's Irish #3* *107a; Wolf Index #1926.

Tunes with this text: Armitage 1944 228-29; Bantock 1930c ii 24-25; Breathnach i 168, *Colleen Dhas Croothe Na Mó;* Bunting 1796 25b #54, *Cailín Deas Crúidhte Na mBó* (title but no text); Bunting 1809 ii 59-61 + Bunting 1840 59-61 + Moffat 1897 240-41, *Cailin Beog Chruite Na Mbo* (in 9/8 phrasing); *Choice Irish Songs* i 104-5 (in 3 × 3/4 phrasing); *Choice Irish Songs* ii 104-5 (in 9/8 phrasing); *Diamond Songster* i 16-17, *Caleendhas Croothenamoe;* EKL 26.1.2 (Susan Reed); *Francis & Day* 1948a 21; *Good Old Songs* ii 40-41 (in 3 × 3/4 phrasing); Goodwin 1956 393a; Grainger #120 + Grainger 1921 #27 (in 3 × 3/4 phrasing); Hansen 157b; *Harding* 39 #119 (instrumental, in 2/4); Hatton 210-11; Haufrecht 1963 60; Hitchcock #305 + Hitchcock iii 178-79; B. Ives 1958 35-36; *JFSS* 6 79b-80 #27, *Cailin deas Chrúiti Na Mó; JFSS* 6 176, *Aingir Gheas Chrúiti Na Mó* (*The Pretty Milkmaid*, with Gaelic text); *JFSS* 6 204; *JIFS* 25 26-28 (texts in Gaelic and in English); *JWFSS* 2 56-57, *Colleen Dhas Cruthen Na Mol;* Kerr xi 26 #243 (instrumentsl, in 9/8); Kidson 1913 186-87; Lampe 1916 38; Leaman 59; Maitland ii 508b (Kidson) + Colles ii 736b (Kidson), *Collen dhas;* McPheeley 106-7; Meehan 100, *Cailin Deas Cruithe na mBo; Minstrel* 128-29, *Caleendhas Croothenamoe;* Munro #49, *Colleen Dhas Cruthen Na Moe* (in 9/8 phrasing); Purphy 129-30; *Musical Bouquet* #2422/3 3b-4a (instrumental); O Lochlainn 1939 114-15, *Cailín Deas Crúite Na Mbo;* O'Neill #102 (instrumental), #103 (instrumental); Page 21-22; *Piano Prize* (in 3× 3/4 phrasing), "as sung by Clara Louise Kellogg;" Roche i #40 (in 9/8 phrasing); Rooney 1918 6-7, *Cailin Deas Crúidte na mbó* (with Gaelic text); J. H. Ryan 8-9; C. Sandburg 1927 40; *Treasure Chest* 1943 25; *Trifet* 1892 108b; Wier 1918 444b + Wier 1924 146 (in 3 × 3/4 phrasing).

Tunes with parody text (*The Pretty Girl Milking Her Goat*): Korson 1938 69-70 + Korson 1949 370-71.

Tune relatives (*The Valley Lay Smiling Before Me,* by Thomas Moore)[all in 9/8 phrasing, usually marked "air: *The Pretty Girl Milking Her Cow*"]: *Choice Irish Songs* ii 22-23; *Gem Selection* 10-11; Graves 1914 19; Hatton 12-13; Hogarth ii 29-32; *Ireland's Songs* 153-54; Lampe 1955 32; T. Moore 130-31; Murphy 79-80; *Musical Bouquet* #1795; Stanford 1895 108-9; Stevenson 1859 257-62.

Tune relatives (others),
Comment, references: Greig *FSB* 164; Greig 1925 xliii-xliv.

Tunes [* indicates half-tune]: Ph. Barry 1939 54; Beethoven N^r 258 28-31 #9, "air: *The pretty girl milking the cow*," the 9/8 phrasing); Behan 1967 74; Breathnach i 166, "air: *Cailín Deaz Cruithe na mBo;*" *British Minstrelsie* iii 144-45 (in 3 × 3/4 phrasing); Cazden 1951a 37c (instrumental); Converse 1887 79c (instrumental, in 9/8); Converse 1888 48 (instrumental in 3 × 3/4); Creighton 1950 110; *Crosby* 266-67, "air: *Caleendhas Croothenamoe*" (in 9/8 phrasing); Dallas 1974 53-54; Doyle 1940 *72 + Fowke 1954 *144 + FSI *46.2.2 (Ed Trickett) + Silverman 1975 i *166a, *The Blooming Bright Star of Belle Isle;* FM *4002B.4, *Bean A'Leanna;* FO 13.1.12; Ira Ford 110c (instrumental, in 2/4); FSI *58.2.4; Gallagher #77; Giblin 9 #3, *Cailin Deas Gruite Na M Bo* (instrumental); Gleadhill 57 (in 3 × 3/4 phrasing); Hughes ii 60-63; Hughes iv 6-7; *JFSS* 2 193; *JFSS 4* 91b, *Llanarom; JFSS* 6 181-82; *JIFS* 6 23; Joyce #164; Manny 268 + J. R. Wilson #22; McPheeley 337 #967 (instrumental); *Minstrel* 128-29, "air: *Ma Caleendhas Croothee—namoe*" (in 9/8 phrasing); *Musical Bouquet* #7853, *Terence's Farewell; Musical Bouquet* #7956/7 2 #1d (instrumental); *NA Ives* *1.6 + ATL *2140.2; *NA Ives* 1.123 + ATL 3130.2; *NA Ives* *1.149 + ATL *3156.7; O'Neill #22 (instrumental); Ord *352 (in 4/4 time); Page 67; Peacock *522; Peacock *598 + Evans *37 + Fowke 1973 *112 + *SO* 7 #2 *18-19, *The Star of Belle Isle;* Petrie #1254; Rooney 1905 68; *Sam Henry* #498, "air: *Cailin deas Cruidthe na mbo;*" *Sam Henry* #654; R. A. Smith 1828a 106 (in 9/8 phrasing); *Spirit* 292, "air: *Cailín Deas Cruitead na mBó;*" Stevenson 1891 130-31 (in 3 × 3/8 phrasing).

32.
The Blind Beggar's Daughter of Bethnell Green

Previously available: none.
Variants: ATL 623.1.
Adaptations: none.
Comment, references: W. Chappell 1959 i 158-60; Dean-Smith Guide; Dixon 60; Greenleaf 71-72; *JAF 35* 357 (Tolman); *JAF 46* 51-68; Laws N 27; Leach 1965 694-95; Purslow 1972 117; Wheatley ii 171-72.
Broadsides, songsters: *Bobbing Around* 237-38; E. W. Cole 366; Davidson ii 274-75; Holloway 478-79 #293, 480-81 #294, 482-83 #295; *Jenny Lind* 129-30 + *New Book of 1000* 129-30; Rollins 26 #210, #211.
Texts [* indicates Part 2]: Bell 51-59; W. Chappell 1859 i 159 + Chilton 12-13 + Duncan 1905 248; W. Chappell 1859 i 160; Dixon 60-66, *66-71; Grover 87-88 + Emrich 1974 163-64; Hadow 15; *JAF 52* 25; *JEFDSS 6* 202-3; Karpeles 1971 188-90; Kidson 1913 28-29; Marzials 17; S. H. Nicholson 28-29 #14; Purslow 1972 6-7; Quiller-Couch 813-24; Rosenberg Index #106; C. J. Sharp 1920 ii 37-39 + Götsch 16, 73-74; Wheatley ii 172-77, *177-81.
Text and tune relatives: ATL 194.10 (Jake Loucks); Karpeles 1974 i 320 A, 322 C.
Tunes relatives: Bayard 24 + Bronson ii 441 #23, Child 93, *Lamkin;* Creighton 1971 97; Doerflinger 142, 143a; Harlow 101; P. Kennedy 1975 791; Kidson 1891 51; Manny 183; Rickaby 150 (from the singing of M. C. Dean).

33.
In Search of Silver and Gold

Previously available: none.
Variants: none.
Adaptations: none.
Comment, references: AFS L55F 6 (Stratman-Thomas); Ph. Barry 1929 145-47; Bronson i 191; Bronson ii 189-91; Child 75, *Lord Lovel;* Coffin 78-79; Cox 1925 78; Cox 1939 i 94-95 #8; A. K. Davis 1925 240-41; Dichter 1941 101; FSA 36F 3-4 (Paton); Gardner 1937 204; Howes 169-72; G. P. Jackson 1937 177-78 #163; *JAF 39* 160; Karpeles 1974 i 713-14 #7; R. Smith 1925 10, 95-96; Spaeth 1948 598; *SS 14* 46 (Gower), 160-61 (Munro); Topic 12T160F B.5 (Lloyd); ZDA 70F 4 (MacColl, Peggy Seeger).
Broadsides, songsters [* indicates comic text]: *Beadle's Half-Dime #1* 15; *Beadle's Olden Time* *13-14; *Book of 1001* iii 159-60; *Bryant* 1861 17-18; Carpenter i 112-13; Davidson #789; *Delaney #18* 26; Dichter i #858, listing of sheet music (1835); *Diprose* 1846 *175-77; Diprose 1865 *141-42; *Dixey* *10-11; *Elton* 290; *Emma Gratton* 67-68; *Formosa Songster* 67-68; *Guiding Star* 84-85; *Gus Shaw* *9; *Nelse Seymour* 29-30; *New Song Book* 20-22; *Patriotic Songster* 145-47; *Singer's Journal #4* 29; *Stonewall Song Book* 70b-71; *Street Literature* *(E. Hodges, London); *Vauxhall* i *40-41; *Wehman's Collection #10* 20.
Texts [* indicates comic text]: AFS L55F 6-8; ATL 565.4, 617.2; Beard 57-59; Bronson ii *193 #10 (Wilkinson), *195 #14 (Scarborough), *196 #16 (Wilkinson), *196-97 #17 (Arnold), *197 #18 (Davis), *198 #20 (Turner), *198 #22 (Barry), *203 #36 (Barry), *213 #61 (Cox); G. G. Carey 1971 97; Combs 1967 204 #20, listing; Gardner 1937 203-4 #5; Grainger #135, #136; LCJ *(Frank); Lee 107; Lyle 54-55; Piper (*); Rainey *14-15; *SS 14* 45-46, 159-60; Topic 12T160B.5 + Topic 12T160F B.5; ZDA 70.2.1-.2 + ZDA 70F 4-5 A, B.
Related text (*The New Ballad of Lord Lovell*),
Comment, references: Belden 1940 53-54 G; Cox 1925 78.
Texts: Belden 1940 53-54 G; Piper; ZDA 70.2.4 + ZDA 70F 5d.
Unrelated text (*Barbara Allen*, comic form): *Davidson* ix 15-16.
Text and tune relatives [* indicates comic text]: AFS L55A.3; *All Time* *58-59; ATL 189.5; Boette 11-13; *Boosey #64* *19-20; Bronson ii 191-208, Group Aa #1-#47; Child v 416 #75; Chilton *16-17, *Joe Muggins;* Chilton 146-47; *Clark's Orphean Warbler* *70-71; Collinson 1946 6-7; *Comic Songster* *62a; Converse 1863 *16-17; *D'Alcorn* i *53b; *Davidson* i *148b; *Davidson* ix *30-31; A. K. Davis 1925 573 A + Hendren 17c; A. K. Davis 1925 573-74 + Hendren 59a-c; FSA 36.1.2 (Frank Proffitt); Gainer 1975 45-46; Gleadhill *304-5; Gledhill 61-65; *Great Comic Volume* i *32a #27; Hadaway *13-14; *Howe* i *9; *Howe* 1864 *26-27; *Howe* 1874 *9a; Howes *169-70, *Joe Muggins;* Howes *170-72; Joyner 41-42; Landeck 1946 42-43; A. Lomax 1967 401 #209 + TLP 1029.1.3; *Musical Bouquet* *#789 + Flanagan *457-58 (with prose interludes); *Musical Bouquet* *#857; Oberndorfer 87b; Ogilvie *174a #196; *Penny Melodist #17;* Petrie #752;

Piper; Piper, *The New Ballad of Lord Lovell;* R. Smith 1925 97-98 A; Rosenberg T82 *3B.1; J. W. Sharp *40-41; Silverman 1975 i *221; *Song Ballads* 16-17 #10; *Song Purpose* 151b; *Songster #1* *48; J. W. Turner i *57b; Virginia Writers Project 11-14; Whitehead 16; Wilkinson *510* 34-35.

Tune relatives (Child 4, *Lady Isabel and the Elf-Knight*): Bronson i 50-54 #25, #28, #31, #32, #33, #34, #36, #37, #38, #40, #41, #42, #43, #45, #46, #47, #48, #50, #51, #52, #53, #54, #56, #59, #60.

(Child 25, *Willie's Lyke-Wake*): Greig 1925 25 + Bronson i 306 #2.

(Child 73, *Lord Thomas and Fair Eleanor*): Bronson ii 93-121 #3, #4, #5, #6, #8, #9, #10, #11, #13-#24, #27, #28, #29, #31, #32, #35-#41, #43-#58, #60-#68; Topic 12T160B.4.

Tune relatives (as instrumental dance tune): *Boosey #5* 16-17 #20, *Lord Lovell's Waltz; Boosey #6* 9a; *Boosey* xii 8c; W. Chappell 1863 27 #71; DLP 112.2.7 (Simmons Family); Howe 1864a 156f; B. Mackenzie #223; *Musical Bouquet #472* 64 #3 (quadrille); *Musical Bouquet #787/8* 5 iv; *Musical Bouquet #795/6* 2, #803/4 5a; *Musical Bouquet #897* 3 #3 (quadrille), #2581/2 4b #3 (quadrille); *Musical Treasury #1177/8* 3b (waltz).

34.
A-Walkin' and A-Talkin'

Previously available: AFS 12309A.10 + EC 329.10; *Neighbors* 1946 22.

Variants: ATL 485.1.

Adaptations: AFS 12312B.7 (De Cormier); Cazden 1958 i 30-31 + Cazden 1978 30-31; SLP 68.1.2 (De Cormier).

Comment, references: Belden 1940 473-74; *CAY 3 #12* 9-11 (E. Brown); Cazden 1958 i 107 + Cazden 1978 107; Cox 1925 425; Dean-Smith Guide, *The Cuckoo;* FSA 2F 9 (Paton); FSA 3F 16-17 (Wilgus); *JAF 30* 349-52 (Kittredge); W. R. Mackenzie 1928 137-38; Opie 1951 139 #121; Randolph i 237; Reeves 1958 98-99; *Sam Henry Index* #479; C. J. Sharp *FSS* iii 79 #72; C. J. Sharp 1932 ii 408 #140.

Broadsides, songsters (*The Unconstant Lovier,* by John H. Collins): J. Andrews + Wolf Index #2398; *Beadle's Dime #12* 39; *Frank Brower* 42; *Singer's Journal #97* 738; *Unsworth* 39-40; *Wehman's Collection #24* 22.

Texts: *All Time* 9; G. Anderson 65-66, 78; B. Arnold 45; Barrett 81 #47; Belden 1940 473-76; Belden 1952 ii 271-74; Boette 88; Botsford 1930 1; Brewster 346-47; T. Burton i 66; Butterworth 12-13; Cambiaire 37, 38, 84; Capitol P8556.2.3; G. G. Carey 1971 102a; Carmer 1942b 169; *CAY 3 #12* 7-8; Combs 1967 227 #183, listing; Copper 1973 291; Cox 1925 425-26; Creighton 1950 142; Davis Index 82-83; Davison 1924 18-19 #19; Downes 99; Eddy 159-60; *EDS 22* 41, *Brigg Fair;* J. Edwards 66; EKL 125.2.5, 125.2.6; Emrich 1974 118; FA 2454.2.3 (Pete Seeger), *The Dove;* Flanders Index 225, A - E; Ira Ford 44; FSA 2.1.5 + FSA 2F 9-10; FSA 3.2.1 + FSA 3F 17 (Edna Ritchie); FSA 33F, listing; FSI 1.2.1 + FSI 1F 10; Gordon *AM* 20.2.26; S. B. Gould 1895 2-4; S. B. Gould 1905 68-69 #33 + Buck 1933 40; S. B. Gould 1974 32-33; Grainger #19; Grover 40; M. E. Henry 255-56, 273-75; G. P. Jackson 1947 #12; *JAF 28* 159; *JAF 39* 149 + Hudson 1937 20; *JAF 45* 105-11; *JAF 52* 10-11; Jameson 1955 17, 20; Jameson 1967 47b, 64-65; *JEFDSS 6* 208; *JFSS 1* 208; *JFSS 3* 90, 223-25; *JFSS 6* 14; *JFSS 8* 16; *JIFS 4* 21, 33; J. Johnson #152; *Joyful Singing* 34; Karpeles 1934 ii 122-24 + Karpeles 1971 245; Karpeles 1973 4; Karpeles 1974 i 623-30, A - I; Kincaid i 20; R. Lloyd 1969 77; J. Lomax 1947 60-61; A. Lomax 1960 217, 218-19; Luboff 130-31, 135; Lunsford 54; McDowell 1947 101b; W. R. Mackenzie 1928 137-38; Malone 1968 55, listing; Matteson 1947 101; A. C. Morris 134-35, 364-66, 366-68; R. O. Morris 22-27; Neely 236-38; Niles 1936 16-17; Nye, *Johnnie and Mollie;* O Lochlainn 1939 150-51; Opie 1951 139 #121; P. Perkins 28; Randolph i 237-39; Reeves 1958 97-99; Reeves 1960 79-81, A - C; RG 150.1.8 (Shirley Collins); Ritchie 1963 255-56 + *Sing 8 #2* 15; Ritchie 1965a 20; E. Robinson 90-91; Rosenberg Index #258; *Sam Eskin* iv 151; Sam Henry #241, #479; C. Sandburg 1927 243-45; Scarborough 1937 274, 280, 313-14; Sedley 118-19; Peggy Seeger 1964 7; *SFQ 3* 204-5; C. J. Sharp 1932 ii 123; C. J. Sharp 1932 ii 177 + Howes 154a + Emrich 1973 534; C. J. Sharp 1961 i 24-25 + *Sam Eskin* i 123; Shearin 24; Silber 1973b 164d; Silverman 1975 i 190b-91; SLP 68J A.2; *SO 8 #1* 22-23 + *RSO #4* 42-43; *SO 15 #5* 13; *Sweet Freedom* 39 + *All Time* 9; Thomas 1931 82, 153b; Thomas 1939 32; Wilkinson i #148, #172, #232, #485; Wyman 1916 62-64; Wyman 1920 1-5; Yolen 130-31.

Unrelated text (*The Unconstant Lover*): Ord 132-33.

Text and tune relatives: ATL 487.2 (Stacy

Bozarth); Purslow 1968 32 (complete form of tune).

Tune relatives (Child 238, *Glenlogie*, all second-half tune forms matching #34): Bronson iii 414-20 #1 - #19.

Tune relatives (complete tune forms, of which #34 would constitute the second half),

(Child 46 Appendix, *The Riddle Song*): *JFSS 3* 114 (Hammond) + Bronson i 377 #3 + VRS 479.1.5 (Alfred Deller); RLP 12-814.2.4 (John Runge).

(Child 238, *Glenlogie*): R. A. Smith iv 78 + Bronson iii 421 #20 + Eyre-Todd 112 + Maver 164 #328 + Moffat 1894 239.

(Child 239, *Lord Saltoun and Auchanachie*): Christie i 10 + Bronson iii 422 (in 4/4 time).

(*Consolation New* or *Consolation B*): Hauser 1848 450b-51; G. P. Jackson 1942 143-44 #131; Rhinehart 38b-39; Walker 58; B. F. White 206; Wyeth ii 105a.

(others),

Comment, references: Bronson i 73 #83; *JFSS 3* 115 (Gilchrist, Broadwood).

Tunes: Brocklebank 12, 21; *Child's Song Book* 40; *EDS* 28 21; Howe 1864a 155i #3, *Old Song* (instrumental); *JFSS 5* 269; *JFSS 8* 11 #8; Joyce #255, #784; Karpeles 1956 44; Karpeles 1974 i 384A + *Novello* vii #1317; Karpeles 1974 i 385 B (in major); Karpeles 1975 ii 41 #36; A. L. Lloyd 1955 15; McPheeley 309 #810 (instrumental); Purslow 1965 60; C. J. Sharp 1920 i 30-31 + Götsch 28a, 91 + B. Warner 20a, 52-53.

Unrelated tunes (*Consolation*): Denson 367; G. P. Jackson 1942 146-47 #135; Jackson 1952 108 #164.

(*The Cuckoo*): Karpeles 1974 i 513 A, *High Germany* (as first half), Karpeles 1974 i 623-24 A+ B (as second half), + C. J. Sharp *FSS* iii 48-50 + Götsch 25b-26, 86-87 + Howes 154b + Karpeles 1975 i 27 #25 + *Novello* vii 19-21 #1321 + C. J. Sharp 1916 82-83 #35 + C. J. Sharp 1920 i 48-49 + C. J. Sharp *Selection* ii 28-30 + *Sing Care Away* iii 10-15 + *Sing Care Away* iv 18-19 + D. Warner 19.

35.
Friends and Neighbors

Previously available: none.
Variants: none.
Adaptations: AFS 19395.2.94 (Joe Hickerson); AFS 12312B.14 (Ben Plotkin); AFS

12312B.16 (Joan Barnhart); Cazden 1958 i 38-39 + Cazden 1978 38-39; Cazden 1963 i 19; SLP 72B.5 (Robert De Cormier).
Comment, references: Cazden 1958 i 113 + Cazden 1978 113.
Broadsides, songsters: none.
Texts: none.
Related texts: (*Farewell to Carter County*): Thomas 1964 175.
Text and tune relatives: ATL 628.3-.4 (Frank Edwards).

Tune relatives (*Nettleton*, with text, *Come, Thou Fount of Every Blessing*),
Comment, references: G. P. Jackson 1933 173-74; McCutchan 108; W. J. Reynolds 34 #313.
Tunes with this text: Alexander 1908 #144; Alexander 1918 #254; Austin 61; Bacon 1907 46; Barbour #8; Beckwith #51; Bliss 74a; Bowen #15; Bradbury 1866 357; *Broadman Hymnal* #190; Carden 72c; Chapman #163; *Christian Hymnal* #35; *Christian Worship* #111; C. H. Churchill #101; J. Clements; Cline 162 #226; R. H. Coleman 1924 #178; R. H. Coleman 1933 #247; Dadmun 19; Date #258; Dawson #338; DLP 112.1.8 (instrumental); Doane 92b; Durand 156 #386; Elderkin 1890 #200; Elderkin 1900 213 #242; *Epworth* i #165; *Epworth* iii #129; Erickson #53; *Evangelical Hymnal* #256; Excell 1889 #163; Excell 1894 #187; Excell 1912 #268; Excell 1918 #55; *Familiar Songs* #65; Gabriel #221; *Galaxy* 328c; *Gipsy Smith* 188; Goodwin 1959 62a; *Happy Voices* 66; *Heart Songs* 506a; E. A. Hoffman #88; Holbrook 333; Hustad #28; *Hymnal* #235; *Hymns & Tunes* 184 #268; *Hymns Christian Life* #160; Ch. Ives 1896 17, 21; G. P. Jackson 1937 127a #101 (from *Primitive Baptist Hymn and Tune Book*, 1902 4); *JAF* 88 273a, 273b; Kirk 160; McCaskey iii 148; McLaughlin #197; *Mennonite Hymnal* #310; *Mennonite Hymnary* #189; *Methodist Hymnal* 1905 14 #19; *Methodist Hymnal* 1939 #23; *Methodist Hymns* 1857 #238; Millard #265; Morehead 228-29; *New Baptist Hymnal* 115 #223; Ogden #225; J. W. Peterson #8; Presley #213; *Revival Echoes* #103; W. J. Reynolds 34 #313; C. H. Richards 1881 190; C. H. Richards 1883 #60; Ch. S. Robinson 328; G. C. Robinson 24; Rodeheaver 1916 #249; Rodeheaver 191- #246; Rodeheaver 1925 #285; Rodeheaver 1939 #121;

Rodeheaver 1945 87a; Rodeheaver 1956 #159; Root 242c; Rosenberg T84 16A.1; Sankey 1894 621 #633; Sankey 1911 #255; *Select Gems* 66 #70; *Seth Parker* #167; A. B. Smith #405; *Songs of Faith* #78; *Songs of Zion* #104; Sweney 1882 i 108a; *Tabernacle Hymns* iii #298; *Tabernacle Hymns* iv #251; Tourjée 161; Winsett 1908 #105; Woodbury 1856 350b.

Tune relatives (other hymns) [*indicates *b* cadence on sixth degree],

(*Female Pilgrim*): Funk 152a + Showalter 152a (from *Harmonia Sacra* of 1832 + Funk's *Christian Lyre* of 1835); Holbrook 343b; *New Sabbath* 172; Phillips i 27; Phillips ii 90-91.

(*The Good Shepherd*): Scudder 74 + *JFSS* 6 38.

(*Hallelujah*)W. J. Reynolds 35a; *Wyeth* ii*112b + *JFSS* 8*93 (from *Wyeth* 1813);

(*Know, My Soul*): Doane 182b #352;

(*Parting Friends*): Cayce #482;

(*Return Again*): Cayce *#646; McCurry *148 (from *Mercer's Cluster*, p. 389); B. F. White *335 + Cooper *335 + Denson *335.

(*Scriptures Fulfilling*): Hauser 1848 333.

Tune relatives (others):

(*The Dying Miner*): FO 21.1.8.

(*The Dying Soldier*): AFS 2331A.

(*Go Tell Aunt Rhody*): G. P. Jackson 1933 174.

(*The Grey Cock*, or *The Lover's Ghost*): *JEFDSS* 7 97 + R. V. Williams 1959 52-53.

(*Nancy of Yarmouth*): *JFSS* 6 37-38.

(*William Hall*): C. J. Sharp 1932 ii 239, 241, 242; Thomas 1931 84; Wyman 1916 100-102.

Unrelated tune (*Female Pilgrim*): G. P. Jackson 1937 208 #205.

36.
A Sport Song

Previously available: AFS 12309A.21 + EC 329.21; AFS 12309B.22 + EC 700.7; *Neighbors* 1944 24.

Variants: AFS 7763A.1.

Adaptations: none.

Comment, references: Belden 1952 iii 4-6; *JAF* 60 7-11 (Yoffie); Laws 1950 266, listing; *JFSS* 4 299-300; W. R. Mackenzie 1928 380; Randolph iii 55; Wilkinson *510* 12-13.

Broadsides, songsters: none.

Sheet music: Dichter i #391, listing.

Texts: C. S. Adams 85-86; Belden 1940 265;

Boette 35; Cobb 79-80; Creighton 1932 46-47 + Fowke 1954 154 + *Sam Eskin* i 76; Davis Index 235-36, A - G; Dorson 410-11; Dyer-Bennett 1971 138-40; Eddy 294-95 B; Emrich 1974 207; FH 5311.2.4 + FH 5311F 11 (from Woodstock, New York); Flanders Index 240 #141, 248 #194; Gardner 1939 425-27; Grover 17; *JAF 18* 55-56; *JAF 24* 342; *JAF 49* 247 #4a; LCJ (Wagner); Linscott 276-78; A. Lomax 1960 28; McIntosh 1935 180-81; E. Moore 215-17; Neal 40-41; Newell 94 #31; Piper (4) + Peterson Index 68; Pound 1922 223-24; Randolph iii 55-60; L. Ring 11; *Ring Ms.* 75-78 #29; Schinhan v 525; Shearin 29, listing; Shekerjian 148-49; Silverman 1975 i 108a; H. Thompson 1940 407-8 (from Philadelphia, New York); Wilkinson *510* 12-13.

Related text (*The Deil's Courtship*): Lyle 104-5.

Related text (*The Keys of Canterbury*): Emrich 1974 34-35; C. J. Sharp 1961 95b + Davison 1924 117-19 #105 + Farnsworth 1909 51-53 + Farnsworth 1917 52 + Götsch 55, 128-29 + Howes 153 + Karpeles 1974 i 484 A + Karpeles 1975 ii 36-37 #32 + Reeves 1958 140-43 + C. J. Sharp 1908, *The Keys of Canterbury* + C. J. Sharp 1916 148-49 #66 + C. J. Sharp *Selection* i 70-71 + C. J. Sharp 1920 ii 110-11 + *Sing Care Away* iv. 34-35 + B. Warner 36; Reeves 1960 169-70.

Related text (*The Keys of Heaven*), **Comment, references:** C. J. Sharp FSS iii 74-75 #63.

Texts and tunes: Ashbee ix 28-29; Broadwood 1893 32-33; Combs 1967 219 #143, listing; C. J. Sharp *FSS* iii 22-25 + *Novello* i 9-10 #957; Spicker 14-15; *University Songbook* 255.

Related text (*Madam, I Have Gold and Silver*), **Comment, references:** O'Shaughnessy 1968 37-38 #12.

Texts: Ashbee ix 6-7; Belden 1940 506-7; Belden 1952 23-27; Brocklebank 25; Broadwood 1893 32-33, 90-91; Butterworth 2-3; R. Chase 1956 146; Copper 1973 262-63; Emrich 1973 555-56; Emrich 1974 230-31; FH 5311.2.3 (from Ulster, New York); FL 5401A.5 + FL 5401J A.5 (Peggy Seeger); FH 5311.2.3 + FH 5311F 10; Flanders 1931 154-55; FO 17.2.6; FSA 2.2.4 + FSA 2F 17-18; FSA 11.1.5 + FSA 11F 7-8; FSA 23.1.4 + FSA 23F 13-14; Gillington 1909b 16-17; Gomme i 320-23; S. B. Gould 1905 44-45 #22; Grainger #250; Grover 18; B. Ives 1962 40-41 + B. Ives 1966 116-18; *JAF 24* 341-42; *JEFDSS 1* 133-34;

JFSS 3 267-68; *JFSS 4* 297-300; Kidson 1916 84; Knox 78-79; J. Langstaff 1969 60-62; N. Langstaff 1970 70-71; A. Lomax 1960 314; *Miramichi Ms.* 16.12b; Munch 90-93; Newell 55-56; O'Shaughnessy 1968 13 #12; Piper; Purslow 1968 71-72, 73; Randolph iii 42-43 B, 53-55; *Ring Ms.* 79 #30 (from Miss Sylvia Van Wagenen, Kerhonkson, New York); C. Sandburg 1927 144; Sedley 41; *SFQ 6* 230-31; C. J. Sharp 1902 126-27; SLP 73B.1; *Song Ballads* 19-20 #13; *Tocher #5* 166-67; Wheeler 1937 64-68.

Related text (*My Man John*),

    Comment, references: NW 239J2 1.4 (Paton); C. J. Sharp *FSS* v 84-85 #114.

    Texts and tunes: *JFSS 2* 88 + Karpeles 1974 i 481-83; NW 239.1.4; C. J. Sharp *FSS* v 32-36 + Farnsworth 1909 36-39 + Karpeles 1974 i 477-80 + Lorenz 105 #155 + C. J. Sharp 1916 150-53 #67 + C. J. Sharp 1920 ii 112-15.

Related text (*No, Sir!*, by A. M. Wakefield),

    Comment, references: *JAF 35* 406 (Kittredge).

    Texts [* indicates text of sequel, *Yes, Sir!*; ** indicates no tune given]: *American Ballad Collection* 9; G. Carey 1971 100a; *CFB #3* 10; Converse 1888 55b; Daughters 131b; *Delaney #23* **26; Emrich 1974 **203-4; FG 3507.1.2f + FG 3507F.1.2 (bawdy parody); FO 21.1.11; Fuson **81; *Gems of Minstrel Songs* i 23; *Harvest* 95-97; Ch. Kennedy 1952 315; Kincaid i 44; LCJ **(Tozier); *Monarch Collection*; E. Moore 217-18; D. H. Morrison i 53-55, *56-60; D. H. Morrison 1894 94-96; D. H. Morrison 1895 *14; Munch 93-94; *Never Grow Old* 149; Piper ** + Peterson Index **60; Reddall 326-27; Shaw; Shaw *; *University Songbook* 236-37; *Wehman's Collection #10* **28, *28, WF 17 238a; Wier 1918a 330a; Wier 1924 243b; Wier 1929 196-97; Wilkinson i #144, #115; J. E. Winner 189- *27-28, 166; S. Winner 1885 *247-28, 251-55; Wolford 73-74; Wyman 1920 101.

Related text (*Once I Loved a Charming Creature*): see notes to #171.

Related text (*A Paper of Pins*),

    Comment, references: Belden 1940 507-9; Fuld 1971 294; Hubbard 378; Leisy 1966 261; Randolph iii 40; Wilkinson *510* 9-11.

    Texts: Agay 364; *All Time* 8; ATL 191.6 (Tom Kelly); ATL 606.12; Beard 384-85; Belden 1940 507-9; Belden 1952 iii 6-9; Bertail 93; Bley 42; Bonar 109-12; Boni

1954 82-83; Brand 1961 70-71; Buford 58; Capitol P8556.1.5; *CFB #3* 12; Cumming 55; Eddy 120-25; Emrich 1973 554-55; Emrich 1974 35-37; Engel 221b; FG 3547.1.6; Flanders 1931 160-61; FSA 23.1.1 + FSA 23F 12; Fuson 82-83; Gainer 1963 #33; Gainer 1975 184-86; Glazer 112-13 + CMS 650B.4 + CMS 650F B.4; Gomme 1909 #1103 9-12; Graeme 80-81 + *Clancy* 1971 80-81; *Greenback Songster* 16-17; Hamer 1967 80; Hansen 154a; Hubbard 378-80; B. Ives 1953 40-41; *JAF 29* 198-99; *JAF 39* 180-82; *JAF 49* 260-62; *JAF 60* 7-8; *JEFDSS 9* 77-78; M. Johnson 46; Kincaid i 34 + Kincaid 1937 53b; Kolb 174-75; Landeck 1944 22; J. Langstaff 1969 18-19; N. Langstaff 1970 18-19; LCJ (Wagner); Leisy 1966 261-62; Leisy 1974 110-11 #109; McDowell 1947 71-72; McIntosh 1974 87-89; M. H. Mason 27; E. Moore 256-59; Neely 192-95, A - B; Newell 51-55; Niles 1936 10-11; Peacock 22-23 + Cass-Beggs 1975 39; Piper; Pound 1922 226-28; Raine 22; Randolph iii 41 A 43-45 C; Reeves 1960 220, 221; Richardson 52-53; L. Ring 6-7; *Ring Ms.* #24; RLP 12-634.2.1; L. Roberts 162-64; *Sam Eskin* iv 150; Scarborough 1937 299-304; *SFQ 6* 224-30; C. J. Sharp 1932 ii 386 + Virginia Writers Project 23-27; Silber 1965 28b; Silverman 1975 i 106a; *Singer's Journal #55* 407, "as sung in several of the public schools"; *Song Ballads* 59-60 #45; Stout 42; C. L. Swan 22-24; Thomas 1931 160-61; Wakefield iii 89-94; Wier 1918b 93; Whittaker 1921 95-97 #31; Wilkinson i #403, #444, #448, #470, #671; Wilkinson *510* 6-8; H. R. Wilson 28-29.

Related text (*The Spanish Lady*, or *O, No, John*),

    Comment, references: Cox 1925 465-66; Leisy 1966 246; Reeves 1958 33-35; C. J. Sharp 1916 xxxv; Topic 12T157F (Lloyd).

    Texts: Beattie 213b; Botkin 1944 804-5; Buck 1916 147; W. Cole 30-31; Eddy 222-23; *EDS 33* 131, listing; *Experimenters* 29; Farnsworth 1909 30-31 + Farnsworth 1917 66a + *Song Ballads* 17-18 #11; FP 21B.3 (Andrew Rowan Summers); Hamer 1973 58; Hansen 116b; I. Hoffman 100; *JAF 35* 405-7; *JFSS 4* 300; Karpeles 1974 i 687-93, A - C; Leisy 1966 246-47; Leisy 1974 102 #101; McCarthy 83-84 (bawdy); A. C. Morris 358-60; Purslow 1965 63; Ratcliff 62-63; Reeves 1958 162-64; Richman 77b; RLP 12-634.2.9; *Sam Henry #532*, *Tarry Trousers*; Sedley 30 (merry);

C. J. Sharp 1961 139-40 (Gardiner); C. J. Sharp *FSS iv 46-47* + *Canadian Boys* 73-75 #34 + H. W. Davies 1931 79 #69 + Davison 1924 110-11 #100 + Lorenz 104-5 #154 + *Novello* ii 46-47 #967; C. J. Sharp 1908, *O, No, John*; C. J. Sharp 1916 154-55 #68 + Götsch 57b, 131 + C. J. Sharp *Selection* i 45-47 + C. J. Sharp 1920 ii 116-17 + B. Warner 35; Shay 1961 154-55; Shekerjian 56-57; Silber 1973b 345a; *Song Purpose* 217d; Stout 44 #29; Surette 36-37 #32; Topic 12T157B.8 + Topic 12T157F B.8; *University Songbook* 236-37; VSD 57.2.6 (Paul Robeson); *Yetties* (60).

Text and tune relatives: Barbeau 21-22; Creighton 1950 199-200 + ATL 2188.2 + *NA Ives* 1.69; Eddy 293-94 A; FH 5311.2.4 (from Woodstock, New York); Gardner 1939 424-25 A; W. R. Mackenzie 1928 380, 408 #158; *NA Ives* 61.1; Newell 94-95 + Botkin 1947 897; Randolph iii 58-59; *Ring Ms.* 75-78 #29 A (from Miss Ellen Curtis, Mabbetsville, New York); Sandburg 1927 71; Vox 632.7.691B (Dyer-Bennett).

Tune relatives: none.

37.
The Bonny Boy

Previously available: none.
Variants: none.
Adaptations: none.
Comment, references: S. B. Gould 1905 28 #106; *JFSS 2* 83 (Broadwood); Reeves 1958 158; Reeves 1960 139-40; Sedley 127; C. J. Sharp 1916 xxxiii #52.
Broadsides, songsters: Cozans i 31; *Hyland* 172; *Ritson Collection: The Cabinet of Love* 6; *Street Literature* (Pitts); *Walton's Treasury* 43a + *Walton* i 163a; *Wolf Index* #177 (a broadside by Wrigley, New York); *Young Lady's Songster*.
Texts: Asch 461.1B (Dyer-Bennett); ATL 484.7; Broadwood 1893 146-47; Cambiaire 39; Eddy 212-13; Gill 1917 28-29; S. B. Gould 1892 216-17 #106 + S. B. Gould 1905 216-17 #106; Graves 1901 127-29 (adapted); *Ireland's Songs* 138-42; *JEFDSS 3* 246; *JFSS 3* 85; Karpeles 1974 i 590-92, B - D; Karpeles 1975 ii 23 #19; Kidson 1915 58b; Kidson 1926 108-9; *LCJ* (Wagner); Petrie 1855 79 + Breathnach ii 198-99 + Moffat 1897 97 + Petrie #452; Petrie #471; Purslow 1965 57; Reeves 1958 158; *Sam Henry* #215; Sedley 126-27 A; C. J. Sharp *FSS* ii 4-5 + Karpeles 1974 i 589 A + C. J. Sharp 1965 190 + C. J.

Sharp 1916 116-17 #52 + C. J. Sharp 1920 i 82-85; C. J. Sharp 1961 iv 169; C. J. Sharp 1908, *My Bonny Boy*; R. V. Williams 1959 209.

Related text (*Cupid's Trappan*),
  Comment, references: *JIFMC 3* 44-50 (Bayard); W. Chappell 1859 ii 555-57; Simpson 151-53.
  Broadsides, songsters: Holloway 49 #35; Roxburghe vii 359-60; W. Chappell 1859 ii 555a.
Related text (*The Grey Hawk*): Brocklebank 14; S. B. Gould 1892 150-51 + S. B. Gould 1905 146-47; Purslow 1965 39; Reeves 1960 139, 140; Sedley 127-28 B.
Text and tune relatives: *JFSS 2* 82-83 #1.
Tune relatives: *JFSS 1* 274; Petrie #698.

38.
I Am a Young Maiden

Previously available: AFS 12309A.22 + EC 329.22; AFS 12309B.21 + EC 700.6.
Variants: none.
Adaptations: none.
Comment, references: none.
Broadsides, songsters: *Walton 132* 82 + *Walton* ii 45.
Texts: Blondahl 119; *EDS 28* 21; *FMJ 3* 26, *Donnybrook Fair*; O'Keeffe 109; O Lochlainn 1939 92, *If I Was a Blackbird*; Reeves 1960 163 #74; *Sam Henry* #79.
Related text (*The Little Sparrow*), **Comment, references:** Belden 1940 477; Cox 1925 419; A. C. Morris 368; C. J. Sharp 1932 ii 128-36, 405 #118.
Related text (*Oh Dear, What Can the Matter Be?*),
  Comment, references: W. Chappell 1859 ii 732; Fuld 1971 398-99; C. Johnson 79; Moffat 1911 212; Opie 1951 248; H. Scott 42; Vinson 110.
Texts [* with the common tune]: *Amateur* *193; *Aquarium Songster*; Armitage 1916 *27; Ashbee x *33; Bertail *88-89; Boni 1954 *74-76; *British Minstrelsie* ii *154-55; Buck 1933 *28; Bullard *64; Callcott *17 #15 (variant text); Cazden 1958 ii *6-7 + Cazden 1973 *6-7; Cazden 22 #27; W. Chappell 1859 ii *732; *Choice Irish Songs* i *70-71; E. W. Cole 36a; Creighton 1971 *179; Daughters *207; Dearmer 1915 *34; *Diamond Songster* ii 16-17, 21-22; *Ernest Newton* *18; Ira Ford *351-52; Fortey 1905 *; *Francis & Day* v *28; Frey 194-*52b-53; Fuld 1971 *398-99; H. F. Gilbert

*13; Goss 1927 *206e; J. Gould iii *108-9; Grant-Schaefer, *sheet music (Boston, 1929); *Guiana Sings* *53a; Hansen *138a; *Heart Songs* *140; *Henderson #2* *13; Hixon 145 (Evans #25936) + Sonneck 304, listings of *sheet music (Philadelphia: Benjamin Carr, 1793); I. Hoffman *71; *Immortalia* *141-46 (bawdy parody); *JAF 28* *169; C. Johnson *79; J. Johnson *#494; N. Langstaff *22-23; Leisy 1974 *99 #97; Lorenz *22a #29; Lynn 1961 *199; McCaskey i *43b; MacMahon i *120-21; Moffat 1911 *212; Oberndorfer *40; Ogilvie *116b-17 #126; Opie 1951 *248-50 #280; Opie 1955 *187; Piper; *Pocket Song Book* *45; Raph *40-44; Ratcliff *164a; Rexford *57; *Ritson Collection: The Royal Songster, or The British Chaunter* 6; Rohrbough 1946 *16a; H. Scott *42-43; *SFQ 6* *257; Shoemaker 83b; Silber 1973 150d; Silverman 1975 i *324a; *Sing Care Away* iii *29b-33; *Singer's Companion* 117; *Singer's Journal #23* 151; *Sociability Songs* *125; *Song Ballads* *23 #16; *Song Purpose* *28; Tobitt *102; *Trifet* 1890 *209c + *Trifet* 1892 *209c; J. W. Turner *55a; Vinson *110-11; Wessels *46-47; E. L. White *125; Whitehead *12-13; Wier 1918a *363a; Wier 1918b *203b; Wilkinson *510* *132-34; Wise 94-95.

Tune relatives (*Oh Dear, What Can the Matter Be?* as instrumental dance tune): Goodwin 1955 i 144b; Guenther 12-13; E. Haywood 6 #1; Hixon 72.28a (1798), listing; Hixon 183.28-.29 + Sonneck 304 (1795), listings; *Howe* 1851a 21c; *Howe* 1851c; Howe 1864a 25g; Holyoke i 34 #17 + Hixon 91.34a (listing) + Mattson 74; Kerr i 28 *#254; Kerr iv 14 #1b; Kerr xii 12h; *Musical Bouquet #795/6* 3b (piano background); *Musical Bouquet #929/30* 3d (piano background); *Musical Bouquet #1690* (piano variations by Charles Grobe); *Musical Bouquet #4382/3* 5a (quadrille); *Musical Budget 5* 638a; *Musical Treasury #498* 200; *New Preceptor* 14c; Riley i 95 *#352; Sonneck 128, 160: listings for *The Gentleman's Amusement* (1794-96) 28-29.

Related text (tune indicated by this title): Engel 216a; *Fairburn* 1830 39 + *Fairburn* 1832 39, *The Loving Quaker*, "air: *O, dear, what can the matter be?*"

Related text (*The Wagoner's Lad*), **Comment, references:** Belden 1952 ii 275-76.

Related text (*What Can the Matter Be?* [Norah form]): Davidson i 244; *Delaney's Irish #2*

15; *Diprose* 1865 487; *Sky-Lark* 204-5; *Vocal Companion* 226-27.

Text and tune relatives: Petrie #455.

Tune relatives (*William and Diana*),

   Comment, references: *JAF 35* 419 (Kittredge); *JFSS 8* 196-98; Laws M 31A.

   Broadsides, songsters: FHE 142 (from a London broadside by Pitts, n d)

   Tunes with this text: Eddy 149-50; Gardner 1939 395-96; *JFSS 8* 146-47, 196-98.

   Texts (others): Fuson 90; Gardner 1937 209-10 + *JAF 35* 420; *NYFQ 5* 91-92; Purslow 1972 110-11.

Tune relatives (*Villikens and his Dinah*),

   Comment, references: Belden 1940 147; Belden 1952 ii 482-83; *CAY I #5* 2-14 (Shoolbraid); P. Davison 24-25; Fuld 1971 603-4; *JAF 29* 190 (Kittredge); Laws M 31B; Wilkinson *510* 78-79.

   Sheet music: *D'Alcorn* i 25 + *JFSS 8* 146-47 + Howes 168, "as sung by Sam Cowell"; Dichter i #461, Boston: Oliver Ditson, ca. 1855; London: Ascherberg, Hopwood & Crew, 185-; London: Campbell, Ransford & Co., 12th ed., 1854 (+ facsimile of title in *Victorian* 18); *Musical Bouquet #452* 71-74 + Wright 668-71, "as sung by F. Robson in *The Wandering Minstrel*" (1853); *Musical Treasury #691* (1851), "as sung by F. Robson."

   Broadsides, songsters (texts only): J. Andrews iii #1; D. E. Appleton, San Francisco: a broadside, by 1859; Ashton 1888 98-100; *Beadle's Dime #3* 24; *Beadle's Half-Dime #17* 10; *Bobbing Around* 9-10 (1851); *Camp Songs* 45-46; *Carry the News* 25; *Delaney #41* 24; *Frank Brower* 57-58; *Singer's Journal #17* 103; *Sol Smith Russell* 1876 59; *Songs of Our Land* ii 70-72; *Street Literature* (Ryle & Co.); Wehman #627; Wolf Index #2461, "sung by Charley White."

Text relative ("Dutched" version): Carpenter i 92-93; A. C. Morris 339-40; *Singer's Journal #17* 103; Stout 54-55.

Tunes with this text: Ashbee ix 72-73; *British Students* 224-25; *CAY I #5* 2-4; Chilton 6-7; Davidson #691; P. Davison 20; Dyer-Bennet 15-16 + Decca 573.24210B + DX 513.1.7 + Dyer-Bennet 1971 48-49; *Francis & Day* iv 40-41; Fuld 1971 603-4; *Great Comic Volume* i 24 #20; Hansen 194; *Henry Russell* 113-14; *Home Melodist a* 18-19 + *Home Melodist b* 18-19; Howe 1877 240a; M. Johnson 16; Kincaid iii 23; Leisy 1966 311; Levy 1971 341-42; Linscott 301-3; *NA Ives* 1.18 + ATL

2147.7; O'Neill 1913 114; *PMLA 39* 479-82
(Beckwith); Randolph i 331-32; Rosenberg
T82 3B; Schinhan iv 263-64 A, C; C. K.
Scott 28-30; H. Scott 64-65; Sedley 211-12;
Shilling Song Book i 98; Spaeth 1926 59-
60; *Trifet* 1890 146a + *Trifet* 1892 146a;
J. W. Turner 5a; *Victorian Tear-Jerkers*
16-18; Wilkinson *510* 75-76.

Tune relatives (*Sweet Betsy from Pike*),

   Comment, references: Fuld 1971 604; Laws B
   9; Leisy 1966 309 (discography); Silber
   1967 14-15.

   Text: First published in *Put's Golden Songster* (San Francisco, 1858) 50-52 + *Pacific
   Song Book* iii 13-16, with indication of
   tune as *Vilikens and His Dinah;* reprinted
   thence, with the tune, in: E. Black 10-11;
   Boni 1947 62-63; Fife 1969 48-49; Lengyel
   ii 22-22A-23; Lingenfelter 42-43; *Miner's
   Songs;* Raph 121-24; Silber 1967 16-17.

   Texts (others) [* with tune]: *Abisch; AFS
   *12310A.11 + EC *702.11 (Grant Rogers);
   AFS *19250.24 (Rogers); Agay *86-87;
   American Cowboy *74-75; Asch *74-75;
   Belden 1940 343-45; *Billy Birch* 38-39; Bot-
   kin 1944 *861-63; Brand 1961 *146-47;
   K. S. Clark 1931 *56-57; CMS 670 *D.5 +
   CMS 670F D.5; S. N. Coleman *30-31;
   Dallin *112-13; Dorson 533-35; Downes
   *156-57; Dwyer *43; Erdei *93 #130;
   FH *5337A.2 (Roger Welsch); Friedman
   *432-34; Glazer *136-37 + CMS 650 *F.2
   + CMS 650F F.2; Green 16; *Hangtown
   Ballads* 26-27; Hansen *182a; Haufrecht
   1959 *70-71; Houston *59; Hubbard *300-
   301; B. Ives 1949 *24-25; B. Ives 1953
   *234-35; M. Johnson *15-16; Kinscella
   *18; Kolb *57-59; Landeck 1946 *36-37;
   D. D. Lawrence *57-58; Leisy 1966 *309-
   11; R. Loyd *38-39; J. Lomax 1934 *424-
   26; J. Lomax 1938 *388-91 + A. Lomax
   1960 *335-36 + A. Lomax 1964 *101;
   Luther *126-27; McConathy *72-74; Matteson 1947 *88-89; Mattson *28 (instrumental); MG *20008B.6 (Earl Robinson);
   ML *54638.2.1 (Susan Reed); E. Moore
   *319-21; Okeh K3 CO *29677 + CL
   *628A.2a; Parker *28-29; P. Perkins *8-9
   (tune in *a – a – a – a* phrase form); Randolph ii *209-10; RLP *12-654.1.2; I.
   Roberts *#30; C. Sandburg 1927 *108-9;
   Shealy *76-77; Sherwin 1932 *42-44; Sherwin 1933 *42-43; Siegmeister 1944b *66-
   67; Silber 1965 *63; Silverman 1975 i *23-
   24; Thomas 1931 *123-25.

Tune relatives (others),

   Comment, references: Ph. Barry 1929 67-69;

Bayard ii 153-7; Cray 174-77; Healy 1962
48-49; *JFSS 8* 146-47 (Gilchrist).

Tunes: Abrahams 85-87; AFS 2324B; J. V.
Allen 105; H. Anderson 51, 74; ATL
182.4, 188.8, 617.4; Barbeau 33; Ph. Barry
1939 81; H. P. Beck 1973 168-69; Behan
1967 98b-99; *BFSSNE #9* 21 + Ph. Barry
1939 57; Blondahl 35, 97, 105; Boardman
6; N. Buchan 1962 38; Cass-Beggs 1963 8-
9; I. Campbell 37; *CAY 2 #3* 13; *CFB #2*
18; Chilton 23; *Clancy* 1964 29, 30; Clayre
38; M. Cohen 73; Copper 1973 292; Cray
96, 98; Creighton 1932 107; Creighton 1932
259 + J. R. Wilson #20f; Cyporyn 126;
Dallas 1974 213-14; Daughters 148; Dawney 42; Dibblee 27; DL 8246.2.4; Doerflinger 126; Doerflinger 217 + J. R. Wilson
#20b; Doyle 1940 69 + Fowke 1960 105-7
+ Fowke 1973 28-29; Doyle 1955 8, 21, 79;
Doyle 1966 49; Dykema #50; R. G. Edwards
1971 167, 186, 194, 209, 239, 278;
Flanders 1931 41; FM 4005A.3; FM
4005A.8; FM 4052.1.9; FM 4052.2.8; *FMJ
1* 330; FO 2.1.1 + Fowke 1970 168; FO
2.1.8; *Folk Song Album* 24-25; Fowke
1954 28, 138; Fowke 1954 180 + Fowke
1972 122; Fowke 1961 162; Fowke 1965 46;
Fowke 1967 72 + Fowke 1970 61; Fowke
1967 156; Fowke 1970 84, 203; Fowke 1973
7, 37; *Francis & Day #1* 6-8; FSA 15.1.10;
FSA 23.1.7; FSC 9.1.2; Galvin 63; Gardner 1937 214-16; Gardner 1939 235, 301,
441; Glazer 1970 132-33; Goodwin 1956
215a; S. B. Gould 1905 80 #40; Graeme
38-39 + *Clancy* 1971 38-39; Graeme 102-3
+ *Clancy* 1971 102-3; Graeme 148-49;
Grainger #44, #280, #282; Greenleaf 127;
Greenleaf 240 + J. R. Wilson #20g;
Greenleaf 327 + J. R. Wilson #20h; G.
Greig 1925 14; Hamer 1967 34; Hamer
1973 77; Harlow 101; Healy 1962 49a, 49b,
49c; Healy 1965 62; Healy 1969 iii 19d;
Hubbard 331; Hugill 421, 462, 466 A, 469
B; Huntington 129; B. Ives 1957 36-37; B.
Ives 1958 60-61; Edw. Ives 1964 35-36;
JAF 18 294 + Ph. Barry 1929 284 D; *JAF
52* 65; *JAF 74* 226; *JFSS 1* 17, 114, 172;
JFSS 3 206-13; *JFSS 6* 267 #55; *JIFS 8* 18;
Joyce #387, #526; P. Kennedy 1975 314,
702; Kincaid 1937 16; Korson 1938 48;
Korson 1938 122 + Botkin 1944 869 +
Korson 1949 454-55 + J. R. Wilson #20j;
Lahey 88, 95; Lingenfelter 210, 332; Long
83, 139, 143; Lynn 114; McCarthy 41;
MacColl 1954 25, 30; W. R. Mackenzie
1928 397 #54; Manny 66 + J. R. Wilson
#20a; Manny 156, 185; *Many Nations* 14;

Miramichi Ms. 15.7, 17.21; A. C. Morris
55, 448; Morton 1970 73 + IRL 12A.2;
Morton 1973 103 #8, 152; *Musical Treasury* #783/4 7b; *NA Ives* 1.22 + ATL
2149.6, 2149.7, 2149.8, 2149.10, 2150.1;
NA Ives 1.33 + ATL 2158.3; *NA Ives* 1.75
+ ATL 2194.1; *NA Ives* 1.80 + ATL
2199.4; *NA Ives 1.85 + ATL 2204.4; NA
Ives* 1.93 + ATL 3100.2c; *NA Ives* 1.94 +
ATL 3101.3; *NA Ives* 1.103 + ATL
3110.3; *NA Ives* 1.108 + ATL 3115.5; *NA
Ives* 1.121 + ATL 3128.3; *NA Ives* 1.150
+ ATL 3157.5; *NA Ives* 61.2, *Chapeau
Boys; NA Ives* 68.4.2.7; *NEF 7* 27, 29-30;
NEF 8 27 + NW 239.2.3; Oberndorfer 88;
O'Donnell 10-11; O'Keefe 48, 61; O Loch-
lainn 1939 2; O'Neill #234; *Orange Stan-
dard* 13; R. Palmer 1974 53; Peacock 98,
118, 123, 443, 594; Petrie #194; *PSB 3*
#258; *PTFLS 6* 158; QC 903.1.8; Ran-
dolph i 270; J. Raven 1971 10; Rickaby 150
+ J. R. Wilson #20k; Ritchie 1965b 58-59;
RLP 12-602.2.1; RLP 12-656.1.6; *Sam
Henry* #161, #620, #783; Sampson 6-7;
C. Sandburg 1950 33-34; H. Sandburg 112;
Scammell 120; Schinhan iv 167 C, 196 F;
Peggy Seeger 1970 37 #21; Pete Seeger
1972 228-29; Silber 1973a 84, 89, 152; Silverman 1966 70; Silverman 1975 i 392;
L. A. Smith 119a; *SO 7 #1* 4; *SO 7 #2* 24-
25; *SO 12 #3* 24; *So 16 #5* 18; Stubbs 31;
Sturgis 26-29; Thurman 13; Topic
12T158A.9; Topic 12T198B.6a; Wheeler
1937 75-80; J. R. Wilson #20; WLP
731.1.6; *Yetties* 66; ZDA 74.2.11, Child
170, *The Death of Queen Jane* (in – – *b – a*
form).
Tune relatives (stretched tune form, with normal form as refrain): *NEF 8* 38-39, *The Bold,
Undaunted Irishman.*
Tune relatives (compressed or condensed form)
[* in 2/4 time]: Collinson 1952 30-34 (in 3/2
time); Fowke 1970 *203; FSA *33.2.4; FSC
9.1.1 (in 4/4 time); Joyce *#300; Kidson
1891 *100; Korson 1938 *364; Larkin *116-
18; A. C. Morris *98.
Tune relatives (as instrumental dance tune,
usually identified by *Villikens* title): Boosey
1862a 4 #14; *Boosey #6* 9b; Howe 1858 84b;
Howe 1859 15b; Howe 1864a 12g; Kerr xii
15e; B. Mackenzie #123; *Musical Bouquet
#462* 21-24 (polka); *Musical Bouquet #472*
66c (in 2/4); *Musical Bouquet #508* 11-14
(waltz, galop); *Musical Bouquet #610* 2b;
Musical Bouquet #897 3 #4 (quadrille); *Musical Bouquet* #1689; *Musical Bouquet*
#2581/2 2b #1 (quadrille); *Musical Treasury*

#705 *[1851]; Musical Treasury* #809/10 4b;
Musical Treasury #831/2 5c-6; *Musical
Treasury* #889/90 6b; *Musical Treasury*
#893/4 2b.
Tune relatives (in 4/4 time),
Comment, references: Ph. Barry 1929 67-69;
BFSSNE #12 2-6 (Barry); C. J. Sharp *FSS*
i 70 #26.
Tunes: Bayard ii 157.8 and 157.9; Bronson i
131 #7; M. H. Mason 24-25 + Bronson i
378 #4.

39.
The Girl I Left Behind

Previously available: none.
Variants: ATL 185.8.
Adaptations: none.
Comment, references: Belden 1952 ii 378-85;
Cox 1925 300; Laws P 1A, 1B; Randolph i
283; *Sam Henry Index* #188.
Broadsides, songsters: *Forget-Me-Not* 220-21
+ *Jenny Lind* 220-21 + *New Book of 1000*
220-21.
Texts: G. Anderson 129-30; ATL 628.6, 628.8;
Belden 1952 ii 378-85; Combs 1967 214 #111,
listing; Davis Index 127-28; Dean 10; G.
Greig *FSNE #83; Grover 41; JAF 48* 351,
listing; *JIFS 19* 66 + Wright 375-76; Ken-
tucky 1938 30; LCJ (Combs); M. Leach 1965
322; McDowell 1937 33-34; Manny 241-42 +
NA Ives 61.4; *MF 13* 148, listing; *Miramichi
Ms.* 15.18; Munch 85-88; *NA Ives* 1.43 +
ATL 2168.1; *NA Ives* 1.51 + ATL 2175.4;
NA Ives 1.97 + ATL 3104.1; O'Keeffe 101;
Ord 45-47; Peacock 449; Piper + Peterson
Index 36; Rainey 32-33; Rosenberg Index
#981; Sam Eskin iv 89; Sam Henry #188;
Schinhan iv 213-14; C. J. Sharp 1932 ii 62-65;
Stekert 1969 N 10; Wilkinson i #110.
Related text (*The Girl I Left Behind Me*),
Comment, references: W. Chappell 1840 i
134-35 #172; W. Chappell 1859 ii 708-11;
Fuld 1971 242-44; H. Johnson 503b; Lins-
cott 79; Moffat 1911 339b.
Broadsides, songsters: *American Songster*
1835 46-47; *Beadle's Half-Dime #39* 1;
Wehman *617* 113; Wolf Index #747, #748.
Texts [* indicates with the common tune,
Brighton's Camp]: Agay *31; Ashbee ix
*62-63; Bacon 1910 *35-37; Bantock 1930c
i *20-21; Beattie *221c; *British Minstrelsie*
iv *50-51; Buck 1916 *82-83; Bunting 1840
*43a #57; *Camp Songs* *11; W. Chappell
1840 ii *85b #172; W. Chappell 1859 ii 708-
11 + *Canadian Boys* *246-47 #149;

Choice Irish Songs ii *96-97; Colum *604; Dallas 1973 *48-49; Dallin *76; Daughters *62; Dolph *507-9; Duncan 1905 *260; J. Farmer *146-47; *Francis & Day* ii *25; Fuld 1971 242-43; Gainer 1963 *#45; Gainer 1975 *173-74; *Gem Selection* *79-80; Goodwin 1956 *479a; Goss 1927 *69; S. B. Gould iv *26-27; Graves 1906 *140-41; Hansen *66b; Hatton *156-57; Hatton i *101; Haynes i *130-31; *Heart Songs* *66-67; Howe 1874 *167c; Howe 1880 *167b; Humphreys *61-62; B. Ives 1958 *92-93; C. Johnson *17; H. Johnson *503-4; Kidson 1913 *86-87; Leaman *57b; McCaskey ii *139; MacMahon ii *60-61 #29; Macmillan *93-94; McPheeley 110-11; Marzials *36; Moffat 1897 *14-15; Moffat 1911 *104; Murphy *44-45; Mursell *38-39; *Musical Bouquet* *#652; *Musical Budget 4* *510-11; *Musical Treasury* #780 *4; *Never Grow Old* *134; S. H. Nicholson 150-51 #77; Noble 1908 *72; Oberndorfer *110-11; Ogilvie *163b #180; *Pacific* ii 38; Page *12-13; *Penny Melodist #4* *; Piper (4) + Peterson Index 36; Raph *26-28; Ratcliff *65b; Reddal *93; Richman *33a; Rooney 1905 *64-65; H. Scott *8-9; C. J. Sharp 1902 #13 *28-29; *Sing Care Away* ii *7; *Sing Care Away* iii *24-29; *Song Purpose* *225c; *Songs Forever* *37-38; Spaeth 1926 *16-17; Spicker *48-49; Stanford 1906a *132-33; Stout 48; Wier 1915 *57b; Wier 1918a *164b.

Tune relative (*Brighton Camp* as instrumental dance tune), **Comment, references:** *EDS* 27 159; Wilkinson *510* 16.

Tunes (commonly identified as *The Girl I Left Behind Me*, as instrumental dance tune): AFS L9B.1; *Arkansas Woodchopper* 1940 52; *Boosey* 1862a 40 #128; Bowers 18; Cazden 1955 14; Chicago Park District 19, 45, 60; FA 2164B.1; Flanders Index 233 #17; Gott 12 #3, 38b; Hadow 118a; *Handy* 1955 64; E. Haywood 35 #7; Howe 1858 10c; Howe 1864a 51i, 61-62 #2; Jarman 7; Karpeles 1951 31b, 55b; P. Kennedy 1951 27 #55; Kerr x 41 #366; Kerr xii 21b; Knorr 12b; Leifer 110; B. Mackenzie #44; Mattson 35; Mayo 98 #3; Muller 32; *Musical Bouquet* #2024/5 5 #4a; *Musical Bouquet* #5367/8 3a; *Musical Bouquet* #7723/4 3 #2; *Musical Treasury* #18/9 75; *Musical Treasury* #22 88b; *Musical Treasury* #831/2 6b-7; *Musical Treasury* #893/4 6b; *Musical Treasury* #929/30 2b (as piano background); O'Neill #299; O'Neill 1907 167 #972;

Price 34; Putney 52; Riley i 95 #349; Rohrbough 1931b 7; Rohrbough 1941 13; Ruth 2c; Ryan 1939 53; F. H. Smith 1955 75; Wilkinson ii #95, #101, #142, #167, #175, #181.

Tunes (*Brighton Camp*, or *The Girl I Left Behind Me*, as tune for Child 20, *The Cruel Mother*): ATL 193.9 ("Dick" Edwards); ATL 618.15 (Frank Edwards).

Tunes (*Brighton Camp*, or *The Girl I Left Behind Me*, for other texts): Behan 1965 11; Behan 1967 112; Blondahl 73; Boardman 19; Breathnach iii 158; Bronson iv 57 #15, 276 #35; *CAY 4* 197; *Child's Song Book* 26; Colum 604 + *CAY 2 #3* 4; Cray 36; Denson 406, *New Harmony* (second half derived); Doyle 1955 52 + Doyle 1966 44; Durlacher 56; R. G. Edwards 1971 164; *Father Kemp* 82; Fife 1969 170; *FMJ 3* 12; Gallagher #75; Garson 112-13; Graeme 176-77; Graves 1914 68 #47; *Handy* 1940 78; Hatton 26-27; Houston 73; *Immortalia* 155-56; *JAF 33* 99-100; *JAF 42* 231; *Jolly Songster* 84; Lampe 1916 96; McIntosh 1941 3, 11; T. Moore 2; Mursell 39; *Musical Treasury* #45, #476; R. Palmer 1974 158; Pittman 9; M. Raven iii 10; RLP 12-631.2.1; C. J. Sharp 1932 ii 363; Silber 1973a 127; R. A. Smith 1828a 74a; Stanford 1906a 133; Stanford 1958 135; Wellman 12; Wier 1924 173b; Wise 79; Wolford 46; Work 172, *Religion is a Fortune*.

Related text (*The Rambling Cowboy*): J. V. Allen 133-34; *American Cowboy* 78-79; K. S. Clark 1932 36; J. Cohen 54; FH 5723C.6 + FH 5723F C.6; Emrich 1974 140-41; A. Lomax 1960 318-19; E. Moore 202-5; Ohrlin 200-201; *SO 20 #1* 15 + Silverman 1975 i 54a; *World's Best* 78.

Unrelated text (*The Girl I Left Behind*): AFS 10505B #35 (Frank Joy).

Text and tune relatives: ATL 618.11 (Frank Edwards); ATL 622.2 (Reuben Edwards); T. Burton i 59-60; *JIFS 19* 46-47; Ord 45-47 (fairly distant).

Tune relatives: see notes to #12.

40.
Petticoat Lane

Previously available: *Neighbors* 1942 25.

Variants: AFS 7755B; ATL 614.13.

Adaptations: Cazden 2958 i 98-99 + Cazden 1978 98-99; Haufrecht 1943 10-11; Haufrecht 1965 i 12-17.

Comment, references: Bronson i 9-10; Cazden

1958 i 119-20 + Cazden 1978 119-20; Child 2;
Coffin 30-31 #2; Flanders 1939 8-11; Friedman xxiii; FSA 15F 9-10 (McElligott); FSA
33F 16-17 (Goldstein); Hendren 107-8;
Jaehde 35-36; *JFSS 3* 12-16 (Broadwood);
JFSS 8 237-50 (Gilchrist); P. Kennedy 1975
656 #300; Opie 1951 108-11 #86; O'Shaughnessy 1971 30-31; RLP 12-627F 4 (Goldstein); C. J. Sharp *FSS* iii 75 #64; Topic
12T160F A.1 (Lloyd); ZDA 67F (MacColl,
Peggy Seeger).

Broadsides, songsters: *Book of 1000* 140; Ph.
Barry 1929 5-8 (a Boston broadside, ca.
1836-37).

Texts: Ashbee x 42-43; ATL 563.11, 565.2;
Barbeau 33; Boni 1947 26-27; G. G. Carey
1971 93; R. Chase 1938 18-19; A. K. Davis
1960 10-13; J. Edwards 58; *Elmore Vincent*
19; Flanders *SR* 7.4.35; F-LFR 100B.8;
Fowke 1954 138; *Francis & Day* 1967 29a;
FSA 15.1.5 + FSA 15F 10; FSA 33.1.5 +
FSA 33F 17-18; Gainer 1975 4-5; Gordon *AM*
15.9.27; F. Graham 1971 29b-30; HTA (2);
G. P. Jackson 1947 #9; *JEFDSS 8* 26; Karpeles 1975 i 14 #12; LCJ (from Albany, New
York); Leisy 1966 51; *MF 13* 141-44; E.
Moore 6-10; *NA Ives* 62.2, *Scarborough
Fair*; *NEF 7* 88-89; Okun 1968 223-24; O
Lochlainn 1965 196; Opie 1951 108-11 #86,
165 #158; Quiller-Couch 43-45; L. Ring 12-13; RLP 12-627.1.4 + RLP 12-627F 4; RLP
12-634.1.4; Peggy Seeger 1960 26; Silverman
1975 i 187b; *SO 12 #5* 27 + *RSO #6* 36; *SO
20 #6* 18a; Topic 12T160A.1b + Topic
12T160F A.1; Whittaker 1921 104-5 #35;
ZDA 67.1.3-.7 + ZDA 67F 3-4, A-D.

Related texts (without the two lovers): Dearmer
1915 33a; *EDS 30* 58; Hamer 1973 27; *JFSS 2*
212-13; *JFSS 3* 274-75; P. Kennedy 1975 656
#300; O'Shaughnessy 1971 1; Reeves 1960
243; C. J. Sharp 1961 iv 119-21 (Gardiner);
Topic 12T160A.1a; C. Wells 71-72; A. Williams 221-22; ZDA 67.1.8 + ZDA 67F 4 F.

Unrelated texts (*Petticoat Lane*): *Delaney's Irish #2* 12; *Faugh-a-Ballagh* 111-13; *Frisky
Irish* 34; *Street Literature* (London: E.
Hodges); *Wehman's Irish #2* 99-100.

Text and tune relatives: ATL 193.11 (Charles
Hinckley); ATL 601.9, 605.4 (James Edwards); ATL 617.1 (Minnie Ward); ATL
628.14 (Reuben Edwards); Ph. Barry 1929 10
+ Bronson i 29 #23 + *JAF 30* 284-85; Flanders 1934 58-59 + Bronson i 28 #45.

Text and tune relatives (with some similarity in
tune contour): Bronson i 19-21 #24, #26,
#27; Schinhan iv 3-4 B + Bronson i 27 #41.

Tune relatives: none.

41.
My Love Is Like a Dewdrop

Previously available: *Neighbors* 1945 22.
Variants: AFS 12312A.15.
Adaptations: Cazden 1958 i 84-85 + Cazden
1978 84-85; Philo 1001B.2 (Margaret MacArthur); SLP 72A.2 (Louise De Cormier).
Comment, references: Cazden 1958 i 118 +
Cazden 1978 118; W. Chappell 1859 ii 734;
JEFDSS 3 253; Karpeles 1974 ii 22; Purslow
1972 124; Randolph iv 236 #751.
Broadsides, songsters: Catnach (reference in
S. B. Gould 1895 97); *Lover's Harmony #23*
183.
Texts: Belden 1940 491-93 + G. P. Jackson
1947 #7; Brune 12-12; G. G. Carey 1971 98b;
Combs 1925 168-69; FHE 170, *Adieu Unto
Cold Winter;* Flanders Index 225, listing;
FSS 49F 17; Gardner 1939 130, 131; S. B.
Gould 1895 96-97, *Farewell He!* HFB 4 27,
listing (Brewster); *JAF 46* 35-36 (Carter);
JAF 52 44 #46 (Treat); *JEFDSS 3* 253;
McDowell 1947 121; Neal 149; Piper (3);
Randolph iv 237 A, 239 D, 240 E, 240-41 F;
Reeves 1960 108-9 #40; *Ring Ms.* 48 #16 +
JAF 66 53-54 #11; *Sam Henry* #479, #504;
Walton's Treasury 7 + Walton i 39, *Let Him
Go, Let Him Tarry.*
Related texts: FHE 70, *Cheer Up, My Heart;*
Kidson 1929 62-63, *Let Him Go.*
Text and tune relatives: Brocklebank 16; FSS
49.2.6 + *SO 24 #4* 24 (Jean Redpath); Purslow 1972 32; Randolph iv 238 B, 239 C, 241-42 G; *Yetties* 57, *Farewell She!*
Tune relatives (*Harry Bail*),
  Comment, references: Fowke 1970 117;
  Laws C 13.
  Tunes with this text: E. C. Beck 1948 219;
  E. C. Beck 1956 142; Fowke 1970 117;
  Gardner 1939 278; Manny 261; *Miramichi
  Ms.* 17.7; *NA Ives* 1.51 + ATL 2175.3;
  NA Ives 62.5.
Tune relatives (*The Manchester Angel*): W.
Chappell 1859 i 734 + J. R. Wilson #25d;
Dallas 1973 71; Topic 12T 147.2.6.
Tune relatives (*Mary Mahoney*): Manny 137 +
J. R. Wilson #25; *NA Ives* 62.5 + Edw. Ives
1964 65.
Tune relatives (*The Winter of '73*): Manny 191;
NA Ives 1.24 + *ATL* 2151.6; *NA Ives* 1.26 +
ATL 2152.3; *NA Ives* 1.42 + ATL 2167.1 +
Edw. Ives 1964 54-55.
Tune relatives (*Zebra Dun*),
  Comment, references: Laws B 16; Ohrlin 54-55.
  Tunes with this text: J. V. Allen 165-68;
  American Cowboy 46-47; Dallin 70; Fife

1969 194; Houston 86; Landeck 1946 40; Larkin 50-51 + Felton 30-31 + Lingenfelter 402; Loesser 202-3; J. Lomax 1938 78-79; ML 54368.2.5 (Susan Reed); Muller 11 (instrumental); Ohrlin 55-57; Sackett 38; Silber 1967 263; Thorp i 144-45; J. White; J. I. White 149-50.

Tune relatives (others) [*tune marked "air: *The Manchester Angel*]: *AT #19* 22, *The Swagman's Dream*; ATL 168.1 #1a; ATL 182.7; Bayard ii 155.1, 155.3, *The Bagaduce*; Behan 1965 91; Bethke #2, *Lasca*; Bethke #47 (Laws J 12); Bronson iv 226 #37, Child 279, *The Jolly Beggar* (in *a – b – a* form); Bronson iv 405 #7, Child 295, *The Brown Girl*; Brune 21; Chilton 63; Christie ii *240; Colum 612; Cox 1939 ii 65, *Joe Bowers*; Crawhall 1965 *34 + F. Graham *15; Creighton 1950 141; Creighton 1971 43, *The Roving Journeyman*; Dallas 1974 207-8; Dibblee 52; Downes 113 (reduction to ¾ time); Dubliners iii 4-5; R. G. Edwards 1972 21, 93; Flanders 1937 14; Flanders 1939 238; R. Ford 1904 78-79; Galvin 45; Gardner 1939 298, 411; Gledhill 75-77; Graeme 26-27 + Clancy 1971 26-27; Grainger 274, #275, #276, #277; *Heart Songs* 408, *Michael Roy* (*b* phrase similar); INT 25014.1.11; B. Ives 1958 44-45; Edw. Ives 1971 221-22; *JFSS 3* 186-87; *JFSS 7* 54 #3; *JIFS 1* 6b; Joyce #55, *The Pretty Girls of Abbeyfeale*; Joyce #153 + Bronson iv 405 #6, Child 295, *The Brown Girl*; Karpeles 1974 i 511 C, 651 A; Karpeles 1974 ii 22, 573a C; Karpeles 1975 ii 75 #70; Kemp 42-43; Kidson 1935 *84-85; Knox 43; Korson 1938 189 + LeMon 33-35 + A. Lomax 1960 130, *The Avondale Mine Disaster*; Leisy 1966 188; Lingenfelter 340; A. L. Lloyd 1952 78, 129; A. L. Lloyd 1967 360; W. R. Mackenzie 1928 403 #113 + J. R. Wilson #25a; Manifold 52; Manny 120 + ATL 2173.1 + *NA Ives* 1.48; Manny 187 + NA Ives 61.2, *A Winter on Renous*; Miramichi Ms. 17.12, 17.14; A. W. Moore 234-35; Morton 1970 17; *NA Ives* 1.12 + ATL 2144.3 + Edw. Ives 1964 96, 174; *NA Ives* 1.57 + ATL 2180.3; *NA Ives* 1.83 + ATL 2202.3; *NA Ives* 1.84 + ATL 2203.4; *NA Ives* 1.93 + ATL 3100.1; *NA Ives* 1.112 + ATL 3119.1; *NA Ives* 1.127 + ATL 3134.1; *NA Ives* 1.128 + ATL 3135.2; *NA Ives* 66.1.1, 66.9.1; O'Donnell 37; O Lochlainn 1939 38; Peacock 159, 354, 897; Piper, *The State of Arkansas*; Polwarth 1966 4; Randolph iv 40; Rickaby 173 (from the singing of M. C. Dean); *Sam Eskin* iv 89; *Sam Henry* #688, #730, #749; Schinhan iv 160, 313; Sedley *222 (dated 1888); *SFQ 5*

139; Silverman 1975 ii 418-19; L. A. Smith 110; Stokoe 162; Thomas 1964 92-94 + J. R. Wilson #25c; J. J. Ward 2; Wilkinson *128* 16b; Wright 224, *John Mitchel;* [See also notes to #42.]

Unrelated tune (*The Fit Comes on Me Now*): W. Chappell 1859 i 176; Simpson 218.

42.
My Good-Looking Man

Previously available: AFS 12309B.23 + EC 700.8.

Variants: none.

Adaptations: FH 5311.1.1 (Barbara Moncure).

Comment, references: Gardner 1939 439; M. Leach 1965 97.

Broadsides, songsters: O'Conor 7; *Singer's Journal #8* 62 + Wolf Index #1503, with indication "air: *Roving Journeyman*"; Wehman #702; Wehman ii 11-12; *Wehman's Irish #2* 80.

Texts: *Dessa Manion* EE 403; FH 5311F 1.1; FO 16.2.14; Gardner 1939 439-40 (from *Detroit News,* 29.4.34); Peacock 302.

Text and tune relatives: M. Leach 1965 96-97; Wilkinson i #637 (tune and title only).

Tune relatives: see notes to #41.

43.
The Jacket So Blue

Previously available: none.

Variants: ATL 183.8.

Adaptations: AFS12312B.4; Cazden 1958 i 76-77 + Cazden 1978 76-77.

Comment, references: Cazden 1958 i 114-15 + Cazden 1978 114-15; R. Ford 1904 214.

Broadsides, songsters: *American Comic Songster* 65-66, *The Bonny Sailor Lad*; a broadside, Boston, 1806 (ref. in Gray 111).

Texts: H. P. Beck 1957 217-18; Belden 1940 301, *The Wagoner*; *CFMJ 3* 28, listing; Creighton 1950 97-100; FHE 428b; Flanders *SR* 5.8.34; FM4006B.24 + FM 4006F 24; R. Ford 1904 212-13; Gray 111-14; G. Greig *FSNE* 105; Grover 57-58; Huntington 276-77; *JFSS 8* 191-92; Karpeles 1974 ii 556-57; Kidson 1891 118-19; Kidson 1927 50-51; *MF 13* 150, listing (2); E. Moore 252-53; *NA Ives* 1.5 + ATL 2139.7; Ord 295-96; *Sam Henry* #644.

Unrelated text (*The Jackets of Blue*, by Alfred Lee): Diprose 1865 160.

Text and tune relatives: ATL 628.12 (Reuben Edwards).

Tune relatives: AFS L61B.8; ATL 182.2, 182.8; Creighton 1950 150, 183; FO 4.2.1, 4.2.2; FSC 10.2.7; FSS 34.2.2; Grover 101; *JFSS 2* 158; Karpeles 1971 83 C, 83D; M. Leach 1965 312; *Miramichi Ms.* 17.16; *NA Ives* 1.12 + ATL 2144.3 + Edw. Ives 1964 96; RG 150.2.6, *Pretty Saro* (Shirley Collins); Wilkinson i #507.
[See also notes to #59, #72].

44.
Fare You Well, My Own True Love

Previously available: *Neighbors* 1948 25.
Variants: AFS 12309A.3 + EC 329.3; ATL 617.8, 625.12.
Adaptations: AFS 12312A.6; Cazden 1958 i 49 + Cazden 1978 49.
Comment, references: Belden 1940 480, 484-85; Cazden 1958 i 112-13 + Cazden 1978 112-13; Cox 1925 87, 413-14; FSA 3F 19-20 (Wilgus); *JAF 30* 304-5 (Kittredge); *JFSS 3* 86-89 (Broadwood); *JFSS 4* 288; A. C. Morris 279; Reeves 1960 214; C. J. Sharp 1932 ii 405 #114.
Broadsides, songsters (*The Unkind Parents*): Roxburghe vii 522 #33, Part 12; notes in Simpson 498, tune in Simpson 496 #314.
(*The True Lover's Farewell*): Ritson Collection: *The New Sadler's Wells Concerts* 4-5.
(*My Own True Love*) 7: *Wehman's Collection #24* 21.
Texts: G. Anderson 30-32; Belden 1952 ii 425-26; Belden 1952 iii 299-304; Boette 67; Brewster 92-96, 348-49; Browne 175; T. Burton i 106-7; Capitol T-700.1.6; L. Chappell 128-29; Combs 1967 227 #189, listing; Davis Index 97-98 (3); Downes 188-89; *Elmore Vincent* 112; Emrich 1973 545-46; *Folk Singers* 26-27; FSA 3.2.4 + FSA 3F 20-21; Fuson 112; Gainer 1975 131-32; M. E. Henry 68, 207, 265; Houston 41; Hudson 1936 170; *JAF 39* 146-49; *JAF 45* 74-78; *JFSS 4* 289-90; *JFSS 5* 174-75; Kentucky 1938 Part 5; Kentucky 1939 i 27, 34; Kincaid ii 24-25; J. Lomax 1941 140-41; McDowell 1947 25-27; A. C. Morris 278-79, 349-50; Randolph iv 265-66; Reeves 1960 213-14; C. Sandburg 1927 3-7, 98-99, 126; H. Sandburg 97-98; Scarborough 1937 315-16; Schinhan v 181-83 #258 B, D, E; Sedley 129-30 A; C. J. Sharp 1932 i 196-98; C. J. Sharp 1932 ii 53, 113-18; C. J. Sharp *Selection* ii 72-73; C. J. Sharp 1920 i 92; C. J. Sharp 1961 i 34-35 (Ham-

mond); Silber 1973b 153c; R. Smith 1928 143; Thomas 1939 34-35; VRS 9078.1.3; E. K. Wells 119-20; I. A. Williams 49b; Wilkinson i #388, #425, #491, #605, #606, #618.
Related text (*My Luve Is Like a Red, Red Rose*, by Robert Burns),
  Comment, references: Dick i 403-4 #152; G. F. Graham ii 29; *JFSS 3* 88-89 (Broadwood); Kinsley iii 1454-56 #453; Stenhouse 362, #402, #403.
  Texts: *American Singer* 59-60; Ashbee ix 40; Bantock 1930b i 6-7; *Beadle's Half-Dime #31* 13 (adaptation); *Beauties of Caledonia* 42-43; Beeton 1865 21, 137 #25; Berggreen 140-41 #91; *Bingley* i 22; *Book of Popular Songs* 187a; *British Minstrelsie* i 147-49; C. Brown 126-27; *Delaney's Scotch #1* 5; Diack ii 102-3; Dick i 137; Ditson 1859 30b-31 + *Gems of Scottish Songs* 30b-31; *Eolian* 13; *Fairburn 1830* 203 + *Fairburn 1832* 203; *Formosa Songster* 90 (adaptation); *Francis & Day* vi 23; *Francis & Day* 1948b 23; Fulcher 173-75; Gleadhill 19; Goodwin 1956 362a; Goss 1927 124; G. F. Graham ii 28-29; J. Greig i 66-68; W. Hamilton 10-11; Hansen 129; Hopekirk 110-12; J. Johnson #402; J. Johnson #403 + *JFSS 3* 88, "old set"; Kinsley ii 734-35 #453; Lampe 1914 62; Lupton 34; *Lyric Gems* 74-75; *Lyric Gems* i 126; McCaskey ii 174; MacCunn 118-19; MacFarren 88-89; Maver 217b #434; Maxfield 96; *Minstrel* 52-53; Moodie 30-31; D. H. Morrison ii 76-82; *Morvan* 24-25; *Musical Bouquet #3611* 3b-4; *Musical Cabinet* 142-43; Nettel 172; *New Musical* ii 183-84 (with a variant tune, "sung by Mr. Sinclair in the opera of *Rob Roy*"); Ogilvie 110a #119; *120 Scotch Songs* 7; Pittman 43; Plumstead 271-73; *Quaver 1844* 95-96; Silber 1973b 140d; *Sing 5* 9; *Sky-Lark* 49; R. A. Smith iii 81; *Song Jewels* 45c; *Trifet 1890* 205c + *Trifet 1892* 205c; Urbani i 66-67; *University Songbook* 144-45; Wier 1918a 305a; Wier 1924 142.
Tunes with this title (instrumental): M. M. Cole 125f (strathspey); Kerr i 25 (waltz); Kerr ii 34 #309 (jig); Kerr iii 8a; Kerr x 6 #27 (strathspey); B. Mackenzie #13; *Musical Bouquet #2059/60* (piano variations by A. Goria); *Musical Bouquet #4636/7* (quadrille).
Related text (*Comic Banjo Song*, by James Unsworth): British Museum Library 11621.h.1 (164).
Related text [and tune] (*My Mary Ann*).

Comment, references: Cox 1925 413; Fowke 1973 205 #48; title included in Stephen Foster's *Song of All Songs* (1863), cf. *NYFQ 25* 25-26 and facsimile in Jordan 33-35.

Broadsides, songsters: J. Andrews iii #14; *Book of Popular Songs* 267a; *Bryant 1857* 16a; *Diprose 1865* 340-41; *Florences* 12-13; *Irish Boy* 12-13; *Johnson's Comic* 17 + *Pacific* iv 17b, "as sung by Master Charley Johnson"; *Prize Song Book* 12; Wolf Index #2181.

Texts: Belden 1952 iii 355-57; *Francis & Day 1967* 4; *Heart Songs* 246; Schinhan v 215-16; Sedley 131 B; Peggy Seeger 1964 51; Silber 1973b 147a; Silverman 1975 ii 258a.

Sheet music, with tune relative of #44: Baltimore, 1856 by Henry McCaffery; *D'Alcorn* i 8b-9, as sung by Sam Cowell; *Musical Bouquet* #1023, *The Yankee Girl's Song: My Mary Anne*, sung by Mrs. Barney Williams and Mrs. W. Florence (1856); *Musical Treasury* #839/40, *My Mary Anne, The Yankee Girl's Song*; *100 Comic Songs* 12; Rimbault iii 28-29 #12, as sung by the Christy Minstrels; *Shilling Song Book* i 39.

Texts with tune relative of #44: Barbeau 41-42 + A. L. Lloyd 1965 40-41 #23; FG 3547.1.1; Fowke 1954 142 + Fowke 1973 116-17; *Heart Songs* 246; *JFSS 3* 89; *JFSS 4* 288; Leisy 1966 227-29; A. Lomax 1960 145-46 + J. Edwards 13; Wier 1918 315b.

Unrelated text (*Sweet Mary Ann*): Harrigan 1883 i 18-20.

Text and tune relatives: Boni 1954 150-151; Haufrecht 1958 39 + Haufrecht 1959 95; Okun 1968 193-94; C. J. Sharp 1932 ii 52-53 C; C. J. Sharp 1932 ii 113 A + J. Edwards 14; C. J. Sharp ii 114-18 B, C, F, G, H, I.

Texts with "English" tune form: Butterworth 20-21; Capitol P8556.1.4; Farnsworth 1909 20-21; FP 2354A.4; *JFSS 3* 86-88; *JFSS 4* 286-87; *JFSS 4* 289-90 + Karpeles 1974 i 508 E; Karpeles 1974 i 505 B, 507 D; A. L. Lloyd 1955 16-17; Purslow 1965 94; C. J. Sharp 1961 i 34-35 + Götsch 25a, 85 + Karpeles 1974 i 506 C + C. J. Sharp 1916 126 #55 + C. J. Sharp 1920 i 22 + C. J. Sharp 1965 95; C. J. Sharp *FSS* ii 26-27 + *JFSS 2* 55 + Karpeles 1974 i 504 A + Karpeles 1975 i 37 #35; C. J. Sharp *FSS* ii 28-29 + *JFSS 2* 57; VRS 1031B.3 (Alfred Deller); R. V. Williams (sheet music of choral setting, London: Curwen & Sons, 1924) + Bikel 134-35 + *Miramichi Ms.* 15.14 + Zanzig #67.

Tune relatives (*Bonnie May*, by Robert Burns,

an adaptation of Child 217, *The Broom of the Cowdenknowes*),

Comment, references: Bronson i 73 #83; Stenhouse 111-12 #110.

Tunes with this text: J. Johnson #110 + Bronson iii 343 #20.

Tune relatives (other Child Ballads),

(*May Colvin*, or Child 4, *Lady Isabel and the Elf-Knight*): Bronson i 73 #82 (from Blaikie Manuscript); Boulton ii 12-14; G. F. Graham 1891 130; Maver 346 #472 (with tune ending altered); R. A. Smith iii 92 + Berggreen 46 #24 + Bronson i 73 #83 + Eyre-Todd 90 + Kinsley 1969 49-51 #12, ZDA 71.1.1 (Ewan MacColl).

(Child 81, *Little Musgrave and Lady Barnard*): C. J. Sharp 1932 i 182 P + Bronson ii 293 #38.

(child 289, *The Mermaid*): Motherwell appendix 30 + Bronson iv 384 #34; Bronson iv 384 #35.

Tune relatives (*My Mary Ann*, as instrumental tune): Boosey 1826b 18 #59; Davidson iv 35 #4b (quadrille); Howe 1864a 203j; B. Mackenzie #217; *Musical Bouquet* #1024 (polka); *Musical Bouquet* #1163/4 4-5 #5 (1857), (quadrille); *Musical Bouquet* #1247/8 2, 5b, 6b (1858) (quadrille); *Musical Treasury* #899/900 5b, 6c (quadrille medley by E. Rayloff); O'Donnell 53.

Tune relatives (*Tribulation*),

Comment, references: G. P. Jackson 1933 142 #43.

Tunes with this text: Carden 46a + G. P. Jackson 1937 100-101 #69; Cayce #424; Davisson 43a; Deason 144a; Hauser 1848 55b; Hauser 1878 81; A. S. Hayden 85b; G. P. Jackson 1933 142 #43; J. B. Jackson 38; R. Patterson 41a; Rhinehart 22b; Walker 119; B. F. White 29b + Denson 29b.

Tune relatives (*The Winter, It Is Past*, by Robert Burns),

Comment, references: Dick i 406 #156; Kinsley iii 1273 #218; Stenhouse 187-88 #200.

Tunes with this text: Davie 95 #57; Dick i 140 #156; *Howe* 188-30; J. Johnson #200 + Hopekirk 152-53; Kinsley i 409 #218; Lampe 1914 85; *Lyric Gems* ii 88; Mac-Cunn 32-33; Oswald x 9b (instrumental); Pittman 67.

45.
The Dens of Yarrow

Previously available (#45 A): *JAF 68* 203-4 (text only); *Neighbors* 1941 7; *NYFQ 8* 248-49 (text only).

Variants (#45 A): AFS 7754B; AFS 7762A.1;
AFS 12309A.1 + EC 329.1; ATL 615.13-.14;
ATL 624.11; *Sam Eskin* i 174. (#45 B): ATL
185.3.

Adaptations (#45 A): AFS 19395.2.90 (Joe Hickerson); Cazden 1949a 23-43 + CRI 117.2.3;
Cazden 1958 i 40-41 + Cazden 1978 40-41;
Haufrecht 1943 23-25; Haufrecht 1965 ii 23-27. INT 13058.2.4 (Peggy Seeger); Landeck
1944 34; Siegmeister 1944a 40; ZDA 74.1.6
+ ZDA 74F 4-5 B (Peggy Seeger).

Comment, references: Abrahams 178 #48; Ph.
Barry 1929 174, 291; Bronson iii 314-15, 328;
Cazden 1958 i 111 + Cazden 1978 111; Child
214, 215; Coffin 129-32; Eyre-Todd 69;
Fowke 1973 214-15 #77, #78; FSA 11F 3
(Parler, Randolph); G. Greig 1925 141-46;
Jaehde 35-36; *JAF 63* 328-35 (Coffin); *JAF 68*
201-9 (Cazden); *JFSS 5* 110-16 (Broadwood,
Gilchrist); M. Leach 1955 568-72; *MF 13*
144-45 (Fowke); *NYFQ 8* 245-66 (Cazden); J.
Reed 143-49; *SFQ 22* 195-200 (Parler); Topic
12T161 A.10 (Lloyd); Veitch ii 173-210;
ZDA 74F 2-4 (Peggy Seeger).

Broadsides, songsters: *Caledonian Musical Repository* 201-2; *96 Old Songs* 171-72; *Orpheus* 1832 342-43; *St. Cecilia* 176.

Texts: Abrahams 124-26; Allingham 11-14;
ALP 111.1.5; Ph. Barry 1929 291-93; Bethke
#36, *The Donny Dims of the Arrow;* N.
Buchan 1973 132-33; P. Buchan ii 193-96;
Christie i 64-67; Cox 1925 137-38; Eddy 69-70 + Wakefield ii 62-64; Flanders 1953 235-37 (from Cadyville, New York); FO 12.1.2
+ Fowke 1973 178-81; FO 12.1.3 + Fowke
1965 62-63; Friedman 99; FSA 11.1.2 + FSA
11F 3-4 (Max Hunter); Gainer 1975 77; Goss
1937 104-6; G. Greig 1925 141-45 + Karpeles
1956 58-59; J. Greig v 198-200; S. C. Hall
229-34; *JEFDSS 5* 77a; Karpeles 1971 95-96;
Kidson 1891 22-23 + Bronson iii 324-25 #36
+ Duncan 1927 221-22 #276; MacColl 1956
4-5 + Asch 48a + Bronson iii 324 #33 +
Clayre 85-86 + MacColl 1965 30 + RLP 12-625.2.1 + RLP 12-625F 5; *MF 13* 141-42,
143-44; E. Moore 104-6; Motherwell ii 126-29; Ord 426-27; Quiller-Couch 416, 786-88;
Ritson 1794 i 223-24, 227-34; J. Roberts 215-17,512-14; Rounder 0017.1.2 (Almeda Riddle) + Rounder 0017F 4-6; Sedley 189-90;
SFQ 22 195-97, 198-200; Silber 1973b 179a +
Silverman 1975 i 277; Topic 12T161A.10 +
Topic 12T161F A.10; ZDA 74.1.5, 74.1.7-.9;
ZDA 74F 3-4.

Related text (*The Braes of Yarrow*, by William
Hamilton [1724]), + Urbani i 28-29 +
Maxfield 87.

Comment, references: Stenhouse 464 #525.

Texts: Ramsay i 235-39 + Bronson iii 326
#39 + *Caledonian Musical Repository*
273-78 + Davie 29 #17 + Eyre-Todd 70
+ J. Johnson #64 + Maver 9b #18 +
Percy 279-82 + Pittman 114 + *Quaver* ii
86-89 + Rimbault 1850 86 + Ritson 1794 i
148-53 #68.

Related text (*The Braes of Yarrow*, by John Logan),

Comment, references: Stenhouse 464 #525.

Texts: Ritson 1794 i 154-55; Stenhouse 464
#525.

Related text (*The Dowie Dens O'Yarrow*, by
Walter Scott): W. Scott iii 173-86 + Bronson
iii 325 #38-#39 + Maver 40 #79.

Related text (*Nae Birdies Sang the Mirky
Hour*, by Robert Burns),

Comment, references: Dick i 409-10 #352.

Texts: Dick i 340-41.

Related text (*Willy's Rare and Willy's Fair*, by
Allan Ramsay),

Comment, references: Bronson iii 329 #5;
Laing 518 #525; Stenhouse 464-65 #525.

Broadsides, songsters: *96 Old Songs* 171-72,
with music by James Hook,"sung by Mrs.
Wrighten at Vauxhall" (1777).

Texts: *British Museum* 108-9; Bronson iii 329
#5; *Caledonian Musical Repository* 270-72; Christie i 64; Eyre-Todd 136; J. Johnson #525; *Lark* 302-3 #357; Maver 208
#416; Ramsay i 139; Ritson 1794 i 142; W.
Thompson ii 110-11.

Unrelates text (*The Braes of Yarrow*, opening
"My bonnie laddie gang wi' me"): *Calliope*
84-85; *Edinburgh Musical Miscellany* 81-83;
Street Literature (London: J. Catnach).

Text and tune relatives: none.

Tune relatives (Child 228, *Glasgow Peggie*):
Bronson iii 370-74, Group Aa #1-#11; Bronson iv 502 #5.1.

(Child 236, *The Laird and the Shepherd's
Daughter*): Ph. Barry 1929 300 + Bronson
iii 406 #26.

(others): N. Buchan 1973 74, *Bonnie Lass
Amongst the Heather;* Manny 248-49,
Herding Lambs Amongst the Heather.

Unrelated tunes (instrumental): Riley i 58 #217,
The Braes of Yarrow; Riley ii 12 #266, *Willie's Rare and Willie's Fair.*

46.
The Bold Soldier

Previously available: *JAF 68* 202 (text only).
Variants: ATL 623.6-.7.

Adaptations: Cazden 1958 i 42-43 + Cazden 1978 42-43.

Comment, references: Belden 1940 103; Belden 1952 287; Bronson i 128, Child 7, *Earl Brand*, Appendix; Cazden 1958 i 108 + Cazden 1978 108; Coffin 37-38, Child 8, *Erlinton;* Cox 1925 375; FSA 27F 24-26 (Paton); *JAF 35* 414 (Kittredge); *JAF 68* 201-9 (Cazden); Karpeles 1974 i 13-16; Laws M 27; Randolph i 303; ZDA 71F 6-7 (MacColl, Peggy Seeger).

Broadsides, songsters: Ashton 1887 164-67; *The Echo* 150; Roxburghe vi 229-33.

Texts: AA 3A.3 (Burl Ives); AFS 12310A.3 + EC 701.3 (Grant Rogers); T. Burton i 47-48; Davis Index 66; Emrich 1974 89-91 A, B; FHE 160; FO 19.2.4; FSA 27.2.5 (Grant Rogers); Grover 92-93; Haring 24-25; Honoré 8; HTA (Salisbury); B. Ives 1953 70-71; Knox 80-81; M. Leach 1965 100-101; *NYFQ* 23 21-22 (from near Suffern, New York); Piper; Purslow 1968 17; Schinhan iv 159-60; Silber 1973b 169b; Silverman 1975 ii 327; H. Thompson 1939 397-99; XTV 62203.4; ZDA 71.2.4 + ZDA 71F 9b.

Text and tune relatives: ATL 194.8 (Jake Loucks); Wilkinson i #43.

Tune relatives: ATL 623.4, *William Cook* (George Edwards); Behan 1965 20; Morton 1973 99 #2.

[See also notes to #119, *The Cordwood Cutter*].

47. The Constant Farmer's Son

Previously available: none.
Variants: ATL 615.9-.10.
Adaptations: none.
Comment, references: *JAF 23* 452-54 (Ph. Barry); *JFSS 5* 123-27; Laws M 33; Morton 1973 163 #17; O'Shaughnessy 1975 70-71 #11; *Sewanee 19* 213-27 (Belden).
Broadsides, songsters: [De Marsan's] *Singer's Journal #25* 62, *The Merchant's Daughter;* Wehman #768.
Texts: Creighton 1962 118; FO 19.1.3; FSA 33F 7, listing; S. B. Gould 1974 54-55; Grainger #274; Grover 56-57; LCJ (Hennesey); Morton 1973 40-41; *NYFQ 5* 96-97; *NYFQ 7* 70 ; O'Shaughnessy 1975 21-22; Piper (2); Pound 1916 20 + Pound 1922 76-78; *Sam Henry* #806; Shearin 10.
Related text (*The Bramble Briar*),
  Comment, references: Belden 1940 109-10; Laws M 32; *PMLA 33* 327-95 (Belden); *Sewanee 19* 213-27 (Belden).

Broadsides, songsters: *Wehman's Collection #28* 23.
Texts: G. Anderson 64-65; Hubbard 49-50; Rosenberg Index #663; *Sewanee 19* 320-22; C. J. Sharp 1932 i 310-16.
Text and tune relatives: none.
Tune relatives: *CAY 3* #5 2-3; Creighton 1962 112; Galvin 21; Karpeles 1934 i 11 + Fowke 1954 162 + Karpeles 1971 235; Karpeles 1934 i 56-58; Karpeles 1971 210; M. Leach 1965 120; O Lochlainn 1939 154, 164; O'Neill #30; Peacock 505.

48. There Was an Old Miser

Previously available: none.
Variants: ATL 190.5.
Adaptations: none.
Comment, references: none.
Broadsides, songsters: none.
Texts: none.
Related texts (incomplete forms): FHE 1, *The Miser's Daughter;* Grainger #284, *It's of an Old Miser;* Karpeles 1974 i 368-69 C; Munch 79-80, *The Old Miser;* NA Ives 1.41 + ATL 2166.5, *In London's Fair City; NYFQ 5* 78, *The Old Miser.*
Related texts (others): Karpeles 1974 i 367-68 B (couple rescued from shipwreck); Karpeles 1974 i 366-67 A (couple perish in shipwreck).
Unrelated text (*The Rich Old Miser*),
  Comment, references: Laws Q 7.
  Texts: Peggy Seeger 1964 71; A. Williams 304, *The Miser.*
Unrelated text (*The Sailor's Misfortune and Happy Marriage,* or *The Press Gang*),
  Comment, references: *JFSS 8* 9-10; Laws N 6.
  Texts: Ashton 1891 #55; Bethke #21; Creighton 1950 146; *JFSS 2* 181-82; *JFSS 8* 9-10 + Karpeles 1974 ii 73-74 A; *JFSS 8* 265-66 + Karpeles 1974 ii 74-75 B; *JFSS 8* 266 + Karpeles 1974 ii 76 C; Karpeles 1971 167-68; M. Leach 1965 106-7; *Sam Henry* #108, *The Rich Merchant's Daughter.*
Unrelated text (*William and Harriet*),
  Comment, references: Laws M 7.
  Texts: Hubbard 61-62.
Text and tune relatives: none.
Tune relatives (*The Bonnet of Blue*): Creighton 1971 99; Huntington 275-76; Kidson 1891 118.

49.
The Lowlands Low

Previously available: none.
Variants: ATL 616.9, 617.10.
Adaptations: none.
Comment, references: Belden 1952 ii 266; *BFSSNE #12* 12-14 (Ph. Barry); *JAF 20* 274; Laws M 34; W. R. Mackenzie 1928 92; Randolph ii 59; C. J. Sharp 1932 ii 397 #52.
Broadsides, songsters: as noted in Laws.
Texts: Belden 1952 ii 266-69; L. Chappell 63-65; Davis Index 54-55; Emrich 1974 93; FHE 307; Flanders *SR* 29.4.34; FO 17.2.5; G. Greig *FSNE #123*; *JFSS 3* 266 + R. V. Williams 1959 106-7; *JFSS 8* 227-29; Karpeles 1971 130-31; Karpeles 1974 i 290-91; W. R. Mackenzie 1919 155a; E. Moore 162-63; Purslow 1965 101; Rosenberg Index #352 + Rosenberg T87 44B.1; *Sam Henry* #113; Schinhan iv 153-54; C. J. Sharp 1961 iv 138 (Gardiner); Wilkinson i #291; Wyman 1920 42-45.
Text and tune relatives: *BFSSNE #12* 12-13 (in *b – b – b – a* form); Creighton 1950 221; Gledhill 57-60; Grover 110-11; Hubbard 51-53; *NA Ives* 1.4 + ATL 2138.8; C. J. Sharp 1932 i 355 F (in *a – a – b – a* form).
Tune relatives: ATL 490.13; *BFSSNE #12* 4c; Blondahl 84; Doyle 1955 72 + Doyle 1966 24; Greenleaf 116 + Doerflnger 283; Grover 70; *Howe* 1878 275; *JFSS 8* 14 #12, 126; M. Leach 1965 52; J. Lomax 1941 324; Peacock 449, 547, 646, 687; Petrie #547, #1243, #1244, #1245; Randolph i 278 B; Ranson 54; Topic 12T140.2.1.

50.
The Banks of Sweet Dundee

Previously available: *Neighbors* 1943 14-15.
Variants: ASCH 560.2 + AFS 12309A.15 + EC 329.15; ATL 616.4.
Adaptations: AFS 12312B.3; Cazden 1958 i 24-25 + Cazden 1978 24-25.
Comment, references: Cazden 1958 i 107-8 + Cazden 1978 107-8; Hannegan 23-26 #51, 34 #72; *JAF 35* 354-56 (Kittredge); Laws M 25; A. L. Lloyd 1967 77-80.
Broadsides, songsters: *Delaney's Scotch #1* 3; De Marsan #21; Peterson Index 98 (broadsides from Dublin, Manchester); *Singer's Journal #5* 37; Wehman i 39; *Wehman's Collection #33* 16; *Wehman's Irish #1* 117.
Texts: AFS 1774B.1; ATl 486.11; ATl 616.5 (James Edwards); ATL 630.8 (Elizabeth Misner); Barrett 78-79; Belden 1940 138; Broadwood 1893 116; Colcord 90; Combs 1939 26-27; Combs 1967 213 #95, listing; Copper 1973 200-201; Cutting 80-82; Davis Index 54; Flanders *SR* 18.3.34, 15.4.34; FO 1.1.9, 20.2.9; R. Ford 1904 78b-81; Grainger #275, #276, #277, #278; Hubbard 54-55; *JAF 52* 9 + Emrich 1974 87-88; Kidson 1891 54-55; Kidson 1927 82-83; A. L. Lloyd 1967 165-66; W. R. Mackenzie 1919 47-48; E. Moore 175-76; Polwarth 1969 15 + F. Graham 1971 26b; Rosenberg Index #63; *Sam Eskin* iv 136; Schinhan iv 341; Peggy Seeger 1960 27; SLP 49A.3; Stout 45a; I. A. Williams 63-64.
Text and tune relatives: none.
Tune relatives (*David and Uriah*): ATL 604.8 (James Edwards); ATL 625.8 (George Edwards).
(*From Thee, Eliza*, by Robert Burns),
Comment, references: Dick i 359-60; Sonneck 73, 151.
Tunes with this text: *British Orpheus* 211-12; Dick i 26; J. Greig i 28-29; Kinsley i 15 #9; Urbani ii 36.
(*Fuller and Warren*): *American Cowboy* 40-41; Big Round Up 3-4; K. S. Clark 1932 34-35; Larkin 127-30; J. Lomax 1938 205-6; E. Moore 361; Sherwin 1933 16-17.
(*Gilderoy*),
Comment, references: Dick i 359-60 #27; Simpson 252-54.
Tunes with this text: Dick i 26 #27; *Edinburgh Musical Miscellany* 240; G. F. Graham ii 46-47; J. Johnson #66; Moffat 1894 142-43; Pittman 148; Ritson 1794 ii 24-25 + *JAMS 3* 134 #28; Peggy Seeger 1960 86 #79; R. A. Smith ii 18; W. Thompson ii 106-7; Urbani i 46-47.
Tunes with this title (instrumental): *Boosey* 1862a 45 #144; *Harding* 17 #51; E. Haywood 54 #18; *Howe* 1851a 39a; *Howe* 1851c 39a; Howe 1858a 55a; P. Kennedy 1951 14 #28 + *Community* iii 7a; Oswald v 20; A. Stuart iv 94-95 + Simpson 253.
(*New Orleans*): Carden 28a; Davisson 23a; Hauser 1848 65; Hayden 89; Hendrickson 12b-13; G. P. Jackson 1937 157 #139 (from *Primitive Baptist Hymn and Tune Book* 1902 255); J. B. Jackson 33; Walker 76.
(*Parting Friends*): Walker 35b + G. P. Jackson 1944 69.
(*The Star of the County Down*): ATL 496.8b-.9; Colum 610; J. Edwards 149; Kerr i 41f (instrumental); O'Keeffe 17; J. J. Ward 9-10.

(*We Be Poor, Frozen Out Gardeners*): W. Chappell ii 748.

Tune relatives (others): ATL 184.4 (George Edwards); ATL 193.10 ("Dick" Edwards); Behan 1965 42; Breathnach i 264; Breathnach iii 218; Broadwood 1893 34-35, 68-69; Broadwood 1893 102-3 + Dearmer 1928 125 # 60; N. Buchan 1962 120; T. Burton i 101; Costello 122 #65; Creighton 1962 19, 166; Creighton 1971 143; J. Edwards 87; *FMJ 2* 349; Fowke 1967 52-53, 182-83; Fox 34-35; Friel 4 #2; Gardner 1939 98; Gledhill 25-27; Grover 203-4; Hannegan #51, *Udhacht Phaidiu Thon-dhealbhaigh;* Henebry 200; Hughes iv 8-13, 34-38; Huntington 133-34; *JEFDSS 7* 99-100; *JEFSS 8* 16; *JFSS 2* 118a + A. L. Lloyd 1967 78a; *JFSS 6* 218; *JIFS 20* 29; Joyce #92; Joyce #405 + Sedley 116, *Oh Love, It Is a Killing Thing;* Karpeles 1975 ii 39 #34; Kemp 42-43; M. Leach 1965 242; MacColl 1963 34; McPheeley 329 #925; *NA Ives* 1.112 + ATL 3119.9; *NEF 7* 64; *NEF 14* 33; O Lochlainn 1939 26 + FSE 21.2.6; O Lochlainn 1939 184; O Lochlainn 1965 4; O'Neill #236, #396, #580; Ord 384 + Clayre 74; Peacock 640; Roche i #38; *Sam Henry* #704, #747; Peggy Seeger 1960 56 #49, *The Banks of Newfoundland;* C. J. Sharp *FSS* i 70 + A. L. Lloyd 1967 51; C. J. Sharp 1932 ii 117 G + *JAMS 3* 133 #29; *Sing 10 #2* 6a (in *a – a – b – a* form); *Sing 10 #2* 7d; SLP 81 A.2; WLP 724.1.5

Tune relatives [half-tunes in *– – b – a* form], (*Brigg Fair*): EDS 22 41; Grainger #200; SL 206.2.19 (Isla Cameron).

(Child 78, *The Unquiet Grave*): Bronson ii 244 #41, 245 #42, #43.

(others): ATL 488.3a-.3b; Brocklebank 10; Doyle 1955 68; Doyle 1966 51; Eddy 231; EKL 125.1.6; FO 3.1.1; Peacock 748 + Fowke 1967 86; Wilkinson i #368.

Tune relatives [condensation in 3/4 time], **Comment, references:** *JFSS 7* 299.

Tunes: Breathnach ii 188, *Youghall Harbour;* Hannegan #72, *Posadh Naomhtha Cana; JFSS 7* 211, *Lá Ile Pádruig; JFSS 7* 215, *Avarán a Wáish; JFSS 7* 218, *Óchal; JFSS 7* 295, *Do Hugus Grá Cléiv Ghoet; JFSS 7* 313, *An Sbérvean Cheaunsa; JFSS 7* 316-17; Karpeles 1975 i 19 #17; O'Neill #473.

Tune relatives [condensation in 6/8 time], (*My Tocher's the Jewel,* by Robert Burns), **Comment, references:** Dick i 414 #186; Kinsley iii 1386-87 #345; Stenhouse 304 #312. **Tunes** with this text: Dick i 166; *Howe* 188-6; J. Johnson #312; Kinsley ii 605; Mac-

Cunn 166; MacFarren 230; Pittman 105; Poston 1956 62-64.

Tune relatives [condensation in 6/8 time] (others): Joyce #597; O Lochlainn 1939 84; Peacock 226, 227; Petrie #387, #1130, #1319.

Unrelated tunes (*The Banks of Sweet Dundee*): Karpeles 1973 25; C. J. Sharp 1965 93-94. [See also notes to #53].

51.
Awake, Awake, Ye Drowsy Sleepers

Previously available (#51 B): *Neighbors* 1942 9.
Variants: none.
Adaptations: AFS 12312B.5; Cazden 1958 i 3 + Cazden 1978 3; Cazden 1962 36; Cazden 1963 i 7; Landeck 1944 48.
Comment, references: AFS L55F 8-9 (Helène Stratman Thomas); Belden 1940 118-19; Cazden 1958 i 107 + Cazden 1978 107; *CEOL 3* 44-46 (Shields); Cox 1925 348; *EDS 27* 49; FHE 103 (Ph. Barry); *JAF 30* 338-43, 361-63 (Kittredge); *JAF 35* 356-57; *JAF 49* 211-13; *JEFDSS 3* 161-64; P. Kennedy 1975 371 #148; Laws G 21, M 4; M. Leach 1955 730-31; Leisy 1966 299-301; *PMLA 36* 565-614 (Baskervill); Randolph ii 53; *SFQ 14* 87-96 (Coffin).

Broadsides, songsters: Wehman #518.
Texts [*indicates *The Silver Dagger* as title]: AFS L55F 8-9; B. Arnold 75; Beard 278-79; Bonar 186-88; Brewster 170-73, A - C; M. E. Bush i *60-61; M. E. Bush ii *63-65; Carlisle *55-56; Christie i 225; J. Cohen 53; Combs 1967 213 #93, listing; Davis Index 56-57, 57-59, 80-81; Eddy 92 A + Wakefield iii 75-76; Emrich 1974 83-84; FHE 48, 50 *151; Flanders *BDN* 3.2.34; Flanders *SR* 28.1.34, 29.7.34; Flanders *SR* *28.10.34 + Flanders Index *251 #121; FSA 22F 10-11; Glass 1976a 22-23; Gordon *AM* 30.3.25; M. E. Henry 259-60; G. P. Jackson 1947 #22; Karpeles 1974 i 329-32, A - D; P. Kennedy 1975 348; Leisy 1966 299-301; McCurry 155b + G. P. Jackson 1952 193; McDowell 1947 41-42; E. Moore 196-97; Ord 89 318-19; Peacock 733-34 + Fowke 1967 30; Rosenberg Index #47, #1285; Rosenberg T86 25A.2; Sedley 48-49; Shearin 23; SLP 74B.5; VRS *9078.1.1 (Baez); Wilkinson i #109, #153, #191, #352, #469, #476, #592, #593.
Related texts (*The Silver Dagger*): Belden 1940 124-26; Belden 1952 258-59; Brewster 211-14, A - B; Combs 1967 211 #76, listing; Cox

1925 350; *EDS 27* 49; Emrich 1974 75-76; Flanders *SR* 24.12.33; Hubbard 66-67; *JAF 25* 282; *JAF 39* 129-32; Leisy 1964 58-59; A. C. Morris 80-81; Neely 161-62; Piper; Pound 1916 17-18 + Pound 1922 121-24; Randolph ii 53-58; E. Robinson 33-35; *Sam Eskin* iv 158; Schinhan iv 149-51 #72; Stekert 1969 N 72;

Text and tune relatives: AFS L55A.4; ATL 182.10; Ph. Barry 1939 83; *Bayard ii 165.3; Brewster 173-74 C; T. Burton ii 91-92; *CFMJ 3* 38b-39; FSA 22.1.1; Gardner 1939 86 B; Hendren 80b, 156a; *JAF 52* 31 #29; A. L. Lloyd 1965 28 #15; W. R. Mackenzie 1928 99, tune 396 #30; A. C. Morris 362-63; *NA Ives* *1.18 + ATL *2147.3; Randolph i 244; Ritchie 1953 1953 46-47; Ritchie 1963 200-201; Scarborough 1937 399 D; Schinhan iv 147-49 A, B, D, E; C. J. Sharp *FSS* iv 56-57 + C. J. Sharp 1916 106-7 #47 + C. J. Sharp 1920 i 72-73; C. J. Sharp 1932 i 358 A, 359 B, 360 C, 362 F, 363 G, 364H, 364 I, 364 J; Sturgis 30-31 + Botkin 1947 859-60; Wilkinson i #364.

Tune relatives with some relationship of text (*The Little Sparrow*): Belden 1940 120-21; C. J. Sharp 1932 i 363.

Tune relatives (others): ATL 615.6, *Arthur Clyde* (James Edwards); FSA 3.2.3; *JFSS 4* 124-26 #4, #6, #7, *The Banks of Sweet Primroses;* Kidson 1891 104, *Johnny Todd;* Kidson 1926 56; J. Lomax 1941 130 + J. Lomax 1947 58-59; Poston 1968 30; Purslow 1972 46; Peggy Seeger 1960 8 #3, *Johnny Todd;* C. J. Sharp 1932 i 373 A, 375 C, *William Taylor;* C. J. Sharp 1932 ii 119, 128-36 (all 18 versions).

Tune relatives (long tune forms of which #51 matches the second half): G. Greig 1925 43e + Bronson i 446 #78, Child 53, *Lord Bateman; JFSS 4* 124-26 #1, #2, #3, *The Banks of Sweet Primroses; JFSS 4* 126 #5, *The Banks of Sweet Primroses* (with variant phrase sequence); C. J. Sharp 1932 i 373-74 B, *William Taylor.*

52.
The Bonny Laboring Boy

Previously available: *Neighbors* 1942 14; *PSB 2 #118.*

Variants: ASCH 560.2 + AFS 12309A.12 + EC 329.12; ATL 623.2-.3

Adaptations: AFS 12312A.7; Cazden 1958 i 22-23 + Cazden 1978 22-23; Haufrecht 1943 16-17; Haufrecht 1945 L-149; SLP 72.1.4.

Comment, references: *CAY 3 #5* 4a (Shoolbraid); Cazden 1958 i 109 + Cazden 1978 109; Fowke 1973 211 #69; P. Kennedy 1975 370-71 #147; Laws M 14 (Irish).

Broadsides, songsters: *Delaney #14* 24; *JFSS 1* 206-7 (from broadside by Such); *Shamrock Shore* 5; *Street Literature* (London: E. Hodges); Wehman #997 (1888); Wehman i 62-63; *Wehman's Irish #2* 51a.

Texts: ATL 626.7 (Charles Seeley); Brocklebank 4; *CAY 3 #5* 2-3; Collinson 1946 16-17; Fowke 1973 160-61; FSA 33F 6, listing; FSE 20.2.1 (Harvey Cox); *JFSS 3* 110-11; Karpeles 1971 216-17; P. Kennedy 1975 347; Kidson 1915 23a; A. L. Lloyd 1967 223; Peacock 564-65; Purslow 1965 9; RG 150.1.9 (Shirley Collins); *Sam Henry* #576; Wright 344.

Related text (*The Bonny Lighter Boy*): C. J. Sharp *FSS* iv 62-64 + Karpeles 1974 i 333-34 + Karpeles 1975 ii 30 #26 + *Novello* ix 7-9 #1409 + C. J. Sharp 1916 112-13 #50 + C. J. Sharp *Selection* ii 18-20 + C. J. Sharp 1920 i 78-79.

Related text (*The Farmer's Boy*),

Comment, references: S. B. Gould i xxx; P. Kennedy 579 #247; Laws Q 30.

Broadsides, songsters: *Amateur* 74-75; *Annie Laurie* 26; *Beadle's Half-Dime #18* 7; *Beadle's Pocket* ii 30-31; Cozans i 12-13; *Delaney #10* 22; *Elton* 150; *Fairburn* 18--298; *Few Days; Frank Brower* 68-69; Hadaway 18-19; *Marsh's Selection* ii 220-21; *Pocket Song Book* 41; *Singer's Journal #16* 95; Wehman ii 62-63; *Wehman's Universal #7* 55; *Young Lady's Songster.*

Texts [*with common tune]: B. F. Baker 1850 *40-41; B. F. Baker 1851 *103; Beard 309-10; Broadwood 1893 *134-35; Dunstan i *40; *Ernest Newton* *7; Fitz 1848 *30-31; FO 14.1.8 + FM 4051.1.4 + FM 4051F 4 + FO 15.2.4; *Francis & Day* iii *40; Gill 1917 *48-49; S. B. Gould i *58-60; Grainger *#244, *#245; Haynes i *150-51; Healy 1967b i 136-37; *Howe* 1878 *241; A. N. Johnson *12-13; P., Kennedy 1975 *555 #247; Kidson 1891 *63-65, *174; Kidson 1926 *100-101; *Labour Party* *49; McCaskey viii *139; McDowell 1947 *82-83; E. Moore *230-31; *Musical Bouquet* *#5943 (1879); *Musical Budget 10* *100-101; S. H. Nicholson *164 #84; *NYFQ 5* 90; L. Ring *14-15; Stout 27-28, A - B; Wilkinson i *628.

Related texts (others): *CFQ 1* 223-24, *The Miner Boy;* Fowke 1960 200-201 + FM 4005A.6 + FM 4005F A.6, *The Railroad*

Boy; Fowke 1970 192-93, *My Jolly Shanty-boy.*

Unrelated text (*The Sun Had Loosed*): D'Urfey i 320-22; S. B. Gould viii 72-73.

Text and tune relatives: ATL 602.4 (Frank Edwards).

Tune relatives [with variant cadence of *b* phrase] (*The Rambling Cowboy*): J. Cohen 54; Lingenfelter 392-93; A. Lomax 1960 318-19; Ohrlin 200-201.

Tune relatives [with variant cadence of *b* phrase] (others): J. Edwards 121; FH 5723A.7, *Utah Carroll;* FSE 21.1.6; Greenlead 233; *JAF 52* 38 #40; A. L. Lloyd 1967 284; *NA Ives* 1.75 + ATL 2194.4b; *NA Ives* 1.123 + ATL 3130.8; Peacock 79, 138, 971; Peacock 372 + Fowke 1967 136; *The Bonny Lighter Boy;* Petrie #351; K. Raven 1974 22; C. J. Sharp 1932 ii 213 B, 214 C (in a – b – a form), 214 D; Silber 1964 72.

Unrelated tunes with "homing" cadences,
  Comment, references: Henry Leland Clarke, "The habitate of homing melody" (personal communication).
  Tunes: Fowke 1970 146, *The Cold Black River Stream; JEFDSS 7* 104, *My Johnny;* Manny 181, *The Wayerton Driver; NA Ives* 1.74, *Byrontown.*

53.
Fair Julian Bond

Previously available: none.
Variants: ATL 624.8-.9.
Adaptations: Cazden 1958 i 26-29 + Cazden 1978 26-29.
Comment, references: *AFSPB 14* 174-76 (Laws); Belden 1940 289; G. G. Carey 1971 105-6; Cazden 1958 i 112 + Cazden 1978 112; Cox 1925 336; G. P. Jackson 1937 124; Laws M 9, M 10 (Irish); McTiernan 26; *UFL 17* 8-9 (Shields).
Broadsides, songsters (Parts I, II, III): *American Songster* 1835 178-90 + *American Songster* 1839 178-90 + *American Songster* 1845 131-45 + *Marsh's Selection* iii 134-34; *American Vocalist* 92-102; *Bobbing Around* 243-52; *Forget-Me-Not* 181-90 + *Jenny Lind* 181-90 + *New Book of 1000* 181-90; (portion in) *Isaiah Thomas* ii 53; Lowens #100 (ca. 1795), #166 (1799), #209 (1801), #371 (1810) and others, listings; *Pearl Songster* 245-54; *Singer's Journal #21* 135; *United States* 114-21; Wolf Index #1987, #1988, #1989.
Broadsides, songsters (portions, condensations): *Delaney's Irish #3* 12; De Marsan

List 16 #75-#78; *Erin-Go-Bragh* 144-49; W. C. Ford #3407, #3408, #3409, #3410 (all prior to 1800); *Howe* 1878 275 + Fireside Library 63b + *Trifet* 1890 180b [with tune]; *Hyland* 118-19, 123-24; O'Conor 86; *Shamrock* 48-50; *Songs of Our Land* i 114-18; *Universal Irish* 90-91; *Walton's Treasury* 40-41 + *Walton* i 156-57; Wehman #389; Wehman *617* 30, 70; *Wehman's Irish #1* 91-93; *Well Known Songs* 67-68.

Texts: Breathnach i 47-49; G. G. Carey 1971 106-9; Carleton i viii-ix; Davis Index 55; FHE 326; Gardner 1939 483, listing of all three Parts; LCJ (Crump); M. Leach 1965 328-29; Meredith 1968 31-32; *PMLA 39* 476 (Beckwith) + M. Leach 1955 743-44 B; Randolph i 418, 419; Rosenberg Index #1556; *Sam Henry* #234; Shearin 13; *UFL 17* 24; Wilkinson i #198.

Unrelated text (*The Colleen Bawn*),
  Broadsides, songsters: *Delaney's Irish #* 25; *Erin-Go-Bragh* 23; *Harry Pell* 28; *Hyland* 85; *Joe English* 29; *Pat Malloy* 71; *Rocky Road* 32-33; *Shamrock* 50b; *Stephen's Fenian* 14-15; *Wehman's Irish #2* 75b.
  Texts [* with common tune]: *Choice Irish Songs* i *3-5; FM *4051.1.7; FO *15.2.7; Goodwin 1956 *394a; *Howe* 1874 *172b + *Fireside Library* *37b + *Howe* 1880 *172b + *Trifet* 1890 *99b + *Trifet* 1892 *99b.
  Variant texts and text titles: *Boosey* iii 13a, *The Colleen Bawn Valse; Boosey* ix 8-9; I. W. W. 5, *Should I Ever Be a Soldier* by Joe Hill, "air: *The Colleen Bawn*"; *Walton's Treasury* 142 + *Walton* ii 33.

Text and tune relatives: Christie ii 144-45; Creighton 1932 152-62; FO 7.1.5, 7.1.6, 19.2.8, 19.2.9; *JAF 24* 340 [tune only is given]; *JFSS 3* 133-36; Joyce #420; J. Lomax 1941 166-68; Petrie #510 + J. R. Wilson #11; Schinhan iv 208-9; C. J. Sharp 1932 ii 81 A, 82 B; Wilkinson i #529 (with tune in a – a – b – a form).

Tune relatives (*The Banks of Sweet Dundee*),
  Comment, references: Karpeles 1973 25; C. J. Sharp 1965 93–94.
  Tunes with this text: Broadwood 1893 116-17; Hubbard 54-55; *JFSS 1* 232; Karpeles 1973 25; Kidson 1891 54; Kidson 1927 82-83; C. J. Sharp 1932 i 399 A, 400 B.

Tune relatives (*The Bonny Laboring Boy*): Brocklebank 4; *JFSS 1* 206a; *JFSS 3* 110-11; Karpeles 1971 216; Kidson 1915 23a; Peacock 564; Purslow 1965 9.

(*The Bonny Lighter Boy*): C. J. Sharp *FSS* iv 62-64 + Karpeles 1974 i 333-34 + Karpeles 1975 ii 30 #26 + *Novello* ix 7-9

#1409 + C. J. Sharp 1916 112-13 #50 + C. J. Sharp *Selection* ii 18-20 + C. J. Sharp 1920 i 78-79.

(Child 7, *Earl Brand*): C. J. Sharp 1932 i 334 C; C. J. Sharp 335 D + Bronson i 137 #23; C. J. Sharp 1932 i 335 F + Bronson i 137 #24, in – – *b* – *a* curtailment; C. J.Sharp 1932 i 337 G + Bronson i 136 #22, in *a* – *b* – *a* curtailment.

(*High Germany*),

Comment, references: Karpeles 1974 i 735.

Tunes with this text: *AT #21* 16; Dallas 1973 79; Davison 1924 134-35 #117; Goss 1927 83; S. B. Gould 1905 44; *JFSS 4* 25b; Joseph 55; C. J. Sharp *FSS* i 42 + Götsch 18a, 76 + Hansen 79a + Karpeles 1974 i 510 B + Loveless 24-25 + C. J. Sharp 1916 127-29 #56 + C. J. Sharp 1920 i 93-95 + D. Warner 12; *Sing 4* 69; *SO 2 #9* 15 + *RSO #3* 52 + Silverman 1975 ii 304b-5.

(*Pilgrim*) [in *a* – *a* – *b* – *a* phrase sequence]: Carden 147; Cayce #353; Hauser 1848 392; Hauser 1878 251; G. P. Jackson 1933 134 #60; G. P. Jackson 1937 124 #98; J. B. Jackson 57; McCurry 117b; Walker 150; B. F. White 201b + Cooper 201b + Denson 201b; Wilkinson i #529.

(*The Sheffield Apprentice*): ATL 628.7 (Charles Seeley); Creighton 1971 45; Karpeles 1974 ii 572 B; C. J. Sharp 1932 ii 66 A, 67 B, 68 D, 68 E.

(*The Traveller*): Rhinehart 119b; Walker 79.

Tune relatives (others): AFS L29A.4, *The Battle of Antietam Creek;* E. D. Andrews 99 #6, *The Happy Journey;* Arthur 20; ATL 627.10, *The Banks of Claudy* (Frank Edwards); ATL 628.13, 629,1-.2, *The Lofty Giant* (Reuben Edwards); Barrett 29; Behan 1965 19; Behan 1967 108; Bethke #21, *The Rich Merchant; BFSSNE #4* 15; Boardman 23; Breathnach i 52, 184; Breathnach ii 49, 70, 138; *CEOL 2 #1* 9; Christie ii 146; J. Cohen 46; Creighton 1932 92 + J. R. Wilson #1e; Creighton 1950 204 A; Creighton 1962 42 + FE 4307B.1; Creighton 1962 49, 128; Creighton 1962 78 + FE 4307B.5; Creighton 1971 71, 74, 220; Dallas 1973 227; Dibblee 23, 110, 120; Doyle 1940 50, *Fishermen of Newfoundland;* R. G. Edwards 1956 72 + R. G. Edwards 1971 80b; R. G. Edwards 1971 103; R. G. Edwards 1972 18; FA 2951B.14, *The State of Arkansas;* Fife 1969 163; FM 4051.1.9; *FMJ 3* 78; FO 13.2.3, 17.2.5; FO 18.1.4 (in 3/4 time); Friel 5 #3; FSA 26.2.7, *The Texas Rangers;* FSI 39.1.2; Gill 1898 2-3 #3, 37 #41; Gill 1917 42-43; Graves 1882 116-17,

The Willow Tree; Greenleaf 100 + Howes 15 + J. R. Wilson #1c; Greenleaf 285 + J. R. Wilson #1a; Greenway 272; Healy 1967 82b; Houston 72; Huntington 54; Edw. Ives 1964 69-70; *JAF 52* 38; *JFSS 1* 106, 118, 124 #40; *JFSS 2* 25 #11; *JFSS 2* 166 + A. L. Lloyd 1967 246; *JFSS 3* 310; *JFSS 5* 85; *JFSS 7* 50, 51, 52, 53, 316; *JFSS, 7* 221, *Thurot; JFSS 8* 41 + A. L. Lloyd 1967 77 + R. V. Williams 1924 38-40, 52-54, 1959 56, *John Barleycorn;* Jolliffe 2; Joyce #326, #499; *JWFSS 2* 118 #71, 119 #72, *Y Ferch O'R Bedlam;* Karpeles 1971 179, 237; Karpeles 1974 i 499-500 D, *The Irish Girl;* Karpeles 1974 ii 49 A, 58-59 B, 167-68 B, 169, 189 B; Karpeles 1974 ii 177 (in *a* – *a* – *b* – *a* form); Korson 1938 191-93 + Korson 1949 386, *The Avondale Mine Disaster;* Lingenfelter 234; A. L. Lloyd 1965 62 #34; J. Lomax 1938 192-93; J. Lomax 1938 283 + J. Lomax 1947 240-41; A. Lomax 1960 322-23; A. Lomax 1967 170; Manny 59 + J. R. Wilson #1; Meredith 1967 122b, 148; Morton 1973 150; *NA Ives 1.70* + *ATL 2189.2; NA Ives 1.103* + *ATL 3110.2* + Edw. Ives 197- [368], *Benjamin Deane; NA Ives 1.142* + *ATL 3149.3; NA Ives 62.6* + Manny 68, *Byrontown; NA Ives 64.6.7, 65.11.1, 65,12.1, 66.8.3, 68.6.10; NA Ives 69.2* + Edw. Ives 1971 65b; Nettel 24 (in *a* – *a* – *b* – *a* form); Ohrlin 140; O'Keeffe 50; O Lochlainn 1965 48; R. Palmer 1972 95; R. Palmer 1973a 10; R. Palmer 1973b 35; Peacock 79, 473, 971; Petrie #1444; Petrie #1525 (*a* phrase only); *PSB 2 #171* + *RPSB* 84, *The Death of Harry Simms;* Randolph ii 177; Randolph ii 272 + A. Lomax 1960 349; Ranson 52; Rickaby 185 + J. R. Wilson #1f; RLP 12-618.2.6, *John Barleycorn* (in *a* – *a* – *b* – *a* form); *Sam Henry* #796; Scarborough 1937 404a (in *a* – *a* – *a* – *a* form); Peggy Seeger 1970 64 #34; Pete Seeger 1964 37; *SFQ 30* 174; C. J. Sharp 1932 ii 215 G, 225 B; C. J. Sharp 1920 ii 90-91; Silber 1964 56; Silber 1973a 147; *Sing 6* 67; *SO 16 #5* 12 + Silber 1963 78-79; *SO 20 #1* 15; Topic 12T147.2.3, *The Manchester Angel;* Whall 113-14; Wright 140; *Yetties* 39.

[See also notes to #124].

54.
Johnny Doyle

Previously available: none.
Variants: ATL 185.2.
Adaptations: none.
Comment, references: Belden 1952 ii 365; Flan-

ders 1939 248-50; *JAF 23* 452-54 (Ph. Barry); *JFSS 5* 142-46; Laws M 2; W. R. Mackenzie 1928 106-7; *NEF 5* 17-18; *UFL 17* 20 (Shields).

Broadsides, songsters: *Big Thing On Ice* 58-59; De Marsan #212; *Singer's Journal #7* 53; *Wehman's Irish #2* 107b; Wolf Index #1138.

Texts: Belden 1952 ii 365-66; T. Burton ii 46-47; Davis Index 64; Flanders *SR* 22.4.34; FHE 269, 339; FSA 22.2.3 + FSA 22F 24; Hubbard 56-57; Hudson 1937 9; *JAF 70* 346 #19; *JIFS 1* 66; Karpeles 1974 i 340-41 A, B; Larson #6; M. Leach 1965 16-17; *MF 13* 147, listing (Fowke); Musick 25 #19; *NA Ives* 1.35 + ATL 2160.6 + *NEF 5* 18-19; *NA Ives* 66.3.1; Peacock 687-90; Petrie #443, #629, #630; Piper + Peterson Index 49; *Sam Henry #137*; *SFQ 8* 163-64; Shearin 27, listing; Wilkinson i #2, #108, #482.

Unrelated text (*Johnny Doyle*, or *The Wild Mustard River*),

    Comment, references: Fowke 1970 109-10; Laws C 5.

    Texts: Fowke 1970 107-10; Manny 306-7.

Text and tune relatives: Karpeles 1971 212-13; O'Neill #476 (instrumental tune with this title); Peacock 689.

Tune relatives: Cazden 1958 ii 62-63 + Cazden 1973 62-63; Darley 21 #48; *JFSS 3* 180-82, 184-85; *JIFS 14* 35a; Joyce #208; Karpeles 1971 39, 40; Manny 308; *Miramichi Ms.* 17.19; Petrie #389.

[See also notes to #13, #46, #91, #119].

55.
The Holland Song

Previously available: none.
Variants: none.
Adaptations: none.
Comment, references: Cox 1925 294; Gray 90; Laws O 39; Sharp 1932 ii 403 #97.
Broadsides, songsters: *Elton* 318-19; W. C. Ford #3307; Lowens 90 #282, listing; *New Book of 1000* 244-45; *Pearl Songster* 56-57; P. S. Smith 22-23.
Texts: ATL 628.7 (Charles Seeley); L. Chappell 140-41; Christie ii 66-67; Creighton 1971 45-46; Davis Index 43; Emrich 1974 129-30; FO 17.2.11; *FST* ii 22-23 #9; Grover 16-17; Karpeles 1974 ii 571-74, A - D; Kincaid iii 18; E. Moore 163-65; *NA Ives* 1.38 + ATL 2163.5; Peacock 709-10; *PTFLS 18* 8-10; *Sam Henry #31*; Schinhan iv 205; Peggy Seeger 1960 87; *SFQ 5* 139-41; C. J. Sharp 1961 ii 88 (R. V. Williams).

Unrelated text (*The Bear on Red Hill*): *Neighbors* 1943 27.
Text and tune relatives: Huntington 192-94; M. Leach 1965 316-17; Ord 421-22.
Tune relatives: *Clancy* 1964 58; *Clancy* 1971 156-57; Joyce #399 + J. R. Wilson #14a; Manny 283 + *NA Ives* 62.5, *The Rose of Britain's Isle*; *NA Ives* 1.108 + ATL 3115.2-.3; *NA Ives* 1.113 + ATL 3120.5; *NA Ives* 1.156 + ATL 3163.3; *NA Ives* 61.2, *The Moncton Tragedy*; *NA Ives* 66.5.6, 66.8.9; Petrie #1243, #1244, #1245.
[See also notes to #4 C].

56.
The Little Cabin Boy

Previously available: *Neighbors* 1943 13-14.
Variants: ATL 618.2-3; ATL 624.5.
Adaptations: none.
Comment, references: none.
Broadsides, songsters: none.
Texts: Christie i 242-43, *William, the Handsome Cabin Boy*.
Text and tune relatives: Stubbs 48.
Tune relatives (*Chesshire*),
    Comment, references: *JFSS 3* 49-50.
    Tune: *JFSS 3* 49b.
(*Idumea*, by Ananias Davisson),
    Comment, references: G. P. Jackson 1933 135 #11.
    Tunes with this text: Carden 38b; Cayce #184; Davisson 33b; Deason 55b; Fillmore 173c; Funk 131b + Showalter 131b; Hauser 1848 224b; Hauser 1878 158; Hayden 1852 121a; Hendrickson 40; G. P. Jackson 1933 135 #11; G. P. Jackson 1937 155-56 #137; J. B. Jackson 36; *JAF 88* 273d; LPS 260-04.2.7; McCurry 55b; M. L. Swan 44; Walker 31a; B. F. White 47b + Cooper 47b + G. P. Jackson 1933 177 #4a.
    Tunes derived from *Idumea*, for other hymn texts: FSA 22.1.8, *The Day Is Past and Gone*; G. P. Jackson 1952 176 #319, *Caroline* (from William Walker's *Christian Harmony* 1866 55); *JAF 88* 173c, *In Sharon's Love*; M. L. Swan 73a, *Oh Sing to Me of Heaven*; Wilkinson 128, *The Day Is Past and Gone*; Wilkinson i #344, *My God, My Life*; Wilkinson i #611, *I Was a Wandering Sheep*.
(Child 289, *The Mermaid*): Callcott 18-19 #16 + Bronson iv 385 #37 + *JFSS 3* 49a, *The Cabin Boy*; Bronson iv 385 #38.

(*Polly on the Shore*): *JEFDSS* 9 195 (P. Kennedy); *JFSS* 7 7-8 (Moeran).
(*The Seeds of Love*): Nettel 82-83 #1, 290.
(*The Sprig of Thyme*): *JEFDSS* 9 190 + Howes 167; *JFSS I* 86 A, 88 B.
(others): JEFDSS 9 72, *George Collins*.

Verse-form relatives with tune distant (*I'll Bid My Heart Be Still*, by Thomas Pringle): A. Campbell i 40-41; G. F. Graham iii 84-85; *Lyric Gems* ii 3b.
(Child 289, *The Mermaid*): Bronson iv 370-86 #1-#5, #7, #9, #17, #19-#24, #26-#33, #40.
(*The Seeds of Love*),

 Comment, references:W. Chappell 1859 ii 520;23 FSA 33F 19 (Goldstein); S. B. Gould 1892 xv #7; S. B. Gould 1905 3-4 #7; Howes 163-67; Karpeles 1974 i 738 #153; Nettel 81-84 (with tune comparison chart); *PMLA 33* 363-65 (Belden); Reeves 1960 229-38; C. J. Sharp *FSS* i 57-58 #1; C. J. Sharp 1965 187; Simpson 116-19.
 Tunes with this text: O. Carey 16-17; W. Chappell 1859 ii 522-23; Chilton 30-31; *FMJ 2* 279; FP 21A.1 (Andrew Rowan Summers); S. B. Gould 1905 36-37; Hamer 1967 14; *JFSS 4* 23 + C. J. Sharp 1920 i 42-44 # C. J. Sharp 1965 102b; *JFSS 4* 23-25 # Karpeles 1974 i 581-83 D, F, G; *JFSS 4* 291-91 + *FST* iii 22-23 #9; *JFSS 8* 19-21 + Karpeles 1974 i 577-78 A; Karpeles 1974 i 577-88, A-N; A. L. Lloyd 1967 183-84; Luboff 120-21; MacMahon i 75-76 #42 + Clayre 17-18 + Howes 163; Sedley 138-39; C. J. Sharp *FSS* i 3-4 + *All Time* 6 + Karpeles 1973 93 + Karpeles 1975 i 22 #20 + C. J. Sharp 1916 76-78 #33 + C. J. Sharp 1920 i 42-44 + VRS 1001A.6 + VRS 1001J A.6; C. J. Sharp 1961 v 216-22 (Merrick); C. J. Sharp 1965 186-87.
(*The Sprig of Thyme*): Boulton ii 202-3; Creighton 1932 53-54 + Creighton 1940 40-41; Farnsworth 1909 62-65; FSA 33.2.2 + FSA 33F 20; S. B. Gould 1892 14-15 #7 + S. B. Gould 1905 14-15 #7; Grainger #122; *JFSS I* 210-11; Kidson 1891 69; Kidson 1926 116-17; O'Shaughnessy 1966 1-6; C. J. Sharp 1961 i 10-11 (Hammond) + C. J. Sharp 1916 79-81 #34 + C. J. Sharp 1920 I 45-47; *Whittier Perkins* 50b + *JAF 22* 79a, *Come All You Maidens Fair*.
(*When Arthur Ruled This Land*, or *King Ar-*

thur Had Three Sons): [see notes to #116, *The Three Rogues*].
(others): W. Chappell 1859 ii 462-63 + Simpson 119 #74, *Hey, Ho, My Honey:* W. Chappell 1859 ii 522-23 + Stokoe 80-81 + W. J. Whittaker 102-3 #34, *The Willow Tree:* S. B. Gould 1974 10, *Adieu to Old England;* Graves 1897 115-58, *O Love, 'Tis a Calm Starry Night;* Hamer 1967 4-5, *Come All You Garners Gay; JFSS 4* 291-92; *JFSS 5* 91 + Karpeles 1974 ii 301-2, *'Tis I Myself Have Done; JFSS 8* 33 + Karpeles 1974 ii 475, *When Jesus Christ Had Lived;* Karpeles 1975 ii 10 #8, *The Briery Bush.*

57.
Betsy B

Previously available: *Neighbors* 1942 33.
Variants: ATL 622.11.
Adaptations: Cazden 1949b #2; Cazden 1958 i 74-75 + Cazden 1978 74-75; Haufrecht 1943 18-19; Haufrecht 1965 ii 1-6.
Comment, references: Belden 1952 ii 253-54; FHE 231A (Ph. Barry); *JAF 12* 245 (Newell); Laws M 20; Purslow 1968 121; Reeves 1960 53; ZDA 75F 2-4 (MacColl, Peggy Seeger).
Broadsides, songsters: ZDA 75F 2-3, 3b.
Texts: ATL 195.9; W. W. Chamberlain 146-47; Combs 1967 213 #94, listing; Davis Index 55; FHE 233, 235; FSE 20.1.7; *JEFDSS 8* 150-51; Karpeles 1974 i 338-39; Lyle 48-49; Reeves 1960 51-55, A - C; Schinhan iv 147; C. J. Sharp 1932 ii 4-5.
Text and tune relatives: ATL 626.3 (James Edwards); Bayard i 82.4; Creighton 1971 123-24; Flanders 1937 10-11; Flanders 1953 9-11; FO 21.1.5; Huntington 201-3 (text from an 1847 ms.); A. C. Morris 136-37; Peacock 666; Purslow 1968 12; Peggy Seeger 1960 29 #26; Wilkinson i #248.
Tune relatives (Child 53, *Young Beichan*): Bronson i 409-64 #1 - #111.
(Child 79, *The Wife of Usher's Well*): Bronson ii 249-64 #4 - #46, #49 - #52; Solomon 26-27.
(Child 132, *The Bold Pedlar and Robin Hood*): Bronson iii 42-45 #5 - #9, #11 - #13; RLP 12-624.2.4 (Ewan MacColl).
(Child 243, *The House Carpenter*): AFS L58A.5 + Bronson iii 464 #78.
(child 272, *The Suffolk Miracle*): Flanders 1953 146 + Bronson iv 88 #7.
(*Bourbon*).

Comment, references: G. P. Jackson 1936 133.

Tunes with this text: Carden 60b; Cayce #575; Funk 159 + Showalter 159; Hauser 1848 8a; G. P. Jackson 1937 132-33 #109; Lewis 56a; *Pilgrim Hymnal* #558; G. C. Robinson 36.

(*Dismission*): Carden 145b; Hauser 1848 8b; G. P. Jackson 1933 134 #4.

(other hymns): Cooper 50b + Denson 32b, *Distress*; Cooper 68a, *Do I Not Love Thee, Lord?*; Hauser 1878 34, *Granada*; *Pilgrim Hymnal* #578, *Peace*.

(*Bold Franklin*): Creighton 1962 145; Creighton 1971 202; Greenleaf 308.

(*Early, Early in the Spring*): Creighton 1962 163; Karpeles 1971 203; Petrie #765; C. J. Sharp 1932 ii 152 B.

(others): ATL 602.11-.12 (James Edwards), *Kate and Her Horns*; Barry 1929 391; Cazden 1961 6; Creighton 1950 67; Creighton 1962 194; Cox 1939 79; EKL 125.1.2; FO 7.1.7 + Fowke 1973 184; FSA 22.2.2; FSI 58.1.6, *Joe Hill's Last Will*; *Heart Songs* 67; *JFSS 2* 156 + A. L. Lloyd 1967 39a; *JFSS 2* 161, 162; *JFSS 3* 55 #20; *JFSS 7* 6; *JFSS 7* 66 + R. Palmer 1974 155; *JFSS 8* 212 #21; A. L. Lloyd 1967 39b; A. Lomax 1960 195; Manny 201 + *NA Ives* 62.4, *Nellie Ray*; Manny 245; Morse 54, *The Song of the World's Last Whale*; Munch 49-50; Nettel 144; Purslow 1965 14, *The Captain's Apprentice*; C. J. Sharp 1932 i 361 D, 361 E; SL 206.1.10, *The Four-Loom Weaver* (Ewan MacColl).

Unrelated tune: Denson 48b, *Kedron*.

58.
The 'Lady Leroy'

Previously available: none.
Variants: ATL 615.7-.8.
Adaptations: none.
Comment, references: Cox 1925 377; Fowke 1965 192-93 #55; FSC 10F 12 (Fowke); Laws N 5; Rickaby 225.
Broadsides, songsters: Gordon *AM* 23.10.26 221-22 [quotation].
Texts: Bayard i 107.1; *CFMJ 3* 28, listing; Davis Index 54; FO 11.1.3, 11.1.4; Fowke 1965 96 + FSC 10F 13 + FSC 10.1.6; Gardner 1939 174 + Wright 361-62; *JAF 29* 180-81; M. Leach 1965 86; *NA Ives* 61.4, 62.5; Peacock 208-9; Piper + Peterson Index 51; *Sam Henry* #214; Shoemaker 72-73; Stekert 1969 B 115; Stout 32-33 #24.

Text and tune relatives: Petrie #389.
Related text with tune relative (*Blue Mountain Lake*, or *The Belle of Long Lake*) [tune form includes *Derry Down* refrain], Chosky 210 #144.
Comment, references: Bronson i 359 #10; Flanders *BDN* 20.1.34 (Eckstorm); Laws C 20; *NYFQ 2* 52-53 (Flanders).
Texts, with tune indicated: Flanders *BDN* 20.1.34; HTA (Aussicker, Plumb); HTA (Lumberman); LCJ (Thayer), *Green Mountain Lake*; *NYFQ 14* 210, listing; H. Thompson 1940 267; Vox 632.2.690B (Richard Dyer-Bennet); F. M. Warner 31 + Silber 1973b.
Texts with tune: Flanders 1939 176-78 + Bronson i 359 #10 [omitting text]; FP 5003.48-6.1.2; J. Lomax 1947 168-69; McLean 75 (F. Warner); *NA Ives* 1.78 + ATL 2197.1g; *NYFQ 2* 53-55; *NYFQ 14* 222-23 + J. Edwards 96-97 + Silverman 1975 ii 408; SLP 82A.1.
Related text with tune relative (*The Little Brown Bulls*),
Comment, references: Laws C 16.
Texts with tunes: Eckstorn 56-58 [text only] + Barry 1939 30; Rickaby 65-68 + Botkin 1944 849.
Related text with tune relative (*Red Iron Ore*),
Comment, references: *JIFMC 3* 95 (Walton); Laws D 9.
Texts with tunes: E. C. Beck 1960 51-53; Dean 12-14 [text only] + A. L. Lloyd 1965 82-83 #50 + A. Lomax 1960 188 + J. Lomax 1934 477 + Rickaby 161-63; FO 8.2.1 + Fowke 1965 140-41; Fowke 1960 216-17 + J. Edwards 98-99 + Silverman 1975 ii 400-401 + *SO 10 #4* 6-7 (a parody by Alan Mills); Fowke 1967 68-70 + FM 4018.1.1; INT 25014.2.5; *JIFMC 3* 95; D. D. Lawrence 10; Luboff 44-45; C. Sandburg 1927 176-77; H. Sandburg 53-54.
Related text with tune relative (others, with refrain): Bayard ii 148.4; Greenleaf 138-39; Harlow 189; Hugill 189, 466b; B. Ives 1956 26 + B. Ives 1962 58-59 + B. Ives 1966 152-53; *JFSS 2* 171 #124; M. Leach 1965 216; J. Lomax 1941 227-28 + A. Lomax 1960 115-16; Peacock 136-37; SLP 81B.4; *Taverners* 18, *'La Pique'*.
Related text with tune relative (others, without refrain): ATL 185.7 (George Edwards); Creighton 1950 232; *JFSS 2* 100 #7 ii; Karpeles 1971 136; M. Leach 1965 346; Peacock 145 + Fowke 1967 66; C. J. Sharp 1961 ii 54-57 (R. V. Williams); WLP 724.2.7.
[See also notes to #120 A, #171.]

59.
The Rich Merchant

Previously available: none.
Variants: ATL 485.6.
Adaptations: none.
Comment, references: Laws M 19.
Broadsides, songsters: Ashton 1888 388-89.
Texts: ATL 188.8; Copper 1973 194-95; Creighton 1950 218 A; Flanders *SR* 16.9.34; Gardner 1939 112-13; Grover 142-43; *JFSS 1* 222-23; *NA Ives* 65.2.7; H. Thompson 1940 392.
Unrelated text (*Jack Monroe*, Laws N 7): Scarborough 1937 205.
Text and tune relatives: ATL 182.2; Creighton 1950 218-20, B - C.
Tune relatives: [see notes to #43 and to #72].

60.
The Dens of Ireland

Previously available: AFS 12309A.11 + EC 329.11.
Variants: ATL 623.11.
Comment, references: none.
Broadsides, songsters: *Isaiah Thomas* iii 46; Rollins #1816, #1817; Roxburghe i 320.
Texts: none.
Related texts, Comment, references:(Child 209, *Geordie*): Coffin 126-27; *SFQ 13* 161-68 (Coffin). (*The Judge and the Jury*): M. E. Henry 142-45 (Ph. Barry). (*The Rich Merchant Man*): Simpson 602-4.
Unrelated text (*The Gems of Ireland*): *Wehman's Iris #2* 30-31; *Wehman's Irish #3* 42.
Text and tune relatives: Joyce #624 [with related title only].
Tune relatives: Breathnach iii 66, 74, 156; Dallas 1974 39-40 (in b-b-b-a form); FO 14.1.8 + FO 15.2.4 + FM 4051.2.5 (in *a-b-b-a* form); Galvin 97; Gardner 1939 66, *Molly Baun* (in *a-b-b-a* form); Graves 1914 #65; Grover 158; Hatton 123; Healy 1967a 12f; *JFSS 2* 255; Joyce 1872 8 #8 + Breathnach ii 230, *Fainne Geal an Lae* [*The Dawning of the Day*]; Joyce #168, #256; Morton 1970 34; *NEF 7* 70; O'Keeffe 95, *The Jackets Green* (in *a - b - b - a* form); O Lochlainn 1939 76; O'Neill #95 + Zimmerman 240; O'Neill #239; Petrie #57; QC 903.1.5; *Sam Henry* #602 (in - - b-a form); *Sam Henry* #757 (in *a-b-b-a* form); *SFQ 30* 177 (in *b-b-b-a* form).

61.
The Pride of Logy Bay

Previously available: *JAF 72* 341, 343 #4.
Variants: ATL 184.7.
Adaptations: none.
Comment, reference: Fowke 1973 204-5; *JAF 72* 310-27 (Cazden).
Broadsides, songsters: none.
Texts: Doyle 1927 68 + Greenleaf 270-71; *NA Ives* 65.2.2.7a.
Text and tune relatives: Doyle 1940 25 + Blondahl 110 + Doyle 1955 59-60 + Doyle 1966 55-56 + Fowke 1973 114-15 + A. Mills 48-49; FSA 33F 9, listing, + text and tune (Sara Cleveland) [personal communication by Pandora Hopkins].
Related text and related tune (*The Maid of Sweet Gartine*),
  Comment, references [personal communication from D. K. Wilgus],
  Broadsides, songsters: *Songs & Recitations* iv (Cork, 1966) 40-41; O'Conor 31; *Universal Irish* 64; *Old "Come All-Ye's": The Finest Collection of Northern Ballads and Folk Poems; Second Enlarged Addition with Many Additional Ditties* (Derry Journal, ca. 1940) 10; *Ireland's Own* 6.4.35 450, 18.6 49 11; broadsides in National Library of Ireland; in Trinity College, Dublin, 22.bb.51 113, CC.M.77, Gall.R.15.34.
  Texts: Irish Folklore Collections, University College, Dublin, *MSS. 184* 264-67; *275* 712-16; *287* 194-97; *613* 68-70; *709* 440-43; *789; MSS. na Scol 187* 76-77; *413* 61-64; *531* 163; *655* 368-70; *108* 188, listing; Macdonagh Collection; *Sam Henry* [#594]: BBC Archive of Recorded Sound, LP 25570; Hume *Ms.* (1845); National Library of Ireland *Ms.* 490; *Ulster Folklore 17* (1971) 3-24, 188-90 (Hugh Shields); Ulster Folk Museum, Hugh Shields Collection T-1969-28; Robin Morton Collection T-26. [Duplicates of many of these are at the Center for the study of Comparative Folklore and Mythology at the University of California, Los Angeles].
Related text and related tune (*The Maid of Sweet Gartine*) [others],
  Broadsides, songsters: *Delaney's Irish #2* 7.
  Tunes with this text: FO 1.1.10; Manny 272-73 + *NA Ives* 61.2; *Miramichi Ms.* 16.5; *NA Ives* 1.53 + ATL 2177.6; *NA Ives* 1.78 + ATL 2197.4; O Lochlainn 1939 44-45; Peacock 375; Petrie #328, #329.
Tune relatives: Fowke 1954 76; Edw. Ives 1964

175-76; P. Kennedy 1975 790; *NA Ives* 1.21 + ATL 2149.5; *NA Ives* 1.71 + ATL 2190.3; Peacock 364.
[See also notes to #4 C].

62.
My Irish Molly-O

Previously available: none.
Variants: none.
Adaptations; none.
Comment, references: Kinkle i 23, listing.
Sheet Music Publications: New York: Jerome H. Remick, 1905; *Francis & Day #26* 14-16 (folio); *Francis & Day* 1948a 10-11 (folio); J. Mills 28 (refrain only).
Broadsides, songsters: *Delaney #42* 12.
Texts: none.
Related text (*Irish Molly-O*),
  Comment, references: Goldberg 250; Mattfeld 266; Shearin 13 (noting Brooke and Rolleston's *Treasury of Irish Poetry*, New York, 1905 15); Spaeth 1948 331.
  Broadsides, songsters: J. Andrews ii #9 + Wolf Index #1057; *Barney Williams; Beadle's Half-Dime #13* 2; *Book of 1001* i 101-2; *Broth of a Boy* 37; *Delaney's Irish #1* 15 + Kimball 173; *Elton* 34; *Father Miller; Formosa Songster* 47-49; *Gipsy's Warning* 15; *Handy Andy* 186- 61-62; *Harry Brown* 32; *Hyland* 92; *Jennie Hughes* 158; *Johnny Brougham* 32; *Kathleen Mavourneen* 42-43; *Lover's Harmony #50* 394; *Pearl Songster* 129-30; O'Conor 52; *Prize Song Book*, Appendix 10-11; *Punch's Comic Songster* 191-92; *Singer's Journal #6* 47; *Universal Irish* 148; Wehman #424; *Wehman's Irish #2* 27a + Wehman 617 113; *Well Known Songs* 24-25.
  Texts: Gardner 1937 213-14 (from Schoharie County, New York); Healy 1967 i 257-58; Joyce #403 (from Patrick W. Joyce, *The Native Music of Ireland, London 1842*); *Kidson 1929 86-87*; LCJ (from Herkimer, New York); A. C. Morris 440-41; Ord 131; Rosenberg Index #674.
  Text with common tune: Joyce #403; [see also notes to #178].
Unrelated texts (*I Wrote Some Letters*): Piper + Peterson Index 43.
(*Molly O*): *Wehman's Irish #4* 19b.
(*My Charming Molly O*): Purslow 1965 58.
(*She's Plain Molly O*, by William J. Scanlan): McPheeley 46-47.
Text and tune relatives: none.
Tune relatives: none.

63.
The Lost Lady

Previously available: none.
Variants: none.
Adaptations: none.
Comment, references: Dean-Smith Index; *JFSS* 2 99-101 #17; P. Kennedy 1975 797 #347, 743-51, 752-62; Laws Q 31; O'Shaughnessy 1968 40-41 #14; W. R. Mackenzie 1928 86.
Broadsides, songsters: as in Laws and others.
Texts: Barrett 43-44; Gillington 1907 12-13; Grainger #44, #281; Grainger 1949 #33 + O'Shaughnessy 1968 16-17 #14; Karpeles 1974 i 325-27, A - C; P. Kennedy 1975 775; *NA Ives* 65.17.10; R. V. Williams 1908 12-15 + C. J. Sharp 1961 ii 54-57.
Text and tune relatives: none.
Tune relatives: Peacock 222.

64.
Fair Fanny Moore

Previously available: *Neighbors* 1943 22.
Variants: ATL 615.4.
Adaptations: none.
Comment, references: *AFSPB 14* 180-81 (Laws); CFC 201F 21-22 (McCulloh); Flanders 1939 234 (Ph. Barry); Laws O 38: Irish; NW 239J3 1.7 (Paton); Randolph ii 64.
Broadsides, songsters: none.
Texts: Abrahams 186, listing; Bayard ii 168.5; Botkin 1949 720-21; CFC 201A.3 + CFC 201F 21-22; FHE 212 + Flanders *SR* 15.4.34; FHE 302; Flanders Index 244 #103, #121, #152; Flanders Index 245 #84; Flanders *SR* 12.8.34, 21.4.35; FSA 33F 7, listing + NW 239.1.7 (Sara Cleveland) + NW 239J3 1.7; Gardner 1939 479, listing; J. Lomax 1938 219-21; *MF 13* 148, listing; *Miramichi Ms.* 15.20; E. Moore 168-69; Piper + Peterson Index 33; Rainey 42; Rosenberg Index #379; Shay 1961 164-65; Sherwin 1933 28-29; Shoemaker 71-72.
Text and tune relatives: *NA Ives* 1.65 + ATL 2185.1; Peacock 610.
Tune relatives: none.

65.
The Lord of Scotland

Previously available: none.
Variants: ATL 613.5, 625.13.
Adaptations: none.
Comment, references: AFS L66F 28 (Alan Jabbour); Bronson ii 60-82; Child 68; Coffin 71-

74; A. K. Davis 1925 182-90; W. R. Mackenzie 1919 185-88; Zielonko 93 ff.

Broadsides, songsters: *Delaney's Scotch #1* 6; *Wehman's Collection #24* 22.

Texts: AFS L66A.1 (Maggie Hammons Parker); B. Arnold 60-61; ATL 563.16, 565.1; P. Buchan i 116-22; M. E. Bush i 75-76; Combs 1967 203 #17, listing; A. K. Davis 1960 113-22; Davis Index, Child 68 (80); Gainer 1975 37-38; Goss 1937 4-5; A. L. Lloyd 1945 20-21; E. Moore 47-51; Quiller-Couch 129-34; J. Roberts 158-62; Rosenberg Index #1598 (12); SLP 73B.3; R. Smith 1925 79-80; Stekert 1969 N 12.

Text and tune relatives: none.

Tune relatives (Child 4, *The Outlandish Knight*): Creighton 1950 4 B + Bronson i 56 #44; Grover 25-26.

Child 49, *The Two Brothers*): Bronson i 396-99, Group D #31-#37 [similar outline, notably #36, #37 (Wilkinson)].

(Child 213, *Sir James the Rose*): Greig 1925 141 #2 + Bronson iii 303 #13.

(Child 240, *The Rantin' Laddie*): Bronson iii 425 #5 + RLP 12-622.2.4 (MacColl).

(Child 243, *The Daemon Lover*): Bronson iii 465 #82.

(Child 250, *Henry Martyn*): *JAF 64* 49 + Hubbard 32.

(Child 289, *The Mermaid*): [see notes to #71].

Tune relatives (*Lisbon*): McCurry 182 + G. P. Jackson 1937 238 #247.

(*Suffering Saviour*): Buchanan 78-79 (from *Christian Lyre* 1842 42-43); Hauser 1848 54b; G. P. Jackson 1942 189 #184 (from *Christian Lyre* 1833 i 42); Neale 17; G. C. Robinson 46a; Woodbury 1856 345c.

(other hymns): Hauser 1878 83, *Suffering Jesus;* Walker 324b, *Intercession;* Wilkinson *510* 18.

Tune relatives (*Peter Gray*),

Comment, references: Damon #48 (with facsimile of sheet music publication, Boston: Oliver Ditson, 1858); Dichter ii #1211, "as sung by Billy Morris"; Spaeth 1948 135.

Tunes with this text: Agay 80; Atkinson 106; Beattie 233b; Bigelow 91; Boni 1947 56-57; Brackett 137b; Carmer 1942b 70-71; *Carmina Princetonia* 44; Cazden 1961 67; Cazden 1962 17; D. C. Chamberlain 189; CMS 650F.1; *College Songs #3* 10; *Comic Songster* 33b; Dallin 122-23; Daughters 267; *Famous College Songs* 51; Foster 113; FP 5003.48-5.1.3 (Pete Seeger); Garretson 44; Glass 1967b 37-38; Glazer 116-17; *Heart Songs* 359b; B. Ives 1949 22-23

+ B. Ives 1953 226-27; Kellogg 19; LCJ; J. Lomax 1941 252 + Kolb 22-23 + *Sam Eskin* i 166; *Most Popular College* 75; *Musical Bouquet #2514/*5; Okeh K3 CO 29844 + CL 628A.5b (Burl Ives); *Sam Eskin* iv 24; Silverman 1975 ii 185b; *Song Purpose* 207b; C. W. Stevens 84; *University of Toronto* 53; Waite 1877 ii 38 + *Northwestern* 38; Wilkinson *510* 53.

Unrelated tunes with this text: Kerr xii 48c (instrumental); *Musical Treasury* + 1213/4.

Tune relatives (others): Converse 1864 20; Creighton 1971 33; DL 8246.2.1; Flanders 1931 168; Flanders 1934 38; FM 4005A.7; Fowke 1954 166-67 (Barbeau); Fowke 1965 48 + FM 4051.2.8 + Wright 53; Fowke 1965 72; Fowke 1973 136; FSI 59.2.3 (in *a – b – b – a* form); G. Greig *FSB* 69; Hatton 138-39 + *Choice Irish Songs* ii 118-19; Haufrecht 1959 96; B. Ives 1962 56-57; *JAF 52* 25-26 #23; *JFSS 1* 256; Joyce #280; Karpeles 1973 4 #1a, #1b; Karpeles 1974 ii 573-74 D; P. Kennedy 1975 555; Kidson 1926 12-13; A. L. Lloyd 1965 64-65 #35; J. Lomax 1934 498; Morton 1973 161 #13 A, *John Barleygrain; Musical Bouquet #2525* 2b (instrumental); *NA Ives* 64.7 + Edw. Ives 1978 [399], *Grand Trunk Wreck;* Ord 317, 400; Ord 352 + Wright 505; Purslow 1968 74; Randolph ii 182; Sedley 158; Peggy Seeger 1970 45 #25; C. J. Sharp 1916 130-31 #57; C. J. Sharp 1961 ii 58-60 (R. V. Williams); C. J. Sharp 1961 107-9, 188-90, 229-30; Silber 1973a 161; Wyman 1920 42-44.

Unrelated tune (*My True Love*): Kidson 1891 46a, 46b.

66.
The Arsenic Tragedy

Previously available: none.

Variants: none.

Adaptations: AFS 12312B.15.

Comment, references: *BFSSNE #12* 14-18 (Jones, Ph. Barry); Emrich 1974 691-92; Laws F 14; Laws 1950 77-78; *NYH 17* 192-205 (Jones); H. Thompson 1940 441-42.

Broadsides, songsters: *Delaney #30* 24; *Wehman's Collection #13* 13.

Texts: Abrahams 185, listing; AFS 1776B.1 (from Gloucester, New Jersey); AFS 14634B.19 (Fred Atwood); *BFSSNE #12* 16b-17 + Emrich 1974 692-93; Burt 11-13; Davis Index 275; FO 4.1.4, 4.1.5; FSA 33F 7, listing; HTA (Cypher); *NYH 17* 203-4.

Related text (*Billy Vite and Nellie Green*),
 Comment, references: *BFSSNE #12* 18 (Ph. Barry).
 Texts [* indicates publication prior to 1845]: *Boosey* xii 6b (instrumental, ca. 1863); *Burton's Comic* * 238-39, "sung by Mr. Hadaway"; Cazden 1961 6; Chilton 122-23; *Clark's Orphean Warbler* 229; *Comical Brown* 24-26; *Concert Room* 43-45; *D'Alcorn #1* 43a; Davidson i 294a; *Fairburn 1823* *167 + *Fairburn 1830* *160 + *Fairburn 1832* *160 + *Harmonist's Preceptor* *164, *Billy Vite, or The Ghost of a Sheep's Head;* Flanders 1931 108-9; *Great Comic Volume* i 37c-38 #33; Hadaway *20-21; *Imperial* 11-12; *Jolly Comic Songster* 192-93; *Musical Bouquet #2581/2* 3a #2 (instrumental quadrille tune); *Musical Cabinet* *25-26 #64 (1822); *Owen Fawcett* 17; Spaeth 1927 198-99.
 Related text (*The Murdered Wife*): *BFSSNE #12* 16a; *NYH 17* 192 (facsimile).
 Text and tune relatives: ATL 185.7 (George Edwards); ATL 192.8 (Tom Kelly); ATL 486.2 (George Edwards); Carmer 1942b 25-26; Flanders 1931 65-68; Gardner 1939 346-48; *JAF 63* 268-70; M. Leach 1965 252-53; A. C. Morris 131-34; *PTFLS 23* 125-27; Randolph ii 121.
 Tune relatives: [see notes to #49].

67.
The "Bold Trellitee"

Previously available: none.
Variants: ATL 625.4.
Adaptations: AFS 12312B.6; Cazden 1958 i 46-48 + Cazden 1978 46-48.
Comment, references: Belden 1940 97-98; Bronson iv 312-14; Cazden 1958 i 108-9 + Cazden 1978 108-9; Child 286, *The Sweet Trinity, or The Golden Vanity;* Coffin 153-55; Friedman 409-11; *JAF 30* 330-31 (Kittredge); C. J. Sharp 1932 ii 395 #41; L. A. Smith 66-67; R. Smith 1928 58-59; Topic 12T161F B.11 (A. L. Lloyd).
Broadsides, songsters: Ashton 1887 201-4; Ashton 1891 #75; Holloway 553-54 #334; *Wehman's Collection #24* (1889) 17.
Songbooks with music: Boni 1947 172-73; Bullen 34-35 + *Canadian Boys* 192-93 #111; Cumming 37; H. W. Davies 36-37 #31; Engel 181-82; Gill 1917 20-21; Goss 1927 74; S. B. Gould 1905 14-15 + *University Songbook* 246-47; Haring 16-17; Kinley 70-71; Moffat 1901 300-301; S. H. Nicholson 136-37

#70; Okun 127-28; O'Shaughnessy 1971 12-13; Raine 6-7; *Scottish Students* 124-25; C. J. Sharp 1902 #17 36-37; Silverman 1975 ii 242; L. A. Smith 66-67 + MacMahon ii 62-63 #30; Stanford 1958 62; Waite 1877 ii 58.
 Texts: Abrahams 143-44; AFS L7A.1 + AFS L7F 31, A - B; *All Time* 14-15; Ashbee ii 2-3; ATL 487.9, 565.6, 606.2; Bayard i 104.2; Bayard ii 150.3, 169.1; Belden 1952 ii 191-95; Bronson iv 315-62; T. Burton i 37-38; T. Burton ii 86-87; M. E. Bush i 88-90; Carlisle 47-51, A - C; R. Chase 1938 20-21; R. Chase 1956 120-21; R. Clements 40-41; CMS 650B.6 + CMS 650F B.6; Cobb 37-39; M. Cohen 1966 64-65; S. N. Coleman 16-17; Creighton 1971 17-21; Dallin 138-39; A. K. Davis 1960 339-43; F. J. Davis 30-31; Dyer-Bennet 1946 7-8; Dyer-Bennet 1971 83-85, 158-59; FA 2319B.1 + FA 2319F B.1; Flanders *SR* 7.1.34, 3.6.34, 4.11.34; Flanders *BDN* 13.1.34; FM 4001B.1; FM 4005B.2 + FM 4005F B.2; FO 9.1.10; Fowke 1965 20-21; Fowke 1973 188; FSA 2.1.4 + FSA 2F B.9; Gainer 1963 #64; Gainer 1975 96-97; Gleadhill 314-15; Gordon *AM* 30.1.26; Gordon *AM* 1.4.27; Goss 1937 184-85; S. B. Gould 1974 44-45; Grainger #118, #119; Grover 138; Hamer 1967 78-79; Ch. Haywood 128-29; HL 500.2.2; INT 13058.2.6 + Peggy Seeger 1964 76-77; B. Ives 1953 42-44 + DL 8245.2.7 + B. Ives 1956 32-33 + B. Ives 1962 62-64 + B. Ives 1966 190-92; Karpeles 1971 107; Keynote K-108.517A (Richard Dyer-Bennet); K. Larson #9; LCJ (Braden); Leisy 1966 128-31; Linscott 136-37; A. L. Lloyd 1965 56-57 #30; A. Lomax 1960 191-92; E. Moore 134-35; Munch 75-77, 153-55; *NA Ives* 1.7 + ATL 2141.5; *NA Ives* 1.18 + ATL 2147.11; *NA Ives* 62.2, 65.17.11; Piper (2); Purslow 1972 37-38; Quiller-Couch 701-2; Reeves 1960 123-24; Ritchie 1965 96-97; Ritchie 1965a 80-81; RLP 12-625.1.4; RLP 199-34.2.1; Rosenberg Index #1361 + Rosenberg T-86 24B.1, 25A.1; *Sam Eskin* iv 25; Schinhan iv 120-24; Peggy Seeger 1960 65; Pete Seeger 1973 214 + *SO 12 #5* 32-33 + *RSO #6* 14-15 + *RSO #7* 24-25 + Silber 1963 19; Shellans 62-63; *Singabout 4 #2* 12-13; Spaeth 1948 596, listing as of 185-; SS 14 55-56, 179-80; Stone 74-76, 77-78; *Tent & Trail* 64; Vox 632.4.693A (Richard Dyer-Bennet); F. M. Warner 51-52; R. V. Williams 1959 46-47.
 Text and tune relatives: ATL 603.1 (James Edwards), with different *a* phrase.
 Text, tune and verse-form similar but lacking the *a* phrase: Bronson iv 335-59 #99-

#105.

Text and tune similar but lacking two opening lines of verse-form: Bronson iv 347-54
#80-#98.

Verse-form and refrain tune similar: Bronson
iv 340-43 #67-#71.

Verse-form similar but not tune relatives:
Bronson iv 337-39 #61, #62, #64; Carlisle
47-49 A, 50-51 B; Christie i 238-39; Cox
1925 169-71 A, B; A. K. Davis 1929 602 D;
Scarborough 1937 185-87 A; C. J. Sharp
1932 ii 285 D, 289 I; Topic 12T161B.11 +
Topic 12T161F B.11.

Tune relatives: [see notes to #117, #134].

68.
Down by the Greenwood Shady

Previously available: *JAF 72* 344 #6; *Neighbors*
1942 12; *NYFQ 4* 36.

Variants: none.

Adaptations: Cazden 1958 ii 104-5 + Cazden
1973 104-5; Cazden 1963 ii 23.

Comment, references: Bronson i 276-78; Cazden 1958 ii 115-16 + Cazden 1973 115-16;
Child 20, *The Cruel Mother;* Coffin 50-51;
Ehrke 56-59; FSA 11F 16; C. J. Sharp 1932 ii
387 #10; Topic 12T160F A.8 (Lloyd); ZDA
66F 3 (MacColl, Peggy Seeger); Zielonko 63,
90ff.

Broadsides, songsters: Fawcett 150-53.

Texts: Allingham 279-80; Arthur 5; ATL 193.9
("Dick" Edwards); ATL 487.10, 490.3, 563.
2; ATL 616.11 (Minnie Ward); ATL 618.5
(Frank Edwards); Bayard i 110.5; Bronson i
278-96; Combs 1967 201 #9, listing; Davis
Index, Child 20; FG 3519.2.1; FHE 39, 115,
162-63, 351, 352; Flanders *SR* 18.2.34; Flanders *BDN* 3.3.34; M. B. Foster 55; FSA
11.2.5 + FSA 11F 16-17; Gainer 1963 #62;
Goss 1937 16-17; INT 14016.2.3 + Peggy
Seeger 1964 18; Lyle 36-38; E. Moore 32-34
(2); *NA Ives* 62.2; Okun 1968 175-76; R. Palmer 1973 67-68; Peacock 804-5; Purslow
1965 22; Quiller-Couch 102-3; M. Raven iii
72; RLP 12-628.2.3; Rosenberg Index #255
(6); *SO 15 #4* 19 + Silverman 1975 i 182b-83;
Stubbs 30; Topic 12T160A.8 + Topic
12T160F A.8; ZDA 66.1.5-.9.

Text and tune relatives: none.

Text and some degree of tune relationship:
Bronson i 290 #38, #39 (Wilkinson); A. K.
Davis 1929 561 C + Bronson i 291 #43;
Gainer 1975 26-27; C. J. Sharp 1932 i 57 C +
Bronson i 291 #42; C. J. Sharp 1932 i 60 H +

Bronson i 291 #40.

Tune relatives: none.

69.
She Perished in the Snow

Previously available: AFS 12309A.14 + EC
329.14; *Neighbors* 1947 15.

Variants: none.

Adaptations: Cazden 1958 i 50-51 + Cazden
1978 50-51.

Comment, references: Cazden 1958 i 121-22 +
Cazden 1978 121-22.

Broadsides, songsters: *Delaney #2* 9; *H. M. S.
Pinafore* 38; *Johnson & Bruno* 9; *Manning &
Drew* 30; Wehman #117; Wehman ii 17.

Texts: AFS 1353A.2; B. Arnold 98; Combs
1967 211 #77, listing; Flanders Index 240
#4; LCJ (Bush); Rosenberg Index #1408 (2);
Wilkinson i #310.

Related text (*The Snow Storm*),

Comment, references: Jordan 81-82; M. R.
Turner 308.

Texts: Jordan 83-86 (facsimile); M. R. Turner
306-8.

Text and tune relatives: none.

Tune relatives: none.

70.
Bright Phoebe

Previously available: *JAF 72* 342 #1; *Neighbors*
1946 23.

Variants: none.

Adaptations: AFS 12312A.4; AFS 12312A.12;
Cazden 1958 i 87 + Cazden 1978 87.

Comment, references: Cazden 1958 i 109 +
Cazden 1978 109; *JAF 72* 341 #1.

Texts: Dean 104, *Sweet Mary Jane;* Huntington 119-29.

Unrelated text (*Bright Phoebus*, by James
Hook),

Comment, references: Purslow 1968 123.

Texts: Purslow 1968 20.

Text and tune relatives: *BFSSNE #3* 6, *The
Down-East Maid;* Creighton 1962 96, 97 +
Bissell 4-7, *Phoebe;* Grover 100, *Sweet
Caroline;* Peacock 434 A + Fowke 1967 120-
21, *Bright Phoebe;* Peacock 435 B (second
half of tune only).

Tune relatives: none.

Unrelated tunes, Comment, references:
(*Fortune, My Foe*): W. Chappell 1859 i 162-
63, 167-68; Simpson 227 #144, 228-31.
(*Greensleeves*): *JAMS 20* 44-45, 46 #12
(John M. Ward).

71.
[The Mermaid]

Previously available: none.
Variants: ATL 626.18.
Adaptations: none.
Comment, references: Ph. Barry 1929 363; Bronson iv 370-71; Child 289; Coffin 157-58; Cox 1925 172; A. K. Davis 1960 344; Dunstan i 57; *JAF 30* 333 (Kittredge); *JFSS 3* 48-51 (Nicholson); W. R. Mackenzie 1928 65.
Broadsides, songsters: Ashton 1891 #41 + Stone 17-18; *Beauty of the Blondes* 146 (a comic parody); *Book of 1001* i 30-31; De Marsan, List 14 #56; *Forecastle Songster* 112-13; *Jenny Lind* 79 + New Book of 1000 79; *Pearl Songster* 155; *Singer's Journal #42* 301; *Street Literature* (J. Catnach, London); Wolf Index #1422.
Texts: Abrahams 83-84; Ashbee ii 15; ATL 613.1; Bronson iv 371-87; Carpenter 80-81; M. Cohen 1966 72-73; Creighton 1950 106-7; Creighton 1971 26; Davis Index, Child 286 (3); A. K. Davis 1960 344-49; Duncan 1927 18-19 #18; FSA 33F 8, listing; Goss 1937 136-37; Hugill 560-61; B. Jackson 119-21 (McCulloh); E. Moore 135-37; Neeser 310-12; RLP 12-814.2.1; Rounder 0017.1.5 + Rounder 0017F 6c; Rosenberg Index #896 (2); Schinhan iv 124-25; Peggy Seeger 1964 54; *SFQ 36* 23-25; L. A. Smith 64-66; H. Thompson 1940 216-17 + H. Thompson 1958 30.
Songbooks with music: S. C. Andrews 41, 56; Armitage 1918 142-43; Blondahl 90; *British Minstrelsie* iii 7-9; Buck 1933 63; *Carmina Princetonia* 7; K. S. Clark 1930 80 #92; K. S. Clark 1931 120; *Columbia University* 50-51; Converse 1888 35-36; Dare 37; F. J. Davis 92-93; H. W. Davies 65 #56; Duncan 1927 266-67; *Ernest Newton* 52-53; *Famous College Songs* 33; Farmer 168-69; Farnsworth 1917 53; N. Foster 122; *Francis & Day* 1952 8-9; Garretson 59b; Goss 1927 118; S. B. Gould vi 74-76; Hadow 72-73; Hansen 124b; *Heart Songs* 360-61; Hills 27; Honoré 24; C. Johnson 156; Kellogg 23; Kerr iii 38d (instrumental); Kinley 84-85; MacMahon i 111-13 #60; Marzials 39; Moffat 1901 56-57; *Most Popular College* 48-49; *Musical Budget 5* 682-83; *Never Grow Old* 108-9; S. H. Nicholson 138 #71; Noble 1908 60-61; Noble 1912 129; *Old Songs* 108; E. A. Palmer 174-77; Posselt 1943 102; Ratcliff 64-65; *Scottish Students* 122-23; C. J. Sharp 1902 44-45 #21; Silverman 1975 ii 247; *Sing Together* 25-26; R. B. Smith 59; *Songs of Columbia* 33; Stanford 1958 24-25; C. W.

Stevens 110; Trident 106-7; *University Songbook* 200-201; Waite 1868 19-20; Waite 1877 ii 47 + *Northwestern* 47; Wrubel 4-5.
Unrelated text (*The Mermaid*): *Musical Bouquet #4672/3* (1871); L. A. Smith 34-36; *Scottish Students* 120-121; *University Songbook* 202-3.
Text and tune relatives: none.
Tune relatives: Ord 317, *The Whaler's Song.* [See also notes to #65].

72.
The Lakes of Col Flynn

Previously available: none.
Variants: ATL 627.1.
Adaptations: none.
Comment, references: *BFSSNE #8* 9-12 (Ph. Barry); Flanders 1939 33-34 (Ph. Barry); P. Kennedy 729 #324; Laws Q 33 (Irish); M. Leach 1955 732-33; *Sam Henry #176.*
Broadsides, songsters: *Delaney's Irish #5* 3; *Hyland* 185; *Shamrock Shore* 5; Wehman #707; Wehman *617* 99 + Kimball 112; *Wehman's Irish #2* 13-14.
Texts: *BFSSNE #8* 9-12 + Ph. Barry 1939 26-27 + Emrich 1974 232-34; Brune 41; *B&S #6* 13; FHE 228, 326; Flanders *SR* 9.9.34; Flanders 1937 23; FSA 33F 8, listing; Gardner 1939 480, listing; Graves 1914 #24; G. Greig *FSNE #114;* Joyce 1872 103 #100 + Joyce #417; Karpeles 1974 i 256-59, A - D; P. Kennedy 1975 708-9; A. C. Morris 437; Piper + Peterson Index 51; Purslow 1968 65; *Sam Henry* 176, *Willie Lennox;* Walton *132* 102a + Walton ii 126.
Related text by Walter Maynard: *Choice Irish Songs* ii 116-17; Hatton 146-47.
Text and tune relatives: Flanders 1939 32-33; *JIFS 9* 15-16.
Derived text with related tunes: Creighton 1962 104, 105.
Tune relatives (*Lovely Jimmie*): Ph. Barry 1939 35; Bayard 58-59; M. Leach 1965 72; O Lochlainn 1939 110.
(*The Pride of Glencoe*): *NA Ives* 1.24 + ATL 2151.8; *NA Ives* 1.53 + ATL 2177.7; *NA Ives* 1.76 + ATL 2195.6 + J. R. Wilson #29a; *NA Ives* 1.77 + ATL 2196.4; *NA Ives* 1.100 + ATL 3107.4; J. R. Wilson #29.
(*The Sioux Indians*),
  Comment, references: Laws B 11.
  Texts with this tune: AFS 5B (Alex Moore); Botkin 1951 743; Cazden 1963 i 5; CMS 670B.4 (Tom Glazer); FH

5337A.3 (Roger Welsch); Fife 1969 122;
FP 5003.48-5.2.7; B. Ives 1953 242-43 +
B. Ives 1962 178-79; Kolb 101-3;
J. Lomax 1938 344-36 + A. Lomax 1964
100; Randolph ii 216; *Sam Eskin* ii; Sil-
ber 1967 34; Silverman 1975 i 16; M. R.
Turner 119-20; :J. Warner 119-20.

Tune relatives (others): Creighton 1962 69;
Fowke 1965 148 + Fowke 1973 126-27;
Greenleaf 73 + J. R. WIlson #29d; Green-
leaf 78 + Colcord 144 + J. R. Wilson #29e,
#29g; Grover 170; Huntington 122; *JAF 14*
297; *When You Grow Old;* Joyce #600;
Manny 243 + ATL 2172.3 + *NA Ives* 1.48;
Manny 292 + J. R. Wilson #29c; *NA Ives*
1.73 + ATL 2192.4 + J. R. Wilson #29b;
NA Ives 62.5, *Green Grow the Rushes;* O
Lochlainn 1939 90; Ord 294; Petrie 1855 i 72;
Rickaby 68 + J. R. WIlson #29f.

73.
Erin's Green Shores

Previously available: none.
Variants: ATL 485.9.
Adaptations: AFS 12312B.2; Cazden 1958 i 86
+ Cazden 1978 86; Cazden 1963 ii 3-4; Hauf-
recht 1963 63.
Comment, references: *AFSPB 14* 179 (Laws);
Cazden 1958 i 111-12 + Cazden 1978 111-12;
Fowke 1965 180-81 #35; FSI 59F 11 (Hicker-
son); Kimball 85-88; Laws Q 27 (Irish); Zim-
merman 178-80.
Broadsides, songsters: *Delaney's Irish #1* 7; De
Marsan #90, marked Johnson's, Philadel-
phia; *Greenback Songster* 65-66; Haly +
Zimmerman 178-179; *Hyland* 98-99; *Kath-
leen Mavourneen* 12; *Mabel Waltz* 21; *Rising
of the Moon* 35; *Shamrock Shore* 2; *Singer's
Journal #6* 42; Wehman #210; *Wehman's
Collection #32* 8; *Wehman's Irish #1* 42;
Wehman #617 107 + Kimball 86-87.
Texts: G. Anderson 79; Creighton 1932 171-72
+ Wright 357; Creighton 1962 164, 165;
Davis Index 123; FO 21.2.7; Fowke 1965 88-
89 + INT 25014.1.1; FSA 33F 7, listing; FSI
59F 11-12; Gardner 1939 479, listing; Grover
203-4; E. Moore 194-95 + Wright 355-56;
Peacock 364; Piper (2) + Peterson Index 32;
Stekert 1969 B 143; Thomas 1931 176-78.
Texts with tune of *The Pretty Girl Milking Her
Cow:* see notes to #31, *The Green Mossy
Banks by the Lea.*
Text and tune relatives: ATL 601.15 (James Ed-
wards); Randolph i 324-25 (stretched tune
form), *Aaron's Green Shores.*

Related (parody) text with related tune (*The
Banks of the Little Eau Pleine,* by William
N. Allen),
Comment, references: Laws 1950 44; Laws C
2; *NEF 5* 78; Rickaby xxiv-xxxviii, 196-98.
Texts with this tune: E. C. Beck 1948 151;
Rickaby 25-29 [as sunb by William N. Al-
len, known as Shan T. Boy] + Botkin
1955 578-79 + Carmer 1942b 192-93 +
R. Lloyd 1969 42-43.
Texts with tune of *The Pretty Girl Milking
Her Cow:* see notes to #31.

Tune relatives (Child 13, *Edward*): AFS
L12A.4.
(Child 78, *The Unquiet Grave*):Bronson ii
241 #28.
(Child 84, *Barbara Allen*): Bronson ii 327 #5
(Child 85, *George Collins*): Bronson ii 402
#33.
(Child 200, *The Gypsy Laddie*): Bronson iii
203 #5, 220-25 #50-#55, #61, #63, #64,
#65, #67.
(Child 283, *The Crafty Farmer*): Bronson iv
289-90 #14-#17.
Tune relatives (*Botany Bay*, Edwards Type 1).
Comment, references: Cray 222-26, 253-54;
R. G. Edwards 1971 10-15; [see also notes
to #100, *The Prisoner's Song*].
Texts with this tune: H. Anderson 18-19;
Ashbee × 9; Brand 1960 18-19 + AFLP
1884 (bawdy parody); *Chapbook 4 #2* 29;
Cray 135 (bawdy parody); R. G. Edwards
1956 23 + R. G. Edwards 1971 10-11; Fin-
ger 129-31 + Boni 1952 247-49; Hansen
29; Long 5-6; MacMahon 1963 #3;
Manifold 22; Meredity 1968 36-37; Mitch-
ell 88-90; Randolph i 374; *This & That* 4a
(collegiate parody); R. Ward 13; Zanzig
#85.
Tune relatives (*Here's Adieu to All Judges and
Juries*): R. G. Edwards 1971 11-12; Gilling-
ton 1911 14-15; Purslow 1972 39; [see also
notes to #100, *The Prisoner's Song*].
Tune relatives (Davis: B. F. White 15; Wyeth ii
81a + Hauser 1848 270a.
(*Dulcimer*),
Comment, references: G. P. Jackson 1937
177-78.
Tunes with this text: Aldrich 18; Doan 200
#389; Funk 65 + Showalter 65; G. P.
Jackson 1937 177 #163 (from *Primitive
Baptist Hymn and Tune Book* 1902 309);
Kirk 216; W. McDonald 1855 212-13;
Methodist Hymnal 1905 #530; *Songs of
Zion* #101; Walker 15.
(*Dunlap's Creek*),

Comment, references: Buchanan xiv-xv; G. P. Jackson 1933 144 #52.

Tunes with this text: Aikin 120b; Aldrich 79; Cayce #650 (from *Baptist Hymn & Tune Book* 1857 106); Deason 44b; Ditson 1869 169c; Fillmore 133a; Hauser 1848 100b; Hauser 1878 98; Hendrickson 15b; G. P. Jackson 1933 144 #52; Kirk 50; Lewis 69a; McCurry 238b; *Methodist Hymns* 1857 347; Rhinehart 50a; Showalter 63; Walker 276a + Buchanan 8-9 #4 + G. P. Jackson 1937 108 #79; Woodbury 1853 98 + Woodbury 1856 98.

(*Ester*): Cayce #491; Cooper 437 + Denson 437 + G. P. Jackson 1933 193b + G. P. Jackson 1937 46 #17.

(*Florence*, with complete tune form): Denson 121 + G. P. Jackson 1937 110 #82.

(*How Lovely the Place*): Knapp 46-47.

(*Imandra New*, with complete tune form): Cayce #459; Hendrickson 71; G. P. Jackson 1942 37 #21.

(*Land of Rest*): Hauser 1878 117 + G. P. Jackson 1937 110a #81.

(*Mount Bither*): Hauser 1878 199; W. McDonald 1855 212-13.

Tune relatives (*The Orphan Girl*),

Comment, references: Abrahams 177-78 #38; Belden 1940 277; Cooper 506; G. P. Jackson 1937 48; C. Sandburg 1927 316; *SO 25 #5* 26.

Tunes with this text: Abrahams 96-98; Belden 1940 278; Boette 61; Brumley ii #18; T. Burton ii 89b; Cooper 506 + G. P. Jackson 1937 48 #19; FSA 32.1.5, parody (Hedy West); Gainer 1963 #15; Gainer 1975 118-19; Kincaid ii 27; McDowell 1947 37-38; *PTFLS 23* 282; C. Sandburg 1927 316-19; H. Sandburg 92b; Scarborough 1937 364 A; Schinhan iv 217 C, 217 F, 218 H; *SO 16 #5* 19 + Silverman 1975 i 150b-51; *SO 25 #5* 27.

Tune relatives (others): Abrahams 54; J. V. Allen 124; Ph. Barry 1939 54, *Sweet Mary Ackland* (with complete tune form); E. C. Beck 1948 51; Blondahl 88; M. E. Bush i 7; Carlisle 81-82; *Chapbook 3 #6* 18-19; *Chapbook 4 #1* 7; *Clancy 1964* 55 + Graeme 116-17 + *Clancy 1971* 116-17; Cox 1939 ii 76, *The Blind Child*; Dallas 1973 224; Doyle 1955 39 + Doyle 1966 48; R. G. Edwards 1971 15, 17, 133; FM 4005B.4; French 39; FSA 32.2.6 (West); Hubbard 86-87, *The Green Mossy Banks of the Lea*; Hamer 1973 16; Huntington 237; *JFSS 2* 6; *JFSS 5* 49-50 + Karpeles 1974 ii 552; Karpeles 1934 ii 13 + Karpeles

1971 226; Karpeles 1971 67, 218; Karpeles 1974 ii 47 B; Keene 8-9; Kincaid ii 32; J. Lomax 1938 266, *The Rambling Gambler*; Peacock 783, 784; *PTFLS 6* 224; Randolph iv 25, 361; Ruth 14 #37; H. Sandburg 155-56; Schinhan iv 218 #149 A, 219 D, 219-20 K; Peggy Seeger 1960 74 #68; *SO 10 #1* 20; *SO 11 #2* 4; TLP 1029.1.1; Topic 12T159A.9.

Unrelated tune (*Hewson, the Cobbler*): W. Chappell 1859 ii 451.

74.
The Ship's Carpenter

Previously available: none.

Variants: ATL 616.1-.2.

Adaptations: Cazden 1958 i 82-83 + Cazden 1978 82-83; Cazden 1963 i 30a.

Comment, references: Ph. Barry 1929 307, 310; Belden 1940 79-80; Bronson iii 429-32; Carlisle 36-37; Cazden 1958 i 122-23 + Cazden 1978 122-23; Child 243; Coffin 138-41; Ehrke 74-77; FA 2951F A.3 (Harry Smith); Fowke 1973 216 #81; S. B. Gould 1905 22 #76; *JAF 30* 325-26 (Kittredge); Leisy 1966 166-68; C. J. Sharp 1932 ii 394 #35; R. Smith 1925 122; R. Smith 1928 57-58; ZDA 67F 4-5 (MacColl, Seeger).

Broadsides, songsters: Ashton 1891 #74 + Stone 178-80, *The Distressed Ship Carpenter*; *Delaney #13* 24; De Marsan #154 [marked J. H. Johnson, Philadelphia] + *JAF 18* 207-9 + *MQ 2* 1 [facsimile] + Wolf Index #908; *Wehman's Collection #7*, listing.

Texts: Abrahams 7-9; AFS 10505B (Celia Kelder) + Bronson iii 438 #16; G. Anderson 50-53; ATL 484.2, 487.3; Boette 9-10; P. Buchan i 209-13; T. Burton i 4-5, 65-66; T. Burton ii 76-78, 105-7; M. E. Bush i 77-79; G. G. Carey 1971 103-4; Carlisle 38-40, A - B; CMS 650A.6 + CMS 650F A.6; Combs 1967 207 #36, listing; Creighton 1971 14-16; Cutting 69-71; Davis Index (2); Dunson 1973 24-25; Dyer-Bennet 1971 89-90; FA 2951A.3 (Clarence Ashley); Flanders *SR* 10.2.35; Flanders 1953 132-33; Fowke 1973 162-63; FP 2364B.4; FSA 22.1.5 + FSA 22F 17-18; FSA 33F 9, listing; Gainer 1963 #52; Gainer 1975 80-81; D. Gilbert 35-36; Gordon *AM* 30.7.23; S. C. Hall 31-36; Hansen 81b; Harrison 22-23; Keynote K-108.518B; Leisy 1964 188-89; Leisy 1966 166-68; A. L. Lloyd 1965 50-51 #27; A. Lomax 1960 132-33; McDowell 1947 2-3; Malone 1968 54, listing; E. Moore 111-13; *NA Ives* 1.7 + ATL 2140.12; *NA Ives* 1.7 + ATL 2141.3; Neal

69-71; Peacock 740-41; Quiller-Couch 123-26; Rainey 18; Reeves 1960 69-71; RLP 12-627.1.2; Sedley 209-10; Peggy Seeger 1964 33 + FL 5401A.3; Pete Seeger 1972 114-15; Pete Seeger 1973 215; Shellans 30-31; Silverman 1975 i 121; SLP 57A.1; R. Smith 1925 123-24; *SO 12 #2* 22-23 + *RSO #5* 24-25 + Silber 1963 75; Topic 12T140.1.5; ZDA 67.2.1 + ZDA 67F 5-6, A - D.

Texts with "ship carpenter" as title or as text element: Belden 1940 86-87 I; Bronson 436-37 #13, 464 #78; Fowke 1973 162-63; FSA 33F 9, listing (Sara Cleveland); Hubbard 28A.

Unrelated text (*The House Carpenter*): Beadle's Olden Time 68-70; Cozans iii 141-43.

Text and tune relatives: AFS 1001A.1 (Captain Pearl R. Nye) + Bronson iii 467 #85; Bronson iii 466 #84 (Wilkinson).

Text with similar verse-form but not the same tune strain: Ph. Barry 1929 304 A; Bronson iii 429-96 #79, #88, #100-#105, #107, #108, #115, #119.

Tune relatives, with matching verse-form (Child 4, *Lady Isabel and the Elf-Knight*): Cox 1939 5, 8; *Sam Eskin* iv 35; C. J. Sharp 1932 i 5 A, 8 D, 9 E, 12 G.

Tune relatives, without matching verse-form (Child 4, *Lady Isabel and the Elf-Knight*): Bronson i 51-52 #28a, #28b; Bronson i 81-99 #103, #104, #105, #107, #108, #110, #111, #112, #114-#120, #122, #123, #126-#131, #133, #134, #136, #138, #140; *JAF 70* 257 #1; Schinhan iv 4-8 A, C, E, G.

(Child 13, *Edward*): Bronson i 241-42 #7-#9.

(Child 74, *Fair Margaret and Sweet William*): Scarborough 1937 390.

(Child 75, *Lord Lovel*): E. Moore 57.

(Child 78, *The Unquiet Grave*): Bronson iv 473 #28.1.

(Child 84, *Barbara Allen*): R. Smith 1925 107-8 A.

(Child 105, *The Bailiff's Daughter of Islington*): G. Greig 1925 84 #1d + Bronson ii 519 #7.

(Child 200, *The Gypsy Laddie*): Bronson iii 203-16 #5, #6, #7, #8, #10, #11, #13, #16, #18, #19, #21, #30, #31, #32, #34, #35, #36.

(Child 217, *The Broom of the Cowdenknowes*): Bronson iii 340-42 #9-#17; *Tocher* #5 164.

Tune relatives (others): ATL 606.6; ATL 614.1-.2 (George Edwards), *The Major's Britches*; Ph. Barry 1939 48; FSA 22.2.6; Hubbard 315; MacColl 1965 55; McIntosh 1974 48; Ritchie 1964 24; Peggy Seeger 1964 35; C. J.

Sharp 1932 McIntosh 1974 48; Richie 1964 24; Peggy Seeger 1964 35; C. J. Sharp 1932 ii 225 C, 330 B, 331 C; Wilkinson i #491.

[See also notes to #134, *The Brats of Jeremiah*].

Tune relatives (complete tune form: *a – b – a – b – c – c – c – b*),

Comment, references: Bronson i 39-40; Bronson iii 198; Dick ii 96-97; G. P. Jackson 1937 58; H. K. Johnson 80; Laing 217-19; Stenhouse 175.

Tunes (Child 56, *Dives and Lazarus*): C. J. Sharp 1932 i 29 A + Bronson ii 21 #10; C. J. Sharp 1932 i 30 B + Bronson ii 20 #9.

(Child 84, *Barbara Allen*): R. Smith 1937 130 + Bronson ii 389 #192.

(Child 200, *The Gypsy Laddie* [*Johnny Faa*]): J. Johnson #181 + Bronson iii 202 #2 + Eyre-Todd 14 + Kinsley 1969 249-50 #66 + Maver 31 #61 + Ritson 1794 ii 176 + R. A. Smith iii 90.

(*Address for All*): Deason 101 + G. P. Jackson 1937 59 #29; Walker 99.

(*Church's Desolation*): Cayce #381; B. F. White 89 + Cooper 89 + Denson 89.

(*Lady Cassilles Lilt*): Dauney 228 #30 + Bronson iii 201 #1 + Goss 1937 95 E.

(*Lord Ullin's Daughter*): H. K. Johnson 332; Ogilvie 150 #163.

(*Louisiana*): Cayce #501; Deason 267; Denson 207 + G. P. Jackson 1942 151 #140; J. B. Jackson 41.

(*Mourner's Lamentation*): Deason 265 + G. P. Jackson 1937 57-58 #28; Hayden 1852 260; G. P. Jackson 1942 151 #140.

(*Wae's Me for Prince Charlie*): Hogg ii 192.

(*others*): J. B. Jackson 112; Ritchie 1965 8; Wilkinson i #101, *Sixteen Next Sunday*.

Tune relatives (*a – b – a – b* portion of complete tune): Bronson iii 202 #3, #4, Child 200, *The Gypsy Laddie*; Fowke 1970 146; G. P. Jackson 1944 277 #293.

75.
The Maid on the Shore

Previously available (#75 A): *Neighbors* 1943 20-21; *YIFMC 3* 74, Ex. 14.

Variants (#75 B): ATL 618.10; ATL 624.10.

Adaptations (#75 A): AFS 12312A.10; Cazden 1958 ii 8-9 + Cazden 1973 8-9; Cazden 1963 ii 30; FSI 65.2.2 (John Roberts, Tony Barrand).

Comment, references: Belden 1940 107;

BFSSNE #7 12-13 (Ph. Barry); Bronson i 336-37; Cazden 1958 ii 120-21 + Cazden 1973 120-21; *CEOL 3* 69-70 (Corcoran); Laws K 27; M. Leach 1955 731; A. Lomax 1960 138 #73; W. R. Mackenzie 1928 74.

Broadsides, songsters: none.

Texts: *BFSSNE* #7 12 + M. Leach 1955 731-32; Gordon *AM* 15.8.27; Grover 154-55 + Emrich 1974 526-28; Karpeles 1971 120-21 D; LCJ (Walsh); W. R. Mackenzie 1919 129; W. R. Mackenzie 1928 74-75 + Friedman 403-4; *MF 13* 146, listing; ZDA 68F 5-6 B.

Text and tune relatives: Belden 1940 107-8; *BFSSNE* #7 12 + Bronson i 345 #26 + Ph. Barry 1939 40-41; *CEOL 3* 68-69; Creighton 1962 41; Creighton 1971 110-11; Greenleaf 63-64 + Bronson i 346 #29 + Fowke 1967 158-59 + A. Lomax 1960 142-43; Grover 154-55 + Philo 1001B.1 (Margaret MacArthur); Hubbard 94-95; Huntington 136-37; Joyce #327 + Bronson i 346 #28; Karpeles 1934 i 30-35 A + Bronson i 345-46 #27 + Karpeles 1971 117-19 A + A. L. Lloyd 1965 32-33 #18; Karpeles 1934 i 36-38 B + Bronson i 346-47 #30 + Karpeles 1971 118-19 B; Karpeles 1971 120 C; Korson 1949 54-55; W. R. Mackenzie 1928 74-75 (tune 394-95 #19 A) + Barbeau 5-6 + Bronson i 344 #25; *NA Ives* 1.72 + ATL 2191.5; Peacock 296; *Sam Eskin* iv 43b; Peggy Seeger 1964 27; *SO 24* #5 29 + Silverman 1975 i 199 (Hedy West, from Folk Variety FV 12008); ZDA 68.2.2 (Peggy Seeger).

Tune relatives (*Drimindown*),

  Comment, references: Breathnach i 43; Bronson iii 179; Bunting 1840 ii 32 #42; Dick i 362 #32, 490-91 #339; *Drimindown*; FE 4307F 1 (Creighton); Hannagan i 21 #45; R. Mason 285; Petrie 1855 114-16; Sonneck 113; Stenhouse 173 #179, 297-98 #303; Zimmerman 56, 205.

  Tunes with this text or title: Creighton 1962 176 + FE 4307A.1, *Drimindoon;* Creighton 1964 280, *Drimindown;* Dibblee 78, *Drimindown;* Hannegan #45, *An Drimin Donn Dilis;* O'Neill #605, #606, *Drium-Fionn Donn Dhileas;* Petrie #81.

  Unrelated tunes, texts and/or verse-forms [* indicates *Drimindown* text]: Boulton 1893 244-47, *Drimin Dhu;* Breathnach i 42-43, *Dhriman Dhoun Deelish;* Breathnach i 208, *Driman Dhoun Dheelish;* Bunting 1840 ii *32 #42, *Drimmin Dubh;* M. M. Cole 25a, *Dimen Dru Deelish;* Delaney's *Irish #3* 3, *Drimendroo;* M. B. Foster 72-73, *Drumion Dubh;* Fraser iii 144-47, *An*

Druimionn Dubh; Graves 1914 57 #41, *Drinann Dhun;* J. Johnson #179 + Bronson iii 181 #7 + Dick i 31 #32, *Druimin Dubh;* H. Johnson #303 + Bronson iii 180 #1 + Eyre-Todd 208 + Maver 180 #360 + R. A. Smith iv 22, Child 191, *Hughie Grame* (with tune *Drimen Duff,* from Oswald); Joyce *#210, *Drimin Dhu Dheelish;* Joyce #371 + Zimmerman 205; Joyce #445, *Druimin Dubh Dilis;* Maver 241a #481, *Druimionn Dhu;* P. McDonald 13 #89, *Druimionn Dubh;* O'Conor 19, *Drimmin Dibh Dheelish;* O'Neill #130, *An Druim-Fhionn Dubh Dhileas;* O'Neill #220 + McPheeley 321 #876, *Druim-Fhionn Dubh Og;* O'Sullivan 143-44, *Druimfhionn Donn Dilis, Drimin Dhonn Deelish;* Oswald viii 12a, *Drimen Duff;* Petrie 1855 115, *Druimfhionn Donn Dilis;* R. A. Smith 1828a *100-101, *Drimin dhu;* *SO 9* #1 3, *Dhrinnin Dhu Dhrinnin;* Varian 115-16, *My Drimindhu,* by James McKowen; Wehman 617 45, *Drimendroo.*

Tune relatives (others): Creighton 1962 26, Child 289, *The Mermaid;* O'Neill #461, *The Sorrowful Maiden* (instrumental).

76.
The Foggy Dew

Previously available: *Neighbors* 1945 21; *NYFQ 10* 216-17.

Variants: none.

Adaptations: AFS 12312A.8 (Robert and Louise DeCormier); Cazden 1958 i 34-35 + Cazden 1978 34-35 + Lusk 8-9; FH 5311.1.3 + FH 5311F 7 (Barbara Moncure); RLP 12-634.2.3 (Milt Okun); SLP 72.2.2 (Robert and Louise DeCormier); *SO 5* #1 6 + *RSO #1* 20 [garbled].

(instrumental form, by Pete Seeger): VRS 9013.1.5.

(to text *Over the Hills,* by Pete Seeger): FP 85/3.1 + Haufrecht 1959 21 + Pete Seeger 1964 100 + Pete Seeger 1965 34-35 + Silber 1963 59 + Silverman 1975 i 142a + *Travelin' On* 78-79; Morse 118 (with variant text); Silber 1973b 147b (text only).

Comment, references: Cazden 1958 i 113 + Cazden 1978 113; *NYFQ 10* 213-17 (Cazden); Peacock 521; RLP 12-634J 2.3 (Okun).

Broadsides, songsters: none.

Texts: Randolph i 397 E.

Related text (*The Foggy, Foggy Dew* or *The Bugaboo*),

Comment, references: Cray 191; Dallas 1974 85-865; *JEFDSS 8* 153 (Lloyd, Shaw); *JFSS 1* 134; P. Kennedy 1975 428 #174; Laws O 3; Leisy 1966 103-6; Reeves 1958 45-57; RLP 12-618J 1.2 (A. L. Lloyd); RLP 12-656J 1.3 (A. L. Lloyd); C. J. Sharp *FSS* i 65 #17; Topic 12T158F A.5 (A. L. Lloyd).

Texts [" indicates tune of # /6]: Arany 63, ATL 614.10 (George Edwards); Brand 1960 54-55 + AFLP 1806.2.5; Britten 1947 20-23 + Haufrecht 1970 52-54; Brune 14c-15; Clayre 10-11; Clifton 42; Combs 1967 183-84; Combs 1967 214 #107, listing; Cray 26-27; Dallas 1974 84-85; Dallin 144-45; Dyer-Bennet 1971 68-70; Emrich 1973 518-19; Engel 175a; Farnsworth 1909 14-15 + *All Time* 16; Flanders Index 219; FO *17.1.3; FSA 33F 7, listing; FSC 62.2.3; FSI 65.1.6 + FSI 65F 5; Glazer 1961 46-47; Goodwin 1956 329a, "traditional"; Hansen 63a; B. Hoffman 16-17; B. Ives 1953 60-61 + B. Ives 1962 22-23; *JEFDSS 8* 152; Joyce *#58; Karpeles 1974 i 410-18; P. Kennedy 1975 400-401 + Topic 12T158A.5; Kidson 1891 167a; Kolb 28-29; Landeck 1946 6-8; C. Leach 123; LL 1341.1.5 (Josh White); Lynn 1963 48 #38; McCarthy 34-35; Morehead 164-65; Nettel 10; *Pocket Song Book* 54; Purslow 1974 31; Raph 387-89; Reeves 1958 111-13; Richman 35b; RLP 12-618.1.2; RLP 12-656.1.3; RLP 12-814.1.4; Sedley 179-80; C. J. Sharp *FSS* i 17 + Karpeles 1974 i 418 + Karpeles 1975 ii 32 #28; C. J. Sharp 1932 ii 174 + J. Edwards 49; Shay 1961 26a; Silber 1973b 159c; Silverman 1966 68-69; Silverman 1975 i 138b-39; R. B. Smith 28; *SO 17 #3* 16; *SO 24 #2* 12-13; Surette 28 #25; VRS 1031B.1 + VRS 1031J 2.1; Wilkinson i #328, #381 C, #533.

Related title (*The Foggy Dew*, as instrumental dance tune),

  Comment, references; Kidson 1890 42-43; *SFQ 6* 7 (Wilkinson); Wilkinson ii #164.

  Tunes: Cazden 1950 60b; Kidson 1890 24a + Kidson 1891 165 + Kidson 1927 78; *SFQ 6* 7; Wilkinson ii #164.

Related texts (*Granuaile*),

  Comment, references: Bunting 1840 i 93 #12; H. Thompson 1958 84-85; Zimmermann 52-55.

  Texts (with unrelated tunes and/or with non-matching verse-forms): Bunting 1840 ii 36a #46; *Delaney's Irish #2* 3, *The Lament of Granu Wail;* Howe 1864a 105d, *Grana Uile;* R. Mason 223 #38; O'Conor 133,

The Lament of Granu Wail; O'Neill #546, *Granu Waile; Universal Songster* iii 286, 348.

  Texts (re American Revolution): Breathnach ii 72, *Grainne Wail;* Flanders 1939 xxii; *Marsh's Selction* ii 16-19; Piper + Peterson Index 38; *Rough & Ready* 197-200; H. Thompson 1958 85-86 + Wright 434-35.

Unrelated texts (*The 'Bugaboo'*): Wehman's Irish #3 45 + Wehman's Irish #4 88. (*The Foggy Dew*): Kidson 1891 165-66 + Kidson 1927 78.

Text and tune relatives: Bunting 1840 ii 109 (tune and title only); *JFSS 3* 295-96; *JIFS 3* 33a (tune in a – a' – b – a' form); O'Neill #185 (tune and title only); Peacock 520-21.

Tune relatives [from Bunting 1840 ii 109], with related text,

  (*The Foggy Dew*, by Alfred P. Graves): Bantock 1930c ii 22-23; *Delaney #73* 24 (tune indicated); Graves 1882 90-92; Haufrecht 1958 68; Lampe 1916 58-59 + Lampe 1955 58; McPheeley 114-15; O'Neill #186 (text indicated); Page 10-11; Surette 57-59 #51; *Treasure Chest* 1943 21; Wise 82-83.

  (*The Foggy Dew*, with new text by Charles O'Neill) [* tune indicated but not notated]: *Dubliners* iii 6-7; J. Edwards 150-51; Graeme 180-81 + *Clancy* 1971 180-81; Kellock *18, "as sung by Hugh MacDonald"; Lusk 9b; *1916 Song Book* *2-3, "tune: *Old Irish Air*"; *Sing 1* 66 (Galvin); *Sing 5* 68; SRL 7624.5.1 (Odetta Gordon); Walton *132* *6-7 + Walton ii *73-74; *Well Known Songs* *15.

  (*The Foggy Dew*, text adaptation by Annie W. Patterson): *Gem Selection* 36-37.

Tune relatives (*The Foggy Dew*, text adaptation by E. H. Milligan): EKL 26.2.2 (Susan Reed); Fox 38-40.

Tune relatives (*The Irish Emigrant*, by William Kennedy): Dibblee 90; Huntington 255 (text from a ms. of 1847); R. A. Smith 1828a 93 + R. A. Smith 1828b 16-17 + Kidson 1913 166-67.

  (*A New Song Called Granuaile*, with tune from Petrie #790): Healy 1969 ii 33; O Lochlainn 1939 6-7, 205; Zimmerman 82-83, 277.

  (*A Shantyman's Life*, complete tune form): Downes 280-81 + Siegmeister 1944b 34-35 (tune from Shoemaker 1931 262); Sandburg 390 + Carmer 1942a 243-244 + Carmer 1942b 37-38 + Horton 19-21.

  (with tune in – – b – a reduction): Barry 1939 60 + Botkin 1947 877-88; Rickaby 43 A + Fowke 1954 66-67 + A. L. Lloyd 1965 84

#51 + Silverman 1975 ii 401b + SLP 71.1.4; Rickaby 45 B (from the singing of M. C. Dean) + FP 19B.1 + *Sam Eskin* i 1-2.

Tune relatives (others, complete tune form),
  Comment, references: *SFQ 6* 7 (Wilkinson); Wilkinson ii #164.
  Tunes: Breathnach i 317; Breathnach iii 212; Creighton 1962 99, 209; Creighton 1962 102 + FE 4307A.10; Gill 1898 81 #91; Hannagan #4, *Bruach na Cairrge Baine [The Brink of the White Rock]*; Healy 1967a 12d; Hughes ii 6-11; *JFSS 6* 141-42; *JFSS 7* 9-10 #7; Jolliffe 73; Joyce #59, *Slieve Elva;* Joyce #296; Karpeles 1974 i 513 A, 515 B, 516 C; M. Leach 1965 192; Peacock 302; Petrie #351, *John O'Reilly;* Petrie #790 + O Lochlainn 6 (text 205), *Poor Old Granna Weal;* C. J. Sharp 1961 ii 63-67 (R. V. Williams); Shoemaker 1931 262, *The Pinery Boy.*

Tune relatives (others, in *a – b – b – a* form),
  Comment, references: Karpeles 1974 i pp vii-xviii.
  Tunes: Barrett 90-91; Breathnach i 158-59, "air: *The Foggy Dew*"; Breathnach ii 184; Creighton 1950 172 A, 174 C; *JFSS 2* 176; *JFSS 2* 214, *John Reilly; JFSS 5* 85-86 + Karpeles 1974 ii 139-40 A + *Sam Eskin* i 74 + C. J. Sharp 1916 198-99 #86 + C. J. Sharp 1920 ii 90-91, *Botany Bay;* Joyce #53; Karpeles 1934 i 67-71; Karpeles 1974 ii 141 B, 142 C; Möller 12-13 #5, *John Riley;* Morton 1973 114 #25; Purslow 1972 114, *Young Reilly; Sam Henry* #240, *Finn Waterside.*

Tune relatives (others, in *– – b – a* form): G. Greig *FSB* 69.
  [See also notes to #65, #72].

Tune relatives (others, in variant tune forms and meters): Christie ii 146, *Low Germany* (in *b – b – b – a* form); Gallagher #6 (in *a – a* form); *JFSS 7* 10-11 #8 (in 3/4 time); Meredith 1968 171 (in *a – b – a* form); Petrie 1855 i 143, *Ar Thaobh na Carraige Báine* (in 6/8 time); C. J. Sharp 1961 i 12-14 (in 3/4 time); Sturgis 32-35 + AFS 14633B.1 (Atwood), *Botany Bay* (in *b – b – b – a* form).

Tune relatives (instrumental): Howe 1864a 107f; O'Neill #485.

77.
Poor and Foreign Stranger

Previously available: none.
Variants: AFS 7754A, *Poor Unworthy Stranger;* AFS 12309A.4 + EC 329.4, *Poor and*
Foreign Stranger; ATL 186.1, *Poor Unworthy Stranger.*

Adaptations: Cazden 1958 i 68-69 + Cazden 1978 68-69; Cazden 1963 ii 28; Landeck 1944 30 (garbled).

Comment, references: Buchanan xxvii; Cazden 1958 i 1920 + Cazden 1978 120; Cooper 492; Denson 457; FSA 3F12 (Wilgus); Glass 1967a 20; Goodwin 1959 492b; G. P. Jackson 1933 250-53 #5; G. P. Jackson 1937 71-72 #40; J. Lomax 1947 330-31; McDowell 1937 48-49; Niles 1950 8; Odum 1909 93 + Odum 1925 137-38; Raph 55; *Renfro Valley #34;* Simon 218; Spaeth 1948 75, listing; J. Warner 43.

Broadsides, songsters: none.

Texts: T. Burton i 91; Davis Index 302; Emrich 1974 380-81; Fuson 208; Ingram 267; Odum 1909 93 + Odum 1925 138, *The Pilgrim's Song;* Rosenberg Index #1153; *Sam Eskin* ii; Silber 1973b 352a; Spaeth 1948 75, listing; Vincent 208; VRS 1031J 2.8.

Unrelated (*Poor Pilgrim*): Dett 169b + G. P. Jackson 1933 271b.

Text and tune relatives: AA 3A.2 (Burl Ives); Abrahams 94-95; Abrams 94a; Agay 58; Boette 80-81, *I Am a Pilgrim and a Stranger;* Boni 1947 34-35; *Broadman Hymnal #74;* Buchanan 66-67; Cayce #714 + G. P. Jackson 1933 251a + G. P. Jackson 1937 70-72 #40 + Joyner 81 + J. Lomax 1947 346-47 + Silverman 1975 ii 76b-77; R. Chase 1956 162-63, 164, 165; CMS 650F.6 (Tom Glazer); Cooper 492; Denson 457; Dett 191 + G. P. Jackson 1933 251b, *The Pilgrim's Song;* FP 5003.48-6.2.6 (Pete Seeger); Gainer 1956 194-95; Gainer 1963 #73, #78; Glass 1967a 20-21; Glazer 1961 149-50; Goodwin 1959 492b; Hansen 83b; Haufrecht 1958 24-25; Haufrecht 1959 94; I. Hoffman 148-49; B. Ives 1953 160-63; James 1955 28; Jameson 1967 30-31; Kentucky 1937 #9 (Charles Seeger); Kentucky 1939 i 18; Kentucy 1939 ii 11; Kolb 216-17; Leisy 1974 112 #111; A. Lomax 1964 78; J. Lomax 1941 37 + *Sam Eskin* i 77b; McDowell 1937 48-49; Manoff 16; ML 2038.2.3 (Paul Robeson); E. Moore 364-65; Morehead 392-93; Niles 1950 8-9; Raph 55-58; Rosenberg T-84 15A.1a; C. Sandburg 1950 47-48; Schinhan v 493; Pete Seeger 1961 15 + Asch 31b + Pete Seeger 1973 181; Shealy 112-13; Silber 1965 144; Simon 218-19; *SO #5* 21 (Horton Barker); *This & That* 38a; Tobitt 46a; M. R. Turner 41-43; VRS 1031B.8 (Alfred Deller); J. Warner 41-43; Wilkinson *128* 3a; H. R. Wilson 54-55;

Winsett 1942 #3 + Brumley 1972 # *Renfro Valley* #34; Zanzig #8.
Tune relatives (*Fulfillment*): Deason 330; McDowell 1937 32; B. F. White 102 + Cooper 102 + G. P. Jackson 1942 #242 + G. P. jackson 1944 196 #72 + G. P. Jackson 1952 168 #300.
Tune relatives (*Parting Friends*),
  Comment, references: *MQ 26* 483-93 (Charles Seeger).
  Tunes with this text: McCurry 101 + G. P. Jackson 1933 250 + J. Lomax 1934 564-65 + [facsimile] *MQ 26* (facing 487).
Tune relatives (others): AFS L7.B.5, *Claude Allen;* Niles 1938 4, Child 4, Lady *Isabel and the Elf-Knight;* Niles 1938 12, *John Riley to Pennsylvania;* Petrie #265, #1222; Schinhan iv 286-87 B, C; Schinhan v 173-74.
Tune relatives [half tunes in *a – a* or *– – b – a* forms] (*The Dear Companion*): C. J. Sharp 1932 ii 109 + *All Time* 51a + Erdei 30 #52 + FSA 3.1.8.
  (*The Drowsy Sleeper*): C. J. Sharp 1932 i 358, 359, 362, 363, 364 H, 364 I, 364 J.
  (*The Little Sparrow*): C. J. Sharp 1932 ii 128-36, A - R.
  (*Man of Constant Sorrow*),
  Comment, references: Abrahams 175 #11.
  Tunes with this text: T. Burton ii 30; FSA 36.2.3 (Frank Proffitt); Hansen 89b; Rosenberg T-89 57A.1; Shellans 26; Wilkinson i #372.
  (others): FSA 2.1.8; *JAF 70* 354 #24; *JWFSS 2* 81 #34, *Dacw Long* [*There's a Ship*]; Randolph i 262; C. J. Sharp ii 26; Wyman 1916 34-37.
Tune relatives in condensed form (*In Old Virginny*): FSA 23.1.11; Ritchie 1953 45; Ritchie 1963 134-35; Ritchie 1965a 16; C. J. Sharp 1932 ii 232 A, 233 C, 234 D.
  (Child 79, *The Wife of Usher's Well*): Bronson ii 249-64 #4-#46, #49-#51.
  (others): Erdei 47 #73, *Christ Was Born in Bethlehem* (in *a – b – b – a* form); M. J. Swan 37, *Hopewell* (in 6/8 time).
  [See also notes to #57, *Betsy B*].
Unrelated Tunes (*Parting Friends*): Cooper 335, 337b; Denson 414b, 521; Walker 35b; B. F. White 308 + Denson 308.

78.
My Home is on the Mountain

Previously available: *YIFMC 3* 72 Ex. 8a [tune only].
Variants: none.

Adaptations: Cazden 1963 ii 15.
Comment, references: none.
Broadsides, songsters: none.
Texts: none.
Text and tune relatives: none.
Related text with related tune (*Farewell, My Dear Brethren*): Boette 78.
Tune relatives,
  Comment, references: Bronson ii 17, Child 56, *Dives and Lazarus*; W. Chappell 1859 ii 747-48, *We Be Poor Frozen Out Gardners*; Christie ii 178; Dick i 359-60, *Gilderoy*; Horn 49-78; G. P. Jackson 1933 146 #64, *Imandra*; G. P. Jackson 1937 49-50 #20, *Paralytic*; G. P. Jackson 1952 67, *Lazarus*; G. P. Jackson 1952 109 #167 (Bayard); *JAMS 3* 120-34 (Bronson); *JAMS 20* 47-52 Ex. 13, Ex. 15 (John M. Ward); *JFSS 2* 115-22 (Kidson, Broadwood); *JFSS 2* 239-42 (Broadwood); *JWFSS 1* 139-42 (H. O. Hughes); A. L. Lloyd 1967 76-83; Maitland #13256 3 (Broadwood); Moffat 1894 142-43, *Gilderoy*; *SFQ 17* 131 #3 (Bayard); Simpson 109, *The Clean, Contrary Way*; Simpson 254, *Gilderoy*; Wilkinson i #319, *Lazarus*; Wilkinson i #326, *My Love Nell*.
Tune relatives [* indicates half-tune],
  (Child 13, *Edward*): Bronson i 247 #24.
  (Child 45, *Dives and Lazarus*): AFS L57.B4 (Aunt Molly Jackson); Broadwood 1893 102 + Bronson ii 22 #13; Bronson ii 21-22 *#11, *#12; RLP 12-627.2.2; Wilkinson i #319.
  (Child 73, *Lord Thomas and Fair Annet*): Bronson ii 144-49 #125, #126, #127, #130, *#131, *#132, *#133, *#134, *#135.
  (Child 78, *The Unquiet Grave*): Brocklebank 10 + Bronson ii 241 #47; Bronson iv 474 *#42.2; Purslow 1965 96 + Bronson ii 244 #41 (with variant *b* phrase).
  (Child 112, *The Baffled Knight*): BFSSNE #12 *12 + Bronson iii 553 *#11.
  (*Blow the Candles Out*): AFLP 1906.1.4 (Oscar Brand); Best 50; Bikel 64-65; Cazden 1963 ii 3; Creighton 1950 214-15; Dallin 53; Disc 609.5020A (Richard Dyer-Bennet); Dyer-Bennet 1971 22-24; J. Edwards 37; *Folk #1* 3; *Folk Song Album* 12-13; *FST ii* 16 #6; Glazer 1961 9; Leisy 1966 36; McCarthy 20-21; *Orpheus* 1749 i 35-36 #49 [text only]; Sedley 54-55 Shekerjian 76-77; Silverman 1975 i 118a; *Sing 1* 61; *SO 7* #1 16 + *RSO #1* 44 + Silber 1963 123.
  (*Christian Farewell*): Funk 199b + Showalter 199b; Hendrickson 86.

(*Come All You Christian Men*): *JFSS 1* 136,
238; *JFSS 2* 115-16; *JFSS 2* 117a + Kar-
peles 1974 ii 494 B; *JFSS 2* 117b + Kar-
peles 1974 ii 496 D; *JFSS 2* 118c +
Dearmer 1928 471 #6.2; *JFSS 2* 119; Kar-
peles 1974 ii 497 E; Karpeles 1975 i 59
#56; C. J. Sharp 1916 212-13 #91 +
Götsch 23a, 82-83 + Karpeles 1956 47 +
Karpeles 1974 ii 495 C + C. J. Sharp 1920
ii 104-5 + C. J. Sharp *Selection* i 13-15 +
Sing Care Away iv 47; C. J. Sharp 1961 i
34 (Hammond); C. J. Sharp 1961 ii 68
(R. V. Williams); C. J. Sharp 1961 iii 102
(Gardiner); C. J. sharp 1965 36 #3 +
JAMS 3 133 #30; C. J. Sharp 1965 36 #4
+ *JAMS 3* 133 #33.

(*Imandra*): Carden 146; Cayce #127; Fillmore 251b; Hauser 1848 316; Hauser 1878
183; Hayden 199b; G. P. Jackson 1933 146
#64 (from Davisson 1820 Supplement 21);
Rinehart 7a; Walker 134 + G. P. Jackson
1942 140 #126.

(*Milton*): J. B. Jackson 84; *MQ 26* [facsimile
facing] 489 (from *Southern Harmony* 1838
[Pumpkintown, Tennessee] 34) + G. P.
Jackson 1952 192-93 #348).

Tune relatives (other hymns): Denson 376 +
G. P. Jackson 1942 69 #50, *Help Me to Sing*;
FR 217.6, *Come to Zion*; Hauser 1848 187a,
New Hope; G. P. Jackson 1937 49-50 #20,
Paralytic; G. P. Jackson 1937 205 #200, *For
Me the Savior Died*; G. P. Jackson 1942 145,
Bellvue; G. P. Jackson 1952 109 #167, *How
Firm a Foundation* (from *The Revivalist*,
1868 #339), G. P. Jackson 1952 112 #173,
Atonement; G. P. Jackson 1952 171 #307,
Happy Time; G. P. Jackson 1952 200 #358,
Praise God, My Friends; J. B. Jackson 45,
New Harmony; *Pilgrim Hymnal* #412 (R. V.
Williams); Walker 78 + G. P. Jackson 1937
82 #51 + A. L. Lloyd 1965 88 #55, *Babe of
Bethlehem*.

(others): Berggreen 140 #90 (instrumental);
Breathnach i 44; Breathnach ii 210; W.
Chappell 1859 ii 748 + R. Palmer 1974
231; Chilton 56; Christie ii 178; Creighton
1950 214 + A. Lomax 1960 146-47;
Creighton 1962 123; D'Urfey v 39; Gill
1898 100 #30 (a Manx hymn); S. B. Gould
1892 142-43 + S. B. Gould 1905 266-27
#111 + S. B. Gould 1974 54-55; Graves
1893 56-59, *Mavourneen Dhu*; Hannegan
#72, *Posadh Naomtha Cana*; Hopekirk
82-83; *JAF 52* 18 #13, 19 #14; *JAMS 3* 133
#28, #29, #30, #32, #33 (Bronson);
JFSS 6 316-17 #77, *Bearta Crúa* [*Sorry
Plight*]; *JFSS 7* 44, *The Prentice Boy*; Jor-

dan 365-66; Joyce #187, *Mary from Black-
water Side*; Joyce #273, *A h-Uiscidhe
Chroidhe na n-Anmann* [*Oh, Whiskey,
Heart of Souls*] (in 6/8 time); Kidson 1916
74, *Labourers Out of Work*; A. L. Lloyd
1967 79; A. Lomax 1960 312-13;
McPheeley 334 #954 (instrumental); *NA
Ives* 62.2, *Green Bushes*; NA Ives 64.6.15;
NYFQ 14 220-21; O'Neill #319 (instru-
mental); Petrie #188, #297, #469, #863,
#867; Purslow 1965 54; Purslow 1968 94;
J. Raven 1971 14; M. Raven iii 25, 98; C. J.
Sharp 1916 104-5 #46 + Karpeles 1974 ii
130 + C. J. Sharp 1920 i 70-71, *Fanny
Blair*; C. J. Sharp 1932 ii 272 + *Sam Eskin*
i 161; Simpson 109, *The Clean, Contrary
Way*; *Sing 10* #2 6b, 7b; *SO 18* #3 30;
Thomas 1964 59-61; Topic 12T198A.5;
Wilkinson i #326, *My Love Nell*; Wilkin-
son i #390, #391; Wright 678b.

(others, in half-tune form): Abrahams 43;
Creighton 1950 121 A; Grainger #193,
#194; *JFSS 8* 30 + Karpeles 1974 ii 503a
C; Matteson 1947 71; Munch 71-72; *NA
Ives* 1.111 + ATL 3118.5; Peacock 755,
875; C. J. Sharp 1932 ii 79; Wilkinson *128*
30b.

Tune relatives (in 3/4 time): *JFSS 5* 171-73;
JFSS 6 223; *JFSS 7* 149; J. Johnson #159
+ Haydn 21 #21, *The Shepherd Adonis*;
Joyce 1872 23 #21, 26 #24.

(in 6/8 time): J. Graham 14-15; Kidson 1929
82-83; J. Raven 1972 19.

(in 9/8 time): Dallas 1974 171-72.

Unrelated tunes (*Lazarus*): C. J. Sharp 1932
ii 29-30, A - B.

(*Milton*): Ditson 1857 145; Jocelin 89.

(*New Orleans*): Hendrickson 18; [see also
notes to #50].

79.
The Resurrection

Previously available: AFS 12309A.9 + EC
329.9; Kimball 40 [text only].

Variants: none.

Adaptations: Cazden 1958 i 70-71 + Cazden
1978 70-71.

Comment, references: Cazden 1958 i 121 +
Cazden 1978 121; G. P. Jackson 1937 32;
JFSS 8 83 (Gilchrist).

Broadsides, songsters: none. Published with
music in Boston, 1842 in *The Wesleyan
Psalmist* 66-67, *Free Salvation*, + Scudder
66-67.

Texts: G. P. Jackson 1937 32 #5; *JFSS 8* 83; Scudder 66-67.
Text and tune relatives: none.
Tune relatives: none.

80.
Heavenly Sunshine

Previously available: AFS 12309B.19 + EC 700.4.
Variants: none.
Adaptations: none.
Comment, references: Benziger 37; R. M. Stone 117; Winsett 1908 #10; Woychuk #11.
Broadsides, songsters: none.
Texts: none.
Unrelated texts: J. Clements #60, *Heavenly Sunshine*; Entwisle #37, *Heavenly sunlight*; *Inspirational Melodies #2* + Stamps #238, *Heavenly Sunshine*.
Text and tune relatives (*Heavenly Sunlight*, by George H. Cook and Henry J. Zelley, complete form): R. S. Arnold, frontispiece; Benziger 37; J. M. Black 1905 #74; Brunk #471; *Broadman Hymnal* #119; *Christian Hymnal* #28; Elderkin 1900 25 #23; Goodwin 1959 116a; J. L. Hall #10; Hustad #403; McCoy #85; Ott #66; Rodeheaver 1939 #103; Rodeheaver 1945 11b; A. B. Smith #291; Stamphill #91; Winsett 1908 #10; Winsett 1948 #1.
Text and tune relatives (*Heavenly Sunlight*, chorus portion only, as set by Charles E. Fuller): *Church of God* #294; J. W. Peterson 1963 #114; Rodeheaver 1956 #210; Woychuk #11.
Tune relatives: none.

81.
My Lord Knows the Way

Previously available: AFS 12309B.19b + EC 700.4b.
Variants: none.
Adaptations: none.
Comment, references: none.
Broadsides, songsters: none.
Texts: none.
Text and tune relatives (*My Lord Knows the Way*, by Sidney E. Cox): J. W. Peterson 1963 #51; J. W. Peterson 1966 #140; Woychuk #312.
Tune relatives (*Bonnie Charlie's Noo Awa'*, or *Will Ye No Come Back Again?*, by Baroness Nairne and Neil Gow Jr.),

Comment, references: Findlay 114-52; J. Greig vi xxix-xxx; *Scottish Students* 325.
Tunes with this text: Boulton 1893 94 #19; Buck 1916 #15; W. Cole 174-75; H. W. Davies 1931 116-17 #99; A. T. Davison 1924 89 #81; Diack i 139; Ditson 1859 61b; Findlay 151-52 [text only]; M. B. Foster 220-221; Fulcher 330-32; *Gems of Scottish Songs* 119; J. Greig vi 318-19; Hansen 206b; Hazlewood 126-27; C. Johnson 25; *Lyric Gems* 92-93; McCaskey i 56; McCaskey 1899 364; MacFarren 225-25; Macmillan 79; A. Mills 1949 46-47; MN C693; D. H. Morrison 1894 247; Nairne 6-7; *120 Scotch Songs* 161; *Pocket Song Book* 8c; *Scottish Students* 325; Stanford 1958 93; Tomlyn 119; *University Songbook* 390-91; Wier 1918a 36a.
Tune relatives (opening phrase, *Wonderful Power in the Blood*, by R. E. Winsett): Winsett 1920 #20.

82.
Wilt Thou Be Made Whole?

Previously available: AFS 12309B.20 + EC 700.5
Variants: none.
Adaptations: none.
Comment, references: none.
Broadsides, songsters: none.
Texts: none.
Text and tune relatives (*Wilt Thou Be Made Whole?* by William J. Kirkpatrick, 1882): Date #431; Elderkin 1900 182 #181; W. P. Hall #34; *Hymns Christian Life* #499; Kirkpatrick 1898 #186; Kirkpatrick 1899 #44; W. McDonald 1885 #72; McLaughlin #158; Sayles 32; Sweney 1882 72-73.
Tune relatives: none.

83.
The Ship of Zion

Previously available: none.
Variants: none.
Adaptations: AFS 12312B.10; Cazden 1958 i 58-59 + Cazden 1978 58-59; Cazden 1963 ii 12-13.
Comment, references: *AFSPB 18* 82-102 [reprinted from: Thomas Wentworth Higginson, "Negro spirituals," in *Atlantic Monthly 19* (1867) 685-94]; W. F. Allen 102; Buchanan xxiii #26; Cazden 1958 i 123 + Cazden 1978 123; Dichter i #1644, listing of sheet music publication, *De Old Ship of Zion* by

Sam Lucas (1881); Ellington, *passim;* M. E.
Henry 419-20; G. P. Jackson 1933 257-58 #8,
296-98; G. P. Jackson 1937 199 #191, 211-
212 #210; G. P. Jackson 1937 212-13, from
Erk and Böhme, *Deutscher Liederbuch,* iii
628-29; *JAF 45* 191-92 (M. E. Henry);
McDowell 1937 47; Odum 1909 78 + Odum
1925 117-18; Pike 192; Scarborough 1925 33-
64, "The Negro's part in transmission"; N. I.
White 93-96; Wilkinson *510* 8.
Broadsides, songsters: none.
Texts [*indicates "North Carolina version"]:
AFSPB 18 96-97 (Higginson); Belden 1952 iii
659-61; Ellington 74c; Hansen 146b; Hauser
1878 *355, The Old Ship;* G. P. Jackson 1933
235 #11; *JAF 41* 566; *JAF 45* 171-72 + M. E.
Henry 419-20; Killion 240-41; Piper, *The
Gospel Ship;* Richardson 71; Rosenberg Index #1089 (6); Schinhan iv 383-87; Silber
1973b 366d; Stekert 1969 N 91; B. F. White
*79 + Cooper *79 + Denson *79 + G. P.
Jackson 1937 *199a #191 (A) + G. P. Jackson 1944 *148 #6; N. I. White 94 A, 95 B;
N. I. White 436, from *The Revivalist* (Troy,
1868) 185 #375.
Related texts, wording more remote: FA
2941B.14 (Huddie Ledbetter; FHE 32-33,
The Old Ship of Zion [from *The Golden Harp*
(Auburn, Maine) 71]; LCJ (Coluzzi); J. B. T.
Marsh 152 #29; Odum 1909 78 + Odum 1925
117-18; Seward 35; *SO 24 #2* 21; N. I. White
96 C.
Unrelated texts (*The Good Ship Zion*): *Christian Harp*
(*The Good Ship Zion*, by Marian Froelich
and G. Froelich): *Happy Voices* 52; Hull
158-59.
(*The Old Ship*, by T. C. O'Kane): Sweney
1881 25 + Sweney 1886 iii 289 #323.
Text and tune relatives [*indicates "Georgia
version]: W. F. Allen #125 + G. P. Jackson
1944 149 #6; Dett 81 + G. P. Jackson 1933
258 #8 (b); Fenner 85b; Hauser 1848 *355 +
Boni 1952 *262-63 + Hauser 1878 *354 +
G. P. Jackson 1933 *257 #8 (a) + G. P. Jackson 1937 *211b-12 #210 (B); McDowell 1937
47; Mansfield 338a + Cook 48a (facsimile);
N. I. White 35; Wilkinson *510* 8.
Tune relatives: Buchanan 48-49, *Saints Bound
for Heaven;* Cooper 388 + Denson 388,
Happy Sailor.

84.
We're Coming, Sister Mary

Previously available: none.
Variants: none.

Adaptations: none.
Comment, references: Spaeth 1948 156.
Broadsides, songsters: *Bryant* 1857 25-27;
E. W. Cole 261a; Diprose 1865 17; Fortey
1905; *Rocky Road* 59-60; *Southern Ethiopian*
84-86 + Negro Forget-Me-Not 185-b 84-86;
[named in], *Song of All Songs,* Wolf Index
#2181 + Jordan 33-35 (facsimile); *Trifet*
1890 227b + *Trifet* 1892 227b [with tune].
Sheet music publications: New York: Firth &
Pond, 1853 (listed in Dichter 1941 153);
Christy 1855, London: C. Sheard (*Musical
Bouquet* #710); London: T. E. Purday, Feb-
ruary 1858; *Musical Bouquet* 1490, ca. 1858,
+ Wade 9-11; *Musical Treasury* #957 (by
July, 1858), re-issued in Davidson's *Fifty
Songs Sung by the Christy Minstrels,* Lon-
don 1859 29b; London: W. Williams & Co.,
January, 1860, "revised edition"; London:
H. & E. Swatton, February 1860; London:
Robert Cocks & Co., March 1860; Rimbault
i 19-20 #8; *Davidson* viii 12-13, 1862; *Christy*
1900 7-8.
Texts: Gardner 1939 483, listing (Rowell Manu-
script); Stout 68-69 #50.
Text and tune relatives: *PTFLS* 6 215-16.
Tune relatives (instrumental): *Boosey* 1862b 17
#53; *Chappell* 1863 8 #14; *Musical Bouquet*
#710 3 #4 (by 1855), #1498 6a, #1702/3 2b-
3; *Musical Treasury* #967/8 4a.

85.
Blossom Time

Previously available: none.
Variants: none.
Adaptations: none.
Comment, references: none.
Broadsides, songsters: none.
Texts: none.
Text and tune relatives: McCaskey i 171 +
McCaskey 1899 137; C. Johnson 132-33.
Tune relatives (*The Wearing of the Green*),
Comment, references: *CAY 3 #3* 4-9 (Shool-
braid); Fuld 1971 628-30; H. K. Johnson
488-90; Lampe 1916 66; Macmillan 99-100;
SFQ 7 89-100, "The career of a revival
hymn" (Hans Nathan); *SFQ 9* 119-25,
"*The Tulip*-the strange adventures, sacred
and profane, of an old Scottish march
tune" (Anne Gilchrist); C. J. Sharp 1902
172; Spaeth 1948 82.
Broadsides, songsters [* indicates "1798"
text]: *Beadle's Half-Dime #12* 4; *Captain
Jinks* 22; *Conner's Irish* 36, *37; *Faugh-a-
Ballagh* 136-37; *Hyland* 104; *Marching*

Through Georgia *21-22, 22-23; O'Connor 69; Piper; *SFQ 9* *119; *Singer's Journal #6* 43; *Stephens* 61-62; *Tony Oakes* 31; *Universal Irish* 139; *Wearing of the Green* 5-6; Wehman *617* 33; Wolf Index #2525, #2526.

Tunes with this text [* indicates "1798" text]: Ashbee iii 41-42; Bacon 138-41; Bantock 1930c i 28-29; Beattie 44; Behan 1965 96; Boni 1952 *286-87; Botsford 1937 *132; Breathnach ii *92-93; J. D. Brown 34-35; Buck 1916 *192-93; *Cavendish #20* *18-19; *CAY 3 #3* 2-3; *Choice Irish Songs* i 52-54; *Clancy* 1964 9; W. Cole 81-83; Dykema #126; Emerson 128-29; *Empire* 45; *Everybody's Favorite* *132-33; *Favorite Songs* 68; Fisher 181-83; *Francis & Day* 1948a 22-23; Fuld 1971 628-30; *Gem Selection* 86-87; Goodwin 1956 391; Graves 1914 *116-17 #78; Haufrecht 1958 62-63; Hesser 112; Howe 1874 186a + *Fireside Library* 36a + Howe 1880 186a + *Trifet* 1890 107a + *Trifet* 1892 107a; *Ireland's Songs* 168-69; B. Ives 1958 116-18; H. K. Johnson 488-90; Lampe 1916 66 + Lampe 1955 64-65; Macmillan 99-100; McCaskey v 169; McPheeley 18-20; Morehead 32-33; Moyes *17; Murphy 110-11; *Musical Bouquet #3660*; *Musucal Budget 6* 810-11; *Never Grow Old* 240-41; Noble 1907 98-99 + Noble 1912 153-54; Oberndorfer 49; *101 Best Songs* #26; Page 70-71; Piper; Raph 162-65; Reddall 84-85; Ricbhman 87; Rooney 1905 *66-67; Rooney 1922 *44-45; *Scottish Students* 70-71; *SFQ 9* *119-20a; C. J. Sharp 1902 *22-23 #11; Silverman 1975 i 388; *Song Purpose* 37; *Songs Forever* 20; *Treasure Chest* 1943 26-27; *Walton's Treasury* *74 + *Walton* i *97; *Walton's Treasure* 75 + *Walton* i 98; Weir 1915 238; Weir 1918 492a; *World's Best* 101; Zimmerman *169-70.

Tunes with this title (instrumental): Brock 10a; Converse 1871 20a; Howe 1864a 107c; Kerr iii 31a; O'Neill #467; S. Winner 1866 5 #2.

Tunes indicated as *Wearing of the Green*, for other texts: Doyle 1966 69; Garretson 21 (3); Glazer 1970 279-80, *The Rising of the Moon;* HTA, *August in July;* I. W. W. 8, 29; Silber 1964 140; *Singabout 2 #1* 5; Vernon 165.

Tune relatives (*Benny Havens, Oh!*): Atkinson 136-37; D. C. Chamberlain 108-9; Garretson 20.

Tune relatives (others): M. Barry 182; Behan 1967 32b-33; Breathnach iii 288; I. Campbell 58-59; A. H. Chase 59; Chilton 162; Downes 130 (first half of tune); Durlacher 270; R. G. Edwards 1971 19, 34, 96, 129; R. G. Edwards 1972 70, 74, 142; Ira Ford 114; J. Greig vi 375-77; Hansen 198a; Healy 1969 iv 16a; Lahey 84; Lingenfelter 496, 548-49; Long 36 (first half of tune); J. B. T. Marsh 198, *In Bright Mansions Above;* Meredith 1955 8; Meredith 1968 138b; *NA Ives* 1.156 + ATL 3163.2; Rimbault iii 14-15 #5 (first half of tune); *SFQ 7* 89, *The Old Church Yard; SFQ 7* 97a, We Are Coming, Father Abraham, by Patrick Gilmore; *SFQ 9* 121, We Are Coming, Father Abraham, "tune: *The Old Granite State*"; *SFQ 9* 124b-25, *Falling of the Leaf; Singabout 5 #3* 6; R. Ward 11.

Tune relatives (others, instrumental): *SFQ 9* 120b, *The Tulip,* by James Oswald; *SFQ 9* 124b-25, *Ballance a Straw.*

86.
The Dying Californian

Previously available: none.
Variants: none.
Adaptations: none.
Comment, references: Belden 1940 350; Cox 1925 232; Dichter #87, sheet music publication, Boston: Oliver Ditson, 1855; Greenleaf 360; G. P. Jackson 1937 38; G. P. Jackson 1942 55; *JAF 26* 359 (Pound); *JAF 35* 365 (Kittredge); Randolph ii 181-82; RLP 12-654J 2.7 (Goldstein).
Broadsides, songsters: *American Dime* i 56-58; J. Andrews i #26; *Beadle's Dime #1* 47; *Beadle's Half-Dime #13* 13; *Beautiful Bells* 47; *Broadway Stage* 17-18; *Delaney #7* 23; *Love & Sentimental* 45-47; *Pacific* v 35-37; *Prize Song Book* 42-43; *Shilling Song Book* i 64; *Singer's Journal #20* 125; Wehman #540; Wehman i 107-8; *Wehman's Universal #11* 82; Wolf Index #540.
Texts: H. P. Beck 1957 177-78; Belden 1940 350-51; Cayce #537; Cox 1925 232-33; Daughters 13; Davis Index 287; Downes 160-61; Eddy 286-87; Emrich 1974 563; Fife 1969 38-41; Gardner 1939 478, listing; Hubbard 217-18; Hudson 1936 221-22; *JAF 35* 364-65 (Tolman); *JAF 39* 139-40; *JAF 48* 381-82 (from New York State); *JAF 56* 106, listing; Laws 1950 263, listing; LCJ (Wagner); McIntosh 1935a 71-75; E. Moore 321-23; Piper (3) + Peterson Index 30; Pound 1922 191-93 (froma manuscript of 1856); Randolph ii 182-84; Rosen berg Index #333 (2); Spaeth 1948 596, listing; B. F. White 410 + Cooper 398b

+ Denson 410 + G. P. Jackson 1933 184-85
+ G. P. Jackson 1937 37-38 #10 + Lingen-
felter 34-35 + RLP 12-654.2.7 (Pat Foster);
Wilkinson i #189, #192.

Related text (*The Dying Californian*, with distinct wording): Creighton 1971 129-30; Hubbard 219; *NYFQ 27* 180-82; H. Thompson
1958 141-42 (from a manuscript copy, no
later than 1856); Wolf Index #541, a broadside by De Marsan.

Related text (*The Dying Message*): Belden 1940
217-18; Hubbard 77; *PTFLS 23* 176-77; Randolph iv 168-70.

Text and tune relatives [resemblance chiefly in
the *b* phrase]: Munch 96-97; Wilkinson i #58
+ G. P. Jackson 1942 55 #36.

Tune relatives (*The Holly and the Ivy*)
[sampling]: CRS 401B.2; Zanzig 1940 #108.

87.
The Rolling Stone

Previously available: *Neighbors 1944 21.*
Variants: ATL 618.9.
Adaptations: Cazden 1958 i 56-57 + Cazden
1978 56-57.
Comment, references: Belden 1940 351; Cazden
1958 i 121 + Cazden 1978 121; Day 88-90,
138-45, 332 #2986; Flanders 1939 107-8; Garland 43-45; Arthur Schrader [personal com-
munication]; *SFQ 37* 331-54 (A. C. Morris).
Broadsides, songsters: none.
Texts: AFS 14634A.20 (Fred Atwood); ATL
563.17 (Lydia Gyderson); Belden 1940 351-
52 + Lingenfelter 18-19; Combs 1967 209
#52, listing; Fuson 100; Garland 44-45; Hub-
bard 307-8; *JAF 35* 408-10; Koehnline 27,
listing; A. Lomax 1960 75; *NYFQ 7* 65-66;
Piper (2) + Peterson Index 70; Randolph ii
214-16, B - D; H. Thompson 1958 139-41;
Wilkinson i #440.
Related texts (*A Dialogue . . . from Don Quix-
ote*, by Thomas D'Urfey): D'Urfey i 88-90;
Mock-Bird 53-55; Purcell 168-74; A. Ramsay
ii 43-45 #44; *Vocal Miscellany* i 100-101
#115.
Unrelated texts (*Don't Leave the Farm, Boys*):
W. W. Partridge 132-33.
(*The Rolling Stone*): FSA 2.2.1 + FSA 2F
13-14 + Ch. Kennedy 1952 201.
(*A Rolling Stone Gathers No Moss*, by Fred-
erick McAvoy): *Dan Nash* 13; *Delaney #6*
21; *Harry Hill 1882* 60; *Musical Bouquet*
#7440 (1889); *Russell* 29; *Ward & Lynch*
8.

(*A Rolling Stone Gathers No Moss*, by J. W.
Bean and Frank Thompson): Goodwin
1956 162.
(*Stay on the Farm*, by James Orr): Ira Ford
361-62; Orr 120-21 + FH 5337B.7 + FH
5337F B.7.
(*'Tis Better to Stay on the Farm*, by J. H.
Tenney): Orr 164-66.
Text and tune relatives: Flanders 1937 32-33;
Flanders 1939 106-7; Gover 59-60; Randolph
ii 213-14 A.
Tune relatives [complete form of the tune
strain]: see notes to #18.

88.
Will You Go Out West?

Previously available: *Neighbors 1943 29.*
Variants: none.
Adaptations: AFS 12312B.13; Cazden 1958 i
54-55 + Cazden 1978 54-55; SLP 72A.5.
Comment, references: Cazden 1958 i 123 +
Cazden 1978 123.
Broadsides, songsters: none.
Texts: AFS 17985 (Clara Heywood);
Shoemaker 59; *Street & Smith 136* 128.
Text and tune relatives: ATL 604.3, 604.5 (Mil-
ler Teeple).
Tune relatives (*Speed the Plough*, by John
Morehead),
Comment, references: *EDS 5* 26-27 (David
Kennedy); Emmerson 1967 194; *William
Litten* 56 (Huntington).
Tunes (instrumental): ATL OT 1539.2d; Bur-
chenal 37; Cazden 1955 34b + Cazden
1950 3c; *Chappell 100* i 5 #12; *Chappell
100* ii 34 #92; *Chappell 1863* 34 #93;
Chicago Park District 32; M. M. Cole 21h;
Dewey 10; Fessenden 130c; Flanders Index 234 #49; Ira Ford 78b; Goodwin 1955 i
156a; Gott 32a; Greenleaf 376 #6; *Harding
3* #15; E. Haywood 50 #6; *Howe 1851a*
29b; *Howe 1851c* 39a; Howe 1858a 58b;
Howe 1864a 41b; Jarman 12; D. Kennedy
1948 18; P. Kennedy 1951 8 #16; Kerr i 24
#6; Kerr ix 15 #6; Linscott 112; Muller
37; *Musical Bouquet* #102 22a #2; *Musical Treasury* #544 145 #4b; *New Preceptor* 24b; *Parlor Companion* 137c; Philo
1001A.1b; Polwarth 1969 45; Robertson
15c; Rollinson 25b; Sonneck 406, listing;
Violin Made Easy 26a; Wilkinson ii #20,
#124; *William Litten* 23b.

89.
The Plains of Illinois

Previously available: none.

Variants: ATL 625.6.

Adaptations: Cazden 1958 i 62-63 + Cazden 1978 62-63 + Rozwenc 115 [text only].

Comment, references: Cazden 1958 i 120 + Cazden 1978 120.

Broadsides, songsters: Wolf Index #2247, *The State of Illinois*.

Texts: none.

Related texts (*Elanoy*): C. Sandburg 1927 162 + Boni 1952 298-99 + Botkin 1955 561-62 + Brand 1961 162-63 + Carmer 1942b 189-90 + CMS 670H.4 + CMS 670F H.4 + Dallin 6-7 + Downes 110-11 + *Folkonvention* + Haufrecht 1958 25-26 + Kinscella 10 + A. Lomax 1960 87-88 + *PSB 3* #276 + H. Sandburg 89 + Silber 1965 58 + Silber 1973b 42c + Silverman 1975 i 17 + Zanzig 1940 #4.

Related texts (*The Banks of the Ohio*): *American Songster* 1845 185-87 + *Book of 1000* 636-37 + *Marsh's Selection* iii 185-87; J. Andrews List 2 #59; Browne 160; Carmer 1942b 170-71; CMS 650F.3; *Delaney #49* 22, © 1888 by Frank Harding; Downes 131; *Forget-Me-Not* 22-23; Jordan 305-7 + Botkin 1955 563-64 + A. Lomax 1960 85a; McMurray 3; Mursell 114; Silverman 1975 i 18b-19.

Related texts (*We'll Hunt the Buffalo*): Barrett 18-19; Gundry 50; Palmer 1974 240-41; Reeves 1960 67; Whall 105-7.

Unrelated text (*The Banks of the Ohio*).

Comment, references: Laws F 5; *SO 7 #4* 3.

Texts: Beard 156-58; Botkin 1955 577; T. Burton ii 101-2, *B & S #3* [7]; Carmer 1942b 168; J. Cohen 154-55; Cyporyn 35, 89; Dunson 1973 110-11; Hansen 14a; M. E. Henry 220-21; *JAF 45* 134; Leisy 1966 21-22; Matteson 1936 44-45; Piper; *Sam Eskin* iv 73; Silverman 1975 i 76a; *Sing 7* 61a, 61b; *SO 7 #4* 3 + *RSO #1* 62 + Silber 1963 39b; VRS 9094.2.1 (Joan Baez); XTV 62202.1 (Joan Baez); ZDA 67.2.7 (Peggy Seeger) + ZDA 67F 7-8 B.

Text and tune relatives: ATL 193.6 ("Dick" Edwards).

Tune relatives: Gardner 1939 96, *Rinordine*. [See also notes to #1].

90.
The Arkansas Traveler

Previously available (#90 A): *Neighbors* 1949 10-12.

Variants: none.

Adaptations: none.

Comment references: Boni 1947 58; Botkin 1944 346-49; Browne 448; Cox 1925 503; Dichter i #356; Fuld 1971 107-8; R. Jackson 262; *JAF 77* 350, "A thousand years before Arkansas" (Cazden); Levy 1971 318-19; Masterson 186-240, 358-76; *PTFLS 18* 11-60 (Vineyard); Rainey 53; Randolph iii 22-23; Spaeth 1948 125-26.

Broadsides, songsters: *Arkansas Traveler* 5-9 [with music] + *PTFLS 18* 12-18; Wehman ii 116-17; *Wehman's Collection #33* 16.

Sheet Music (with conversation, by Mose Case): Boston: Oliver Ditson, 1862-63, + facsimiles in Dichter 1956, Levy 1971 330, R. Jackson 10-13.

(as instrumental tune): Louisville: W. C. Peters, 1847, + facsimile in Masterson 220.

(prints by Currier & Ives, 1952): reproductions in Masterson, frontispiece and facing 186.

Texts: Beard 494-97; Browne 449-50; Combs 1967 231 #226, A - B; Cox 1925 503-5; Flanders *SR* 12.5.35; M. E. Henry 129-30; LCJ [fragments]; Masterson 220-32 (12); *PTFLS 18* 18-42; Randolph 1955 114; Shoemaker 250-54.

Text and tune relatives: ATL 196.10; Botkin 1944 346-49; J. Cohen 1964 232-35; Converse 1865 90-96; FA 2412.1.6 (Pete Seeger); Ira Ford 46, 188-92; FP 5003.48-6.2.1 (Pete Seeger); Hitchcock iv 6-7; Levy 1971 331-32; Loesser 54-55; J. Lomax 1934 267-71; Luther 147-48; Randolph iii 23-25; S. Winner 1866 26; S. Winner 1885 227-28.

Text (synopsis as song text, by David Stevens) **and tune relatives:** Boni 1947 58-59; R. Delaney 3-10; M. Johnson 14; Keene 35-36; Kincaid iii 37; D. D. Lawrence 107; Silber 1973b 33a [tune indicated]; Silverman 1975 i 14a.

Text with other tune forms: M. Cohen 1966 16-17 (first half of tune only); L. Roberts 133-34 (with unrelated tune fragment).

Tune relatives (as instrumental tune, or otherwise without text of the *cante-fable*):

Comment, references: Cox 1939 ii 87; Dichter 1941 139-40.

Tunes: AFS 12311A.19 + EC 326.19 (Grant Rogers); *Arkansas Woodchopper* 1940 12; ATL 186.6.B2-.B3 (Walden Van Wagner); Burchenal i 58; Calhoun 26; Cazden 1955 8a + Cazden 1950 3b; Chicago Park District 10; M. M. Cole 4c; *Community* iv 3c; Converse 1887 121; Cox 1939 ii 87; DLP 112.1.1; Durlacher 48; *Everybody's Favor-*

ite 147-48; Flanders Index 239 #139, 240 #165; Gardner 1939 214, *The Lowlands Low* (first phrase of tune); Goodwin 1955 151b; Gott 36a; Handy 1955 54a; *Harding* 60 #190; Howe 1858a 53b; *Howe 1859* 11a; Jarman 2; D. Kennedy 25; Kerr i 22 #5; Kinscella 40 (first half of tune); Kirkell 45; Krassen 44; Leifer 101; Masterson, facing 220; MH 1072A (Ralph Page); *Musical Bouquet* #2475 4b #5; L. Owens 1950 45; Putney 34; Rollinson 27b; Rosenberg T82 6B.3b; Ryan 1926 13; Ryan 1939 100; H. Sandburg 6a (first half of tune); Pete Seeger 1973 74-75; F. H. Smith 1939 12; F. H. Smith 1955 64; Wilkinson ii #43, #119, #192; S. Winner 1866 52b.

91.
The Days of 'Forty-Nine

Previously available: *Neighbors* 1946 25.
Variants: ATL 616.7-.8.
Adaptations: none.
Comment, references: CFC 301F 16 (Harlan Daniel); Dwyer 9; Laws 1950 163; Lengyel i 29; J. Lomax 1947 161-62; Randolph ii 221; Silber 1967 93-99; SLP 82J A.3 (Goldstein); Zimmerman 30.
Broadsides, songsters: *Barney & Rickey* 48-49; *Charles Schofield* 46-47; *Delaney* #66 23; *Great Emerson* 53-57; *Wehman's Universal* #12 95.
Texts: J. V. Allen 157-59; CFC 301B.6 + CFC 301F 16; *Clampers* 20-21; CMS 650F H.6; CMS 670F D.l; Gordon *AM* 9.10.24; Gordon *NYT* 15.1.28; *Hangtown Ballads* 44-45; HTA (Clark); Hubbard 297-99; *JAF 28* 7-8 (J. Lomax); Lengyel i 29; Lengyel ii 58-59; *MF 21* 253-54; Piper + Peterson Index 27; Sherwin 1932 12-13; Silber 1973b 285a; Wilkinson i #314.
Text sequel (*The Good Old Days of '50, '1 and '2*): *Popular California Songs* + Silber 1967 99; *California Checklist* 21; Dwyer 191-92 + Lingenfelter 560.
Related texts (*The Year of '29*): Zimmerman 30.
(*The "Date" of 'Thirty-Nine*): Neeser 326b-28.
Text and tune relatives: AFS 3363A, 3365A; *American Cowboy* 60-61; Asch 32-33; ATL 602.1, 602.2, 605.5 (James Edwards); *Big Round up* 76-77; Bingham 1-5; E. Black 53-55 + Botkin 1951 735-36 (tune in *a–a–b–a* form); K. S. Clark 1932 26-27; CMS 650H.6; CMS 670D.l; J. Davis 44; Dwyer 189-90 + Lingenfelter 558-59; Flanders 1937 38-39; Kinscella 19 (tune in *a–a–b–a* form); J.

Lomax 1938 378-81; J. Lomax 1947 180-83; Randolph ii 221-22; Silber 1967 97-98; SLP 82.1.3; *SO 2* #9 8-9 + *RSO* #5 10-11 + Silber 1963 64-65 + Silber 1965 60-61 + Silverman 1975 i 14b-15; *Treasure Chest* 1935 36-37.
Tune relatives: *Tip Top* 1935 44; [ee also notes to #119.]

92.
The Jolly Thrasher

Previously available: *Neighbors* 1946 22-23.
Variants: ATL 183.7.
Adaptations: Cazden 1958 i 91 + Cazden 1978 91.
Comment, references: Belden 1952 iii 89-90; Dean-Smith 1954 91; Dick i 503 #361; Dixon 148; *JAF 30* 353-55 (Kittredge); *JFSS 1* 79; P. Kennedy 1975 581-82 #253; Purslow 1968 139; Randolph i 436 #127; Simpson 782-83, *The Two English Travelers*.
Broadsides, songsters: Holloway 253 #159 (B); Roxburghe vii 328-30.
Texts: ATL 563.7 + *JAF 52* 60 (Lydia Gyderson); Belden 1952 iii 90; Bell 1857 98-100; Broadwood 1893 68-69 + Reynardson 28-29; Cobb 71; Copper 1971 274-75 + *FSN* 19.2.3; Cox 1939 i 70-71, 72; Dixon 148-51; Emrich 1974 773-74; Flanders 1931 156-59 [version B is from *Green Mountain Songster* of 1823]; Gardner 1937 208; *JAF 30* 353; *JFSS 1* 79; *JFSS 2* 198-99; *JFSS 3* 302-4; *JFSS 5* 200-202; J. Johnson #372 + Dick i 349 #361; Karpeles 1974 ii 209-10, A-B; P. Kennedy 1975 562; LCJ (Crump); Nettel 187; Ord 48-49; Piper + Peterson Index 49; Purslow 1968 87; Randolph i 436 #127; *Sam Henry* #622; C. J. Sharp 1961 iii 130-32 (Gardiner); C. J. Sharp 1961 v. 188-89 (Merrick); Stokoe 118-19; Stubbs 52-53; H. Thompson 1958 178-79; I. A. Williams 70b-71.
Related texts (*The Contented Peasant*): *Blossoms* 12.
(*The Thrasher*): Fairburn 1809 42-43.
Text and tune relatives: ATL 619.6 (Frank Edwards).
Tune relatives (fairly distant): Creighton 1962 108; Peacock 944 A; Peacock 147 B + Fowke 1954 48-49.

93.
The Rock Island Line

Previously available: *JAF 72* 343 Ex. 3 (tune only); *Neighbors* 1947 22.

Variants: none.

Adaptations: Cazden 1958 i 52-53 + Cazden 1978 52-53; SLP 72.2.1 (Robert De Cormier).

Comment, references: Cazden 1958 i 121 + Cazden 1978 121; Fowke 1970 52-53, 56-57; FSC 10F 19 (Fowke); *NA Ives* 1.139 + ATL 3146.3.

Broadsides, songsters: none.

Texts: E. C. Beck 1956 233-35, *The East Jordan Line;* Creighton 1932 252-53, *The Fox River Line;* FM 4001F A.6, *The Keith and Hiles Line;* FSC 10F 20, *The Rock Island Line;* Manny 169-70, *The Scantling Line; Miramichi Ms.* 17.1, *The Rock Island Line* (Arthur MacDonald); *NA Ives* 1.63 + ATL 2183.2, *The Scantling Line; NA Ives* 1.64 + ATL 2184.1, *The Scantling Line; NA Ives* 1.139 + ATL 3146.3 *The Scantling Line; NA Ives* 61.2, 68.3.1, *The Scantling Line;* Stekert 1969 B 96.

Related text (*The State of Arkansas*),
  Comment, references: AFS L7F 35A; Belden 1940 424; Cox 1925 359; FSC 10F 8-9 (Fowke); FSI 59F 9 (Hickerson); Laws H 1; J. Lomax 1947 227-28; Randolph iii 25-26; Thorp i 195-218 (Fife).
  Broadsides, songsters: Wehman #1239; *Wehman's Collection #32* 22.
  Texts: AFS L7.B4 + AFS L7F 35A; G. Anderson 235; Belden 1940 424-26; Belden 1952 iii 382-85; Botkin 1944 316-17; Brewster 265-67 + Friedman 434-36; Browne 451-54, A-B; Combs 1967 211 #78, listing; Cox 1925 239-41; Davis Index 142; Dean 8-9 + Wright 543; Dorson 402-3; Downes 286-87; Dunson 1973 44-45; FA 2951B.14 (Kelly Harrell); FSA 33F 9, listing; FSI 59.1.3 + FSI 59F 9-10 (Joe Hickerson); Gordon *AM* 3.1.27; Hudson 1936 208; *JAF 26* 173; LCJ (Krauch); J. Lomax 1938 283-85; J. Lomax 1947 240-41; A. Lomax 1960 322-23; McDowell 1947 88-89; Masterson 255-68 (11); Milburn 184-87; E. Moore 385-86; Neely 210-12; Piper + Peterson Index 75; *PSB 3* #228 + *RPSB* 22-23; *PTFLS 23* 226-28; Randolph iii 25-33; *Sam Henry* #674; Schinhan v. 230; C. J. Sharp 1932 ii 238; Silber 1973b 46a; Silverman 1975 i 20; Stekert 1969 B 28, N 40; Thomas 1931 152-53; Thomas 1964 176-77; *Weavers Song Book* 142-45; Welsch 49-50.
  Related Text (*'Way Out in Idaho*): AFS L61A.6 + AFS L61F 5-6; Botkin 1953 440-41; Gordon *AM* 20.10.23; Lingenfelter 78-79; J. Lomax 1941 269-70 + Emrich 1974 666-67.
  Related texts (others): Armitage 1926 233,

The Range of the Buffalo; FSC 10.1.4 + FSC 10F 9-10, *Muskoka;* Joyce #406, *The Spalpeen's Complaint;* M. Leach 1965 236, *The Riverhead Line;* Peacock 768-69, 770-71, *The Riverhead Line.*

Unrelated text (*The Rock Island Line*): AFS L8.B5; AFS L50.2.1; Brand 1961 58-59; DL 8413.1.7; EKL 301/2b.7c; FA 2014A.1 (Huddie Ledbetter); FA 2941B.18 (Huddie Ledbetter); FA 2942C.3 (Huddie Ledbetter); FP 20.2.7 (Huddie Ledbetter); Grafman 94-95; Hansen 162a; Haufrecht 1959 116-17; Landeck 1969 64-65; Leisy 1966 282-85; Leisy 1974 16 #115; J. Lomax 1959 74-75 + A. Lomax 1964 128; Lynn 1961 150 + Lynn 1963 51 #97; Okum 1968 95-96; Shealy 110-11; *SO 2* #8 9 + *RSO #3* 23 + Silber 1973b 102a; VRS 9010.1.5 (The Weavers); *Weavers Song Book* 12-13.

Text and tune relatives: Fowke 1970 50-51 A + FSC 10.2.2, *The Rock Island Line;* Fowke 1970 51-52 B, *The Rock Island Line;* Fowke 1970 54-56, *The New Limit Line;* FM 4001A.6, *The Narrow Gauge Line* (Warde H. Ford); *NA Ives* 1.78 + ATL 2197.2, *The Rock Island Line.*

Tune relatives (Child 12, *Lord Randall*): Bronson i 217 #76, #77, #78.

(Child 169, *Johnny Armstrong*),
  Comment references: Bronson iii 140; Ritson 1794 ii 7-9; Simpson 401-3; Stenhouse 335-36 #356.
  Tunes with this text or title: Bronson iii 140-41 #1-#3; J. Johnson #356 + Kinsley 1969 520-25 #106; Oswald ii 75 + Simpson 401; Ritson 1794 ii 7-13; Stenhouse 336.

(*Christ in the Garden*): Hayden 240 + G. P. Jackson 1942 29 #13 B; G. P. Jackson 1942 29 #12 A (from Day's *Revival Hymns,* Boston, 1842 48); J. Knapp 24; Neale 48.

(*The Dreary Black Hills*): AFS L49.1.1 (Alan Lomax); J. Davis 45; Fife 1969 65; Glass 1967a 48-49; D. D. Lawrence 83; Silber 1967 151; M. R. Turner 125; J. Warner 125.

(*The Green Bushes*),
  Comment, references: Dick i 503 #361; *JFSS 8* 112-13 (Broadwood, Gilchrist); Kidson 1913 168; O'Shaughnessy 1975 77-78 #20; Stenhouse 344 #372.
  Tunes with this text: *D'Alcorn #1* 58a; *Charley Fox* 1863 64 (parody text); Chilton 97; Creighton 1932 38 + Creighton 1940 20-21 + Loveless 22-23; W. Cole

42-43; *Davidson* i 25a; Howe 1864a 101i
(instrumental); *Ireland's Songs* 84-87;
B. Ives 1958 33; *JFSS 8* 112, 113a; *JFSS
8* 177 (in *a – a' – b – a'* form); Kidson
1913 168-69; *Musical Treasury* #92
(1845); J. W. Turner 11a.
(The Little Brown Bulls),
    Comment, references: AFS L55F 20-22;
    AFS L56F 6 (E. C. Beck); Laws C 16.
    Tunes with this text: AFS 5A (Emory De
    Noyer); AFS 2356B, 3281B, 3287B;
    AFS L56B.1; ATL 169.1.1b, 169.2.1a +
    E. C. Beck 1941 92; E. C. Beck 1948 66-
    67; E. C. Beck 1956 67-71; E. C. Beck
    1960 24-28 (with *Down, Derry Down* re-
    frain); FP 19B.3 (Sam Eskin); J. Lomax
    1941 224-26; Rickaby 68 B, 225.
(Todlin Hame),
    Comment, references: Stenhouse 258
    #275.
    Tunes with this text: M. B. Foster 193; J.
    Johnson #275; MacFarren 108 (with
    new text).
Tune relatives (others, with tune in *a – b – b – a*
form): Behan 1965 12; *British Minstrelsie* i
26-27 + MacMahon ii 108-9 #55 (for
Thomas Moore's *The Meeting of the Waters*, "air: *The Old Head of Dennis*"); N.
Buchan 1973 53, 104; T. Burton i 35; M. E.
Bush ii 20; *Chapbook 3 #4* 6; *Chapbook 4 #3*
3; R. Chase 1938 152-53; Copper 1973 194–
95; Creighton 1932 226; Creighton 1950 146;
Creighton 1962 192; Creighton 1971 99; Dallas 1974 41, 48; Dibblee 98; *EDS 26* 39; Flanders 1953 155; FM 4053.2.3, *The Pride of
Kildare*; FO 9.2.11, 13.1.2; FO 14.1.7 +
Fowke 1967 186 + FM 4005A.2; Fowke
1967 190; Fowke 1970 87; Fowke 1972 110-
11; R. Ford 1904 212 (in *b – b – b – a* form);
Giblin 7 #11, *Boughleen Bawn* (instrumental); Gillington 1911 8-9; G. P. Jackson 1942,
98, *Lead Me to the Rock*; *JEFDSS 3* 191,
The Old Head of Dennis; *JFSS 1* 222; *JFSS 8*
177; Joyce 1872 73; P. Kennedy 1975 300,
397, 414-15; Knox 16; J. Lomax 1934 438-39
+ A. Lomax 1964 104; Luboff 135;
McPheeley 340 #988, *A Stranger in Cork*;
NA Ives 1.70 + ATL 2189.1; O Lochlainn
1939 30; O'Neill #38, #222; O'Neill #326,
The Forlorn Stranger; R. Palmer 1972 61;
Peacock 882, 963, 998; Petrie #740; Ran-
dolph ii 36 E; Ritchie 1963 121; Ritchie 1971
50; RLP 12-648.1.3; *Sam Henry* #542, #720;
Sam Henry #821, "tune: *The Green
Bushes*"; C. Sandburg 1950 102-3; Scar-
borough 1925 63; Schinhan iv 22, 209-10;
Schinhan v 159 Ba, 159 Bb, 171 Ai, 517-19;

C. J. Sharp 1932 ii 206 C; *Singabout 5 #1* 3;
SO 12 #3 14; *Tip Top* 1935 45; TLP 1047.1.1
(Blanche Wood); Topic 12T157B.7; Topic
12T158B.10; *UFL 18* 37.
Tune relatives (in *a – a' – b – a'* form),
    Comment, references: FH 5723F C4; Powell
    27-28.
    Tunes of this form (*The Railroad Corral*): see
    notes to #94, *Haul In Your Bowline.*
    Tunes of this form (others): Arthur 11; Bley
    76; R. Chase 1956 142 + *SO 7 #4* 14-15;
    Chapbook 5 #1 13; K. S. Clark 1934 40-41;
    J. Edwards 114; EKL 26.1.1 (Susan
    Reed); FH 5723C.4, 5723D.7 (Harry Jack-
    son); Flanders 1937 28; Ira Ford 44, 126;
    FP 2364B.3 (Andrew Rowan Summers);
    FP 5003.48-5.1.1 (Pete Seeger); FSA
    32.2.2, 32.2.5 (Hedy West); S. B. Gould
    1905 46; Hudson 1937 5, 6; INT 14016.2.1
    (Peggy Seeger); P. Kennedy 1975 187;
    Landeck 1946 25; Lingenfelter 376; Mac-
    Coll 1965 33; Manny 279 + FM 4053.2.1;
    A. C. Morris 360; Niles 1934 20; Oswald
    viii 20a, *Kennet's Dream;* Polwarth 1969
    1; Powell 29-32; Randolph i 271; Randolph
    iii 321; RG 150.1.1, *Sweet England* (Shir-
    ley Collins); Ritchie 1971 50; RLP 12-
    654.1.1 (Pat Foster); Ruth 8 #17
    (instrumental); Peggy Seeger 1960 63 +
    WLP 724.1.3 (A.: L. Lloyd), *Farweel to
    Tarwaithie;* Peggy Seeger 1970 43 #24;
    Pete Seeger 1961 21; C. J. Sharp *FSS* ii 42-
    43 + Karpeles 1974 ii 575; Thede 55b, 156
    (instrumental); VRS 1001B.6, *Sweet Eng-
    land* (Alfred Deller); WLP 724.1.3
Tune relatives (in *a – a'* or *– – b – a'* half-tune
form): AFS L28A.4; J. V. Allen 90, 163; Botkin 1937 206; Bronson i 200 #20; Brumley i
#40; Calhoun 57; *Carson J. Robison* 32;
Cazden 1961 73; Cazden 1962 8; Cazden
1963 i 9; Cumming 57b; Cyporyn 141; Dolph
361-62; Erdei 41 #65; Fife 1969 13; FP
5003.48-6.2.5 (Pete Seeger); FSI 2.1.1
(Howie Mitchell); FTS 3016.1.4 (Gordon
Bok); B. Ives 1962 166-67 + B. Ives 1966 59-
60; *JAF 28* 129; Kincaid i 20; Leisy 1966 289;
Loesser 232-33; J. Lomax 1934 170-73;
J. Lomax 1938 166, 372-73; J. Lomax 1938
163-64 + Botkin 1944 855; Luther 44; Piper,
I Wrote My Love a Letter; PSB 2 #164 +
RPSB 17; *PTFLS 7* 153; *PTFLS 23* 235, 278;
Randolph ii 35 D; Randolph iii 134, 135, 251,
260; L. Roberts 109-10; C. Sandburg 1927
307 A + C. Sandburg 1950 53; C. Sandburg
1927 307 B; Scarborough 1937 429 E.; Peggy
Seeger 1964 20; Pete Seeger 1961 69; Shellans 54; M. J. Swan 52a; Thede 156; Thomas

1931 128; VRS 9107.1.1 (Cisco Houston);
Wilkinson i #575; Wilkinson *128* 14b; Zanzig
1940 #19.

Tune relatives (others, with time variants of
tune): FSI 58.2.3 (Joe Hickerson), in 4/4
time; Graves 1893 13-16, *The Roving Pedlar*,
in five-measure phrase "Gaelic meter"; G. P.
Jackson 1947 #16, in $a - a' - b - a - a'$ form;
Joyce #531, in transformed ¾ time; O Loch
lainn 1939 74, in 9/8 time; O'Neill #38 +
McPheeley 336 #966, in five-measure
phrases).

Unrelated tune (*The Green Bushes*, "English"
or *other tune form),

  Comment, references: S. B. Gould 1905 13-14
    #43; Kidson 1891 47-48; C. J. Sharp *FSS* ii
    66-67 #34; C. J. Sharp 1916 xxx #40 +
    C. J. Sharp 1920 i xxi #24.

Text (*The Green Bushes*) with unrelated
tune: ATL 485.3 (George Edwards);
Breathnach ii 108; Broadwood 1893 170-
71; Cazden 1951b 31a (instrumental); Copper 1973 *241-42; Gillington 1911 4-5;
S. B. Gould 1892 *90-91 #43 + S. B.
Gould 1905 *86-87 #43; Grainger #100,
#282; Grainger 1921 #25 (Passacaglia);
Hamer 1967 42; *JFSS 1* 66, 90; Karpeles
1974 i 595-96, A - D; Karpeles 1975 i 23
#21; O'Shaughnessy 1975 39; Petrie #222,
#223, #368, #603; Petrie #370 + *JIFMC
3* 49g (Bayard); Polwarth 1966 25 + Polwarth 1970 22; Poston 1968 26-27 (Kidson); Purslow 1965 38; *Sam Henry* 143;
C. J. Sharp *FSS* ii 16-17 #34 + C. J. Sharp
1916 92-93 #40 + C. J. Sharp 1920 i 58-59;
C. J. Sharp 1961 iv 170; F. Stuart 34.

94.
Haul in Your Bowline

Previously available: none.
Variants: none.
Adaptations: none.
Comment, references: Wyld 75-107.
Broadsides, songsters: none.
Texts: J. Lomax 1934 462-63, from *Buffalo
News* 5.11.33; J. Lomax 1934 465-66, from
Auburn, New York; *NYFQ 14* 219-20 (F.
Warner); H. Thompson 1940 246, from Buf-
falo, New York.
Related text (*Haul on the Bowline*),
  Comment, references: AFS L26F 4 (Emrich);
    Colcord 38-39; Emrich 1973 465; Leisy
    1966 156-58; Linscott 139-40.
  Texts: AFS 2531B.2; AFS L26A.1; Bone 38-

39; Bullen 30a; *Canadian Boys* 223 #131;
M. Cohen 1966 77; Colcord 38-39; Creighton 1962 144; Dallin 139b; F. J. Davis 35;
Doerflinger 5, 9; Emrich 1973 466; *Ernest
Newton* 50; FM 4006B.19; Grainger #159;
Greenleaf 338 + Cass-Beggs 1975 35; Harlow 95-96; *Heart Songs* 459; G. Hitchcock
8; Hugill 354-57; B. Ives 1956 71b; *JFSS 5*
314-15; King 12b; Kinley 92; LCJ (Jacobs,
Jobson); Leisy 1966 156-58; Linscott 139-
40; Lynn 1961 204; Oberndorfer 67a; Rat-
cliff 134; *Sam Eskin* 14a; Sampson 50;
C. J. Sharp 1914 42-43 + *Novello* #262 2-3
#1271a + *Sing Care Away* iv 62a; Shay
1924 132; Siegmeister 1944b 13; Silber
1973b 87b; Silverman 1975 ii 253b; SL
206.1.1; SLP 80A.1 (Lloyd, MacColl);
L. A. Smith 13, 14; *Song Purpose* 153a;
F. Stuart 64-65, *Haul Away the Bowline;*
Terry 1919 i 10-11; Terry 1921 i 58;
Trevine 13; Wier 1918 190.

Text and tune relatives: none.
Tune relatives: see notes to #93.
Tune relatives [in $a - a' - b - a'$ form] with
related text (*The Railroad Corral*): *American
Cowboy* 76-77; K. S. Clark 1932 5 + Lingen-
felter 376-77; Dallin 147; Downes 274-75;
Fife 1969 208; Goodwin 1956 172b; J. Lomax
1938 42-43; Mursell 80; RLP 12-631.1.4
(Merrick Jarrett); Sackett 1961 24; Sires 22-
23; Tobitt 62; *Treasure Chest* 1935 11.

95.
Bound for the Stormy Main

Previously available: none.
Variants: ATL 625.3.
Adaptations: none.
Comment, references (*The Greenland Fishery*):
Belden 1940 104; Fowke 1967 49; Hunting-
ton 9-13; Laws K 21; *NEF 8* 29; NW 239J2-3
1.6 (Paton); Peacock 148.
("brave boys"): *JFSS 2* 243; *JFSS 7* 87-88;
JFSS 8 182-86.
(*Cupid's Trepan*): W. Chappell i 555-57;
JIFMC 3 44-50 (Samuel P. Bayard); Simp-
son 151-53 [See also #37].
Broadsides, songsters: Ashton 1888 265-67;
Ashton 1891 #83; M. Leach 1955 707-8 (a
broadside by Pitts); *Singer's Journal #34*
237.
Texts: ATL 198.1 (John W. Ford); Belden 1940
104-5 + Emrich 1974 496-97; Best 127; *B &
S #4* [4]; CMS 650G.4 + CMS 650F G.4
(Tom Glazer); M. Cohen 1966 132-33; Col-
cord 147-48 + Friedman 401-3 + B. Ives

1953 148-49 + B. Ives 1956 18-19 + B. Ives 1962 80-81 + Silverman 1975 ii 241 + *SO 1* #*10* 11 + *RSO* #*1* 19; Collinson 1946 26-27; Cumming 36; Dallin 20-21; Eckstorm 226-27 A + H. P. Beck 1973 174-75 (from *Sea Stories Magazine*, February 1926); FP 911.1; FSI 46.2.6 (Ed Trickett); Gleadhill 239; S. B. Gould 1895 56-57; S. B. Gould 1974 50-51; Harlow 223-27; Huntington 9-10, 11-12; *JFSS 8* 179; Karpeles 1971 157-58; Karpeles 1974 ii 295-96 B, C; Keynote K 102.533B; Knox 36-37; Lawson 59-60; A. L. Lloyd 1967 279; J. Lomax 1941 89; J. Lomax 1941 214 + A. Lomax 1960 61; Luboff 30-31; Mursell 58-59; *NYFQ 27* 139-40; Peacock 147-48 + Fowke 1967 48-49; Quiller-Couch 841-42; Reeves 1960 134-36; Peggy Seeger 1970 45 #25; C. J. Sharp *FSS* iii 54-55 + Karpeles 1974 ii 294-95 A + Karpeles 1975 i 50 #47 + *Novello* ii 10-11 #963 + C. J. Sharp *Selection* ii 38-39; *Sing 7* 75; SLP 57B.2 (Pete Seeger); SLP 65A.3 (Milt Okun); SLP 81A.3 (Lloyd, MacColl); L. A. Smith 45; *Taverners* 11; *University Songbook* 208-9; *Weavers Song Book* 125-27; Whall 71-73; Yolen 170-71.

Unrelated texts (*Greenland*): *JFSS 1* 101-2; A. L. Lloyd 1955 + Peggy Seeger 1960 64 + WLP 724.2.8; Ord 317.

Text and tune relatives (in *c – c – c – a – d* form): *NEF 8* 29-30 + NW 239.1.6 (Gale Huntington).
(in *a – b – c – a – d* form): *JFSS 2* 243 + Clayre 64-65 + J. Edwards 118-19 + R. V. Williams 1959 50-51 + WLP 724.1.1 (A. L. Lloyd); Purslow 1974 37.

Tune relatives (in *a – b – c – a – d* form): *JFSS 7* 87a, 87b, *I Am a Brisk Lad;* Purslow 1972 89, *The Sheep Stealer.*
(in *a – b – c – d* form),
(Child 77, *Sweet William's Ghost*): Karpeles 1971 52-54 B, 54 C, 54 D.
(Child 209, *Geordie*): *JFSS 4* 332c + Bronson iii 279 #26; *JFSS 4* 333a + Bronson iii 278 #22; *JFSS 4* 333b + Bronson iii 279 #27; *JFSS 4* 333c + Bronson iii 275 #12.
(in *c – c – c – d* form),
(Child 77, *Sweet William's Ghost*): Karpeles 1971 56 H, 57 I.
(Child 209, *Geordie*): *JFSS 1* 164 + Bronson iii 286 #45; *JFSS 2* 208b + Bronson iii 280 #29; *JFSS 4* 332a + Bronson iii 280 #32; *JFSS 4* 332b + Bronson iii 279 #28.

96.
The Stagecoach Driver's Lad

Previously available: AFS 12309B.9 + EC 699.9.

Variants: none.

Adaptations: none.

Comment, references: Fowke 1970 36; Greenleaf 322; G. Greig *FSNE* #99; P. Kennedy 1975 532 #228; Topic 12T159F B.9 (A. L. Lloyd).

Broadsides, songsters [* indicates with tune]: *Barney & Rickey* 1875 176; *Billy Cotton* *40-41; *Comic Songster* *14b; *Harry Hill* 52; *Henry O'Richmond* 18-19; *James H. McGuire's Jim, the Carter Lad Songster* (1870) *5-6; *Jolly Old Clown* 15; *Lew Benedict* 19; *Little Lotta* 20-21; *Wehman's Universal* #*15* 117.

Sheet music: *Board of Music Trade* 67, listing; Boston: *Cundy* #85, 1871; London: J. & W. Chester, 1951, *Joe, the Carrier Lad;* London: J. McDowell & Co., n. d.; New York: E. H. Harding, 1870.

Texts: ATL 486.13; Copper 1973 244-45; G. Greig *FSNE* #99; Hamer 1967 68-79; *Sam Henry* #171; Topic 12T159F B.9.

Related texts (*Joe, the Coster Lad*): G. Davies 6; *Moet & Shandon* 13.

Related texts (the refrain text of #96 as an insert in versions of #2, *Cutting Down the Pines*): Dibblee 38-39; Eckstorm 25-27; FH 5323.2.1 + FH 5323F 5; Fowke 1970 34 A, 34-35 B, 35 C; Greenleaf 321-22 + A. L. Lloyd 1965 42-43 #24; *NA Ives* 1.10 + ATL 2143.1; *NA Ives* 1.28 + ATL 2154.4; *NA Ives* 1.29 + ATL 2154.6; Peacock 750-51.

Text and tune relatives: Collinson 1951; *Comic Songster* 14b; *James H. McGuire* 5-6; P. Kennedy 1975 512-13 + Topic 12T159 B.9 (tune of refrain only); McCaskey 1899 86.

Tune relatives: See notes to #118, *The Terrier Dog.*

97.
Life Is a Toil

Previously available: none.

Variants: none.

Adaptations: none.

Comment, references: Belden 1952 iii 367; Fowke 1961 136; A. Lomax 1960 133; Silber 1963 78; *SO 6* #*4* 28 + *RSO* #*1* 28.

Broadsides, songsters: *Comical, Topical* 90-91; *It's Naughty* 6-7.

Texts: Belden 1952 iii 367-68; CMS 670F A.5; LCJ (Moore); A. C. Morris 194.

Related text (*The Old Man's Lament*): A. Lomax 1960 375.

Text and tune relatives: CMS 670A.5 (Tom Glazer); *Francis & Day* 1967 + FA 2338 (O'Bryant); Glazer 1970 149-51; Keene 19-20; Kincaid iii 13; P. Perkins 44-45; Schinhan v 223-24; *SO 6 #4* 28-29 + Fowke 1961 136-37 + A. Lomax 1960 133-34 + *RSO #1* 28-29 + Silber 1963 78 79.

Tune relatives: [see #106, *Two Little Girls in Blue*, opening phrase].

98.
Last Winter Was a Hard One

Previously available: *Neighbors* 1941 9 + *Sam Eskin* i 175.

Variants: AFS 7762A; ATL 186.2.

Adaptations: Cazden 1958 i 66-67 + Cazden 1978 66-67; FSI 59.1.2 (Joe Hickerson); SLP 72.2.4 (Robert and Louise De Cormier).

Comment, references: Cazden 1958 i 117 + Cazden 1978 117; FSI 59F 7-8 (Hickerson).

Broadsides, songsters (*When McGuiness Gets a Job*): *Billy Barry* 10-11, "as sung by Johnny Roach"; *Delaney #67* 24; *Emerald Four* 16-17, "as sung by Johnny Roach"; *Hen Graham* 19; *Johnny Roach* 1881 3-4; *Lawell & Drew* 24-25; *Murphy & Mack* 36-37, "as sung with tremendous success by Johnny Roach"; *Murphy & Miles* 24-25; *Pat Rooney* 188- 52; *Rentz-Santley* 42-43; Wehman 617 78; *Wehman's Irish #2* 35b-36.

Texts: Dean 89-90 + Wright 499; FSI 59F 8.

Text and tune relatives: *NA Ives* 1.148 + ATL 3155.5.

Tune relatives (Child 20, *The Cruel Mother*): *JFSS 3* 70 #2 + Bronson i 279 #4.

(Child 68, *Young Hunting*): Ph. Barry 1929 122 + Bronson ii 78 #36 + E. K. Wells 152b; C. J. Sharp 1932 i 101 A + Bronson ii 78 #35.

(Child 100, *The Knight and the Shepherd's Daughter*): BFSSNE #9 7 + Bronson ii 541 #12, #13; G. Greig 1925 89 #1a + Bronson ii 541 #14.

(*The Rejected Lover*): FSI 2.2.3 (Howie Mitchell); Gainer 1963 #51; RLP 12-634.1.9 (Ellen Stekert); C. J. Sharp 1932 ii 96 A, 97 B, 98 C, 100 E, 100 F, 101 H, 102 I, 102 J; VRS 9094.1.6 (Joan Baez); XTV 62203.6. Wilkinson i #6.

(others): ATL 186.6, *Rock Hill;* Ph. Barry 1939 17; Beethoven Nr. 257 5-7 #2, *Sunset;* Botkin 1951 748-49; Dolph 6-8 + Lingenfelter 279-80; M. B. Foster ii 187,

The Sun Rises Bright; FSI 58.1.4, *Rolling of the Stones;* Morton 1973 120, *The Wee Tailor from Tyrone; Tocher #3* 70, *The Beggar Man.*

99.
In the Days When I Was Hard Up

Previously available: *Neighbors* 1946 21 + Kimball 167b [text only].

Variants: none.

Adaptations: none.

Comment, references: none.

Broadsides, songsters: *Banner Songster* 36; *Beadle's Dime #5* 53; *Book of Popular Songs* 273-74; G. M. Clark 1871 9; G. M. Clark 1872 12-13; *Delaney #10* 24 + Kimball 168; *Gus Shaw* 56-57; *Heart & Home* 68-69; *Nightingale Songster* 68-69; *Singer's Journal #7* 50; Wehman *#732; Wehman's Universal #7* 51; Wolf Index *#1035* (broadsides by J. Andrews, De Marsan, Johnson).

Texts: Chilton 63; Healy 1967 i 149-50; Kimball 166, 167a.

Related text: Randolph iv 361-62, *Hard Up and Broken Down.*

Related text elements (*County Jail*): Gardner 1939 357. [See also notes to #169].
(*Song of All Songs,* by Stephen Foster): Jordan 33-35 (facsimile).

Text and tune relatives: none.

Tune relatives (Child 26, *The Three Ravens,* *Billy McGee Magar* derivative): *American College* 247; Best 26; Bronson i 310-12 *#3-#7; College Songs #3* 19; A. K. Davis 1960 86; R. G. Edwards 1972 76; Ira Ford 449; Goodwin 1956 203b; *Heart Songs* 485a; Honoré 113; Leisy 1966 31; Lorenz 114 *#181; Most Popular College* 81; *Never Grow Old* 74; Noble 1908 70; RLP 12-814.1.9 (John Runge); Rodeheaver 1928 118a; *Scottish Students* 268; Thurman 121; *University of Toronto* 71 + Macmillan 150-51; Waite 1868 26; Waite 1877 ii 33; Waite 1890 78; Wilkinson i *#464;* Wilkinson *510* 28.
(*For Bales,* or *Johnny, Fill Up the Bowl*),

    Comment, references: Dichter 1941 121; FA 2354F 2.6 (Ellen Stekert); Fuld 1971 639-41; Randolph ii 284; Spaeth 1948 154.

    Broadsides, songsters: *Harry Pell* 33-34; V. B. Lawrence 397b; Wolf Index *#1140.*

Tunes with this text: CMS 660G.4 (Tom Glazer); Dolph 297-98; FA 2354.2.6 (Ellen Stekert); Glass 1968 192-93;

O'Neill #468 + McPheeley 305 #787 (instrumental); Randolph ii 284-87.

(*John Anderson, My Jo*),

Comment, references: W. Chappell 1859 ii 770-71; Dauney 259-60 #7; Dick i 425; Dick ii 105; *EDS 4* 30 (Stuart); R. Ford 1900 198-204; G. F. Graham i 129; G. F. Graham 1891 23; W. Hamilton 195 #13; Haufrecht 1970 140-41; H. Johnson 399-400; Kinsley iii 1334-35 #302; Moffat 1894 103; Stenhouse 243-45 #260.

Sheet music: Boston: Russell & Tolman 1851, "as sung by Jenny Lind."

Tunes with this text: *Amateur* 126-27; *Annie Laurie* 25; H. Anderson 69b; *Beauties of Caledonia* 12-13; Beeton 1865 5, 131 #9; *Boston Musical Miscellany* 162-64; *British Orpheus* 334; C. Brown 176-77; *Caledonian Musical Repository* 105-7; Dauney 219a #7; *Davidson* i 238b; Davie 28 #16; H. W. Davies 48-51 #40; Dempster 22-23; Diack i 80; Dick i 189 #212; Ditson 1859 7b; Emerick 151-53; *Empire* 17b; Farmer 1909 114-15; Fitz 1848 169; *Francis & Day* iv 27; Fulcher 32-33; *Gems of Scottish Songs* 55b-56; *Gentle Annie #2* 15; Gleadhill 52; Goodwin 1956 369a; G. F. Graham 1891 22-23; J. Greig i 56-57; A. Hamilton 8-9; W. Hamilton 16; Haufrecht 1970 138-39; Haydn 2 #2; Haynes ii 65; *Heart Songs* 378-79; Hickok 10-11; Hitchcock #173; Hitchcock ii 126-27; Hopekirk 71-72; *Howe* 1864b 33; *Howe* 188- 112; C. Johnson 36; H. Johnson 399-400; J. Johnson #260; Kidson 1913 57; Kinsley ii 528-29 #302; Lampe 1914 46; *Lyric Gems* 52-53; *Lyric Gems* i 149; MacCunn 12-13; MacFarren 8-9; MacMahon ii 85 #42; Maver 11a #21; *Minstrel* 113-15; Mitchison 204; Moodie 64-65; D. H. Morrison i 346; Morvan 40; *Musical Bouquet #428* 73-74; *Never Grow Old* 143; *Nightingale* 72-75; Ogilvie 105b #116; *120 Scotch Songs* 27; *Penny Melodist #2*; Pittman 72; Plumstead 31-32; Reddall 161; Rimbault 1850 64b-65; *Scottish Songs* 50-51; Sedley 249-50; C. J. Sharp 1902 164-65; *Silver Chord* 54; *Singer's Companion* 72-74; *Sky-Lark* 300-301; J. T. Smith 30; R. A. Smith i 42a + Berggreen 80 #49; *Song Jewels* 42b; *Songs Forever* 13; *Songster's Favourite Companion* 63-65; A. Stuart v 114-15; Tomlyn 42-43; *Vocal Companion* 394-95; Vornholt 12b; Wier 1924 197; Wilkinson i #395; *World's Best* 129.

Tunes identified by this title, for other texts: Barke 142-43 (bawdy); A. Campbell ii 33b; *Charmer* i 114-15, 119, 285, 348-49; V. B. Lawence 220, 239; McCarthy 50 (bawdy); *Masque* 285-86 (bawdy); Ramsay i 59; Ramsay i 162-63 + *Lark* 209-11 #285; *Sing 7* 74 (bawdy); Joe Wilson 91-92, 325-26, 383-84.

Tunes identified by this title, instrumental: *Boosey* 1862a 50 #161; *Chappell* 1863 23 #57; Converse 1871 31a; *Howe* 1864a 112g; Jewett 25c; J. Kennedy 1 (flute variations); Kerr iii 6d; Kerr v 12; B. Mackenzie #265; *Musical Bouquet* #2648 (piano variations by Charles Grobe); Oswald iv 22-23; *Violin Made Easy* 30d; Woodbury 1853b 24 #38.

(*Johnny, I Hardly Knew Ye*),

Comment, references: Leisy 1966 193-98.

Tunes with this text: Behan 1965 35; Clayre 66-67; Bikel 192-93; Dallas 1973 109-10; J. Edwards 177; *Folk #3* 12; Glazer 1970 183-85; Graeme 31-33 + *Clancy* 1971 31-33; Hughes iii 38-42; B. Ives 1958 82-83; *Johnny, I Hardly Knew Ye Songster* [tune indicated]; Leisy 1964 180-81; Leisy 1966 195-96 + Leisy 1974 74 #70; *Little Lotta* 72-73; *Lomir Ale Singen* 96; Luboff 294-95; Okun 1968 23-25; Silverman 1975 ii 292a; J. J. Ward 55-56.

(*Pat Works on the Railway*): [See notes to #174, *The Bluestone Quarries*].

(*When Johnny Comes Marching Home*),

Comment, references: J. Burton i 8; Cray 242-43; Dichter 1941 118; FA 2188F 22 (Hermes Nye); Fuld 1971 639-41; R. Jackson 285; NW 202F 5-6 (Charles Hamm); Spaeth 1948 154; Wolf Index #2524.

Sheet music: Boston: Henry Tolman, 1863, in Dichter 1956 (facsimile) + R. Jackson 233-36 (facsimile); London: *Musical Bouquet* #3794.

Broadsides, songsters [without tune]: *Ben Cotton* 26-27; *Charlie Monroe* 25-26; *Dr. J. L. Thayer* 25-26; *Harry Pell* 12; *Hooley* 1863 29.

Tunes with this text: C. B. Adams 33-34; Agay 136; Armitage 1918 47; Beattie 18; Boni 1952 196-97; Buck 1916 196; Buck 1933 77; *Buckley* 25; Butler 71-72; *Canadian Boys* 248-49 #150; Cazden 1962 26; CMS 660F.4 (Tom Glazer); Dolph 357-58; Downes 188-89; Dykema #9; *Em-*

pire 18a; *Everybody's Favorite* 73b; FA 2188A.4 (Hermes Nye); *Favorite Songs* 11a; *Folk #2* 34; Ira Ford 322-23; *Francis & Day* ii 38; Frey 1941 64; Frey 1942 91; Frey 194- 66a; Frey 1948 91; Fuld 1971 639-41; Garson 82-83; Hansen 200a; Haufrecht 1959 49; *Heart Songs* 484; Hesser 167; B. Hoffman 30-31; Horton 42-43; *Howe* 1872 107a; Humphreys 70-71; B. Ives 1962 308-9 + B. Ives 1966 205-7; Leaman 29b; Leisy 1974 155 #155; Lingard 75-76; R. Lloyd 134; A. Lomax 1960 98; Lorenz 125 #225; Lynn 1961 82-83; MacLean 15; Marrocco 302-3 #120; J. Mills 5; Mursell 131b; Nelson 40; S. H. Nicholson 154 #79; Noble 1908 28; NW 202.2.5; Oberndorfer 111b; *101 Best Songs* #15; *Penny Melodist* #3; Raph 250-52; Ratcliff 60-61; Rodeheaver 1928 34b; *Scottish Students* 282-83; Pete Seeger 1973 166-67; Serposs 223; Shealy 192; Silber 1964 94; Silber 1965 26; Silverman 1975 ii 323b; *Song Purpose* 246; *Songs Forever* 57; Vornholt 6a; Wier 1915 229; Wier 1918 516a; Wier 1931 168; Wilkinson i #327.

    Tunes identified by this title, not notated: Stekert 1969 B 53; Joe Wilson 92-93, 371-72.

    Tunes identified by this title, instrumental: Jarman 33i; Kerr i 28 #6; Kerr xii 12i, "Scottish"; Kirkell 69; *Musical Bouquet* #3823 (piano variations by Charles Grobe).

Tune relatives (others): S. C. Andrews 14-15, *The Animals Went In One by One*; Bronson i 228 #3, *Billy Boy* variant of Child 12, *Lord Randall* (tune similar to *John Anderson, My Jo*); Bronson iv 170 #56, *Dandoo* form of Child 277, *The Wife Wrapt in Wether's Skin* (tune similar to *When Johnny Comes Marching Home*); N. Buchan 1962 86; N. Buchan 1973 41; A. Campbell ii 33b; Cass-Beggs 19— 30a; Catcheside-Warrington iii 6-7; CFC 301B.8 + CFC 301F 17 (Glenn Ohrlin); Cray 142-43; Creighton 1962 148; CS 54 (Malvina Reynolds), *The Judge Said*; D'Urfey vi 251-52, *Put In All*; Ernest Newton 71; Fowke 1969 82-83 #150; E. Haywood 32 #24d (instrumental); *JEFDSS 4* 119a; *JFSS 8* 210 + Bronson i 228 #3; Karpeles 1975 i 5 #5; J. Johnson #481 + Dick i 348 + *JFSS 8* 212, *The Maid Gaed to the Mill;* King 25; M. Leach 1965 150; A. Lomax 1967 361; Mackay i 77 + Lingenfelter 301; G. S. Morris 12-13; Moyer #34; Ohrlin 132-

33; *Pocket Song Book* 61, *The Animals Went In One by One;* Silverman 1966 58, 60; Terry 1931 30-31; Topic 12T159B.1; Waite 1887 72, *The Ark:* J. J. Ward 66-67.

100.
The Prisoner's Song

Previously available: Kimball 177-78 [text only]; *NYFQ 16* 92-93.
Variants: none.
Adaptations: none.
Comment, references: Beard 372; Belden 1952 iii 416-17; T. Burton ii 62; Freeman 202, listing; *JEMFQ 11* 95-103 (Haden); W. R. Mackenzie 1928 303; Malone 1968 56, 58, 230; Malone 1975 72-75; *NYFQ 16* 90-92 (Cazden); Randolph iv 226-28; *Sam Henry* #746; C. Sandburg 1927 146, 216-18.
Broadsides, songsters: none.
Texts: G. Anderson 230; Belden 1952 iii 416; Combs 1967 227 #192, listing; Cox 1939 ii 71-72; *FSA 33F* 7, *Seven Long Years in State Prison*, listing; M. E. Henry 327; Kimball 176a, 176-77; W. R. Mackenze 1919 149; Pound 1916 34; C. Sandburg 1927 218-19, *Seven Long Years in State Prison;* H. Sandburg 57, *Seven Long Years;* Scarborough 1937 348-49 C.
Related text (*Botany Bay*, Edwards Type I),
    Comment, references: Manifold 28.
    Texts: H. Anderson 18-19; Ashbee x 9; DL 8245.2.2 (Burl Ives); R. G. Edwards 1956 23; Finger 129-31 + Boni 1952 247-49; Hansen 29; Long 5-6; MacMahon 1963 #3; Manifold 22; Mitchell 88-90; Randolph i 374; Silber 1973b 67c; *Singabout Songster* 12b; R. B. Smith 18.
    Text parody (*If I Had the Wings of a Caterpillar*): *This & That* 4a; Zanzig 1940 #85.
Related text (*Farewell to All Judges and Juries*),
    Comment, references: Purslow 1972 124-25.
    Broadsides, songsters: Ashton 1888 364-65.
    Texts: Gillington 1911 14-15; Hamer 1967 49, *Sweet Swansea; JFSS 1* 135 + Scarborough 1937 346; Merrick 44-46 + C. J. Sharp 1961 v 228; Purslow 1972 39; D. Stewart 15-16.
Related text (*Meet Me by Moonlight Alone*, by Joseph Augustus Wade),
    Comment, references: Belden 1952 iii 411; S. B. Gould iv iii; H. Johnson 374-75; Maitland v 265, 385-86.
    Sheet music and other publications with music: Wrexham: Alaw, n. d.; New York:

Firth & Hall, n. d., "as sung by J. B. Tay-lor"; Bantock 1914 203-4; Boston: Hitch-cock #286; *Cavendish #21* (188-)14-15; Hitchcock iii 138-39; Kerr iii 34a (instru-mental); McCaskey v 128; *Musical Bou-quet #3319*, ca. 1864; *Musical Carcanet* (1832) 16-17; Ogilvie 79b #87; *Shower of Pearls* 124-25; *Silver Chord* 124-25; S. Winner 1885 68-69.

Texts: *American Singer* 12; *Beadle's Old time* 34-35; Beeton 1865 29; Briegel 1934 42; E. W. Cole 39c; Davidson 1854 21-22; *Fireside* 114-15; Gleadhill 218; Hatton i 28-29; H. Johnson 374-76; *Pacific* i 39; *Pacific* ii 20a; *Quaver* 1844 134-35; *Shilling Song Book* ii 90; Stout 87-88 #64.

Text parodies: Prest ii 227, *Meet Me Next Sunday Alone; Few Days* 154-55, *Meet Me at Sunrise Alone.*

Related text (*Meet Me in the Moonlight* adapta-tion, with images of prison, "I wish I had someone to love me," ship on the ocean, wings of an angel),

  Comment, references: T. Burton ii 62; Beard 370; Randolph iv 226; C. Sandburg 1927 216-17.

  Texts: Beard 370-71; Belden 1952 iii 411-16; T. Burton i 60-61; T. Burton ii 62-63; Clif-ton 27; Cox 1939 193-94; Davis Index 285; *Elmore Vincent* 143; Fuson 143; Gordon AM 1.1.27; *Musical Budget 8* 115-16 (1884); Neely 239-40; Odum 1926 83-84; Randolph iv 226-28; Richardson 55; C. Sandburg 1927 216-17; Scarborough 1937 347 A, 347-48 B, 349 D, 350 E, 350-51 F; Schinhan v 246; Stout 49b #35.

Related text (*Oh! Had I the Wings of a Dove*, by Charles Jefferys and L. Devereaux) [* in-dicates with tune]: *Book of Words* 57; Ditson 1857 *264-65 [a vocal quartet arrangement by William H. Oakes, from his *Sabbath Eve-nings* (1840)]; Hadaway 140-41; Hitchcock iii *254-55; Howe 1858 *85a (instrumental); McCaskey vii *45b; *Musical Bouquet* *#7658; Ogilvie *16a #13; *Sentimental Songs* 96-97; *Souvenir Minstrel* 9; Trifet 1890 *214b; S. Winner 1885 *296; Woodbury 1856 *320.

  Text used as refrain (*Wings of a Dove*): Malone 1968 255, listing; Work 129.

Related text (*The Prisoner's Song*, by Guy B. Massey),

  Comment, references: Engel 96a; Goldberg 255; Mattfeld 405; Randolph iv 226; Spaeth 1948 445-46.

  Sheet music: New York: Shapiro, Bernstein & Co., 1924.

Texts with tunes: Edison 51459 (Vernon Dalhart); Engel 96a; *Thirty-Three* 2-3.

Related text (parody: *Seven Long Years I've Been Married*): Gardner 1939 132; Shay 1961 190-91.

Related text (*The Ship That Never Returned*, by Henry C. Work),

  Comment, references: Dichter 1941 151; Spaeth 1948 157.

  Sheet music: Chicago: Root & Cady, 1865; *Musical Bouquet #4230*; *Thirty-Three* 18-19.

  Texts: R. G. Edwards 1971 283-84; Randolph iv 140-41; C. Sandburg 1927 146; W. J. Smith 38-39; Spaeth 1927 138.

Text and tune relatives: Creighton 1932 309; W. R. Mackenzie 1928 303, tune 403-4 #121; McDowell 1947 59; *Sam Henry #746, The Gaol Song*; Scarborough 1937 347 A, tune 449 + Emrich 1974 124 [text only]; Schinhan v 246-47; *Thirty-Three* 12-13, *Locked Up in Prison*, by Jimmie Burns and George Brown.

Tune relatives (*Can I Sleep in Your Barn To-night, Mister?*): FA 2365.1.3; Kanawha 313.1.3 (Grant Rogers); *Carson J. Robison* 60-61 + *Tip Top 1936* 60-61; W. J. Smith 10-11.

Tune relatives (*On the Banks of the Old Rari-tan*): Atkinson 186; D. B. Chamberlain 227; *Collegiate* 153; C. W. Johnson 148.

Tune relatives (*Red River Valley*),

  Comment, references: Fife 1969 157; Fuld 1971 457; Kallman 160, Leisy 1966 276-78; WF 23 163-71, "*The Red River Valley* re-examined" (Fowke).

  Sheet music (*In the Bright Mohawk Valley*, by James J. Kerrigan): New York: How-ley, Haviland & Co., 1896.

  Tunes with this text: Agay 182; *American Cowboy* 10-11; Barbeau 7-8, *Remember the Red River*; Best 39; *Big Round Up* 29; Boni 1947 146-47; Briegel 7; Brumley 1970 i #5; Carmer 1942b 177-78; *Carson J. Robison* 18-19 + *Tip Top 1936* 18-19; K. S. Clark 1930 68 #84; K. S. Clark 1932 78; K. S. Clark 1934 53; *Cowboy Tom* 5; Daughters 130-31; Downes 324-25; R. Evans 10; *Everybody's Favorite* 182-83; FA 2365.2.5; Fife 1969 157; FO 13.1.6, 17.1.8; Fowke 1964 88-89 + Leisy 1966 276-78; Frey 1941 164-65; Frey 1942 88; Frey 194- 54; Frey 1948 88; Fuld 1971 457; Goodwin 1956 170; Goss 1927 147; Hansen 159a; Haufrecht 1958 33 + Haufrecht 1959 37; B. Ives 1962 218-20 + B. Ives 1966 161-63; Keene 49; T. Kennedy 44; Kins-cella 15; J. Lomax 1947 220-21; Luther

197-98; McLean 84; *Many Nations* 32a,
Remember the Red River; J. Mills 71; E.
Moore 372-73; Morehead 154-55; Nelson
134-35; P. Patterson 46-48 + J. Lomax
1938 298-99; *Pocket Song Book* 47; *Powder River* 8-9; Randolph iv 203; Raph 379-82; Richman 69a; C. Sandburg 1927 130;
Pete Seeger 1973 192, 193; Shealy 176;
Sherwin 1944 58 59; Silverman 1975 i 31b;
W. J. Smith 7-9; Stekert 1969 N 58, listing;
Tent & Trail 80; *Thirty-Three* 8-9; *This & That* 39; Thurman 97b-98; *24 Mountain Songs* 14; Vornholt 7b; Welsch 32-34;
H. R. Wilson 45-46; Wise 48; *World's Best* 4-5; Zanzig 1940 #5.

Tune relatives (others): Cazden 1955 12b; Durlacher 70; Fife 1969 279; Kirkell 31; Kraus 55; Larkin 106-7; M. Leach 1965 142; Leifer 51; Price 88; Putney 79; Randolph iv 365; Schinhan v 265; *SO 2 #3* 11.

101.
The Poor Man's Family

Previously available: Kimball 107-8 [text only];
Neighbors 1948 26; *PSB 3* #269 + *RPSB* 44-45; *YIFMC 3* 72 #8c [tune only].

Variants: none.

Adaptations: none.

Comment, references: Foner 239-42; Kimball 106; *Neighbors* 1948 26; *PSB 3* #269 + *RPSB* 45.

Broadsides, songsters: W. H. Arnold 15 + Kimball 106-7; *Delaney* #64 24; Foner 239, 242 (facsimiles); *Harrigan & Braham* 1886 40;
Harrigan & Hart 1875 58; *Harrigan & Hart* 1878 11; *Peter J. Downey* 53; Wehman #396 + Greenway 236.

Texts: Dean 82-83; A. Lomax 1967 119; *HYFQ 14* 208, listing.

Related texts (*He's Only a Workingman*):
James O'Neil 1882 26.

(*The Workingmen's Strike*): Fred Roberts 25, "as sung by the Original Shamrock Four"; *Shamrock Four* 8.

Text and tune relatives: none.

Tune relatives,

Comment, references: Ph. Barry 1939, notes to 28, 33, 62; A. L. Lloyd 1967 50-51, 77-79; O'Neill 1922 120b.

(*The Banks of Newfoundland*): Colcord 169 + A. Lomax 1960 59-60; *JFSS 5* 300;
Hugill 412; Peacock 854.

(Child 92, *The Lowlands of Holland*): Healy 1967a 66d; Hughes ii 70-75 + Bronson ii 423 #10; *JIFS 2* 31, 32; Joyce 1972 69 #68

+ Joyce #404 + Bronson ii 423-24 #11;
C. J. Sharp 1932 i 200 + Bronson ii 424 #12 + *SFQ 1* 23b.

(others, complete tune form): Bayard 11,
The Old Oak Tree; Breathnach ii 142;
Breathnach iii 48, 76, 240, 246; *CAY 2 #2* 8; *CEOL 1 #3* 13; *CEOL 2 #1* 8; *CEOL 3* 112; *Choice Irish Songs* ii 114; Creighton 1962 6, 71, 95, 103; Creighton 1971 87, 95;
R. G. Edwards 1956 126; Fowke 1967 80-81 + Fowke 1970 104; FSA 33.2.1, 33.2.3;
FSE 7.1.2; FSS 34.1.7; Hatton 207; Hugill 411; Edw. Ives 1964 33-34; *JFSS 2* 173;
JFSS 3 287; *JFSS 5* 60 + Karpeles 1974 ii 548-49; Joyce 1872 98 #96; Joyce #393,
#562, #608, #626; P. Kennedy 80, 355,
699; A. Lomax 1960 136 (from an Irish source); Meredith 1968 172; Moeran 1950 6-8; *NA Ives* 1.32 + ATL 2157.4; *NA Ives* 1.37 + ATL 2162.6; *NA Ives* 62.2, *The Bells of Shandom*; Noraidh 38; O Lochlainn 1939 4, 162; O Lochlainn 1965 14;
O'Neill #96, #164, #396; Petrie 1855,
Supplement 16; Petrie #37, #193, #202,
#322, #323, #648; QC 903.2.6; *Sam Henry* #626; *Sing 10 #2* 7a; SLP 80A.5;
Steeleye Span 54-57.

(others, in *a - a'* half-tune form): *All Time* 21;
JFSS 6 130; *JFSS 8* 16 #14; Karples 1971 141 B; A. Lomax 1960 136; Manny 151;
NA Ives 1.100 + ATL 3107.3; Ritchie 1953 15.

(others, in *--b-a'* half-tune form): [See notes to #22, *Johnny Riley*].

(others, in 3/4 time): Costello 98 #55, 102 #56; *JFSS 5* 60; *Acquittal of Thomas Holoran*; Joyce #362, #561, #776; O Lochlainn 1939 26; O Lochlainn 1965 150,
The Manchester Martyrs; O'Neill #473;
Petrie #75, #252, #1069.

(others, in 6/8 time): Breathnach iii 68;
O'Neill #242, #397, #428; O'Neill 1913 120, *Mo Mhuirnin na Gruaige Baine* [*My Fairhaired Darling*]; Petrie #1340.

102.
The Ragged Coat

Previously available: none.
Variants: none.
Adaptations: none.
Comment, references: D. Gilbert 146-53;
Spaeth 1948 173.
Broadsides, songsters: Ashton 1888 382-84; J.
Auner + Wolf Index #1950; *Charley Monroe* 14-16; *Concert Room* 45-48; *Dr. J. L.*

Thayer 14-15; *Greenback Songster* 87-88; *Harry Hill* 63-65, "as sung by Charlie Sanford"; *Henderson #10* 78; *J. M. Berry* 1856 18-20; *Johnson's Comic* 13-15 + Dwyer 179-80 + *Pacific* iv 13-15; *J. S. Berry* 61-63; *Nat Austin* 18-19; *Ned Turner* 47-48; *Popular California Songs #1*, a broadside by J. W. Sullivan, San Francisco; *Singer's Journal #7* 52; *That's the Style* 47; *Tony Pastor* 1862 29-30 + *Tony Pastor* ix 29-31; *Uncle True* 138-40; *Wehman #650; Wehman* i 121-22.
Texts: none.
Related text (*Shabby Genteel*),
    Sheet music: *Board of Music Trade* 115, listing; Boston: Oliver Ditson 1870; Cincinatti: John Church Co., 1870; *Cundy #83*.
    Texts [* indicates with tune]: *Central Park* *46-47; *Delaney #47* 21; *Harry Richmond* 1869 60-61; *Howe* 1874 *48a + *Trifet* 1890 *49a + *Trifet* 1892 *49a; *Lookout Mountain; Lydia Thompson* *26-27; *Sol Smith Russell* 1869 44-45; *Song Jewels* 30a; Spaeth 1927 54-55.
Text and tune relatives: none.
Tune relatives: none.

103.
Poor, but a Gentleman Still

Previously available: none.
Variants: none.
Adaptations: none.
Comment, references: D. Gilbert 151-52.
Broadsides, songsters: *Delaney #41* 24; *Murphy & Morton* 26; *Wehman #246; Wehman* i 53; *Wehman's Collection #28* 16; *Wm. J. Scanlan* 24.
Texts: Piper + Peterson Index 67; Randolph iv 349-50, from a manuscript copy; Shellans 84; Stekert 1969 B 146, listing.
Related text (*The Norway Bum*, by Joe Scott): Edw. Ives 1978; *NA Ives* 1.36 + ATL 2162.3; *NA Ives* 1.142 + ATL 3149.4.
Text and tune relatives: none.
Tune relatives: none.

104.
When I Leave These Earthly Shores

Previously available: AFS 12309B.13 + EC 699.13.
Variants: none.
Adaptations: none.

Comment, references: none.
Broadsides, songsters: none.
Texts: none.
Tunes: none.

105.
The Black Sheep

Previously available: none.
Variants: none.
Adaptations: none.
Comment, references: CFC 201F 11a, 16a (McCulloh); *Delaney #18* 7; Malone 1968 285.
Broadsides, songsters: *Delaney #18* 7.
Sheet music: New York: Howley, Haviland & Co., 1897; Feist 12-15 [with different tune].
Texts: AFS 920B, 2357A; Brumley i *#54; CFC 201A.6 + CFC 201F 22-23; Davis Index 76-77 (2); Feist 12-15; Fuson 79-80; HTA (Young); LCJ; Malone 1968 285, listing; *MF 13* 150, listing (Fowke); *NA Ives* 1.66 + ATL 2185.4; *NA Ives* 1.88 + ATL 2205.4; *NYFQ 5* 98-99; Piper & Peterson Index 19; Shearin 33, listing; Spaeth 1927 173-74.
Text and tune relatives: none.
Tune relatives (*The Fatal Wedding*),
    Comment, references: Belden 1940 141-42; Belden 1952 ii 629; J. Burton i 150-51; D. Gilbert 267-70; Greenleaf 368; Spaeth 1926 172; Spaeth 1948 266-67.
    Broadsides, songsters: *Delaney #59* 23.
    Texts: Belden 1940 141-42 A; Dichter ii #162, listing of sheet music publication, 1893; Marks 232, listing; Mattfeld 208, listing; Pound 1922 140-42.
    Tunes with this text: Belden 1940 143 B; Greenleaf 368; Randolph iv 278; Schinhan iv 303, 304 #452, 304-5 #453; Spaeth 1927 172-73.
Tune relatives (others): Gardner 1939 349, *Nat Goodwin;* Hubbard 100, *Jack and Joe; NEF 5* 60 + ATL 2165.2 + *NA Ives* 1.39, *When the Battle It Was Won.*

106.
Two Little Girls in Blue

Previously available: AFS 12309B.12 + EC 699.12.
Variants: none.
Adaptations: none.
Comment, references: J. Burton i 152; D. Gilbert 275; M. Leach 1965 168; Marks 263; Randolph iv 338; Spaeth 1926 199-200; Spaeth 1948 269-70.

Broadsides, songsters: Engel 242-43; Fortey 1894, 1896, 1897; *Harrigan & Braham 189-;* *Harrigan & Braham* 1894; Wehman #1340; Wehman 1916.

Sheet music: New York: Spaulding & Kornder, 1893 + Charosh 282-85 (facsimile); London: Chas. Sheard & Co., 1894; *Francis & Day* #13 13-14 + *Francis & Day* i 12-13 + *Sixty Variety Songs* 26-27.

Texts: K. S. Clark 1930 127 #165; HTA (Effler); M. Leach 1965 168; *NYFQ 5* 98-99; Piper; Randolph iv 338-39; Stout 57-58.

Related text (parody): *N. C. Bostock.*

Text and tune relatives [*indicates tune of refrain only]: Bonar 158-59; Browne 383-84 A, 385-86 B; Brumley ii #1; Buford 160; K. S. Clark 1930 127 #166; Goodwin 1956 14a; L. O. Smith *8b-9a; Spaeth 1926 n*199-200; *Tunes Dad Whistled* 2-3.

Related text and tune (*After the Ball*, by Charles K. Harris),

  Comment, references: Boni 1952 35-39; Freeman 11; Fuld 1955 8; Fuld 1971 87a; Harris 58-61.

  Sheet music: Milwaukee: Chas. K. Harris & Co., 1892 + Freeman 10 + Fremont 1-5 (facsimile) + Fuld 1955 31 (facsimile title page) + Harris 58-61; London: *Francis & Day* i 5-7 + *Sixty Variety Songs* 13-15.

  Texts with tunes [*indicates tune of refrain only]: Agay 195-97; Boni 1952 39-40; Boni 1960 77-80; Browne 329-30; Brumley i #50; K. S. Clark 1930 127 #165; Freeman *11; Frey 1942 *2 + Frey 1943 *84 + Frey 194-*14 + Frey 1948 *2; Fuld 1971 87a; Gamse 58-61; Goodwin 1956 4a; Hansen *213b; I. Hoffman 4-7; MacLean 79; Morehead *106-7; Nelson 86; Stern *20-21; *World's Best* 37.

  Text (parody) **with tune** (*After the Ball*): R. G. Edwards 1972 191.

Related text and tune (*Two Little Kangaross*): R. G. Edwards 1972 134.

Tune relatives (others) [*indicates tune comprising first and last phrases of the stanza portion]: Dolph 34-36 + Lingenfelter 290-91; Hubbard *405 + Lingenfelter *245; Lingenfelter 170-71; Silber 1967 *76; *WF 17* *233, *235a. [also see #97, *Life Is A Toil*].

107.
The Lazy Club

Previously available: none.
Variants: ATL 184.8, 185.1.
Adaptations: none.

Comment, references: none.

Broadsides, songsters [*tune indicated as *Green Grow the Rushes, O*]: Bob Slaven 30-31; *Book of Popular Songs* *251-53; De Marsan *#237; *Electric Three* 54-55; *Elton* 159, "tune: *Regent Street*"; *Harrison's Comic* 40-42, "tune: *The Doctor's Boy*"; *Singer's Journal #20* *122; *That's the Style* *38-39; *Tony Pastor* ix 41-42; Wolf Index #1232.

Texts: none.

Text and tune relatives: none.

Tune relatives (*Beulah Land*, by Edgar Page Stites and Jno. R. Sweney),

  Comment, references: Austin 26-27; Ohrlin 249-50 #9 (Harlan Daniel).

  Tunes with this text: Austin 27; Bacon 1907 83-84; J. M. Black 1900 #168; *Broadman Hymnal* #114; Chapman 98; Cline 129 #187; J. A. Davis #63; Elderkin 1890 #226; Elderkin 1898 #219; Elderkin 1900 216 #257; *Epworth Hymnal* i #276; Excell 1912 #66; Excell 1918 #118; Goodwin 1959 32a; C. Johnson 198, "German tune"; Kinsburg 138; Leiper 311b-12; Lindsay 178; McCaskey ii 11; McCaskey 1899 19a; McCoy #282; Morehead 328-329; Peloubet #31; *Revival Echoes* #75;Rodeheaver 1916 #40; Rodeheaver 191- #64; Rodeheaver 1925 #154; Sankey 1894 436a #608; A. B. Smith #310; Sweney 1882 i (1878) 69; Sweney 1882 ii (1880) 25; Sweney 1888 #146; *Tabernacle* iii #182.

Tune relatives (derivatives from *Beulah Land*),

  (*Alberta Land*): Fowke 1960 209a.

  (*Dakota Land*): CFC 301B.2a (Glen Ohrlin) + CFC 301F 13 + Ohrlin 22-24; Lingenfelter 476-77.

  (*Harvest Land*): Lingenfelter 491-92.

  (*Kansas Land*): Lingenfelter 462 A, 463 B.

  (*Prairie Land*, by William W. Smith): Fowke 1960 209b; MacLeod 80-82.

  (*Saskatchewan*),

    Comment references: Fowke 1960 208-9.

    Tunes with this text: Cass-Beggs 1963 14-15; Fowke 1960 210-11 + Fowke 1972 120-21 + *Young Canada* 37-38; FW 3001B.24 (Alan Mills); Ohrlin 25-27.

  (*Sweet Nebraska Land*): FH 5337A.8 (Roger Welsch); Lingenfelter 460-61.

Tune relatives (*Oats, Peas, Beans and Barley Grow*),

  Comment, references: Gomme ii 12-13; Mattson 49; *SFQ 6* 192-94; Wilkinson *510* 14.

  Tunes with this text: Bertail 60; Bley 80; Bullard 102b-103; Cazden 1962 11; Erdei 68 #97; Geri 54; *JAF 49* 251-52; Marsh 38;

McIntosh 1948 59-60; McIntosh 1974 95; Neal 34; *Nightingale* (1850) 28-29; Noble 1912 121b-22; O'Shaughnessy 1966 46-53 (a variant in minor); Price 110-11; Rohrbough 1931a 4; H. Sandburg 14b; Schinhan v 514-15 B; L. Warner 40b-41; Welsch 287-88; Wessells 39b; Wier 1918b 82b-83; Wilkinson i #474; Wilkinson *510* 14; Winn 181.

Tune relatives (others): Botkin 1937 173, 174; Cazden 1974 8-9, *Monday I Asked My Neighbor to Play; Champagne Charlie* 1867 66-68, *The Way the Money Goes* [tune indicated]; Erdei 69 #98; Fowke 1969 14 #6; *Handy* 1940 7; *JAF 24* 301, *Consolation Flowing Free;* Linscott 47, 231; Matteson 1947 47; Mattson 49b, *Baltimore* (instrumental); *Musical Bouquet* #21 83d, *Moll in the Wad* (instrumental); Price 24; Ritson 1813 iii 53-56, *To Cupid on Valentine's Day;* Sackett 1961 173, *The Miller and Three Sons.*

Unrelated tunes (text derivatives of Beulah Land): Sackett 1961 143-44, *Kansas Land;* C. Sandburg 1927 280-81, *Dakota Land;* Silber 1967 234, *Dakota Land.*

(*Oats, Peas, Beans*): FHR-04.1.5; Gomme ii 1a, 1b, 2a, 2b; Gomme 1909 16; Newell 81.

108.
The Mule Song

Previously available: Kimball 171 [text only].
Variants: none.
Adaptations: Cazden 1958 i 80-81 + Cazden 1978 80-81.
Comment, references: Cazden 1958 i 118 + Cazden 1978 118.
Broadsides, songsters: *Bob Slaven* 50; *Harrigan & Hart* 1882a 52; *Hyde & Behman* 14; *Sam Devere* 10; *Wehman's Collection #10* 2, "tune: *Never Take the Horseshoe from the Door*".
Texts: H. Thompson 1940 227.
Relates texts (*Never Take the Horseshoe from the Door,* by Edward Harrigan and Dave Braham),
   Broadsides, songsters: *Barnum* 8; *Coup* 40; *Dan Nash* 21; *Dayton* 1882 50; *Dick Sands* 24; *Harrigan & Hart* 1882b 46; *Harry Woodson* 52; *Hi Henry* 31;l *Jay Rial* 15; *Johnny Patterson* 8; *Johnny Roach* 1881 42; *Merchant* 6; *Murray & Murphy* 43; *Pat Rooney* 188- 43; *Tony Pastor* 1881 51.
   Sheet music: New York: Wm. A. Pond, 1880 + Dichter 1941, listing; London: *Musical Bouquet* #6646, 1882; (in folio), Harrigan i 12-14.

Texts: E. C. Beck 1948 285-86; Goodwin 1956 112 [with tune]; Kimball 170; Stekert 1969 B 50.
Unrelated text (*Keep the Horseshoe Over the Door,* by J. P. Skelly): Garson 21-23; *Trifet* 1886 45a; *Trifet* 1890 45a.
Related texts (*The Bay Mule*): Leavitt 36; Manchester & Jennings 6; Russell 33.
   (Donker songs): *JAF 38* 171-77; *SFQ 8* 178-79.
   (*My Sweetheart's the Mule in the Mines*),
     Comment, references: Goldstein 1-14 (George Korson).
     Texts: Emrich 1974 579a; Fowke 1960 64; FP 5003.48-6.1.6 (Pete Seeger) + Dallin 149 + Glazer 1970 235-36 + Mursell 63 + Pete Seeger 1964 38 + Silber 1973b 27c + Silverman 1966 51 + Silverman 1975 ii 194b + *SO 7 #1* 12a.
   (*Old Thompson's Mule,* by Thomas P. Westendorff): Browne 418-19; Goodwin 1956 223a; Honoré 108-9; Pound 1922 213-14; Randolph 1955 674-75; Rosenfeld 56-57.
   (*Whoa, Mule, Kicking Mule,* or *Simon Slick*) [*instrumental tune only]: AFS *L20A.3; Brewster 335-38; Browne 552-55; Combs 1967 223-24 #176, A-B; Cornell 5-6; Cyporyn 79; DD 102.1.7 + DD 102F 12-13; Duggan *97; Emrich 1974 66-68; FP 710.1.4; *Hamlin Wizard Oil;* Harbin #38; Hubbard 349-50; Justus 32-33; A. C. Morris 190-91; Odum 1925 154-55; Odum 1926 177-80; *PTFLS 5* 167; Peggy Seeger 1960a *9; Ruth Seeger 1950 62'63; Shellans 76-77; Thede *130a; Yolen 34-35.
other mule songs) [*instrumental tunes]: Boette 143; DD 102.1.8 + DD 102F 13b; Felton 72-73; Kincaid ii 13; *NA Ives* 62.6, *Mule Song;* Possett 1943 75b; *PSB 2* #126; C. Sandburg 1927 400; Ruth Seeger 1950 64; Thede*129.
Text and tune relatives: none.
Tune relatives: Felton 72-73; Larkin 106-7; J. Lomax 1938 48a, 98-99; Schinhan v 497-98; Welsch 15-16.

109.
Puttin' On the Style

Previously available (#109 A): *Neighbors* 1945 20; *SO 5 #1* 26-27 (1955) + *RSO #1* 6-7. (#109 B): AFS 12309A.16 + AFS 12311A.1 + EC 329.16 + EC 703.1.
Variants: AFS 12311A.2 + EC 703.2; AFS 12311A.3 + EC 703.3; AFS 19250.5.
Adaptations: Cazden 1958 i 26-27 + Cazden

1978 26-27 [the form assigned to TRO by Abelard-Schuman prior to its book publication, and © by TRO, 1957].

Derivatives from this source, with acknowledgement variously to Ernie Sager, to Norman Cazden, to the Camp Woodland Collection, to *The Abelard Folksong Book* and/or to TRO: AFS 12312A.9 (David Hess, Susan Pragan and Carl Rodman [all age 10], at Camp Woodland, August 1946); AFS 12312A.16 (Robert and Louise De Cormier, 25 March 1955); AFS 12312B.9 (Camp Woodland counselor group, 20 August 1957); Brand 1961 50-51, with credit to Norman Cazden and to Melody Trails [TRO]; Cazden 1962 30, with notice of © by Melody Trails [TRO]; M. Cohen 1966 86-87, with acknowledgement to Camp Woodland; Decca 9-30409 (Rudy Hanson); Haufrecht 1959 104-5, with credit to Norman Cazden and notice of © by Melody Trails [TRO]; Kanawha 313.1.5 (Grant Rogers), with acknowledgement to Ernie Sager; RLP 12-603.9 (Milt Okun), with acknowledgment and notes by Norman Cazden; Pete Seeger 1961 68 + FC 7028 + FP 728.2 + Pete Seeger 1973 89, with acknowledgements to Ernie Sager and to Norman Cazden; Serposs 132-33, arr. by Milt Okun, with acknowledgment to Norman Cazden and © notice by Melody Trails [TRO]; Sheet music publication, New York: Melody Trails, 1957, with additional text as sung by Lonnie Donegan, + Mercury 71181.X45; Sheet Music publication, London: Essex House, 1957, with variant text as sung by Dickie Valentine, + London 45-1756; Sheet Music publication, München: Essex-Musikvertrieb, 1958, with the title *Gib Doch Nicht So An* and a German adaptation of the text by Gustav Auerbach; Sheet Music publication, München: Ralph Maria Siegel Musik Edition, 1958, in a band arrangement by Ulrich Sommerlatte; Silber 1963 68, with acknowledgment to Ernie Sager and to derivation from *SO 5 #1; Sing 2 #1* 3, with note of its derivation from the singing of Pete Seeger and from *SO 5 #1; SO 5 #1* (1955) 26-27 + *RSO #1* 6-7, with acknowledgement to Camp Woodland and erroneous attribution to George Edwards.

Derivatives from this source, issued 1957 or later, but without acknowledgment: ABC 45-9747.1 (The Neighbors); M. Cohen 1967 70 (with new text); DL 8413.1.1 (The Gateway Singers); EKL 142 (The Shanty Boys); Harrison 18-19; Leisy 1966 266-68; Leisy 1974 112-13 #112; Shealy 203-5; Silber 1973b 24a (text only); Silverman 1966 16-17; Silverman 1975 i 343.

Comment, references: Cazden 1958 i 120 + Cazden 1978 120; Cox 1925 514; Leisy 1966 266; Randolph iii 229; RLP 12-603 J.9 (Cazden); *Sing 2 #1* 3; SLP 49F B 3 (Goldstein)

Broadsides, songsters: none.

Texts: Browne 429 A, 430 B, 430-31 C; Cox 1925 514-15; A. K. Davis 1949 148, listing; *Folkonvention;* HTA (Grant); LCJ (Constanz); Piper + Peterson Index 68; Pound 1916 62 #19, summary; Randolph 230 B; *WF 24* 240, listing.

Related text (*Folks That Put On Airs,* or *Some Folks Put On Airs*),

Comment, references: *Beadle's Pocket* i 36; Dichter 1941 143; Spaeth 1948 160.

Sheet music: New York: Lee & Walker, 1863; (in folio), *Minstrel Songs* 1882 64-66 + [with additional verses] *Minstrel Songs* 1910 64-66; [title only, included in] Stephen Foster: *Song of All Songs* (1863) [facsimile in Jordan 35].

Broadsides, songsters [*indicates with tune]: *Beadle's Pocket* i 36; *Beauty of the Blondes* 76; *Bryant 1863* 22; *Clown's Songster* *26; *George Christy* 16-17; *J. M. Berry* (1856) 50-51; *Nelse Seymour* 48-49; *Singer's Journal #23* 146; *Tony Pastor 1862* 31-33 + *Tony Pastor* ix 31-33; *Wehman #563; Wehman* iii 17; Wolf Index #2181.

Texts [* indicates with tune]: Goodwin 1956 *329a; Mattfeld 114, listing; Wier 1929 *236-37.

Tune relatives; Rimbault ii 11-13 #4, *Kiss Me Quick and Go.*

Related text (*Putting on Airs,* or *You've Got To Put On Airs*),

Sheet music (as noted in Dichter i #1011): Chicago: H. M. Higgins, 1860.

Broadsides, songsters: *Banner Songster* 29; *Beadle's Dime #16* 20-21; *Beadle's Half-Dime #35* 2; *Beadle's Pocket* i 13-15; *Bob Hart* 57-58; *Hague's Minstrels* 74.

Texts: Brewster 332-33; Davis Index 148; Randolph iii 230-31; Rosenberg Index #1169.

Related text (*The Rising Generation*),

Broadsides, songsters: *Good-Bye, John* 12-13; Wolf Index #2015 (De Marsan).

Related text (*We'll Have To Get the Style*),

Broadsides, songsters: *Beadle's Dime #20* 5; *Beadle's Half-Dime #39* 10.

Related text elements ("put on style"): Doerflinger 261-62; Edw. Ives 1964 70-71; Manny 68-69; Welsch 114.

Text and tune relatives: AFS 4200B.3 (Warde H. Forde); *Arkansas Woodchopper* 1932 61-62 + *Dessa Manion* F 51; Browne 431-32 D; Randolph iii 229-30 + SLP 49B.3 (Ellen Stekert); Sheet music publication, New York: Shapiro, Bernstein, 1926.

Tune relatives (*Charles Guiteau*),

  Comment, references: Hubbard 252; Laws E 11; Randolph ii 29, 118.

  Texts with this tune [* indicates half-tune]: AFS L29 B.3 (Bascom Lamar Lunsford); B. Arnold *113; *CFB #3* 22; L. Chappell *188; Dunson 1973 48-49; FA 2951C.16 (Kelly Harrell); M. E. Henry 332; Hubbard 252; A. Lomax 1960 273; Luther 246-47; A. C. Morris 72; *NA Ives* 1.12 + ATL 2143.9; *NA Ives* 1.17 + ATL 2146.4; Randolph ii 29, 31, 32; Rosenberg T-83 10B.3; Sackett 1961 159-60; Schinhan iv 288, 289; Silber 1965 91; Silverman 1975 i 83b.

  Related texts with this tune (*My Name Is John R. Birchall*),

    Comment, references: FM 4005F A.4 (Fowke); Fowke 1965 189-90; Laws E 11.

    Texts with this tune: Burt 226-28; FM 4005A.4; Fowke 1965 126-27; Randolph ii 118.

  Related texts with this tune (others) [* indicates half-tune]: Belden 1940 407, 409-10; Burt 164; Lingenfelter 448; E. Moore *349; Randolph ii 115, 119; *WF 17* 236.

Tune relatives (*Guy Reed*),

  Comment, references: Flanders 1939 58; Edw. Ives 1978 [201-240]; Laws C 9; *NEF* 5 63-68.

  Texts only: Gray 24-28; Manny 104 [with distinct tune, see notes to #145].

  Texts with this tune: Flanders 1939 55-58; *NA Ives* 1.39 + ATL 2164.4; *NA Ives* 1.60 + ATL 2180.6 + Edw. Ives 1978 [240]; *NA Ives* 1.96 + ATL 3103.3 + Edw. Ives 1978 [201]; *NA Ives* 1.123 + ATL 3130.4; *NA Ives* 57.1.10, 62.4, 63.1, 64.7.1, 64.9.1, 64.9.3, 65.15.1, 65.17.5, 65.19.4, 65.22.2, 66.10.5.

Tune relatives (*The Lakes of Ponchartrain*),

  Comment, references: Laws H 9.

  Tunes with this text: AFS L55B.7; ATL 486.7 (George Edwards); ATL 601.10-.11 (James Edwards); ATL 621.9, 621.11 (Reuben Edwards); FA 2354.2.4 (Ellen Stekert); Larkin 46-48 (cowboy adaptation); Lingenfelter 430; Manny 256; *NA*

Ives 1.18 + ATL 2147.5; *NA Ives* 1.74 + ATL 2193.4; Randolph iv 413.

Tune relatives (*A Life on the Ocean Wave*, by Epes Sargent and Henry Russell),

  Comment, references: Dichter i #1809; H. Johnson 130; M. R. Turner 105-6.

  Sheet music publications: New York: Hewitt & Jaques, 1838; New York: Firth & Hall, 1838; London: *Musical Bouquet* #76 109-12; London: *Musical Treasury* #40 (1845), #566 (185-).

  Tunes with this text: Armitage 1916 80; Bardeen 1888 40-41; *D'Alcorn #2* 46a; *Davidson #40*; *Davidson* i 353; Dolph 290-92; *Empire Book* 110a; Ira Ford 33, 408-9; *Gems of Song* 144-47; Gleadhill 276-77; Goodwin 1956 178; Hansen 108c; Haynes i 38-40; *Heart Songs* 431; Hesser 92; *Howe* 1878 258; H. Johnson 131-36; W. M. Lawrence 58; Lovett 54; McCaskey iii 35; McCaskey 1899 146; Morehead 138-39; *Never Grow Old* 102-3; Ogilvie 148 #161; *Old Songs* 102; *Penny Melodist #30*; Reddall 38-39; *Trifet* 1890 164a + *Fireside Library* 22a + *Trifet* 1892 164a; E. L. White 178; Wier 1918 260a.

  Tunes with parody or variant text [* tune indicated but not notated]: Allan *48a, *A Life on the Vicksburg Hills*; *Band of Hope* 23; Fowke 1972 118; Glass 1968 211-13, *A Life on the Vicksburg Bluff*; *Pacific* i *8-9, *A Life by the Cabin Fire*; Paskman 209-11.

  Tunes (as instrumental or dance tunes): Cazden 1950 14b + Cazden 1955 32; Chicago Park District 62; Duggan 76; Dwyer 95 (from a Sacramento, California violin primer of ca. 1850); Ira Ford 33a; *Handy* 1955 100; Hesser 193; Howe 1851b 12c; Jarman 9; Kerr i 28 #2; Kerr xii 13d; Kirkell 81; Knorr 10a; B. Mackenzie #19; *Musical Bouquet* #21 83c, #298 38.3, #684 3b, #5116/7 4.3a; *Musical Bouquet* #998/9 (piano fantasie by William Dressler, Opus 40, 1856); *Musical Treasury* #137 100-101 #3 (1846); *Musical Treasury* #1006 (piano fantasia); Piper; Rohrbough 1931b 2 (quadrille); Ruth #113c; Ryan 1939 58.

Tune relatives (*Little Nell of Narragansett Bay*, by George F. Root),

  Sheet music publications: New York: Firth & Pond, 1860 + *Ada Holding Miller* Tear Jerker #13; London: *Musical Bouquet* #3498 (ca. 1864).

Broadsides, songsters: Wolf Index #204.

Texts only: Brewster 345; Dean 119; Laws 1950 264, listing; Neely 226-27.

Tunes with this text: Hubbard 121; Edw. Ives 1978 [226]; Spaeth 1927 30-31.

Tune relatives (*Rosie Nell,* or *Swinging in the Lane,* by Charles Carroll Sawyer),

Texts only: *Champagne Charlie* 1868 36; *Mabel Waltz* 34; *Walking Down Broadway.*

Tunes with this text: C. Sandburg 1927 114-15; H. Sandburg 42.

Tune relatives (*The State of Arkansas*): AFS L7.B4; AFS 35 + Botkin 1944 316-17 (Charles Seeger); Schinhan v 230.

Tune relatives (others) [* indicates half-tune]: Bethke #54, *I'm Just a Common Lumberhick* (from Adirondack region, New York); Brewster 336-37, *Simon Slick;* Cazden 1961 72, *Row de Dow de Dunfer;* K. S. Clark 1932 70-71 + Lingenfelter 350, *The Cowboy's Christmas Ball;* Cyporyn 83, *Jimmie Brown, the Newsboy;* Doerflinger 251, *Tom Dixon;* Downes *399; Durlacher 44-45; R. G. Edwards 1971 112, *Widgegoara Joe;* Fife 1969 108; FSA 26.2.8, *This Old Time Religion;* Kraus 73; Lengyel ii 124 A, *San Francisco Fog;* J. Lomax 1959 *33 (Huddie Ledbetter); J. Lomax 1959 *37, *The Shreveport Jail* (Huddie Ledbetter); Manifold 128-29, *Widgegoara Joe; NA Ives* 65.10.1, *John Ladner;* Putney 81; Randolph i 344, *Lone the Plowboy;* Randolph ii 115, *The Bald Knobber;* Randolph i 344, *Lone the Plowboy;* Randolph ii 115, *The Bald Knobber;* Randolph iii 228, *Sparking Sunday Night;* Schinhan v 290 #432, *Boil Them Cabbage Down;* Thomas 1964 165-66; Thomas 1964 *234 + Glazer 1970 *14-16 + A. Lomax 1967 *196-97, *T. V. A. Song; Tip Top* 1935 23, *In 1983.*

Unrelated tunes (*Sparking Sunday Night*): Mammoth 56-57; Trifet 1890 10a; J. W. Turner 61b.

110.
Brennan on the Moor

Previously available: *Neighbors* 1943 16-17.
Variants: ATL 614.7-.8.
Adaptations: Cazden 1958 i 72-73 + Cazden 1978 72-73; Haufrecht 1963 56-57.
Comment, references: AFS L55F 12 (Hélène Stratman Thomas); Belden 1940 284-86; Cazden 1958 i 109 + Cazden 1978 109; FM 4001F A.9 (Sidney Robertson Cowell); Healy 1965 118-19; Jolliffe 27-33; P. Kennedy 1975 725-26 #315; Laws L 7; Leisy 1966 42; McTiernan 82-83; *SO 12 #1* 8-9 + *RSO #5* 60-61.

Broadsides, songsters: *Dan Nash* 1882 36-37; *Delaney's Irish #1* 13; *Faugh-a-Ballagh* 27-29; *Four Eccentrics* 22-23; *Hyland* 137-38; *Kathleen Mavourneen* 22-23; *Street Literature* (T. Birt, London); *Universal Irish* 77-78; *Walking Down Broadway* 28-29; *Walton* ii 186-87; Wehman #133; Wehman i 107; *Wehman's Collection #28* 24; *Wehman's Irish #1* 106; Wolf Index #200.

Texts: AFS L55F 12-14; G. G. Carey 1971 114a; Emrich 1974 707-8; Farnsworth 1909 6-7 + C. J. Sharp 1916 52-53 + C. J. Sharp *Selection* i 8-9; FM 4001F A.9; R. Ford 1904 245-46; FSA 33F 6, listing; Gillington 1907 7-9; Healy 1965 119-21; HTA (2); Karpeles 1974 ii 167-68 B; P. Kennedy 1975 697-98; Kidson 1891 124 + Friedman 371-74; Kidson 1927 56-57; LCJ (3); McTiernan 82-83; *MF 13* 147, listing; *NA Ives* 1.23 + ATL 2150.8; NA Ives 1.150 + ATL 3157.4; Nettel 135-36; *NJ 12 #7* 28-30; Piper + Peterson Index 20; C. J. Sharp *FSS* i 52-53 + Karpeles 1974 ii 166-67 A + Karpeles 1975 i 44-45 #42; Shoemaker 242-43; Silber 1973b 325; Stubbs 18-19; Varian 272-74; Wilkinson i #312.

Related texts (*Dick Turpin, My Bonny Black Bess*),

Comment, references: Belden 1952 ii 356-57; Emrich 1974 703; FSA 15F 18-19 (McElligott); FSC 10F 27-28 (Fowke); Hamer 1973 44; *JFSS 3* 315-16; Karpeles 1974 ii 616 #244; P. Kennedy 1975 736; Laws L 8, L 9, L 10; W. R. Mackenzie 1928 311-14; Miles, *passim;* F. Stuart 125.

Texts: Ashton 1888 366-67; Cutting 73-74; Emrich 1974 703-4; FHE 319; Fife 1969 15-17; FSA 15.2.3 + FSA 15F 19-20; FSC 10.2.7 + FSC 10F 28-29; Grainger #180; Hamer 1967 6-7; Hamer 1973 44; Hubbard 260; *JFSS 2* 279-81; Karpeles 1974 ii 164-65, A - B; P. Kennedy 1975 724; Kidson 1926 60; J. Lomax 1938 217-20; E. Moore 155-56; Ohrlin 67; Philo 1001A.3; Purslow 1965 25; J. T. Ramsay 180-82; *SO 25 #4* 9; Stekert 1969 B 137; A. Williams 99-101.
[see also notes to #117, Tune relatives: *Turpin Hero*].

Related texts (others): H. Anderson 90-94, *Charlie Quantrello;* Eckstorm 332-34, *Bracey on the Shore;* J. Lomax 1938 144-46 + A. Lomax 1960 347, *Charlie Quantrello.*

Text and tune relatives: AFS L49.1.4 (Alan Lomax); AFS L55A.7; Asch 24-25; ATL 629.5 (Reuben Edwards); Breathnach iii 258-59; *Clancy* 1964 46-47 + CS 8448.1.6; Creighton 1950 236-37; FM 4001A.9;

Gledhill 80-84; Grover 129-30; Hansen 31a; B. Ives 1953 52-54 + B. Ives 1958 85-87 + B. Ives 1962 10-12; Jolliffe 27, 29-31; Joyce #379; Leisy 1966 43-44; J. Lomax 1941 317-18 *Miramichi Ms.* 15.13; *NA Ives* 65.6.2; O'Keeffe 25-26 [tune separately in end insert]; O Lochlainn 1965 144-47; C. J. Sharp 1932 ii 170-72; Silber 1963 122-23; *SO 12 #1* 8-9 + *RSO #5* 60-61 + Silverman 1975 i 61.

Tune relatives: H. Anderson 91, 99; Creighton 1932 179; R. G. Edwards 1956 36, 72; Fowke 1970 143; Galvin 48 + *SO 6 #2* 10; HTA, *The Kerry Recruit;* B. Ives 1953 94-95; B. Ives 1962 251-52; Edw. Ives 1978 [185], *Howard Carey;* Keynote K-102.534A; J. Lomax 1938 144 + A. Lomax 1960 347; Manny 254; Ohrlin 67; O Lochlainn 1939 126; Peacock 66; Randolph i 356; Randolph ii 81, 82; Ritchie 1971 70-71; C. J. Sharp 1932 i 377; Silber 1973a 124; Thomas 1931 152-53.

111.
The Three Jolly Butchers

Previously available: none.
Variants: none.
Adaptations: none.
Comment, references: Belden 1952 ii 269-71; Broadwood 1908 119; Cox 1925 302; Flanders 1939 240-44; *JFSS I* 174-176; Laws L 4; M. Leach 1965 161; Peacock 818; C. J. Sharp 1932 ii 398 #60.
Broadsides, songsters; Roxburghe vii 59-61 + Flanders 1939 241-44, *The Three Worthy Butchers of the North;* Roxburghe vii 62-63 + Holloway 384 #235.
Texts: Belden 1952 ii 270-71, A - B; Brand 9161 100-101; Creighton 1932 208-9; Davis Index 39; Emrich 1974 587-88; FA 2319A.2 + FA 2319F A.2 (Pete Seeger); Flanders *SR* 28.10.34; Flanders 1937 14-15; Gordon *AM* 23.4.26; S. B. Gould 1892 50-51; Healy 1969 iii 72-73; HTA; Karpeles 1971 132-35; Karpeles 1974 i 274-79, A - H; Karpeles 1975 i 42 #40; M. Leach 1965 160; Lyle 58-59; E. Moore 156-57; Nettel 133-34; Opie 1955 161; Peacock 817-18; Purslow 1965 89; Reeves 1958 215-16; Rosenbert Index #1403; *Sam Henry #185; Singabout 6 #1* 11-13; Wilkinson i #206.
Text and tune relatives: ATL 617.5-.7 (George Edwards); ATL 624.4 (George Edwards); SATL 628.9 (Charles Seeley); A. C. Morris 386 [distant]; Schinhan iv 154 #80.
Tune relatives [in a complete *a - b - b - a* form] Gardner 1939 261, 399; Edw. Ives 1964 106-

7; Edw. Ives 1971 64b-65 + *NA Ives* 68.2, *Prince Edward's Isle, Adieu;* Edw. Ives 1971 160 + *NA Ives* 65.13 + *NA Ives* 68.3, *The Callaghan Murder;* Edw. ives 1971 170 + *NA Ives* 70.2, *The Millman-Tuplin Murder;* Edw. Ives 1971 209 + *NA Ives* 70.4, *The Crooked Rib;* Manny 289; *Miramichi Ms.* 16.20; R. Palmer 1973a 40; Peacock 202, 690, 973; Randolph ii 33, 36.

112.
The Wild Irish Boy

Previously available: none.
Variants: none.
Adaptations: none.
Comment, references: none.
Broadsides, songsters; *Barney & Rickey* 162, "as sung by Miles Morris"; *Delaney's Irish # 1* 5; *Donnybrook Fair* 50; Eaton *# 6* 38; *Harry Richmond* 42-43; *Johnny, I Hardly Knew Ye* 63-64; *My Father Sould Charcoal* 37; *Norah O'Neal* 8-9; *O'Conor* 26; *Rising of the Moon* 19; *Wearing of the Green* 21-22; Wehman *#* 374; Wehman *617* 9; *Wehman's Irish #1* 51a; Wolf Index *#* 2643 (a broadside by Wrigley, New York).
Texts: HTA (McConnaughy) + Kimball 79 (from Iowa); LCJ (from Paris Hill, New York); Wright 201 (from an unidentified broadside copy).
Unrelated texts (*The Bonny Irish Boy*),
  Comment, references: Laws P 26.
  Texts: Greenleaf 192; Peacock 560-61.
  (*The Wild Irish Boy*): *New Musical* i 248-49; *Songs of Our Land* ii 102.
Text and tune relatives: none.
Tune relatives: O'Neill #326, *The Forlorn Stranger.*
[See also notes to #93, *The Rock Island Line*].

113.
The Wild Colonial Boy

Previously available: none.
Variants: none.
Adaptations: none.
Comment, references: H. Anderson 90-94; Ph. Barry 1939 100; *BFSSNE #12* 5 (Ph. Barry); R. G. Edwards 1971 19-25; FM 4001F A.8 (Cowell); R. W. Gordon *AM* 20.12.25 191-92; Jolliffe 47-51; Laws L 20; M. Leach 1965 149; Meredith 1960; *Sam Henry #750; Singabout 2 #1* 4-5; Topic 12T123J 2.1 (Lloyd).

Broadsides, songsters: *Songs & Recitations* 50-51; *Walton 132* 50-51 + *Walton* ii 120-21.

Texts [* indicates Australian or Irish form with refrain lines]: H. Anderson *91; ATL 486.3 (George Edwards); E. C. Beck 1948 268-69; E. C. Beck 1956 241-43; H. P. Beck 1957 98-99; I. Campbell *58-59; Cumming *24-25; R. G. Edwards 1956 *35 + R. G. Edwards 1971 ᵗʰ19-21 #1; R. G. Edwards 1971 23-24 #4, *24-25 #5, 25b #6; Emrich 1974 70-75; FHE 109 + Flanders *SR* 6.3.34 + Ph. Barry 1939 63; FM 4001F A.8; FO 5.2.7, 5.2.9; *Francis & Day* 1967 *24-25; Friedman 374-75; FSA 33F 9, listing; R. W. Gordon *AM* 20.12.25; Hanson *205; Jolliffe *50-51; LCJ; J. Lomax 1941 320-21; Long *24-25; MacMahon 1963 *#5; Manifold *52-54; Meredith 1968 *72, *124, *148; *MF 13* 147, listing; *NA Ives* 1.3 + ATL 2138.2; *NA Ives* 1.36 + ATL 2162.2; *NA Ives* 62.2, 64.6.6; Okun 1968 121-23; Piper + Peterson Index 46; Silverman 1975 i 56-57; *Singabout 2 #1* *5; *Singabout 3 #3* *6; *Singabout Songster* *72b-74, A - B; R. B. Smith *92-93; *SO 3 #3* *4-5 + Silber 1973b *201a; Stekert 1969 B 138; D. Stewart *39-40; R. Ward *74-75; J. R. Wilson 54-55.

Related text (Bold Jack Donahue),

    Comment, references: R. G. Edwards 1971 18; Laws L 22; W. R. Mackenzie 1928 306; Meredith 1960.

    Broadsides, songsters: *Barney & Rickey* 105; *Delaney's Irish #2* 21; De Marsan #287; O'Conor 22-23; Wehman #751; *Wehman's Irish #2 48; Wehman's Irish #4* 12.

    Texts [* indicates tune relative of #113]: ATL 187.6B, 187.7A (Chauncey Blackmore); E. C. Beck 1941 237-38 + E. C. Beck 1948 270-71; E. C. Beck 1956 244-46; R. G. Edwards 1971 18-19; Emrich 1974 304-5; J. Lomax 1938 209-12; Long 20-22; W. R. Mackenzie 1928 306-7; *NEF 8* 38-40; *Sam Eskin* iv 117; *Sam Henry* *#765 + Wright *421; *Singabout Songster* 10b-11; R. Ward 44-45; E. K. Wells 304-5.

    (Johnny Troy),

    Comment, references: FA 2354F 1.5 (Stekert); Laws L 21.

    Texts [* indicates tune relative of #113]: E. C. Beck 1941 235-36; FA *2354.1.5 + FA 2354F 1.5 (Ellen Stekert); Gardner 1939 329-30; M. E. Henry 178-79.

    (*The Wild Montana Boy*): J. Lomax 1938 167-68.

Text and tune relatives: *BFSSNE #8* 18 + Ph.

Barry 1939 63; *Clancy* 1964 13; J. Edwards 172-73; R. G. Edwards 1971 21b #2 + R. G. Edwards 1972 25 (in *b - b - b - a* form); R. G. Edwards 1971 22-23 #3; Flanders 1931 130-31; FM 4001A.8; FO 5.2.8; Gardner 1939 326-27; Lahey 76-77; M. Leach 1965 148-49; Manny 304-5 + J. R. Wilson #5a; Meredith 1968 255; *NA Ives* 1.5 + ATL 2139.11; *NA Ives* 1.96 + ATL 3103.1, *NA Ives* 1.139 + ATL 3146.5; *NA Ives* 61.3, 66.12.3; *Sam Henry* #750; Shealy 124; Topic 12T123.2.1 (Margaret Barry).

Tune relatives (*The Banks of the Gaspereaux*): Manny 49 + *NA Ives* 62.4; *NA Ives* 1.78 + ATL 2197.3; *NA Ives* 1.96 + ATL 3103.2.

(*Caroline of Edinborough Town*): *BFSSNE #12* 3b; Linscott 183 + J. R. Wilson #5g; *NA Ives* 1.85 + ATL 2204.2; Randolph i 240; Schinhan iv 207 #124.

(*The 'City of Baltimore'*): Creighton 1932 117; Manny 224 + J. R. Wilson #5 + *NA Ives* 1.52 + ATL 2177.1.

(*The Enniskillen Dragoon*): Eddy 316; FSE 21.1.5 (Bill Meek); Graeme 156-57; Graves 1914 54 #38; Joyce #399; Kerr i 41c; O'Neill #411; Petrie #547; *Sam Henry* #98a, #631; J. J. Ward 8-9.

(*The Jam on Gerry's Rock*): Creighton 1950 267; Doerflnger 238 (Woody Guthrie).

(*My Bonny Irish Boy*): Greenleaf 192 + J. R. Wilson #5f; Hubbard 136; Peacock 562 B.

(*Prince Edward Isle, Adieu*): Edw. Ives 1964 46-47 + ATL 2155.7 + Fowke 1960 108-9 + Fowke 1973 40 + *NA Ives* 1.29; Edw. Ives 1971 64a + ATL 2156.9 + *NA Ives* 1.31; *NA Ives* 1.1 + ATL 2136.1.

(*The 'Stately Southerner'*): Ph. Barry 1929 xxix a; Colcord 122 + J. R. Wilson #5m; Creighton 1950 270 B; Doerflnger 131 + J. R. Wilson #5k; FH 5323.1.6 (Edward Ives); Harlow 177; Sampson 62-63; C. F. Smith 87 + J. R. Wilson #5n (in *a – b – a – a* form).

Tune relatives (others): AFS L56A.4; ATL 183.3, 183.4; Behan 1965 7; Behan 1967 95; Belden 1940 138; *BFSSNE #11* 12; Blondahl 46, 57; Breathnach i 224-25, 244, 293; Breathnach ii 112; Broadwood 1893 116-17; N. Buchan 1973 115; Burt 12; Copper 1973 200-201; Costello 91 #50; Creighton 1962 198; Dallas 1974 80; Doerflnger 214 + J. R. Wilson #5b; Doerflnger 241; Doyle 1940 48 + Doyle 1955 46 + Doyle 1966 34 + Fowke 1973 44; Doyle 1955 42, 72; Eddy 264; *EDS 33* 99; R. G. Edwards 1972 114; FA 2354.1.5; FM 4005B.1; *FMJ 3* 8; FO 4.1.6; *Folk #2* 30;

Fowke 1960 76; Fowke 1965 24 + FM 4051.2.7; Fowke 1970 121 + FM 4052.2.6; Fowke 1970 154; FSC 9.1.3; FW 8744.1.1; Galvin 55; Gill 1898 79 #88; Grainger #274, #275, #276, #277; Greenleaf 283 + J. R. Wilson #5e; Hamer 1967 62; Hamer 1973 64; Healy 1962 107; Healy 1969 iii 16c; Henebry 123; Hughes ii 101-4; B. Ives 1953 96-97; Edw. Ives 1971 187-88 + *NA Ives* 69.1; *JAF 52* 9-10; Joyce #298, #303; Karpeles 1974 i 532 B; P. Kennedy 1975 363; Kidson 1891 152 (in *a – a – b – a* form); Kidson 1926 82-83, *High Germany;* Kidson 1927 28-29 (in *a – a – b – a* form); M. Leach 1965 124; Levy 1967 256-57, *The Raging Canal;* Manny 86, 283; Manny 126 + ATL 2192.5 + FM 4053.2.5 + *NA Ives* 1.73; Meredith 1968 40; E. Moore 175-76; Morton 1970 3; *NA Ives* 1.97 + ATL 3104.3; *NA Ives* 1.101 + ATL 3108.2; *NA Ives* 1.102 + ATL 3108.3; *NA Ives* 1.110 # ATL 3117.4; *NA Ives* 1.125 + ATl 3132.3; *NA Ives* 1.129 + ATL 3136.5; *NA Ives* 1.140 + ATL 3147.1; *NA Ives* 61.4, *Patrick O'Donnell; NA Ives* 64.6.1, 66.3.5, 66.4.1; *NEF 7* 32; O'Keeffe 23; O Lochlainn 1939 198; O'Shaughnessy 1975 21, 35; Peacock 842, 905, 931; Petrie 1855 91; Petrie #28 + J. R. wilson #50; Petrie #48; *Powder River* 11; Ranson 56; K. Raven 1974 25; Rickaby 79 + J. R. Wilson #5j; Rickaby 157 + J. R. Wilson #5i; RLP 12-602.1.4 + WLP 731.1.4, *The Hills of Donegal;* RLP 12-648.1.3; *Sam Eskin* iv 92; SIF 1001.1449B.6; Silber 1967 121; Silber 1973a 130; SLP 49A.3; Wyld 89, *The Raging Canal;* Zimmerman 271.

Unrelated tune (*Fainne Geal an lae*): Joyce 1872 8.

114.
The Boston Burgular

Previously available: AFS 12309B.11 + EC 699.11.

Variants: AFS 10505B.27.

Adaptations: none.

Comment, references: AFS L14F 67A (Emrich); Brewster 223; Cox 1925 296; R. G. Edwards 1972 17; Friedman 220-23; FSA 2F 15 (Paton); Laws L 16 B; Marks 226, listing as of 188-; Randolph ii 37; *SO 9 #4* 12-13 + *RSO #6* 32-33; Spaeth 1948 243-44.

Broadsides, songsters: *Book of Songs & Ballads* 179-80; *Delaney #58* 23; Wehman ii 29; *Wehman's Universal #7* 52.

Texts: Belden 1952 ii 555-56A; Brewster 223-

24; Buford 42-43; G. G. Carey 1970 61-62; Combs 1967 212 #91, listing; Cox 1925 296-97 + Emrich 1974 712-13; Cox 1939 i 89; Davis Index 280-82 (14); Finger 88-89; Flanders Index 247 #136; Friedman 222-23; FSA 33F 6, listing; R. W. Gordon *AM* 30.3.24; R. W. Gordon *NYT* 52; G. Greig *FSNE* #132, *The Boston Smuggler;* HTA (5); Hubbard 250-51; B. Ives 1958 56-57; Karpeles 1974 ii 141 B, 142 C; Ch. Kennedy 1952 170-71 + Ch. Kennedy 1954 303-4; Larson #15; LCJ (4); Malone 1968 46, listing; *MF 13* 147, listing; Neal 55; *NYFQ 14* 210, listing; Piper (2) + Peterson Index 22; Randolph ii 37; Rosenberg T-84 13B.4; Rosenberg Index #126 (8); *Sam Henry* #202; Shay 1961 162-63; Silber 1973b 67a; Silverman 1975 i 63; *SO 9 #4* 12-13 + *RSO #6* 32-33; Stekert 1969 B 136; *Walton 132* 19 + *Walton* i 12-13.

Related text (*Botany Bay,* Edwards Type 2), **Comment, references:** *AT #19* 5; Cox 1925 296; R. G. Edwards 1971 12-13; *JFSS 5* 85-86.

Texts: AFS 14633B.11; H. Anderson 19-20; *AT #19* 5; Barrett 90-91 + R. Palmer 1974 242; Chilton 126-27; R. G. Edwards 1956 24-25; R. G. Edwards 1971 12-13; R. G. Edwards 1972 18; Flanders 1937 44-45; Flanders 1939 253-54; Friedman 222-23; Haufrecht 1963 64; *JFSS 5* 85-86 + Karpeles 1974 ii 139-40 A + C. J. Sharp 1916 198-99 #86 + C. J. Sharp 1920 ii 90-91; Lahey 26-27; *Sam Eskin* i 74; *Sam Henry* #691; Silverman 1975 ii 385b; *Singabout 5 #3* 8-9; D. Stewart 7-8; Sturgis 32-35.

Related texts (local adaptations and parodies)[* indicates tune of #114]: AFS 67A + AFS L14A.3 + AFS L14F 67A, *Frank James;* W. W. Chamberlain 195, *The Bowling Green Burglar;* J. Cohen *148-49 + Silverman 1975 i *62, *The Louisville Burglar;* FSA 2.2.3 + FSA 2F 16-17, *The Louisville Burglar; NA Ives* 64.6.19, *The Bangor Burlgar;* PTFLS 26 133 (cowboy parody).

Unrelated text (*The Female Smugglar*): Bryant 1857 10-11; Copper 1973 234-35; *Delaney #14* 26; De Marsan #107; *Dime Melodist* 23; *Gus Shaw* 18-19; Shay 1961 132-33; *Singer's Journal #29* 194; Whall 27-29.

Text and tune relatives [* indicates half-tune form]: C. S. Adams 119-20; AFS *14633B.10 (Atwood); ATL 184.6 (George Edwards); Bayard 56; *Chapbook 2 #5* 19; Creighton 1932 206; Dibblee 73; Eddy *204-6; R. G. Edwards 1972 17-18; Gardner 1939 335-36; Hubbard 249-50; M. Leach 1965 254-55; J. Lomax 1938 203-5; McDowell 1947 86-87;

Meredith 1968 64-65, 96-97, 257-58; *NA Ives* 1.18 + ATL 2147.7; *NA Ives* 1.105 + ATL 3112.2; *NA Ives* 1.139 + ATL 3146.4; *NEF 8* 43; *Old Time Hits* 6-8; R. Palmer 1973a 75; *PTFLS 23* 105-7; Scarborough 1937 433 A, 434-35 E; Schinhan iv 281-82; Spaeth 1926 178-79.

Tune relatives [* indicates half-tune form]: Dallas 1973 230; FM 4051.1.8, *The Bunch of Water Cresses;* Fowke 1960 200-201; Fowke 1970 192; Kolb *52-54 + Lingenfelter *325, *Pretty Boy Floyd* (Woody Guthrie); *NA Ives* 1.61 + ATL 2181.5; Peacock *869.
[See also #152, *The Three Huntsmen*].

115.
The 'Flying Cloud'

Previously available: none.
Variants: none.
Adaptations: none.
Comment, references: Colcord 140-43; Doerflinger 138-39, 334-35; FM 4001F B.4 (Cowell); Friedman 411; FSC 10F 13-15 (Fowke); Hugill 585-86; *JAF 35* 390-92 (Kittredge); *JAF 66* 123-33, "The riddle of *The 'Flying Cloud'*" (H. P. Beck); Laws K 28 (Irish); Rickaby 223; Whall 77.
Broadsides, songsters: Gray 116-23 (from *Boston Transcript*, 30.12.1916); *Wehman's Collection #42* 12.
Texts: Belden 1940 128-31 + Emrich 1974 509-12; *CAY 4* 43; *Elmore Vincent* 54-55; FHE 337-38; Flanders Index 227, 249 #154; FM 4001F B.4; FSC 10F 15-17; R. W. Gordon *AM* 11.8.26 206-7; HTA (Norton); *JAF 35* 370-72; *JAF 48* 351, listing; M. Leach 1965 156-58; *MF 13* 146, listing; *NA Ives* 1.6 + ATL 2140.3; *NYFQ 14* 207; Peacock 842-45; Piper + Peterson Index 34; Rosenberg Index #411 (2); Stekert 1969 B 21.
Text and tune relatives: Bayard 15-16, 45-46; H. P. Beck 1957 247-51; Colcord 141-43; Creighton 1932 126-30 (tune fragmented); Doerflinger 136-39; Finger 84-87; FM 4001B.4; Fowke 1973 34-36; Friedman 411-15 (tune from a manuscript copy of Phillips Barry); FSC 10.1.7; Gledhill 49-55; Hugill 586a; *JAF 66* 130-33; *NA Ives* 1.69 + ATL 2188.7; *NA Ives* 1.111 + ATL 3118.7; *NA Ives* 65.13.11; *NEF 8* 35-37; Rickaby 145-49 + Botkin 1944 845-47; Peggy Seeger 1960 60 + *SO 19 #2* 20-21; Shay 1961 210-12 + (tune) J. Lomax 1934 504-5; SLP 80B.4 (Lloyd, MacColl).
Tune relatives: Broadwood 1893 136-37;

Creighton 1932 187, 326; Doyle 1940 34, *Fanny's Harbour Bawn;* Doyle 1940 38, *The Spanish Captain;* Doyle 1955 48; FM 4005A.5; FO 2.2.6 + Fowke 1970 127; FO 4.1.8, 4.2.5; Fowke 1970 131; FSC 62.2.5; Grover 125; Henebry 90, 91; *JAF 52* 9; Morton 1973 114 #26; *NEF 5* + ATL 2161.4 + *NA Ives* 1.36; Peacock 816; Petrie #418, #419, #420; Ranson 46; *SO 6 #2* 10; *SO 16 #6* 8.

116.
The Three Rogues

Previously available: none.
Variants: none.
Adaptations: none.
Comment, references: Belden 1940 268; Belden 1951 ii 458; Damon #6, *JAF 35* 350-51 (Tolman, Kittredge); P. Kennedy 1975 681 #307; Randolph i 416; Wilkinson *510* 93-96.
Broadsides, songsters [*indicates two added stanzas]: *Beadle's Dime #12* *39; *Beadle's Half-Dime #31* *7; *Broadway Stage* *69; *It's Naughty* 6-7; *Singer's Journal #41* *293; *Stonewall* 36; *Universal Book* ii 42.
Texts: Armitage 1926 416b-17; ATL 622.9 (Elizabeth Misner); Belden 1940 268-69; Belden 1952 ii 458-59; L. Chappell 185 + *Sam Eskin* i 135a; Cox 1925 480-81; Davis Index 136-37 (6); FA 2367F 4b; Flanders 1931 103; Flanders Index #38, #134; M. E. Henry 191; Hubbard 373; *JAF 29* 167-68; *JAF 35* *350; E. Moore 149-50; Neely 189-90; Piper + Peterson Index 37; Pound 1922 234-35; Rosenberg Index #1410.
Related text(*King Arthur Had Three Sons*) [* indicates related tune]: *Aquarium Songster;* Ashbee viii *12 (parody text); Broadwood 1893 *20-21 + Ashbee x *20-21 + Bantock 1914 *53-54 + Buck 1916 *110-11 + *Canadian Boys* *84-85 #40 + H. W. Davies *55 #45 + Goss 1927 *96-97 + Maitland *#13243 (1915) + S. H. Nicholson *58-59 #29 + *Scottish Students* *225; Fortey 1897, 1898; *JAF 29* 167; Karpeles 1974 ii 371 B; P. Kennedy 1975 664-65; M. H. Mason *7 + Purslow 1968 *62; *Quaver 1858* 287 + *JAF 30* 348-49; C. J. Sharp *FSS* iii 10-11 + Karpeles 1974 ii 370 A + *Novello* iii #988 + C. J. Sharp 1916 180-81 #80 + C. J. Sharp *Selection* i 70 + *Sing Care Away* iv 38; Stubbs 42; *Vocal Library* 406 #1080; W. J. Whittaker 126-27 #45; Wilkinson *510* 91 A; A. Williams 194.

Unrelated text (*When Arthur First in Court Be-gan*, by Thomas Deloney),

Comment, references: W. Chappell 1859 i 199; Mann 323.

Texts: Mann 323-26.

Related text (*When Arthur First in Court Be-gan*, by George Coleman the Younger): *Clark's Orphean Warbler* 194; *Musical Treasury* #369 (1848), glee setting; *Quaver* 1844 52-53; J. W. Sharp 187; *Universal Songster* i 80.

Unrelated text (*When Good King Arthur Ruled This Land*): Bertail 100; Bullard 23b; Crane 32; *Ernest Newton* 103b; *Howe* 1874 13b + *Trifet* 1890 13b + *Trifet* 1892 8c; Lee 108a; *Song Jewels* 25b; C. Wells 1902 73 + C. Wells 1936 879a; Wier 1918b 77b.

Text and tune relatives: Agay 40; *Amateur* 109; Boette 44; Brand 1961 135; M. Cohen 1966 138-39; Damon #6 + Boni 1952 252-53 + Botkin 1947 841; Dyer-Bennet 1949 22-23; Eddy 197, 198; Erdei 83 #115; FA 2367.1.4 (Kevin Roth); FC 7625.2.2 (Robin Christenson); Haufrecht 1959 92; HL 500.1.5; *Howe* 1878 261; M. Johnson 59; Kellogg 121; Linscott 213-14; R. Lloyd 30-31; A. Lomax 1960 11-12; Mursell 26; Piper; Randolph i 416; *Ring Ms.* #26 + *JAF* 66 47-48; Sackett 1961 171-72 [refrain tune only]; *Sam Eskin* iv 10, 20a; Schinhan iv 246; Silverman 1975 i 220; *Trifet* 1890 167c + *Trifet* 1892 162d; J. W. Turner 30b; H. R. Wilson 9-10; Zanzig 1940 #1.

Tune relatives (*Gin Sling*): Goodwin 1956 164; Hills 45; Honoré 27; Waite 1868 24.

(*What Was Your Name in the States?*): E. Black 1; Boni 1952 307; *Hangtown Ballads* 23; Lengyel i 31A; *Miners*; RLP 12-654 (Pat Foster); C. Sandburg 1927 106 + Botkin 1944 861 + Lingenfelter 313.

(others): Cazden 1961 68, *Tanglefoot Sue*; N. C. Gould 135 #176, *Jubilee*; *Harmonist* 312 #270, *Syria*; *Heart Songs* 491, *The Glorious Fourth*; W. McDonald 156, *Dalston* (first half of tune); C. J. Sharp *FSS* i 3-4 + *All Time* 6 + Karpeles 1973 93 + Karpeles 1975 i 22 #20 + C. J. Sharp 1916 76-78 #33 + C. J. Sharp 1920i 42 + VRS 1001A.6, *The Seeds of Love*; *Whittier Perkins* 50b + *JAF* 22 79a, *Come All You Maidens Fair* [*The Sprig of Thyme*].

117.
The Old Spotted Cow

Previously available (#117 A): *Neighbors* 1943 25-26.

Variants (#117 B): ATL 617.9 [in major, but with refrain in minor, recorded 1938[; ATL 624.6 [all in minor, recorded 1938].
(#117 C): AFS 10505 B #32.

Adaptations (#117 A): Cazden 1949a 44-66 #3 + CRI 117.2.4; Cazden 1958 i 78-79 + Cazden 1978 78-79; Cazden 1963 ii 24; Haufrecht 1943 20-22; Haufrecht 1967 ii #3.
(#117 C): FH 5311.1.5 + FH 5311F 7-8 (Harry Siemsen).

Comment, references: Bronson iv 282; Cazden 1958 i 118-19 + Cazden 1978 118-19; Child 283; Coffin 151-52; Flanders iv 138-41; *JAF* 30 367-69 (Kittredge); Laws L 1; Laws 1957 71-77; M. Leach 1965 165-66; ZDA 70F (MacColl, Peggy Seeger).

Broadsides, songsters: as noted by Laws; add: *The Crafty Ploughboy*, a broadside in British Museum Library 1876 e.2 + facsimile in M. Raven iii 99.

Texts [* indicates tune of *Down, Derry Down*]: ATL 192.1 (Tom Kelly); ATL 565.8-.10; Belden 1952 ii 188-90; Combs 1967 212 #89, listing; FHE 131; FHE 132-33, 389, *The New Hampshire Bite*; Flanders *SR* 28.10.34; FO 5.2.2; HTA; Hubbard 263-64; M. Leach 1965 162-66; *MF* 13 147, listing; E. Moore *131-33; R. Palmer 1971 60-61; Peacock 36-38 B, C; Purslow 1968 19; *Sam Henry* #51; C. Sandburg 1927 *118-19 + Bronson iv *300 #37; Silverman 1975 i 384; H. Thompson 1940 163-64 + H. Thompson 1958 22-24; *Tocher* #4 106-7.

Related text (*The Rich Merchant's Daughter*): Peacock 226-28 A, B.

Unrelated text (*The Yorkshire Bite*): Kidson 1890 17b.

Text and tune relatives: ATL 630.9, 630.12 (Elizabeth Misner of Pepacton, New York); Ph. Barry 1929 410 + Bronson iv 297 #31, *The New Hampshire Bite*; Bronson iv 290-93 Group Ca #18, #19, #20, #21, #24; Bronson iv 294-99 Group Cb #25-#35; Flanders *SR* 4.2.34 + Flanders 1937 26 + Bronson iv 296 #29 + Flanders 1939 97 (the version sung by George Edwards of Burlington, Vermont); Flanders iv 139-75: 142 A, 154 E, 160 G, 167 J, 171 L, 174 O; FO 5.2.1; *Lyre*; Peacock 33-35 A; Piper; ZDA 70.1.2 (Peggy Seeger); ZDA 70.1.3 (Ewan MacColl).

Tune relatives (*The Bear at Grand River*, by Lawrence Doyle): Dibblee 111; Edw. Ives 1971 47 + *NA Ives* 65.13, 68.3, 70.6 (half-tune form); Edw. Ives 1971 49 + *NA Ives* 68.5, 69.4, 70.9; Edw. Ives 1971 51-52 + *NA Ives* 68.5; *NA Ives* 69.2.

(*The Cobbler*): [See notes to #138, The Jolly Boatswain].

(*O Good Ale, Thou Art My Darling*),
Comment, references: W. Chappell 1859 ii 660; S. B. Gould vii xix-xx.
Tunes with this text: Buck 1916 143; W. Chappell 1859 ii 661; S. B. Gould vii 60-61; Moffat 1911 110.

(*Turpin Hero*). A. Campbell 62-63; W. Chappell 1959 ii 661 + W. G. Whittaker ii 4-5; Grainger #180; Hansen 135b; Moffat 1901 160; S. H. Nicholson 51 #25; RG 150.1.7 (Shirley Collins); *Sam Eskin;* Peggy Seeger 1960 83; C. J. Sharp 1902 146-47 #69; F. Stuart 126-27.

(others): Bethke #34, *I Had a Little Girl;* W. Chappell 1859 ii 660, *Hathersage Cocking;* Christie ii 4-5; Doerflinger 111, *The Big Five Gallon Jar;* R. G. Edwards 1972 26, *Turpin and the Lawyer; FST* i 9 #7; Grainger #178, #179; Healy 1965 121; *JFSS 2* 226, *Anson's Race Horse; JFSS 3* 131-32, *The Devil; JFSS 3* 253-54 #3, *My Father Was a Good Old Man; JFSS 3* 315 #45 + R. V. Williams 1959 78, *On Monday Morning; JFSS 8* 131a, *The Young Damsel; JFSS 8* 131b, *The Devil;* Joyce #418, *Bold Captain Frenzy;* Moeran 1924 5-11, 20-23; R. Palmer 1973 40; Petrie #183, #184; Ruth Seeger 1950 28 + *SO 11 #3* 15 + *RSO #5* 37, *The Little Brown Dog;* C. J. Sharp 1961 iv 158-60 + Karpeles 1974 ii 261 A, *Anson's Race Horse;* C. J. Sharp *FSS* ii 46-47, *The Irish Bull; Sing 2* 6.

118.
The Poor Chronic Man

Previously available: none.
Variants: none.
Adaptations: Cazden 1958 ii 40-41 + Cazden 1973 40-41.
Comment, references: Cazden 1958 ii 121-22 + Cazden 1973 121-22; Cazden 1961 iii-iv; *CEOL 1 #4* 14 (Hugh Shields).
Broadsides, songsters: Healy 1967 i 265-66, *A New Song Called The Connaught Man's Trip to Belfast* (reprinted from an unidentified broadside); Healy 1969 iii 124-25, *A New Song Called The Connaught Man's Trip to Dublin* (reprinted from an unidentified broadside).
Texts: none.
Related texts (*A-Roving*): [See notes to #142, *Missie Mouse*].

(*Jock Hawk's Adventures in Glasgow*): N. Buchan 16 (from a Greig ms.); Ord 278-79; Peggy Seeger 1960 101 #92; *Sing 7* 106.

(*The Shirt and the Apron*),
Comment, references: Laws K 42.
Texts: Creighton 1932 226-27; DL 8245.1.5 (Burl Ives); Droke 70-71; Greenleaf 222-23; Hugill 376-77.
Texts with related tune: *CEOL 1 #4* 12-14.
(others): Cazden 1958 ii 94-95 + Cazden 1973 94-95, *My Ducksie Has Fled;* Greenleaf 110-11, *The Gold Watch; NYFQ 14* 205, *Snake Hill Jail.*
Unrelated texts: O'Conor 149, *The Athlone Landlady;* Wehman 617 41, *The Town of Athlone.*
Text and tune relatives: none.
Tune relatives [* indicates first half of tune]: ATL 484.1; E. C. Beck 1941 52, with tune in ATL 169.4.1b, *Budd Lake Plains; CEOL 1 #4* 12-14, *Betsy McLean; Comical Brown* 17-18; Creighton 1932 265, *In the Month of October;* Creighton 1950 214-15, *When a Man's in Love;* FO 13.1.3 + Fowke 1970 66 + FM 4052.2.3, *The Basketong;* Fowke 1970 69, *MacDonald's Camp;* Fowke 1970 178, *I Went to the Woods;* FSC 10.2.3; Greenleaf 138, *Paddy and the Whale;* Hubbard 260, *My Bonny Black Bess;* Edw. Ives 1964 74-75, *The Old Prowler;* Joyce #594, *Barney Is in Prison;* J. Lomax 1941 200-201, *The True Paddy's Song;* R. Mason 65 (in shifted phrase sequence); *NA Ives* 1.104 + ATL 3111.4; *NA Ives* 65.13.8; O'Neill #525, *The Old Head of Denis;* Peacock 83, *Old Grandma Hones;* Petrie #740, *Rory O'Moore;* Petrie #823, *In My First Proceedings; Sam Henry* *#230, *Nae Bonny Laddie tae tak' Me Awa'; Topic* *12T159A.6, *Green Brooms.*
[See also notes to #166, *The Newburgh Jail*].

Verse-form relatives without tune: E. C. Beck 1941 84-85; E. C. Beck 1948 91-92; E. C. Beck 1956 230-33.

119.
The Cordwood Cutter

Previously available: none.
Variants (#119 A): ATL 185.4-.5.
(#119 B): ATL 623.12.
Adaptations: AFS 12312A.14; Cazden 1949b 2-16 #1; Cazden 1958 i 14-15 + Cazden 1978 14-15; SLP 72.2.3.
Comment, references: Cazden 1958 i 110 +

Cazden 1978 110; FM 4052F 10 (Fowke); Fowke 1970 174-75; Laws C 19; SLP 72J B.3 (Cazden).

Broadsides, songsters: *Delaney #23* 26; *Wehman's Collection #10* 27.

Texts: Belden 1952 iii 397-99; Cox 1925 404; Cutting 21; Flanders *BDN* 10.3.34; Flanders *SR* 25.2.34; FM 4052F 10-11; FO 10.1.5; HTA; *NA Ives* 1.154 + ATL 3161.4; RLP 12-648.2.4; Shoemaker 54-55; Stekert 1969 B 16; H. Thompson 1940 263-64.

Text and tune relatives: ATL 187.8-.9 (Chauncey Blackmore); Bayard 35 (in – – *b′* – *a* form); Fowke 1970 173-75; Fowke 1973 78-79 + FM 4052.2.5; Grover 176-77; J. Lomax 1941 231-32; McDowell 1947 96-97; *SO 18 #2* 16; Wilkinson i #514.

Tune relatives: ATL 184.5 (George Edwards); ATL 190.2 (Walt Wermouth) [only the *a* phrase is similar]; ATL 190.4 (George Swarthout); *BFSSNE #2* 8 (in 3/4 time); *BFSSNE #4* 13; *BFSSNE #12* 4b; Blondahl 63 [distant]; Creighton 1932 284 + FW 8744.2.7 + A. Lomax 1960 144 + McLean 46; Creighton 1962 112 [distant]; R. G. Edwards 1971 12-13; Flanders 1939 29; Flanders 1953 240; Fowke 1970 81; R. Ford 1904 59; Gardner 1939 157, 173; Grainger #192 + *JFSS 3* 184-85; Greenleaf 233; Hubbard 362; *JFSS 1* 142; *JFSS 2* 198; Joyce #208, #333; Karpeles 1974 i 653 C; Knox 43-44; M. Leach 1965 208 [distant], 258 [close]; J. Lomax 1941 200, 320-21; *NEF 8* 25; Nettel 150; Peacock 679, 709; Petrie #808; RLP 12-820.2.5 (Sean Tracy); Peggy Seeger 1960a 69, 87; C. J. Sharp 1932 i 401 C (in *b – b – b – a* form); SLP 81B.5 (in 6/8 time); *SO 14 #6* 41; *Whittier Perkins* 42d, *My Dearest Jewel* [*b* phrases and final a phrase related]; Wilkinson i #348.

[See also notes to #13, #46, #54, #91.]

120.
Lather and Shave

Previously available (tunes of #120 A and #120 B separately, with composite text): *Neighbors* 1944 23-23; *NYFQ 4* 34-35.

Variants: none.

Adaptations (#120 A): FSI 39.1.4 (Joe Hickerson); Haufrecht 1945 L 150. (#120 B): Cazden 1958 i 96-97 + Cazden 1978 96-97.

Comment, references: Cazden 1958 i 117 + Cazden 1978 117; FSI 39F 8-9 (Hickerson); P. Kennedy 1975 532 #227; Laws Q 15 (Ir-

ish); *Neighbors* 1944 22; *NYFQ 4* 34-35; *PTFLS 9* 185 (Piper).

Broadsides, songsters: J. Andrews iii #23; Auner; *Beadle's Dime #3* 40; *Beadle's Half-Dime #4* 5; *Delaney's Irish #3* 11; De Marsan #235 + Wolf Index #1229; *Jennie Hughes* 8; *Pacific* iv 57b-59; *Singer's Journal #7* 51; *Street Literature* (E. Hodges, London); *Tony Pastor* ix 71-72; Wehman #349; *Wehman's Irish #1* 104-5.

Texts: Ph. Barry 1939 30; Beard 302-3; E. C. Beck 1956 240-41; FSA 33F 8, listing; FSI 39F 9-10; Gardner 1939 483, listing; *JAF 45* 159-61 + M. E. Henry 409-10; P. Kennedy 1975 510-11; LCJ (Wagner); Meredith 1968 211-12; A. C. Morris 446-47; *NA Ives* 66.8.4; Piper + Peterson Index 55 + *PTFLS 9* 185-86; C. J. Sharp 1932 ii 276 #200 [refrain only]; Shoemaker 134; Stout 134-35 #106; Wilkinson *510* 127.

Related text (*The Monkey as Barber*),
Comment, references: Laws Q 14.
Texts: Creighton 1950 239; Knox 73; *NEF 8* 44-46.

(*Monkey Turned Barber*, by David Humphrey): Ch. Kennedy 1954 29-30.

Text and tune relatives (#120 A): Creighton 1962 136. (#120 B): none.

Tune relatives (#120 A: tune strain of *Down, Derry Down*, but with variant refrain text or syllables) [* tune indicated but not notated],

(*The Lumberman's Alphabet*): Manny 265 + FM 4053.1.1 + J. R. Wilson #21; *Miramichi Ms.* 15.5; *NA Ives* 1.42 + ATL 2166.7; *NA Ives* 1.50 + ATL 2174.4; *NA Ives* 1.54 + ATL 2178.4; *NA Ives* 1.67 + ATL 2186.1; *NA Ives* 61.1.1. [See also notes to #3.]

(*The San Francisco Rag Picker*, "air: *Lather and Shave*"): *California Checklist* *129, listing; Lengyel ii *142; Lingenfelter *517-18; Wolf Index *#2063 (a broadside by T. C. Boyd).

(*When Johnny Went Plowing for Kearon*): Dibblee 19; Edw. Ives 1971 122 + *NA Ives* 68.5; Edw. Ives 1971 127 + *NA Ives* 69.1.

(others); Barrett 16-17; *Chapbook 3 #3* 25; Downes 66-67; Gledhill 41-42; Greenleaf 128 + J. R. Wilson #33c, *Paddy and the Whale*; *Imperial* *188-89; Karpeles 1974 ii 362; M. Leach 1965 216; *Miscellanea* i 29, 121; *NA Ives* 1.5 + ATL 2139.5; *NA Ives* 1.61 + ATL 2181.8; *Pacific* i *54-55, *California Legislature*; Prest ii 33, *I Don't Care If I Do*; Silverman 1966 88; *SLF #2* 20; SLP 80B.2.

Tune relatives (#120 B, *Up in a Balloon*),
  Comment, references: R. Lloyd 1969 182-84;
  Spaeth 1926 72.
  Tunes with this text (credits noted): *Album
  Comique* (G. W. Hunt); *Comic Songster*
  11; *Comical, Topical* 152-53; *Cundy #1* +
  Fireside Library 40a + *Howe* 1874 40a +
  Trifet 1890 40a + *Trifet* 1892 40a (W. H.
  Sanderson); *Cundy #14, Up in a Balloon
  Polka Redowa* (Harry Clifton); Hitchcock
  #29 + Hitchcock i 230 (Eugene Ray-
  mond); Jordan 155-57 (facsimile of sheet
  music issue by Wm. A. Pond Co., New
  York; H. B. Farnie); Levy 1971 349 (text
  by George Leybourne); R. Lloyd 1969
  182-84 (H. B. Farnie, G. W. Hunt); *Lydia
  Thompson* 4-5; Spaeth 1926 27-73 (H. B.
  Farnie, G. W. Hunt); S. Winner 1885 286-
  87.
Unrelated tunes (*Dumbledum Deary*),
  Comment, references: *EDS 35* 99.
  Tunes (*Lather and Shave*): Meredith 1968
  211; Wilkinson *510* 127.
  (*Richard of Taunton Dean*) [* tune indicated, not notated]: Ashbee ix 2-3; Barrett *86 #50; Moffat 1901 165; S. H.
  Nicholson 60-61 #30; SL 206.2.26; Wilkinson i #663; Woodgate 1951 62-63.

on *Ice* 22-23; Bryant 1864 24-25; *Delaney's
Irish #1* 19; *Guiding Star* 65; *Harry Pell*
21-22; *Howe* 1874 182 + *Trifet* 1890 105 +
Trifet 1892 105 (all with music); *Joe English* 58-59; O'Conor 136; *Paddy's the Boy*
25-26; *Singer's Journal #7* 55; *Tony Pastor* ix 19-20; *Tony Pastor* 1872 26-27; *Walton's Treasury* 28-29 + *Walton* i 48-49;
Wearing of the Green 10-11; *Wehman's Irish #1* 55.
Texts: *Clancy* 1964 33 + CS 8448.2.1;
Downes 366-68; Eldridge 32; FO 9.2.7,
9.2.8, 16.2.8; Goodwin 1956 32; Healy
1965 32-33; Hubbard 315; Ch. Kennedy
1952 45-47; Kimball 183 (listing of a Catskill text); LCJ (8); McPheeley 100; Piper;
Silber 1965 118-19; *Sing 5* 38; *SO 11 #2* 6-7
+ *RSO #5* 52-53 + Silber 1973b 232a +
Silverman 1975 ii 182b-83; Trident 58-59.
Related texts (others): Goodwin 1956 45, *Mike
McCarty's Wake;* Goodwin 1956 51, *Dooli-
gan's Ghost.*
Unrelated text (*Paddy Malone*): H. Anderson
129-31.
Text and tune relatives [some degree of resem-
blance in partial tune forms]: R. G. Edwards
1972 193a; Randolph 236.
Tune relatives: none.

121.
Pat Malone

Previously available: none.
Variants: none.
Adaptations: none.
Comment, references: FSA 15F 21-22 (McEl-
ligott); Laws Q 18 (Irish); Randolph iii 236;
Wright 551-604, "The stage Irishman."
Sheet music: New York: H. W. Petrie, c 1893;
London: Chas. Sheard & Co., 189-.
Broadsides, songsters: *Delaney's Irish #4* 14;
Fortey 1898.
Texts: R. G. Edwards 1972 193a; FO 9.2.9,
9.2.10; FSA 15.2.8 + FSA 15F 22-23; Hub-
bard 318-19; LCJ (Kemmerer); *NA Ives*
62.6; Piper + Peterson Index 33; Randolph
iii 236-37.
Related text (*Tim Finnegan's Wake*),
  Comment, references: Healy 1965 33-34;
  Hubbard 315; Ch. Kennedy 1952 45; Laws
  Q 17; McTiernan 47.
  Sheet music: New York: Wm. A. Pond Co.,
  1864.
  Broadsides, songsters: *Beadle's Dime #10*
  12; *Beadle's Half-Dime #6* 10; *Big Thing*

122.
Ol' Mickey Brannigan's Pup

Previously available: none.
Variants: none.
Adaptations: none.
Comment, references: Ira Ford 430-32; Wolf Index #2181.
Sheet music (reprint, with credits): Honoré 84-
85; title in Tony Pastor's *Song of Songs*, fac-
simile in Wolf Index, frontispiece iii.
Broadsides, songsters [* indicates with tune]:
Comical Brown *3 (with credits); *Delaney
#11* 23; *Delaney's Irish #2* 17; *Gus Phillips*
14; *Hatfield Brothers* 28; *James O'Neil* 188-
14; *J. H. Conroy* 41; *John Conroy* 20;
Johnny Roach 1879 7; *Murphy & Morton* 59,
"as sung by Johnny Roach"; *Pat Rooney*
188- 19; *Walton 132* 76a; *Walton* i 145-46;
J. J. Ward *28-29; *Wehman 617* 99;
Wehman's Irish #4 72a; *Wehman's Univer-
sal #17* 131.
Texts: Bethke #7 + Philo 1022.1.5; Buford
178; LCJ (Trumbull, Walsh, others).
Text and tune relatives: none.
Tune relatives: none.

123.
The Terrier Dog

Previously available: none.
Variants: none.
Adaptations: none.
Comment, references: FSI 2F 6 (Paton).
Broadsides, songsters: *Electric Three* 30; *Pat Reilley* 56; *Sweeney & Ryland* 51; *Yankee Robinson* 5.
Texts: FSI 2.1.6 + FSI 2F 6-7.
Related text (*The Twenty Pound Dog*): Dean 68-69.
Text and tune relatives: none.
Tune relatives (*Jim, the Carter Lad*): P. Kennedy 1975 512-13. [See also notes to #96].

124.
The Rich Man's Daughter

Previously available: none.
Variants: ATL 615.3.
Adaptations: Cazden 1958 ii 20-21 + Cazden 1973 20-21; RLP 12-603.10 (Milt Okun).
Comment, references: Bronson i 362; Cazden 1958 ii 115 + Cazden 1973 115; RLP 12-603.10 (Cazden); Child 1, 46; Child v 216 #46; Coffin 59-60; FSA 3F 7 (Wilgus); Jaehde 61-62; Jamieson ii 162; Opie 1951 386-88 #478, *The Riddle Song;* RLP 12-603J.10 (Cazden); Topic 12T160F B.1 (Lloyd).
Broadsides, songsters: none.
Texts: AFS 4196B.1; ATL 601.4 (James Edwards); Bronson i 363-75; FHE 359; Flanders 1953 43-46; Gainer 1975 29; Jamieson ii 154-65; Karpeles 1971 39-41; A. L. Lloyd 1965 52-53 #28; E. Moore 35-38 (2); *NA Ives* 1.155 + ATL 3162.3; *NA Ives* 1.158 + ATL 3165.5; RLP 12-628.1.5 + RLP 12-628F 7; *Sam Eskin* v; *Sam Henry* #681; Sedley 37-38; *SS 9* 14-17; Topic 12T160B.1 + Topic 12T160F B.1.
Related texts (*The Riddle Song*),
  Comment, references: Bronson i 376; Opie 1951 386-88 #478.
  Texts: Abrams 88a; Agay 372; Arany 62; *Bixby #4* 49, *Perri Merri Dictum Domine;* Boette 36; Brand 1961 43; Brocklebank 12; Bronson i 377-83; T. Burton i 88; Capitol T700.2.3 (Tennessee Ernie Ford); Cazden 1962 27; Cazden 1963 i 2; Chosky 172 #62; Creighton 1950 163 + Fowke 1954 136-37; Cumming 56b; Erdei 52 #79; Fowke 1972 96-97; FSA 3.1.3 + FSA 3F 7-8; Hansen 85a; B. Ives 1957 24-25; Jameson 1955 16; Jameson 1967 46-47; *JFSS 3* 114 (Ham-

mond) + Bronson i 377 #3 + VRS 479.1.5; Landeck 1946 12-13; N. Langstaff 46-47; Leisy 1974 114 #113; Manoff 6; M. H. Mason 23, 24-25; Matteson 1947 64-65; McIntosh 1935 177-78; ML 54368.2.4; Morehead 178-79; Nettel 224-25; *Novello* vi #232 14-15 #1133 (Hammond); *Novello* vii #268 12 #1318 + C. J. Sharp 1932 ii 191 C; Oberndorfer 85b; Okeh K3 CO 29678 (Burl Ives); Okun 1968 45-46; Opie 1951 386-88 #470; Reeves 1960 161; RLP 12-814.2.4 (John Runge); Rosenberg Index #168; Shay 1961 126; Shelton 146-47; Silber 1965 30a; Tobitt 162b; *Tocher #1* 23; J. Warner 105; Wilkinson *510* 103-4; Wise 35.
Related texts (*Tum Balalaika*): Bikel 57-59; DL 8413.2.5 (The Gateway Singers); EC 334.11 (Chaim Plotkin); *Lomir Ale Singen 54; PSB 2* #136 + *RPSB* 19; Rubin 58-59; Pete Seeger 1964 68-69; *SO 6* #4 32-33.
Text and tune relatives: ATL 604.2, 604.16 (Frank Edwards); ATL 629.3 (Reuben Edwards); Creighton 1950 22-23 A + Bronson i 371 #19; Creighton 1950 23-24 B + Bronson i 372 #20 + *JEFDSS 6* 84; Gardner 1939 139-40 + Bronson i 373 #24; Korson 1949 35-36 + Bronson i 374 #25.
Tune relatives: [See notes to #53, *Fair Julian Bond*].

125.
Kate and Her Horns

Previously available: *Neighbors* 1946 24.
Variants: ATL 485.7-.8.
Adaptations: Cazden 1958 88 90-91 + Cazden 1973 90-91; FHR-04.1.6 (John Roberts).
Comment, references: Bronson i 409-10; Cazden 1958 ii 118-19 + Cazden 1973 118-19; FHR-04J 1.6; Flanders 1939 123; *JAF 35* 387 (Kittredge); Laws N 22; W. R. Mackenzie 1919 146-49; W. R. Mackenzie 1928 325-27.
Broadsides, songsters: *Bobbing Around* 212-15; W. C. Ford #3199; *Forget-Me-Not* 145-47 + *Jenny Lind* 145-47 + *New Book of 1000* 145-47; *Isaiah Thomas* i 76, i 47; Roxburghe viii 430-31.
Texts: AFS 1463A.15 (Fred Atwood); ATL 602.11-.12 (James Edwards); Combs 1925 157-58 + Combs 1967 137-38; Combs 1967 213 #101, listing; Cutting 74-76; Emrich 1974 176-77; Flanders *SR* 13.5.34; Hubbard 111-13; Shearin 30; H. Thompson 1940 413-16 (from Glens Falls, New York); H. Thompson 1958 69-71 (from a New York manuscript of 1841-56).

Related text (*Poor Nell and the Chimney Sweep*): Karpeles 1974 ii 100-102 A, 102 B, 103 C.

Text and tune relatives: none.

Tune relatives (Child 53, *Young Beichan* or *Lord Bateman*),

  Comment, references: Bronson i 417-19; *JFSS 3* 55 (Broadwood).

  Tunes with this text: Bronson i 417-26 Group *Aa* #10 - #12, #16 - #34; Bronson i 426-40 Group *Ab* #70 - #86b; Bronson i 454-57 Group *Ac* #95 - #99; *JFSS 8* 27 + Karpeles 1974 i 345 B; Karpeles 1971 46 C.

Tune relatives (others): Creighton 1971 121-22, 127-28; Flanders 1931 133; Gainer 1975 151; *JEFDSS 9* 194; *JFSS 1* 220; *JFSS 2* 97; *JFSS 3* 55 #20; *JFSS 5* 128; Karpeles 1974 i 602 G, *The Brisk Young Lover*; P. Kennedy 1975 715; *NEF 8* 23; *Pilgrim Hymnal* #455.

126.
The Roving Irishman

Previously available: none.

Variants: none.

Adaptations: Cazden 1958 ii 98-99 + Cazden 1973 98-99.

Comment, references: Cazden 1958 ii 122 + Cazden 1973 122; Fowke 1965 181-82; FSC 10F 3-4 (Fowke); P. Kennedy 1975 800-801 #353; C. Sandburg 1927 312-13; Topic 12T159F A.2 (Lloyd).

Broadsides, songsters: *Bobbing Around* 210-12, *The Roving Pedlar*; Delaney #23 + C. Sandburg 1927 312-13, *The Gamboling Man*; *Marsh's Selection* ii 122-23, *The Roving Irishman*; *Wehman's Collection #10* 27, *The Gamboling Man*.

Texts: Belden 1940 374-75, *The Guerrilla Boy*; Bethke #23 + Philo 1022.2.4, *The Roving Cunningham*; Bethke #51, *The Roving Ash-law Man*; Clifford 18-20, *The Rambling Irishman*; Creighton 1971 43, *The Roving Journeyman*; Dean 124-25, *The Roving Irish-man*; FSC 10F 4-5, *The Rambling Irishman*; S. B. Gould 1892 16-17 #8 + *Folk #1* ii + S. B. Gould 1905 16-17 #8, *The Roving Journeyman*; S. B. Gould 1974 92-93; LCJ (Harrigan), *The Roving Journeyman*; LCJ, *Charlie Cunningham* (from Malone, New York); Randolph iv 358-59 B, *The Gamboling Man*; Reeves 1958 186, *The Roving Journeyman*; Rickaby 81 + Fowke 1954 76-77, *Ye Maidens of Ontario*; *SFQ 8* 176-77 + A. C. Morris 443-44, *The Jolly Irishman*; Shearin 13, *The Roving Irish Boy*; D.

Stewart 65, *Dennis O'Reilly*; Topic 12T159F A.2, *The Roving Journeyman*; Wright 416 (from an unidentified broadside).

Related texts (*Neuve Chapelle*): Sam Henry #528.

Related texts (*The Roving Gambler*),

  Comment, references: Belden 1952 iii 374-77; Laws H 4; RLP 12-643J 1.1 (Goldstein).

  Texts: Abrahams 185, listing H 4; Beard 268-69; Belden 1952 iii 79 B; Botkin 1944 889; Brewster 342-44; Brunswick 2923 (Vernon Dalhart); Capitol T700.2.1 (Tennessee Ernie Ford) + Veal 29-31 #15; *Carson J. Robison* 42-43 + *Tip Top* 1936 23; *CFB #3* 7b; W. W. Chamberlain 201; CMS 670C.2 + CMS 670F C.2 (Tom Glazer); Columbia C186.6.38484b; Davis Index 125-26 (6); Downes 346-47; *Elmore Vincent* 30-31; FSA 32.1.6 + FSA 32F 10-11 (Hedy West); Fuson 131; Hansen 158b; B. Ives 1949 32-34; *JAF 39* 134-35; Leisy 1964 100-101; Leisy 1966 286-88; J. Lomax 1934 150-51 + A. Lomax 1964 113; Niles 1963 17; Okeh K-3 + CL 628A.10b (Burl Ives); Piper; *PTFLS 23* 183-85; Randolph iv 356-58 A, 359-60 C; RLP 12-643.1.1 (Logan English); L. Roberts 108-9; Rosenberg Index #1222 (6); *Sam Eskin* iv 36; Shay 1961 22; Silber 1973b 54a; Silverman 1975 ii 330a; SLP 9A.3 (Cisco Houston); Stekert 1969 N 59; *Twenty-Four* 13.

Unrelated texts: Graves 1893 13-16, *The Roving Pedlar*; Wehman *617* 115, *The Roving Irish Boy*.

Text and tune relatives: ATL 602.14 (James Edwards); ATL 628.5 (Frank Edwards); Creighton 1971 43, *The Roving Journeyman* (distant); Fowke 1965 92-93 + FSC 10.1.1 + Wright 414-15, *The Rambling Irishman*; P. Kennedy 1975 781 + Topic 12T159A.2, *The Roving Journeyman*; MacColl 1968 46-47, *The Rambling Irishman*.

Tune relatives: Creighton 1971 138-39, *The Rocks of Scilly*.

Unidentified tune title (*The Roving Journey-man*): Croker 162-64, *The Carrigaline Goalers Defeated*; *Singer's Journal #8* 62 + Wolf Index #1503, *My Good-Looking Man*.

127.
The Islands of Jamaica

Previously available: none.

Variants: ATL 614.11-.12.

Adaptations: Cazden 1958 ii 46-47 + Cazden 1973 46-47.

Comment, references: Cazden 1958 ii 117 + Cazden 1973 117; Flanders 1939 29; O Lochlainn 1965 152.
Broadsides, songsters: none.
Texts: Creighton 1932 73-74; FE 4307F 5-6.
Text and tune relatives: ATL 191.10 (Tom Kelly); Creighton 1962 142 + FE 4307A.9; Flanders 1939 27-39; M. Leach 1965 224-25 (in - -*b-a* form); Manny 239-40; *NA Ives* 1.77 + ATL 2196.3 (from New Brunswick); *NA Ives* 1.113 + ATL 3120.1 (from New Brunswick); *NA Ives* 66.4.6 (from Maine); Peacock 218-19 A, 220-21 B; Peacock 222-23 C (in - -*b-a* form).
Tune relatives (*Benjamin Deane*): Creighton 1962 169; *JAF 72* 53; *NA Ives* 1.2 + ATL 2137.1 + Edw. Ives 197- [318]; *NA Ives* 1.11 + ATL 2143.7; *NA Ives* 1.24 + ATL 2151.4 + Edw. Ives 197- [366]; *NA Ives* 1.123 + ATL 3130.1; *NA Ives* 1.154 + ATL 3161.1; *NA Ives* 62.2, 65.4.2, 65.14.1; *NEF 5* 55-56 + ATL 2164.3 + *NA Ives* 1.38.
Tune relatives (others): Behan 1965 61; Dibblee 97; Doerflinger 283; Edw. Ives 1971 65b + *NA Ives* 69.2; Edw. Ives 1971 66 + *NA Ives* 68.5; M. Leach 1965 182, 226; Manny 108 + J. R. Wilson #16; Meredith 1968 122a, 164; *Miramichi Ms.* 16.4, 16.17, 17.12; Morton 1973 127; *NA Ives* 1.43 + ATL 2168.1, *The Girl I Left Behind*; *NA Ives* 1.72 + ATL 2191.1; *NA Ives* 1.108 + ATL 3115.6; *NA Ives* 1.128 + ATL 3135.3, *The Winter of '83* (Nick Underhill), "tune: *Benjamin Deane*"; *NA Ives* 1.131 + ATL 3138.1, *Howard Carey*; O Lochlainn 1939 88; O Lochlainn 1939 154 + J. R. Wilson #16a; Peacock 192; Ranson 18; *Sing 1* 87 (Lloyd); *SO 10* #4 28-29 + *RSO* #5 26-27 + *Sing 7* 67, *The Handsome Cabin Boy*.
Tune relatives (others, partial similarity): Bethke #18, #23, #44, #51, (*a* phrase); O Lochlainn 1965 40 (*b* phrase); Peacock 560, 969 (*b* phrase).

128.
Where Are You Going, My Pretty Fair Maid?

Previously available: none.
Variants: ATL 627.2.
Adaptations: Cazden 1958 ii 42-45 + Cazden 1973 42-45.
Comment, references: Cazden 1958 ii 122 + Cazden 1973 122; Cox 1925 394; S. B. Gould

1905 21 #73; *JFSS 4* 291 (Broadwood); Laws O 17; O'Shaughnessy 1968 36-37 #11; Reeves 1958 128; C. J. Sharp 1932 ii 406 #127; Topic 12T157F B.1 (Lloyd).
Broadsides, songsters: [as in Laws O 17].
Texts: G. Anderson 121; Belden 1952 iii 21-23; Bikel 60-61; Butterworth 16-17; *Clancy 1971* 44-45; W. Cole 14-15; Cox 1925 394; Dallas 1973 68-70; Dunson 1968 74-75; Eddy 188-90; Emrich 1974 205-6; *FMJ 2* 288a; R. Ford 1904 99-102; Gundry 42 (including Cornish test); Hubbard 147; *JFSS 6* 7; Kidson 1926 2; E. Moore 213-14; P. Perkins 95 (adapted); Reeves 1958 126-28; Reeves 1960 238-39; Rosenberg Index #1256 (5); *Sam Henry* #152, #793; Schinhan v 205-8; C. J. Sharp 1932 ii 156-57 A; C. J. Sharp 1965 193c-94; Silverman 1975 i 119b; Topic 12T157F B.1; Wilkinson i #47, #101, #337, #369.

Related texts (*The Farmer's Daughter*),
Comment, references: Cox 1925 392; Hubbard 148-49; Opie 1951 281-83 #317; C. J. Sharp 1916 xxxi #44.
Broadsides, songsters: *American Singer* 243a; *American Vocalist* 110; *Book of 1001* i 160; *British Students* 202-4; *College Songs* #3 24; *Dilly Burn*; *Francis & Day* iv 35; *Good Old Songs* ii 113-14; *Howe* i 27; *Howe* 1874 27a + *Trifet* 1890 27a + *Trifet* 1892 25a; *Marsh's Selection* ii 208; *Mocking Bird* 93; *Northern & Eastern* 250-51; *Penny Melodist* #112 (with attribution of text to J. Kenney); *Souvenir Minstrel* 87; *Sport's Own*; *Stephens* 10b; *Tony Pastor* 1873 17; J. W. Turner 8c; *Universal Songster* 1832 119-20; *Vauxhall* i 6-7.
Texts: AFS 10505B.31 (Celia Kelder); Bertail 114; Bonar 114-17; *Boosey* xii 7c (instrumental tune); Brune 15c; Buck 1933 25a; Bullard 8, 38b; Cazden 1958 ii 35 + Cazden 1973 35; Chilton 28-29; Cozans i 29b; Cox 1939 i 83-84; Crane 48-49; *D'Alcorn #1* 79a; A. T. Davison 1922 39 #68; Dearmer 1915 58a; *Ernest Newton* 99; *FMJ 2* 290a; R. Ford 1904 137b-38; Gainer 1975 150; Grainger #289, #290; *Great Comic Volume* 30a #25; Hansen 201b; Knox 82; Mansion 86-87; McCarthy 106-7; McCaskey iii 46; McDowell 1947 13; A. Mills 1949 77; Moffat 1904 8; Moffat *50* 11; R. O. Morris 1-4; *Musical Bouquet* #2192, ca. 1862; *Musical Bouquet* #4883/4 2b (instrumental); *Musical Treasury* #574 1-2, ca. 1850; Ogilvie 81 #91; Opie 1951 281-83 #317; J. W. Sharp i 6-7; *Song Ballads* 70-71 #62; Tobitt 52b; W. G. Whittaker i 8-9;

Wier 1918b 215b; Wilkinson i #213, #265; Wilkinson *510* 16.

Related texts Child 200, *The Gypsy Laddie*, opening: Bronson iii 204 #7; Bronson iii 242-49 #112, #114, #117, #119, #120, #122, #125, #126.

Related texts (*How Old Are You*, as children's game song): Ruth Seeger 1948 56-57.

Related texts (*The Milkmaid*, or *Dabbling in the Dew*),

    Comment, references: Cazden 1958 ii 122 + Cazden 1973 122; Cox 1925 392; C. J. Sharp 1916 xxxi #44.

    Texts: Cazden 1958 ii 3 + Cazden 1973 3; Cox 1925 392; C. J. Sharp 1916 100-101 #44.

Related texts (*My Pretty Little Maid*),

    Comment, references: Cazden 1958 ii 121 + Cazden 1973 121.

    Texts: Cazden 1958 ii 35 + Cazden 1973 35.

Related texts (*The Pretty Girl Milking Her Cow*): [see notes to #31, *The Green Mossy Banks by the Lea*].

Related texts (*A Waukrife Minnie*, by Robert Burns),

    Comment, references: Dick i 414; Stenhouse 280 #288.

    Texts: Dick i 167; J. Johnson #288; Kinsley ii 539 #311; Maver 207a #413.

Related texts (*Weavily Wheat*): J. Lomax 1934 292-93 B.

Text and tune relatives: ATL 619.5 (Frank Edwards); Creighton 1950 164; Creighton 1962 32; Creighton 1971 44; Dallas 1973 54-55; FSE 20.1.1 (Harry Cox); S. B. Gould 1892 154-55 #73 + S. B. Gould 1905 150-51 #73 (with censored text); S. B. Gould 1974 14-15 [collected in 1889]; Grainger #125 + #132 [#129 notably similar]; Grainger 1912 #8 + O'Shaughnessy 1968 12 #11 + *Sing Care Away* iv 11; Hamer 1973 75-76; Holst 17 #14 (R. V. Williams); *JFSS* 2 269a, 269b, 270; *JFSS* 4 291; Karpeles 1974 i 422-49, A - H; Kidson 1926 2-3; Peacock 286; Petrie #774; Poston 1968 4-5 (Kidson); Purslow 1968 104; C. J. Sharp *FSS* ii 4-5 + H. W. Davies 43 #36 + Farnsworth 1909 8-9 + Götsch 30b-31, 96 + Karpeles 1956 45 + Karpeles 1975 i 31 #29 + C. J. Sharp 1916 138-40 #44 + C. J. Sharp *Selection* i 32-33 + C. J. Sharp 1920 i 104-6 + R. V. Williams 1924 1-4, 18-21; *SO 26* #6 7a (with rôles reversed); Topic 12T157B.1.

Tune relatives: *JFSS* 2 38-39 #3 + Karpeles 1974 i 695-96, *Jack, the Jolly Tar*; C. J. Sharp 1914 3, *Leave Her, Johnny* (with condensed second portion).

129.
Katey Morey

Previously available: none.

Variants: ATL 625.9.

Adaptations: Cazden 1951b 8a [tune only]; Cazden 1958 ii 32-34 + Cazden 1973 32-34; RLP 12-603.11 (Milt Okun).

Comment, references: Bronson ii 547-58; Cazden 1958 ii 119 + Cazden 1973 119; Child 112; Coffin 103-4; *JAF 35* 385 (Tolman); *JAF 35* 387 (Kittredge); Laws N 24; McTiernan 12; RLP 12-603J.11 (Cazden).

Broadsides, songsters: [as listed by Laws].

Texts: H. P. Beck 1957 110-12; Bethke #37 + Philo 1022.1.2; Eddy 64-65 + Bronson ii 563 #39 + Wakefield i 15-16; Emrich 1974 174-75; McTiernan 12; Shoemaker 130-32; H. Thompson 1940 411-12 + H. Thompson 1958 9-11; Wilkinson i #279; ZDA 66.2.9.

Text and tune relatives: ATL 182.3; ATL 615.16 (James Edwards); Bronson ii 561-63 #34-#38; Gardner 1939 393-94 + Bronson ii 562 #36 + *Sam Eskin* i 134.

Tune relatives (Child 214, *The Braes of Yarrow*): Bronson iii 321 #26, #27.

130.
A Bold Brave Bonair

Previously available: none.

Variants: ATL 618.4-.5, 626.1.

Adaptations: Cazden 1958 ii 92-93 + Cazden 1973 92-93; RLP 12-603.3 (Milt Okun).

Comment, references: Belden 1940 239-44; Belden 1952 iii 24-25; Cazden 1958 ii 114 + Cazden 1973 114; FSA 23F 17-18 (Wilgus); P. Kennedy 1975 434 #185; Laws P 14; RLP 12-603J.3 (Cazden); Topic 12T158F B.5 (Lloyd).

Broadsides, songsters: Roxburghe ix 70-71.

Texts: Abrahams 23-25; *All Time* 10; ATL 619.7-.8; Behan 1967 72-73, *The Bold Balladeer*; Belden 1952 iii 24-25; Boette 40; Brocklebank 21; T. Burton i 95; T. Burton ii 31; M. E. Bush ii 73-75; Churchill 36-38, 39; J. Cohen 1964 68-69; Combs 1939 20-21; Combs 1967 214 #112, listing; Copper 1973 210-11; Cox 1939 i 78-79, 80-81, 82; Davis Index 43 (3); Eddy 230-31; *EDS 26* 39; Emrich 1974 231-32; FA 2367.2.1 + FA 2367F 4e; FHE 71; Fife 1969 7; FM 4005B.1 + FM 4005F B.1; FSA 23.1.10 + FSA 23F 18; Gainer 1963 #31; Gainer 1975 122-23; Honoré 8; *JAF 70* 346-47; Jameson 1955 6a; Jameson 1967 40; *JFSS* 2 254; *JFSS* 5 11-15; Jolliffe 65-66; Karpeles 1971 232-33; Kar-

peles 1974 i 654-49, A-F; Karpeles 1975 i 25
#33; P. Kennedy 1975 414-15 #185; Ken-
tucky 1939 i 21; Kinscella 3; J. Lomax 1938
183 + A. Lomax 1960 382-83, *The Wild Rip-
pling Water;* McCarthy 77-78; *MF 13* 148,
listing; E. Moore 211-12; Musick 25 #6;
Niles 1934 22-23 # Niles 1963 5; O'Shaughnessy 1971 2-3; Peacock 594; Piper (2) +
Peterson Index 39; *PTFLS 7* 167-68 (cowboy
variant); Purslow 1965 60; Rainey 13-14;
Reeves 1958 85-87; Ritchie 1971 31-32;
Rosenberg Index #1009 (12); Rounder
0017.2.5 + Rounder 0017F 8a; C. Sandburg
1927 136-37 A; H. Sandburg 56; Sedley 16-
17; *SFQ 2* 154-55; *SFQ 36* 27-29; C. J. Sharp
1932 ii 194 E + Karpeles 1973 36 + A. L.
Lloyd 1965 59 #32; Silber 1973b 166b; Silverman 1975 i 165; F. H. Smith 1939 29;
R. B. Smith 64-65; *SO 16 #4* 29; Stubbs 16-
17; Topic 12T158B.5 + Topic 12T158F B.5;
Wales 1971 32-33 + *Yetties* 58; F. M. Warner 41-42; E. K. Wells 222; Wilkinson i
#507; Wilkinson *128, The Nightingale;*
H. R. Wilson 12; Wyman 1916 71 + *Song
Ballads* 57-58 #43; Zanzig 1940 #20.

Text and tune relatives: none.

Tune relatives (*The Whistle*),
 Comment, references: Dick i 431-32 #229;
  Laing 362-63 #314; Stenhouse 305-6 #314.
 Tunes with this text: Dick i 204; J. Johnson
  #314.
Tune relatives (others): ATL 486.9, *The White
 Fawn* (bawdy), (George Edwards); Creigh-
 ton 1962 126, *Three English Rovers.*

131.
Old Shoes and Leggings

Previously available: none.
Variants: none.
Adaptations: none.
Comment, references: Belden 1940 264; Belden
 1952 iii 17; Cox 1925 489; FSA 15F 14-15
 (McElligott); Gardner 1939 413; P. Kennedy
 1975 333 #139; Randolph i 291; Peggy See-
 ger 1960a 6 #9, C. J. Sharp 1932 ii 404 #108;
 Stenhouse 377 #416; Topic 12T127F A.7
 (Lloyd).
Broadsides, songsters: *Lark* 292 #328; *Musical
 Miscellany* iii 110; *Orpheus* iii 90 #158; *Uni-
 versal Songster* ii 247.
Texts: Belden 1940 264; Belden 1952 iii 17-20;
 Bell 1857 237; Brewster 255-56; Christie ii
 96-97; Cox 1925 489; Creighton 1950 190-91;
 Davis Index 173; Dixon 237; Dunson 1973
 34-35; Eddy 132-35; FA 2951B.9 (Eck Dun-

ford); FHE 362; R. Ford 1904 142-43; M. B.
Foster 155; FSA 15.1.11 + FSA 15F 15;
Gardner 1939 413-14; G. Greig *FSNE* #149;
Hammond 65; M. E. Henry 301-2; Hubbard
152-53; *JAF 28* 158; *JAF 29* 188; *JEFDSS 3*
130-31; J. Johnson #416 + Maver 237b
#474; Karpeles 1974 ii 24-26, A-C; P. Ken-
nedy 1975 316 #139; Kidson 1891 92; LCJ;
Leodhas 41-42; J. Lomax 1941 132-34; M. H.
Mason 33b; Matteson 1947 30-31; E. Moore
253-54; A. C. Morris 376-78; P. Perkins 39-
40; *PTFLS 23* 217; Purslow 1965 65; Randolph i 291-94; Schinhan v 9-10; Peggy
Seeger 1960a 11 #9 + Peggy Seeger 1970 6-
7; C. J. Sharp 1932 ii 93-95; Shoemaker 17-
8; Stout 30; Topic 12T157A.7 (Jeannie
Robertson); Wilkinson i #35, #64, #564;
Wilkinson *510* 29; A. Williams 73; I. A. Williams 2-3; R. V. Williams 76.

132.
The Long Eddy Waltz

Previously available: none.
Variants: none.
Adaptations: none.
Comment, references (1. Discussion re bawdy,
 merry and obscene genres of traditional
 song): Barke 23-36; Cazden 1958 ii 1-2 +
 Cazden 1973 1-2; *Chapbook 4 #3* 7-19 (Legman); Cray xi-xxxv; B. Jackson 45-61, "A
 sampling of bawdy ballads from Ontario"
 (Edith Fowke).
 (2: Examples of opening narrator patterns),
  (a) Narrator drops out: Laws 1957 J 9, M
   12, O 22, O 27, O 31, Q 26.
  (b) Narrator plays rôle: Laws 1957 K 17,
   K 40, L 24, N 33, N 34, N 35, N 36, N
   37, N 40, N 41, O 7, O 13, P 2, P 15, P
   16, P 18, P 19, P 40, Q 13, Q 27.
Broadsides, songsters: none.
Texts: none.
Text and tune relatives: none.
Tune relatives: none.

133.
The Little Scotch Girl

Previously available: none.
Variants: ATL 624.7.
Adaptions: Cazden 1958 ii 10-11 + Cazden
 1973 10-11; RLP 12-603.7 (Milt Okun); ZDA
 75.1.7 + ZDA 75F 5 B (Peggy Seeger).
Comment, references: Bronson iv 257-77, 511;
 Cazden 1958 ii 119-20 + Cazden 1973 119-
 20; Child 281; Coffin 150-51; G. Greig 1925

230; RLP 12-603J.7 (Cazden); RLP 12-624F 6 (Goldstein); Topic 12T161F B.10 (Lloyd); ZDA 75F 4-5 (MacColl, Peggy Seeger).

Broadsides, songsters: none.

Texts: Bell 1857 75-77; P. Buchan i 270-73; FHE 419 + Ph. Barry 1929 338-39; Flanders iv 137; R. Ford 1904 277-80; G. Greig 1925 232-33 #1a + Bronson iv 266-67 #19 + MacColl 1956 19 + MacColl 1965 52-53 + RLP 12-624.1.1 + RLP 12-624F 6 + Pete Seeger 1972 116-18 + ZDA 75.1.6 (Ewan MacColl) + ZDA 75F 5A; Lyle 64-66; McCarthy 54-56; *Sam Henry* #201; Sedley 20-22; Topic 12T161B.10 + Topic 12T161F B.10.

Text and tune relatives: ATL 189.9 (Reuben Edwards); ATL 193.8 ("Dick" Edwards); ATL 626.8 (Charles Seeley).

Tune relatives: none.

134.
The Brats of Jeremiah

Previously available: none.

Variants: none.

Adaptations: Cazden 1958 ii 50-51 + Cazden 1973 50-51.

Comment, references: Bronson iii 198; Cazden 1958 ii 114-15 + Cazden 1973 114-15; G. S. Jackson 196-97.

Broadsides, songsters (*Unhappy Jeremiah*) [*followed by text of sequel, *Happy Hezekiah;* ** with air indicated as *Polly Clover*]: *Beadle's Dime #3* *44; *Beadle's Half-Dine #8* *13; *Book of 1001* iii **199-200; *Clark's Orphean* **210-11; *Elton* 111 + G. S. Jackson 196-97; *Lover's Harmony #22* 170; *Pearl Songster* 167-68; *Tony Pastor* ix *66-67; Wolf Index *#2403 (broadsides by Auner, Andrews).

Texts: ATL 565.14 (Lydia Gyderson); Cutting 50-51.

Related text (*Rocking the Cradle*): Healy 1969 iv 120-22 (from an undated broadside); A. Lomax 1960 375; Randolph iii 118-19; *Street Literature* (a broadside by E. Hodges, London).

Text and tune relatives: none.

Related texts and tunes (*Devilish Mary*): Randolph iii 188; C. J. Sharp 1932 ii 200 A. (others): Flanders 1931 91, *Lie Low;* Glassie 157, *The Bachelor's Song.*

Tune relatives (similar half-tune forms with similar refrain): Hubbard 315, *Tim Finnegan's Wake;* Morton 1973 121, *Marrow Bones;* J. W. Turner 16, *Mary Blane.* [See also notes to #74, *The Ship's Carpenter*].

Unspecified tune (*Unhappy Jeremiah*): Bailey, *The Rush to Coromandel; Good-Bye, John* 12-13; *The Rising Generation; Harrison's Comic* 54, *The Yankee Volunteer;* Wolf Index #2015, *The Rising Generation* (a broadside by De Marsan).

135.
The Wife Who Was Dumb

Previously available: AFS 12309A.8 + EC 329.8; *YIFMC 3* 72 Ex. 8b [tune only].

Variants: ATL 623.5.

Adaptations: Cazden 1958 ii 72-73 + Cazden 1973 72-73.

Comment, references [*indicates discussion of the tune]: Belden 1952 ii 452-53; Cazden 1958 ii 123 + Cazden 1973 123; W. Chappell 1840 i *165-66 #220; W. Chappell 1859 i *117-20; W. Chappell 1859 ii *770-71; Dean-Smith 1957 *52, *Goddesses;* Dick i *424-25; S. B. Gould ii vi; Haufrecht 1970 *141; *JAF 66* 48; *JAMS 3* *120-34 (Bronson); *JAMS 20* *47-49 Ex. 13, *I Would I Were in My Own Country* (Ward); *JAMS 20* *49-52 Ex. 15, *John Anderson, My Jo—Paul's Steeple—Goddesses* (Ward); P. Kennedy 1975 *477 #199; Laws Q 5; Lampe 1955 *31; Lee *71-72; Moffat 1897 *136-37; Moffat 1901 *1 2-3; Simpson *331-35, *I Am the Duke of Norfolk;* Simpson *351-53; Stenhouse *243-45; Stokoe *194, *The Oak and the Ash;* Wilkinson 510 *59.

Broadsides, songsters: *Antidote* 77-78; Ashton 1887 319-21; *Bella Union* 7-8; De Marsan #87 (marked: J. Andrews, New York); W. C. Ford #2989; Holloway 97 #67, 98 #68; *Orpheus* iii 137-39 #231; M. Raven iii 94 [facsimile]; Roxburghe iv 355-59; *Wehman's Collection #33* 10, "by O. Whittlesey."

Sheet music: Dichter i #451, listing of publication, Boston: Oliver Ditson, ca. 1873, [as sung] "by Mrs. J. M. Russell."

Texts: Breathnach iii 6-8; Cobb 57-59; Davis Index 161 (7); Eddy 214-15; Farmer 202-3; R. Ford 1904 32-34; Gardner 1937 199-200 (from Conesville, New York); Hubbard 238-39; P. Kennedy 1975 456; Korson 1949 56; E. Moore 224-25; A. C. Morris 379-81; *NA Ives* 64.7.18; S. H. Nicholson 44-45 #21; Randolph iii 118-20; *Ring Ms.* 64-66 #25 + *JAF 66* 48-49 (from Clinton Corners, New York); Schinhan v 242, 243; *SFQ 5* 181-82 + *JAF 57* 282-83; Wilkinson i #212; Wilkinson 510 53-54.

Text and tune relatives: ATL 604.11 (James Edwards); ATL 617.3 (Minnie Ward); ATL 618.13, 619.1 (Frank Edwards); Botsford 1937 118-19; W. Chappell 1859 i 120 + R. Palmer 1971 52-53; D'Urfey iii 274, 276-77 + Glass 1967b 24-25 + T. Wood 10-11 + W. G. Whittaker iv 2-3; S. B. Gould ii 54-56; Joyce #389 + J. R. Wilson #32a; MacMahon i 47-48 #25; Moffat 1897 136-37; Moffat 1901 102-3.

Tune relatives (*Backslider*): Hauser 1848 197b; G. P. Jackson 1952 148 #257 (from *Columbian Harmony* 1825 83).

(*Consolation A* [in condensed tune form]),

    Comment, references: Buchanan xiv #3.

    Tunes with this text: Buchanan 6-7 #3; Carden 25b + Marrocco 249 #93; Cayce #118; Davisson 28a; Hauser 1848 58a; Heaton #25; Hendrickson 14b-15; G. P. Jackson 1942 146-47 #135; J. B. Jackson 21; Rhinehart 16b; Showalter 106b; Walker 17b + *All Time* 40a; B. F. White 50a + Cooper 50a; *Wyeth* ii 20a.

(*Hiding Place*): Carden 29b; Davisson 30a; Ditson 1857 219b; Funk 77b + Showalter 77b (from *Harmonia Sacra* of 1832); Hayden 249b; G. P. Jackson 1942 54 #35 (from *Day's Revival Hymns* 71); J. B. Jackson 34; Leavitt i 162; Neale 71; Rhinehart 17a; Woodbury 1853 54c; *Wyeth* ii 22b.

(*Primrose* [tune in major]): Denson 47; Hayden 17b; G. P. Jackson 1942 172 #165.

(other hymns): Funk 219b + Showalter 219b, *Exultation* (from *Harmonica Sacra* of 1832); G. P. Jackson 1952 114 #178, *Impartial Song* (from Jeremiah Ingalls, *Christian Harmony* 1805 35); *Wyeth* ii 98b, *Happiness*.

Tune relatives (*The Cruiskeen Lawn*),

    Comment, references: W. Chappell 1859 ii 770-71; G. P. Jackson 1952 114; Moffat 1897 136-37; Stanford 1895 222-25.

    Broadsides, songsters [texts only]: *American Singer* 156 [with refrain in Gaelic]; M. J. Barry 65; *Beadle's Half-Dime #15* 4; *Book of Irish Songs* 7; *Burton's Comic* 112; *Singer's Journal #23* 148; *Songs of our Land* ii 7-8; *Universal Irish* 17; *Universal Songster* 1832 154-55; Wehman *617* 79; *Wehman's Collection #29* 5.

    Tunes with this text: Bantock 1930c ii 18-19; Behan 1967 31-32; Bingley ii 156-57; *British Minstrelsie* i 62-64; *Cavendish #20* 15; *Choice Irish Songs* i 134-35; W. Cole 62-63; Colum 609; J. Edwards 82-83; FO 15.2.10 + FM 4051.1.12 +

Fowke 1965 16-17; *FST* iv 30-31, *An Cruiscin Lan*; *Gem Selection* 84-85; Gleadhill 77; Goodwin 1956 381a, "traditional"; Graeme 171-72 + *Clancy* 1971 171-72, *Cruiscín Lán*; Graves 1914 153 #99; Hatton 86-88; *Hitchcock #194*; Hitchcock ii 46-47; Hogarth ii 105-12; Howe ii 71; *Howe* 1874 71b; *Ireland's Songs* 182-84; B. Ives 1958 49-51; *JIFS 13* 13b [tune in major]; Lampe 1955 39; *Musical Bouquet #2446*; *Musical Treasury #1262*; Ogilvie 117b #127; *Old Songs for the Pianoforte* 50-52 #16; Page 6-7; Rooney 1905 36-37; *Songster #1* 37.

    Tunes with this title (instrumental): *Boosey* 1862a 21 #69; Converse 1887 68b; *Harding* 63 #200; *Howe* 1846a 49c; Kerr xii 25a; *Musical Bouquet #2406/7 3* #2(quadrille), #2421 3c-4a (waltz), #2422/3 3a (galop); *New Preceptor* 11g; O'Neill #254.

(*The Little Man and the Little Maid*, by Charles Sedley),

    Texts only: G. A. Stevens (1771) 287-88 #221.

    Tunes with this text: *British Museum* 266-67; *D'Alcorn #1* 64a; Howe 1874 29a + *Fireside Library* 64a + *Trifet* 1890 29a + *Trifet* 1892 17a; Lupton 42c; *96 Old Songs* 103; Simpson 335 #211; *Song Jewels* 46a.

(*A North Country Lass*, or *I Would I were in My Own Country*),

    Comment, references: W. Chappell 1859 ii 456-58; *JAMS 20* 47-48 (Ward); Simpson 351-53; Stokoe 194.

    Tunes with this text: W. Chappell 1859 ii 457-58; *FMBS #2* 14; *Folk #1* 10; Weckerlin 51-54 #14.

(*The Oak and the Ash*),

    Comment, references: Bantock 1914 xx #27; H. K. Johnson 80; Lee 71-72.

    Tunes with this text: Ashbee iii 14-15; Bantock 1914 44-45 #27; Bantock 1930a ii 18-19; Buck 1916 142; Catcheside-Warrington iv 8; *Cavendish #21* 28, "seventeenth century"; W. Cole 34-35; H. W. Davies 84 #72; *Ernest Newton* 19; Götsch 32a, 98; H. K. Johnson 81; Lee 72c; Loomis 114-15; MacMahon ii 120-21 #61; Möller 38-39 #19; *Musical Bouquet #4275*; Ratcliff 67; Rohrbough 1946 4; *Sing Together* 70-71; Stanford 1958 15; *University Songbook* 242-43; VRS 479.1.6 (Alfred Deller); W. J.

Whittaker 72 #20 + Stokoe 14; Wier 1918a 370b.

(*Old King Cole*),

Comment, references: W. Chappell 1840 i 40 #16; W. Chappell 1859 ii 633-35.

Tunes with this text: Bertail 28; Buck 1933 48-49; Bullard; Cazden 1961 102; Cazden 1966 14-27 #3; W. Chappell 1840 ii 8b #16 + W. Chappell 1859 ii 635 + T. Wood 104-5; Crane 56; A. T. Davison 1922 48 #81; Goodwin 1956 244, "traditional"; Kinley 24-25; Loomis 40; Mansion 48-49; Moffat 1904 45; *Musical Budget 5* 714-15; R. Perkins iii 16-17; Ratcliff 167; *Scottish Students* 242-43; *Sing Together* 84-85; Weckerlin 144-47 #36; Wessells 50-51; Whitehead 190-91; W. G. Whittaker i 10-11; Wilkinson *510* 172; Woodgate 1951 132-34.

Tunes with this title (instrumental): *Chappell 100* ii #93; E. Haywood 34 #4.

Tunes with related text (*Der Rebbe Elimelach*): Bikel 164-66; *Lomir Ale Singen* 70-71; *Songs to Keep* 53 + MacMahon i 122-23.

(*The Scow on Cowden Shore*, by Larry Gorman): Doerflinger 234-35; Edw. Ives 1964 62-63 + Manny 171 + J. R. Wison #32.

(*Child 10, The Two Sisters*): Bronson i 167-69 #55—#60.

(*When the Lumberman Comes Down*): Fowke 1970 159; *NA Ives* 63.12 + *NEF 5* 69; *NEF 2* 58.

(*Yn Nyffryn Clwyd, or The Vale of Clyde*): Beethoven Nr. 263 51-52 #19; *British Minstrelsie* iii 76-77, *Dyffryn Clwyd*, "old Welsh air"; E. T. Davies 65; Gibbon 35, "air "*Dyffryn Clwyd*"; Graves i 18-20; Graves 1928 224-25; Moffat 1906 83; J. Parry 172-73 [with new text]; Richards 132-33, "air: *Yn Nyffryn Clwyd*"; Stanford 1958 220; J. L. Williams 18-20.

(others): E. C. Beck 1948 29-30 [tune in major]; Breathnach ii 179, "air: *The Cruiscín Lán*"; W. Chappel 1840 ii 105 #220; Chilton 182; Clayre 28; Dean-Smith 1957 69, *Goddesses;* Dearmer 1928 97 #46; D'Urfey iii 274, *Bacchus's Health;* D'Urfey vi 247, *A Broad as I Was Walking; EDS 27* 39; Foner 31c-34, *A Song for the Bank Men* (1834), "air: *The Kroos-Keen Lawn*"; Fowke 1970 159 + FM 4052.1.1; Gallagher #43 [half-tune]; Gallagher #87; Galvin 101; Haufrecht 1970 141; Huntington 172-73; *JAMS 20* 49 Ex. 13, 51-52 Ex. 15; P. Kennedy 1975 498, *The Buchan Miller;* Kerr x 20 #170, *The Gaberlunzie*

Man; Lee 71a, 72b; Manny 54; Moffat 1897 136-37; T. Moore 156, *Song of the Battle;* Murphy 88-89, "air: *Cruiskeen Lawn*"; R. Palmer 1974 269; Reynardson 4 (Broadwood); *Sam Eskin* v, *The Sheepstealer* (in 6/8 time); Peggy Seeger 1960a 92 #84 (second half of tune, refrain); Simpson 332 #210, *Paul's Steeple;* Simpson 352 #225, *Goddesses;* Stevenson 1891 240-41.

136.
Tinnama Clinnama Clinchama Clingo

Previously available: *Neighbors* 1943 15.
Variants: none.
Adaptations: none.
Comment, references: Bronson iv 143-45; Child 277; Coffin 146-48; Cox 1939 i 99 #13; FSA 3F 5-6 (Wilgus); FSA 32F 4 (Lloyd); *HFB #4* 41-48 (Jansen).
Broadsides, songsters: none.
Texts: Boette 19-20; M. E. Bush i 80-81; *CFB #2* 4-5; Combs 1967 207 #39, listing; FHE 276; FO 9.1.11; FSA 3.1.2 + FSA 3F 6-7; FSA 32.1.1 + FSA 32F 4-5; Gainer 1963 #66; Gainer 1975 90-91; *JEFDSS 3* 120; E. Moore 124-26; *TFB 8* 74.
Text and tune relatives: Flanders 1953 221 + Bronson iv 164 #45 + Flanders iv 91 J.
Related verse-form and refrain: B. Arnold 110 + Bronson iv 166 #48; Randolph i 187 + Bronson iv 167 #51; Schinhan iv 113 A + Bronson iv 162-63 #41; Schinhan iv 113 C + Bronson iv 163 #42b; WF 26 272 + Bronson iv 165 #47.
Tune relatives: none.

137.
The Devil and the Farmer's Wife

Previously available: *Neighbors* 1948 24-25 [text adapted].
Variants: none.
Adaptations: AFS 12312A.13, 12312A.17; Cazden 1958 ii 74-75 + Cazden 1973 74-75.
Comment, references: Bronson iv 174-76; Cazden 1958 ii 115 + Cazden 1973 115; Child 278; Coffin 148-50; Dixon 210; *JAF 30* 329-30 (Kittredge); NW 239J 1.2 (Paton); Stekert 1961, "*The Farmer's Curst Wife*, a modified historical-geographical study"; Topic 12T161F B.7 (Lloyd).
Broadsides, songsters: Roxburghe v 367, *How the Divell was guld by a scould;* Walton's *Treasury* 134-35.

Texts: AA 3A.6 (Pete Seeger); ATL 189.3 (Reuben Edwards); ATL 198.3; Barbeau 19-20; Bell 1857 204-5; Bethke #4 + Philo 1022.1.8 (Ted Ashlaw); Boette 5-7; Brand 1961 105; T. Burton ii 72-73; M. E. Bush i 82-85, A - B; I. Campbell 10-11; G. G. Carey 1971 105a; R. Chase 1938 23-24 (Wilkinson); CL 628B.2 (Burl Ives); CMS 650F.7 + CMS 650F F.7 (Tom Glazer); J. Cohen 12-13; C 186.8.38485 (Burl Ives); Combs 1967 208 #40 C; Dallin 126-27; A. K. Davis 1960 316-27 (8); Decca 573.24209A (Richard Dyer-Bennet); Dixon 210-11; DL 8080.1.1 (Burl Ives); Dunson 1973 26-27; FA 2951A.5 (Bill and Belle Reed); FHE 117, 298; FO 9.1.9; M. B. Foster 91; FSA 15.1.2 + FSA 15F 6-7 (Lawrence Older); FSA 17.1.6 (Hobart Smith); FSA 22.2.1 + FSA 22F 22-23; Gainer 1963 #67; Gainer 1975 92-93; Haufrecht 1959 25; Healy 1962 63; B. Ives 1949 8-9; B. Jackson 117-19 (McCulloh); *JEFDSS 8* 27; Karpeles 1975 i 16 #4; Kimball 134; A. Lomax 1964 43; McDowell 1947 61-62; Masterson 297-98; Middlebury #1 2.4; E. Moore 127-28; *NA Ives* 1.84 + ATL 2203.2; *NYFQ 7* 75, listing; R. Palmer 1971 50-51; Peacock 265-67 (3); P. Perkins 110-11; *PSB 2* #152 + *RPSB* 18; Purslow 1965 24; Ritchie 1953 22; Ritchie 1965 31 + EKL 125.2.1; L. Roberts 99-100; Rosenberg Index #388 (9); *Sam Eskin* iv 18, 90, 146; Sedley 222-23; Peggy Seeger 1960b 8; Pete Seeger 1961 58 + FA 2319B.3 + FA 2319F B.3; *SFQ 4* 157-58 + E. C. Beck 1956 191-92; Shellans 18-19; Silber 1965 38; Silverman 1975 ii 218; Stekert 1969 B 24; *Sweet Freedom* 86-87 + *All Time* 53 (from the Pearl R. Nye Collection of *Songs from the Ohio-Erie Canal*); Topic 12T161B.7 + Topic 12T161F B.7; *Weavers Song Book* 134-35.

Related text (*The Carle of Kellyburnbraes*, by Robert Burns),
  Comment, references: Dick i 486-87 #331; Kinsley iii 1404 #376; Stenhouse 350-52 #379.
  Texts: Burns 408-9; Dick i 312-13; G. Greig 1925 220 + Bronson iv 200 #48; Jamieson i 305-8; J. Johnson #379; Kinsley ii 644-46 #376; Kinsley 1969 634-36 #135.
Text and tune relatives,
  (with some degree of tune resemblance): AFS 1B (Horton Barker); ATL 195.2 (Jake Loucks); Bronson iv 184 #15, 185 #17, 187 #21, 200 #50, 201 #51, 208 #64; Downes 228-29 (Siegmeister); Fowke 1973 174-75; Hubbard 40-41 A.
  (with similar refrain and verse-form): AFS

L58B.2 + Bronson iv 210 #67; ATL 604.4 (James Edwards); DX 513.1.8 (Sam Hinton); Harlow 70-71, *A fal de lal day*. [See also notes to #142].

138.
The Jolly Boatswain

Previously available: none.
Variants: ATL 625.5.
Adaptations: Cazden 1958 ii 82-83 + Cazden 1973 82-83.
Comment, references: Cazden 1958 ii 118 + Cazden 1973 118; Flanders 1939 125; Greenleaf 112; Laws Q 8; A. C. Morris 371; Purslow 1968 122.
Broadsides, songsters: as cited by Laws.
Texts: AFS 3665A.1, from New Jersey; Cobb 54-55; Combs 1967 216 #120, listing; Davis Index 158 (2); Droke 71-73; Emrich 1974 225-26; Flanders *SR* 10.3.35; Gardner 1939 482, listing; D. Gilbert 36-37, dated 186- or 187-; Hubbard 228-29; Peacock 306-10 (3); Purslow 1968 16; Reeves 1958 83-84; Rosenberg Index #115; *SFQ 8* 173-74 + A. C. Morris 371-72; Wilkinson i #271.
Related texts (*The Charleston Merchant*): M. E. Bush ii 76; Churchill 52-53; Cox 1939 i 75-77; Keynote K-108.519A (Richard Dyer-Bennet); LCJ (Lyons).
(*The Cooper of Norfolk*),
  Comment, references: Simpson 777-780, tune 778.
  Texts: Holloway 60-61 #44; *Roxburghe* i 99-104; *Seventy-Nine* 60-63 #12.
(*The Dog in the Closet*),
  Comment, references: Laws Q 11.
  Texts: Belden 1952 ii 444-45; Flanders 1939 123-25.
(*The Major's Britches*),
  Comment, references: Laws Q 10.
  Texts: ATL 614.1-.2 (George Edwards); H. P. Beck 1957 268-70.
(*The Trooper and the Tailor*): [See #139].
Text and tune relatives [* indicates complete tune form of which #138 is a half-tune with refrain]: L. Chappell 93-94; Fowke 1973 168-69; *JAF 52* 64-65 (from New Jersey); Karpeles 1974 ii *1-2; Nye, *The Clever Skipper*; Peacock *310-11 C; *Sam Henry* #604; C. J. Sharp 1932 i *338-39 A, 339-40 B.
Related texts with related tunes (The Cobbler) [* indicates complete tune forms],
  Comment, references: P. Kennedy 1975 476-77 #197; O'Shaughnessy 1975 87-88; Topic 12T158F A.12 (Lloyd).
  Texts and tunes: *B&S* #6 *12; Copper 1973

*224-26; JFSS 2 *156-57; JFSS 3 *253-54
#4; Karpeles 1974 ii *3 A + Topic
12T158A.12; Karpeles 1974 ii *3 B, *4 C,
4-5 D; P. Kennedy 1975 453-54; O'Shaughnessy 1975 *58; Purslow 1972 *15-16.

Tune relatives (complete tune forms); [See
notes to #117, *The Old Spotted Cow*].
(half-tune + refrain forms): Eddy 106, 110,
111, *Jack, the Sailor;* Gardner 1939 165;
LCJ (Braden), *Green Willow Tree; NA
Ives* 62.2, *There Was a Little Man; NYFQ
14* 215; C. J. Sharp *FSS* iii 12-13 + C. J.
Sharp 1916 174-75, *The Crabfish;* C. J.
Sharp 1932 i 392 L; C. J. Sharp 1961 ii 92-
94 (R. V. Williams).

Related drawing (*Be a Good Boy*): *Universal
Songster* i 145.

139.
The Trooper and the Tailor

Previously available: none.
Variants: none.
Adaptations: Cazden 1958 ii 12-15 + Cazden
1973 12-15; RLP 12-603.5 (Milt Okun).
Comment, references: Cazden 1958 ii 122 +
Cazden 1973 122; Morton 1973 174-75 #50;
P. Kennedy 1975 478 #200; RLP 12-603J.5
(Cazden).
Broadsides, songsters: none.
Texts: Copper 1973 125-26, 270-71; Dallas 1973
96-97, *The Bold Trooper; JFSS 8* 274-75, *The
Groggy Old Tailor;* Karpeles 1974 ii 16-17 A;
P. Kennedy 1975 457, *The Game Cock;* M.
Leach 1965 286, *Tiddy the Tailor;* Morton
1970 80 + IRL 11B.1, *The Wee Croppy
Tailor;* Morton 1973 144-45, *The Wee
Croppy Tailor;* Peacock 243-44 A, *The Bold
Trooper;* Peacock 245-46 B, *The Bold
Trooper;* Peacock 247-48 C, *The Croppèd
Tailor;* Purslow 1965 6, *The Bold Tropper.*
Related texts: [See notes to #138, *The Jolly
Boatswain*].
Text and tune relatives: none.
Tune relatives: none.

140.
Will, the Weaver

Previously available: AFS 12309B.27 + EC
700.12.
Variants: ATL 190.7.
Adaptations: none.
Comment, references: Cazden 1958 ii 123-24 +

Cazden 1973 123-24; Laws Q 9; W. R. Mack-
enzie 1928 328-29.
Broadsides, songsters: *Sam Sharpley* 22-23.
Texts: Abrahams 186, listing; ATL 486.4
(George Edwards); ATL 488.1, 490.14; Bel-
den 1952 ii 477-78; R. Chase 1956 184-85;
Davis Index 158 (3); Emrich 1974 226-27;
W. C. Ford 3405, 3406; FHE 140; Flanders
SR 5.11,33, 3.3.35; Isaiah Thomas ii 41;
NYFQ 14 210, listing; Purslow 1965 99;
Rosenberg Index #1548; *Sam Henry* #682;
SFQ 33 117-19 (Lumpkin); C. J. Sharp 1932
ii 208-9; *SO 14* #6 31; Stekert 1969 B 61 N 5.
Text and tune relatives: Bayard ii 157.6; Brews-
ter 360-61; Cazden 1958 ii 76-77 + Cazden
1973 76-77; Gainer 1963 #36; Gainer 1975
146-47; M. E. Henry 304-5; Hubbard 230-31;
JAF 63 265-66; Karpeles 1974 ii 14-15;
Miramichi Ms. 15.6; *NA Ives* 61.2, 62.4;
Ritchie 1953 41-43; Scarborough 1937 237-
38, tune 418; Schinhan iv 258; C. J. Sharp
1932 ii 207; Stubbs 83; Wilkinson i #509.
Tune relatives: none.

141.
The Old Woman from Boston

Previously available: none.
Variants: none.
Adaptations: none.
Comment, references: AFS L66F 32 (Jabbour);
Belden 1940 237-38; Belden 1952 ii 450-52;
Brewster 281; Cox 19235 464; Fowke 1967
155; FSA 15F 11 (McElligott); FSC 10F 7
(Fowke); *JAF 29* 179 (Kittredge); *JAF 35* 385
(Tolman); Karpeles 1971 277-78 #39; P.
Kennedy 1975 482 #208; Laws Q 2; Morton
1973 170 #35; *NEF 5* 75 (Edw. Ives);
Peacock 264; Reeves 1958 205; *Sam Henry
Index* #174 (Huntington); C. J. Sharp 1932 ii
397 #55; Wolford 93-94; ZDA 71F 4-5 (Mac-
Coll, Peggy Seeger).
Broadsides, songsters: none.
Texts: AFS 14262A.7 + AFS L66B.3 + AFS
L66F 33 (Maggie Hammons Parker); ATL
170.9 #3a, 171.7 #3a; ATL 628.15 (Reuben
Edwards), *The Old Woman from Trenton;*
Belden 1940 238b-39; Belden 1952 ii 450-52;
Boette 63 + Gainer 1963 #35, *Singa Hipsy
Doodle;* Brewster 281-82; T. Burton ii 110; I.
Campbell 13; G. G. Carey 1971 101b; *CEOL
a #4* 8-9; *Chapbook 2 #4* 27; L. Chappell 79-
80; *Clancy* 1964 18-19; Clemens 32; Combs
1967 216 #119, listing; Cox 1925 464; Creigh-
ton 1962 122; Creighton 1971 158-59; Davis
Index 164-65; Decca 573.24209B (Richard

Dyer-Bennet); Dyer-Bennet 1946 44-45; Dyer-Bennet 1971 63-65; Eddy 90-91; R. G. Edwards 1972 120; Emrich 1974 222-23; Flanders *SR* 21.12.34; FO 9.2.2, 9.2.3, 9.2.4, 9.2.5, 13.1.7; FSA 15.1.7 + FSA 15F 11-12 (Lawrence Older), *The Old Woman from Yorkshire;* FSA 33F 8, listing; FSC 10.1.1 + FSC 10F 7-8 + Fowke 1967 154-55; FSE 20.2.4; Gainer 1975 148-49; G. Greig *FSNE #13, The Wily Auld Carle;* HTA; Hubbard 224-26; Hughes iv 66-71; *JAF 29* 179a, 179b-80; *JAF 40* 40; *JEFDSS* 7 197-99 + Karpeles 1974 ii 43-44 A; Karpeles 1971 151-52; Karpeles 1974 ii 44B; Karpeles 1975 ii 62 #57; P. Kennedy 1975 465-66; LCJ (Link), *The Old Woman from Trenton;* M. Leach 1965 282-83; Leisy 1964 176-77; Linscott 255-58; J. Lomax 1941 176 + A. Lomax 1960 512; McDowell 1947 67; McIntosh 1974 35-36; E. Moore 218-20, *Johnny Sands* [sic!]; Morton 1973 89-90, *Marrow Bones;* Musick 27 #23; *NA Ives* 1.7 + ATL 2140.11; *NA Ives* 1.148 + ATL 3155.3; Neely 151-52; *NEF* 5 75-76 + *NA Ives* 63.12; Peacock 261.64; P. Perkins 74-75 [with rôle reversal]; Polwarth 1970 10; Powell 34-37 (Wilkinson); *PTFLS 10* 165; *PTFLS 23* 207-9; Purslow 1965 55 + *EDS 27* 150; Rainey 9b-10; Randolph iv 248; Reeves 1958 204-5; *Sam Eskin* iv 99, *The Old Woman from Trenton; Sam Henry* #174; Scarborough 1937 239-40; Schinhan iv 240-42 #182, #359, #360; C. J. Sharp 1932 i 348; Silber 1973b 173a; Silverman 1975 i 177; *Steeleye Span* 51-52; Wilkinson i #201, #202, #289, #387, #409, #516; Wolford 93-94; ZDA 71.1.6, 71.1.7 + ZDA 71F 5-6.

Related texts (*Johnny Sands,* by John Sinclair),
  Comment, references: Belden 1940 237-39; Damon #30; Dichter #410; Friedman 451-52; *JAF 29* 178 (Kittredge); Laws Q 3; Randolph iv 246; Spaeth 1948 88.
  Broadsides, songsters: *Americam Dime* ii 33-34; *Annie Hindle* 21-22; *Billy Birch* 26-27; *Comic Songster* 57b; *Dan Kelly* 55-56; *Delaney #72* 23; *Delaney's Irish #2* 22; *Diprose* 1865 172; *Granite Songster* 49; *Henderson #11* 84; *Home Melodist* 49-50; *Howe* i 23b; *Howe* 1874 23b + *Trifet* 1890 23b + *Trifet* 1892 23b; *Jardin Mabille* 82-83; *Johnny Wild* 71-72; *MacLagan* 31; *Shilling Song Book* i 74; *Singer's Journal #4* 31; *Tony Pastor* viii 48-49; J. W. Turner 21b; *Wehman's Universal #12* 91.
  Sheet music: Boston: Oliver Ditson, 1842 (facsimile in Damon #30); Boston: Oliver Ditson, 1848? (facsimile of title in Levy

1971 32-33); London; Duff & Hodgson (reference in *MacLagan* 31).
  Texts: Arthur 17; Belden 1940 238a; Belden 1952 ii 448-49; Brewster 262-64, A - C; *British Minstrelsie* iv 22-24; Carpenter i 269-70 + Carpenter 1858 31-32 + Carpenter 1864 137-38; *CFB #3* 11; E. W. Cole 142b; Copper 1973 88, 222-23; Eddy 89; Emrich 1974 223; Flanders Index 221; FO 9.2.6; Goodwin 1956 109; Hamer 1973 39; Haynes ii 122-23; *Heart Songs* 42-43; Hudson 1936 198-99; *JAF 28* 174; *JAF 29* 179; *JAF 49* 235-36; *JAF 60* 204; Knox 66-67; LCJ (from Mindenville, New York); Levy 1971 32-33; LPS 260-01.1.4; Luther 108-9; McCaskey ii 168-69; Neely 175-76; *NYFQ 14* 210, listing; Ogilvie 114-15 #124; Ord 93; Piper (2); Pound 1922 114-16, A - B; *PTFLS 6* 223; Purslow 1968 60; Randolph iv 246-49; Shay 1961 158-60; Stout 65-68 #49; ZDA 71.1.8 + ZDA 71F 6b.

Text and tune relatives: none.
Tune relatives (*The Son of a Gambolier*),
  Comment, references: *Delaney #74* 22; Fuld 1955 63; Fuld 1971 515-16; Spaeth 1926 88-92.
  Tunes with this text or partial parody: Fuld 1971 515-16; Goodwin 1956 199; *Hold the Ford* 24-27 (by Alfred B. Sedgwick); C. Leach 115; Posselt 62b; C. Sandburg 1927 44; *Sam Henry #741;* Silverman 1975 ii 336; Spaeth 1926 88-90; *World's Best* 28-29.
  Tunes with college parodies: Brackett 142-43; D. C. Chamberlain 211b; *College Songs* 18; Garretson 63-65; Haufrecht 1970 206-11 (Charles Ives); Honorê 46-47; Kellogg 44-45; *Most Popular College* 38-39; Northwestern 50-52; Richman 56b; *University of Toronto* 64-65.
Tune relatives (*Dunderbeck's Sausage Machine*): Brand 1961 84; J. Cohen 117; Ehret 363-37; Spaeth 1926 90b.
  (*The Man Who Waters the Worker's Beer,* by Paddy Ryan): *CAY 2 #1* 13; Glazer 1970 209-10; *Labour Party* 15; *Pocket Song Book* 71; *PSB 3* #227; Silverman 1975 ii 189; *Walton* i 88.
  (*A Rambling Wreck from Georgia Tech*); *Collegiate* 58-59; Fuld 1955 63; E. A. Palmer 113, *A Hulluvan Engineer.*
  (*Teency Weency Spider* [distant]): Beattie 211c; Bley 81; Erdei 85 #119; FP 710.2.4 (Pete Seeger); Ruth Seeger 1948 126; Thurman 56, *Imsey Wimsey Spider;* Yolen 202.

(others): Ash 60-61, *Joe Bowers;* Asch 69; *AT #19* 11; ATL 168.7 #1b, 169.5 #1b, 170.1 #1a, 170.4 #1a; Brand 1960 24-25 + AFLP 1906; Bronson i 379 #10, *The Riddle Song;* Brune, tunes 8d; Chilton 176-77; Cray 58, 122; Dallin 10; Dawney 40; Dibblee 25, 31; Dolph 38-39; Durlacher 50; R. G. Edwards 1956 94 + R. G. Edwards 1971 101, R. G. Edwards 1971 140; Fife 1969 30; *Francis & Day* 1967 34, *Joe Bowers;* FSC 62.2.6; Glazer 1970 256-57; Kincaid 1937 51-53, *Zebra Dun;* Lingenfelter 507; *NA Ives* 1.88 + ATL 2207.2; *NA Ives 1.91 + ATL 2207.5; NA Ives* 64.6.9, 65.11.5; *NEF 5* 26 + ATL 2162.4 + *NA Ives* 1.36; NW 239.2.20 (Grant Rogers), *I'll Hit the Road Again;* E. A. Palmer 129, 178; R. Palmer 1971 58-59; *Powder River* 32, 34; *PSB 1* #18; *Ruff-Stuff* 10-11; Sampson 68-69; Shellans 44; Silber 1964 64-65; Silber 1973a 111; Silverman 1966 90; *Singabout 3 #3* 6; *SO 2 #4* 3; Spaeth 1926 90-92; Trident 12-13, 166-67; VRS 9094.1.5 (Joan Baez).

142.
Missie Mouse

Previously available: *Neighbors* 1941 8.
Variants: ATL 185.6
Adaptations: Cazden 1958 i 88-90 + Cazden 1978 88-90; FC 2997 (Haufrecht); Haufrecht 1943 6-7; SLP 68.1.4 (Robert and Louise De Cormier); Haufrecht 1965 i 9-11.
Comment, references: Belden 1940 494-95; Belden 1952 iii 154-56; *CAY 2 #9* 12-14 (Schoolbraid); Cazden 1961 iii-v; Dean-Smith Guide; Gardner 1939 455-59; *JAF 35* 394-99 (Kittredge); *JAF 52* 125-27 (Grace Smith); *JEFDSS 5* 38-40 (Gilchrist); *JFSS 8* 38-40, "A note on refrains of British ballads" (Gilchrist); P. Kennedy 1975 674-75 #294; Kidson 1890 29; Leisy 1966 234; W. R. Mackenzie 1928 373-74; NW 239J 1.1 (Paton); Opie 1951 177-81; *PTFLS 5* 5-48, "Some Texas versions of *The Frog's Courtin'*" (L. W. Payne, Jr.); Randolph i 402-10; *SFQ 26* 97-106 (Cuccinello); C. J. Sharp 1932 ii 413 #220, #221; Topic 12T198F A.7 (Lloyd); Wilkinson *510* 43-51; Yolen 116; ZDA 73F 6-7 (MacColl, Peggy Seeger).
Broadsides, songsters: *AFSPB 12* 140-41, *The Marriage of the Frogge and the Mouse* (facsimile of Thomas Ravenscroft, *Melismata,* of 1611) + W. Chappell 1859 i 88 + V. Jackson 32 + T. Wood 95; W. C. Ford #3120; 96

Old Songs 57, *The Frog and the Mouse;* Rollins 45 #435 (1580): *A most Strange weddinge of the ffrogge and the mowse; Street Literature* (E. Hodges, Ryle & Co.).
Texts: Abrahams 45-47; AFS L12B.1; Agay 12-13; *All Time* 76; G. Anderson 260-61; Beard 235-36; Bley 62-63; Boette 91-93, A—B; Bonar 104-6 A; Bullard 22-23; G. G. Carey 1971 113; R. Chase 1938 7 9; Chosky 187 #90; Cobb 187-91; S. N. Coleman 20-22; Combs 1967 218 #136 (8); Creighton 1950 250-54; Creighton 1971 178; Davis Index 208-14 (45); Duncan 226-27 #280; Dyer-Bennett 1971 74-76; Erdei 56-57 #84; Flanders 1931 122; Flanders 1953 11-13; Flanders *SR* 6.5.34, 6.1.35; Fowke 1954 170; FP 701.2.5 (Pete Seeger); FP 710.1.6 (Pete Seeger); Gainer 1975 162-63; Glass 1967a 56-58; D. Gordon 27-29; R. W. Gordon *AM* 20.4.25; R. W. Gordon *NYT* 86; Gundry 47; B. Ives 1953 24-25; Jameson 1967 69; *JEFDS 7* 105; *JIFS 4* 22, *Uncle Rat; JWFSS 1* 178; Kidson 1913 72-73; J. Langstaff 1955; N. Langstaff 64-66; Leisy 1974 38b-39 #34; Loesser 48-49; M. H. Mason 8, 9; E. Moore 251-52; *NA Ives* 1.41 + ATL 2166.4; *NA Ives* 66.9.2; R. Palmer 1971 6-7; *PTFLS 23* 255-56; Rimbault 1851 87-94; *Ring Ms.* 47-50 #19, #20; L. Roberts 194-95; Rosenberg Index #426 (20); Scarborough 1937 245-46; *SFQ 36* 29-32; C. J. Sharp 1902 *A Book of British Song* #49; Shelton 184-85; Shoemaker 268; SLP 68J A.4; *Songs to Keep* 5; Sturgis 18-21; Talley 190-95; Topic 12T198 A.7c; *True Blue* 82; Virginia Writer's Project 16-19; VRS 1031B.2 + VRS 1031J 2.2; Wessels 34-35; Wilkinson i #66, #382, #383, #543, #599; Wilkinson *510* 35-42; H. R. Wilson 26-28; Winn 58-59; Wyman 1916 29; Wyman 1920 93; Yolen 116-17; ZDA 73.2.5.-.8 + ZDA 73F 7-8.
Related texts (Amo Amas, by John O'Keefe): Buck 1916 4; Carpenter 1864 154-55; *Nightingale* 9; *Scottish Students* 55; *Songster's Repostiory* 279; *Vocal Library* 390 #1039.
(Heigho, Says Rowley),
   Comment, references: *JAF 35* 397-98 (Kittredge); P. Kennedy 1975 674 #294; Kidson 1890 29.
   Broadsides, songsters [*indicates inclusion of the usual tune]: *Banner Songster* 53-54; Carpenter 1858 71-72; *D'Alcorn #1* *46-47; *Davidson* i *166-67; FHE 300-301, from *The Yankee Songster's Pocket Companion,* Gardiner, Maine 1824; *Great Comic Volume* ii *52 40;

Isaiah Thomas i 32, i 69; *KFQ* 9 *#1* 50
(reproduction of a Boston broadside,
ca. 1813); *Musical Cabinet* *20-21 #64;
Musical Repertory 52-54; *Nightingale*
*172; *Oliver* 28-29; *Penny Melodist*
*#20; *Singer's Companion* *172-73;
J. W. Turner *6a; *Vocal Library* 648
#1758.

Sheet music: Dichter i #387, listing of publication, Boston: Parker & Ditson, ca.
1840.

Texts: ATL 192.2.3 (Chauncey Blackmore); Barbeau 35-36; Bertail 34-35;
Bonar 107-9 C; Buck 1933 49b; Crane
24-25; Dominion 1280B.3; FH 5311.1.6;
S. B. Gould 1905a 88-89; H. K. Johnson
434; Karpeles 1974 ii 385-89, A-D; Karpeles 1975 i 65 #62; W. R. Mackenzie
373-74, 407 #155; MacMahon i 56-57 #
30; A. Mills 1949 20-21; Moffat *50* 13;
Opie 1951 177-81; Topic 12T198A.7d.

Parody texts: *American Star* 109-10,
Heigho! Says Thimble; American Star
158-59, *Alderman Gobble; Imperial* 263-
64, *Heigho! Says Neddy; Imperial* 343-
44, *Dash My Vig; Oliver* 40, *Heigho!
Says Thimble;* Prest i 91, *Heigho! So
Merrily; SMP* iii 121, *Heigho! Says
Thimble; SMP* iv 2, *Aha! Says Alder-
man Gobble; Universal Songster* iii 84,
*The Hungry Goat and the Cottage
Couch, or Heigho Says Winny;* Univer-
sal Songster iii 139, *"You're a Rum Sort
of Ghost," says Horatio; Universal
Songster* iii 268, *The Old Maid and the
Tom Cat.*

Tune only, as instrumental dance tune:
Boosey xii 9a; *Boosey* 1862a 8 *#25; Musical Bouquet #473* 65 *#4b (quadrille).*

(*Keemo Kimo*),

Broadsides, songsters: *Dime Melodist* 26-
27; *Street Literature* (E. Hodges; Ryle
& Co.); Wehman i 86.

Sheet music: *Musical Bouquet #804*
(1855); *Musical Treasury #839/40 6-8
(1858).*

Texts [*indicates with common tune]:
Abrahams *44-47; FC *7625.2.9; Ira
Ford *106b, 418-19, 450-51; Odum 1926
187; *Scottish Students* *310-11; *SO 26
#1* 31, *King Kong Kitchie Kitchie Ki-
Me-O;* Wier 1929 70-71.

(*The Young Man's Song*): Flanders 1939
180.

Text and tune relatives: none.

Tune, verse-form, refrain relatives,

1. **Tune and verse-form relatives** (Child 10,

The Twa Sisters),
(Comment, references): Bronson i 143-
44.
(Similar tune opening but longer verse-
form): *All Time* 20-21; Boette 164;
Bronson i 153-63 #27, #28, #29,
#35, #36, #39, #40, #41, #59; A.
Mills 1949 64-65.
(Similar verse-form): Bronson i 169-70
#61, #62, ##64, #68.
(Similar tune and similar verse-form):
AFS L7.A5 (Horton Barker) +
Bronson i 150 #67 + *SO 13 #2* 4;
Woodgate 1956 106-7.

2. **Verse-form relatives** (Child 277, *The Wife
Wrapt in Wether's Skin*): Bronson iv
162-68 #40, #41, #42, #42a, #45, #47,
#48, #51, #54. [See also notes to
#136, *Tinna Clinnama Clinchama
Clingo*].

3. **Tune, verse-form, refrain form and non-
sense syllable pattern** (Child 278, *The
Farmer's Curst Wife*),
(Similar verse-form): Bronson iv 199-
200 #47 (from a cylinder recording
by Phillips Barry); Bronson iv 202-3
#55.
(Similar refrain form and nonsense-
syllable pattern): Bronson iv 202-3
#55, 207-8 #63; Cutting 71-72; W. R.
Mackenzie 1928 64.
(Similar refrain form and refrain tune):
FA 2354.1.6 (from Cohocton, New
York: tune very similar to #142, but
with Rowley-type refrain); Hubbard
40-41. [See also notes to #137, *The
Devil and the Farmer's Wife*].

4. **Other similarities in refrain forms and syllable patterns,**
(Similar refrain form and similar refrain
tunes, for text relatives of #142):
Creighton 1932 194-95; Gardner 1939
455-57 A.
(Similar refrain forms and nonsense
syllable pattern, for other texts):
Harlow 70-71, *I Met a Girl in Portland Street.*

5. Disregarding the refrain, **similar verse-
forms and similar tunes** for text relatives of #142),
(Similar verse-forms): *FST 3* 24-25
#10; Hubbard 386-87 A, 388-89 C; B.
Ives 1962 54-55; Kincaid i 16; McIntosh 1974 49-51; *PTFLS 5* [Payne ar-
ticle] 33-34 #12 "type C", 34 #13
"type D", 45-46 #41 "type F"; Randolph i 405-7 E, 408-9 G, 410 I; Scar-

borough 1925 48, 48-50; Ruth Seeger 1948 116-17; N. I. White 218.

(Similar verse-forms and similar tunes): Brewster 229 B, 237 F; S. N. Coleman 20-22; Cox 1939 174 A, 177 C, 178-79 D; Creighton 1950 250-51 A; Creighton 1971 176-77; Eddy 137-38 A; Frey 1941 177; Gardner 1939 457 58 B; Glazer 1961 51-52; Haufrecht 1959 29; M. E. Henry 395-96 C; B. Ives 1953 24-25; M. Johnson 7; Kolb 168-69; Landeck 1944 36-37; Leisy 1966 234; Linscott 200; Petrie #647; *PTFLS* 5 [Payne article] 35-43 #14-#20; Randolph i 404 C; Raph 29-31; Richardson 78-79; C. Sandburg 1927 143; Scarborough 1925 46-48; Scarborough 1925 50-52 (for *Old Bangum*); Scarborough 1937 245-46 A, 420; Schinhan v 89 E, 91 CC, 92-93 EE; Pete Seeger 1961 56; C. J. Sharp 1932 ii 312 A, 315 D, 316 E, 317-18 F, 318 G, 319 H, J, K; *SO 12 #3* 18-19; Thomas 1931 154.

6. **Similar tune and verse-form** (*A-Roving*),
   Comment, references: AFS L26F 9 Emrich; C. F. Smith 59; Wilkinson i #313.
   Tunes with this text: Abrams 20a; AFS L26A.5; *All Time* 15b, *All 'Round My Hat;* Armitage 1926 180; Asch 18-19; Ashbee ix 36-37; Brand 1961 143; Brune, tunes 6b; Bullen 11 [only the refrain is similar]; Cazden 1958 ii 24-27 + Cazden 1973 24-27 + RLP 12-603.1 (Milt Okun); Chilton 4 [text adapted]; CL 948.2.1; M. Cohen 1966 78 [text adapted]; Colcord 83; Cray 18-19; F. J. Davis 68-69; DL 8413.1.2; Doerflinger 56; Ehret 44-45; Elson 1702-3; *Ernest Newton* 46; FA 2312.1.9 (Alan Mills); Farnsworth 1909 100-101; Finger 156-57; *Francis & Day* 1952 18-19; Goss 1927 16; Grainger #153; Hansen 9a [second half only]; Harlow 49-51; Hazlewood 90-91; Heaton 24-25; Hille 16-17; G. Hitchcock 17-19; Hugill 48-52; *Immortalia* 132-37 (bawdy); B. Ives 1953 114-15 + B. Ives 1956 104-5 + B. Ives 1962 70-71; *JFSS 2* 245; King 23; Kolb 120-21; *Labour Party* 44; MacMahon i 134-35 #71; Mitchell 34-35; *Most Popular College* 68; *Northwestern* 74; *Pocket Song Book* 2-3; Ratcliff 130-31; Richman 36a; Sampson 12-

13; *Scottish Students* 130; C. J. Sharp 1914 28-29 + *Novello #263* 12-13 #1285 + C. J. Sharp *Selection* ii 22-23 + *Sing Care Away* iv 58; Shay 1961 76-77; Silber 1965 36; Silverman 1975 ii 274; *Sing Together* 77a; SL 206.1.2; C. F. Smith 60-61; Terry 1921 ii 6 7, 8 9; Trevine 2 3; *University Songbook* 206-7; Waite 1877 ii 74; Waite 1890 96; Whall 61-62; Wier 1918a 24b; Wilkinson i #313; Woodgate 1951 52; Wrubel 26-27.

7. **Similar tune, verse-form and related refrain** (*Lukey's Boat*): Blondahl 44-45 ("Aha! fala fala me riddle-I-day"); Creighton 1932 274 ("Aha, doodle I day"); Doyle 1940 71 + Doyle 1955 40 + Doyle 1966 43; Fowke 1954 46-47; Greenleaf 254-55; A. Mills 1958 28-29.

8. **Tune relatives** for the final refrain, complete form (*Nancy Dawson*),
   Comment, references: W. Chappell 1840 i 94 #98; W. Chappell 1859 ii 718-20; S. B. Gould viii p. vii; *JEFDSS* 5 31-40; Rabson 36-37.
   Texts only: G. A. Stevens 235-36 #181 (1771).
   Tunes with this text: W. Chappell 1840 ii 49c #98; W. Chappell 1859 ii 719; *Gardens* [a London broadside, ca. 1770]; S. B. Gould viii 50-51; M. H. Mason 13; O'Shaughnessy 1975 45, *Howden Fair;* R. Palmer 1973a 26 #1; Rabson 36-37 (from *The Universal Magazine*, London, October 1760 208); C. J. Sharp 1902 120-21 #56; Silber 1973a 150; Simpson 503-4; *Sing Care Away* i 49b; Vernon 18 [new text].
   [A broadside of text and tune, late eighteenth century, in Morrison Library, University of California at Berkeley, M1619.C654].
   Tunes (instrumental): *Boosey #6* 8a; *Chappell 1863* 28 #73; *Chappell 100* ii 7 #18; Emmerson 116; Keller 1974 34a; Keller 1975 38; *Musical Bouquet #435* 8 #5; *Musical Bouquet #472* 65 #4c; *Musical Budget 7* 953b; *New Preceptor* 20d; Riley i 93 #242; Roche ii #313; *Whittier Perkins* 47e.

9. **Tune relatives** for the final refrain, comprising first section of *Nancy Dawson*, with full cadence, (*The Mulberry Bush*),

Comment, references: Fuld 1971 378;
SFQ 6 187 (Cox).

Tunes with this text: Bertail 90; Bley
9; Buchtel #79; Buck 1933 35b;
Bucke i 31; Bullard 106a; Crane
10; Dearmer 1915 79; *Everybody's
Favorite* 64a; Ira Ford 257; Fowke
1969 16 #8; Fuld 1971 378; Gillington 1913 5; Goldstein 111; Gomme
i 404; *JAF 33* 113-14 #33; Kidson
1916 75; Mansion 41-42; C. G.
Marsh 14; Moffat *50* 32a; Neal 38;
Newell 86; Noble 1912 119b-20;
Poston 1961 40; Ratcliff 157; H.
Sandburg 9; *SFQ 6* 187; Wessels
19; Whitehead 200; Wier 1915
186a; Wier 1918a 303b; Wier 1918b
108b; Wilkinson *510* 19, 36; Winn
172; Wolford 56; Woodgate 1956
76-77.

(*Gathering Nuts in May*): Beckwith 49
#39; Buck 1933 11b; Dearmer 1915
69; Erdei 86 #120; Gillington 1909a
14; Gomme i 424; *JAF 31* 178 #6;
Kidson 1916 31; C. G. Marsh 64;
Miscellanea i 73; Newell 236; Poston
1961 36; Randolph iii 373.

(*I Saw Three Ships A-Sailing*): Buck
1933 62b; Bucke i 35; A. T. Davison
1922 20 #24; Dearmer 1915 21 #20;
Dearmer 1928 36 #18; Karpeles 1974
ii 478 B; Kidson 1916 16-17; *Novello
#245* 14-15 #1180 (C. J. Sharp) +
Karpeles 1974 ii 477 A + Karpeles
1975 i 58 #55; Poston 1961 128;
Poston 1965 8-9; Tobitt 166-69; D.
Warner 47; W. G. Whittaker i 2-3;
W. J. Whittaker 116-17 #41.

(others) [* indicates instrumental tune]:
C. B. Adams 54; *All Time* 18a, *Dash-
ing Away with the Smoothing Iron*;
E. D. Andrews 135 #71; Arany 8;
Bardeen 1875 20b; Bertail 39, 95,
101; Browne 541; Bucke i 39; Bullard
106b; *Canadian Boys* 47 #21; *CAY 3
#11* 7, 11; R. Chase 1949 48; R.
Chase 1956 189; Creighton 1950 262,
264; *Crosby* 1812 266-67, *The Great
Booby*; Dearmer 1928 7 #3; Downes
234; Durlacher *46; *EDS 31* 64; R. G.
Edwards 1971 271; *Everybody's Fa-
vorite* 61a, *Lazy Mary*; *Everybody's
Favorite* 63a; Farnsworth 1909 96;
Fitz 1846 26; Geri 48; Gillington
1909a 4; Gillington 1909b 2-3, 4, 13,
18-19; Gillington 1913 1-2, 7-8;
Goldstein 107; Gomme i 9, 369;

Gomme ii 196, 197, 228a, 233a, 233b,
233d; Gomme 1909 #937 2; Graeme
82-83 + *Clancy* 1971 82-83; *Handy*
1940 8; *Howe* 1864a *9k; *JAF 25* 271
#4; *JAF 44* 7a, 8; *JEFDSS 9* 87; Jus-
tus 40, 46, 48; Kerr iv *16a #4; Kidson 1916 10, 25, 61; Kirkell *77;
Kraus 87; Levy 1971 305; C. G.
Marsh 100; McCaskey iv 101 #1;
McConathy 273b; McIntosh 1948 50,
53, 56a; Muir 23; Neal 46, 47; Neely
195; Newell 96 #32, 243, 244; Nutt i
42; Nutt ii 57-60; O'Sullivan 29;
W. A. Owens 5; *Penny Melodist
#21, The Wonderful Eater*, by L. M.
Thornton; Price 98, 108, 122, 138; M.
Raven ii 54; Rohrbough 1931a 5;
SFQ 6 191, 201, 208, 241; C. J. Sharp
1908 ii 4-5; C. J. Sharp 1932 ii 248,
Billy Grimes; L. O. Smith 36b, 37b;
Society of Brothers 2-3; Sumner 18,
21a; M. J. Swan 91 + G. P. Jackson
1942 169 #162, *Lancaster* [tune in
minor]; *University Songbook* 75, *The
Bait of the Average Fisherman*; Wessels 18a; W. J. Whittaker 114-15 #40,
118-19 #42; Wier 1918a 231b; Wier
1918b 88b, 95; Wilkinson i #450,
#678; Winn 17; Wolford 30; Wood-
gate 1956 106-7.

143.
The Old Tobacco Box

Previously available: none.

Variants: none.

Adaptations: Cazden 1949B #4 (instrumental);
Cazden 1951a 18a (instrumental); Cazden
1955 32a; Cazden 1961 88; Silber 1973b 242a
[text only].

Comment, references: . Kennedy 1975 796; Silber 1973b 18 [re adaptations]; Spaeth 1948
73.

Broadsides, songsters: *Delaney #1* 2; *Wehman's Collection #24* 10.

Texts: C. S. Adams 131; E. C. Beck 1941 241,
Old Geezer; Brewster 353; FA 2187B.5 +
FA 2187F 15; Flanders 1931 50; Gardner
1939 483, listing; Ch. Kennedy 1952 187-88;
Kimball 165; Kincaid ii 17; LCJ (Donovan,
Scudder, Smyth, and five others); Linscott
243-44; Piper; *Ring Ms.* 124 #56; Silber 1964
32; C. L. Swan 112; *WF 24* 240, listing; N. I.
White 401.

Text and tune relatives: Ira Ford 38; Kentucky
1937 41; W. M. Lawrence 87; C. Sandburg

1927 432-33; Silverman 1975 ii 191; Wilkinson i #659; Wilkinson ii #1, #30; Wilkinson *128* 28b.

Tune relatives (*An Maidrín Ruádh, or The Little Red Fox*): Bunting 1840 ii 98a #129.

(*Do-Si Ballinet*): Cazden 1955 32a, 32b.

(*Down in a Coal Mine*): A. L. Lloyd 1952 125 + R. Palmer 1974b 52; Luboff 34-35; J. Raven 1972 29.

(*Let Erin Remember the Days of Old*, by Thomas Moore, "air: *The Little Red Fox*"): Bantock 1930c ii 8-9; Breathnach i 347; *British Minstrelsie* iv 136-37; Buck 1916 117; *Choice Irish Songs* i 72-73; W. Cole 60-61; Emerick 199-201; Graves 1928 39-40; Hatton 20-21; *Howe 1874* 199a + *Trifet 1890* 112a + *Trifet 1892* 112a; *Ireland's Songs* 27-29; H. K. Johnson 225-26; Lampe 1955 38; MacMahon ii 98-99 #50; McCaskey i 38; McCaskey 1899 160; McPheeley 9; T. Moore 62; D. H. Morrison ii 335; D. H. Morrison 1895 201; Murphy 55-56; *Musical Bouquet* #1761; S. H. Nicholson 84-85 #44; Stanford 1895 36-38; Stanford 1906a 112; Stanford 1958 114; Stevenson 1891 87-92.

(*The Little Beggarman*): Graeme 164-66 + Clancy 1971 164-66.

(others): *FST 3* 26-27 #11; Gallagher #57 (half-tune); Joseph 60; McCarthy 52 (first half of tune); R. A. Smith 1828a #76.

(instrumental) [* indicates title of *The Little Beggar Man* or *The Little Red Fox*): *Boosey 1862a* *29 #94; *Cavendish* #20 *24-25; Cazden 1951a 18a, 26a; Cazden 1955 32a; *Folk #1* *19; *Howe 1864a* *107i; McPheeley 278 #674, 316 #848; O'Neill *#390, #1748; O'Neill 1907 #921; *SFQ 6* 8-9 (Wilkinson); Wilkinson ii 198.

Unrelated tunes (*The Little Red Fox*): Breathnach i 342; W. Cole 68-70.

144.
Ta-ra-ra Boom, Hooray!

Previously available (#144 B): *Neighbors 1941* 10b.

Variants: none.

Adaptations: Haufrecht 1942 4-5; Haufrecht 1972 7-8.

Comment, references: Botkin 1937 142-43 #5; Botkin 1954 259.

Broadsides, songsters: none.

Texts: Botkin 1937 143 B, C; *Goldenseal 2 #3* 12; LCJ (Barnard); LCJ (R. C. Smith); Randolph iii 207 #452.

Related texts (*I Got a House in Baltimo'*): Work 241a.

Text and tune relatives [* tune by reference or refrain indication only]: Botkin 1937 143 A; Botkin 1937 *144 D; Botkin 1954 *259; C. L. Swan *133.

Tune relatives (*Ta-ra-ra-ra Boom-der-é* or *Ta-ra-ra Boom-de-ay*),

Comment, references: Boni 1952 23; J. Burton i 129-31; Fuld 1955 72; Fuld 1971 570-71; D. Gilbert 206-7; Goldberg 260, listing; M. Knapp 176; Levy 1971 182-83; M 481.246 iii #15, clippings; Mattfeld 202, listing; Spaeth 1948 258-59.

Broadsides, songsters: *Delaney #1* 8; *Fortey* 1894, 1905; Wehman #1259.

Song publications with music: Agay 190-91; Arany 12b-13; Boni 1952 23-25; De Vore 41; *Francis & Day* ii 10-11; *Francis & Day's Album* v 6-7; Fremont 299-301; Frey 1942 60-61 + Frey 1948 60-61; Fuld 1971 570; Gamse 146-47; Goodwin 1956 2; Hansen 183b; *Hitchcock* 1891 22-24; Lupton 2-3; M 481.246 i #10, *Boom Ta-Ra*; M 481.246 iii #15, *Ta-ra-ra-ra Boom-der-é*; MacLean 76-77; Ogilvie 100-101 #111; Spaeth 1926 164-65; Wilk 3; J. E. Winner 1894 186-88; *World's Best* 44-45.

Related texts (*I'm the Man that Wrote Ta-ra-ra Boom-de-ay*): Randolph iii 142-44; Wehman #1309.

Tune relatives (with dance calls): AFS 12311B.6 + EC 327.6 (Grover Hornbeck); Cazden 1955 13a [adaptation]; *Neighbors* 1941 10 (George Van Kleeck).

(with other texts): R. G. Edwards 1971 68-69; I. W. W. 3-4 + Lingenfelter 494-95 [tune indicated].

145.
The Lofty Giant

Previously available: none.

Variants: none.

Adaptations: none.

Comment, references: G. Greig *FSNE* #149; *JEFDSS 4* 113-21, "The song of marvels (or lies)" (Gilchrist); *JEFDSS 6* 15; Randolph iii 47; Topic 12T198F A.5 (Lloyd); R. V. Williams 1959 125.

Broadsides, songsters: none.

Texts: ATL 628.13, 629.1-.2 (Reuben Edwards); T. Burton ii 83; Cazden 1961 44-45; Cox 1925 47-49; *EDS 27* 82; Flanders 1934 20-21 *The Big Jeest*; WC Ford #3317; S. B. Gould 1974 74-75; G. Greig *FSNE* #149;

Hudson 1936 275; *Isaiah Thomas* i 40, ii 8; *JAF 4* 269-70; *JAF 40* 9; *JEFDSS 6* 1 + R. V. Williams 1959 101; *JEFDSS 6* 14-15; *JFSS 5* 292; Karpeles 1971 247-48; Knox 68-69; M. Leach 1965 278-79; Manny 258-60 + *NA Ives* 61.4; *NA Ives* 1.71 + ATL 2190.5; *NA Ives* 1.81 + ATL 2200.6; Peacock 24-25, 26-27, 28-29; Randolph iii 48, 49; Richardson 52; Topic 12T198A.5; *WF 20* 110-11.

Related texts (*Banbury Lying Song*): Farnsworth 1909 40-41 + Götsch 60a, 134b-35 + *Sam Eskin* i 58; Karpeles 1975 ii 64 #59; J. Langstaff 1969 88; *Novello* iii #212 6-7 #986 (C. J. Sharp) + Karpeles 1956 49 + *Sing Care Away* iv 30; Reeves 1958 69; D. Stewart 252.

(*Fooba Wooba*),

    Comment, references: W. Chappell 1859 i 76; *JEFDSS 4* 118-20 (Gilchrist); Simpson 776-77.

    Texts: Cazden 1961 90; *Cool Burgess* 27, *Flewy, Flewy; Deuteromelia* 68-69 + *CAY 2 #1* 3 + W. Chappell 1859 i 76 + Rimbault 1851 115-17 + Simpson 777 #518; Hudson 1936 274; *Harry Woodson* 1877 41, *Flewy, Flewy; JAF 39* 195; *JEFDSS 4* 118, 119a, 120; Randolph iii 200; Richardson 97 + A. Lomax 1960 260; C. Wells 1902 74-76; Wilkinson *510* 107-8.

(*Nottingham Fair*): AFS L20B.2; *All Time* 56; ATL 606.14; *Bob Hart* 25; Cazden 1961 4, *Danbury Fair*; Combs 1967 219 #139, listing; Creighton 1950 240-41; *Delaney #14* 26; J. Edwards 216; EKL 125.1.2 (Jean Ritchie); M. Leach 1965 276 B; *Pammelia* 17 #30; Randolph iii 201-3 + Emrich 1974 16-17; Ritchie 1953 30-33 + Ritchie 1963 105-7 + Ritchie 1965a 11 + Ritchie 1971 79 + *SO 25 #2* 20-21; C. J. Sharp 1932 ii 270; Silverman 1975 i 192a; *Singer's Journal #8* 61; *Universal Book* iv 29; Wolf Index #811, #1711; Wyman 1920 9.

(*The Swapping Song*),

    Comment, references: P. Kennedy 1975 683-85 #312; C. J. Sharp 1932 ii 413 #271.

    Texts: *All Time* 74; Belden 1952 ii 471-74; Botsford 23-24; Brand 1961 166; Cambiaire 78; Cazden 1961 28; *CFMJ 3* 43b; R. Chase 1956 174-75; Chosky 176 #68; Combs 1967 223 #174, listing; Cox 1939 ii 49-50, 51; Decca 573.2421 1A (Richard Dyer-Bennet); Dyer-Bennet 1971 152-54; Eddy 215-17; Flanders Index 247 #56; S. B. Gould 1905a 106-7; Horton 5-

6; B. Ives 1962 50-51 + B. Ives 1966 177-79; Jameson 1967 70-71; Karpeles 1974 ii 383-84, A - C; Karpeles 1975 ii 65 #60; Ch. Kennedy 1954 184-85; P. Kennedy 1975 670; Kincaid i 39; J. Langstaff 1960; LCJ (Batte, Faust); M. H. Mason 16a; Raine 11; Richardson 48-49; Ritchie 1964 12-13 + Ritchie 1965 7; L. Roberts 100-101; *Sam Eskin* iv 159; Schinhan iv 255-56; C. J. Sharp 1932 ii 307-9; Sturgis 7-9; C. L. Swan 52; Wilkinson i #561, #676; Wilkinson *510* 141-42; H. R. Wilson 42-43; Wyman 1920 13 + *Song Ballads* 63-64 #49.

(others): Boardman 20-21, *The Lancashire Liar*; Flanders 1934 30-33, *A True Story*; Moffat 1904 55, *When I Was a Little Girl*; O'Sullivan 173-74, *Amhrán na mBréag* [*Song of Lies*].

[See also notes to #151, *The Darby Ram*].

146.
The Knickerbocker Line

Previously available: none.

Variants: none.

Adaptations (combining #146 A and #146 B): AFS 12312B.8; AFS 19250.10 (Laura Stein); Cazden 1958 i 94-95 + Cazden 1978 94-95; Cazden 1961 74; FH 5257.2.7 (Pete Seeger, Ed Renahan); *Neighbors* 1944 26 (Cazden); SLP 72.1.3 (Robert and Louise De Cormier); *SO 7 #2* 6-7.

Comment, references (*The Knickerbocker Line*): Cazden 1958 i 117 + Cazden 1978 117; *EDS 24* 38 (Peter Kennedy); Fowke 1965 193-94; P. Kennedy 1975 728 #323; Meredith [a private communication to *Sing Out,* 10.9.57]; O'Shaughnessy 1975 78-79 #21; Peggy Seeger 1960a 52 #54; SLP 72J A.3 (Cazden).

(The Knickerbocker Stage Co.): Botkin 1956 133, The Knickerbockers; Botkin 1956 209-12, The Bowery; Botkin 1956 321-54, stories of stage driver life; Jenkins 231; *NYCD* 1857-1866; *NYHSQB 22* (1938) 125-29, "Omnibus lines in New York City in 1855."

(James Unsworth): Reynolds 25; Reynolds, photos facing 190, 192; Wittke 235-36. [See also notes to #44, *Comic Banjo Song*].

Broadsides, songsters (*The Stage Driver*): Billy Birch 18-19; Unsworth 11-12.

Texts: *Singabout Songster* 38b.

Derived texts (*George Henry*): Waite ii 22 + *Northwestern* 22.

(*The Pioneer Stage Driver*),
    Comment, references: Lingenfelter 57.
    Texts: *Clampers* 17; Lengyel ii 74; Lingenfelter 56-57, *The Overland Stage Driver*, "tune: The *High Salary Driver of the Denver City Line*."

Related texts (*The Broadway Stages*): Converse 1864 27-28.

(*The City Railroad Car*): Budworth 57-58.

(*The Great Northern Line*): Lahey 60-61; Meredith 1968 273 + *Singabout 4 #4* 7 + *Singabout Songster* 32b-33.

(*The Soda-Water Man*, by James Unsworth): De Marsan #378; *Unsworth* 1859 52.

(*Waiting for a Broadway Stage*): *Broadway Stage* 2-3.

Related refrain texts [* indicates tune relative of #146 A]: E. C. Beck 1956 226-27, *Camp Seven Song;* FG *3507.1.1c (Sam Larner) + FG 3507F 4, *The Dogger Bank;* Gill 1917 8-9, *The Collier Lads;* J. Lomax 1934 28-29, *Ten Thousand Miles from Home;* J. Lomax 1934 461, *Erie Canal Song;* Peggy Seeger 1960a *61, *The Dogger Bank.* [See also notes to #2, related texts (*Cruise of 'The Bigler'*)].

Text and tune relatives (#146 A): *EDS 24* 38 + P. Kennedy 1975 707-8 + *Singabout 4 #4* 6; Grainger #216 [tune and title only]; Meredith 1968 195; *NA Ives* 1.159 + ATL 3166.5; O'Shaughnessy 1975 78-79 #21; Peggy Seeger 1960a 61.

Tune relatives (#146 A) [* tune indicated but not notated]: Joe Wilson *241-42, *Sally Lee; Tommy Armstrong *38-40, *Corry's Rat.* [See also notes to #2, *Cutting Down the Pines*].

Text and tune relatives (#146 B): none.

Tune relatives (#146 B) (*Itisket, Itasket*),
    Comment, references: Chosky 138 #13; Fuld 1971 113-14; Mattfeld 521.
    Tunes with this text: ATL 181.3.17b, *Tattle Tale* (from New York City); Bley 51; Botkin 1944 806; Brand 1961 147; Bullard 101b; Cazden 1974 6-7 #2; Chosky 150 #13; Downes 232; Erdei 4 #8, 6 #11; Fowke 1969 11 #3; Fuld 1971 113-14; W. M. Lawrence 25; Marsh 16; Newell 169 (from New York); Noble 1912 120b; W. A. Owens 7; Silverman 1975 i 348b; Welsch 283-84; Wessels 24; Wier 1918b 85a; Winn 176-77; Wolford 59.

Tune relatives (#146 B) (others): Botkin 1944 799; Chosky 148 #7, 149 #9, 151 #14, 151 #15; Erdei 3 #6, 4 #7, 12 #24; Ira Ford 254; Fowke 1969 11 #2, 26 #19; Goldstein 115;

JWFSS 2 45, "as nursery penillion"; M. Knapp 60, "the traditional melody of abuse"; McQuillen ii 43 (instrumental); E. Parry 6; Poston 1961 24; J. Warner 19a.

Unrelated tune (*The Knickerbocker Polka*, by C. Burckhardt): *Boosey* i 10-12.

147.
Lookit over Yonder

Previously available: AFS 12309B4 + EC 699.4.

Variants: none.

Adaptations: Cazden 1961 89; FH 5311.2.6 (Barbara Moncure).

Comment, references (*The Old Gray Goose*): Damon #41, with facsimile of the sheet music publication of 1844; Dichter #1645, listing of the same; Spaeth 1948 592.

Broadsides, songsters (*The Old Gray Goose*) [* with tune as in sheet music; ** with "new" tune or "tune as sung by the Christy Minstrels"]: *Beadle's Half-Dime #27* 3; *Davidson* iii **31; *Elton* 316; *Ethiopian Glee Book #2* **79 + *Boni* 1952 **294-95 + *Emerick* **210-12 + R. Lloyd 1959 **96; *Howe* 1877 *226b + *Trifet* 1890 *135b + *Trifet* 1892 *135b; *I Want to See* 53; *Musical Treasury* **#904; *Negro Forget-Me-Not* 185-a 98; *Negro Melodist* 33-34; *White's Serenaders* **5; Wolf Index #810.

Tune relatives (instrumental): *Boosey* 1862b **49 #160; *Howe* 1859 **17c; B. Mackenzie **#204.

Texts: Chosky 167 #51; Flanders *SR* 28.1.34; Piper + Peterson Index 38; Wilkinson i #493.

Related texts (*Cum Plung-Gum*): *Bob Hart* 23; *Mammoth* 89-90.

(*There's No One Like Jesus*): Odum 1909 61a + *JAF 41* 572 #30 + Odum 1925 93.

Unrelated texts (*The Grey Goose*),
    Comment, references: J. Lomax 1936 108-10; *SFQ 18* 165-74, "The flight of the Grey Goose" (John Greenway); *SO 3 #11* 8-9 + *RSO #7* 52-53.
    Texts and tunes: AFS 15A + A. L. Lloyd 1965 85 #52; AFS L3.B.5, L53.2.4; Brand 1961 81; *CAY 4* 185b-86; Dallin 89; Erdei 110 #150; FA 2941B.13 (Huddie Ledbetter); FP 4.2.1 (Huddie Ledbetter); FP 20.2.6 (Huddie Ledbetter); FP 710.2.3 (Pete Seeger); B. Ives 1962 126-27; J. Langstaff 1969 89; J. Lomax 1959 27; MJV 59.1.1 (Burl Ives); *SFQ 18* 171-73; Shelton 180; Silverman 1975 ii

32a; *Sing 4* 34a; J. Warner 49-50; Yolen 152-53.
(*The Old Gray Goose*): Creighton 1950 257.
Text and tune relatives: none.
Tune relatives (*The Baptists*, by Larry Gorman [refrain portion]): Edw. Ives 1964 38-39 + ATL 2163.6 + *NA Ives* 1.38; *NA Ives* 1.31 + ATL 2157.3.
(Child 214, *The Dewy Dens of Yarrow*): Flanders 1953 236 + Bronson iii 327 #42.
[See also #155, *John Styles and Susan Cutter*].

148.
Sally Come Up

Previously available: none.
Variants: none.
Adaptations: none.
Comment, references: Dichter 1941 150; Dichter i #1656; Lengyel i 107-17.
Broadsides, songsters [* indicates with tune]: *Beadle's Dime* #15 62; *Beadle's Half-Dime* #34 10; *Billy Birch* 29-30; *Bob Hart* 52-53; *Bryant* 1861 42-43; *Bryant* 1863 40-41; *Bryant* 1864 12-14; *Buckley* *95; *California Checklist* 129 (a broadside by T. C. Boyd, San Francisco); *Comic Songster* *12-13; *Davidson* iii *1-3; *Eaton* #6 39-40; *Formosa* 57-58; *Fortey* 1905, "new version"; *Howe* 1874 *38-39 + *Howe* 1877 *201 + *Howe* i *38-39; *Mammoth* 32, 86; *Singer's Journal* #29 195; Wehman #692; Wehman ii 42-43; Wolf Index #2056 (broadsides by De Marsan and by Wrigley).
Sheet music, folios: Boston: Oliver Ditson, 1863 (listed in Dichter 1941 150); Boston: Russell & Patee, 1869 (listed in Dichter i #1635, with facsimile title page in Marks, facing 38); *Heart Songs* 206-7; London: *Musical Treasury* #993/4 (1859); *Minstrel Songs* 1882 148-49; New York: Henry Tolman, 1862; Wier 1918a 430a + Wier 1929 230 + Wier 1931 190.
Texts: Piper + Peterson Index 71-72; LCJ (from New York City).
Related texts, adaptations: Dodgson 813, *The Mock Turtle's Song;* Fortey 1905, "new version"; *Street Literature* (a London broadside by Ryle & Co.); Joe Wilson 37-38, 100-101.
Text and tune relatives: none.
Tune relatives (instrumental): *Davidson* iv 21a, 23b (quadrille); *Howe* 1864a 135a, *Sally Come Up Schottische; Musical Treasury* #1177/8 2a (waltz); *Musical Treasury* #1189/90 4-5 #3.

149.
Simple Little Nancy Brown

Previously available: none.
Variants: AFS 10505B.34 (Frank Joy, recorded 10.7.50 by Sam Eskin).
Adaptations: Cazden 1958 ii 86 + Cazden 1973 86; Cazden 1961 57; FH 5311.1.4 + FH 5311F 7-8 (Harry Siemsen).
Comment, references: Cazden 1958 ii 122 + Cazden 1973 122.
Broadsides, songsters (*Fol de Rol Dol*): Delaney #59 22.
Sheet music (*Fol de Rol Dol*, by Harry Williams and Egbert Van Alstyne): New York: Jerome H. Remick & Co., 1905.
Texts: none.
Unrelated text titles (*Nancy Brown*, by J. C. Quant and W. G. Parkinson): *Musical Budget 7* 1102-3.
(*Nancy Brown*, by Clifton Crawford),
    Comment, references: Kinkle ii 756 #388; Marks 251; Spaeth 1948 315.
    Texts and tunes: Wilk 47.
(*Nancy Brown* [a musical], by Frederick Ranken and Henry Hadley),
    Comment, references: Kinkle i 14, ii 662 #247.
(*Nancy Brown*): Lynn 1963 20 #31.
Text and tune relatives: none.
Tune relatives (*Gabhaid Sinn an Rathad Mòr*, or *Stewart's March*, words by John Breck McKendrick): A. C. MacLeod 70-72; Moffat 1907 74-75; Robertson 153c (instrumental); C. Stewart 40-42; Thomson 33-36.
(*Ka Foozle-Um*, by S. Oxon),
    Comment, references: Cray 212-13; Spaeth 1948 166.
    Broadsides, songsters: *Beadle's Half-Dime* #9 9; *Engel* 200a; *Henderson* #4 28; *Owen Fawcett* 13; *Tony Pastor 201* 22-23.
    Texts: Spaeth 1926 148-49 (with a distinct tune by Frederick Blume).
Related texts (*Abdulla Bulbul Ameer*, by Percy French),
    Comment, references: Fuld 1971 82; Goodwin 1956 240b; Healy 1966 4-10.
    Texts [* indicates with usual tune]: Best *56-57; Brand 1961 *78; Brune *12b, 6b; *Canadian Boys* *278-79 #165; *Columbia University* 112-13; Cray 70 (bawdy parody); Dallin *2-3; Donnell *38; *Everybody's Favorite* *157b; French *9-10; Fuld 1971 *84; Goodwin 1956 *240b; Hansen *2; Healy 1966 5-7, *8-9; C. Leach *82-83; E. A. Palmer *218-23; Posselt *86; C. Sand-

burg 1927 *344-45; *Scottish Students* *244-45; Shay 1961 *3; Silverman 1975 ii *216-17; Spaeth 1926 *145-46; Thurman *9-10; *Treasure Chest* 1936 *46-47; Trident 26-27; Wrubel *12-13.

(*The Maid of Phillippopolis*): Cazden 1961 64-65, *Tell-a-me-True;* Converse 1888 100-101; Honoré 30-31; Rosenfeld 42-43.

(*Zuleika*, by Andrew B. Stirling and Alfred Doyle) [** indicates bawdy parody]: Brand 1960 *86-87 + AFLP **1806.1.1; *Delaney #38* 20; *Immortalia* **50-54.

Tunes with this text [* indicates instrumental tune, ** indicates bawdy parody]: Bigelow 108; Brand 1960 **20-21 + AFLP **1884; Brand 1961 54-55; S. N. Coleman 122-23; Cray **72-73, *Kathusalem; Empire Book* 126-27; Hitchcock #90 (1869); Hitchcock i 103; Kerr i *20 #15, *Kafoozalum* (Highland Schottische); C. Leach 86-87; Lynn 1961 34-35; *Musical Bouquet #3810/1* *3b-4a, *The Bam-Boo-Zle-em Polka; Musical Bouquet* *#3827, *It's All Bamboozle-'Em* (piano variations by Charles Grobe); Nettleinghame **66b; Niles 1929 23-26 (parody text); *Songs for Harvard* 95-96; *Songs of Columbia* 50.

(*London Bridge*),

Comment, references: Fuld 1971 337; *SFQ 6* 231-33 (Cox).

Tunes with this text: Bertail 37; Bley 7; Buchtel #81; Bullard 100a; Cazden 1974 10-11 #4; Creighton 1971 173; Dearmer 1915 70a; Erdei 74 #105; Farnsworth 1909 83-84; Ira Ford 262; Fowke 1969 30 #24; Fuld 1971 337; Geri 50; Gillington 1909a 18; Goldstein 109; Gomme i 192, 333-350; Gomme 1909 #926 2, 4; Jones 181b; Kidson 1916 6; Linscott 35-36; Mansion 70-71; C. G. Marsh 32; Newell 209 [text only], 253; Noble 1912 119a; Nutt ii 15; P. Perkins iii 6a; Ritchie 1965a 14; *Sam Henry #48g, Broken Bridges;* Schinhan v 532a; L. O. Smith 36a; L. Warner 40a; Welsch 295; Wessels 45; Wier 1918b 88a; Wilkinson *510* 1; Woodgate 1956 117.

(*Will You Go to Sheriffmuir*),

Comment, references: Brander 192-93; *CAY 1* #6 10-11 (Shoolbraid); G. F. Graham iii 111; J. Greig i p. iv; Thomson 33-36.

Tunes with this text [* indicates instrumental tune]: *Boosey* 1862a *51 #164; *Commu-*

nity iii *4a, *Ka-foo-zalum;* G. F. Graham iii 110-11; Hogg i 149 + *CAY 1* #6 9c + J. Greig i 64-65; P. Kennedy 1951 *20 #40, *London Bridge (Ka-foo-zalum);* Kidson 1913 156-57; MacColl 1965 85; Maver 88b #176; S. H. Nicholson 82 #42; Oswald vi *10b-11; R. A. Smith i 18a.

Unrelated tunes (*Sheriffmuir*): Chambers 60-62; J. Johnson #282; Ritson 1794 ii 56-57 #116. [See also notes to #1, *A Shantyman's Life*].

(others),

Comment, references (as *penillion* tune): *JWSS 2* 46b; J. Parry vi 1.

Tunes: Beckwith 32 #26, 46-47 #37a, 47-48 #37b; Behan 1965 58; Boette 103; *British Students* 245, *To the Old Road We Will Hie;* N. Buchan 1962 136; Dallas 1973 178; Durlacher 106a; Gillington 1909b 20-21 #16; Gomme i 33a, 92; Gomme ii 102; Gomme 1909 #1112 14-15; Kidson 1916 26, 58; M. Raven iii 102, *Hark, the Robbers;* Whyte #42; ZDA 66.1.4, Child 10, *The Twa Sisters.*

150.
If I Were as Young as I Used to Be

Previously available: *Neighbors* 1950 32.
Variants: none.
Adaptations: none.
Comment, references: none.
Broadsides, songsters: *Hamlin Wizard Oil, Not so Young as I Used to Be.*
Texts (*Uncle Joe*): Flanders *SR* 5.5.35; LCJ (Olmsted); LCJ (from Bisby Lake, New York); Piper (dated 1884).
Text and tune relatives (*Uncle Joe*): Gerry 160-62; Kincaid 1937 56; D. H. Morrison i 32-33.
Tune relatives: none.
Unrelated tune (*Uncle Joe*, a dance tune variant of *Miss McLeod's Reel*): J. Cohen 80-81; Ira Ford 47b; N. Langstaff 18-19; J. Lomax 1941 58 + A. Lomax 1960 228; L. Owens 1949 32a; L. Owens 1950 127; Ruth 6 #13; Silverman 1975 i 354a; Thede 100.

151.
The Darby Ram

Previously available: none.
Variants: none.
Adaptations: Cazden 1961 87.
Comment, references [* on nursery forms, **

on bawdy forms]: Brewster 319; Cray **180-82; Dean-Smith Guide; *FMBS #2* 8-13, "T'owd Tup" (P. and G. Smith); *JEFDSS* 5 23-30, "*The Old Tup* and its ritual" (Gatty); P. Kennedy 1975 679 #304; Legman **424-25; Leisy 1966 80-82; Nettel 32; Opie 1951 *145-46 #129; Randolph i 398; Reeves 1958 103; RLP 12-618J 1.1 (Lloyd); C. J. Sharp 1932 ii 408 #141; Topic 12T198F B.9 (Lloyd); Wilkinson *510* 111-12.

Broadsides, songsters: A broadside, before 1800, in the Julian Marshall Collection, Houghton Library, Harvard University; *Orpheus* 1832 86-87.

Texts [** indicates bawdy version]: ATL 606.4; Bantock 1930a ii 16-17; Beard 229-30; Belden 1952 ii 439-40; Brewster 319-21, A - B; Broadwood 1893 44-47 + Bantock 1914 57-58 + Loveless 40-41 + Maitland #13241 (1921) + C. J. Sharp 1902 88-89 #411; *B&S #3* [12]; I. Campbell 74-75; L. Chappell 182; R. Chase 1956 134-36; Collinson 1946 12-13; Combs 1967 219 #138, listing; Cray **17; Creighton 1950 241-42 + Bissell 14-15; Cutting 72-73; Davis Index 134-36 (18); Dibblee 97; Emrich 1974 17-18; Flanders Index 218 (9); Flanders Index 248 #18, #96, #197; Flanders Index 250 #201; *Folk #2* 9-10, *Little Tup;* R. Ford 1904 124-25; FP 711.1.4 (Pete Seeger); *Francis & Day #26* 40; FSA 15.2.12 + FSA 15F 26 (Lawrence Older); FSI 65.2.1 + FSI 65F 6; Fuson 58; Hamer 1967 21; Hamer 1973 51-52, The Old Tup; M. E. Henry 175-78; HTA (7); Hudson 1936 127, 273-74; Hugill 437-38; *JAF 18* 51; *JAF 36* 377; *JAF 39* 173; Karpeles 1974 ii 375-77, A - B; Karpeles 1975 i 66 #63; Keynote K-108.517B.2 (Richard Dyer-Bennet); LCJ (Harrigan); LCJ (Mills); Legman **424 (a fragment); J. Lomax 1941 104-7 + A. Lomax 1964 24; Luboff 230-31; Lynn 1961 200; McCarthy **30-31; Meredith 1968 112-13; Nettel 33-34; S. H. Nicholson 140 #72; *NYFQ 7* 75; Opie 1951 145-46; Opie 1955 205; Peterson Index 27; *PMLA 39* 478 (Beckwith); *PTFLS 5* 157-59; *PTFLS 23* 230-31; Reeves 1958 102; Reeves 1960 92; RLP 12-618.1.1 (A. L. Lloyd); L. Roberts 101-2; Peggy Seeger 1964 20; Shekerjian 42-43; Shoemaker 266b; Silber 1973b 404c; Silverman 1975 ii 181, *Birmingham Bull; Singabout 1 #4* 16 + *Singabout Songster* 5a; P. S. Smith 28-31, *The Old Tup; SO 7 #4* 6-7; Stekert 1969 B 1, N 29; H. Thompson 1940 153; Topic 12T198B.9; D. Warner 39b; *WF 24* 239, listing; Wilkinson i #173, #231,

#392, #664, #674a; Wilkinson *510* 111-12; Yolen 49-51.

Related texts (*The Great Meat Pie*): Chilton 34-36; Leisy 1974 47 #93.

(*The Great Sea-Snake*),

Broadsides, songsters: *Clark's Orphean* 277-78; Hadaway 7-9; *Quaver 1844 319-21; Wm. E. Burton* 86-87.

(*Oh, Didn't He Ramble*),

Comment, references: Beard 231-33.

Texts: AFS 2358B; Bayard ii 153.9, *The Sea Serpent;* Kinkle i 11, listing; Mattfeld 250, listing; Silber 1965 136.

(*The Wonderful Crocodile*),

Comment, references: Creighton 1950 230-32; P. Kennedy 1975 673 #292; *Sam Henry Index* #231 (Huntington).

Broadsides, songsters: Ashton 1888 147-49; *Clark's Orphean* 227.

Texts: Broadwood 1893 184-85; Creighton 1932 122-23 + Ch. Haywood 33; FHE 55; Flanders 1931 168-70; Flanders 1934 38-40; Gardner 1939 469-70; G. Greig *FSNE #14;* B. Ives 1953 154-55 + B. Ives 1956 8-9 + B. Ives 1962 56-57; P. Kennedy 1975 646-47; J. Lomax 1934 498-500; Meredith 1968 134-35; Purslow 1965 20; QC 903.2.7 (LaRena Clark); *Sam Henry* #231 + R. Palmer 1971 48-49; C. J. Sharp 1902 #20. *Singabout 1 #3* 10-11 + *Singabout Songster* 75-76; Yolen 178-81.

(*The Wonderful Telescope*): *Pacific* iv 35-37, "air: *The Wonderful Crocodile*".

Text and tune relatives [** indicates bawdy text form]: AFS L12B.6; Asch 80a; *AT 3 #3* 11; Brand 1960 **34-35 + AFLP **1806.2.6; Brand 1961 112; Brewster 319 A; Dominion 1280B.6 (Alan Mills); Erdei 59 #86; Flanders 1934 24-26 + Botkin 1947 887-88 + *Sam Eskin* i 83 + *Songs to Keep* 7; Friedman 441-42; Gardner 1939 463 C; Hamer 1973 70-71, *The Derby Tup;* Hubbard 390-91 A; *Immortalia* **60-70; Karpeles 1974 ii 378 C; P. Kennedy 1975 660-61; Lahey 49; Manifold 97; Meredith 1968 120-21; A. Mills 1949 28-29; *NA Ives* 1.41 + ATL 2166.6; *NA Ives* 1.73 + ATL 2192.3b; O'Shaughnessy 1971 10-11; Randolph i 398 A; Ritchie 1963 38-40; Schinhan iv 234-35 B; Silverman 1975 ii 195a; *Sing 9 #1* 14- 15; *The Old Tup; Singabout 4 #4* 3.

Tune relatives (Child 112, *The Baffled Knight*): ATL 193:7 ("Dick" Edwards); ATL 616.15, 616.16 (George Edwards); ATL 619.2 (Frank Edwards); ATL 629.8 (Reuben Edwards); Bronson ii 557-59

#23, #24; Peggy Seeger 1960a 29a; ZDA 66.2.8 (Peggy Seeger).

(*Blow, Ye Winds of the Morning*): A. Bush 1-2; *Chapbook 4 #3* 18-19; Chosky 206 #135; CMS 650A.7 (Tom Glazer); Colcord 187 + Botkin 1944 829-31 + J. Lomax 1947 144-45; DL 8245.2.3 (Burl Ives); FA 2312.2.6 (Alan Mills); FG 3507.1.2b (Ewan MacColl); Fowke 1960 112; Fowke 1965 142 + FM 4051.1.3 (O. J. Abbott); Gibbon 69; Glazer 1961 13; S. B. Gould 1905a 34-35 #16 + Buck 1933 2; Hansen 23b; B. Ives 1953 146-47 + B. Ives 1956 22; A. L. Lloyd 1955 11; *Sing 1* 70; *Sing Together* 97a; *SO 2 #12* 8-9 + Cumming 39 + *RSO #3* 28-29 + Silber 1963 69; Trident 96; Whall 21-22 + Loveless 18; *World's Best* 77.

(Child 283, *The Crafty Farmer*): Bronson iv 293 #22.

(*Dove of Peace*): Deason 59b; Hauser 1848 149a; G. P. Jackson 1952 116 #183, *Pensive Dove* (from *Ancient Harmony Revived*. 6th ed., 1858 75); Walker 89a.

(Child 279, *The Jolly Beggar*): Bronson iv 216-17, Group A, Appendix #7, #8, #9.

(Child 110, *The Knight and the Shepherd's Daughter*): Bronson ii 537-39 #3, #6.

(Child 274, *Our Goodman*): Bronson iv 105 #13, #14; Bronson iv 125 #50; Linscott 260-61 + J. R. Wilson #26a; Silverman 1966 84.

(*Swinging in the Lane*): *NA Ives* 1.72 + ATL 2191.3; Schinhan v 461 #729.

(Child 277, *The Wife Wrapt in Wether's Skin*, "Dandoo" form): AFS 11457B.7 + Bronson iv 168 #54.

(others): Ashbee viii 19; H. P. Beck 1957 267; Brand 1960 88-89 + AFLP 1824. . ; Broadwood 1893 70; Bronson i 232 #17 (C. J. Sharp); *Chapbook 3 #3* 32; R. Chase 1956 110; Chosky 184 #84, 186 #89; Cox 1925 532 #165b + *Sam Eskin* i 187a; Cox 1939 207; Cray 34; Dallin 14-15; R. G. Edwards 1972 161; FH 5314A.11 (Margaret MacArthur); Fife 1969 8; Fowke 1965 14-15 + Arthur 7 + FM 4051.1.3 (O. J. Abbott), *The Barley Grain*; FSC 62.1.1, *Campbell, the Drover;* Garretson 41; Gledhill 13-14; Graves 1897 110-12; Graves 1906 153; P. Kennedy 1975 452; J. Lomax 1934 354; Manifold 126; Meredith 1968 248, 268; NW 239.2.4; Ord 73; Randolph iv 398; Richmond 80-81; Ritchie 1963 108; Ritchie 1971 80; *Sam Eskin* v, *The Ball of Kinniemuir;* Schinhan v 420-21 #681; Peggy Seeger 1960a 101 #92; C. J.

Sharp 1961 iv 146-48 + C. J. Sharp 1920 i 98-99, *My Boy Willie* (with opening phrase repeated); *Singabout 1 #3* 17; *Singabout 1 #4* 7; *SO 5 #3* 27; *SO 12 #4* 33b; Waite 1868 49; Wilkinson i #195; WLP 724.1.4.

Unrelated tunes (*Dove of Peace*): G. P. Jackson 1952 143 #242; McCurry 71-72.

152.
The Three Huntsmen

Previously available: AFS 12309B.18 + EC 700.3.

Variants: none.

Adaptations: none.

Comment, references: Belden 1940 246-47; Belden 1952 iii 460-63; Botkin 1947 839-40; Cox 1925 478-79; Damon #33; Flanders 1939 128-29 (Ph. Barry); Karpeles 1974 ii 628 #331; P. Kennedy 1975 680-81 #306; RLP 12-618J 2.1 (Lloyd); C. J. Sharp 1932 ii 412-13 #214; Topic 12T198F B.1 (Lloyd); Wilkinson *510* 155-56.

Broadsides, songsters (*Cape Ann*): *Davidson* ii 317; *Granite Songster* 22-23.

(*Choice of Inuentions*): Flanders 1939 129; Opie 1951 421-23 #525 [facsimile of a broadside of 1632]; Roxburghe i 104-10.

(others): *Barney & Rickey* 46-47, "sung by Garnella Brothers"; *Murphy* 1883 52-53; Offord 66-68.

Sheet music (*Cape Ann*): Damon #33 [facsimile] + Glass 1967a 15-17 + A. Lomax 1960 12-13.

Texts: Agay 76-77, *Cape Ann;* B. Arnold 88-89; Belden 1940 246-47; Belden 1952 iii 460-63; Cazden 1961 54-55; L. Chappell 174-75; J. Cohen 184; M. Cohen 1966 98-99; Creighton 1932 201-3; Davis Index 198 (7); A. T. Davison 1924 40-41 #41; Eddy 208-9; Farmer 186-87; Flanders 1931 125-26; Flanders 1934 28-29; Flanders 1939 128-29; FSA 33F 9, listing; Fuson 183-84; Gordon *AM* 10.9.25; S. B. Gould 1905a 50-51; J. Graham 6-7; Hamer 1973 37-38; B. Ives 1962 4-5 + B. Ives 1966 185-87; *JAF 3* 242-43; *JAF 27* 71-72; *JAF 49* 233-34; Karpeles 1974 ii 390-93, A - C; Karpeles 1975 ii 66 #61; P. Kennedy 1975 663; Linscott 290-92; A. C. Morris 415; E. Moore 249-50; *NA Ives* 1.120 + ATL 3127.6; NA Ives 62.5, *Porkypine;* NW 239.2.4; Piper + Peterson Index 78; *PTFLS 6* 255-56; Purslow 1965 90; Randolph i 328; RLP 12-618.2.1 (A. L. Lloyd); Rosenberg Index #1405; *Sam Eskin* iv 83; Ruth Seeger

1950 36-37; *Sam Henry* #185; Silverman 1975 ii 180; Topic 12T198B.1; C. Wells 1902 70-71; C. Wells 1936 878b; *WF 24* 29, listing; Wilkinson i #471; Wilkinson *510* 155-56; Yolen 190-91.

Related texts (*A National Quarrel*, by Thomas D'Urfey): D'Urfey ii 77-78.

(*Paddy's Dream*),

Broadsides, songsters: *Bishop Buckley; Faugh-a-Ballagh* 106-8; *Murphy* 52-53; *Wehman's Irish #2* 83-84.

Texts: Creighton 1971 156-57; *Miramichi Ms.* 15.16.

Text and tune relatives: none.

Tune relatives: [See notes to #114, *The Boston Burgular*].

Unrelated tunes (*Choice of Inventions*),

Comment, references (*Under and Over*): Simpson 723 #476.

153.
Happy, Frisky Jim

Previously available: AFS 12309B.24 + EC 700.9

Variants: none.

Adaptations: Cazden 1961 40.

Comment, references: none.

Broadsides, songsters: *Shimer & West* 20-21.

Texts: Peterson Index 34; Randolph iii 180-81.

Related texts (*De Boss ob Delaware*): *Beadle's Half-Dime #25* 7.

(*Go Away, Go Away, Don't Come Nigh*): *Handy Andy* 36.

(*Hoop-la!*): *Beadle's Half-Dime #41* 14; *Delehanty & Hengler* 44; *Jennie Hughes* 187-23.

Text and tune relatives: Knox 55; Piper.

Tune relatives (*I've Got Something to Be Thankful For*): *Francis & Day #* 230-31.

154.
The Barefoot Boy

Previously available: AFS 12311A.7 + EC 703.7.

Variants: none.

Adaptations: none.

Comment, references: Cazden 1961 iii-v.

Broadsides, songsters: none.

Texts: *Folkonvention; LCJ (France)*; Randolph iii 204-5 B.

Related texts (*Crazy Dixie*): Cazden 1961 34-35, *Dixieland;* S. N. Coleman 120-21; *Delaney #33* 24 + C. Sandburg 1927 342, "written by Andy Lee"; *Musical Bouquet*

#2241, *Dixey's Land*, "sung by Buckley's Serenaders"; *Musical Bouquet* #2456/7 + *Great Comic Volume* i 12-13 #11, *My Betsy* (by C. Sloman); *Musical Treasury* #1203/4, *On the Sands* (by J. Caulfield); Yolen 80-81.

(*A Horse Named Bill*): Asch 36; Brand 1961 44-45; Cazden 1961 98; C. Sandburg 1927 340-41 + C. Sandburg 1950 88-89; *SO 12 #2* 9 + *RSO #6* 23 + Silverman 1975 ii 170a; *Tent & Trail* 36a; Winn 154-55; Yolen 28-30.

(*Midnight on the Ocean*): Brand 1961 189; Cazden 1961 63; Downes 331; Harbin #74, *The Train Pulled in the Station;* M. Knapp 98b; Piper + Peterson Index 46; Randolph iii 203; C. L. Swan 129.

(*The Queer Little Man*): *American Comic Songster* 102-3; Ashton 1888 105-7; *Can Can* 60-62; Cazden 1961 18; *Fairburn 1823* 159; *Fairburn 1830* 87; *Fairburn 1832* 87; *Frank Van Hess* 60-62; *Howe 1874* 60-61 + *Trifet 1890* 55-56; *Laughing Songster* 15-16; *Paddy Kelly* 53-54; *Pauline Markham* 25; *Singer's Journal #40* 286; *Sol Smith Russell 1876* 69; *Vocal Library* 543 #1464; *Vocal Lyre* 109-10.

(*Tim Queer*): *Billy Birch* 45-46; *Goose Hangs High* 24-25; *Harrison's Museum* 12-13; *Nightingale* 120-21; *Singer's Companion* 120-21.

(*A Yard of Pudding*): Cazden 1961 7; *Concert Room* 37-38; *Jolly Comic* 241-43; *Quizzical Songster* 3-4.

(others): *Beadle's Dime #18* 46, *Yankee Wonders;* Cazden 1961 71, *My Dove; Francis & Day #6* 32-33, *In a Dark and Dreary Sky; James Gray* 34, *Never Put Off till Yesterday What You Can Do the Day Before; Johnny Cross* 5, *The Flutamagilder; Nonpareil* 121-22, *A Bundle of Truths;* Randolph iii 203-4, *I Was Born in Jersey City, Texas.*

Unrelated text (*The Barefoot Boy*, by John Greenleaf Whittier, with music by Clayton Johns): Tomlins 2.

Text and tune relatives: none.

Tune relatives (Child 10, *The Twa Sisters*): Bronson i 181 #90.

(*When the Work's All Done This Fall*),

Comment, references: Belden 1952 ii 618-19; FH 5723F C.8 (Goldstein); Edw. Ives 1978 177; Laws B 3; J. Lomax 1938 76; Malone 1968 148; Philo 1022J 2.6 (Bethke).

Tunes with this text: Abrahams 78-79; J. V. Allen 160-62; *American Cowboy*

56-57; *Arkansas Woodchopper* 1932 40-41; Bethke #45 + Philo 1022.2.6; *Big Round Up* 68-69; *Carson J. Robison* 18-19; K. S. Clark 1932 66; K. S. Clark 1934 36-37; Dallin 142-43; J. Davis 62; *Everybody's Favorite* 94-95; FH 5723C.8 (Harry Jackson); Fife 1969 220; Frey 1941 174-75; Goodwin 1956 173b; Keene 22-23; Kincaid ii 36-37; J. Lomax 1938 74-76 + Lingenfelter 432-33; LPV 522.2.1; Luther 205-6; RLP 12-631.1.2 (Merrick Jarrett); C. Sandburg 1927 260-62; Silverman 1975 i 34-35; W. J. Smith 36-37; *Tip Top* 1935 62; *Treasure Chest* 1935 10.

(others): ATL 191.5, 191.7; E. C. Beck 1948 144; E. C. Beck 1956 187; Bethke #33, *Cousin Nellie*; A. H. Chase 45; Cyporyn 50; Durlacher 62; R. G. Edwards 1956 90; Kraus 79; Larson #12; Manny 135; *Miramichi Ms.* 15.15; E. Moore 297-98; *NA Ives* 62.4, *Will a Monkey Climb a Tree*; Ohrlin 107, 117; SLP 82B.4 (Milt Okun); J. White 26-27; J. I. White 194.

(instrumental): Cazden 1951b; Muller 30; *Neighbors* 1946 27b.

155.
John Styles and Susan Cutter

Previously available: AFS 12309B.10 + EC 699.10.
Variants: none.
Adaptations: none.
Comment, references: none.
Broadsides, songsters: none.
Texts: none.
Text and tune relatives: none.
Tune relatives: [See notes to #147, *Lookit over Yonder*].

156.
A Home in the Catskills

Previously available: none.
Variants: none.
Adaptations: none.
Comment, references: none.
Broadsides, songsters: none.
Texts: none.
Tunes: none.

157.
Catskill Valley

Previously available: AFS 12309A.18 + EC 329.18; AFS 12309B.3 + EC 699.3.
Variants: none.
Adaptations: none.
Comment, references: none.
Broadsides, songsters: none.
Texts: none.
Tunes: none.

158.
Tobasco

Previously available: AFS 12309B.15 + EC 699.15.
Variants: none.
Adaptations: none.
Comment, references: none.
Broadsides, songsters: none.
Texts: none.
Text and tune relatives: none.
Tune relatives: [See notes to #41, *My Love Is Like a Dewdrop*].

159.
The Hills of Last Chance

Previously available: AFS 12309A.19 + AFS 12309B.1 + EC 329.1 + EC 699.1
Variants: ATL 194.1
Adaptations: AFS 12312B.17 (Dick Baumann).
Comment, references: none.
Broadsides, songsters: none.
Texts: none.
Text and tune relatives: none.
Tune relatives: [See notes to #6, *The Flat River Raftsman*, and to #38, *I Am a Young Maiden*].

160.
The Rainbow to Heaven

Previously available: none.
Variants: none.
Adaptations: none.
Comment, references: none.
Broadsides, songsters: none.
Texts: none.
Text and tune relatives: none.
Tune relatives (*Over the Hills to the Poorhouse*, by George L. Catlin and Dave Braham),
Comment, references: R. G. Edwards 1972 175.

Tunes with this text: R. G. Edwards 1971 173; R. G. Edwards 1972 175; *Musical Bouquet* #6139; *24 Mountain Songs* 2-3.

161.
I'm Sad When I Cry

Previously available: AFS 12309A.20 + AFS 12309B.2 + EC 329.20 + EC 699.2.
Variants: none.
Adaptations: none.
Comment, references: none.
Broadsides, songsters: none.
Texts: none.
Related texts (with pattern of "I eat when I'm hungry"),
  Comment, references: JAF 30 345 (Kittredge).
  Texts: Belden 1940 376 B, C; Cox 1925 279; Eckstorm 61; Fowke 1970 203; Korson 1938 364; J. Lomax 1934 218-19 + Botkin 1944 855-57; Randolph ii 317-18; C. Sandburg 1927 307 A; C. J. Sharp 1932 ii 213 B.
Text and tune relatives: none.
Tune relatives: none.

162.
Kintey Coy at Samsonville

Previously available: none.
Variants: none.
Adaptations: none.
Comment, references (#162): none. ("Kintey Coy"): FH 5311F 1 (Tyrell).
Broadsides, songsters: none.
Texts: none.
Text and tune relatives: none.
Tune relatives: none.

163.
The Buck Sheep—The Hesleys

Previously available: none.
Variants: none.
Adaptations: none.
Comment, references (on "insult songs"): Edw. Ives 1964 167-79, "The satirical song tradition"; *JIFMC 14* 65-69 (Edw. Ives).
Broadsides, songsters: none.
Texts: none.
Unrelated texts (epitaphs): *BFSSNE #3* 19 (Fannie Hardy Eckstorm), *Captain Cook*;

Edw. Ives 1964 57, *Larry Gorman and Mr. Teazle;* Edw. Ives 1964 206 #9, *Bob Christie; NYFQ 5* 70 (Harold Thompson), *The Traveler and Farmer Beezil; NYFQ 16* 294 (Pierre De Nio), *Boney Quillen and Mr. "Keesel."*
Text and tune relatives: none.

Tune relatives (Casey Jones),
  Comment, references: Beard 170-71; Belden 1952 iii 510-12; Botkin 1944 241-46; Botkin 1949 382-87; Droke 90; Emurian 15-18; L. Freeman 195; Fuld 1955 17; Fuld 1971 165; *JAF 78* 235-37; Laws G 1; A. Lomax 1960 553-57; A. Lomax 1964 127; J. Lomax 1934 34-42; *SO 7 #3* 28-29; Spaeth 1948 266-67; *WF 32* 77-103.
  Traditional texts [* indicates with related tune]: FSI *58.2.1 (Joe Hickerson); *JAF 24* 257, 351-52 (Odum); *JAF 26* 165-67 (E. C. Perrow); A. Lomax 1960 *553-57; A. Lomax 1964 *127; J. Lomax 1934 *39-42; Odum 1925 207-8; Odum 1926 126.
  Sheet music (as re-written by Lawrence Siebert and Eddie Newton): Los Angeles: Southern California Music Co., 1909; copy in *Ada Holding Miller*, Transportation #30; facsimile of title cover in Wilk 76a.
  Broadsides, songsters: *Delaney #58* 6; Pound 1922 133-34, from *The Railroad Man's Magazine*, May 1918.
  Texts only: Dorson 404-5; Hubbard 364-65; A. C. Morris 109-10.
  Tunes with this text (by Lawrence Siebert and Eddie Newton): Boni 1947 142-44; Botkin 1944 245-46; Brumley ii #6; T. Burton ii 57-58; CMS 670E.2 (Tom Glazer); Loesser 208-9; Mitchell 148-51; Morehead 202-4; Neely 168-71 + A. Lomax 1960 564-65; Scarborough 1925 249-50; Pete Seeger 1973 228; Sherwin 1943 4-6; SLP 9A.5 (Pete Seeger); Spaeth 1926 120-22; Victor 20502 (Vernon Dalhart).
  Parody text (*Casey Jones,* by Joe Hill) [* indicates with related tune]: *CAY 3 #9* *7, 9-10; FA *2039.2.3 (Joe Glazer); FH *5285.2.2 (Almanac Singers); Fowke 1961 43; Glazer 1970 *44-47; Greenway 186; I. W. W. 1; Lingenfelter *82-83; A. Lomax 1967 *92-93; *PSB 1* #6; Pete Seeger 1972 *89-91; Stavis *8-10.

Tune relatives (others): Cray 50; Durlacher 58; Fahs 91 (instrumental); Lingenfelter 146-47; Randolph ii 19a; Schinhan v 131 #114; *SFQ 6* 104; *SO 4 #7* 17.

164.
The Southwood Girls

Previously available: none.
Variants: none.
Adaptations: none.
Comment, references: none.
Broadsides, songsters: none.
Texts: none.

Related texts (*Lanigan's Ball*) [* indicates with common tune],
> **Sheet music:** *Musical Bouquet* *#3911/2.
> **Broadsides, songsters:** *Beadle's Dime #10* 12; *Beadle's Half-Dime #6* 8; *Bryant 1864* 30-31; *Charley Monroe* 6-7; *Comic Songster* *8a; *Converse 1863* *36; *Delaney's Irish #1* 24; *Dick Martz* 54-55; *Diprose 1865* 486; *Guiding Star* 59; *Harry Pell* 15-17; *Howe 1874* *19b + Howe* i *19b + Trifet 1890* *19b + Trifet 1892* *19b; *Irish Broadsides #38* (Dublin: Brereton, n. d.); *J. J. Ward* 19-20; *J. S. Berry* 63-65; *Lanigan's Ball* 2-3; *Ogilvie* *140-41 #151; *Paddy's the Boy* 21-22; *Wearing of the Green* 12-13; *Wehman 617* 89; *Wehman's Irish #3* 26-27.
> **Texts:** *Goodwin 1956* *43b; *Healy 1965* 7-8; *Healy 1969* iii 30-31; *O'Lochlainn 1939* *104-5; *Spaeth 1927* *222-24; *Walton's Treasury* 5-6 + *Walton* i 36-37.
> **Tunes** only (instrumental): *Cazden 1950* 26a; *M. M. Cole* 68i; *Jarman* 17e; *P. Kennedy 1954* 43b; *O'Neill* #858.
(*The Picnic at Groshaut*),
> **Comment, references:** Edw. Ives *1971* 19-34.
> **Texts:** Edw. Ives *1971* 20-22.
(*Tim Finnegan's Wake*),
> **Comment, references:** Laws Q 17.
> **Texts:** [see notes to #121, *Pat Malone*].
(*The Tipperary Christening*),
> **Sheet Music:** *Musical Bouquet* #7499 (1889).
> **Broadsides, songsters:** *J. H. Conroy* [title song]; *Wehman 617* 113.
> **Texts:** *Healy 1965* 6-7.
(others): *Bryant 1864* 65-66, *Mrs. McLaughlin's Party; Healy 1969* iii 25-28, *The Wedding Anone in Glenchree; NA Ives* 65.13.4, *The Irish Jubilee.*

Text and tune relatives: none.

Tune relatives: [See notes to #2, *Cutting Down the Pines*].

165.
The Monticello Jail

Previously available: *NYFQ 16* 97-98.
Variants: none.
Adaptations: none.
Comment, references: Kimball 183; *NYFQ 16* 96-97 (Cazden).
Broadsides, songsters: none.
Texts: none.
Text and tune relatives: none.
Tune relatives (*In Soho on Saturday Night*): Korson *1949* 432-33. (*Up in a Balloon*): [See notes to #120 B, *Lather and Shave*].

166.
The Newburgh Jail

Previously available: *NYFQ 16* 101-2.
Variants: none.
Adaptations: AFS 12312B.18 (Joe Hickerson); AFS 19251.40 (Alan McKnight, Jan Evers); Cazden *1958* i 64-65 + Cazden *1978* 64-65.
Comment, references: Cazden *1958* i 118 + Cazden *1978* 118; *NYFQ 16* 101 (Cazden).
Broadsides, songsters: none.
Texts: none.
Text and tune relatives (refrain only): *JEFDSS* 8 201 + Karpeles *1974* ii 107 B; Karpeles *1974* ii 108 C, 109 D, 109 E, 110 F; Purslow *1972* 67; C. J. Sharp *FSS* i 10-11 #5 + *JFSS* 2 48 + Karpeles *1974* ii 106 A.
Tune relatives: [See #118, *The Poor Chronic Man*].

167.
Sing-Sing

Previously available: *NYFQ 16* 95.
Variants: none.
Adaptations: none.
Comment, references: NYFQ 16 94-95 (Cazden).
Broadsides, songsters: none.
Texts: none.
Unrelated texts (*Dear Sing-Sing*): LCJ.
Text and tune relatives: none.
Tune relatives: [See notes to #12, *As I Went Down to Port Jervis*].

168.
The Albany Jail

Previously available: AFS 12309A.13 + EC 329.13; *NYFQ 16* 100-101.
Variants: none.

Adaptations: none.

Comment, references: Fowke 1965 188-89 #48, *The Soo St. Mary's Jail; NJ 12 #7* 16-17 (Cazden); *NYFQ 16* 99-100 (Cazden).

Broadsides, songsters: none.

Texts: none.

Unrelated texts (*The Albany Jail*): Thompson 1940 229 + Kimball 151.

Text and tune relatives: Fowke 1965 120-21 + Fowke 1967 188-89, *The Soo St. Mary's Jail.*

Tune relatives: [See notes to #178, *I Walk the Road Again*].

169.
The Delhi Jail

Previously available: AFS 12309B.7 + EC 699.7; AFS 12309B.8 + EC 699.8; *NYFQ 16* 99.

Variants: none.

Adaptations: FH 5311.2.7 (Harry Siemsen) + FH 5311F 11-12.

Comment, references: *NYFQ 16* 98-99 (Cazden).

Broadsides, songsters: none.

Texts: none.

Related texts (*County Jail*),

 Broadsides, songsters: O'Conor 121-22; *Old Clown* 26-27; *That's the Style* 12-13; Wehman *617* 34; *Wehman's Collection #12* 4; *Wehman's Irish #3* 71-73; *Yankee Robinson* 48-49.

 Texts: *American Cowboy* 69; Frey 194-137b; Gardner 1939 357; LCJ (Busti); LCJ (Manion); LCJ (Welch); Peterson Index 21.

 (*Cryderville Jail*): Houston 55 + AA 3A.8 + Glazer 1970 65-66 + Leisy 1964 154-55 + J. Lomax 1934 138-43 + A. Lomax 1967 72-73 + *RSO #2* 24 + *Sam Eskin* iv 74, 81 + Silverman 1975 ii 349 + *SO 2 #5* 14.

 (*Mount Holly Jail*): ATL 487.4, 490.11; *JAF 52* 67.

 (*Portland County Jail*): Botkin 1951 777-78; Milburn 176-77; Piper; *Sam Eskin* iv 38; C. Sandburg 1927 214-15 + Lingenfelter 323; H. Sandburg 23.

 (others),
  Comment, references: HTA (Luria, p. 17).
  Texts: Asch 88; Carlisle 107-9, *Hard Times in Boston Jail;* Flanders 1953 25-27, *Old Kingston [R. I.] Jail;* HTA (Luria, p. 9), *Clinton County Jail; JAF 48* 339-40, *Hard Times in Lancaster Jail;* Randolph ii 32-37, *The Dallas County Jail; SO 6 #1* 39; H. Thompson 1940 229 + Kimball 151, *The Albany Jail.*

Unrelated text (*The Delhi Jail*),

 Comment, references: Christman 204-241; Evers 413-32; Monroe, passim.

 Texts: Christman 220-21 + Cazden 1958a 14 #7.

Text and tune relatives: none.

Tune relatives with related text (*Turkey in the Straw*),

 Comment, references [including history of *Old Zip Coon*]: AFS L65F A.6 (Burl Hammons); Boette 114; J. Burton i 6; Damon #30, with facsimile of sheet music publication of *Old Zip Coon* (1834); Dichter i #1672, listing of same, "sung by Mr. Bob Farrel, the original Zip Coon"; FSI 35F 1-2 (Michael Cooney); Goldberg 36; R. Jackson 258-60, facsimile of sheet music publication (ca. 1835); R. Lloyd 80-82; Mattfeld 47; Randolph ii 353; Spaeth 1948 72; Trident 39; Wilkinson *510* 36-37.

 Tunes with related text: Agay 66-67; Bley 72-73; Boni 1947 66-68; Brumley 1973 ii #12; CMS 650H.4 + CMS 650F H.4; Combs 1967 232 #245, listing; Ira Ford 59, 435-38; Frey 1941 145; Frey 194- 133; Green 2; Hansen 189b; Harbin #56, #75; Horton 8-10; Hurst 190-91; B. Ives 1953 196-98 + B. Ives 1962 154-55; *JAF 49* 234-35; M. Johnson 23; Loesser 108; A. Lomax 1960 95-96; Morehead 166-67; Mursell 93; Neal 42-43; Nelson 145; Randolph ii 353-55; C. Sandburg 1927 94-97; Silber 1965 19; Silverman 1975 i 350; L. O. Smith 22a, part 2; *World's Best* 74b-75.

 Tune relatives (*Old Zip Coon*): Boette 114; K. S. Clark 1930 104 #111; Downes 144-45; *Empire Book* 54-55; *Favorite songs* 128; Ira Ford 413-14; Hazlewood 72-73; *Howe 1877* 222a; Levy 1967 91; Loesser 106-7; Lupton 20b; Marrocco 263-64 #105; *Minstrel Songs* 120-21; *Musical Treasury #522* (1849); *Song Jewels* 13a; Spaeth 1926 18-19; Trifet 1890 131a + Trifet 1892 131a; Wier 1918a 463b + Wier 1929 193-94 + Wier 1931 180-81.

 (other texts)[* indicates first part of tune only]: C. S. Adams 132; C. S. Adams *140; AFS 12311B.7 + EC 327.7 (with dance calls by Grover Hornbeck); Cazden 1961 59; A. H. Chase 63; K. S. Clark 1934 5-6; Denson *401, *Cuba;* Durlacher 54; Dykema #58; R. G. Edwards 1971 74a, 74b; FA 2187B.5; FH 5314B.4; Fife 1969 54; *JAF 24* 306; *JAF 25* 269; Keene 5; Kincaid ii 17; A. Lomax 1960 334; A. Lomax 1967 278; Manifold 140; Manny 124 [second half of tune, condensed] + FM

4053.2.5 + Fowke 1973 68 + FW 8744. . ;
Peat 130; Randolph iii 158a, 158b; C. J.
Sharp 1932 ii *367.

(others, as instrumental dance tune)[* indicates first part of tune only]: AFS
19393.2.56 (John Coss); AFS 7759A.2
(Harry Robinson); AFS 12310B.5 + EC
325.5; AFS 12310B.6 + EC 325.6; AFS
12310B.38 + EC 326.19; AFS 14732A.7,
14733A.1; AFS L65A.6 (Burl Hammons);
Artley 54; Bennett 80; Bertail *118; Boette
114, listing; *Boosey* 1862b 36 #118; Burchenal i 20; Cazden 1950 43a; Cazden 1955
26b; Chicago Park District 33; *Community*
i 11c; Converse 1887 101b; DLP 112.2.3;
Everybody's Favorite 148b; Fahs 101;
Flanders Index 239 #17, 240 #165; Fuld
1971 591-92; Geri *64; Guenther 21;
Handy 1955 69; *Howe* 1851a 43c; Howe
1851b 12a; *Howe* 1851c 43c; Howe 1858a
58d; *Howe* 1859 15c; Howe 1864a 44a; D.
Kennedy 1948 21; P. Kennedy 1954 9b;
Kerr xii 41c; Kinscella 42c-43; Kirkell 63;
Knorr 19b; Kraus 48; Leifer 85; Messer 17
#52; Muller 14; O'Neill #1520; O'Neill
1907 #739; Paskman 109; Price *48; Putney 45; Rohrbough 1931b 22; Rollinson
22a; Ruth 8 #18; Ryan 1926 20; Ryan 1939
108; H. Smith 1955 85; Wilkinson ii #116;
Wilkinson *510* 34-35.

Distantly related tune (*The Rose Tree*)
[sampling],

Comment, references: G. P. Jackson 1937
119; Schinhan iv 250; Wilkinson *510* 36-37.

Tunes with this text (*A Rose Tree in Full
Bearing*): Aimwell 7; Barron 272-73; *Old
Songs for the Pianoforte* 23 #11.

Tunes (*Grandmother's Advice*, by A. N.
Johnston)[first half of tune],

Comment, references: Belden 1952 ii 467-
68; Cox 1925 469; Randolph i 383.

Tunes with this text: Creighton 1962 36;
Cox 1939 85; Eddy 300-301; Ira Ford
316-17; *Heart Songs* 302-3; *Home
Melodist* 44-45; Linscott 243-45; Ran-
dolph i 383-84; Richardson 4-6; Scar-
borough 1937 374-75, tune 457b;
Schinhan iv 250 A, 251 C, 251-52 F;
Shilling Song Book i 93; SLP 49.1.2
(Ellen Stekert); Spaeth 1927 160; *Trifet*
1890 245-46; J. W. Turner 28.

(*I'd Mourn the Hopes That Leave Me*, by
Thomas Moore): Hatton 34, "air: *The
Rose Tree*."

(*There Is a Land of Pleasure*): Cayce #304;
Hauser 1848 399; Hauser 1878 212; J. B.

Jackson 165 + G. P. Jackson 1933 166a +
G. P. Jackson 1937 118.

(others): E. C. Beck 1948 316; Creighton
1932 185, *Tim Finnigan's Wake;* FM
4052.1.3; Fowke 1965 34 + FM 4051.2.1;
Fowke 1965 68; Fowke 1970 45.

(others, instrumental): Cazden 1951a 16a;
Cazden 1951b 14a; Joyce #460; P. Kennedy 1951 28 #58; T. Wood 134 #132.

[See also #143].

170.
The Chichester Boys

Previously available: none.
Variants: none.
Adaptations: none.
Comment, references: Evers 343-51 (on Zadok
Pratt); Evers 439-41 (on Chichester); *Neigh-
bors* 1942 21.

Broadsides, songsters: none.
Texts: none.

171.
John Whipple's Mill

Previously available: none.
Variants: ATL 485.11-.12, *John Hopper's Hill*
(George Edwards).
Adaptations: AFS 12312B.11; Cazden 1958 i
102-3 + Cazden 1978 102-3; Cazden 1963 i 8;
Neighbors 1951 11-12.

Comment, references: Cazden 1958 i 116 +
Cazden 1978 116; Fowke 1970 78; *NEF* 7 29.
Broadsides, songsters: none.
Texts: *NEF* 7 29-31, *John Thompson's Mill*.
Text and tune relatives [*tune indicated but not
notated]: Fowke 1970 176-77, *Shannelly's
Mill; NYFQ* 11 *133-35, *Shannel's Mill;*
Shoemaker *69-71, *John Hopper's Mill*.
Tune relatives (*Down, Derry Down*),

Comment, references: Bronson i 354-55;
Bronson iv 25; W. Chappell 1840 i 136
#174; W. Chappell 1859 i 348-53;
O'Shaughnessy 1975 83-84 #28; R. Palmer 1974 331; Rabson 93-94; Simpson
172-76.

(Child 45, *King John and the Bishop of
Canterbury*)[*tune indicated and probable, but not notated]: Bronson i 355-60
#1, #2, #3, #6, #7, #9, #10, #11; Hollo-
way *358-59 #223A, *King John and the
Abbot of Canterbury;* Ritson 1813 ii 317-
20, tune in Ritson 1813 iii 299-300; H.
Thompson 1958 *5-7 (from a New York
manuscript of 1841-56).

(Child 250, *Henry Martyn*): Bronson iv 37-41, Group Ab #32-#40; Bronson iv 509 #34.1, #34.2; Cazden 1959 20b-21 #2b; DL 8080.1.2 (Burl Ives); Hendren 152-53; O'Shaughnessy 1975 43; RLP 12-627.2.2; *SO 12 #4* 11 + Leisy 1964 96-97 + Silverman 1975 ii 256; Topic 12T161B.3; VRS 1031B.7 (Alfred Deller).

(Child 283, *The Crafty Farmer*): Bronson iv 299-302 #35, #36, #37, #39, #40, #41; E. Moore 131-33.

(*A Cobler There Was*, by Richard Leveridge)[*tune by indication only]: *American Songster* 1798 *35-36; *Calliope* 248-49; W. Chappel 1840 i 37-38; W. Chappell 1840 ii 5 #9, #9b; *Charmer* i *107-8; *Columbian Songster* *9-10 #6; *Comic Scrapbook* [a broadside sheet with the tune]; *Fairburn* 1830 *343; *Gay* ii 40-41 #56; *Great Comic Volume* iii 9 #6; *Howe* 1874 46b + *Fireside Library* 56c + *Howe* ii 46b; *Leveridge* ii 28-30; *Masque* *68-70 #66; *Merry Musician* ii 163-64; *Musical Entertainer* 36; *Musical Miscellany* ii 170-71, "set by Mr. Leveridge"; *Orpheus* i *5 #5; *Ramsay* ii *157-58; *Ritson* 1813 i 164-65, tune in Ritson 1813 iii 299-300; *Singer's Journal* #58 *429; *Song Jewels* 23c; *Vocal Library* *56 #158; *Vocal Music* *338-39 #1257.

(*Cod Liver Oil*) [*tune by indication only]: Asch 64-65; Blondahl 28; Brand 1961 63; *Delaney* #72 *24; FG 3532.1.2 (Alan Mills) + FG *3532F 2b; *Geo. Jarvis* #25, "as sung by Johnny Roach"; Greenleaf 316; B. Ives 1957 26-27; *NA Ives* 1.80 + ATL 2199.1c (Alan Mills); *NA Ives* 61.3 (Alan Mills); J. Lomax 1941 116-17; Silverman 1975 ii 160.

(*Cutting Down the Pines*, with double-length stretched tune, no refrain): [see #2, #146 A, #164].

(*Dennis Bulgruddery*, by George Colman and Charles Dibdin)[*tune by indication only]: Carpenter 1864 *63-64 + Carpenter i *195-96; *Delaney's Irish #4* *23; *Diamond Songster* ii *36-38; G. S. Jackson *166-67 (from *The Yankee Songster's Pocket Companion*, Gardiner, Maine, 1824); *New Musical Cabinet* ii 165-66; *Oliver* *51-52; *Singer's Journal* #57 *421; *Wearing of the Green* *17-18.

(*Whistle, Daughter, Whistle*, with stretched tune form in 4/4 time, without refrain): FL 5401A.1 (Peggy Seeger); Joyce 1872 27; Karpeles 1974 ii 21 B; Karpeles 1975 i 72 #69; P. Perkins 59; Peggy Seeger 1964 84;

C. J. Sharp *FSS* iii 20-21 #62 + Karpeles 1974 i 20 A + C. J. Sharp 1916 134-35 #59 + C. J. Sharp 1920 i 100-101.

(others, with tune given, no refrain): ATL 602.8, *Johnny Riley* (James Edwards); Broadwood 1893 65; Creighton 1940 25-27 + Creighton 1950 165 A; Creighton 1950 195 A, 197 B; Eddy 93 C; Gill 1898 80 #89; *JEFDSS 3* 63; *JFSS 1* 202 I; *JFSS 2* 100, 209; *JFSS 3* 278-79 #21; *JFSS 6* 3; Karpeles 1971 136; Karpeles 1974 i 321 B, 672 B, 672-73 C; Karpeles 1974 ii 247 A, 248 B; A. L. Lloyd 1967 365; *NA Ives* 1.53 + ATL 2178.1; *NA Ives* 1.141 + ATL 3148.3; *NA Ives* 62.6, *Sarah's Young Man; NEF 8* 40-42, *The Fit Comes on Me Now* [doubled tune]; Peacock 368 B; P. Perkins 97; Purslow 1968 66, 114; Sedley 182 B; C. J. Sharp 1920 ii 37-39; C. J. Sharp 1961 iii 54-57 (R. V. Williams) + *Novello* #261 16-17 #1268; SL 206.1.12. [See also notes to #58, *The "Lady Leroy"*].

(others, with tune and refrain given): ATL 627.3 (Frank Edwards); E. C. Beck 1956 228-30; Bethke #24, *Beaver River;* Bethke #49, *Miner's Hill;* A. Campbell 65; W. Chappell 1859 i 350 + R. Palmer 1974 204; *Crosby* 1812 235-39, 239-41; Dallas 1974 222; *Davidson* i 262b; Dibblee 108; R. G. Edwards 1971 176, 282; FH 5279.1.5, *The World Turned Upside Down* (Arthur F. Schrader); Fowke 1960 44-45; Fowke 1970 76; B. Ives 1953 80-81; Edw. Ives 1964 91-92 + ATL 2144.5 + *NA Ives* 1.13; Edw. Ives 1971 132-33 + *NA Ives* 69.2, *Bud Jones; JAF 22* 73; *JFSS 8* 277 #16; A. L. Lloyd 1967 344; McCarthy 48; McIntosh 1974 52; *Merry Musician* iii 156-57; *Musical Miscellany* i 94-96; *Musical Miscellany* vi 136-41; *Musical Treasury* #795/6 5c-6a; *NA Ives* 1.78 + ATL 2197.1h; *New Merry Companion* 146-7; R. Palmer 1973 32; Purslow 1972 2; Purslow 1974 38-39; Rabson 14-19; Randolph iii 20; Peggy Seeger 1960 68; Silber 1973a 67; Vinson 26-27.

[See also notes to #120 A, *Lather and Shave*, for tune relatives with variant wording of the refrain].

Tune relatives indicated and probable, not notated: *American Comic Songster* 23-24; *American Star* 94-96; *Arkansas Traveler* 52-53, *Twelve Parsons;* E. C. Beck 1948 121-22; *Burton's Comic* 174; Carpenter i 164-65, 167-68, 175-76; *Charmer* i 191-92, *Who Has Ever Been to Paris; Charmer* i 227; *Charmer* ii 68-69, 229, 293-94; *Concert Room* 13-14; Croker 220, *Johnny Adair;* Dixon 148-151, *The*

Nobleman's Generous Kindness; Dublin Comic 37-38; *Eighteenth Century* 263, *The Modern Tradesman* [a broadside]; *Every-Day* 133-36, *The Seven Naval Victories; Fairburn* 18-- 297; *Fairburn* 1830 155, *The Parson and the Quaker;* J. S. Farmer ii 178-80, *The Button Hole;* Flanders *BDN* 30.1.34, *The Belle of Long Lake; Goldfinch* 55-56, *A Bundle of Proverbs; Hooley* 43-44; *J. M. Berry* 1856 16-17, *The Parson and the Quaker; Joe English* 69-70; *Lanigna's Ball* 53-54; *Laughing Songster* 162-63; *Lingard* 103-4; *Masque* 55-57 #56, 213-14 #223, 232-33 #242, 308-9 #313; *Musical Miscellany* vi 136-41; *96 Old Songs* 29, 144; *NYFQ 14* 211b (Warner) *Oliver* 70, 189-90; *Orpheus* i 256-58 #387; *Orpheus* ii 141-42 #211, 142-44 #212; *Orpheus* iii *Orpheus* 1832 157-60, *Clio Grub at Brighton; Pacific* i 54-55, *California Legislature;* Ritson 1813 ii 187-89; *Salisbury Square* 2, *Bung Your Eye; Songster's Repository* 215-16, 237-38; G. A. Stevens 253-55 #177, *The Sea Voyage;* G. A. Stevens 292-94 #224, 348-49 #259; H. Thompson 1940 267; *Tony Pastor* vi 45-47; *Tony Pastor* vii 24-25; *Tony Pastor* viii 13, 32-33; *Tony Pastor* ix 22-23; *Universal Songster* i 157, *Craniology,* 302, *The Sentimental Cobbler,* 307, *One Nation,* 344, *Cobbler à la Française,* 380, *King Richard and Lady Anne; Universal Songster* ii 14, *The Soldier's Alphabet,* 44, *Tom Stitch, the Tailor,* 187, *Paddy's Description,* 399-400, *The Parson and the Quaker,* 421, *Paddy's Courtship; Universal Songster* iii 100, *To Be Sure,* 203, *Horns,* 247, *A Budget of Blunders,* 313, *The Hunt of the Gods,* 387, *Come, Fill the Bumper; Vocal Magazine* 98 #363, *The Cordelier; Vocal Miscellany* i 2-3 #2, 72-73 #88, 122-23 #136, 131 #147, 206-7 #230; *Wm. E. Burton* 123, 174-75. [See also notes to #154, Related Text: *The Queer Little Man*].

Unrelated tunes designated as *Down, Derry Down* or equivalent, notated,

(*Yonder Stands a Charming Creature*)[*tune indicated]: *Comic Scrapbook* [a broadside with the tune, ca. 1720], *The Bashful Maid;* J. S. Farmer ii *196-97; *Musical Miscellany* iii 172-73; *Orpheus* iii *399 #582; *Vocal Miscellany* i *34 #42.

(*A Yorkshire Tale,* or *A Parson There Was,* by Richard Leveridge): Crawhall 1864 140 (from *The Fisher's Garland* for 1840); *Leveridge* ii 28-30; *Merry Musician* ii 97-99; *Musical Miscellany* iii 76-80.

(others): AFS 4196 + Bronson i 357 #4, *King John and the Bishop;* W. Chappell

1840 ii 86b #174; Crawhall 1965 77; Gardner 1939 379 + Bronson i 357-58 #5, *King John and the Bishop;* Howe 1864a 106f (an instrumental tune, with title: *Dennis Bulgruddery*); *JAF 64* 43-44 + Bronson i 360 #12 + Hubbard 10-12, *King John and the Bishop;* Karpeles 1974 ii 363; Kidson 1929 110-11, *Joe Muggins;* J. Lomax 1938 256; *NA Ives* 1.122 + ATL 3129.3, *The Little Brown Bulls;* R. Palmer 1974 173, 279.

Unrelated tunes designated as *Down, Derry Down* or equivalent, not notated, but the text could not be made to fit the tune strain of #171: Diprose 1865 148, *Pat and His Cat;* D'Urfey iv 179 + J. S. Farmer i 109-12, *The Maid of Tottenham* [dated 1666]; *Fairburn* 1832 3, *The Cricketeer;* J. S. Farmer ii 214-16, *The Butcher; Masque* 219-20 #229, *What Mean You;* Silber 1973b 177; G. A. Stevens 276-77 #215 + *Masque* 50-51 #53, *A Taylor There Was; Universal Songster* ii 272, *Billy Snip,* 412, *A Glass of Gin; Universal Songster* iii 124, *The Wheel of Life.*

172.
The D. & H. Canal

Previously available: AFS 12309B.17 + EC 700.2.

Variants: none.

Adaptations: none.

Comment, references (#172): none.

(Canal songs): Wyld 75-107.

(The D. & H. Canal): *NYFQ 6* 260-67 (Benner); L. C. Wood 88 [photo].

Broadsides, songsters: none.

Texts: none.

Related texts: [See #173, *Sarah Jane*].

Text and tune relatives: [See #173].

Tune relatives (*Pop Goes the Weasel*),

Comment, references: Dichter 1941 149; Fuld 1971 440-41; R. Jackson 279; Randolph iii 368; *SFQ 6* 246-47 (Cox); Spaeth 1948 133; Wilkinson *510* 14.

Sheet music: New York: Berry & Gordon, 1853 [facsimile title in Levy 1971 244]; New York: Stephen B. Gordon, 1859 [facsimile in R. Jackson 176-79].

Tunes with this text: Agay 93; Bertail 136; Bley 48; Boni 1952 302-3; Brumley ii #37; Buck 1933 73a; Bullard 14a; Cazden 1961 33; Cazden 1962 23; Dwyer 31; Ira Ford 40; Fuld 1971 440-41; Garson 72-73; Goldstein 113; Haufrecht 1958 17; HTA (from Doris Grant, Fredonia, New York); B. Ives 1953 104-5 + B. Ives 1962 270-71;

JAF 33 119 #37a; *JAF 38* 213-14; Landeck 1944 32; N. Langstaff 115; W. M. Lawrence 24; C. G. Marsh 86; Neal 20-21; *NEF 8* 60; Price 86; Randolph iii 368-69; Raph 131-33; H. Sandburg 127b; Silverman 1975 i 372 a; J. W. Turner 3a; Wessells 41; Wier 1918b 56a; Winn 100-101; Wolford 83b-84 (second half of tune); *World's Best* 26a; Yolen 88-89.

(others); E. Black 18; A. H. Chase 14; Converse 1864 33; Durlacher 42, 84; Fife 1969 36; *Gold Diggers* 16-17; Goodwin 1956 39; B. Ives 1956 66; Lengyel i 19-19A; Levy 1971 245; Lingenfelter 28-29; Lovett 62; C. G. Marsh 70; *NA Ives* 65.13.6; J. W. Turner 21a.

(others, as instrumental dance tune): Bowers 29; Burchenal i 22; Cameron 30; Cazden 1950 3a; Cazden 1955 6a (George Van Kleeck); M. M. Cole 24f; *Everybody's Favorite* 150-51; Flanders Index 234 #165; Gott 29a; *Handy* 1940 85; E. Haywood 12 #18; Howe 1858a 67a; Howe 1858b 33; *Howe* 1859 #27a; Howe 1864a 42g; Karpeles 1951 4a; P. Kennedy 1951 20 #39, in 2/2 time; Kerr xii 38e; Kinscella 42a; Knorr 23b; Leifer 73; Mattson 33; Mayo 101 #7; Muller 31; *Musical Bouquet* #409 (with description of dance); *Musical Bouquet* #431 86b-87 (polka); *Musical Bouquet* #437 16-17, #610 4c, #620 4c #1047 4; *Musical Bouquet* #1688 (piano variations by Charles Grobe); *Musical Budget* x 68a; *Musical Budget* xi 12a, 13a; *Musical Treasury* #659 1; *Musical Treasury* #671 (polka, mazurka); *Musical Treasury* #734 4c; *Musical Treasury* #1154; Rohrbough 1941 10; Rosenberg T83 10B; Ruth 3 #3; Wilkinson ii #44, #75, #171, #176; Wilkinson *510* 14 (second half of tune).

173.
Sarah Jane

Previously available; none.
Variants: none.
Adaptations: FH 5311.2.5, *The D. & H. Canal* (from a Kingston, New York newspaper of 1850) (Barbara Moncure).
Comment, references: FH 5311F 11a.
Broadsides, songsters (*The Jersey Lovers*): *Beau Monde* 79-80.
Texts: FH 5311F 11b.
Related texts (*Peter Gray*): [See notes to tune relatives, #64, *The Lord of Scotland*].

Text and tune relatives: [See #172, first stanza].
Tune relatives: [See notes to #172, *The D. & H. Canal*].

174.
The Bluestone Quarries

Previously available: none.
Variants: FH 5311.1.2.
Adaptations: none.
Comment, references (#174): FH 5311F 7.
(Bluestone quarrying in the Catskills): Evers, facing 585 [painting of a local quarry, by Marie Siemsen]; *NYFQ 13* 92-99, "Blue gold of the Catskills" (Harold Harris); *NYFQ 18* 86-107, "Bluestone lore and bluestone men" (Alf Evers).
Broadsides, songsters: none.
Texts: FH 5311F 7.
Text and tune relatives: none.
Tune relatives (*Pat Works on the Railway*),
  Comment, references: Fowke 1961 84-85; J. Lomax 1947 250-51 #76; Peggy Seeger 1960 36 #37.
  Broadsides, songsters: *Mac Dill Darrell* 43-44.
  Tunes with this text: Asch 91; Boni 1947 150-51; Brand 1961 113; Cazden 1962 64; Cazden 1963 ii 9; Chosky 211 #146; CMS 650H.1 (Tom Glazer); CMS 670E.1 (Tom Glazer); Dallin 28-29; Downes 284-85; Fowke 1961 84-85; FP 5003.48-6.1.3 (Pete Seeger); Glazer 1961 114-15; Hille 32; Honoré 61; Houston 66; B. Ives 1953 232-33 + B. Ives 1962 168-69; Loesser 206-7; J. Lomax 1934 22-24 + Landeck 1944 58 + J. Lomax 1947 270-71 + Siegmeister 1944b 72-73 + Wright 540; Kolb 199-200; McConathy 69-70; Sherwin 1943 28; Silber 1965 81; Silverman 1975 ii 413; *Travelin' On* 74-75; VRS 9013.1.4 (The Weavers); J. Warner 115-17; Zanzig #11.
  (others): [See notes to #99, *In the Days When I Was Hard Up*].
Unrelated tunes (*Poor Paddy Words on the Railway*): Best 11b; MacColl 1954 20 + Peggy Seeger 1960 42; MacColl 1954 21.

175.
Shore Around the Grog

Previously available: none.
Variants: none.
Adaptations: none.
Comment, references (#175): Ph. Barry 1939

96#5; FA 2354F 2.8 (Stekert); Goldstein 1966 24-26 (Stekert); Manny 159.

(Rafting on the Delaware): L. C. Wood 1934 5-73, 181-232; L. C. Wood 1950 23-44.

Broadsides, songsters: none.

Texts: FA 2354F 2.8; H. Thompson 1940 280; L. C. Wood 1934 208; L. C. Wood 1950 25.

Related texts (*The Shanty Song*): Eckstorm 60 + Ph. Barry 1939 17; *NA Ives* 1.69 + ATL 2188.4; F. M. Warner 74.

Text and tune relatives: ATL 188.3a, 188.3d (George Swarthout); Carmer 1942b 72; FA 2354.2.8 (Ellen Stekert).

Tune relatives with related text (*Jock Hawk's Adventures in Glasgow*): Peggy Seeger 1960 101.

(*Peelhead*): Manny 158-59 + J. R. Wilson #26, 81-82; *NA Ives* 1.44 + ATL 2169.1; *NA Ives* 1.73 + ATL 2192.1; *NA Ives* 61.2.

Tune relatives (others); [See notes to #151, *The Darby Ram*].

176.
The Babcock Bedtime Story

Previously available: none.

Variants: none.

Adaptations: none.

Comment, references (#176): none.

(The *cante-fable*): *AFSPB 14* 139-50, "The cante-fable in decay" (Halpert).

(Whirling): *NYFQ 8* 301-6, "Whirling and applejack in the Catskills" (Studer).

Broadsides, songsters: none.

Texts: none.

Text and tune relatives: none.

Tune relatives (*Loch Lomond*),

Comment, references: R. Ford 1900 275-81; R. Ford 1904 146-48; G. Greig *FSNE* #91; J. Greig iii p. xxv.

Tunes with this text: Armitage 1918 406-7; Armitage 1926 436; Bacon 50-51; Bantock 1930b ii 28-29; Beattie 36a; Boni 1947 80-81; *British Minstrelsie* ii 58-59; Buck 1916 124-25; Buck 1933 56; *Canadian Boys* 102-3 #49; Cazden 1959 21b #26; Christie i 278-79 (with additional phrases by Christie); Davie 76-77 #47; H. W. Davies 1931 61 #52; A. T. Davison 1922 76 #116; A. T. Davison 1924 92-93 #84; Diack i 28-29; DX 513.2.3c; Dykema #102; Elson 1722-23; *Empire Book* 37a; *Ernest Newton* 32; *Experimenters* 31; Eyre-Todd 30-31, 32-33; R. Ford 1904 145-47; Foster 164-65; Fran-

cis & Day i 36; *Francis & Day* 1906 100-101; Frey 1943 112b; Fuld 1971 336-37; *Gems of Scottish Songs* 219; H. F. Gilbert 18-19; Goss 1927 110; G. F. Graham 1891 394-95; J. Greig iii 352-53; *Guiana Sings* 40; A. Hamilton 4-5; Hansen 113a; Haufrecht 1958 48-49; Haufrecht 1959 87; Haufrecht 1963 48; *Heart Songs* 216-17, 406-7; Hesser 116-17; B. Hoffman 34-35; I. Hoffman 104-5; Hopekirk 20-23; C. Johnson 38; *Labour Party* 25; Lampe 1914 18-19; Levermore 60-61 #26; Loomis 136-37; Lorenz 26a #36; *Lyric Gems* 112-13; McCaskey 1899 342a; MacLean 109; MacLeod i 10-12; MacMahon i 105-7 #58; Macmillan 72-73; Marshall 250-51; J. Mills 74; Morehead 84-85; *Morvan* 34-35; S. H. Nicholson 74-75 #38; Oberndorfer 45; *101 Best Songs* #63; *120 Scotch Songs* 100-101; *Pocket Song Book* 44; Ratcliff 19; Richman 24a; I. Roberts #12; *Sam Eskin* ii; *Scottish Songs* 26-27; C. J. Sharp 1902 #74 158-59; Silverman 1975 i 280b-81; *Sing Care Away* ii 14-15; J. T. Smith 60; *Song Purpose* 30a; Spicker 72-74; Surette 46-47 #42; Thomson 171-74; Tomlyn 54-55; VSD 58.4.6 (Paul Robeson); Whitehead 42-43; Wier 1918a 273a; Wier 1924 158; Willan ii 44-46; Woodgate 1951 52; *World's Best* 111.

(Child 10, *The Twa Sisters*): T. Gordon 98.

(Child 25, *Willie's Lyke-Wake*): Bronson i 306 #2, #4; RLP 12-625.1.3.

(Child 193, *The Death of Percy Reed*): Bronson iii 184.

(Child 199, *The Bonny House of Airlie*): Bronson iii 194-95 #8-#11; FG 3519.2.3 (Lucy Stewart).

(Child 219, *The Gardener*): Bronson iv 501 #8.1.

(others): *CFB #3* 5; Davie 32-33 #19; Durlacher 258 A; FA 2164B.5 (Wallace House); Putney 94; *Sam Henry #193*, #511; *SS 14* 49-50, 176-77.

(others, as instrumental dance tune): Durlacher 260 A; Kerr ii 45 #407; Kerr iii 30a, *The Braes of Binnorie*; Kerr xii 3c.

177.
The Tall Pine Tree,
or
The Samsonville Song

Previously available: AFS 12309B.14 + EC 699.14; *Neighbors* 1950 29.

Variants: AFS 10505B.28 (Celia Kelder).
Adaptations: none.
Comment, references: *Neighbors* 1950 28.
Broadsides, songsters: none.
Texts: none.
Related text (*The Old Pine Tree*, or *Nancy Bell*),
  Comment, references: Dichter ii #1207.
  Broadsides, songsters: *American Dime* i 34-35; J. Andrews iii #83; *Beadle's Half-Dime #17* 2; *Big Thing on Ice* 93; *Christy & White* ii 69; *Christy's Panorama* 114; *Delaney #11* 22; De Marsan #285; *James A. Bland* 49; *Singer's Journal #5* 37; *Wehman's Universal #20* 159.
Text and tune relatives: none.
Tune relatives: none.

178.
I Walk the Road Again

Previously available (texts and tunes): *Neighbors* 1942 13; *NJ 12 #9* 23-24; *PSB 1 #29.*
  (texts only): FSI 59F 10-11; LCJ (Eastman); NW 239J6 2.10.
Variants: AFS 7755A.1 (1944); ATL 629.9-.10 (1938).
Adaptations: AFS 12312A.5 (John Cohen); AFS 19251A.48 + AFS 19394.1.72 (Pete Seeger) + ATL OT 5141.48 (Pete Seeger); AFS 19395.1.85 (Joe Hickerson); Cazden 1958 i 4-5 + Cazden 1978 4-5; J. Edwards 204-5; FSI 59.1.4 (Joe Hickerson); Haufrecht 1943 12-13; Haufrecht 1944; Haufrecht 1963 24-25; Haufrecht 1965 ii 7-10; Lusk 5-6 + NW 239.2.10, *I'll Hit the Road Again* (Grant Rogers) [text only]; SLP 72.1.1 (Robert DeCormier); *SO 5 #1* 9 + *RSO #1* 66 + Silverman 1975 ii 355 [garbled].
Comment, references (text and tune): AFS 7755A.2 (Ben Botkin, George Edwards); Cazden 1958 i 114 + Cazden 1978 114; FSI 59F 10 (Hickerson); *JAF 72* 329 Table 1 B, 332 Table 2 B, 315 #6, 320 #32, 335 Table 3 B (Cazden); NW 239J6 2.10 (Paton); SLP 72J A.1 (Cazden).
  (tune): *BFSSNE #11* 12 (Ph. Barry); Joyce #403; *NJ 12 #7* 12-21, *12 #8* 23-28, *12 #9* 19-24, "I walk the road again and again" (Cazden); Purslow 1972 64; Wilkinson i #235.
Broadsides, songsters: none.
Texts: none.
Related texts (*The National Line*): R. W. Gordon *AM* 10.9.23.
  (*The Rock Island Line*): [See #93].
Text and tune relatives: none.
Tune relatives (*The Good Old State of Maine*,

by Larry Gorman): Edw. Ives 1964 103-4 + ATL 2152.2 + *NA Ives* 1.25; Manny 99 + FM 4053.2.2 (James Brown) + *NA Ives* 62.5; *Miramichi Ms.* 15.16; NW 239.2.2 (James Brown).
(*The Hat Me Father Wore*, by Edwin Ferguson) [* tune by reference only]: *Barney & Rickey* *115; FO 16.2.15; Grover 178; McPheeley 70-71; O'Neill *#195; Wilkinson i #171.
(*Howard Carey*, by Joe Scott): *NA Ives* 1.137 + ATL 3144.5 + Edw. Ives 1978 [185]; *NA Ives* 67.3.1.
(*Irish Molly-O*),
  Tunes with this text: Breathnach i 56; FO 18.1.8; Joyce #403.
  Tunes with reference to this title (*Jim Jones*): H. Anderson 1955 21-22; *AT #19* 12-13; R. G. Edwards 1956 28 + R. G. Edwards 1971 4; Lahey 32; Long 1964 13; Manifold 12.
  Tunes by reference to this title (others) [* indicates tune not notated]: Breathnach i 60; Breathnach ii 100-101; Breathnach iii 148, 151; Dwyer 166; *Miscellanea* i 65 #5; Murphy 67-88 + *Rising of the Moon* *18 + *Wearing of the Green* *62-63, *The Green Above the Red*, by Thomas Davis; Murphy 71, *Rising of the Moon*; Pacific iii *11-12 + E. Black 8-9 + *Put's Golden* *48-49, *I Often Think of Writing Home*; R. Palmer 1974 89; Silber 1967 111-13; D. Stewart 17-18.
(*Lonely Waterloo*): *JAF 67* 134 + Peacock 1007-8 A; M. Leach 1965 306; *NA Ives* 1.6 + ATL 2140.9, *Bloody Waterloo*; *NA Ives* 1.150 + ATL 3157.3; Peacock 1008 B.
(*The Munroe Murder*): Creighton 1971 186-87; *NA Ives* 1.22 + ATL 2150.2; *NA Ives* 1.149 + ATL 3156.1.
(*Patrick Sheehan*): *BFSSNE #11* 12 + Ph. Barry 1939 33; Morvan 25; Purslow 1972 64.
(*The State of Arkansas*): FSI 59.1.3 (Joe Hickerson); J. Lomax 1938 283 + J. Lomax 1947 240-41; *PSB 3 #228* + *RPSB* 22-23; *Sam Henry #674*; *Weavers Song Book* 142-43.
(*The Turfman from Ardee*, by Patrick Akins) [* indicates tune not notated]: RLP 12-602.1.5 (Margaret Barry); Topic 12T123.1.4 (Margaret Barry); *Walton's Treasury* *189; WLP 731.1.5 (Margaret Barry).
(others): AFS 3398B, *The 'Cromwell'*; H. Anderson 1955 94; ATL 616.5, *The Banks of Sweet Dundee* [in major] (James Ed-

wards); ATL 621.3, *Dixie's Sunny Land;*
BFSSNE #11 11 + Ph. Barry 1939 62,
Daniel Sullivan; CEOL 3 49-50 (Shields),
The Poulshone Fisherman; Creighton
1932 96-97, *The Rose of Britain's Isle;*
Creighton 1932 165-66, *Down by the Tan-*
Yard Side; Creighton 1962 78 + *CAY 4* 23,
A Maid I Am in Love; Creighton 1962 147,
The Banks of the Nile; Creighton 1962 185,
The Springhill Mine Disaster (1891);
Creighton 1971 156-57, *Johnny Bull, Irish-*
man, and Scotchman; Dibblee 65, 69, 103,
105; R. G. Edwards 1956 38, *Bushranger*
Jack Power; FMJ 1 82, *Drumallachie;*
FMJ 3 23; FO 17.1.3; *Folk #2* 7; Fowke
1965 94-95, *The Twelfth of July;* Fowke
1965 134-35 + FHR-04.1.1 + FM 4052.2.9
(Jim Doherty) + Fowke 1970 206, *Save*
Your Money While You're Young; FSC
62.1.3 (Margaret Christl, Ian Robb);
Fowke 1970 131-32, *The River through the*
Pine; Fowke 1970 150-51, *Young Conway;*
Gallagher #10; Greenleaf 288; Healy
1967a 52g, 128d; Hughes iii 16-18; B. Ives
1958 58; *JFSS 7* 52a, 52b, 316; Karpeles
1971 173-75, *The Rose of Britain's Isle;* P.
Kennedy 1975 363 i; Kidson 1891 173b,
The Banks of Sweet Dundee; M. Leach
1965 122-23, *Pat O'Donnell* M. Leach
1965 230-31, *Canadee-I-O;* A. L. Lloyd
1967 356-57, *Johnny Seddon;* Meredith
1956 6; Meredith 1968 191; Moeran 1950 1-
5; Morton 1973 111 #21, 128; *NA Ives* 1.55
+ ATL 2178.5, *Oh No, Not I; NA Ives*
62.2, *Skibbereen; NA Ives* 64.6.6, *The*
Wild Colonial Boy; O'Neill #195, *The*
Bonny Labouring Boy; O'Neill #577,
Sheridan of Coolcanig; Ranson 102, *The*
Poulshone Fisherman; Rickaby 167, *Lake*
Huron's Rock-Bound Shore; C. J. Shapr
FSS iv 62-64 #102 + Karpeles 1974 i 333-
34 + Karpeles 1975 ii 30 #26 + *Novello* ix
7-9 #1409 + C. J. Sharp 1916 112-13 #50
+ C. J. Sharp *Selection* ii 18-20 + C. J.
Sharp 1920 i 78-79, *The Bonny Lighter*
Boy; Stanford 1901 116-17; Thomas 1931
152-53; *Tocher #12* 156; Topic 12T157B.5,
My Darling Ploughman Boy; Whall 113-
14, *Shakings;* Wilkinson i #343, *The Rebel*
Soldier.
(others, with tune condensation in 3/4 time):
  Karpeles 1971 161, 191 A, 192 B, 193 C;
  Noraidh 47, *An Ceannaí Bán.*
(others, as instrumental dance tune): Giblin
  7 #13; Henebry 268; Howe 1864a 103c;
  Kerr i 41i; Kerr xii 23f.

List of Sources

This list of sources expands the concept of bibliographical reference.

All references are listed in a single alphabet. This alphabetical sequence therefore includes entries by author, by editor, by title, by publisher, by name of periodical, by record number or by other archives number.

Where several editions of the same published or recorded work have been issued, the date of the edition used for reference is cited first.

All titles are italicized. When such titles serve for main headings in the alphabetical listing, initial *A* or *The* is disregarded.

Author's or editor's names beginning with Mc or with M' are alphabetized as if they began with Mac.

Entries of songsters or of other collections that lack an assignable author name are usually made by title. Where a songster or other volume is essentially the presentation of a publisher, or where it is most easily located that way, it is listed under the publisher's name.

Notably for songsters, where proper names (of writers, performers, publishers or place names) appear as the opening of a title entry, they are placed in the alphabet just as given in that title. Thus *Charlie Monroe's Clown Song Book* is alphabetized under C for Charlie, not under Monroe.

Where a secondary or cross-reference entry seems useful, it is given in brackets at its normal alphabetical position, with an indication of its short title.

Each listing of an entry that contains notated music, though not necessarily for all of its contents, is preceded by an asterisk [*].

Each listing of a recorded source is preceded by a dagger sign [†].

With entries of recordings, notice is taken of any significant printed commentary or text, such as in an accompanying booklet or on a record jacket. The author of such commentary is identified (in parentheses).

For a few titles, of which copies may be difficult to locate, libraries or other repositories are identified, and call numbers are supplied where they seem useful.

Each entry in the list of sources is preceded by an assigned short title reference term, which is used in the discussion matter and in the end Notes. Most often, this short title consists of the last name of the author or editor, or of the last name of the first author or editor listed. Title entries are supplied with an appropriate abbreviation as short titles, as *Charlie Monroe*.

Where there is more than one title listed for the same author or editor name, its year of publication is appended, as Fowke 1961. Should such an added date not suffice, it is further distinguished by subscript letters, as 1954a, 1954b.

To replace such date, some other distinguishing feature is used for certain short titles. These may consist of the volume numbers of a multi-volume work, or of the # sign for a work whose contents are commonly identified by their item numbers.

Where the same last name occurs for more than one author or editor, distinguishing initials, as R. A. Smith, R. B. Smith, are added to the short title, though without change of their alphabetical placement under Smith. In a few instances, as for Pete Seeger, Peggy Seeger, Ira Ford, the full name serves better.

For a few entries, some identifying designation other than date or volume is joined to the short title, in italics. Thus R. W. Gordon *AM* refers to the columns contributed by Robert W. Gordon to *Adventure Magazine*.

Where printed publications are in more than one volume, the short title form observes the distinction among the volumes merely by lower-case Roman numerals, as Bronson iv. Such usage frequently obviates the addition of a publication date, which is given in full with the complete title. For the few multi-volume works that have continuous pagination, as Peacock, the volume numbers are accordingly omitted.

The short title for periodicals consists of their common abbreviations, given in italics, in the same form as for other title entries. Thus *JAF* suffices for *Journal of American Folklore*.

An entry that identifies a syllabus, annotated listing or description of a collection or repertory is assigned the uniform term Index in its short title.

Because this seems the simplest means for retrieval of their information, the short titles of disc recordings consist of the record letters and numbers, placed in their normal alphabetical position. The full identity of the disc(s) is then entered, normally in the form of a title, with the performer's name following (in parentheses). Thus the short title FM 4051 identifies the disc titled *Irish and British Songs from the Ottawa Valley*, sung by (O. J. Abbott), and issued by Folkways Records as its disc numbered FM 4051. Performer's names are generally omitted from miscellaneous compilations.

AA 3, 4 †*The Asch Recordings, 1939-1945, Vol. 2.* 2 discs, booklet (Charles Edward Smith). Asch AA 3, 4.

ABC 45-9747 †*The Neighbors.* ABC-Paramount 45-9747.

Abisch *Roz Abisch; Boche Kaplan. *Sweet Betsy from Pike* [an illustrated children's book]. New York: MacCall Publishing Co., 1970.

Abrahams *Roger D. Abrahams; George A. Foss. *A Singer and Her Songs:* Almeda Riddle's book of ballads. Louisiana State University Press, 1970.

Abrams *Freda Morrill Abrams. *Work and Sing.* 2nd ed., Delaware, Ohio: Coöperative Recreation Service, 1948.

Ada Holding Miller *The Ada Holding Miller Collection of Sheet Music.* Special Collections, University of Iowa Library, Iowa City.

C. B. Adams *Carrie B. Adams. *The Chimes of Yesterday.* Cincinnati: John Church Co., 1919.

C. S. Adams *Charles S. Adams. "New Hampshire folklore." Master's Thesis, Indiana University, 1968.

AFLP 1806 †*Bawdy Songs and Barroom Ballads, Vol. 2* (Oscar Brand). Audio-Fidelity AFLP 1806.

AFLP 1906 †*Bawdy Songs and Barroom Ballads, Vol. 1* (Oscar Brand). Audio Fidelity AFLP 1906.

AFS †*Archives of Folk Song* [recordings numbers], Library of Congress.

AFS L †*Archive of Folk Song:* Folk Music of the United States. [A series of LP discs issued by the Music Division Recording Laboratory of the Library of Congress].

AFSPB American Folklore Society Publications, Bibliographical Series.

Agay *Denes Agay. *Best Loved Songs of the American People.* Garden City, New York: Doubleday, 1975.

Aikin *J[esse] B. Aikin. *The Christian Minstrel.* 104th ed., Philadelphia etc.: T. K. Collins, 1858.

Aimwell *Absalom Aimwell. *The Philadelphia Songster, Part 1:* being a collection of choice songs such as are calculated to please the ear. Philadelphia: John M'Culloh, 1789.

Alaw *Owain Alaw. *Cwrddwyn Wrth Oleu Y Lloer [Meet Me by Moonlight Alone].* Wrexham: R. Hughes, n.d.

Album Comique *The Album Comique.* Cleveland: S. Brainard & Sons, C. 1875.

Aldrich *Jonathan Aldrich. *The Sacred Lyre.* Boston: Andrew F. Graves, 1858.

Alexander 1908 *Charles McCallon Alexander. *Alexander's Gospel Songs.* New York: Fleming H. Revell Co., 1908.

Alexander 1918 *Charles M[cCallon] Alexander; May Whittle Moody. *Northfield Hymnal No. 3.* East Northfield, Mass.: The Northfield Schools, 1918.

All Time *Songs of All Time.* Revised ed., Delaware, Ohio: Coöperative Recreation Service, 1957. (1st ed., 1946).

Allan Francis D. Allan. *Allan's Lone Star Ballads:* a collection of Southern patriotic songs. Galveston, Texas: J. D. Sawyer, 1874.

J. V. Allen *Jules Verne Allen. *Cowboy Lore.* San Antonio, Texas: The Naylor Press, 1933.

W. F. Allen *W. F. Allen; C. P. Ware; L. McK. Garrison. *Slave Songs of the United States.* New York, 1867.

Allingham William Allingham. *The Ballad Book.* London: Macmillan, 1864.

ALP 111 †*The Arkansaw Traveller's Heritage Music.* Arkansaw Traveller Folk Theatre ALP 111.

Amateur *The Amateur's Song Book, Part First.* New York: Nafis & Cornish; Boston: Elias Howe, Jr., 1843.

American Ballad Collection *American Ballad Collection.* Boston: Oliver Ditson, 1885.

American Comic Songster The American Comic Songster. New York: J. G. Shaw, 1834.

American Cowboy *American Cowboy Songs.* New York: Robbins Music Corp., 1936.

American Dime i - ii The American Dime Song Book. 2 Vols., Philadelphia: Fisher & Bro., 1860.

American Musical Miscellany *The American Musical Miscellany.* Northampton, Mass.: 1798. (Facsimile reprint, 1972).

American Singer The [American] Singer's Own Book. 30th ed., Philadelphia: Key & Biddle, 1855. (1st ed., 1834).

American Songster 1798 The American Songster. New-York: Samuel Campbell, 1798.

American Songster 1835 The American Songster. Baltimore: John Kenedy, 1835.

American Songster 1839 The American Songster. New York: Nafis & Cornish, 1839.

American Songster 1845 The American Songster. Philadelphia: W. A. Leary, 1845.

American Star The American Star. Richmond: Peter Cottom, 1814. (2nd ed., 1817).

American Vocalist The American Vocalist, or the American Singer's Own Book. New-

York: Richard Marsh, 1856.

American War Songs American War Songs. Reprint, 1871. (1st ed., Philadelphia: National Society of the Colonial Dames of America, 1925).

G. Anderson Geneva Anderson. "A Collection of ballads and songs from East Tennessee." Master's Thesis, University of North Carolina, 1932.

H. Anderson *Hugh Anderson. *Colonial Ballads*. Ferntree Gully, Victoria: 1955.

E. D. Andrews *Edward Deming Andrews. *The Gift to be Simple*. J. J. Augustin, 1940. (Reprint, New York, 1962).

J. Andrews i - iii John Andrews [printer]. *List of Songs* [3 sets, each consisting of 100 broadside sheets]. New York, 1858. [In Music Division, New York Public Library].

S. C. Andrews S. C. Andrews. *The American College Songster*. Ann Arbor, Michigan: Sheehan & Co., 1876.

Annie Hindle The Annie Hindle Songster. New York: Frederick A. Brady, 1869.

*Annie Laurie *The Annie Laurie Melodist.* New York: Robert M. De Witt, 1860.

Antidote An Antidote against Melancholy. London, 1884.

Aquarium Songster The Aquarium Songster. London: W. S. Fortey, 189-. [not paginated].

Arany *Cornel Arany. *We're Having a Party.* (Music for Millions, Vol. 24). New York: Consolidated Music Publishers, 1959.

*Arkansas Traveler *The Arkansas Traveler's Song Book.* New York: Dick & Fitzgerald, 1864.

*Arkansas Woodchopper 1932 *The Arkansas Woodchopper's World's Greatest Collection of Cowboy Songs.* Chicago: M. M. Cole, 1932.

*Arkansas Woodchopper 1940 *Arkansas Woodchopper Square Dance Calls.* Chicago: M. M. Cole, 1940.

Armitage 1916 *M. Teresa Armitage. *Junior Laurel Songs*. Boston: C. C. Birchard & Co., 1916.

Armitage 1918 *M. Teresa Armitage. *The Laurel Unison Book*. Boston: C. C. Birchard, 1918.

Armitage 1926 *M. Teresa Armitage. *Senior Laurel Songs*. Boston: C. C. Birchard, 1926.

Armitage 1944 *M. Teresa Armitage: Peter W. Dykema; Gladys Pitcher; David Stevens; J. Lilian Vandevere. *Our Land of Song*. Boston: C. C. Birchard, 1944.

B. Arnold *Byron Arnold. *Folksongs of Alabama*. University of Alabama Press, 1950.

R. S. Arnold *Robert S. Arnold; W. Oliver

Cooper; Olen S. Payte; J. W. Payte. *Heavenly Sunlight*. Jefferson, Texas: National Music Co., 1958.

Arthur *Dave Arthur; Toni Arthur. *Songs for Singing Folk*. London: Galliard, 1970.

Artley *Malvin Newton Artley. "The West Virginia country fiddler: an aspect of the folk music tradition in the United States." D. F. A. dissertation, Chicago Musical College, 1955.

Asch *Moses Asch. *104 Folk Songs*. New York: Robbins Music Corp., 1964.

Asch 461 †*Ballads* (Richard Cyer-Bennett). Asch 461.

Asch 560 †*Ballads* (George Edwards). Asch 560.

Ashbee i - x *C. R. Ashbee; Janet E. Ashbee. *The Essex House Song Book, [or] the Song book of the Guild of Handicraft*. 10 Vols., London: n.d.

Ashton 1887 John Ashton. *A Century of Ballads*. London: Elliot Stock, 1887. (Reprint, 1968).

Ashton 1888 John Ashton. *Modern Street Ballads*. London, 1888.

Ashton 1891 John Ashton. *Real Sailor Songs*. London: Leadenhall Press, 1891.

*AT *Australian Tradition*, 1964-. [Folk Lore Society of Victoria, New South Wales].

[*Athole Collection*] *The Athole Collection of the Dance Music of Scotland*. [see; James Stewart Robertson].

Atkinson *Robert W. Atkinson; Ernest Carter. *Songs of the Eastern Colleges*. New York: Hinds & Noble, 1901.

ATL †*Archives Tape Library* [recordings numbers]. Indiana State University, Bloomington, Indiana.

Auner A. W. Auner [printer]. *Broadside Sheets* [undated and un-numbered]. Philadelphia. [Collection in Music Division, New York Public Library].

Austin *Arthur Austin. *The Family Book of Favorite Hymns*. New York: Funk & Wagnalls, 1950.

Bacon 1907 *Dolores Bacon. *Hymns that Every Child Should Know*. New York: Doubleday, Page & Co., 1907.

Bacon 1910 *Dolores Bacon. *The Children's Library: Songs*. New York: Doubleday, Page & Co., 1910.

Bailey *Rona Bailey; Herbert Roth. *Shanties by the Way*. Christchurch, New Zealand: Whitcombe & Tombs, 1967.

Baker 1850 *B. F. Baker; L. H. Southard.

The Boston Melodeon, Vol. 3. Boston: Elias Howe, 1850.

Baker 1851   *B. F. Baker; L. H. Southard. *The School Chimes.* Boston: Wilkins, Carter & Co., 1851.

*Band of Hope   *Band of Hope Melodies.* New York: American Temperance Union, 1860.

Banner Songster   The Banner Songster. New York: American News Co., 1865.

Bantock 1914   *Granville Bantock. *One Hundred Songs of England.* Boston: Oliver Ditson, 1914.

Bantock 1930a i - ii   *Granville Bantock. *The Songs of England.* 2 Vols., London: W. Paxton & Co., 1930.

Bantock 1930b i - ii   *Granville Bantock. *The Songs of Scotland.* 2 Vols., London: W. Paxton & Co., 1930.

Bantock 1930c i - ii   *Granville Bantock. *The Songs of Ireland.* 2 Vols., London: W. Paxton & Co., 1930.

Barbeau   *Marius Barbeau; Arthur Lismer; Arthur Bourinot. *Come A-Singing! Canadian Folksongs.* Ottawa: National Museum of Canada Bulletin No. 107, 1947.

Barbour   *Clarence A. Barbour. *Fellowship Hymns.* New York: Association Press, 1923.

Bardeen 1875   *C. W. Bardeen. *The Song Budget.* Syracuse, New York: C. W. Bardeen, 1875. (2nd ed., 1895).

Bardeen 1888   *C. W. Bardeen. *The Song Century.* Syracuse, New York: C. W. Bardeen, 1888. (2nd ed., 1896).

[Baring-Gould]   Sabine Baring-Gould [see: S. B. Gould].

Barke   James Barke; Sydney Goodsir Smith. *Robert Burns's The Merry Muses of Caledonia.* London: W. H. Allen 1965.

Barney Williams   Barney Williams' Songster. New York: Fisher & Bro., 18--.

Barney & Rickey   Barney & Rickey's Irish Songster. New York: A. J. Fisher, 1875.

Barnum   [P.T.] Barnum's Great Clown Songster. New York: Popular Publishing Co., 1880.

Barron   *G. I. Barron. *English Musical Repository.* Edinburgh: Oliver & Co., 18--.

M. J. Barry   Michael Joseph Barry. *The Songs of Ireland.* Dublin, 1845.

Ph. Barry FMA   *Phillips Barry. *Folk Music in America.* Works Progress Administration Federal Theatre Project National Service Bureau Publication No. 80-S, June 1939.

Ph. Barry 1929   *Phillips Barry;Fannie Hardy Eckstorm; Mary Winslow Smith. *British Ballads from Maine.* Yale University Press, 1929.

Ph. Barry 1939   *Phillips Barry. *The Maine Woods Songster.* Cambridge, Mass.: Powell Printing Co., 1939.

Bayard   *Samuel P. Bayard. *Folk Tunes from the Phillips Barry Collection.* June, 1942. [A manuscript at Widener Library, Harvard University, 27256.155.193. Duplicate at Northeast Folklore Archives, University of Maine (Orono)].

B&S   *Ballads & Songs,* 1964-. [A magazine published at irregular intervals at Salford, Lancashire].

Beadle's Dime   Beadle's Dime Song Books, #1 - #28. New York: Beadle & Co. or Beadle & Adams, 1859-1871. [#21 ff. bear individual titles and are so listed].

Beadle's Half-Dime   Beadle's Half-Dime Songsters, #1 - #43. New York: Beadle & Adams, 1878-79.

Beadle's Olden Time   Beadle's Dime Songs of the Olden Time. New York: Beadle & Co., 1863.

Beadle's Pocket i - iii   Beadle's Dime Pocket Songster. 3 Vols., New York: Beadle & Co., 1865.

Beard   Anne Winsmore Beard. "The personal Folksong collection of Bascom Lamar Lunsford." M. A. Thesis, Miami University, 1959.

Beattie   *John W. Beattie, et al. *The New Blue Book of Favorite Songs.* Chicago: Hall & McCreary, 1941.

Beau Monde   The Beau Monde Songster. New York: Fisher & Denison, 1872.

*Beauties of Caledonia   *The Beauties of Caledonia, or Gems of Scottish Song.* Boston: Oliver Ditson, 1845.

Beautiful Bells   The Beautiful Bells Songster. New York: Robert M. De Witt, 1870.

Beauty of the Blondes   The Beauty of the Blondes Songster. New York: Robert M. De Witt, 1870.

E. C. Beck 1941   *Earl Clifton Beck. *Songs of the Michigan Lumberjacks.* University of Michigan Press, 1941.

E. C. Beck 1948   *Earl Clifton Beck. *Lore of the Lumber Camps.* University of Michigan Press, 1948.

E. C. Beck 1956   *Earl Clifton Beck. *They Knew Paul Bunyan.* University of Michigan Press, 1956.

E. C. Beck 1960   *Earl Clifton Beck; Virginia Goodin. *Songs of the Lake and Forest.* Ann Arbor: Edwards Brothers, 1960.

H. P. Beck 1957   *Horace P. Beck. *The Folklore of Maine.* Philadelphia: Lippincott, 1957.

H. P. Beck 1962 *Horace P. Beck. *Folklore in Action:* Essays for discussion in honor of MacEdward Leach. American Folklore Society, 1962.

H. P. Beck 1973 *Horace P. Beck. *Folklore and the Sea.* Wesleyan University Press, 1973.

M. W. Beckwith *Martha Warren Beckwith; Helen H. Roberts. *Folk-Games of Jamaica.* Poughkeepsie, New York: Vassar College, 1922.

P. Beckwith *Paul Beckwith. *Hymns.* Chicago: Inter-Varsity Press, 1947.

Beethoven *Ludwig Van Beethoven. *Werke*, Serie 24, Bd. 23: *Lieder*, Nr. 257-63. Leipzig: Breitkopf & Härtel, 1882. (Reprint, 1949).

Beeton 1865 *Beeton's Book of Songs.* London: S. O. Beeton, 1865.

Beeton 1872 *Beeton's Song Book*: National Collection. London: Ward, Lock & Tyler, [ca.] 1872.

Behan 1965 *Dominic Behan. *Ireland Sings.* London: Essex Music Co., 1965.

Behan 1967 *Dominic Behan. *The Singing Irish.* London: Scott Solomon, 1967.

Belden 1940 *Henry M. Belden. *Ballads and Songs Collected by the Missouri Folk-Lore Society.* University of Missouri Studies 15 #1, 1940. (Reprint, 1966).

Belden 1952 ii - iii Henry M. Belden; Arthur Palmer Hudson. *North Carolina Folklore*: The Frank C. Brown Collection, Vol. 2: *Folk Ballads*; Vol. 3: *Folk Songs*. Duke University Press, 1952.

Bell 185- Robert Bell. *Early Ballads.* London: Charles Griffin & Co., 185-.

Bell 1857 Robert Bell. *Ancient Poems.* London: John W. Parker & Sons, 1857.

Bella Union Bella Union Melodeon Songster. San Francisco: D. E. Appleton, 1860.

Ben Cotton Ben Cotton's Own Songster No. 2. San Francisco: D. E. Appleton, 1864.

Bennett *David Parker Bennett. "A study in fiddle tunes from western North Carolina." Master's Thesis, University of North Carolina, 1940.

Benziger *Barbara Benziger; Eleanor Dickinson. *That Old Time Religion.* New York: Harper & Row, 1975.

Berggreen *A. P. Berggreen. *Engelske, Skotske og Irske Folke-Sange og Melodien.* 2nd ed., Kjöbenhavn: C. A. Reitzels Forlag, 1862.

Bertail *Inex Bertail; Walt Kelly. *Complete Nursery Song Book.* New York: Lothrop, Lee & Shepard, 1947.

Best *Dick Best; Beth Best. *Song Fest.* Reprint, New York: Crown Publishers, 1957. (1st ed., 1948).

Bethke *Robert Bethke. *Bunkhouse Singers and Barroom Bards*: Adirondack woods singers. [forthcoming; tapes of field recordings, via personal communication; numberings tentative].

BFSSNE *Bulletin of the Folksong Society of the Northeast, #1 (1930) - #12 (1937). Reprint in one volume, American Folklore Society, 1960.

Bigelow *William P. Bigelow. *Amherst College Songs.* Amherst Alumni Council, 1926.

*Big Round Up *The Big Round Up of Cowboy Songs.* New York: Amsco, 1934.

Big Thing on Ice The Big Thing on Ice Songster. New York: Robert M. De Witt, 1869?

Bikel *Theodore Bikel. *Folksongs and Footnotes.* New York: Meridian Books, 1960.

[Bill Hardey] *Bill Hardey's Songs of the Gay Nineties. [see: Frey 1942].

Billy Barry Billy Barry's Budget of Fun Songster. New York: Popular Publishing Co., 1883?

Billy Birch Billy Birch's Ethiopian Melodist. New York: Dick & Fitzgerald, 1862.

Billy Cotton Billy Cotton's Ethiopian Songster. New York: Frederick A. Brady, 1870.

Billy Holmes Billy Holmes' Comic Vocal Lyrics. New York: Dick & Fitzgerald, 1866.

Bingham *Seth Bingham. *Five Cowboy Songs.* New York: H. W. Gray, 1930.

*Bingley i - ii *Bingley's Select Vocalist.* 2 Vols., London: J. Bingley, 185-.

Bishop Buckley Bishop Buckley's Comic Songs. Boston: F. A. Searle, 1865.

Bissell *Keith Bissell. *Six Maritime Folksongs, Set 1.* Scarborough, Ontario: Berandol Music Co., 1970.

*Bixby i - v *Bixby's Home Songs, #1 - #5.* New York: S. M. Bixby, 189- - 1907.

E. Black *Eleanora Black; Sidney Robertson. *The Gold Rush Song Book.* San Francisco: The Colt Press, 1940.

J. M. Black 1898 *James M. Black. *The Chorus of Praise.* New York: Eaton & Mains, 1898.

J. M. Black 1900 *J[ames] M. Black; C. C. McCabe. *Praise and Promise.* Chicago: R. R. McCabe & Co., 1900.

J. M. Black 1905 *James M. Black. *Songs of Faith and Hope.* Cincinnati: Jenkins & Graham, 1905.

Bley *Edgar S. Bley; Margaret Chase. *The Best Singing Games for Children of All Ages.* New York: Sterling Publishing Co.,

1957.

Bliss *P[hillip] P[aul] Bliss. *Gospel Songs.* Cincinnati: John Church Co., 1874.

[Blond] *Anthony Blond [pseud.]. *Bawdy Ballads.* London: Music Sales Corp., 1970. [see: Cray].

Blondahl *Omar Blondahl. *Newfoundlanders, Sing!* St. John's, Newfoundland· E. I. Bonnel Associates, 1964.

Blossoms The Blossoms of Harmony. London: R. Harrild, 1803.

Board of Music Trade Board of Music Trade of the United States of America. *Complete Catalogue of Sheet Music and Musical Works for 1870.* Reprint, New York, 1973.

Boardman *Harry Boardman; Lesley Boardman. *Folk Songs and Ballads of Lancashire.* New York: Oak Publications, 1973.

Bobbing Around The Bobbing Around Songster. Philadelphia: Fisher & Bro., 1851.

Bob Hart Bob Hart's Plantation Songster. New York: Dick & Fitzgerald, 1862.

Bob Slaven Bob Slaven's Over the Neighbor's Fence Songster. New York: Popular Publishing Co., 1882.

Boette *Marie Boette. *Singa Hipsy Doodle and Other Folk Songs of West Virginia.* Parkersburg, W. Va., 1971.

Bonar *Eleanor Jean Bonar. "A collection of ballads and popular songs, Iowa and Appalachian." M.A. Thesis, University of Iowa, 1930.

Bone *David W. Bone. *Capstan Bars.* New York, 1932.

Boni 1947 *Margaret Bradford Boni; Norman Lloyd. *The Fireside Book of Folk Songs.* New York: Simon & Schuster, 1947.

Boni 1952 *Margaret [Bradford] Boni; Norman Lloyd. *The Fireside Book of Favorite American Songs.* New York: Simon & Schuster, 1952.

Boni 1954 *Margaret [Bradford] Boni; Norman Lloyd. *The Fireside Book of Love Songs.* New York: Simon & Schuster, 1954.

Boni 1960 *Margaret [Bradford] Boni; Norman Lloyd. *Songs of the Gilded Age.* New York: Golden Press, 1960.

Book of Irish Songs Book of Irish Songs by Samuel Lover and others. Philadelphia: A. Winch, 1860.

Book of 1000 The Book of a Thousand Songs. New York: Richard A. Marsh, 1844.

Book of 1001 i - iii Book of 1001 Songs, or Songs for the Million. 3 Parts [paginated separately], New York: Wm. H. Murphy, 1848?

Book of Poetry The Book of Poetry of the

Hutchinson Family. Boston: Franklin Printing House, 1858.

Book of Popular Songs The Book of Popular Songs. Philadelphia: G. G. Evans, 1860.

Book of Songs & Ballads Book of Songs and Ballads, New York: Hurst & Co., 188-.

Book of Words The Book of Words of the Hutchinson Family, 2nd ed., Boston: J. S. Potter & Co., 1855.

*Boosey # *Boosey's Musical Cabinet.* [A series of vocal and instrumental music folios, #1 - #216]. London: Boosey & Co., 1861-81.

*Boosey i - xv *Boosey's Monthly Violinist:* A miscellany of the newest music. 15 Vols., London: Boosey & Co., 1861-63.

*Boosey 1862a *Boosey's 200 English, Irish and Scotch Melodies* arranged for the violin. London: Boosey & Sons, 1862.

*Boosey 1862b *Boosey's 200 Christy Minstrels' Melodies* arranged for the violin. London: Boosey & Sons, 1862.

*Boosey 1869 *Boosey's Instrumental Library No. 7:* 100 National Melodies, Irish and Scotch, for the violin. London: Boosey & Co., 1869.

*Boston Musical Miscellany *The Boston Musical Miscellany.* Boston: J. T. Buckingham, 1811.

Botkin 1937 *Benjamin A. Botkin. *The American Play-Party Song.* Reprint, New York, 1963. (1st ed., 1937).

Botkin 1944 *Benjamin A. Botkin. *A Treasury of American Folklore.* New York: Crown Publishers, 1944.

Botkin 1947 *Benjamin A. Botkin. *A Treasure of New England Folklore.* New York: Crown Publishers, 1947.

Botkin 1949 *Benjamin A. Botkin. *A Treasury of Southern Folklore.* New York: Crown Publishers, 1949.

Botkin 1951 *Benjamin A. Botkin. *A Treasury of Western Folklore.* New York: Crown Publishers, 1951.

Botkin 1953 *Benjamin A. Botkin. *A Treasury of Railroad Folklore.* New York: Crown Publishers, 1953.

Botkin 1954 *Benjamin A. Botkin. *Sidewalks of America.* New York: Bobbs-Merrill Co., 1954.

Botkin 1955 *Benjamin A. Botkin. *A Treasury of Mississippi Folklore.* New York: Crown Publishers, 1955.

Botkin 1956 Benjamin A. Botkin. *New York City Folklore.* New York: Random House, 1956.

Botsford 1930 *Florence Hudson Botsford.

Songs of the Americas. New York: G. Schirmer, 1930.

Botsford 1937 *Florence Hudson Boulton. *The Universal Folk Songster.* New York: G. Schirmer, 1937.

Boulton ii - iii *Harold Boulton; Malcolm Lawson. *Songs of the North.* 9th ed., 3 Vols. London: The Leadenhall Press, 188-. [For i, see MacLeod i].

Boulton 1893 *Harold Boulton; Arthur Somervell. *Songs of the Four Million.* 3rd ed., London: J. B. Cramer & Co., 1893.

Bowen *C. A. Bowen. *The Cokesbury Worship Hymnal.* New York and Nashville: Abingdon-Cokesbury Press, 1938.

Bowers *Ethel Bowers. *Musical Mixers and Simple Square Dances.* New York: National Recreation Association, 1937.

Brackett *A. Wendell Brackett, et al. *University of Washington Songs.* 2nd ed., New York: Hinds, Hayden & Eldredge, 1924.

Bradbury i - iii *William B[atchelder] Bradbury. *The New Golden Trio.* [3 Vols. in one, comprising:
  i *The New Golden Chain;*
  ii *The New Golden Shower;*
  iii *The Golden Censer*].
New York: William B. Bradbury, 1866.

Brand 1960*Oscar Brand. *Bawdy Songs and Backroom Ballads.* New York: Dorchester Press, 1960.

Brand 1961 *Oscar Brand. *Folksongs for Fun.* New York: Berkeley Books, 1961.

Brander *Michael Brander; Jimmie Macgregor. *Scottish and Border Battles and Ballads.* London: Seeley Service & Co., 1975.

Breathnach i - iii *Padraig Breathnach [pseud. for P. A. Walsh]. *Songs of the Gael.* [With tunes in Tonic-Sol-Fa notation]. 3 Vols., Dublin: Browne & Nolan, 1918-21. (1st ed. of Vol. i issued in 12 numbers, Dublin, 1915.)

Brewster *Paul G. Brewster.*Ballads and Songs of Indiana.* Indiana University Publications, Folklore Series No. 1, 1940.

Briegel 1933 *George F. Briegel. *44 Old Time Mormon and Far West Songs.* New York: Geo. F. Briegel, 1933.

Briegel 1934 *Breigel's All Star Collection of Cowboy Ballads and Far West Songs.* New York: George F. Briegel, 1934.

British Minstrelsie i - iv *British Minstrelsie.* 4 Vols., Edinburgh: T. C. & E. C. Jack, 1899.

*British Museum *The British Museum, or the Edinburgh Musical Miscellany,* Edinburgh: Oliver & Boyd, 1814.

*British Orpheus *The British Orpheus.* Stourport: George Nicholson, 18--,

*British Students *The British Students' Song Book.* London: Bayley & Ferguson, 1913.

Britten *Benjamin Britten. *Folk Song Arrangements, Vol. 3: British Isles.* London: Boosey & Co., 1947.

*Broadman Hymnal *The Broadman Hymnal.* Nashville, Tennessee: The Broadman Press, 1940.

Broadway Stage Waiting for a Broadway Stage Songster. New York: Robert M. De Witt, 1868.

Broadwood 1893 *Lucy E. Broadwood; J. A. Fuller Maitland. *English Conty Songs.* London: The Leadenhall Press, 1893.

Broadwood 1908 *Lucy E. Broadwood. *English Traditional Songs and Carols.* London, 1908.

Brock *John Brock. *Morris Dance Tunes.* London: English Folk Dance & Song Society, 1973.

Brocklebank *Joan Brocklebank; Biddie Kindesley. *A Dorset Book of Folk Songs.* London: English Folk Dance & Song Society, 1948.

Bronson i - iv *Bertrand Bronson. *The Traditional Tunes of the Child Ballads.* 4 Vols., Princeton University Press, 1959-72.

Broth of a Boy The Broth of a Boy Songster. New York: Robert M. De Witt, 1870.

C. Brown *Colin Brown. *The Thistle: a Miscellany of Scottish Song.* London & Glasgow: William Collins, 1883.

J. D. Brown *James Duff Brown; Alfred Moffat. *Characteristic Songs and Dances of all Nations.* London: Bayley & Ferguson, 1901.

Browne *Ray B. Browne. "Alabama folk songs." Dissertation (English), University of California at Los Angeles, 1956.

Brumley 1972 *Albert E. Brumley. *All-Day Singin' and Dinner on the Ground.* Camdenton, Missouri, 1972.

Brumley i - ii *Albert E. Brumley. *Songs of the Pioneers.* 2 Vols., Camdenton, Missouri, 1970-73.

Brune *John A. Brune. *The Roving Songster.* London, 1959.

Brunk *J[ohn] D. Brunk. *Church and Sunday School Hymnal.* Scottdale, Pennsylvania: Mennonite Publishing House, 1902.

Brunswick 2923 †*The Roving Gambler* (Vernon Dalhart). Brunswick 2923.

Bryant 1857 *Bryant's Power of Music.* New York: Robert M. De Witt, 1857.

Bryant 1861 *Bryant's Songs from Dixie.* New York: Robert M. De Witt, 1861.

Bryant 1863 *Bryant's Cane Brake Refrains.* New York: Robert M. De Witt, 1863.

Bryant 1864 *[Dan] Bryant's New Songster.* New York: Robert M. De Witt, 1864.

[*Bryant's Minstrels*] [see: William L. Hobbs].

N. Buchan 1962 *Norman Buchan. *101 Scottish Songs.* Glasgow: William Collins Sons, 1962.

N. Buchan 1973 *Norman Buchan; Peter Hall. *The Scottish Folksinger.* London: William Collins, 1973.

P. Buchan i - ii Peter Buchan. *Ancient Ballads and Songs of the North of Scotland.* 2 Vols., Edinburgh: William Patterson, 1875. (1st ed., 1828).

Buchanan *Annabel Morris Buchanan. *Folk Hymns of America.* New York. 1938.

Buchtel *Forrest L. Buchtel. *100 Songs You Remember.* Chicago: Neil A. Kjos Music Co., 1946.

Buck 1916 *Percy C. Buck. *The Oxford Song Book, Vol. 1.* London, 1916.

Buck 1933 *Percy [C.] Buck. *The Oxford Nursery Song Book.* Oxford University Press, 1933. (2nd ed., 1961).

Bucke i *Lilian E. Bucke. *The Songs of the Children, Set 1.* London: Joseph Williams, 1923.

Buckley *Buckley's [Serenaders] Melodist.* Boston: Henry Tolman & Co., 1864.

Budworth Budworth's New Comic Ethiopian Songster.* New York: Frederick A. Brady, 1861.

Buford Mary Elizabeth Buford. "*Folk songs of Florida and Texas.*" M. A. Thesis (English), Southern Methodist University, 1941.

Bullard *Carrie Bullard. *The Most Popular Mother Goose Songs and Other Nursery Rhymes.* New York: Hinds, Hayden & Eldredge, 1910.

Bullen *Frank T. Bullen; W. F. Arnold. *Songs of Sea Labour (Chanties).* London: Orpheus Music Publishing Co., 1914.

Bunting 1796 *Edward Bunting. *A General Collection of the Ancient Irish Music.* Dublin, 1796. [Facsimilar reprint included in Bunting 1969, separately paginated].

Bunting 1809 i - ii *Edward Bunting. *A General Collection of the Ancient Music of Ireland.* 2 Vols., London, 1809. [Facsimile reprint included in Bunting 1969, separately paginated].

Bunting 1840 i - ii *Edward Bunting. *A Collection of the Ancient Music of Ireland.* 2 Vols., Dublin: Hodges & Smith, 1840. [Facsimile reprint included in Buting 1969, separately paginated].

[Bunting 1969] *Edward Bunting. *The Ancient Music of Ireland.* [Facsimile reprint of the three collections of 1840, 1809 and 1796 in that sequence]. Dublin: Walton's, 1969.

Burchenal *Elizabeth Burchenal. *American Country Dances, Vol. 1: Contra Dances.* New York: G. Shirmer, 1918.

Burns Robert Burns. *Complete Poetical Works.* Cambridge Edition, Houghton Mifflin, 1897.

[Burns] *Robert Burns. *The Scots Musical Museum.* [see: James Johnson #].

[Burns] *Robert Burns. *Poems and Songs.* [see: James C. Dick; James Kinsley; Robert Laing; William Stenhouse].

[Burns 1800] Robert Burns. *The Merry Muses of Caledonia.* 1st ed., 1800. [see: James Barke].

Burt *Olive Woolley Burt. *American Murder Ballads.* New York: Citadel, 1964.

J. Burton i - ii Jack Burton. *The Blue Book of Tin Pan Alley.* 2 Vols., 2nd ed., Watkins Glen, New York: Century House, 1962.

T. Burton i - ii *Thomas G. Burton; Ambrose N. Manning; Annette L. Wolford. *The East Tennessee State University Collection of Folklore: Folksongs.* 2 Vols., Johnson City: East Tennessee State University Press. 1967-69.

Burton's Comic [W. F.] Burton's Comic Songster.* Philadelphia: James Kayjun & Bro., 1838.

A. Bush *Alan Bush. *Variations, Nocturne and Finale on an English Sea-Song,* for Piano and Orchestra, Opus 60. 2-Piano Score, London: Novello & Co., 1973.

M. E. Bush i - ii *Michael E. Bush. *Folk Songs of Central West Virginia.* 2 Vols., Ravenswood, W. Va., 1969-70. [Library of Congress M1629.B955.F6].

Butler *Charles Buteer. *The Silver Bell.* Boston: Henry Tolman & Co., 1864.

Butterworth *George Butterworth. *Folk Songs from Sussex.* London: Augener, 1912.

C 186 †*The Return of the Wayfaring Stranger* (Burl Ives). Columbia Album C 186.

Caledonian Musical Repository The Caledonian Musical Repository.* London: B[enjamin] Crosby, 1806.

Calhoun *Cecil Warner Calhoun. "Selected instrumental folk music of south central Kentucky." M. A. Thesis, University of Iowa, 1941.

California Checklist Checklist of California Songs.* Archive of California Folk Music, Works Projects Administration, University of California [Berkeley] Department of Music, 1940.

[*California Songster*] *The California Song-ster*. San Francisco: D. E. Appleton, 1855. [see: *Pacific Song Book* i].

Callcott *Maria Hutchins Callcott; William Hutchins Callcott. *The Child's Own Singing Book*. London: Cramer, Addison & Beale, 1843.

Callender *Callender's Original Colored Minstrel Songster*. New York, 1882.

Calliope *Calliope: or, The Vocal Enchantress*. London: C. Elliot & T. Kay, 1788.

Cambiaire Celestin Pierre Cambiaire. *East Tennessee and Western Virginia Mountain Ballads*. London: The Mitre Press, 1934.

Cameron *Iain Cameron. *Corrie Voices:* Folk Songs of the Gael. London: Folk Press, n.d.

A. Campbell *Alexander Campbell. *Albyn's Anthology*, or a select collection of the melodies and vocal poetry peculiar to Scotland and the Isles. 2 Vols. in 1, Reprint: Norwood Editions, 1973. (1st ed., 1816).

I. Campbell *Ian Campbell. *Come Listen*. London: Ginn & Co., 1969.

Camp Songs *Camp Songs*. Boston: Oliver Ditson, 1861.

Can Can The Can Can Songster. New York: Fisher & Denison, 1868.

Canadian Boys *Songs for Canadian Boys*. Toronto: Macmillan, 1932.

Capitol P8556 †*I Know My Love* (Salli Terri). Capitol P8556.

Capitol T700 †*This Lusty Land* (Tennessee Ernie Ford). Capitol T700.

Captain Jinks Captain Jinks Songster. New York: Robert M. De Witt, 1868.

Captain Kelly Captain [Patrick] Kelly's Songster. New York: Frederick A. Brady, 1870.

Carden *Allen D. Carden. *The Missouri Harmony*, with Supplement. New Ed., Cincinnati: E. Morgan & Son, 1837. (1st ed., 1820).

G. G. Carey 1970 *George G. Carey. *Maryland Folklore and Folklife*. Cambridge, Maryland: Tidewater Publications, 1970.

G. G. Carey 1971 George G. Carey. *Maryland Folk Legends and Folk Songs*. Cambridge, Maryland: Tidewater Publications, 1971.

O. Carey *Olive Carey. *Ten English Folk-Songs*. London: J. Curwen, 1915.

Carleton William Carleton. *Willy Reilly and his Dear Coleen Bawn*. 3 Vols., London: Hope & Co., 1855.

Carlisle *Irene Jones Carlisle. "Fifty ballads and songs from northwest Arkansas." M. A. Thesis, University of Iowa, 1941.

Carmer 1942a *Carl Carmer. *America Sings*. New York, 1942.

Carmer 1942b *Carl Carmer; Albert Sirmay. *Songs of the Rivers of America*. New York: Farrar & Rinehart, 1942.

Carmina Princetonia *Carmina Princetonia*. 2nd ed., New York: W. H. Stelle, 1873.

Carpenter 1858 J[oseph] E. Carpenter. *The Modern Song Book*, or book of modern songs. London: G. Routledge & Co., 1858.

Carpenter 1864 J[oseph] E. Carpenter. *The Funny Man's Song Book*. London: Routledge, Warne & Routledge, 1864.

Carpenter 18— Joseph E. Carpenter. *Sailor Songs:* A new naval song book. London: Frederick Warne & Co., n.d.

Carpenter i - ii Joseph E. Carpenter. *The Comic and Humorous Song Book*. 2 Parts [Part 2 bears separate running title: *The Humorous Song Book*], London: Routledge, Warne & Routledge, 1864.

Carry the News Carry the News to Mary Songster. New York: Robert M. De Witt, 1871.

Carson J. Robison *Carson J. Robison's World's Greatest Collection of Mountain Ballads and Old-Time Songs*. Chicago: M. M. Cole, 193-.

Cass-Beggs 19— *Barbara Cass[-Beggs]; Helen Freeman, *Awake and Sing!* Toronto: Fellowship for a Christian Social Order, n.d.

Cass-Beggs 1963 *Barbara Cass-Beggs; Richard Johnston. *Eight Songs of Saskatchewan*. Toronto: Canadian Music Sales, 1963.

Cass-Beggs 1975 *Barbara Cass-Beggs. *Canadian Folk Songs for the Young*. Vancouver: J. J. Douglas, 1975.

Catcheside-Warrington i-iv *C. E. Catcheside-Warrington. *Tyneside Songs*. 4 Vols., Newcastle-on-Tyne: J. G. Windows, 1911-13. (2nd ed., 1927-29).

Cavendish # *The Cavendish Music Books* [a numbered series of vocal and instrumental music folios]. London: Boosey & Co., 1878-.

CAY *Come All Ye* [Journal of the Vancouver Folk Song Society], 1972-.

Cayce *C. H. Cayce. *The Good Old Songs*. 28th ed., Thornton, Arkansas: Cayce Publishing Co., 1967. (1st ed., 1913?).

Cazden 1949a *Norman Cazden. *Three Ballads from the Catskills*, Opus 52, for small orchestra. Privately Printed, New York, 1949.

Cazden 1949b *Norman Cazden. *Songs from the Catskills*, Opus 54, for symphonic band. Privately printed, New York, 1949.

Cazden 1950 *Norman Cazden. *Reels, Jigs and Squares* : 200 Dance Tunes. Privately printed, New York, 1950.

Cazden 1951a *Norman Cazden. *Traditional Dances*. Privately printed, New York, 1951.

Cazden 1951b *Norman Cazden. *Olden Time Dances*. Privately printed, New York, 1951.

Cazden 1955 *Norman Cazden. *Dances from Woodland*. 2nd ed., Bridgeport, Connecticut, 1955. (1st ed., New York, 1945).

Cazden 1958 i - ii *Norman Cazden. *The Abelard Folksong Book*. 2 Vols. in 1, separately paginated, New York: Abelard-Schuman, 1958.

Cazden 1958a *Norman Cazden; Norman Studer. *Dingle Hill* [a play with music]. New York: MCA Music Corp., 1958.

Cazden 1959 *Norman Cazden. *Good Old Songs for Piano*, Opus 64. Privately printed, Bridgeport, Connecticut, 1959. (Revised ed., 1976).

Cazden 1961 *Norman Cazden. *A Book of Nonsense Songs*. New York: Crown Publishers, 1961.

Cazden 1962 *Norman Cazden. *American Folksongs for Piano*. Stamford, Connecticut: Jack Spratt Music Co., 1962.

Cazden 1963 i - ii *Norman Cazden. *American Folksongs for Two Recorders*. 2 Vols., New York: Associated Music Publishers, 1963.

Cazden 1966 *Norman Cazden. *Three Traditional Songs*, Opus 61. Privately printed, Lexington, Mass., 1966.

Cazden 1973 *Norman Cazden. *Merry Ditties*. New York: Bonanza Books, 1973.

Cazden 1974 *Norman Cazden. *Sing, Learn and Play*. 3rd ed., Bangor, Maine, 1974. (1st ed., 1955).

Cazden 1978 *Norman Cazden. *A Catskill Songbook*. Fleischmanns, New York: Purple Mountain Press, 1978.

Central Park *The Central Park Show Songster*. New York: Robert M. De Witt, 1872.

CEOL *CEOL* [A Journal of Irish Music], 1963-.

CFB *Colorado Folksong Bulletin*, 1962-.

CFC 201 †*Green Fields of Illinois*. (Booklet, ed. by Judith McCulloh). University of Ilinois Campus Folk Song Club CFC 201.

CFC 301 †*The Hell-Bound Train* (Glenn Ohrlin). Booklet. University of Illinois Campus Folk Song Club CFC 301.

CFMJ *Canadian Folk Music Journal*, 1973-.

D. B. Chamberlain *David B. Chamberlain; Karl P. Harrington. *Songs of All the Colleges*. New York: Hinds & Noble, 1900.

W. W. Chamberlain William Woodrow Chamberlain. "Folk music of the Kentucky barrens." Ms. at Music Library, Stanford University: ML 3551.C443, 194-.

Chambers *Robert Chambers. *The Songs of Scotland Prior to Burns*. Edinburgh & London: W. & R. Chambers, 186-.

Champagne Charlie 1867 *Champagne Charlie Songster*. New York: Dick & Fitzgerald, 1867.

Champagne Charlie 1868 *Champagne Charlie and Coal Oil Tommy Songster*. San Francisco: D. E. Appleton & Co., 1868.

Chapbook *Chapbook* [Scotland's Folk-Life Magazine], 1964-.

Chapman 1904 *J. Wilbur Chapman. *Songs of Praise No. 1*. Philadelphia: Presbyterian Board of Publication, 1904.

Chapman 1906 *J. Wilbur Chapman; E[dwin] O. Excell. *Winona Hymns*. Philadelphia: The Westminster Press, 1906.

Chapman Sisters The Chapman Sisters Songster. New York: Robert M. De Witt, 1870.

L. Chappell Louis W. Chappell. *Folk-Songs of Roanoke and the Albemarle*. Morgantown, W. Va.: The Ballad Press, 1939.

W. Chappell 1840 i - ii *William Chappell. *A Collection of National British Airs*. 2 Vols., London: Chappell & Co., 1840.

W. Chappell 1859 i - ii *William Chappell. *Popular Music of the Olden Time*. 2 Vols., Reprint, New York: Dover Books, 1965. (1st ed., London: Chappell & Co., 1859).

Chappell 100 i - ii *Chappell's One Hundred Hornpipes, Strathspeys, Reels, Jigs, & Country Dances*. 2 Vols., London: Chappell & Co., 1859, 1872.

Chappell 1863 *Chappell's One Hundred Popular Airs for the German Concertina*. London: Chappell & Co., 1863.

[Chapple] *Joe Mitchell Chapple. *Heart Songs Dear to the American People*. [see: *Heart Songs*].

Charles Schofield Charles Schofield's Flashes Songster. New York: Popular Publishing Co., 1883.

Charley Fox 1858 *Charley Fox's Bijou Songster*. Philadelphia: A. Winch, 1858.

Charley Fox 1863 *Charley Fox's Minstrel's Companion* [with music ed. by Frank B. Converse]. Philadelphia: Fisher & Bro., 1863.

Charley Monroe Charley Monroe's Clown Song Book. Philadelphia: R. F. Simpson, 1861.

Charmer i - ii *The Charmer*: a choice collection of songs. 2 Vols., Edinburgh: J. Yair,

1751.

Charosh *Paul Charosh; Robert A. Fremont. *More Favorite Songs of the Nineties* [62 facsimiles of sheet music]. New York: Dover Books, 1975.

A. H. Chase *Ann Hastings Chase. *The Singing Caller*. New York: Association Press, 1951.

R. Chase 1938 *Richard Chase. *Old Songs and Singing Games*. University of North Carolina Press, 1938.

R. Chase 1949 *Richard Chase. *Hullabaloo and Other Singing Folk Games*. Boston: Houghton Mifflin, 1949.

R. Chase 1956 *Richard Chase. *American Folk Tales and Songs*. New York: Signet Key Books 1956.

Chicago Park District *Chicago Park District. *Folk Tunes, Including Square and Round Dances and Specialties*. Works Progress Administration Illinois Writers Project, 1942.

Child *Francis James Child. *The English and Scottish Popular Ballads*. 5 Vols., Reprint, New York: Dover Books, 1965. (1st ed., Boston and New York: Houghton Mifflin, 1882-94).

Child's Song Book *The Child's Song Book*. Boston: Richardson, Lord & Holbrook, 1830.

Chilton *Charles Chilton; Robin Beaumont. *Victorian Folk Songs*. London: Essex Music Co., 1965.

Choice Irish Songs i - ii *Choice Irish Songs*. 2 Vols., Boston: White-Smith Music Publishing Co., 1892, 1906.

Chosky *Lois Chosky. *The Kodaly Method*. Englewood Cliffs, New Jersey: Prentice-Hall, 1974.

Christian Harp *The Christian Harp and Sabbath School Songster*. Singer's Glen, Virginia: Joseph Funk's Sons, 1869.

Christian Hymnal *Christian Hymnal*. Hesston, Kansas: Church of God in Christ, Mennonite, 1959.

Christian Worship *Christian Worship*. St. Louis, Missouri: The Bethany Press, 1941.

Christie i - ii *William Christie. *Traditional Ballad Airs*. 2 Vols., Edinburgh: 1876, 1881.

Christman Henry Christman. *Tin Horns and Calico:* a decisive episode in the emergence of democracy. New York: Henry Holt & Co., 1945.

Christy 1854 *Christy & White's Ethiopian Melodies Part 2: White's New Illustrated Melodeon*. Philadelphia, 1854.

Christy 1855 *Edwin Pearce Christy; Henry C. Work. *We Are Coming, Sister Mary*. London: C. Sheard, 1855.

Christy 1857 *Christy's Panorama Songster*. New York: William B. Murphy, 1857.

Christy 1860 *Christy's Minstrels Melodies* [A collection of sheet music publications under various imprints, London, ca. 1860, at British Museum Library].

Christy 1900 *Christy Minstrel Songs, First Book*. London: Boosey & Co., ca. 1900.

Church of God *Hymnal of the Church of God*. Anderson, Indiana: The Warner Press, 1971.

C. H. Churchill *Clinton H. Churchill. *Tabernacle Service Songs*. Buffalo, New York: Churchill Tabernacle, 193-.

S. Churchill *Stuart Churchill; Harry Robert Wilson. *Sing a Folk Song*. New York: Plymouth Music Co., 1957.

CL 628 †*The Wayfaring Stranger* (Burl Ives) [a re-issue with additions of Okeh K-3]. Columbia CL 628.

CL 948 †*Songs of the Sea* (Norman Luboff Choir). Columbia CL 948.

Clampers *What Was Your Name in the States? The Clamper's Book of Balladry or Hewgagiana*, issued by the Order of E. Clampus Vitus, Goat Island, 1939.

Clancy 1964 *The Clancy Brothers & Tony Makem Song Book*. New York: Oak Publications, 1964.

Clancy 1971 *The Clancy Brothers & Tony Makem's The Irish Songbook*. New York: Music Sales Corp., 1971.

G. M. Clark 1871 George M. Clark. *Original and Selected Comic and Sentimental Songs*. Montpelier, Vermont: 1871.

G. M. Clark 1872 George M. Clark. *Drifting with the Tide Song Book*. Montpelier, Vermont: Argus & Patriot Printing House, 1872.

K. S. Clark 1930 *Kenneth S. Clark. *The "Everybody Sing" Book*. New York: Paull-Pioneer Music Co., 1930.

K. S. Clark 1931 *Kenneth Sherman Clark. *Songs of the Campus*. New York: Paull-Pioneer Music Co., 1931.

K. S. Clark 1932 *Kenneth S. Clark. *The Cowboy Sings*. New York, 1932.

K. S. Clark 1934 *Kenneth S. Clark. *The Happy Cowboy*. New York: Paull-Pioneer Music Corp., 1934.

Clark's Orphean Warbler [W. M.] *Clark's Orphean Warbler*. London: W. M. Clark, 185-.

Clayre *Alasdair Clayre. *100 Folk Songs and New Songs*. London: Wolfe Publishing Co., 1968.

136

Clemens   Samuel L. Clemens. *Life on the Mississippi*. New York: Harper & Brothers, 1911. (1st ed., 1874).

J. Clemens   *John Clements. *Hymns for the Master*. Philadelphia: Wesleyan Publishing Co., 1908.

R. Clements   Rex Clements. *Manavilins: A Muster of Sea-Songs, 1890-1910*. London: Heath Cranton, 1928. (Reprint, Norwood Editions, 1975).

Clifford   *Teresa Clifford; Havelock Nelson. *An Irish Folksinger's Album*. London: J. Curwen & Sons, 1957.

Clifton   *Bill Clifton. *150 Old-Time Folk and Gospel Songs*. Burke, Virginia: Bluegrass Unlimited, 195-.

Cline   *C. C. Cline. *Popular Hymns*. Covington, Kentucky: Guide Publishing Co., 1885.

Clown's Songster   *The Clown's Songster*. New York: Robert M. De Witt, 1871.

CMS 650, 660, 670   †*The Musical Heritage of America* (Tom Glazer). 12 discs in 3 vols., CMS Records 650, 600, 670.

Cobb   Lucy Maria Cobb. "Traditional ballads and songs of eastern North Carolina." Master's Thesis, University of North Carolina, 1927.

Coffin   Tristram P. Coffin. *The British Traditional Ballad in North America*. Philadelphia: The American Folklore Society, 1950. [Bibliographical Series, Vol. 2].

J. Cohen   *John Cohen; Mike Seeger. *The New Lost City Ramblers Song Book*. New York: Oak Publications, 1964.

M. Cohen 1966   *Mike Cohen. *101 Plus 5 Folk Songs for Camp*. New York: Oak Publications, 1966.

M. Cohen 1967   *Mike Cohen. *To Hell with Skiing*. New York: Oak Publications, 1967.

Colcord   *Joanna C. Colcord. *Songs of American Sailormen*. Reprint, New York: Oak Publications, 1964 [with variant pagination]. (1st ed., 1938).

E. W. Cole   E. W. Cole. *The Thousand Best Songs in the World*. London: Hutchinson & Co., [187-].

M. M. Cole   *M. M. Cole [publisher]. *One Thousand Fiddle Tunes*. Chicago: M. M. Cole, 1940.

W. Cole   *William Cole. *Folk Songs of England, Ireland, Scotland and Wales*. Garden City, New York: Doubleday, 1961.

R. H. Coleman 1924   *Robert H. Coleman. *Harvest Hymns*. Philadelphia: The Judson Press, 1924.

R. H. Coleman 1933   *Robert H. Coleman. *The American Hymnal*. Dallas, Texas: Robert H. Coleman, 1933.

S. N. Coleman   Satis N. Coleman; Adolph Bregman. *Songs of American Folks*. New York: John Day, 1942.

College Songs   *College Songs*. New York: Richard A. Saalfield, 1888.

College Songs #3   *College Songs, No. 3*. New York: Academic Music Co., 1907.

Collegiate   *Collegiate Song Book:* the world's greatest collection of college songs. Chicago: M. M. Cole, 1930.

Colles i - v   *H. C. Colles. *Grove's Dictionary of Music and Musicians*. 3rd ed., 5 vols. New York: The Macmillan Co., 1927.

Collinson 1946   *Francis M. Collinson; Francis Dillon. *Songs from the Countryside* featured in *Country Magazine*. London: W. Paxton & Co., 1946.

Collinson 1951   *Francis [M.] Collinson. *Joe, the Carrier Lad*. London: J. W. Chester, 1951.

Collinson 1952   *Francis M. Collinson; Francis Dillon. *Folk Songs from Country Magazine*. London: W. Paxton & Co. 1952.

Collinson 1966   *Francis [M.] Collinson. *The Traditional and National Music of Scotland*. Nashville, Tenn.: Vanderbilt University Press, 1966.

Colum   *Padraic Colum. *A Treasury of Irish Folklore*. 2nd rev. ed., New York, 1967. (1st ed., 1954).

Columbia University   *Columbia University Songs*. Boston: Oliver Ditson, 1904.

Columbian Songster   The Columbian Songster. Nathaniel Heaton, 1799.

Combs 1925   Josiah H. Combs. *Folk Songs du Midi des États-Unis*. Paris: Les Presses Universitaires de France, 1925.

Combs 1939   *Josiah H. Combs; Keith Mixon. *Folk Songs from the Kentucky Highlands*. New York: G. Schirmer, 1939.

Combs 1967   Josiah H. Combs; D. K. Wilgus. *Folk-Songs of the Southern United States*. University of Texas Press, 1967.

Comic Scrapbook   *Comic, Drinking and Hunting Songs [Scrapbook]*. [A collection of broadside sheets, including music]. Music Division, New York Public Library: Drexel 4109.

Comic Songster   *The Comic Songster*. Boston: Oliver Ditson, 1870.

Comical Brown   *Comical [William B.] Brown's Songster*. Boston: White-Smith, 1885.

Comical, Topical   *Comical, Topical and Mottoe Songs*. New York: Richard A. Saalfield, ?1887.

Community i - vii *Community Dance Manuals*. 7 Vols., London: English Folk Dance & Song Society, 1949-1967.

Concert Room The Concert Room Songster. Philadelphia: A. Winch, 1860.

Conner's Irish Conner's Irish Songster. San Francisco: D. E. Appleton & Co., 1864.

Converse 1863 *[Frank B. Converse]. *Frank Converse's Old Cremona Songster*. New York: Dick & Fitzgerald, 1863.

Converse 1865 *Frank [B.] Converse. *Banjo Instructor*. New York: Dick & Fitzgerald, 1865.

Converse 1871 *Frank B. Converse. *The Banjoist*. New York. William A. Pond Co., 1871.

Converse 1887 *Frank B. Converse. *Analytical Banjo Method*. New York: S. T. Gordon & Son, 1887.

Converse 1888 *Frank B. Converse. *Converse's Banjo Songs*. New York: S. T. Gordon & Son, 1888.

Cook *Harold E. Cook. *Shaker Music*. Bucknell University Press, 1973.

Cool Burgess Cool Burgess's Oh! Don't Get Weary, Children Songster. New York: A. J. Fisher, 1877.

Cooper *W. M. Cooper et al. *The B. F. White Sacred Harp*. Re-issue, Troy, Alabama: Sacred Harp Book Co., 1949. (1st ed., 1902).

Cooper 1971 *Bob Copper. *A Song for Every Season*. London: Heineman, 1971.

Copper 1973 *Bob Copper. *Songs and Southern Breezes*. London: Heineman, 1973.

Cornell *Prof. H. H. Cornell's Collection of Latest Songs with Valuable Recipes and Instructions How to Become a Ventriloquist and Magician*. San Francisco: J. R. Brodie & Co., 1886.

Costello *Eileen Costello. *Amráin Mhuighe Seóla:* Traditional folk-songs from Galway and Mayo. Dublin: The Talbot Press, 1923.

Coup [W. C.] Coup's Monster Clown Songster. New York: Popular Publishing Co., 1881.

Cowboy Tom *Cowboy Tom's Round Up Book. New York, 1933.

[Cowell] *120 Comic Songs Sung by Sam Cowell. [see: *D'Alcorn #1*].

Cox 1925 *John Harrington Cox. *Folk Songs of the South*. Reprint, New York: Dover Books, 1967. (1st ed., Harvard University Press, 1925).

Cox 1939 i - ii *John Harrington Cox. *Traditional Ballads and Folk-Songs, Mainly from West Virginia*. Works Progress Administration Federal Theatre Project National Service Bureau Folk-Song and Folklore Department, 1939. (Reprint, with variant pagination in 1 vol., for American Folklore Society: George W. Boswell, 1964).

Cozans [Phillip J. Cozans, publisher]. *Forget-Me-Not Songster* [a compilation of four sections with continuous pagination, comprising:
  i. *Select Songs,*
  ii. *The Deck & Port Songster,*
  iii. *Brother Jonathan, or the American Boy's Songster,* and
  iv. *Robin Hood and Captain Kidd's Songster*].
New York: Philip J. Cozans, 1845?

Crane *Walter Crane. *The Baby's Opera*. London: Frederick Warne & Co., n.d.

Crawhall 1864 *Joseph Crawhall. *A Collection of Right Merrie Garlands for North Country Anglers*. Newcastle-on-Tyne: George Rutland, 1864.

Crawhall 1965 *Joseph Crawhall. *A Beuk O' Newcassel Songs*. Newcastle Upon Tyne: Harold Hill, 1965.

Cray *Ed Cray. *The Erotic Muse*. New York: Oak Publications, 1968.

Creighton 1932 *Helen Creighton. *Songs and Ballads from Nova Scotia*. Toronto: J. M. Dent, 1932. (Reprint, New York: Dover Books, 1966).

Creighton 1940 *Helen Creighton; Doreen [H.] Senior. *Twelve Folk Songs from Nova Scotia*. London: Novello & Co., 1940.

Creighton 1950 *Helen Creighton; Doreen H. Senior. *Traditional Songs from Nova Scotia*. Toronto: The Ryerson Press, 1950.

Creighton 1962 *Helen Creighton. *Maritime Folk Songs*. Toronto: The Ryerson Press, 1962.

Creighton 1964 *Helen Creighton; Calum MacLeod. *Gaelic Songs from Nova Scotia*. Ottawa: National Museum of Canada, Bulletin No. 198, 1964.

Creighton 1971 *Helen Creighton. *Folksongs from Southern New Brunswick*. Ottawa: National Museum of Canada, 1971.

CRI 111.2 †Herbert Haufrecht. *Square Set for String Orchestra* (Orchestra of Accademia di Santa Cecilia—Roma). Composers Recordings Inc. CRI 111.2.

CRI 117.2 †Norman Cazden. *Three Ballads for Orchestra*, Opus 52 (Oslo Philharmonic Orchestra). Composers Recordings Inc. CRI 117.2.

Croker Thomas Crofton Croker. *The Popular Songs of Ireland*. London: Henry Colburn, 1839.

Crosby 1808 *[Benjamin] Crosby's Irish Mu-

sical Repository. London: [B. Crosby], ca. 1808.

Crosby 1812 *[Benjamin] *Crosby's English Musical Repository*. London: B. Crosby, [1812].

CRS 401 †*Christmas Carols in Cambridge, Volume 1* (Harvard Glee Club and Radcliffe Choral Society, cond. by G. Wallace Woodworth). Cambridge Records CRS 401.

CS 54 †*The Judge Said* (Malvina Reynolds). Cassandra Records CS 54.

CS 8448 †*The Clancy Brothers & Tommy Makem*. Columbia CS 8448.

Cumming *Alistair C. Cumming. *Folk Songs for School, Home, Camp, Anywhere*. Wellington, New Zealand: A. H. & A. W. Reed, 1968.

Cundy # *Cundy's Five Cent Series of Popular Music* [a numbered series of sheet music issues, #1 - #112]. Boston: W. H. Cundy, 1869-71.

Cutting Edith B. Cutting. *Lore of an Adirondack County*. Cornell University Press, 1944.

Cyporyn *Dennis Cyporyn. *The Bluegrass Songbook*. New York: The Macmillan Co., 1972.

Dadmun *J. W. Dadmun. *the Melodeon*. Boston: J. P. Mager, 1860.

D'Alcorn # *D'Alcorn's Musical Miracles* [a series of 20 vocal and instrumental music folios]. London: H. D'Alcorn, 1876.

Dallas 1973 *Karl Dallas. *The Cruel Wars:* 100 soldier's songs. London: Wolfe Publishing Co., 1973.

Dallas 1974 *Karl Dallas. *One Hundred Songs of Toil*. London: Wolfe Publishing Co., 1974.

Dallin *Leon Dallin; Lynn Dallin. *Folk Songster*. Dubuque, Iowa: Wm. C. Brown, 1967.

Damon # *S. Foster Damon. *Series of Old American Songs* [reproduced in facsimile]. Brown University Library, 1936.

Dan Kelly Dan Kelly's Songster. New York: Frederick A. Brady, 1869.

Dan Nash 1881 *Dan Nash's New Original Barney the Guide Songster*. New York: Popular Publishing Co., 1881.

Dan Nash 1882 *Dan Nash's I'm Proud I'm an Irishman's Son Songster*. New York: Popular Publishing Co., 1882.

Dare *George S. Dare. *Everybody's Song Book*. New York: A. S. Barnes, 1938.

Darley *Arthur Darley; P. J. McCall. *Feis Ceoil Collection of Irish Airs*. Dublin, 1914.

Date *Henry Date. *Pentecostal Hymns, No. 1 and No. 2 Combined*. Chicago: The Hope Publishing Co., 1898?

Daughters *Daughters of the Utah Pioneers. *Pioneer Songs*. 1932.

Dauney *William Dauney. *Ancient Scottish Melodies*. [A discussion and transcription from lute tablature of the *Skene Ms.* of ca. 1615-30]. Edinburgh: The Maitland Club, 1838.

Davidson 1854 George Henry Davidson. *Modern Song Book*. London: George H. Davidson, 1854.

*Davidson i - ii *Davidson's Universal Melodist*. 2 Vols., London: G. H. Davidson, 1847, 1849.

*Davidson iii - x *Davidson's Musical Library*, Vols. 3-10. London: G. H. Davidson, 1861-62.

*Davidson # *Davidson's Musical Miracles:* One hundred twenty songs of Ireland. [Numbered listings follow p. 64]. London: G. H. Davidson, 1965.

Davie *Cedric Thorpe Davie; George McVicar. *The Oxford Scottish Song Book*. Oxford University Press, 1969.

E. T. Davies *E. T. Davies; Sydney Northcote. *Caneuon Cenedlaethol Cymru* (*The National Songs of Wales*). London: Boosey & Co., 1959.

G. Davies *Gwilym Davies. *A Hampshire Collection* [of songs]. [London, 1974].

H. W. Davies *H. Walford Davies. *The New Fellowship Song Book*. 2nd ed., London: Novello & Co., 1931. (1st ed., London: J. Curwen & Sons, 1915).

A. K. Davis 1929 *Arthur Kyle Davis. *Traditional Ballads of Virginia*. Harvard University Press, 1929.

Davis Index Arthur Kyle Davis. *Folk-Song of Virginia:* an index and classification. Duke University Press, 1949. (Reprint, New York, 1965).

A. K. Davis 1960 *Arthur Kyle Davis. *More Traditional Ballads of Virginia*. University of North Carolina Press, 1960.

F. J. Davis *Frederick J. Davis; Ferris Tozer. *Sailor's Songs* or "Chanties." 3rd ed., London: Boosey & Co., n.d.

J. Davis *Joe Davis. *Tip Top Songs of the Roaming Ranger*. New York: Tip Top Publishing Co., 1935.

J. A. Davis *John A. Davis; Jno. R. Clements. *Songs of Redemption and Praise*. Chicago: Bilhorn Brothers, 1906.

A. T. Davison 1922 *Archibald T. Davison; Thomas Whitney Surette. *140 Folk-Tunes*

(Concord Series No. 3). 2nd ed., Boston: E. C. Schirmer, 1922.

A. T. Davison 1924 *Archibald T. Davison; Thomas Whitney Surette; Augustus D. Zanzig. *A Book of Songs* (Concord Series No. 14). Boston: E. C. Schirmer, 1924.

P. Davison *Peter Davison. *Songs of the British Music Hall*. New York: Oak Publications, 1971.

Davisson *Ananias Davisson. *Kentuck Harmony*. 5th ed., Harrisenburg, Virginia, 1826. (1st ed., 1815; Reprint, Minneapolis, 1976).

Dawney *Michael Dawney. *The Iron Man: English occupational songs*. London: Stainer & Bell, 1974.

Dawson *W. J. Dawson. *The American Hymnal*. New York: The Century Co., 1913.

Day Cyrus Lawrence Day; Eleanore Boswell Murrie. *English Song-Books 1651-1702*. Oxford University Press, 1940.

Dayton 1881 *The Dayton's Songster*. New York; A. J. Fisher, 1881?

Dayton 1882 *The Dayton's Letter-Carrier Songster*. New York: Popular Publishing Co., 1882.

DD 102 †*Dulcimer: Old Time and Traditional Music* (Ralph Lee Smith et al). Booklet. Skyline Records DD 102.

Dean Michael C. Dean. *The Flying Cloud*. Virginia, Minnesota, 1922. (Reprint, 19--).

Dean-Smith Guide Margaret Dean-Smith. *A Guide to English Folk Song Collections, 1822-1952*. Liverpool and London: English Folk Dance & Song Society, 1954.

Dean-Smith 1957 *Margaret Dean-Smith. *Henry Playford's The English Dancing Master:* facsimile of the 1st edition of 1651. London: Schott & Co., 1957.

Dearmer 1915 *Percy Dearmer; Martin Shaw. *Song Time*. London: J. Curwen & Sons. 1915.

Dearmer 1928 *Percy Dearmer; Ralph Vaughan Williams; Martin Shaw. *The Oxford Book of Carols*. Oxford University Press, 1928.

Dearmer 1929 *Percy Dearmer; Ralph Vaughan Williams; Martin Shaw. *Songs of Praise for Boys and Girls*. Oxford University Press, 1929.

Deason *John Deason; O. A. Parris [William Walker's] *The Christian Harmony*. New edition: The Christian Harmony Publishing Co.: 1958. (1st ed., 1866).

Decca 9-30409 †*Puttin' On the Style* (Rudy Hanson). Decca 9-30409.

Decca 573 †*The Twentieth Century Minstrel* (Richard Dyer-Bennet). Decca 573.

Decca 574 †*Kentucky Mountain Ballads* (Cousin Emmy). Decca 574.

R. Delaney *Robert Delaney *The Arkansaw Traveler*. Boston: E. C. Schirmer Music Co., 1934.

Delaney # *Delaney's Song Books, #1 - #89*. New York: William H. Delaney, 1892-1922. (Music Division, New York Public Library, Microfilm *ZB 1, 2).

Delaney's Irish # *Delaney's Irish Song Books, #1 - #5*. New York: William H. Delaney, 188-.

Delaney's Scotch #1 Delaney's Scotch Song Book #1. New York: William H. Delaney, 1892.

Delehanty & Hengler Delehanty & Hengler's Song and Dance Book. New York: Robert M. De Witt, 1874.

De Marsan # Henry De Marsan and others [publishers]. *American Songs and Ballads* [a numbered collection of 467 broadsides issued in New York and Philadelphia ca. 1860]. Music Division, New York Public Library, *MP-U.S.

Dempster *William R. Dempster. *The Beauties of Vocal Melody*. Boston: J. H. Wilkins & R. B. Carter, 1842.

Denson *Owel W. Denson, et al. *The Original Sacred Harp Supplement, Denson Revision*. Cullman, Alabama: Sacred Harp Publishing Co., 1960.

Dessa Manion *The Dessa Manion Music Collection*. Ms. at Special Collections, University of Iowa Library, Iowa City, Ms C 218.

Dett *Nathaniel R. Dett. *Religious Folk-Songs of the Negro*. Hampton Institute Press, 1927.

Deuteromelia *Deuteromelia* [or Part 2 of *Pammelia*]. London: William Barley, 1609. (Ms. copy at Music Devision, New York Public Library, Drexel 4211).

De Vore *Nicholas De Vore. *Fifty Famous Favorites*. New York: Richmond-Robbins, 1922.

Dewey *Monica Dewey; Walter Bergman. *English Dance Tunes*. London, 1953.

Diack i - ii *J. Michael Diack. *The Scottish Orpheus Collection*. 2 Vols., London: Paterson's Publications, 1949.

Diamond Songster i - ii *The Diamond Songster*. 2 Vols., Baltimore, 1812.

Dibblee *Randall Dibblee; Dorothy Dibblee. *Folksongs from Prince Edward Island*. Summerside, P.E.I., 1973.

Dichter 1941 Harry Dichter; Elliot Shapiro. *Early American Sheet Music*. New York,

1941.

Dichter i - ii Harry Dichter. *Handbook of American Sheet Music.* 2 Vols., Philadelphia: Harry Dichter, 1947, 1953.

Dichter # *Harry Dichter. *Musical Americana:* 100 great American songs. [A numbered series in 2 vols. of original sheet music issues]. Philadelphia, 1956.

Dick i - ii *James C. Dick. *The Songs of Robert Burns* (1903) and *Notes on Scottish Songs by Robert Burns* (1908). Reprint in 1 Vol., Folklore Associates, 1962.

Dick Martz Dick Martz's Sensational Songster. New York: Ornum & Co., 1871.

Dick Sands Dick Sands' Irish Jig, Clog and Dance Book. New York: Popular Publishing Co., 1880.

*Dime Melodist *The Dime Melodis.* New York: Beadle & Co., 1859.

Diprose 1846 Diprose's Comic Song Book. London: J. Diprose, 1846.

Diprose 1865 J. Diprose. *The Red, White and Blue Monster Song Book.* London: J. A. Berger, ca. 1865.

Disc 609 †*Love Songs* (Richard Dyer-Bennet). Disc Album 609.

Ditson 1857 *Oliver Ditson [publisher]. *Continental Harmony.* Boston: Oliver Ditson, 1857.

Ditson 1859 *Oliver Ditson [publisher]. *100 Songs of Scotland.* Boston: Oliver Ditson, 1859.

Ditson 1869 *Oliver Ditson [publisher]. *The American Tune Book.* Boston: Oliver Ditson, 1869.

Dixey [E. F.] Dixey's Thoro'bred Songster. Philadelphia: A. Winch. 1869.

Dixon James Henry Dixon. *Ancient Poems, Ballads and Songs of the Peasantry of England.* London: Percy Society, 1846. (Reprint, Rowman & Littlefield, 1976).

DL 8080 †*Coronation Concert* (Burl Ives). Decca DL 8080.

DL 8245 †*Down to the Sea in Ships* (Burl Ives). Decca DL 8245.

DL 8246 †*Women* (Burl Ives). Decca DL 8246.

DL 8413 †*Puttin' On the Style* (Gateway Singers). Decca DL 8413.

DLP 112 †*Stone County Dulcimer* (The Simmons Family). Dancing Doll Records DLP 112.

Doane *W. Howard Doane; E. H. Johnson. *The Baptist Hymnal.* Philadelphia: American Baptist Publication Society, 1883.

Dodgson [Charles Lutwidge Dodgson]. *The Complete Works of Lewis Carroll.* New

York: Modern Library, 1936.

Doerflinger *William Main Doerflinger. *Songs of the Sailor and Lumberman.* New York: Macmillan, 1972. (Rev. ed. of his *Shantymen and Shantyboys,* New York, 1951).

Dominion 1280 †*Folk Songs for Young Folk* (Alan Mills). Dominion Records 1280.

*Don Messer *Don Messer's 'Way Down East Fiddlin' Tunes.* Toronto: Gordon V. Thompson, 1948.

Donnell *William B. Donnell; John T. Walker. *The Columbia College Song Book.* Boston: Oliver Ditson, 1896.

Donnybrook Fair The Donnybrook Fair Songster. New York: Robert M. De Witt, 1872.

Dorson Richard M. Dorson. *Buying the Wind.* University of Chicago Press, 1964.

Downes *Olin Downes; Elie Siegmeister. *A Treasury of American Song.* New York, 1940.

Doyle 1927 Gerald S. Doyle. *The Old Time Songs and Poetry of Newfoundland.* St. John's: The Family Fireside, 1927.

Doyle 1940 *Gerald S. Doyle. *Old Time Songs and Poetry of Newfoundland.* 2nd ed., St. John's, 1940.

*Doyle 1955 *Gerald S. Doyle. Old Time Songs of Newfoundland.* 3rd ed., St. John's, 1955.

Doyle 1966 *Gerald S. Doyle. *Our Newfoundland Songs.* 4th ed., St. John's: Gerald S. Doyle, 1966.

Dresser *[Paul Dresser]. *The Songs of Paul Dresser.* New York: Boni & Liveright, 1927.

Drimindown Drimindown [a bibliography of Joseph Hickerson], Library of Congress, 1968.

Dr. J. L. Thayer Dr. J. L. Thayer's Clown Song Book. Philadelphia: R. F. Simpson, 1861.

Droke Maxwell Droke. *Bawdy Ballads and Lusty Lyrics.* Indianapolis: Droke House, 1950. (1st ed., 1935).

Dublin Comic Songster The Dublin Comic Songster. Dublin: James Duffy, 1841.

*Dubliners i - iii *The Dubliner's Song Album.* 3 Vols., London: Scott Solomon Productions, 1967.

Duggan *Anne Schley Duggan; Jeanette Schlottman; Abbie Rutledge. *Folk Dances of the United States and Mexico.* New York: A. S. Barnes, 1948.

Duncan 1905 *Edmondstoune Duncan. *The Minstrelsy of England.* London: Augener, 1905.

Duncan 1927 Edmonstoune Duncan. *Lyrics from the Old Song Books.* New York: Harcourt Brace, 1927.

Dunson 1968   *Josh Dunson; Ethel Raim. *Grass Roots Harmony*. New York: Oak Publications, 1968.

Dunson 1973   *Josh Dunson; Ethel Raim. *Anthology of American Folk Music*. New York: Oak Publications, 1973.

Dunstan   *Ralph Dunstan. *Lyver Canow Kernewek (The Cornish Song Book)*. Reprint, London: Ascherberg, Hopwood & Crew, 1974. (1st ed., 2 Vols., Padstow: Lodenek Press, 1929).

Durand   *Silas H. Durand; P. G. Lester. *Hymn and Tune Book* for use in Old School or Primitive Baptist churches. Greenfield, Indiana: D. H. Goble, 1886.

D'Urfey i - vi   *Thomas D'Urfey. *Wit and Mirth, or Pills to Purge Melancholy*. 6 Vols. in 3, Reprint from the edition of 1719-20, New York: Folklore Library Publishers, 1959. (1st ed. by Henry Playford, 1698-1706).

Durlacher   *Ed Durlacher; Ken MacDonald. *Honor Your Partner*. New York: Devin-Adair Co., 1949.

Dwyer   *Richard A. Dwyer; Richard E. Lingenfelter; David Cohen. *The Songs of the Gold Rush*. University of California Press, 1964.

DX 513   †*America's Musical Heritage*. MCA Records DX 513.

Dyer-Bennet 1946   *Richard Dyer-Bennet. *The 20th Century Minstrel*. New York: Leeds Music Corp., 1946.

Dyer-Bennett 1971   *[Richard Dyer-Bennet]. *The Richard Dyer-Bennet Folk Song Book*. New York: Simon & Schuster, 1971.

Dykema   *Peter W. Dykema; Will Earhart; Hollis Dann; Osbourne McConathy. *Twice 55 Plus Community Songs*. Reissue, Boston: C. C. Birchard, 1929. (1st ed., 1919).

Eaton #   Thos. H. Eaton. *Penny Song Books #1 - #9*. [issued irregularly, with varying imprints, not paginated], 186-.

EC   †[Earliest Copy]. [Tapes from the Camp Woodland Collection of Folk Music of the Catskill Mountains]. Archives of Traditional Music, Indiana University.

Eckstorm   Fannie Hardy Eckstorm; Mary Winslow Smith. *Minstrelsy of Maine*. Boston: Houghton Mifflin, 1927.

Eddy   *Mary O. Eddy. *Ballads and Songs from Ohio*. New York: J. J. Augustin, 1939.

Edinburgh Musical Miscellany   *The Edinburgh Musical Miscellany*. 2nd ed., Edinburgh: Mundell & Son, 1804.

Edison 51459   †*The Prisoner's Song* (Vernon Dalhart). Edison 51459. (Re-issue, Bluebird B-10578).

[Edith Fowke Collection]   †Edith Fowke Tape Collection [see: FO 1 - 94].

Edmunds   *John Edmunds. *A Williamsburg Songbook*. New York: Holt, Rinehart & Winston, 1964.

EDS   *English Dance and Song, 1936-*.

J. Edwards   *Jay Edwards; Robert Kelley. *The Coffee House Songbook*. New York: Oak Publications, 1966.

R. G. Edwards 1956   *Ron G. Edwards. *The Overlander Songbook*. 1st ed., Victoria, New South Wales, 1956.

R. G. Edwards 1971   *Ron G. Edwards. *The Overlander Songbook*. Adelaide: Rigby, 1971.

R. G. Edwards 1972   *Ron G. Edwards. *australian Folksongs*. Queensland, 1972.

Ehret   *Walter Ehret. *It's Song Time*. New York: Sam Fox Publishing Co., 1965.

Ehrke   Konrad Ehrke. "Das Geistermotiv in den schottischenglischen Volksballaden: ein Beitrag zur Geschichte der Volksdichtung." Dissertation: Königlichen Universitäts Marburg, 1914.

Eighteenth Century   *Eighteenth Century Songs & Ballads* [a collection of broadsides]. Morrison Library, University of California at Berkeley, M1619.C652.

EKL 26   †*Old Airs from Ireland, Scotland and England* (Susan Reed). Elektra EKL 26.

EKL 125   †*Jean Ritchie*. Elektra EKL 125.

EKL 142   †*Puttin' On the Style* (The Shanty Boys). Elektra EKL 142.

EKL 301/2   †*Leadbelly*: the Library of Congress Recordings (Huddie Ledbetter). Booklet (Alan Lomax). Elektra EKL 301/2.

Elderkin 1890.   *Geo[rge] D. Elderkin. *The Finest of the Wheat*. Chicago: R. R. McCabe & Co., 1890.

Elderkin 1898   *Geo[rge] D. Elderkin et al. *The Bow of Promise*. Chicago: R. R. McCabe & Co., 1898.

Elderkin 1900   *Geo[rge] D. Elderkin; Jno. R. Sweney; W[illiam] J. Kirkpatrick; H. L. Gilmour; F. A. Hardin. *Songs of the Century*. Chicago: Geo. D. Elderkin Publishing Co., 1900.

Eldridge   *Annetta Eldridge; Ruth F. Richardson. *Stunt Songs for Social Sings*. Franklin, Ohio: Eldridge Entertainment House, 1923.

Electric Three   *The Electric Three Songster*. New York: Popular Publishing Co., 1882.

Ellington   *Charles Linwood Ellington. "The

Sacred Harp tradition of the South: its origin and evolution." Dissertation, Florida State University, 1969.

Elmore Vincent *Elmore Vincent's Lumber Jack Songs. Chicago: M. M. Cole, 1932.

Elson *Louis C. Elson; Nicholas De Vore. *Old Favorites* (Modern Music and Musicians for Vocalists, Vol. 6). New York: The University Society, 1918.

Elton Elton's Songs and Melodies for the Multitude, or Universal Songster. [Internal sectional and running titles from presumed earlier separate issues: Elton's Song Book; Elton's Illustrated Songster]. New York: T. W.Strong, 1848?

Emerald Four The Emerald Four Songster. New York: Popular Publishing Co., 1880.

Emerick *Albert G. Emerick. Songs for the People, Vol. 1. Philadelphia: Geo. B. Zieber & Co., 1848. (Re-issued: Philadelphia, J. & J. L. Gihon, 1849; Boston, Oliver Ditson, 1852).

Emerson *L. O. Emerson. Merry Chimes. Boston: Oliver Ditson, 1865.

Emma Grattan Emma Grattan's Lancashire Lass Songster. New York: Fisher & Denison, 1871.

Emmerson 1967 George Emmerson. Scotland through Her Country Dances. New York: Transatlantic Arts, 1967.

Emmerson 1971 *George S. Emmerson. Rantin' Pipe and Tremblin' String. Montréal: McGill-Queen's University Press, 1971.

Empire Book*The Empire Book of Favourite Songs. Oakville, Ontario: Frederick Harris & Co., n.d.

Emrich 1973 *Duncan Emrich.Folklore on the American Land. Boston, 1973.

Emrich1974 Duncan Emrich. American Folk Poetry. Boston: Little, Brown & Co., 1974.

Emurian Ernest K. Emurian. Living Stories of Favorite Songs. Boston: W. A. Wilde Co., 1958.

Engel Lyle Kenyon Engel. 500 Songs that Made the All-Time Hit Parade. York: Bantam Books, 1964.

Entwisle *J. Howard Entwisle; Powell G. Fithian; Adam Geibel; R. Frank Lehman. Evangelistic Edition of Heavenly Sunlight. Philadelphia: MacCalla & Co., 1901.

Eolian *The Eolian Songster. Cincinnati: U. P. James, 1832.

Epstein *Dena J. Epstein, Sinful Tunes and Spirituals: Black folk music to the Civil War. University of Illinois Press 1977.

Epworth Hymnal i - iii *The Epworth Hymnal. No. 1, New York: Phillips & Hunt, 1885;

No. 2, New York; Hunt & Eaton, 1891; No. 3, edited by J[ames] M. Black, New York: Eaton & Mains, 1900.

Erdei *Peter Erdei; Katalin Komics. 150 American Folk Songs. New York: Boosey & Hawkes, 1974.

Erickson *J. Irvin Erickson, et al. The Covenant Hymnal. [The Evangelical Covenant Church of America]. Chicago: Covenant Press, 1973.

Erin-Go-Bragh *The Ernest Newton Community Song Book. London: Keith Prowse Publishing Co., 1927.

[Eskin] *Sam Eskin Collection. [see: Sam Eskin].

Ethiopian Glee Book #2 *The Ethiopian Glee Book #2. Boston: Elias Howe, 1848.

Evangelical Hymnal *The Evangelical Hymnal. Cleveland: Board of Publications of the Evangelical Church, 1921.

R. Evans *Robert Evans; Craig Davidson. Song to a Seagull. Toronto: The Ryerson Press, 1970.

Evers Alf Evers. The Catskills, from Wilderness to Woodstock. Garden City, New York: Doubleday & Co., 1972.

Everybody's Favorite *Everybody's Favorite Songs. New York: Amsco Music Sales, 1933.

Every-Day The Every-Day Song Book. New York: Leavitt & Allen, 18--.

Excell 1889 *E[dwin] O. Excell. Triumphant Songs #2. Chicago: E. O. Excell, 1889.

Excell 1894 *E[dwin] O. Excell. Triumphant Songs #4. Chicago: E. O. Excell, 1894.

Excell 1912 *E[dwin] O. Excell; William E. Biederwolf. Make Christ King. Chicago: The Glad Tidings Co., 1912.

Excell 1918 *E[dwin] O. Excell. Hymns and Sacred Songs. Chicago: Hope Publishing Co., 1918.

Experimenters *Songbook for Experimenters. Delaware, Ohio: Coöperative Recreation Service, 1960.

Eyre-Todd *George Eyre-Todd. Ancient Scots Ballads with the Traditional Airs to Which They Were Wont to Be Sung. London: Bayley & Ferguson, [1894].

FA 2014 †Leadbelly Legacy, Vol. 2 (Huddie Ledbetter). Folkways FA 2014.

FA 2039 †The Songs of Joe Hill (Joe Glazer). Folkways FA 2039.

FA 2163, 2164 †Ballads of the War of 1812 (Wallace House). Booklet (Moses Asch). 2 discs, Folkways FA 2163, 2164.

FA 2187, 2188 †*Ballads of the Civil War* (Hermes Nye). Booklets. 2 discs, Folkways FA 2187, 2188.

FA 2312 †*Songs of the Sea* (Alan Mills et al). Booklet (Edith Fowke). Folkways FA 2312.

FA 2319 †*American Ballads* (Pete Seeger). Booklet. Folkways FA 2319.

FA 2354 †*Songs of a New York Lumberjack* (Ellen Stekert). Booklet. Folkways FA 2354.

FA 2365 †*Mountain Music Played on the Autoharp*. Booklet (Mike Seeger). Folkways FA 2365.

FA 2367 †*Kevin Roth Sings and Plays the Dulcimer*. Booklet. Folkways FA 2367.

FA 2412 †*Concert at Carnegie Hall* (Pete Seeger, Sonny Terry). Folkways FA 2412.

FA 2454 †*The Rainbow Quest* (Pete Seeger). Booklet. Folkways FA 2454.

FA 2941, 2942 †*Leadbelly's Last Sessions* (Huddie Ledbetter). 2 discs, Folkways FA 2941, 2942.

FA 2951 †*American Folk Music, Vol. 1*. Booklet (Harry Smith). Folkways FA 2951.

Fahs *Lois S. Fahs. *Swing Your Partner:* Old time dances of New Brunswick and Nova Scotia. Sackville, New Brunswick: Mount Allison University, 1939.

Fairburn 18-- *Fairburn's Collection of Songs*. London: J[ohn] Fairburn, n. d.

Fairburn 1809 *Fairburn's Laughable Songster and Fashionable Quizzer*. London: John Fairburn, 1809.

Fairburn 1823 *Fairburn's Everlasting Songster*. London: J[ohn] Fairburn, 1823.

Fairburn 1830 *Fairburn's British Songster or New Vocal Library*. London: J[ohn] Fairburn, 1830.

Fairburn 1832 *Fairburn's (London) Brilliant Songster*. London: J[ohn] Fairburn, 1832.

Familiar Songs *Familiar Songs of the Gospel*. Fort Wayne, Indiana: E. A. K. Hackett, 190-.

Famous College Songs *Famous College Songs*. New York: Jos. W. Stern & Co., 1906.

J. Farmer *John Farmer. *Gaudeamus:* a selection of songs for colleges and schools. London, 1917. (1st ed., 1890).

J. S. Farmer i - v *John S. Farmer. *Merry Songs and Ballads Prior to the Year A. D. 1800*. 5 Vols., New York: Cooper Square Publishers, 1964.

Farnsworth 1909 *Charles H. Farnsworth; Cecil J. Sharp. *Folk-Songs, Chanteys and Singing Games*. London: Novello & Co., [1909].

Farnsworth 1917 *Charles S. Farnsworth.

Grammar School Songs. New York: Charles Scribner's Sons, 1917.

Father Kemp *Father Kemp's Old Folks Concert Music*. Boston: Oliver Ditson, 1874.

Father Miller *Father Miller's Comic Songster*. New York: Thomas G. Booth, 187-. [Not paginated].

Faugh-a-Gallagh *The Faugh-a-Ballagh Song Book*. New York: P. J. Kenedy, 1877.

Favorite Songs *Favorite Songs of the People*. Philadelphia: Theodore Presser Co., 1927.

Fawcett F. Burlington Fawcett. *Broadside Ballads of the Restoration Period*: The Osterley Park Ballads. London: John Lane, 1930.

FC 2997 *Herbert Haufrecht. *Missy Mouse and Mister Frog* [choral setting]. New York: Edwin H. Morris, 1951, FC 2997.

FC 7028 †*Camp Songs* (Pete Seeger and group). Folkways FC 7028.

FC 7625 †*You Can Sing It Yourself, Vol. 2* (Robin Christenson). Folkways FC 7625.

FE 4307 †*Maritime Folk Songs*. (Booklet: Helen Creighton). Folkways FE 4307.

Feist *Leo Feist. *Popular Songs Folio No. 2*. New York: Leo Feist, 1902?

Felton *Harold W. Felton. *Cowboy Jamboree*. New York, 1951.

Fenner 1901 *Thomas P. Fenner; Frederick G. Rathbun; Bessie Cleaveland. *Cabin and Plantation Songs*. 3rd ed., New York: The Knickerbocker Press, 1901. (1st ed., 1874).

Fenner 1924 *Thomas P. Fenner. *Religious Folk Songs of the Negro*. Hampton, Virginia: The [Hampton] Institute Press, 1924. (1st ed., 1874).

Fessenden *L. G. Fessenden. *The Modern School for the Violin*. Boston: Oliver Ditson, 1853.

Few Days *The Few Days Songster*. Philadelphia: Fisher & Bro., 185-.

FFMA *Folklore and Folk Music Archivist*, 1959-.

FG 3507 †*Now is the Time for Fishing* (Sam Larner). Booklet (Ewan MacColl, Peggy Seeger). Folkways FG 3507.

FG 3519 †*Lucy Stewart*. (Booklet: Goldstein). Folkways FG 3519.

FG 3532 †*Songs, Fiddle Tunes and a Folktale from Canada* (Alan Mills, Jean Carrignan). Booklet. Folkways FG 3532.

FG 3547 †*Through Streets Broad and Narrow* (Karen James). Booklet. Folkways FG 3547.

FH 5257 †*Fifty Sail on Newburgh Bay* (Pete Seeger, Ed Renahan). Folkways FH 5257.

FH 5279 †*American Revolutionary War Songs* (Arthur F. Schrader et al). Booklet.

Folkways FH 5279.

FH 5285 †*Talking Union* (Almanac Singers). Folkways FH 5285.

FH 5311 †*Folksongs of the Catskills* (Barbara Moncure, Harry Siemsen). Booklet. Folkways FH 5311.

FH 5314 †*Folk Songs of Vermont* (Margaret MacArthur). Booklet. Folkways FH 5314.

FH 5323 †*Folksongs of Maine* (Sandy Ives). Folkways FH 5323.

FH 5337 †*Sweet Nebraska Land* (Roger Welsch). Booklet, Folkways FH 5337.

FH 5723 †*The Cowboy*: his songs, ballads and brag talk (Harry Jackson). Booklet (Kenny Goldstein). Folkways FH 5723.

FHE *The Fannie Hardy Eckstorm Collection of Folksongs.* [Ms. Box #61).23-.27 at Special Collections, Fogler Library, University of Maine (Orono). Listing in *NEF 16* 88-104].

FHR-04 †*Mellow with Ale from the Horn* (John Roberts, Tony Barrand). Front Hall Records FHR-04.

[Fife 1966] †Austin E. Fife; Alta Fife; Naunie Gardner. [*Thorp's Songs of the Cowboys (1908)*. See: Thorp i].

Fife 1969 *Austin Fife; Alta Fife; Mary Jo Schwab. *Cowboy and Western Songs.* New York: Clarkson N. Potter, 1969.

Fife 1970 Austin Fife; Alta Fife. *Ballads of the Great West.* Palo Alto: American West Publishing Co., 1970.

Fillmore *A[ugustus] D. Fillmore. *Harp of Zion.* Cincinnati: R. W. Carroll & Co., 1865.

Findlay Jessie P. Findlay. *The Spindle-Side of Scottish Song.* New York: E. P. Dutton & Co., 1902.

Finger *Charles P. Finger. *Frontier Ballads.* New York, 1927.

Fireside The Fireside Song Book. Leavitt & Allen, 18--.

Fireside Library *The Fireside Library: 162 Popular Songs. Augusta, Maine: P. O. Vickery, 1895.

Fisher *William Arms Fisher, *Sixty Irish Songs.* Boston: Oliver Ditson, 1915.

Fitz 1846 *Asa Fitz. *The Primary School Song Book.* Boston: Wm. B. Fowle & N. Capen, 1846.

Fitz 1848 *Asa Fitz. *The Parlor Harp and Boston Social Melodist.* Boston: John P. Jewett & Co., 1848.

FL 5401 †*Courting and Complaining Songs* (Peggy Seeger). Jacket Notes. Signet FL 5401.

Flanagan John T. Flanagan; Arthur Palmer Hudson. *Folklore in American Literature.*

Evanston, Illinois: Row, Peterson & Co., 1958.

Flanders 1931 Helen Hartness Flanders; George Brown. *Vermont Folk Songs and Ballads.* Brattleboro: Stephen Daye Press, 1931.

Flanders *BDN* Helen Hartness Flanders; Fanny Hardy Eckstorm. *New England Folk Songs*: a scrapbook of columns in the *Bangor Daily News*, 1933-34. [Widener Library, Harvard University, 27256.31.14].

Flanders *SR* Helen Hartness Flanders. *New England Folksongs*: a scrapbook of columns in the *Springfield [Vermont] Republican*, 1933-35. [Widener Library, Harvard University, 27256.31.14.10].

Flanders 1934 *Helen Hartness Flanders. *A Garland of Green Mountain Song.* Northfield, Vermont, 1934.

Flanders 1937 *Helen Hartness Flanders; Helen Norfleet. *Country Songs of Vermont.* New York: G. Schrimer, 1937.

Flanders 1939 *Helen Hartness Flanders; Elizabeth Flanders Ballard; George Brown; Phillips Barry. *The New Green Mountain Songster.* Yale University Press, 1939.

Flander Index Helen Hartness Flanders. "Index of ballads and folk-songs in the Archive of Vermont Folk-Songs at Smiley Manse, Springfield, Vermont." *Vermont Historical Society Proceedings*, N. S. 8 (1940), 214-51. [# refers to recorded items].

Flanders 1953 *Helen Hartness Flanders; Marguerite Olney. *Ballads Migrant in New England.* New York, 1953.

Flanders i - iv *Helen Hartness Flanders. *Ancient Ballads Traditionally Sung in New England.* 4 Vols., University of Pennsylvania Press, 1960-65.

F-LFR 100 †*On the Mountains High* (Margaret MacArthur and family). Living Folk Records F-LFR 100.

Florences Songs of the Florences. New York, 1860.

FM 4001 †*Wolf River Songs* [collected in Wisconsin, Wyoming and California]. Booklet (Sidney Robertson [Cowell]). Folkways FM 4001.

FM 4002 †*Songs of Aran*, edited by Sidney Robertson Cowell. Folkways FM 4002.

FM 4005 †*Folksongs of Ontario.* Booklet (Edith Bowke). Folkways FM 4005.

FM 4006 †*Folk Music from Nova Scotia.* Booklet (Helen Creighton). Folkways FM 4006.

FM 4051 †*Irish and British Songs from the Ottawa Valley* (O. J. Abbott). Booklet

(Edith Fowke). Folkways FM 4051.

FM 4052 †*Lumbering Songs from the Ontario Shanties.* Booklet (Edith Fowke). Folkways FM 4052.

FM 4053 †*Folksongs of the Miramichi.* Booklet (Louise Manny). Folkways FM 4053.

FMBS *Folk Music, Ballads & Songs,* New Series, 1965-.

FMJ *Folk Music Journal,* 1965-.

FO 1 - 94 †*Edith Fowke Tape Collection.* Scott Library, York University, Toronto, Ontario.

Folk *Folk* [a series issued at irregular intervals by E[nglish] F[olk] D[ance &] S[ong Society] Publications, London, 1962-.

Folk Singers *The Folk Singers Song Bag.* New York: Sanga Music, 1962.

Folk Song Album *The Folk Song Album* popularized by Alan Lomax and The Ramblers. London: B. Feldman & Co., 1957.

Folkonvention *[Songs of the] Folkonvention* Collected by the Southern Illinois Chapter. Greenville, Illinois: Rackensack Folklore Society, 1974.

Foner *Philip S. Foner. *American Labor Songs of the Nineteenth Century.* University of Illinois Press, 1975.

Ira Ford. *Ira Ford. *Traditional Music of America.* New York, 1940.

R. Ford 1900 Robert Ford. *Song Histories.* Glasgow & Edinburgh: William Hodge & Co., 1900.

R. Ford 1904 *Robert Ford. *Vagabond Songs and Ballads of Scotland.* 2nd ed., Paisley: Alexander Gardner, 1904. (1st ed., 2 Vols., 1899, 1901.)

W. C. Ford Worthington Chauncey Ford. "Broadsides, ballads & c. printed in Massachusetts, 1639-1800." *Massachusetts Historical Society, Collections,* Vol. 75, 1922.

Forecastle Songster The Forecastle Songster.* New York: Nafis & Cornish, 1849.

Forget-Me-Not The Forget-Me-Not Songster.* New York: Nafis & Cornish, 1842.

Formosa The Formosa Songster.* New York: Popular Publishing Co., 1881.

Fortey 1894-1905 W. S. Fortey [Printer-publisher]. *A Collection of Favorite Songs* [A monthly series of word sheet folders, not paginated and with many duplications]. London: W. S. Fortey, 1894-1905.

M. B. Foster *Miles B. Foster. *The Songs of Scotland.* London: Boosey & Co., 187-.

N. Foster *Norman P. Foster; James S. Hamilton; Elijah R. Williams. *Songs of Amherst College.* Amherst, Massachusetts, 1906.

Four Eccentrics The Four Eccentrics Songster.* New York: Popular Publishing Co., 1881.

Fowke 1954 *Edith Fowke; Richard Johnston. *Folk Songs of Canada.* Waterloo, Ontario: Waterloo Music Co., 1954.

Fowke 1960 *Edith Fowke; Alan Mills; Helmut Blume. *Canada's Story in Song.* Toronto: W. J. Gage, [1960].

Fowke 1961 *Edith Fowke; Joe Glazer. *Songs of Work and Freedom.* Reprint, Garden City, New York, 1961. (1st ed., 1960).

Fowke 1965 *Edith Fowke; Peggy Seeger. *Traditional Singers and Songs from Ontario.* Folklore Associates, 1965.

Fowke 1967 *Edith Fowke; Richard Johnston. *More Folk Songs of Canada.* Waterloo, Ontario, 1967.

Fowke 1969 *Edith Fowke. *Sally Go Round the Sun.* Toronto, 1969.

Fowke 1970 *Edith Fowke; Norman Cazden. *Lumbering Songs from the Northern Woods.* (Memoirs of the American Folklore Society, Vol. 55). University of Texas Press, 1970.

Fowke 1972 *Edith Fowke; Bram Morrison. *Canadian Vibrations.* Toronto: Macmillan, 1972.

Fowke 1973 *Edith Fowke. *The Penguin Book of Canadian Folk Songs.* Harmondsworth: Penguin Books, 1973.

Fox *Charlotte Milligan Fox. *Songs of the Irish Harpers.* London: Bayley & Ferguson, 1910.

FP 3 †*Darling Corey* (Pete Seeger). Folkways FP 3.

FP 4 †*Huddie Ledbetter Memorial Album, Vol. 1.* Folkways FP 4.

FP 19 †*Logger's Songs and Sea Shanties* (Sam Eskin). Booklet. Folkways FP 19.

FP 20 †*Songs to Grow On, Vol. 2.* Folkways FP 20.

FP 21 †*Seeds of Love* (Andrew Rowan Summers). Folkways FP 21.

FP 43 **A Pete Seeger Sampler.* Folkways FP 43.

FP 85/3 †*Love Songs for Friends and Foes* (Pete Seeger). Folkways FP 85/3.

FP 701 †*American Folk Songs for Children* (Pete Seeger). Folkways FP 701.

FP 710 †*Birds, Beasts, Bugs and Little Fishes* (Pete Seeger). Folkways FP 710.

FP 711 †*Birds, Beasts, Bugs and Bigger Fishes* (Pete Seeger). Folkways FP 711.

FP 728 †*Camp Songs* (The Song Swappers). Folkways FP 728.

FP 911 †*The Song Swappers.* Folkways FP

911.

FP 2364 †*The Unquiet Grave* (Andrew Rowan Summers). Booklet. Folkways FP 2364.

FP 5003 †*Frontier Ballads* (Pete Seeger). Folkways FP 5003.

FR 217 †*Shaker Folk Songs*. Shaker FR 217.

Francis & Day # *Francis & Day's [Comic Song] Annual*, 1891-.

Francis & Day i - vi *Francis & Day's Community Song Album*. 6 Vols., London: Francis, Day & Hunter, 1931-35.

Francis & Day Album i - xi *Francis & Day's Album of Famous Old Songs*. 11 Vols., London: Francis, Day & Hunter, 1913-17.

Francis & Day 1906 *Francis & Day's Standard Folio of 100 Best Songs*. London: Francis, Day & Hunter, 1906.

Francis & Day 1948a *Francis & Day's Community Book of Irish Songs*. London: Francis, Day & Hunter, 1948.

Francis & Day 1948b *Francis & Day's Community Book of Scottish Songs*. London: Francis, Day & Hunter, 1948.

Francis & Day 1952 *Francis & Day's Book of Sea Songs & Shanties*. London: Francis, Day & Hunter, 1952.

Francis & Day 1967 *Francis & Day's Folk Songs*. London: Francis, Day & Hunter, 1967.

[*Frank B. Converse*] [see Converse].

Frank Brower *Frank Brower's Black Diamond Songster*. New York: Dick & Fitzgerald, 1863. [Also included in *Universal Book of Songs and Singer's Companion* ii].

Frank Van Ness *Frank Van Ness's Free and Easy Songster*. New York: Fisher & Denison, 1868.

Fraser i - iii *Marjory Kennedy Fraser; Kenneth Macleod. *Songs of the Hebrides*. 3 Vols., London: Boosey & Co., 1909-21.

Fred Roberts *Fred Roberts's Latest and Greatest Songster*. New York: Popular Publishing Co., 1882.

Freeman *Larry Freeman. *The Melody Lingers On: 50 Years of Popular Song*. Watkins Glen, New York: Century House, 1951.

Fremont *Robert A. Fremont. *Favorite Songs of the Nineties* [facsimile reproductions of sheet music publications]. New York: Dover Publications, 1973.

French *Percy French. *The Irish Troubadour*. London: Keith Prowse Music Publishing Co., 1963.

Frey 194- *Hugo Frey. *Merrily We Sing*. New York: Leo Feist, 194-.

Frey 1941 *Hugo Frey. *Robbins Mammoth Collection of American Songs*. New York: Robbins Music Corp., 1941.

Frey 1942 *Hugo Frey. *Bill Hardey's Songs of the Gay Nineties*. New York: Robbins Music Corp., 1942.

Frey 1943 *Hugo Frey. *Geoffrey O'Hara Golden Treasury Song Book*. New York: Robbins Music Corp., 1943.

Friedman *Albert B. Friedman. *The Viking Book of Ballads*. New York: Viking Press, 1946.

Friel *Redmond Friel. *The Paterson Irish Song Book*. London: Paterson's Publications, 1957.

Frisky Irish *The Frisky Irish Songster*. New York: Dick & Fitzgerald, 1862.

FSA 2 †*Joseph Able Trivett*, Tennessee. Booklet (Sandy Paton). Folk-Legacy FSA 2.

FSA 3 †*Edna Ritchie*, Kentucky. Booklet (D. K. Wilgus). Folk-Legacy FSA 3.

FSA 11 †*Ozark Folksongs and Ballads* (Max Hunter). Booklet. (Mary Celestia Parler, Vance Randolph). Folk-Legacy FSA 11.

FSA 15 †*Adirondack Songs, Ballads and Fiddle Tunes* (Lawrence Older). Booklet (Peter E. McElligott). Folk-Legacy FSA 15.

FSA 17 †*Hobart Smith*. Booklet (Sandy Paton). Folk-Legacy FSA 17.

FSA 22, 23 †*The Traditional Music of Beech Mountain, North Carolina*. Booklet (Sandy Paton). 2 Vols., Folk-Legacy FSA 22, 23.

FSA 26 †*Girl of Constant Sorrow* (Sarah Ogan Gunning). Booklet (Archie Green). Folk-Legacy FSA 26.

FSA 27 †*Songmaker of the Catskills* (Grant Rogers). Booklet. Folk-Legacy FSA 27.

FSA 32 †*Old Times and Hard Times* (Hedy West). Booklet (West, Lloyd). Folk-Legacy FSA 32.

FSA 33 †*Ballads and Songs of the Upper Hudson Valley* (Sara Cleveland). Booklet (Goldstein). Folk-Legacy FSA 33.

FSB 19 †*English Shepherd and Farming Songs* (Bob and Ron Copper). Booklet (Bob Copper). Folk-Legacy FSB 19.

FSC 9 †*Marie Hare*. Folk-Legacy FSC 9.

FSC 10 †*The Rambling Irishman* (Tom Brandon). Folk-Legacy FSC 10.

FSC 62 †*The Barley Grain for Me* (Margaret Christl, Ian Robb). Folk-Legacy FSC 62.

FSE 7 †*The Man of Songs* (Paddy Tunney). Booklet (Sean O Doyle). Folk-Legacy FSE 7.

FSE 20 †*Traditional English Love Songs* (Harry Cox). Booklet (P. Kennedy, Collinson). Folk-Legacy FSE 20.

FSE 21 †*Traditional and Original Songs of Ireland* (Bill Meek). Booklet. Folk-Legacy

FSE 21.

FSI 1 †*Fleming Brown*. Booklet (Sandy Paton). Folk-Legacy FSI 1.

FSI 2 †*Howie Mitchell*. Booklet (Sandy Paton). Folk-Legacy FSI 2.

FSI 35 †*Michael Cooney, or The Cheese Stands Alone*. Booklet. Folk-Legacy FSI 35.

FSI 39 †*Folk Songs and Ballads* (Joe Hickerson). Booklet. Folk-Legacy FSI 39.

FSI 40 †*Tune for November* (Gordon Bok). Folk-Legacy FSI 40.

FSI 46 †*The Telling Takes Me Home* (Ed Trickett). Folk-Legacy FSI 46.

FSI 58, 59 †*Drive Dull Care Away* (Joe Hickerson). Booklets. 2 Vols., Folk-Legacy FSI 58, 59.

FSI 65 †*Dark Ships in the Forest* (John Roberts, Tony Barrand). Booklet. Folk-Legacy FSI 65.

FSS 34 †*Ballads and Songs of Scotland* (Norman Kennedy). Booklet (Peter Hall). Folk-Legacy FSS 34.

FSS 49 †*Frae My Ain Countrie* (Jean Redpath). Booklet. Folk-Legacy FSS 49.

FST i - v *Folk Song Today* [a series of booklets issued at irregular intervals]. London: E[nglish] F[olk] D[ance &] S[ong] S[ociety], 1965-70.

FTS 3016 †*Gordon Bok*. Verse-Forecast FTS 3016.

Fulcher *John Fulcher. *Lays and Lyrics of Scotland*. London: Swan & Co., n. d.

Fuld 1955 James J. Fuld. *American Popular Music, 1875-1950*. Philadelphia: Musical Americana, 1955.

Fuld 1971 *James [J.] Fuld. *The Book of World Famous Music*. Revised and enlarged ed., New York: Crown Publishers, 1971. (1st ed., 1966).

Funk *Joseph Funk. *The New Harmonia Sacra* [of 1832]. Shenandoah Valley: Joseph Funk & Sons, 1959.

Fuson Harvey H. Fuson. *Ballads and Songs of the Kentucky Highlands*. London, 1931.

FW 3001 †*O Canada!* (Alan Mills). Booklet (Edith Fowke). Folkways FW 3001.

FW 8744 †*Songs of the Maritimes* (Alan Mills). Booklet. Folkways FW 8744.

Gabriel *Cha[rle]s H. Gabriel. *Joyful Praise*. Cincinnati: Jennings & Graham, 1902.

Gainer 1963 *Patrick W. Gainer. *West Virginia Centennial Book of 100 Songs*. West Virginia University Press, 1963.

Gainer 1975 *Patrick W. Gainer. *Folk Songs from the West Virginia Hills*. Grantsville, W.

Va.: Seneca Books, 1975.

Galaxy *Galaxy of Song*. Philadelphia: Thomas Hunter, 1883.

Gallagher *Elizabeth Gallagher; Carlo Peroni. *Irish Songs and Airs*. Toms River, New Jersey: Elizabeth Gallagher, 1936.

Galvin *Patrick Galvin. *Irish Songs of Resistance*. New York: The Folklore Press, 1956.

Gamse *Albert Gamse. *World's Favorite Songs of the Gay Nineties*. New York: Ashley Publications, 1962.

Gardens *Songs of the Gardens*, c. 1770. [A bound collection of broadsides at Morrison Library, University of California at Berkeley, M1740.S657].

Gardner 1937 *Emelyn Elizabeth Gardner. *Folklore from the Schoharie Hills*. University of Michigan Press, 1937.

Gardner 1939 *Emelyn Elizabeth Gardner; Geraldine Jencks Chickering. *Ballads and Songs of Southern Michigan*. Reprint, Folklore Associates, 1967. (1st ed., 1939).

[Gardiner] *George B. Gardiner; Gustav Holst. *Folk-Songs from Hampshire*. London: Novello & Co., 1909. [see: C. J. Sharp 1961 iii].

Garland Hamlin Garland. *A Son of the Middle Border*. New York, 1925. (1st ed., 1917).

Garretson *Ferd[inand] V. D. Garretson. *Carmina Yalensia*. Enlarged ed., New York: Taintor Brothers, Merrill & Co., 1873. (1st ed., 1867).

Garson *Eugenia Garson; Herbert Haufrecht. *The Laura Ingalls Wilder Songbook*. New York: Harper & Row, 1968.

Gay i - ii *John Gay. *The Beggar's Opera*. [2 books in 1, i: Introduction by John Doughty, and text reproduced from the 3rd edition, London: John Watts, 1729, as reprinted, London: Daniel O'Connor, 1922; ii: Musical Supplement, reproduced from the 3rd edition, London: John Watts, 1729; separately paginated]. New York: Dover Publications, 1973.

Gems of Song *The Gems of Song*. Boston: Elias Howe, 1846.

[Gem Selection, Scottish] *Gem Selection of Scottish Songs*. [see: Tomlyn].

Gem Selection *The Gem Selection of Songs of Ireland*. Dublin: Valentine & Sons, 19--.

Gems of Minstrel Songs i - ii *Gems of Minstrel Songs*. 2 Vols.,? New York: W. F. Shaw, 1882.

Gems of Scottish Songs *Gems of Scottish Songs*. Boston: Oliver Ditson, 1894.

Gentle Annie i - ii *Gentle Annie Melodist*. 2 Vols., Boston: Oliver Ditson Co., 1859.

Geo. Jarvis Geo. Jarvis's Boat's A-Going Over Songster. New York: Popular Publishing Co., 1882.

George Christy George Christy's Essence of Old Kentucky. New York: Dick & Fitzgerald, 186-.

Geri *Frank H. Geri. *Illustrated Games and Rhythms for Children*. New York: Prentice Hall, 1955.

Gerry *H. E. Gerry. *Camp Fire Entertainment and True History of Robert Henry Hendershot*. San Francisco, 1895.

Gibbon *John Murray Gibbon. *New World Ballads*. Toronto: The Ryerson Press, 1939.

Giblin *P. J. Giblin. *Collection of Traditional Irish Dance Music*. Dublin: Piggott & Co., 1933. (1st ed., 1928).

D. Gilbert Douglas Gilbert. *Lost Chords*. Garden City, New York: Doubleday, 1942.

H. F. Gilbert *Henry F. Gilbert. *One Hundred Folk-Songs*. Boston: C. C. Birchard, 1910.

Gill 1898 *W. H. Gill. *Manx National Music*. London: Boosey & Co., 1898.

Gill 1917 *W. H. Gill. *Songs of the British Folk*. London: J. Curwen & Sons, 1917.

Gillington 1907 *Alice E. Gillington. *Eight Hampshire Folk Songs*. London: J. Curwen & Sons, 1907.

Gillington 1909a *Alice E. Gillington. *Old Hampshire Singing Games and Trilling the Rope Rhymes*. London: J. Curwen & Sons, 1909.

Gillington 1909b *Alice E. Gillington. *Old Surrey Singing Games and Skipping Rope Rhymes*. London: J. Curwen & Sons, 1909.

Gillington 1911 *Alice E. Gillington; Dowsett Sellars. *Songs and Poems of the Open Road*. London: Joseph Williams, 1911.

Gillington 1913 *Alice E. Gillington. *Old Dorset Singing Games*. London: J. Curwen & Sons, 1913.

*Gipsy Smith *Gipsy Smith's Mission Hymnal*. New York: Bigelow & Main co., 1906.

Gipsy's Warning The Gipsy's Warning Songster. New York: Robert M. De Witt, 1867.

Glass 1967a *Paul Glass; Louis C. Singer. *Songs of the Hill and Mountain Folk*. New York: Grosset & Dunlap, 1967.

Glass 1967b *Paul Glass; Louis C. Singer. *Songs of Town and City Folk*. New York: Grosset & Dunlap, 1967.

Glass 1968 *Paul Glass. *Singing Soldiers*. New York, 1968. (1st ed., 1964).

Glassie *Henry Glassie; Edward D. Ives; John F. Szwed. *Folksongs and Their Makers*. Bowling Green University Press, 1972.

Glazer 1961 *Tom Glazer. *A New Treasury of Folk Songs*. New York, 1961.

Glazer 1970 *Tom Glazer. *Songs of Peace, Freedom and Protest*. New York: David McKay Company, 1970.

Gleadhill *T. S. Gleadhill. *Songs of the British Isles*. London: Swan & Pentland, 1876.

Gledhill *Christopher Gledhill. *Folk Songs of Prince Edward Island, First Series*. Charlottetown, P. E. I.: Square Deal Publishers, 1973.

Götsch *Georg Götsch. Englisches Liederbuch. Wolfenbüttel: Möseler Verlag, 1953.

Gold Diggers The Gold Digger's Song Book. Marysville, California: Daily Herald, 1856.

*Goldenseal *Goldenseal* [A periodical issued by the State of West Virginia], 1975-.

Goldfinch The Goldfinch: a collection of love, comic, naval, patriotic and sentimental songs. Falkirk: A. Johnston, 1835.

Goldstein Kenneth S. Goldstein; Robert H. Byington. *Two Penny Ballads and Four Dollar Whiskey*. Hatboro: Pennsylvania Folklore Society, 1966.

Gomme i - ii *Alice Bertha Gomme. *The Traditional Games of England, Scotland and Ireland*. Reprint, 2 Vols., New York: Dover Publications, 1964. (1st ed., London, 1894, 1898).

Gomme 1909 *Alice B[ertha] Gomme; Cecil [J.] Sharp. *Children's Singing Games*. (Novello's School Songs). London: Novello & Co., 1909-12.

Good-Bye John Good-Bye John Songster. New York: Frederick A. Brady, 1870.

[*Good Old Songs* i - ii] *The Good Old Songs we Used to Sing*. [see: J. C. Haynes].

Goodwin 1955 i - ii *George Goodwin. *Song Dex Treasury of World-Famous Instrumental Music*. 2 Vols., New York: Song Dex, 1955.

Goodwin 1956 *George Goodwin. *Song Dex Treasury of Humorous and Nostalgic Songs*. New York: Song Dex, 1956.

Goodwin 1959 *George Goodwin. *Song Dex Treasury of Hymns*. New York: Song Dex, 1959.

Goose Hangs High The Goose Hangs High Songster. New York: Robert M. De Witt, 1866.

D. Gordon *Dorothy Gordon. *Sing It Yourself*. New York: E. P. Dutton, 1928.

R. W. Gordon AM Robert Winslow Gordon. *Old Songs that Men Have Sung* [a collection of articles in *Adventure Magazine*, 10 July 1923 to 15 October 1927]. Music Division, Library of Congress.

R. W. Gordon *NYT* Robert Winslow Gordon. *Folk-Songs of America* [a collection of articles from *The New York Times Magazine,* 1927-28]. Works Progress Administration Federal Theatre Project National Service Bureau Folksong and Folklore Department Publications, 1938.

T. Gordon *Thomas Gordon. *Scotish Ballads* (1793) [a manuscript at Widener Library, Harvard University; duplicate at Music Division, New York Public Library, *MO (Scottish)].

Goss 1927 *John Goss. *Daily Express Community Song Book.* London: London Express Newspaper, 1927.

Goss 1937 John Goss. *Ballads of Britain.* London: John Lane, 1937.

Gott *George C. Gott. *Old Familiar Dances.* Boston: Oliver Ditson, 1890.

N. D. Gould *Nathaniel D. Gould. *National Church Harmony.* Boston: Gould, Kendall & Lincoln, 1836. (1st ed., 1833).

S. B. Gould 1892 *Sabine Baring-Gould; H. Fleetwood Sheppard. *Songs of the West.* 2nd ed., London: Methuen & Co., 1892. (1st ed., 4 Vols., 1890).

S. B. Gould 1895 *Sabine Baring-Gould; H. Fleetwood Sheppard. *A Garland of Country Songs.* London, 1895.

S. B. Gould i - viii *Sabine Baring-Gould. *English Minstrelsie.* 8 Vols., Edinburgh: T. C. & E. C. Jack, 1895-97.

S. B. Gould 1905a *Sabine Baring-Gould; Cecil J. Sharp. *English Folk-Songs for Schools.* London: J. Curwen, [1905].

S. B. Gould 1905b *Sabine Baring-Gould; H. Fleetwood Sheppard; F. W. Bussell; Cecil J. Sharp. *Songs of the West.* New edition, London: Methuen & Co., 1905.

S. B. Gould 1974 *Sabine Baring-Gould; Gordon Hitchcock. *Folk Songs of the West Country.* London: Keith Prowse, 1974.

Graeme *Joy Graeme; Robert DeCormier. *The Irish Songbook* collected, adapted, written and sung by the Clancy Brothers and Tommy Makem. Toronto: The Macmillan Co., 1969.

Grafman *Howard Grafman; B. T. Manning. *Folk Music U.S.A.* New York: Citadel Press, 1962.

F. Graham 1965 *Frank Graham. *Tyneside Songs.* Newcastle Upon Tyne: Harold Hill & Son, 1965.

F. Graham 1971 *Frank Graham. *The Geordie Song Book.* Newcastle Upon Tyne: Frank Graham, 1971.

G. F. Graham i - iii *George Farquhar Graham. *The Songs of Scotland.* 3 Vols., Edinburgh: Wood & Co., 1848-49.

G. F. Graham 1891 *George Farquhar Graham; J. Muir Wood. *The Popular Songs and Melodies of Scotland.* London and Glasgow, 1891.

J. Graham *John Graham. *Dialect Songs of the North.* London: J. Curwen & Songs, 1910.

Grainger # *Percy Grainger; Rose Grainger. *Collection of English Folksongs, Sea Chanties, etc.* [Hektographed, 1907]. Music Division, New York Public Library.

Grainger 19— *Percy Aldridge Grainger. *British Folk-Music Settings* [a numbered series of arrangements, issued separately]. London: Schott & Co., 1911-49.

Granite Songster The Granite Songster. Boston & New York: C. Holt, Jr., 1847. (1st ed., 1841).

Grant-Schaefer *G. A. Grant-Schaefer. *Oh, Dear! What Can the Matter Be?* Boston: Arthur P. Schmidt Co., 1929.

Graves 1882 *Alfred Percival Graves; C. Villiers Stanford. *Songs of Old Ireland.* London: Boosey & Co., 1882.

Graves 1893 *Alfred Percival Graves; C. Villiers Stanford. *Irish Songs and Ballads.* London: Novello, 1893.

Graves 1894 *Alfred Percival Graves. *The Irish Song Book.* London: T. Fisher Unwin, 1914. (1st ed., 1894).

Graves 1897 *Alfred Percival Graves; Charles Wood. *Irish Folk Songs.* London: Boosey & Co., 1897.

Graves 1901 *Alfred Percival Graves; C. Villiers Stanford. *Songs of Erin.* London: Boosey & Co., 1901.

Graves i - ii *Alfred Percival Graves; J. Lloyd Williams; Arthur Somervell. *Welsh Melodies.* 2 Vols., London: Boosey & Co., 1907, 1909.

Graves 1928 *Alfred P[ercival] Graves. *The Celtic Song Book.* London: Ernest Benn, 1928.

Gray Roland Palmer Gray. *Songs and Ballads of the Maine Lumberjacks.* Harvard University Press, 1924.

Great Comic Volume i - iii *Great Comic Volume of [121] Songs* [A compilation in three parts, separately titled and paginated]. London: C. Sheard, 186-.

Great Emerson The Great Emerson New Popular Songster. San Francisco: White & Bauer, 1872.

Green *Paul Green. *Texas Songbook.* New York: Samuel French, 1967.

Greenback Songster The Greenback Song-ster. Philadelphia: Simpson & Co., 1867.

Greenleaf *Elisabeth Bristol Greenleaf; Grace Yarrow Mansfield. *Ballads and Sea Songs of Newfoundland.* Harvard University Press, 1933.

Greenway John Greenway. *American Folk-songs of Protest.* New York, 1960. (1st ed., 1953).

G. Greig *FSB* Gavin Greig. *Folk-Song in Buchan.* (*Transactions of the Buchan Field Club,* Vol. 9, 1906-7). Reprint, Folklore Associates, 1963.

G. Greig *FSNE* Gavin Greig. *Folk-Song of the Northeast.* [A collection of articles contributed to the *Buchan Observer,* Dec. 1907 to June 1911]. Reprint, Folklore Associates, 1963. (1st ed., 2 Vols., 1909, 1914).

G. Greig 1925 *Gavin Greig; Alexander Keith. *Last Leaves of Traditional Ballads and Ballad Airs.* Aberdeen: The Buchan Club, 1925.

J. Greig *John Greig. *Scots Minstrelsie.* 6 Vols., Edinburgh, 1892.

[Grove] *[George] *Grove's Dictionary of Music and Musicians.* (1st ed., London, 1890. [see Colles i - v and Maitland i - v].

Grover *Carrie B. Grover; Ann L. Griggs. *A Heritage of Songs.* Norwood Editions, 1973.

Guenther *Felix Guenther. *Swing Your Partner!* New York: Mercury Music Corp., 1944.

Guiana Sings *Guiana Sings. Delaware, Ohio: Coöperative Recreation Service, 1959.

Guiding Star The Guiding Star Songster. New York: Beadle & Co., 1865.

Gundry *Inglis Gundry. *Canow Kernow: Songs and Dances from Cornwall.* Federation of Old Cornwall Societies, 1966.

Gus Phillips Gus Phillips's Oofty Gooft Song-ster. New York: Popular Publishing Co., 1880.

Gus Shaw Gus Shaw's Comic Song and Reci-tation Book. New York: Dick & Fitzgerald, 1860.

Hadaway T[homas] H. Hadaway. *Hadaway's Select Songster.* Philadelphia: Gihon & Kucher, 1840.

Hadow *W. H. Hadow. *Songs of the British Islands.* London: Curwen & Sons, 1903.

Hague's Minstrels Hague's Minstrels Song-ster. Liverpool: Matthews Bros., 1873.

J. L. Hall J. Lincoln Hall; C. Austin Miles; C. Harold Lowden, et al. *New Songs of the Gospel Nos. 1, 2 & 3 Combined.* Philadel-phia: Hall-Mack Co., 1909.

S. C. Hall Samuel C. Hall. *The Book of Brit-ish Ballads.* London: Henry C. Bohn, 1853.

W. P. Hall *William Phillips Hall; J. Wilbur Chapman; W. S. Weeden. *Christian Hymns No. 1.* Philadelphia: Hall-Mack Co., 1899.

Hamer 1967 *Fred Hamer. *Garner's Gay.* London: English Folk Dance & Song Soci-ety, 1967.

Hamer 1973 *Fred Hamer. *Green Groves.* London: English Folk Dance & Song Soci-ety, 1973.

A. Hamilton *Adam Hamilton. *The Scottish Orpheus.* Edinburgh: Paterson & Sons, 1901.

W. Hamilton *William Hamilton. *The Select Songs of Scotland.* Glasgow: W. Hamilton, 1848.

Hamlin Wizard Oil Humorous and Sentimen-tal Songs as sung throughout the United States by Hamlin's Wizard Oil Concert Troupe. Chicago: Hamlin Wizard Oil Co., 188-, [Not paginated].

[Hammond] *H. E. D. Hammond; Cecil J. Sharp. *Folk-Songs from Dorset.* London: Novello & Co., 1908. [see: Sharp 1961 i].

[Hammond] *H. E. D. Hammon; Cecil J. Sharp. *Folk-Songs for Schools.* London: Novello & Co., 1908. [see: *Novello* viii #269].

Handy 1940 *Handy Play Party Book. Dela-ware, Ohio: Coöperative Recreation Ser-vice, 1940.

Handy 1955 *Handy Square Dance Book. Dclawarc, Ohio: Coöperative Recreation Service, 1955.

Handy Andy 185- Handy Andy's Budget of Songs. New York: Wm. H. Murphy, 185-.

Handy Andy 186- Handy Andy Dime Song Book. New York: Robert M. De Witt, 186-.

Hangtown Ballads *Hangtown Ballads, Nevada City, California: The Forty-Niner, 1949.

Hannagan i - iii *Margaret Hannagan; Seamus Clandillon. *Londub An Cairn* [Songs of the Irish Gaels]. 3 Vols., London: Humphrey Milford, 1927.

Hannegan *Margaret Hannegan; Seamus Clandillon. *Songs of the Irish Gaels.* Oxford University Press, 1927.

Hansen *Charles Hansen; Warren Conway. *400 Super Song Fest.* New York: Folk World, 1973.

Happy Voices *Happy Voices: New Hymns and Tunes.* New York: American Tract So-ciety, 1865.

Harbin Elvin G. Harbin. *Paradology.* Nash-ville, Tennessee: Cokesbury Press, 1930.

Harding *[Frank] *Harding's Collection of 200 Jigs, Reels and Country Dances.* New York: Richmond-Robbins, 1915. (1st ed., 1891).

Haring *Lee Haring. *The Gypsy Laddie: Anglo-American folk songs for 5-string banjo.* New York: Hargail Music Press, 1961.

Harlow *Frederick Pease Harlow. *Chanteying Aboard American Ships.* Barre, Massachusetts, 1962.

Harmonist *The Harmonist:* being a collection of tunes from the most approved authors; adapted to every variety of metre in the *Methodist Hymn-Book.* New York: G. Lane and P. O. Sanford, for the Methodist Episcopal Church, 1841.

Harmonist's Preceptor *The Harmonist's Preceptor, or Universal Vocalist.* London: J. Fairburn, n.d.

Harrigan & Braham i - ii *Harrigan & Braham's Popular Songs.* 2 Vols., New York: Wm. A. Pond, 1883, 1892.

Harrigan & Braham 1886 *Harrigan & Braham's Songs from The Leather Patch.* New York: Popular Publishing Co., 1886.

Harrigan & Braham 189- *Harrigan & Braham's Dan's Tribulation Songs.* New York: Henry J. Wehman, 189-.

Harrigan & Braham 1894 *Harrigan & Braham's Notoriety Songs.* New York: Henry J. Wehman, 1894.

Harrigan & Hart 1878 *Harrigan & Hart's Down Broadway Gallant 69th Songster.* New York: A. J. Fisher, 1878.

Harrigan & Hart 1882a *Harrigan & Hart's McSorley's Inflation Songster.* New York: Popular Publishing Co., 1882.

Harrigan & Hart 1882b *Harrigan & Hart's Mordecai Lyons Songster.* New York: Popular Publishing Co. #219, 1882.

Harris *Charles K. Harris. *After the Ball: Forty Years of Melody.* New York: Frank-Maurice Inc., 1926.

Harrison *Richard Cortland Harrison. *Choice Folk Songs.* New York: Hargail Music Press, 1965.

Harrison's Comic [W. B.]*Harrison's Comic Songster.* New York: Dick & Fitzgerald, 1849. (re-issued with the same title, and also with variant title: *Harrison's Museum Songster,* same pagination, New York: Dick & Fitzgerald, 1862).

Harry Brown *Harry Brown's Moonlight Walk Songster.* New York: Ornum & Co., 187-.

Harry Hill 1870 *The Harry Hill Songster.* New York: Ornum & Co., 1870.

Harry Hill 1882 *Harry Hill's Greatest Song-ster.* New York: Popular Publishing Co., 1882.

Harry Pell *Harry Pell's Ebony Songster.* New York: Dick & Fitzgerald, 1864.

Harry Richmond 1869 *Harry Richmond's Call Her Back and Kiss Her Songster.*1869.

Harry Richmond 1870 *Harry Richmond's Not for Joseph Songster.* New York Dick & Fitzgerald, 1870.

Harry Woodson 1877 *Harry Woodson's Gwine Back to Dixie Songster.* New York, 1877.

Harry Woodson 1880 *Harry Woodson's Goodbye, Liza Songster.* New York: Popular Publishing Co., 1880.

Harvest *Harvest of Minstrel Songs.* Boston. White-Smith, 1884.

Harvey A. S. Harvey. *Ballads, Songs and Rhymes of East Anglia.* Norwich, 1936.

Harwell *Richard B. Harwell. *Confederate Music.* University of North Carolina Press, 1950.

Hatfield Brothers *The Hatfield Brothers' Pride of Mayo Songster.* New York: Popular Publishing Co., 1883.

Hatton i - ii *J. L. Hatton. *The Songs of England.* 2 Vols., London: Boosey & Co., n.d.

Hatton *J. L. Hatton; J. L. Molloy. *The Songs of Ireland.* New and Englarged Edition, London: Boosey & Co., n.d.

Haufrecht 1942 *Herbert Haufrecht. *Square Set* for String Orchestra. New York: Associated Music Publishers, Inc. 1942.

Haufrecht 1943 *Herbert Haufrecht. *Folk Songs of the Catskills* [collected and arranged with piano accompaniments]. Manuscript reproduction, © 1943 by Herbert Haufrecht. [Copy at American Music Center Library, New York City].

Haufrecht 1944 *Herbert Haufrecht. *Walkin' The Road* for band. New York: Leeds Music Corp. 1944.

Haufrecht 1945 *Herbert Haufrecht. *The Bonny Laboring Boy; Lather and Shave; Wild Americay* (choral settings). New York: Leeds Music Corp. 1945.

Haufrecht 1953 *Herbert Haufrecht. *Boney Quillen:* Opera-Pantomine in Three Scenes. New York: Broude Brothers, 1953.

Haufrecht 1956 *Herbert Haufrecht. *A Woodland Serenade* for woodwind quintet. Rongwen Music Inc.: New York: 1956.

Haufrecht 1958 *Herbert Haufrecht. *109 Folk Songs and Ballads.* New York: Remick Music Co., 1958.

Haufrecht 1959 *Herbert Haufrecht. *Folk Sing.* New York: Hollis Music.

Haufrecht 1963 *Herbert Haufrecht. *'Round the World Folk Sing*. New York: Hollis Music Co., 1963.

Haufrecht 1965 *Herbert Haufrecht. *Folksongs of the Catskills* Composers Facsimile Edition. Ms 1965.

Haufrecht 1970 *Herbert Haufrecht. *Folk Song Settings by Master Composers*. New York: Funk & Wagnalls, 1970.

Hauser 1848 *William Hauser. *The Hesperian Harp*. Philadelphia: T. K. & P. G. Collins, 1848.

Hauser 1878 *William Hauser; Benjamin Turner. *The Olive Leaf*. Wadley, Georgia: William Hauser and Benjamin Turner, 1878.

Hayden 1835 *A. S. Hayden. *Introduction to Sacred Music*. Pittsburgh, 1835. (1st ed., 1818).

Hayden 1852 *A. S. Hayden. *The Sacred Melodeon*. Philadelphia: T. L. Collins, 1852.

Haydn *Franz Joseph Haydn. Werke, Reihe XXXII: *Volkslieder Bearbeitungen*, Bd. I Nr. 1 - 100; *Schottische Lieder*. München: G. Henle Verlag, 1961.

Haynes i - ii *J. C. Haynes. *The Good Old Songs We Used to Sing*. 2 Vols., Boston: Oliver Ditson, 1887, 1895.

Hayward H. Richard Hayward. *Ulster Songs and Ballads*. London, 1925.

Ch. Haywood *Charles Haywood. *Folk Songs of the World*. New York: The John Day Co., 1966.

E. Haywood *Ernest Haywood; Ernest Newton. *Country Dances*. London: Keith Prowse Publishing Co., 1929, 1933.

Hazlewood *Rex Hazlewood; John Thurman; A. Mackintosh. *The Second Gilwell Camp Fire Book*. London: C. Arthur Pearson, 1962.

Healy 1962 *James N. Healy. *The Second Book of Irish Ballads*. Cork: The Mercier Press, 1962.

Healy 1965 *James N. Healy. *Ballads from the Pubs of Ireland*. Cork: The Mercier Press, 1965.

Healy 1966 *James N. Healy. *Percy French and His Songs*. Cork: The Mercier Press, 1966.

Healy 1967 *James N. Healy. *Irish Ballads and Songs of the Sea*. Cork: The Mercier Press, 1967.

[Healy 1968] [see: O'Keeffe].

Healy i - iv *James N. Healy. *The Mercier Book of Old Irish Street Ballads*. 4 Vols., Cork: The Mercier Press, 1967-69.

Heart & Home The Heart and Home Songster. New York: Dick & Fitzgerald, 1862.

*Heart Songs *Heart Songs Dear to the American People*. Boston: Chapple Publishing Co., 1910. (Re-issue, Cleveland: World Publishing Co., 1950).

C. Heaton *Charles Huddleston Heaton. *Hymnbook for Christian Worship*. St. Louis, Missouri: The Bethany Press, 1970.

P. Heaton *Peter Heaton; Maria Bird. *Songs Under Sail*. London: Burke, 1963.

Henderson# Henderson and Halbert's Original Singer's Journal. [A periodical, probably issued fortnightly, of unspecified time-span, ca. 186-. #2 - #14 are included on microfilm *ZB 138 at Music Division, New York Public Library, intermixed with issues of De Marsan's *Singer's Journal*, but the continuous pagination and the contents are not the same. Some issues bear the title *Singer's Journal*].

Hendren *J. W. Hendren. *A Study of Ballad Rhythm*. Princeton University Press, 1936.

Hendrickson *George Hendrickson. *The Union Harmony*. Mountain Valley, Virginia: Joseph Funk & Sons, 1848.

Henebry *Richard Henebry. *A Handbook of Irish Music*. Dublin: Cork University Press, 1928.

Hen Graham Hen Graham's Just Arrived from Harrisburg Songster. New York: Mrs Pauline Leider, 1881.

M. E. Henry *Mellinger Edward Henry. *Folk-Songs from the Southern Highlands*. New York: J. J. Augustin, 1938.

[Sam Henry] [see: *Sam Henry* and Sam Henry Index].

Henry O'Richmond Henry O'Richmond's Never Push a Man Songster. Philadelphia: A. Winch, 1870.

*Henry Russell *Henry Russell's 100 Copyright Songs*. London: C. Sheard, 186-.

[Henry Russell 1876] *Henry Russell's Songs and Scenas. London: H. D' Alcorn, 1876. [see: *D'Alcorn's Musical Miracles* #2].

[*Hesperian Harp*] *The Hesperian Harp*. [see: Hauser 1848].

Hesser *Ernest G. Hesser; Bessie Shipman Dustman. *Treasure Chest of Songs*. New York: American Book Co., 1932.

HFB Hoosier Folklore Bulletin, 1942-.

Hickok *J[ohn] H[oyt] Hickok. *The Social Lyrist* [with tunes in shape-notes]. Harrisburg, Pennsylvania: W. Orville Hickok, 1840. (2nd ed., 1843).

Hi Henry Hi Henry's Premium Minstrel Songster. New York: Popular Publishing Co., 188-.

Hille *Waldemar Hille. *The People's Song*

Book. New York, 1948.

Hills *William H. Hills. *Student's Songs.* Boston: Rand Avery, 1880. (13th ed., 1887).

G. Hitchcock *Gordon Hitchcock. *The Shell Book of Sea Chanties.* Brighton, Sussex: E. H. Freeman, 1952.

Hitchcock # *Hitchcock's Half Dime Series of Music for the Million. [Individual sheet music issues, #1 - #462]. New York: B. W. Hitchcock, 1868-71.

Hitchcock i - iv *Hitchcock's Collection of Old and New Songs.* 4 Vols., New York: Hitchcock's Music Store, 1881.

Hitchcock 1891. *Hitchcock's Comic Song Casket. New York: B. W. Hitchcock, 1891.

Hixon Donald L. Hixon. *Music in Early America:* a bibliography of music in Evans. Metuchen, New Jersey: The Scarecrow Press, 1970.

HL 500 †*Yankee Legend* (Bill and Gene Bonyun). Heirloom HL 500.

H.M.S. Pinafore The *H. M. S. Pinafore Songster.* New York: Popular Publishing Co. #24, 1879?

Hobbs William L. Hobbs. *Complete [Dan] Bryant's Minstrels Songs and Programme for One Year,* Vol. 3 [only]. New York: T. B. Harrison, 1860-61.

B. Hoffman *Brigitte Hoffman. *Folk Songs of Britain and America.* München: Max Hueber Verlag, 1965.

E. A. Hoffman *Elisha A. Hoffman. *Best Hymns.* Chicago: Evangelical Publishing Co., 1894.

I. Hoffman *Irwin Hoffman. *Everybody's Favorite Second Book of Songs.* New York: Amsco Music Publishing Co., 1948.

Hogarth i - ii *George Hogarth. *The [Illustrated] Book of British Song.* 2 Vols., London: James S. Virtue, n.d.

Hogg i - ii *James Hogg. *The Jacobite Relics of Scotland.* 2 Vols., Edinburgh: William Blackwood, 1819, 1821.

Holbrook *J. P. Holbrook et al. *The Baptist Praise Book.* New York: A. S. Barnes & Co., 1871.

Hold the Fort Hold the Fort Songster. New York: Robert M. DeWitt, 1876.

Holloway John Holloway. *The Euing Collection of [408] English Broadside Ballads.* (Facsimile reprints). University of Glasgow Publications, 1971.

Holst *Imogene Holst; Ursula Vaughan Williams. *A Yacre of Land*: Sixteen folk-songs from the Ms. Collection of Ralph Vaughan Williams. Oxford University Press, 1961.

Holyoke i - ii *Samuel Holyoke. *The Instru-mental Assistant.* 2 Vols., Exeter, New Hampshire, 1800, 1807.

Home Melodist a - b *The Home Melodist. a, Boston: Oliver Ditson, 1859. b, San Francisco: A. Kohler, 1859.

Honoré *Lockwood Honoré. *Popular College Songs.* Cincinnati: John Church Co., 1891.

Hook *[James] Hook. *Woodland Mary.* London: William Dale, n.d. [Included in a miscellaneous collection of sheet music at Boston Public Library, M 481.246].

Hooley 1863 Hooley's Opera House Songster. New York: Dick & Fitzgerald, 1863.

Hooley 1865 Hooley's High Daddy Songster. New York: Robert M. De Witt, #41, 1865.

Hopekirk *Helen Hopekirk. *Seventy Scottish Songs.* Boston: Oliver Ditson, 1905.

Horn *Dorothy D. Horn. *Sing to Me of Heaven.* University of Florida Press, 1970.

Horton *John Horton. *The American Song Book.* Leeds: E. J. Arnold & Sons, n.d.

Houston *Cisco Houston. *900 Miles.* New York: Oak Publications, 1965.

Howe 1851a *Howe's School for the Violin. Boston: Oliver Ditson, 1851.

Howe 1851b *Elias Howe [under pseud., Gumbo Chaff]. *The Complete Preceptor for the Banjo.* Boston: Oliver Ditson, 1851.

Howe 1851c *[Elias] Howe's School for the Flageolet. Boston: Oliver Ditson, 1851.

Howe 1858a *Elias Howe. *Leviathan Collection of Instrumental Music.* New York: S. T. Gordon, 1858.

Howe 1858b *Elias Howe. *Young America's Collection of Instrumental Music.* Boston: H. Tolman & Co., 1858.

Howe 1859 *[Elias] Howe's New American Banjo School, Abridged Edition.* Boston: Russell & Tolman, 1859.

Howe 1864a *Elias Howe. *The Musician's Omnibus, Complete.* Boston: Elias Howe, 1864.

Howe 1864b *[Elias] Howe's Songs and Ballads of Olden Time, No. 1.* Boston: Elias Howe, 1864.

Howe 1872 *[Elias] Howe's 100 Sentimental Songs.* Boston: Elias Howe, 1872.

Howe 1874 *[Elias] Howe's 500 Sentimental, Comic, Scotch and Irish Songs.* Boston: Elias Howe, 1874.

Howe i - ii *[Elias] Howe's 100 Comic Songs, #1 - #2.* Boston: Elias Howe, 1877.

Howe 1877 *[Elias] Howe's 100 Ethiopian Songs.* Boston: Elias Howe, 1877.

Howe 1878 *[Elias] Howe's 100 Old Favorite Songs.* Boston: Elias Howe, 1878.

Howe 1880 *[Elias] *Howe's 100 Irish Songs.* Boston: Elias Howe, 1880.

Howe 188- *[Elias] *Howe's 100 Songs of Scotland,* with accompaniments for piano or organ. Boston: Elias Howe, [188-].

Howes *Frank Howes. *Folk Music of Britain and Beyond.* London: Methuen & Co., 1969.

HTA *Harold Thompson Archives [a manuscript collection, chiefly from New York State sources. Items are not paginated; some are identified by name of collector, others by category]. Fenimore House Library, New York State Historical Society, Cooperstown.

Hubbard *Lester A. Hubbard; Kenly W. Whitelock. *Ballads and Songs from Utah.* University of Utah Press, 1961.

Hudson 1936 Arthur Palmer Hudson. *Folksongs of Mississippi.* University of North Carolina Press, 1936.

Hudson 1937 *Arthur Palmer Hudson; George Herzog. *Folk Tunes from Mississippi.* New York: Works Progress Administration Federal Theatre Project National Play Bureau, 1937.

Hughes 1903 *Herbert Hughes; Padraig mac Aodh O'Neill; Seosamh mac Cathmhaoil. *Sons of Uladh.* Belfast, 1903.

Hughes i - iv *Herbert Hughes. *Irish Country Songs.* 4 Vols., London: Boosey & Co., 1909.

Hugill *Stan Hugill. *Shanties from the Seven Seas.* London and New York, 1961.

Hull *Asa Hull. *The Jeweled Crown.* New York: Asa Hull, 1891.

Humming Bird The *Humming Bird Songster.* Philadelphia: Fisher & Bro., 18--.

Humphreys *Henry S. Humphreys. *Songs of the Union.* Cincinnati: Willis Music Co., 1961.

Huntington *Gale Huntington. *Songs the Whalemen Sang.* Barre, Massachusetts, 1964.

[Huntington 1977] *Gale Huntington. *William Litten's Fiddle Tunes, 1800-1802.* [See: *William Litten*].

Hurst *Jack Hurst. *Nashville's Grand Ole Opry.* New York: Harry N. Abrams, 1975.

Hustad *Donald P. Hustad. *Hymns for the Living Stream.* Carol Stream, Illinois: Hope Publishing Co., 1974.

[Hutchinson Family] [see: *Book of Poetry; Book of Words*].

Hyde & Behman *Hyde & Behman's Two Johns Combination Songster.* New York: Popular Publishing Co., 188-.

Hyland *Hyland's Mammoth Hibernian Songster.* Chicago, 1901.

Hymnal *The *[Presbyterian] *Hymnal.* Philadelphia, 1934.

Hymns Christian Life *Hymns of the Christian Life.* Harrisburg, Pennsylvania: Christian Publications, 1962. (1st ed., 1891).

Hymns & Tunes *Hymns and Tunes for Public and Private Worship.* Elkhart, Indiana: Mennonite Publishing Co., 1890.

Immortalia *Immortalia Volume Three: Ribald Songs.* New York: Hart Publishing Co., 1971.

Imperial The *Imperial Comic Song Book.* Glasgow: Cameron & Ferguson, 1877. [Part 2, continuing the same pagination, bears the separate title: *The Merry Lad's Comic Song Book*].

Ingram Tom Ingram; Douglas Newton. *Hymns as Poetry.* London: Constable & Co., 1956.

Inspirational Melodies #2 *Inspirational Melodies No. 2.* Nashville, Tennessee: National Baptist Young People's Union of America Board, 1929.

INT 13058 †*A Song for You and Me* (Peggy Seeger). Prestige-International INT 13058.

INT 14016 †*The Best of Peggy Seeger.* Prestige-International INT 14016.

INT 25014 †*Ontario Ballads and Folksongs.* (Fowke). Prestige-International 25014.

Ireland's Songs *Ireland's Songs.* London: Boosey & Co., 1915.

Irish Boy The *Irish Boy and Yankee Girl Songster.* New York: Dick & Fitzgerald, 1860.

Irish Broadsides A Collection of [Irish] *Broadside Songs.* [A bound volume at Morrison Library, University of California at Berkeley, M1744.C56].

[*Irish Comic Songster*] [See: *Songs of Our Land* 185- ii].

[*Irish Melodies*] [*Irish Melodies by Thomas Moore*: see *Songs of Our Land* 1852 iii].

IRL 11, 12 †*Folksongs Sung in Ulster,* collected by Robin Morton. 2 Vols., Mercier IRL 11, 12.

Isaiah Thomas i-iii *Isaiah Thomas Collection*: Boston, ca. 1812-14, 3 vols., American Antiquarian Society, Worcester, Mass.

It's Naughty *It's Naughty but It's Nice Songster.* New York: Robert M. De Witt #110, 1871.

B. Ives 1949 *Burl Ives. *Favorite Folk Ballads.* New York, 1949.

B. Ives 1953 *Burl Ives. The *Burl Ives Song*

Book. New York, 1953.

B. Ives 1956   *Burl Ives. *Sea Songs.* New York, 1956.

B. Ives 1957   *Burl Ives. *At Home with Burl Ives.* New York: Leeds Music Corporation, 1957.

B. Ives 1958   *Burl Ives. *Irish Songs.* New York, 1958.

B. Ives 1962   *Burl Ives. *Song in America.* New York, 1962.

B. Ives 1966   *Burl Ives. *More Burl Ives Songs.* New York, 1966.

Ch. Ives 1896   *Charles Ives. *Quartet No. 1 (1896), "A Revival Service."* New York: Peer-International Music Corp., 1961.

Edw. Ives 1964   *Edward D. Ives. *Larry Gorman.* Indiana University Press, 1964.

Edw. Ives 1971   *Edward D. Ives. *Lawrence Doyle.* Orono, Maine, 1971.

Edw. Ives 1978   *Edward D. Ives. *Joe Scott: the woodsman songmaker.* University of Illinois Press 1978.

I Want to See   I want to See the Old Home *Songster.* Clinton Taylor De Witt, 1877.

I. W. W.   [Industrial Workers of the World]. *Songs of the Workers.* 8th ed., Cleveland: I. W. W. Publishing Bureau, 1914.

Jack Reeve   Jack Reeve's Comic Songster. London: E. Lloyd, 1835. [not paginated].

Jack Tar   Jack Tar's Songster. Philadelphia: Fisher & Bro., 1851.

B. Jackson   *Bruce Jackson. *Folklore and Society:* essays in honor of Benj[amin] A. Botkin. Hatboro, Pennsylvania: Folklore Associates, 1966.

G. P. Jackson 1933   *George Pullen Jackson. *White Spirituals in the Southern Uplands.* Reprint, New York, 1965. (1st ed., 1933).

G. P. Jackson 1937   *George Pullen Jackson. *Spiritual Folk-Songs of Early America.* Reprint, New York, 1964. (1st ed., 1937).

G. P. Jackson 1942   *George Pullen Jackson. *Down-East Spirituals and Others.* 2nd ed., New York: J. J. Augustin, 1953. (1st ed., 1942).

G. P. Jackson 1944   *George Pullen Jackson. *White and Negro Spirituals.* New York: J. J. Augustin, 1944.

G. P. Jackson 1947   *George Pullen Jackson; Charles Faulkner Bryan. *American Folk Music.* Boston: C. C. Birchard & Co., 1947.

G. P. Jackson 1952   *George Pullen Jackson. *Another Sheaf of White Spirituals.* University of Florida Press, 1952.

G. S. Jackson   *George Stuyvesant Jackson.

Early Songs of Uncle Sam. Boston, 1933.

J. B. Jackson   *John B. Jackson. *The Knoxville Harmony.* Madisonville, Tennessee: D. & M. Shields & Co., 1838.

R. Jackson   *Richard Jackson. *Popular Songs of Nineteenth-Century America* [64 facsimiles]. New York: Dover Books, 1976.

V. Jackson   *Vincent Jackson. *English Melodies from the 13th to the 18th Century.* London: J. M. Dent & Sons, 1910.

Jaehde   Walter Jaehde. "Religion, Schicksalsglaube, Vorahnungen, Träume, Geister und Rätsel in den englisch-schottischen Volksballaden." Dissertation, Vereinigten Friedrichs-Universität, Halle-Writtenberg, 1905.

JAF   *Journal of American Folklore,* 1888-.

James A. Bland   James A. Bland's De Golden Wedding Songster. New York: Popular Publishing Co., #114, 1880.

James Gray   James Gray's I'm a Man You Don't Meet Every Day Songster. New York: Popular Publishing Co., 1883.

James H. McGuire   James H. McGuire's Jim the Carter Lad Songster. New York: Frederick A. Brady, 1870.

James O'Neil 188-   James O'Neil's Gilhooley, Your Coat is Half-Mast Songster. New York: Popular Publishing Co., 188-.

James O'Neil 1882   James O'Neil's Oh, Mr. Flannigan Songster. New York: Popular Publishing Co., 1882.

Jameson 1955   *Gladys V. Jameson. *Wake and Sing.* New York: Associated Music Publishers, 1955.

Jameson 1967   *Gladys V. Jameson. *Sweet Rivers of Song.* Berea, Kentucky: Berea College, 1967.

Jamieson i - ii   Robert Jamieson. *Popular Ballads and Songs.* 2 vols., Edinburgh: Archibald Constable & Co., 1806, 1808.

JAMS   *Journal of the American Musicological Society,* 1948-.

Jardin Mabille   The Jardin Mabille Songster No. 2. New York: Fisher & Denison, 1869.

Jarman   *Harry E. Jarman. *Old Time Fiddlin' Tunes.* Toronto, 1938.

Jay Rial   Jay Rial's Ideal Uncle Tom's Cabin Song Book. San Francisco: Frances, Valentine & Co., 1883.

JEFDSS   *Journal of the English Folk Dance and Song Society,* 1934-64.

JEMFQ   John Edwards Memorial Foundation Quarterly, 1965-.

Jenkins   Stephen Jenkins. *The Greatest Street in the World.* New York: G. Putnam's Sons, The Knickerbocker Press, 1911.

Jennie Hughes 187- *Jennie Hughes' Dolly Varden Songster.* New York, 187-.

Jennie Hughes 1874 *Jennie Hughes' Rose of Erin Songster.* New York: Robert M. De Witt, 1874.

Jennie Lind *The Jennie Lind Forget-Me-Not Songster.* New York: Richard Marsh, 184-.

Jewett *Jewett's National Violin Teacher.* Boston: Oliver Ditson, 1859.

JFSS *Journal of the Folk Song Society* (London), 1890-1931.

J. H. Conroy *J. H. Conroy's Tipperary Christening Songster.* New York: Popular Publishing Co., #217, 1882.

J. H. Ryan *J. H. Ryan's Dublin Bard Songster.* New York: Clinton T. De Witt, 1877.

JIFMC *Journal of the International Folk Music Council*, 1949-68.

JIFSS *Journal of the Irish Folk Song Society*, 1904-.

J. M. Berry [*J. M.*] *Berry's Comic Songs.* Philadelphia: A. Winch, 1856.

Jocelin *Jocelin. The Chorister's Companion*, 1792.

Joe English *Joe English's Irish Comic Songster.* New York: Dick & Fitzgerald, 1864.

John Conroy *John Conroy's Tit-A-Ta Songster.* New York: Popular Publishing Co., 1881.

Johnny Brougham *Johnny Brougham's Exile of Erin Songster.* New York: Ornum & Co., 187-.

Johnny Cross *Johnny Cross's Flutamagilder Songster.* New York: Frederick A. Brady, 1869.

Johnny, I Hardly Knew Ye *Johnny, I Hardly Knew Ye Songster.* New York: Frederick A. Brady, 1870.

Johnny Patterson *Johnny Patterson's Great London Circus Songster.* New York: Popular Publishing Co., 188-.

Johnny Roach 1879 *Johnny Roach's That Kid of Mine Songster.* New York: Popular Publishing Co., #25, 1879.

Johnny Roach 1881 *Johnny Roach's When McGuinness Gets a Job Songster.* New York: Popular Publishing Co., #95, 1881.

Johnny Wild *Johnny Wild's What Am I Doing Songster.* New York: Dick & Fitzgerald, 1868.

A. N. Johnson *A. N. Johnson; Josiah Osgood; J. C. Johnson. The Normal Song Book.* Boston: George P. Reed & Co., 1861.

C. Johnson *Clifton Johnson. Songs Everyone Should Know.* New York, 1908.

C. W. Johnson *Charles W. Johnson. Songs of America and Homeland.* New York, 1906.

H. K. Johnson *Helen Kendrick Johnson. Our Familiar Songs and Those Who Made Them.* New York, 1881.

J. Johnson # *James Johnson [publisher]. The Scots Musical Museum* [edited by Robert Burns]. 6 Vols. in 1, reprint [from the edition of 1853], Hatboro, Pennsylvania: Folklore Associates, 1962. (1st ed., Edinburgh, 1787-1803). [See also: Laing, Stenhouse].

M. Johnson *Margaret Johnson; Travis Johnson. Early American Songs.* New York, 1943.

Johnson & Bruno *Johnson and Bruno's Tom Big Bee Bay Songster.* New York: Popular Publishing Co., #10, 1878.

[*Johnson's Comic*] *Johnson's Comic Songster* (1858), re-issued as *Johnson's Original Comic Songster #1* (1864). [See: *Pacific Song Book* iv].

[*Johnson's New Comic*] *Johnson's New Comic Songster* (1859), re-issued as *Johnson's New Comic Songster #2* (1863). [See: *Pacific Song Book* v].

Jolliffe *Maureen Jolliffe. The Third Book of Irish Ballads.* Cork: The Mercier Press, 1970.

Jolly Comic Songster *The Jolly Comic Songster.* Philadelphia: Fisher & Bro., 1851.

Jolly Miller *The Jolly Miller Songster.* The Northwestern Miller, ca. 1905.

Jolly Old Clown *The Jolly Old Clown's Songster.* New York: Robert M. De Witt, 1872.

Jolly Songster *Jolly Songster.* Chicago: Laird & Lee, 1894.

Jones *Bessie Jones; Bess Lomax Hawes. Step It Down.* New York: Harper & Row, 1972.

[*Jones Archives*] *The Louis C. Jones Folklore Archives.* [See: LCJ].

Jordan *Philip D. Jordan; Lillian Kessler. Songs of Yesterday* [containing sheet music in facsimile]. Garden City, New York, 1941.

Joseph *Nathan Joseph; Eric Winter. New English Broadsides.* New York: Oak Publications, 1967.

Joyce 1872 *Patrick Weston Joyce. Ancient Irish Music* [a re-issue of 1st ed. of 1872]. Dublin, 1906.

Joyce 1906 *Patrick Weston Joyce. Irish Peasant Songs.* London: Longmans Green, 1906.

Joyce # *Patrick Weston Joyce. Old Irish Folk Music and Songs.* Dublin: Hodges, Figgis & Co., 1909.

Joyful Singing *Joyful Singing.* Delaware,

Ohio: Coöperative Recreation Service, 194-.

Joyner *Charles W. Joyner. *Folk Song in South Carolina*. University of South Carolina Press, 1971.

J. S. Berry *J. S. Berry's Flying Trapeze Songster*. New York: Robert M. De Witt, 1868.

Justus *May Justus. *The Complete Peddler's Pack*. University of Tennessee Press, 1967.

JWFSS *Journal of the Welsh Folk Song Society*, 1909-.

Kallman Helmut Kallman. *A History of Music in Canada, 1534-1914*. University of Toronto Press, 1960.

Kanawha 313 †*Ballads and Fiddle Tunes* (Grant Rogers). Kanawha 313.

Karpeles 1934 i - ii *Maud Karpeles; Ralph Vaughan Williams. *Folk Songs from Newfoundland*. 2 vols., Oxford University Press, 1934.

Karpeles 1951 *Maud Karpeles; Kenworthy Schofield. *A Selection of 100 English Folk Dance Airs* for melodic instruments. London: English Folk Dance & Song Society, [1951].

Karpeles 1956 *Maud Karpeles. *Folk Songs of Europe*. London: Novello & Co. [for the International Folk Music Council], 1956.

Karpeles 1971 *Maud Karpeles. *Folk Songs from Newfoundland*. London: Faber & Faber, 1971.

Karpeles 1973 *Maud Karpeles. *An Introduction to English Folk Song*. Oxford University Press, 1973.

Karpeles 1974 i - ii *Maud Karpeles. *Cecil Sharp's Collection of Folk Songs*. 2 vols., Oxford University Press, 1974.

Karpeles 1975 i - ii *Maud Karpeles. *The Crystal Spring*. 2 vols., Oxford University Press, 1975.

Kathleen Mavourneen The *Kathleen Mavourneen Songster*. New York: Robert M. De Witt, 1872.

Keene *Hank Keene. *Hill-Billy, Mountaineer and Cowboy Songs*. New York: Crawford & Co., 1932.

Keller 1974 *Kate Van Winkle Keller. *Giles Gibbs, Jr.: His Book for the Fife* [Ellington, Connectiicut, 1777]. Hartford: Connecticut Historical Society, 1974.

Keller 1975 *Kate Van Winkle Keller; Ralph Sweet. *A Choice Selection of American Country Dances of the Revolutionary Era, 1775-1795*. New York: Country Dance and Song Society, 1975.

Kellock William Kellock. *The Rebels Ceilidh Song Book*. Glasgow: Scottish National Party, 195-.

Kellogg *Francis B. Kellogg; Thomas G. Shepard. *Yale Songs*. 3rd ed., New Haven, 1889. (1st ed., 1882).

Kemp *Willie Kemp. *Kerr's Cornkister's: Bothy Ballads*. Glasgow: James S. Kerr, 1950.

Ch. Kennedy 1952 Charles O'Brien Kennedy; David Jordan *American Ballads: Naughty, Ribald and Classic*. New York: Fawcett Publications, 1952.

Ch. Kennedy 1954 Charles O'Brien Kennedy. *A Treasury of American Ballads*. New York, 1954.

D. Kennedy 1948 *Douglas Kennedy. *English Country Dances of Today*. New York: Country Dance Society of America, 1948. [1st English edition, 1947].

D. Kennedy 1965 *Douglas Kennedy; Helen Kennedy. *Square Dances of America*. London: English Folk Dance and Song Society, 1965.

J. Kennedy *Joseph Kennedy. *The Amateur's Souvenir, or the Flutist's Own Book*. Philadelphia: G. E. Blake, 1845.

P. Kennedy 1951 *Peter J. Kennedy. *The Fiddler's Tune Book: 100 traditional airs*. London: English Folk Song & Dance Society, 1951.

P. Kennedy 1954 *Peter Kennedy. *The Second Fiddler's Tune Book*. London: English Folk Dance & Song Society, 1954.

[P. Kennedy 1965] *Peter Kennedy. *Folk Songs Today #1*. [See: *FST*].

P. Kennedy 1975 *Peter Kennedy; Raymond Parfrey. *Folk Songs of Britain and Ireland*. London: Cassel, 1975.

T. Kennedy *Tom Kennedy; George B. McConwell; Dick Sanford. *Radio Rube's Collection of Hill Country Ballads and Comic Songs*. New York: Nattrass-Schenk, 1933.

[Kennedy-Fraser] [See: Marjory Kennedy Fraser].

Kentucky 1937 *[Kentucky]: United States Works Progress Administration. *Songs* collected by workers of the Federal Music Project in Boyd, Floyd and Rowan Counties, 1937-38.

Kentucky 1939 i - ii *[Kentucky]: United States Works Progress Administration Federal Music Project, Kentucky. *Folk Songs from East Kentucky*. 2 vols., 1939.

[*Kentucky Harmony*] *The Kentuck Harmony*. [See: Ananias Davisson].

Kerr i - xii *James S. Kerr [publisher]. *Collec-

tion of Merry Melodies for the Violin. 12 Vols., Glasgow: James S. Kerr, 1920.

Keynote K-102 †*Early American Ballads* (John and Lucy Allison). Keynote K-102.

Keynote K-108 †*Ballads and Folk Songs* (Richard Dyer-Bennet). Keynote K-108.

KFQ Keystone Folklore Quarterly, 1956-.

Kidson 1890 *Frank Kidson *Old English Country Dances.* London: William Reeves, 1890.

Kidson 1891 *Frank Kidson. *Traditional Tunes.* Reprint, New York, 196-. (1st ed., Oxford, 1891).

Kidson 1913 *Frank Kidson; Martin Shaw. *Songs of Britain.* London: Boosey & Co., 1913.

Kidson 1915 *Frank Kidson; Mary Neal. *English Folk-Song and Dance.* Cambridge, 1915.

Kidson 1916 *Frank Kidson; Alfred Moffat.*100 Singing Games.* London: Bayley & Ferguson, 1916.

Kidson 1926 *Frank Kidson. *A Garland of English Folk-Songs.* London: Ascherberg, Hopwood & Crew, 1926.

Kidson 1927 *Frank Kidson; Ethel Kidson; Alfred Moffat. *Folk-songs of the North Countree.* London, 1927.

Kidson 1929 *Frank Kidson; Ethel Kidson; Alfred Moffat. *English Peasant Songs.* London: Ascherberg, Hopweed & Crew, 1929.

Killion *Ronald G. Killion; Charles T. Waller. *A Treasury of Georgia Folklore.* Atlanta, 1972.

Kimball Marilyn Kimball. "George Edwards, Catskill folksinger." Master's Thesis, State University of New York at Oneonta, 1966.

Kincaid i - iii *Bradley Kincaid. *Favorite Old Time Songs and Mountain Ballads.* 3 vols., 1928-30.

Kincaid 1937 *Bradley Kincaid. *Favorite Mountain Ballads and Old Time Songs.* New York: Southern Music Publishing Co., 1937.

King *Stanton H. King. *King's Book of Chanties.* Philadelphia: Oliver Ditson Co., 1918.

Kingsbury *F. G. Kingsbury. *Hymns of Praise.* Chicago: Hope Publishing Co., 1922.

Kinkle i - iv Roger D. Kinkle. *The Complete Encyclopedia of Popular Music and Jazz, 1900-1950.* 4 vols., New Rochelle, New York: Arlington House, 1974.

Kinley *Ethel A. Kinley. *A Song Book.* Toronto: Clark, Irwin & Co., 1940.

Kinloch George Ritchie Kinloch. *The Ballad Book.* Reprint, Edinburgh, 1891. (1st ed., 1827).

Kinscella *Hazel Gertrude Kinscella. *Folk Songs and Fiddle tunes of the U. S. A.* New York: Carl Fischer, 1959.

Kinsley i - iii *James Kinsley. *the Poems and Songs of Robert Burns.* 3 vols., Oxford: Clarendon Press, 1968.

Kinsley 1969 *James Kinsley. *The Oxford Book of Ballads.* Oxford: Clarendon Press, 1969.

Kirk *Edward N[orris] Kirk. *Songs for Socal and Public Worship.* Revised ed., Boston: Henry Holt, 1864.

Kirkell *Miriam H. Kirkell; Irma K. Schaffnit. *Partner's All—Places All!* New York: E. P. Dutton & Co., 1949.

Kirkpatrick 1898 *Wm. J. Kirkpatrick; H. L. Gilmour. *Pentecostal Praises.* Philadelphia: Hall-Mack Co., 1898.

Kirkpatrick 1899 *Wm. J. Kirkpatrick; H. L. Gilmour; Chas. A. Tushingham. *Songs of Praise and Victory.* Philadelphia: Pepper Publishing Co., 1899.

J. Knapp *Jacob Knapp. *Revival Melodies.* Boston: John Putnam, 1842.

M. Knapp *Mary Knapp; Herbert Knapp. *One Potato, Two Potato: the secret education of American children.* New York: W. W. Norton & Co., 1976.

Knorr *Frederick Knorr; Lloyd Shaw. *Cowboy Dance Tunes.* Caldwell, Idaho: Caxton Printers, 1946.

Knox *Winifred I. Knox. "Folksongs from the Olympic Peninsula and Puget Sound." M. S. Thesis, Juilliard School of Music, 1945.

[*Knoxville Harmony*] *The Knoxville Harmony.* [See: John B. Jackson].

Koehnline William Angus Koehnline. "A study of folksongs of the western United States reflecting Western life." M. A. Thesis (English), University of North Carolina, 1949.

Kolb *Sylvia Kolb; John Kolb. *A Treasury of Folk Songs.* New York, 1948.

Korson 1938 *George Korson. *Minstrels of the Mine Patch.* University of Pennsylvania Press, 1938.

Korson 1943 *George Korson. *Coal Dust on the Fiddle.* University of Pennsylvania Press, 1943.

Korson 1949 *George Korson. *Pennsylvania Songs and Legends.* University of Pennsylvania Press, 1949.

Krassen *Miles Krassen. *Appalachian Fiddle.* New York: Oak Publications, 1973.

Kraus *Richard G. Kraus. *Square Dances of Today.* New York: A. S. Barnes & Co., 1950.

Labour Party *The Labour Party Song Book.* 2nd ed., London: Labour Publications Department 1955. (1st ed., 1933).

Lahey *John Lahey; Estelle Sheehan. *Great Australian Folk Songs.* Hill of Content Publishing Co., 1965. (Reprint, New York, 1965, with variant title: *Australian Favorite Ballads*).

Laing *David Laing. *Additional Illustrations of the Lyric Poetry and Music of Scotland* [a supplement to: William Stenhouse, *The Scots Musical Museum, Volume Two*, and included with it in the same reprint volume with separate pagination]. Reprint, Hatboro, Pennsylvania: Folklore Associates, 1962.

Lampe 1914 *J. Bodewalt Lampe. *Songs of Scotland.* New York: Jerome H. Remick & Co., 1914.

Lampe 1916 *J. Bodewalt Lampe. *Songs of Ireland.* New York: Remick Music Co., 1916.

Lampe 1955 *J. Bodewalt Lampe. *Folk Songs of Ireland* [largely a re-issue of Lampe 1916] (Music for Everyone, No. 9). New York: Remick Music Corp., 1955.

Landeck 1944 *Beatric Landeck. *Git on Board.* New York: Edward B. Marks, 1944.

Landeck 1946 *Beatric Landeck; Charity Bailey. *Songs My True Love Sings.* New York: Edward B. Marks, 1946.

Landeck 1969 *Beatrice Landeck; Elizabeth Crook. *Wake Up and Sing.* New York: Edward B. Marks, 1969.

J. Langstaff 1955 *John Langstaff; Feodor Rojankovsky. *Frog Went a-Courtin'.* New York: Harcourt, Brace, 1955.

J. Langstaff 1960 *John Langstaff. *The Swapping Boy.* New York: Harcourt, Brace, 1960.

J. Langstaff 1969 *John Langstaff. *Hi! Ho! the Rattlin' Bog.* New York: Harcourt, Brace & World, 1969.

N. Langstaff *Nancy Langstaff; John Langstaff. *Jim Along, Josie.* New York: Harcourt, Brace, Jovanovich, 1970.

Lanigan's Ball *The Lanigan's Ball Comic Songster.* New York: Dick & Fitzgerald, 1863.

Lark *The Lark.* London: John Osborn, 1740.

Larkin *Margaret Larkin. *The Singing Cowboy.* Reprint, New York, 1963. (1st ed., 1931).

Larson *Kenneth Larson. "Songs of eastern Idaho." Graduate paper, University of Utah, 1950. [Copy at Archive of Folk Song, Library of Congress].

Laughing Songster *The Laughing Songster.* Glasgow: Cameron & Ferguson, 1877.

Lawell & Drew *Lawell and Drew's Muldoon's Boarding House Songster.* New York: Popular Publishing Co., #109, 1881.

D. D. Lawrence *Dorothea Dix Lawrence. *Folklore Songs of the United States.* New York: George F. Briegel, 1959.

V. B. Lawrence *Vera Brodsky Lawrence. *Music for Patriots, Politicians and Presidents:* harmonies and discords of the first hundred years. New York: Macmillan, 1975.

W. M. Lawrence *W. M. Lawrence; O. Blackman. *The Riverside Song Book.* Boston: Houghton Mifflin, 1893-

Laws A - I, or Laws 1950 G. Malcolm Laws. *Native American Balladry.* American Folklore Society Bibliographical Series, Vol. 1, 1950.

Laws J - Q, or Laws 1957 G. Malcolm Laws. *American Balladry from British Broadsides.* American Folklore Society Bibliographical Series, Vol. 8, 1957.

Lawson Cecil C. Lawson. *Naval Ballads and Sea Songs.* London: Peter Davies, 1933.

LCJ *Louis C. Jones Folklore Archives.* [A manuscript collection, chiefly from New York State sources; items are not paginated; some are identified by name of collector, others by category]. Fenimore House Library, New York State Historical Society, Cooperstown.

C. Leach *Clifford Leach. *Bottoms Up!* New York: Paull-Pioneer Music Corp., 1933.

M. Leach 1955 MacEdward Leach. *The Ballad Book.* New York: Harper & Bros., 1955.,

M. Leach 1965 *MacEdward Leach. *Folk Ballads and Songs of the Lower Labrador Coast.* [Music transcriptions by Bruno Nettl]. Ottawa: National Museum of Canada, 1965.

Leaman *George L. Leaman. *American Airs.* New York: Edwin H. Morris & Co., 1943.

Leavitt *Leavitt's Minstrels Songster.* New York: Popular Publishing Co., 188-.

J. Leavitt i - ii *Joshua Leavitt. *The Christian Lyre.* 2 vols., New York: Jonathan Leavitt, 1830, 1831.

Lee *Edward Lee. *Music of the People.* London: Barrie & Jenkins, 1970.

Legman G. Legman. *The Horn Book:* studies in erotic folklore and bibliography. New Hyde Park, New York: University Books, 1964.

Leifer *Fred Leifer; Manny Blanc. *The Official Li'l Abner Square Dance Handbook.* The Toby Press, 1953.

Leiper *Maria Leiper; Henry W. Simon. *A Treasury of Hymns*. New York: Simon & Schuster, 1953.

Leisy 1957 *James F. Leisy. *Abingdon Song Kit*. New York: Abingdon Press, 1957.

Leisy 1964 *James F. Leisy. *Hootenanny Tonight*. Greenwich, Connecticut: Fawcett Publications, 1964.

Leisy 1966 *James F. Leisy. *The Folk Song Abecedary*. New York, 1966.

Leisy 1974 *James F. Leisy. *The Good Times Songbook*. Nashville, Tennessee: Abingdon Press, 1974.

LeMon *Melvin LeMon; George Korson. *The Miner Sings*. New York: J. Fischer & Bro., 1936.

Lengyel i - ii *Cornell Lengyel. *History of Music in San Francisco*. 12 vols. [including:
  i. *Music of the Gold Rush Era*.
  ii. *A San Francisco Songster*].
Works Progress Administration Northern California San Francisco, 1939-42.

Leodhas *Sorche Nic Leodhas; Evaline Ness. *A Scottish Songbook*. New York: Holt, Rinehart & Winston, 1969.

Leveridge i - ii *[Richard] Leveridge. *A Collection of Songs with the Musick*. 2 vols., London, 1727.

Levermore *Charles Herbert Levermore. *The American Song Book*. Boston: Ginn & Co., 1917.

Levy 1967 *Lester S. Levy. *Grace Notes in American History*. University of Oklahoma Press, 1967.

Levy 1971 *Lester S. Levy. *Flashes of Merriment*. University of Oklahoma Press, 1971.

Lew Benedict Lew Benedict's 2.4-1/4 Songster. Philadelphia: Merrihew & Son, 1870.

Lewis *Freeman Lewis. *The Beauties of Harmony*. Pittsburgh: Johnson & Stockton, 1835.

Lindsay *Louis F. Lindsay; Ja[me]s N. Clemmer; John R. Sweney; W[illia]m J. Kirkpatrick. *Hymn-Songs*. Philadelphia: John J. Hood, 1895.

Lingard *William H. Lingard. *On the Beach at Long Branch Songster*. New York: Dick & Fitzgerald, 1868.

Lingenfelter *Richard E. Lingenfelter; Richard A. Dwyer; David Cohen. *Songs of the American West*. University of California Press, 1968.

[*Linnet*] *The Linnet*. [See: *Orpheus* 1749 i].

Linscott *Eloise Hubbard Linscott. *Folk Songs of Old New England*. New York: MacMillan, 1939.

Little Lotta Little Lotta Songster. New York: Fisher & Denison, 1868.

LL 1341 †*A Josh White Program*. London LL 1341.

A. L. Lloyd 1945 Albert L. Lloyd. *Corn on the Cob*. London: Fore Publications, 1945.

A. L. Lloyd 1952 *A[lbert] L. Lloyd. *Come All Ye Bold Miners*. London, 1952.

A. L. Lloyd 1955 *A[lbert] L. Lloyd; Alan Bush. *Twenty Sing for Pleasure Songs*. London: Joseph Williams, 1955.

A. L. Lloyd 1965 *A[lbert] L. Lloyd. *Folk Songs of the Americas*. London: Novello & Co. (for the International Folk Music Council), 1965.

A. L. Lloyd 1967 *A[lbert] L. Lloyd. *Folk Song in England*. New York: International Publishers, 1967.

R. Lloyd *Ruth Lloyd; Norman Lloyd. *The American Heritage Songbook*. New York: American Heritage Publishing Co., 1969.

Loesser *Arthur Loesser. *Humor in American Song*. New York, 1942.

A. Lomax 1960 *Alan Lomax. *The Folk Songs of North America in the English Language*. Garden City, New York, 1960.

A. Lomax 1964 *Alan Lomax. *The Penguin Book of American Folk Songs*. Baltimore: Penguin Books, 1964.

A. Lomax 1967 *Alan Lomax; Woody Guthrie; Pete Seeger. *Hard Hitting Songs for Hard-Hit People*. New York: Oak Publications, 1967.

J. Lomax 1934 *John A. Lomax; Alan Lomax. *American Ballads and Folk Songs*. New York: MacMillan, 1934.

J. Lomax 1936 *John A. Lomax; Alan Lomax. *Negro Folk Songs* as sung by Leadbelly. New York: MacMillan, 1936.

J. Lomax 1938 *John J. Lomax; Alan Lomax. *Cowboy Songs and Other Frontier Ballads*. New York: Macmillan, 1938. (1st ed., 1910).

J. Lomax 1941 *John A. Lomax; Alan Lomax; Ruth Crawford Seeger. *Our Singing Country*. New York: Macmillan, 1941.

J. Lomax 1947 *John J. Lomax; Alan Lomax; Charles L. Seeger; Ruth Crawford Seeger. *Folk Song U. S. A*. New York: Duell, Sloane & Pearce, 1947.

J. Lomax 1959 *John A. Lomax; Alan lomax; Hally Wood. *Leadbelly*: a collection of world-famous songs by Huddie Ledbetter. New York: Folkways Music Publishers, 1959.

*Lomir Ale Singen *Lomir Ale Singen*, New York: Jewish Music Alliance, 1956.

London 45-1756 †*Puttin'On the Style* (Dickie Valentine). London 45-1756.

London Melodist The London Melodist or Songster's Companion [running title, London Vocalist]. London: Deprose & Co., 183.

Long *Lionel Long; Graham Henkin. *Favourite Australian Bush Ballads*. Adelaide, 1964.

Lookout Mountain Lookout Mountain Songster. Chattanooga, Tennessee: Chattanooga Medicine Co., n.d. [not paginated].

Loomis *Harvey Worthington Loomis. *The Lyric Song Book*. New York: Frank D. Beattys & Co., 1908.

Lorenz *Ellen Lane Lorenz; Harry C. Eldridge. *Get-Together Songs*. New York: Lorenz Publishing Co., 1935.

Love & Sentimental The Love and Sentimental Songster. New York: Dick & Fitzgerald, 1862.

Loveless *Kenneth Loveless; Imogen Holst. *A Jubilee Book of English Folk-Songs*. Oxford University Press, 1958.

Lover's Harmony # The Lover's Harmony, #1 - #50. London: Pitt's 184-.

Lovett *Benjamin B. Lovett. *Good Morning*: music, calls and directions for old-time dancing as revived by Mr. and Mrs. Henry Ford. 4th ed., Dearborn, Michigan, 1943.

Lowens Irving Lowens. *A Bibliography of Songsters Printed in America before 1821*. Worcester, Massachusetts: American Antiquarian Society, 1976.

LPS 260-01 †*Excerpts from the Young Folks' Glee Book, Boston, 1856*. American Music Group LPS 260-01.

LPS 260-04 †*Hymns, Fuguing Tunes and Anthems from the Original Sacred Harp*. American Music Group LPS 260-04.

LPV 522 †*Authentic Cowboy Songs and their Western Folklore* (ed. by Fred G. Hoeptner). RCA Victor LPV 522.

Lubin *Ernest Lubin. *Awake, Awake*. Arranged for voice and piano. New York: G. Schimer, 1949.

Luboff *Norman Luboff; Win Stracke. *Songs of Man*. Englewood Cliffs, New Jersey: Prentice-Hall, 1965.

Lunsford *Bascom Lamar Lunsford; Lamar Stringfield. *Thirty and One Folk Songs from the Southern Mountains*. New York: Carl Fischer, 1929.

Lupton *F. M. Lupton [publisher]. *156 Popular Songs*. (People's Handbook Series, No. 3). New York: F. M. Lupton, 1893.

Lusk *Bob Lusk. *Irish Music of the Catskills and Mid Hudson Valley*. Ulster County Council for the Arts, 1978.

Luther *Frank Luther. *Americans and Their Songs*. New York: Harper & Bros., 1942.

Lydia Thompson *The Lydia Thompson Songster. New York: Robert M. De Witt, 1869.

Lyle *E. B. Lyle. *Andrew Crawfurd's [1827] Collection of Ballads and Songs*. Edinburgh: The Scottish Text Society, 1975.

Lynn 1961 *Frank Lynn. *Songs for Singin'*. San Francisco: Leisy & Co., 1961.

Lynn 1963 *Frank Lynn. *The Beer Bust Songbook*. San Francisco: Fearon Publishers, 1963.

Lyre *The Lyre [a collection of some 38 individual broadsides, with tunes; numbering erratic, extent of the series not evident; a bound collection is at Boston Public Library, **M143.6]. Leith: R. W. Hume, 18--.

Lyric Gems *Lyric Gems of Scotland. Bayley & Ferguson, n. d.

Lyric Gems i - ii *The Lyric Gems of Scotland. 2 vols., Glasgow: John Cameron, 1856.

M 481.246 i - iii *Collection of Popular Songs [a miscellany of sheet music publications]. 3 vols., at Boston Public Library **M 481.246.

Mabel Waltz The Mabel Waltz Songster. New York: Robert M. De Witt, 1868.

McCarthy *Tony McCarthy. *Bawdy British Folk Songs*. London: Wolfe Publishing Co., 1972.

McCaskey i - viii *J. P. McCaskey. *Franklin Square Song Collection*. 8 vols., New York, 1884-92.

McCaskey 1899 *J. P. McCaskey. *Favorite Songs and Hymns* for school and home. New York: Harper & Brother, 1899.

MacColl 1954 *Evan MacColl. *The Shuttle and the Cage*. New York: Hargail Music Press, 1954.

MacColl 1956 *Ewan MacColl. *Personal Choice* of Scottish folksongs and ballads. New York: Hargail Music Press, 1956.

MacColl 1968 *Evan MacColl; Peggy Seeger.*The Ewan MacColl and Peggy Seeger Songbook*. New York: Oak Publications, 1963.

MacColl 1965 *Ewan MacColl. *Folk Songs and Ballads of Scotland*. New York: Oak Publications, 1965.

MacColl 1963 *Ewan MacColl; Peggy Seeger. *I'm a Freeborn Man*. New York: Oak Publications, 1968.

McConathy *Osborne McConathy, et al. *American Music Horizons*. New York: Silver Burdett & Co., 1951.

McCoy *Otis L. McCoy. *Songs of Prayer and Praise*. Cleveland, Tennessee: Tennessee Music & Printing Co., 1940.

MacCunn *Hamish MacCunn. *Songs and Ballads of Scotland*. Edinburgh: Paterson & Sons, [1891].

McCurry *John G. McCurry. *The Social Harp*. Facsimile reprint, University of Georgia Press, 1973. (1st ed., Philadelphia: T. K. Collins, Jr., 1855).

McCutchan Robert Guy McCutchan. *Hymn Tune Names:* their sources and significance. Nashville, 1957.

MacDill Darrell *MacDill Darrell Dime Melodist No. 1*. New York: Robert M. De Witt, 1860.

P. McDonald *Patrick McDonald. *A Collection of Highland Vocal Airs*. Reprint, Norwood, 1973. (1st ed., Edinburgh, 1784).

W. McDonald 1855 *W. McDonadl; S. Hubbard. *The Wesleyan Sacred Harp*. Boston: John P. Jewett & Co., 1855.

W. McDonald 1885 *W. McDonald; Joshua Gill; Jno. R. Sweney; W. J. Kirkpatrick. *Songs of Joy and Gladness*. Boston: McDonald & Gill, 1885.

McDowell 1937 *Lucien L. McDowell. *Songs of the Old Camp Ground*. Ann Arbor: Edwards Bros., 1937.

McDowell 1947 *Lucien L. McDowell; Flora Lassiter McDowell. *Memory Melodies*. Smithville, Tennessee, 1947.

MacFarren *G[eorge] A[lexander] MacFarren, *Old Scottish Ditties*. London: Chappell & Co., [186-?].

McGill *Josephine McGill. *Folk-Songs of the Kentucky Mountains*. New York: Boosey & Co., 1917.

McIntosh 1935a David S. McIntosh. "Some representative southern Illinois folk-songs." M. A. Thesis (Music), University of Iowa, 1935.

McIntosh 1935b David S. McIntosh. *Some Representative Southern Illinois Folk Songs*. Iowa City, 1935.

McIntosh 1941 *David S. McIntosh. *Singing Games and Songs of Southern Illinois*. Delaware, Ohio: Coöperative Recreation Service, 1941.

McIntosh 1948 *David S. McIntosh. *Sing and Swing*. Southern Illinois University, 1948.

McIntosh 1974 *David S. McIntosh. *Folk Songs and Singing Games of the Illinois Ozarks*. Southern Illinois University Press, 1974.

Mackay i - ii *Charles Mackay; J. Pittman; Colin Brown. *The Songs of Scotland*. 2 vols., London: Boosey & Co., 1877.

B. Mackenzie i - iii *B. Mackenzie. *Companion for the German Concertina*. 3 vols., London: B. Williams, 1861.

W. R. Mackenzie 1919 W[illiam] Roy Mackenzie. *The Quest of the Ballad*. Reprint, New York: Haskell House, 1966. (1st ed., 1919).

W. R. Mackenzie 1928 *William Roy Mackenzie. *Ballads and Sea Songs from Nova Scotia*. Harvard University Press, 1928.

[*Mackney*] *Mackney's Forty Comic Songs*. [See: *Great Comic Volume*, iii].

[Mackney] *E. W. Mackney. *Seventeen Songs*. [See: *Davidson* iii].

MacLagan [T.] *MacLagan's Musical Age Songster*. London: The Music Publishing Co., n. d.

McLaughlin *G. A. McLaughlin; J. M. Harris; Wm. J. Kirkpatrick. *The Golden Trumpet*. The Christian Witness Co., 1906.

McLean *Don McLean. *Songs and Sketches of the First Clearwater Crew*. Croton-on-Hudson, New York: North River Press, 1970.

MacLean *Douglas Maclean. *Song Session:* a community song book. New York: Remick Music Co., 1953.

A. C. MacLeod *A. C. MacLeod; Harold Boulton; Malcolm Lawson. *Songs of the North*. 9th ed., 3 vols., London: The Leadenhall Press, 188-. [For vols. ii - iii, see: Boulton].

M. A. Macleod *Margaret Arnett MacLeod. *Songs of Old Manitoba*. Toronto: The Ryerson Press, 1959.

MacMahon i - ii *Desmond MacMahon. *The New National and Folk Song Book*. 2 vols., London: Thomas Nelson & Sons, 1938, 1939.

MacMahon 1963 *Desmond MacMahon. *Sundowner's Song Book:* Australian traditional songs. Oxford University Press, 1963.

Macmillan *Ernest Macmillan. *A Canadian Song Book*. London and Toronto: J. M. Dent & Sons, 1929.

McMurray *Vance McMurray. *Home Songs*. Oxford, Ohio: Vance McMurray, 1937.

McPheeley *James McPheeley. *More than 1000 Songs and Dances of the Irish People*. New York: Hansen House, 1976.

McQuillen Bob McQuillen. *Bob's Note Book:* Jigs, Reels and other tunes. 3 vols., Dublin, New Hampshire, 1976-78.

McTiernan *Ellen Mary McTiernan. "Irish ballads and songs in America." M. A. Thesis, Cornell University, 1945.

Maitland i - v *J. A. Fuller Maitland. *Grove's Dictionary of Music and Musicians.* 2nd ed., 5 vols., New York: The Macmillan Co., 1911. (1st ed., 1890).

Maitland # *J. A. Fuller Maitland; Lucy E. Broadwood. *English County Songs* [a series of separate sheet music issues]. London: J. B. Cramer & Co., 1915-.

Malone 1968 Bill C. Malone. *Country Music U.S.A.* University of Texas Press, 1968. (Memoirs of the American Folklore Society, Vol. 54).

Malone 1975 Bill C. Malone; Judith McCulloh. *Stars of Country Music.* University of Illinois Press, 1975.

*Mammoth *The Mammoth Songster.* Boston: G. D. Russell & Co., 1866.

Manchester & Jennings Manchester & Jennings Eccentric Character Songster. New York: Popular Publishing Co., 187-.

Manifold *John S. Manifold. *The Penguin Australian Song Book.* Harmondsworth: Penguin Books, 1964.

Mann *Francis Oscar Mann. *The Works of Thomas Deloney* [d. 1600]. Oxford: The Clarendon Press, 1912.

Manning & Drew Manning & Drew's Character Change Songster. New York: Popular Publishing Co., 1882.

Manny *Louise Manny; James Reginald Wilson. *Songs of Miramichi.* Fredericton, New Brunswick: Brunswick Press, 1968.

Manoff *Tom Manoff. *The Music Kit Scorebook.* New York: W. W. Norton, 1976.

Mansfield *D. H. Mansfield. *The American Vocalist.* Revised ed., Boston: W. J. Reynolds & Co., 1849.

Mansion *Horace Mansion; Anne Anderson. *Old English Nursery Songs.* New York: Brentano, ?1926.

*Many Nations *Songs of Many Nations.* Delaware, Ohio: Coöperative Recreation Service, 1941. (12th ed., 1962).

Marching through Georgia Marching through Georgia, and The Wearing of the Green Songster. 5th ed., San Francisco: D. E. Appleton & Co., 1867. (1st ed., 1865).

Marks Edward B. Marks. *They All Sang.* New York: Viking Press, 1934.

Marrocco *W. Thomas Marrocco; Howard Gleason, *Music in America:* an anthology from the landing of the Pilgrims to the close of the Civil War, 1620-1865. New York: W. W. Norton & Co., 1964.

C. G. Marsh *Cheser Geppert Marsh. *Singing Games and Drills.* New York: A. S. Barnes, 1925.

J. B. T. Marsh *J. B. T. Marsh. *The Story of the Jubilee Singers* with their songs. Boston: Houghton Mifflin & Co., ?1880.

Marsh's Selection i - iii *Marsh's Selection, or Singing for the Million* [a compilation of several sections that appear to have also been issued separately; sectional or running titles include: *Popular Songs; The Lady Washington Songster; American Songster*]. 3 vols., New York: Richard Marsh, 1854.

Marshall *Leonard B. Marshall. *The Halcyon Song-Book.* New York: Silver Burdett, 1909.

Marzials *Theo[dore] Marzials; Walter Crane. *Pan-Pipes.* 2nd ed., London: F. Warne & Co., n. d.

M. H. Mason *M. H. Mason. *Nursery Rhymes and Country Songs.* London: Letzler & Co., 1877.

R. Mason *Redfern Mason. *The Song Lore of Ireland.* New York, 1910.

Masque The Masque. London: Richardson & Urquhart, 1768.

Masterson James R. Masterson. *Tall Tales of Arkansas.* Boston: Chapman & Grimes, 1943.

Matt Peel Matt Peel's Banjo. New York: Robert M. De Witt, 1859.

Matteson 1936 *Maurice Matteson. *Beech Mountain Folk-Songs and Ballads.* New York: G. Schirmer, 1936.

Matteson 1947 *Maurice Matteson. *American Folk-Songs for Young Singers.* New York: G. Schirmer, 1947.

Mattfeld Julius Mattfeld. *Variety Music Cavalcade 1620-1950.* New York: Prentice-Hall, 1952.

Mattson *Donald E. Mattson; Louis D. Walz. *Old Fort Snelling Instruction Book for the Fife.* St. Paul: Minnesota Historical Society, 1974.

Maver *Robert Maver; George Alexander. *Genuine Scottish Melodies.* Glasgow: Robert Maver, 1866.

Maxfield *W. H. Maxfield. *Fifty Gems of Scottish Song.* London, 190-.

Mayo *Margot Mayo. *The American Square Dance.* New York: Oak Publications, 1964. (1st ed., 1943).

Meehan *C. P. Meehan. *The Poets and Poetry of Munster.* 3rd ed., Dublin: James Duffy & Sons, n. d. (1st ed., 1849).

*Mennonite Hymnal *The Mennonite Hymnal.* Newton, Kansas: Faith and Life Press, 1969.

*Mennonite Hymnary *The Mennonite Hymnary.* Berne, Indiana: General Conference of the Mennonite Church of North America,

1940.

Merchant Merchant's Gargling Oil Songster. Lockport, New York, 188-.

Mercury 71182 †*Puttin' On the Style* (Lonnie Donegan). Mercury 71181 X45.

Meredith 1955 *John Meredith. *Songs from the Kelly Country.* Sydney: Bush Music Club, 1955.

Meredith 1956 *John Meredith. *Songs from Lawson.* Sydney: Bush Music Club, 1956.

Meredith 1960 *John Meredith. *The Wild Colonial Boy:* The life and times of Jack Donahue, 1808?-1830. (Studies in Australian and Pacific History, No. 2). Sydney: The Wentworth Press, 1960.

Meredith 1968 *John Meredith; Hugh Anderson. *Folk Songs of Australia.* Sydney, 1968.

[Merrick] *W. Percy Merrick; Ralph Vaughan Williams; Albert Sobins. *Folk Songs from Sussex.* London: Novello & Co., 1912. [See: C. J. Sharp 1961 v].

[*Merry Lad*] *The Merry Lad's Comic Song Book.* [See: *Imperial Comic Song Book*, Part 2].

Merry Musician i - iv *The Merry Musician; or, A Cure for the Spleen.* 2nd ed., 4 vols., London: J. Walsh, 1730.

Methodist Hymnal 1905 *The Methodist Hymnal.* Cincinnati: Jennings & Graham, 1905.

Methodist Hymnal 1939 *The Methodist Hymnal.* Methodist Publishing House, 1939. (1st ed., 1932).

Methodist Hymns 1857 *Hymns for the Use of the Methodist Episcopal Church.* New York: Carlton & Porter, 1857.

MF *Midwest Folklore*, 1951-.

MG 20008B †*Americana* (Earl Robiunson). Mercury MG 20008B.

MH 1072 †*The Arkansas Traveler* (Ralph Page Orchestra). Folk Dancer MH 1072.

Middlebury #1 †*Eight Traditional British-American Ballads* from the Helen Hartness Flanders Collection [Flanders 1953] at Middlebury College. Middlebury College #1.

Milburn George Milburn. *The Hobo's Hornbook.* New York, 1930.

Miles Henry Downes Miles. *The Life of Richard Palmer* [1706-1739]; better known as Dick Turpin; the notorious highwayman and robber; including his numerous exploits, adventures and hairbreadth escapes, trial and execution; with notices of many of his contemporaries. London: T. White, 1839.

Millard *Harrison Millard, et al. *Gospel Melodies.* New York: S. T. Gordon & Son, 1885.

A. Mills 1949 *Alan Mills; Arthur Morrow. *The Alan Mills Book of Folk Songs and Ballads.* Montreal: Whitcombe & Gilmour, 1949.

A. Mills 1958 *Alan Mills; Kenneth Peacock. *Favourite Songs of Newfoundland.* Toronto, 1958.

J. Mills *John Mills. *Sing and Be Happy.* New York: Mills Music Corp., 1941.

Miners *Miner's Songs of '49 from Put's California Songster of 1855.* Grass Valley, California: Noolcam Co., 1948. [not paginated].

Minstrel *The Minstrel* [Lowens #423]. Baltimore: P. Lucas, 1812.

Minstrel Folio *Minstrel Folio.* New York: Richard A. Saalfield, 1885.

Minstrel Songs 1882 *Minstrel Songs, Old and New.* Boston: Oliver Ditson, 1882.

Minstrel Songs 1910 *Minstrel Songs, Old and New.* Boston: Oliver Ditson, 1910.

Miramichi Ms. *Miramichi Ms.* [a notation by Norman Cazden of tunes, with titles only, of the songs and ballads presented at the Ninth Annual Miramichi Folk Songs Festival held at Newcastle, New Brunswick, 15-17 August 1966; copies now in the possession of James Reginald Wilson and at Northeast Folklore Archives, NA 1008.

Micellanea i - iii *Miscellanea* [of the Rymour Club, Deinburgh], 1907-. (Reprint, 3 vols.: Norwood, 1973).

[*Missouri Harmony*] *The Missouri Harmony.* [See: Carden].

Mitchell *Donald Mitchell; Roderick Bliss. *The Faber Book of Children's Songs.* London: Faber & Faber, 1968.

MJV 59 †*Animal Fair* (Burl Ives). Columbia MVJ 59.

ML 2038 †*Swing Low, Sweet Chariot* (Paul Robeson). Columbia ML 2038.

ML 4941 †*Irish Folk Songs* (ed. by Seamus Ennis, Alan Lomax, Robin Roberts and Brian George). Booklet. Columbia ML 4941.

ML 54638 †*Susan Reed in Folk Songs.* Columbia ML 54638.

MN C 693 *Collection of Miscellaneous [Eighteenth Century]Vocal and Instrumental Music* [including some handwritten additions]. Music Division, New York Public Library *MN C 693

Mock-Bird Mock-Bird: American and English songs, ballads, glees &c. Baltimore: Warner and Hannah, 1805.

Mocking Bird The Mocking Bird Songster. Philadelphia: John B. Perry 1856.

Möller *Heinrich Möller. *Englische und Nordamerikanische Volkslieder.* Mainz: B.

Schott's Söhne, n. d.

Moeran 1924 *Ernest J. Moeran. *Six Folk Songs from Norfolk.* London: Augener, 1924.

Moeran 1950 *Ernest J. Moeran. *Songs from County Kerry.* London: Augener, 1950.

Moet & Shandon The Moet and Shandon Songster. New York: Robert M. De Witt, #116, 1870.

Moffat 1894 *Alfred Moffat. *The Minstrelsy of Scotland.* 4th ed., London, 1894.

Moffat 1897 *Alfred Moffat. *Minstrelsy of Ireland.* London: Augener, 1897.

Moffat 1901 *Alfred Moffat. *The Minstrelsy of England.* London: Bayley & Ferguson, 1901.

Moffat 1904 *Alfred Moffat; Frank Kidson. *75 British Nursery Rhymes.* London: Augener, 1904.

Moffat 1906 *Alfred Moffat. *The Minstrelsy of Wales.* London: Augener, 1906.

Moffat 1907 *Alfred Moffat. *The Minstrelsy of the Scottish Highlands.* London: Bayley & Ferguson, 1907.

Moffat 1911 *Alfred Moffat; Frank Kidson. *English Songs of the Georgian Period.* London: Bayley & Ferguson, 1911.

Moffat 50 *Alfred Moffat. *Fifty Nursery Rhymes.* London: Ascherberg, Hopwood & Crew, n. d.

*Monarch Collection *The Monarch Collection of Music.* Springfield, Massachusetts: Monarch Music Co., 1883. [not paginated].

Monroe John Duncan Monroe. *The Anti-Rent War in Delaware County.* Privately printed, New York, 1940.

Moodie *William Moodie. *Our Native Songs.* Glasgow: David Bryce & Son, n. d.

A. W. Moore *A. W. Moore. *Manx Ballads.* Douglas, Isle of Man: G. & R. Johnson, 1896.

E. Moore *Ethel Moore; Chauncey O. Moore. *Ballads and Folksongs of the South West.* University of Oklahoma Press, 1964.

T. Moore *Thomas Moore. *Moore's Irish Melodies.* Revised ed., Boston: Oliver Ditson, 1893.

Morehead *James Morehead; Albert Morehead. *Best Loved Songs and Hymns.* Cleveland: World Publishing Co., 1965.

Morison Samuel Eliot Morison. *John Paul Jones: a sailor's biography.* Boston: Little, Brown & Co., 1959.

A. C. Morris *Alton Chester Morris. *Folksongs of Florida.* University of Florida Press, 1950.

G. S. Morris *G. S. Morris. *Kerr's Buchan*

Bothy Ballads, Book 1. Glasgow: James S. Kerr, 1956.

R. O. Morris *R. O. Morris. *Six English Folk-Songs.* Oxford University Press, 1929.

Morrison i - ii *D[aniel] H. Morrison. *The Treasury of Song for the Home Circle.* 2 vols., Philadelphia: Hubbard Brothers, 1882, 1884.

Morrison 1894 *D[aniel] H. Morrison. *The World's Sweetest Songs.* Chicago: Monarch Book Co., 1894.

Morrison 1895 *D[aniel] H. Morrison. *Cyclopaedia of Favorite Songs.* Philadelphia: The World's Musical Association, 1895.

Morse *Jim Morse; Nancy Mathews. *The Sierra Club Survival Songbook.* San Francisco: The Sierra Club, 1971.

Morton 1970 *Robin Morton. *Folksongs Sung in Ulster.* Cork: The Mercier Press, 1970.

Morton 1973 *Robin Morton. *Come Day, Go Day, God Send Sunday.* London, 1973.

*Morvan *The Morvan Collection of Scottish Songs.* Glasgow: Mozart Allen, n. d.

*Most Popular College*Most Popular College Songs.* Hinds, Noble & Eldridge, 1904

Motherwell i - ii William Motherwell. *Minstrelsy, Ancient and Modern.* 2 vols., Boston: William D. Ticknor & Co., 1846.

Motherwell 1873 William Motherwell. *Minstrelsy, Ancient and Modern.* Reprint, Detroit, 1968 (from the New Edition, Paisley: Alexander Gardner, 1873).

Moyer *Harvey P. Moyer. *Songs of Socialism.* 3rd ed., Chicago: Brotherhood Publ. Co., 1906. (1st ed., 1905).

Moyes *Andrew Moyes. *Songs from Ireland's History.* Glasgow: Glasgow Folk Centre, n. d.

*MQ *The Musical Quarterly, 1915-.

Muir *Willa Muir. *Living with Ballads.* London: The Hogarth Press, 1965.

Muller *Al Muller. *All-American Square Dances.* New York: Paull-Pioneer Music Corp., 1941.

Munch *Peter A. Munch. *The Song Tradition of Tristan da Cunha.* Bloomington: Indiana University Folklore Institute Monographs #22, 1970.

*Munro # *Munro's Musical Library, #1 - #49.* ?London, 1878-80.

Murphy The Murphy's Dan Donahue Songster. New York: Popular Publishing Co., 1883.

Murphy *M. J. Murphy. *The National Songs of Ireland.* Cincinnati: John Church Co., 1892.

*Murphy & Mack Murphy & Mack's Dan

McCarty's Party Songster. New York: Popular Publishing Co., #157, 1881.

Murphy & Miles Murphy & Miles' Gentlemen from Kerry Songster. New York: Popular Publishing Co., #257, 1882.

Murphy & Morton Murphy & Morton's Katy Ann O'Brien Songster. New York: Popular Publishing Co., #33, 1879.

Murray & Murphy Murray & Murphy's O'Reilly's Party Songster. New York: Popular Publishing Co., 186-.

Mursell *James L. Mursell, et al. *Music for Living in Our Country*. Morristown, New Jersey: Silver Burdett Co., 1956.

*Musical Bouquet # *The Musical Bouquet* [a numbered series of vocal and instrumental sheet music publication; #1-#78 issued by J. Bingley & W. Strange, ca. 1846-55; #79-#8016 issued by C. Sheard, 1855-88]. London: The Musical Bouquet Office, 1846-88.

*Musical Budget *The Musical Budget* [a periodical series of vocal and instrumental sheet music folios]. London: Hart & Co., 1881-.

*Musical Cabinet *Musical Cabinet:* a selection of all the new and fashionable songs. Charlestown, Massachusetts, 1822.

*Musical Carcanet *The Musical Carcanet*. New York: Collins & Hannay, 1832.

*Musical Entertainer *The Musican Entertainer*. Reprint, London: The Sudbrook Press, n. d. (1st ed., 1737).

*Musical Miscellany i - vi *The Musical Miscellany*. 6 vols., London: John Watts, 1729.

Musical Repertory The Musical Repertory. Augusta, Maine: Hallowell Bookstore, 1811.

*Musical Treasury # *The Musical Treasury* [a number series of vocal and instrumental sheet music issues, #1-#1304; some bear variant series title, *Davidson's Musical Treasury;* from 1860, publisher is given as The Music Publishing Co.]. London: G[eorge] G. Davidson, 1845-62.

Musick *Ruth Ann Musick. *Ballads, Folk Songs and Folk Tales from West Virginia*. West Virginia University Library, 1960.

My Father Sould Charcoal My Father Sould Charcoal Songster. New York: Robert M. De Witt, #90, 1870.

Nairne *Caroline, Baroness Nairne; Findlay Dun. *Lays from Strathearn*. Edinburgh: Paterson & Sons, 184-?

NA Ives †Northeast Archives of Folklore and Oral History: The Edward D. Ives Collection [consisting of tape recordings, with their transcriptions, of interviews and of song texts in English, at the University of Maine (Orono); *NA Ives* tapes 1.1-1.160 are duplicated as ATL 2136-3167 at the Archives of Traditional Music, Indiana University (Bloomington)].

Nancy Till Nancy Till's Songster. Philadelphia: Fisher & Bro , 184-

Nat Austin Nat Austin's Comic and Sentimental Song Book. ?Boston, 186-.

N. C. Bostock N. C. Bostock's New Edition Song Book. London: McGlennon's Song Book Office, 1897.

Neal *Mabel Evangeline Neal. "Brown County [Indiana] songs and ballads." M. A. Thesis, Indiana University, 1926.

Neale *R. H. Neale; H. W. Day. *Revival Hymns* set to some of the most familiar and useful Revival Tunes, many of which have never before been published. Boston: Musical Visitor Office, 1842.

Ned Turner Ned Turner's Bones & Tambourine Songster. New York, 1869.

Neely *Charles Neely. *Tales and Songs of Southern Illinois*. Menasha, Wisconsin: George Banta, 1938.

Neeser Robert W. Neeser. *American Naval Songs and Ballads*. Yale University Press, 1938.

*NEF *Northeast Folklore*, 1958-.

Negro Forget-Me-Not 185-a The Negro Forget-Me-Not Songster. Philadelphia: Turner & Fisher, 185-.

Negro Forget-Me-Not 185-b The Negro Forget-Me-Not Songster [contents not identical with those of the preceding]. Philadelphia: Fisher & Bro., 185-.

Negro Melodist The Negro Melodist. Cincinnati: U. P. James, 186-.

*Neighbors *Neighbors*, 1941-60 [a booklet issued annually by Camp Woodland at Phoenicia, New York, and devoted largely to highlights of its Folk Festivals of the Catskill Mountains; imprint varies: *Folk Festival of the Catskills, The World Is a Neighborhood*].

Nelse Seymour Nelse Seymour's Big Shoe Songster. New York: Dick & Fitzgerald, 1863.

Nelson *David Nelson. *120 American Songs*. New York: Robbins Music Corp., 1967.

Nettel *Reginald Nettel. *Sing a Song of England*. London: Phoenix House, 1954.

Nettleinghame *F. T. Nettleinghame. *More Tommy's Tunes*. London: Erskine McDonald, 1918.

Nettleton *Asahel Nettleton. *Zio's Harp; or,*

A New Collection of Music. New Haven: N. & S. S. Jocelyn, 1824.

Never Grow Old *Songs that Never Grow Old.* New York: Syndicate Publishing Co., 1909.

New Baptist Hymnal *New Baptist Hymnal.* Nashville, Tennessee: The Broadman Press, 1926.

New Book of 1000 *New Book of a Thousand Songs for the Million, or Complete Singer's Own Book.* New-York: Richard A. Marsh, 185-.

[*New Comic & Sentimental*] [De Marsan's] *New Comic and Sentimental Singer's Journal* [a variant title]. [See: *Singer's Journal*].

[*New Harmonia Sacra*] *The New Harmonia Sacra. [See: Funk].*

New Merry Companion *The New Merry Companion or Vocal Remembrancer.* London: Wallis & Stonehouse, 177-.

New Musical Cabinet i - ii *The New Musical and Vocal Cabinet.* 2 Vols., London: Thomas Kelly, 1820.

New Preceptor *A New and Complete Preceptor for the Violin.* Albany, New York: Oliver Steele, 18--.

New Sabbath *The New Sabbath Hymn and Tune Book.* New York: Mason Brothers, 1866. (1st ed., 1859).

New Song Book *The New Song Book.* Hartford, Connecticut: S. Andrus & Son, 1851. (Copyright 1835 by Ezra Strong).

Newell *William Wells Newell. *Games and Songs of American Children.* Reprint, New York: Dover Publications 1963. (1st ed., 1883).

C. Nicholson *[Charles] *Nicholson's Selection of Beauties for the Flute.* London: J. Fentum, 182-.

S. H. Nicholson *Sydney H. Nicholson. *British Songs for British Boys.* London: Macmillan & Co., 1927.

Nightingale *The Nightingale, or Jenny Lind Songster.* New York: Stringer & Townsend, 1850.

Nightingale Melodies *Nightingale Melodies, or Jenny Lind Minstrel.* 2nd ed., New York: G. & S. Bunce, 1850.

Nightingale Songster *The Nightingale Songster.* New York: Dick & Fitzgerald, 1863.

Niles 1929 *John Jacob Niles. *Songs My Mother Never Taught Me.* New York, 1929.

Niles 1934 *John Jacob Niles. *Songs of the Hill-Folk.* New York: G. Schirmer, 1934.

Niles 1936 *John Jacob Niles. *More Songs of the Hill-Folk.* New York: G. Schirmer, 1936.

Niles 1938 *John Jacob Niles. *Ballads, Love Songs and Tragic Legends.* New York: G. Schirmer, 1938.

Niles 1945 *John Jacob Niles. *The Anglo-American Ballad Study Book.* New York: G. Schirmer, 1945.

Niles 1950 *John Jacob Niles. *The Shape-Note Study Book.* New York: G. Schirmer, 1950.

Niles 1963 *John Jacob Niles. *John Jacob Niles Song Book* for the guitar. London: Chappell & Co., 1963.

1916 Song Book *The Nineteen Sixteen Song Book.* Dublin: Irish Book Bureau, n. d.

96 Old Songs *96 Old Songs* [a bound collection of late eighteenth century broadsides at Morrison Library, University of California at Berkeley, M1619 C63].

NJ *Northern Junket* [Keene, New Hampshire], 1948-.

Noble 1907 *Gilbert Clifford Noble. *The Most Popular National Songs.* New York: Hinds, Noble & Eldredge, 1907.

Noble 1908 *Gilbert Clifford Noble. *The Most Popular Home Songs.* Revised ed., New York, 1908. (1st ed., 1906).

Noble 1912 *Gilbert Clifford Noble. *The Most Popular Songs for Every Occasion.* New York: Hinds, Hayden & Eldredge, 1912.

Nonpareil *The Nonpareil.* Baltimore: John S. Horton, 1836.

Norah O'Neill *The Noral O'Neill Songster.* New York: Robert M. De Witt, #10, 1868.

Noraidh *Liam de Noraidh. *Ceol ón Mumhain.* Baile Atha Cliath, Ireland: Clóchomhar, 1965.

Northern & Eastern *The Northern & Eastern Songster.* Boston: Charles Gaylord, 1835.

Novello i #201 (1908), ii #202 (1908), iii #212 (1909), iv #213 (1909), v #222 (1910), vi #232 (1912), vii #268 (1922), viii #269 (1908), ix #274 (n.d.), #245 (1913), #261 (n.d.), #262 (n.d.), #263 (n.d.), *Novello's School Songs* [a series of octavo booklets under the general editorship of William G. McNaught; the individual booklets include nine volumes, titled variously *Folk Songs of England* or *Folk Songs for Schools;* among those, Set vi was edited by Ralph Vaughan Williams, Set viii by H. E. Hammond and Cecil J. Sharp, and the others by Cecil J. Sharp; four additional volumes lacking "set" numbers and bearing individual titles were edited by Cecil J. Sharp]. London: Novello & So., 1908-22.

Nutt i - ii *David Nutt. *Children's Singing Games.* 2 Vols. London, 1894.

NW 202 †*Songs of the Civil War* (ed. by

Charles Hamm). Booklet. New World Records NW 202.

NW 239 †*Brave Boys:* New England traditions in folk music. Jacket notes (Sandy Paton). New World Records NW 239.

NYCD New York City Directory.

Nye *Captain Pearl R. Nye; Cloea Thomas. *Scenes and Songs of the Ohio-Erie Canal.* Columbus: Ohio State Archaeological and Historical Society, 1952. [not paginated].

*NYFQ *New York Folklore Quarterly,* 1942-.*

NYH New York History, 1922-.

NYHS New York Historical Society Collection of Photographs.

NYHSQB New York Historical Society Quarterly Bulletin, 1917-.

Oberndorfer *Max Oberndorfer; Anne Oberndorfer. *The New American Song Book.* Chicago: Hall & McCreary, 1933.

O'Conor Manus O'Conor. *Old-Time Songs and Ballads of Ireland.* New York: Popular Publishing Co., 1901.

O'Donnell *John C. O'Donnell. *The Men of the Deeps.* Waterloo, Ontario: Waterloo Publishing Co., 1975.

Odum 1909 Howard W. Odum. "Religious folk-songs of the Southern Negroes." Dissertation, Clark University, 1909. (Reprint of summary in *American Journal of Religious Psychology and Education 3* (1909) 265-365).

Odum 1925 Howard W. Odum; Guy B. Johnson. *The Negro and His Songs.* University of North Carolina Press, 1925.

Odum 1926 *Howard W. Odum; Guy B. Johnson. *Negro Workaday Songs.* University of North Carolina Press, 1926.

Offord William Offord. *Comic and Sentimental Song Book.* Brooklyn, New York: W. Offord, 1865.

Ogden *W. A. Ogden. *Gathered Jewels.* Toledo, Ohio: W. W. Whitney, 1886.

Ogilvie *Frank B. Ogilvie. *Two Hundred Old-Time Songs.* New York, 1896. (Re-issued, 1924).

Ohrlin *Glenn Ohrlin; Harlan Daniel. *The Hell-Bound Train.* University of Illinois Press, 1973.

O'Keeffe *Daniel O'Keeffe; James N. Healy. *The First Book of Irish Ballads.* Revised ed., Cork: The Mercier Press, 1968.

Okeh K-3 †*The Wayfaring Strangers* (Burl Ives). Okeh K-3.

Okun *Milt Okun. *Something to Sing About.* New York: Macmillan, 1968.

Old Clown *Old Clown's Whoa, January! Songster.* New York: Robert M. De Witt, #14, 1870.

*Old Songs for the Pianoforte *Old Songs for the Pianoforte* [a bound collection of sheet music, dated 1823-31, at Music Division, New York Public Library, Drexel 4156].

*Old Songs *The Old Songs We Love So Well.* New York: North American Music Publishing Co., 1909.

*Old Time Hits *Old Time Hits of the Gay Eighties and Nineties* [folio]. New York: Edward B. Marks, 1928.

Oliver Oliver's Comic Songs. Edinburgh, 18-.

O Lochlainn 1939 *Colm O Lochlainn. *Irish Street Ballads.* London: Constable & Co., 1939. (Reprint, New York, 1960).

O Lochlainn 1965 *Colm O Lochlainn. *More Irish Street Ballads.* Dublin, 1965.

[*100 Comic Songs*] *100 Comic Songs. [See: J. W. Turner].

*101 Best Songs *101 Best Songs.* 49th ed., Chicago: The Cable Co., 1951.

[*120 Comic Songs*] *120 Comic Songs sung by Sam Cowell. London: H. D'Alcorn, 1876. [See: *D'Alcorn's Musical Miracles #1*].

*120 Scotch Songs *120 Scotch Songs.* Winnepeg: Whaley, Royce & Co., n. d.

[*1000 Fiddle Tunes*] *1000 Fiddle Tunes. [See: M. M. Cole].

O'Neill # *Capt. Francis O'Neill. *O'Neill's Music of Ireland.* Chicago: Lyon & Healy, 1903. (Reprint, The Bronx, New York, 197-).

O'Neill 1907 *Capt. Francis O'Neill. *The Dance Music of Ireland.* Chicago: Lyon & Healy, 1907. (Reprint, Dublin, 197-).

O'Neill 1913 *Capt. Francis O'Neill. *Irish Minstrels and Musicians.* Chicago: Lyon & Healy, 1913.

O'Neill 1922 *Capt. Francis O'Neill. *Waifs and Strays of Gaelic Melody.* Dublin, 1922.

Opie 1951 Iona Opie; Peter Opie. *The Oxford Dictionary of Nursery Rhymes.* Oxford: Clarendon Press, 1951.

Opie 1955 Iona Opie; Peter Opie. *The Oxford Nursery Rhyme Book.* Oxford: Clarendon Press, 1955.

*Orange Standard *Orange Standard:* Eighteen selected songs. Glasgow: Mozart Allen, n. d.

Ord *John Ord. *The Bothy Songs and Ballads.* Paisley: Alexander Gardner, 1930.

[*Original Sacred Harp*] *The Original Sacred Harp.* [See: Denson].

*Orpheus 1749 i - iii *Orpheus: a collection of
1974 of the most celebrated English and

Scotch songs, in three volumes [separately titled:
   i. *The Linnet;*
   ii. *The Thrush;*
   iii. *The Robin*[.
London: C. Hitch and I. Osborn, 1749.

Orpheus 1832 *Orpheus, or The Concert Room Companion.* London: H. A. Arliss, 1832.

Orr   *James L. Orr. *Grange Melodies.* Philadelphia: Geo. S. Ferguson Co., 1902.

O'Shaughnessy 1966   *Patrick O'Shaughnessy. *Seven Lincolnshire Folk Songs* [from manuscripts of Percy Grainger]. Oxford University Press, 1966.

O'Shaughnessy 1968   *Patrick O'Shaughnessy. *Twenty-One Lincolnshire Folk-Songs* [mostly from manuscripts of Percy Grainger]. Oxford University Press, 1968.

O'Shaughnessy 1971   *Patrick O'Shaughnessy. *More Folk Songs from Lincolnshire* [from manuscripts of Percy Grainger]. Oxford University Press, 1971.

O'Shaughnessy 1975   *Patrick O'Shaughnessy. *Yellowbelly Ballads* [from manuscripts of Percy Grainger]. Lincoln: Lincolnshire and Humberside Arts, 1975.

O'Sullivan   *Donal O'Sullivan. *Songs of the Irish.* Dublin: Browne & Nolan, 1960.

Oswald i - xii   *James Oswald. *The Caledonian Pocket Companion.* 12 Vols. 1743-59. [Bound copy in one volume at Folger Shakespeare Library, M1738.05].

Ott   *Albert Ott; Charles P. Jones. *Old Camp Meetin' Church of the Air Songs.* Dallas, Texas: Albert Ott, 1938.

Owen Fawcett   Owen Fawcett's Paul Pry Songster. Philadelphia, 1869.

L. Owens 1949   *Lee Owens; Viola Ruth. *American Square Dances of the West and Southwest.* Palo Alto, California: Pacific Books, 1949.

L. Owens 1950   *Lee Owens; Viola Ruth. *Advanced Square Dance Figures of the West and Southwest.* Palo Alto, California: Pacific Books, 1950.

W. A. Owens   *William A. Owens. *Swing and Turn:* Texas play party games. Dallas, Texas: Tardy Publishing Co., 1936.

Pacific i - v *The Pacific Song Book* [a compilation of five songsters, with separate titles and pagination, 1854-59:
   i. *The California Songster* (1st ed., 1855);
   ii. *Put's Original California Songster* (1st ed., 1854);
   iii. *[Put's] Golden Songster* (1st ed., 1858);

   iv. *Johnson's Comic Songster* (1st ed., 1858, later issued as *Johnson's Original Comic Songster #1,* 1864);
   v. *Johnson's New Comic Songster* (1st ed., 1859, later issued as *Johnson's New Comic Songster #2,* 1863)].
San Francisco: D. E. Appleton, 1861. [Bound copy at Bancroft Library, University of California at Berkeley, F855.3.S63].

Paddy Kelly Paddy Kelly's Irish Comic Songster. New York: Frederick A. Brady, 1869.

Paddy's the Boy Paddy's the Boy Songster. New York: Dick & Fitzgerald, 1867.

Page   *N. Clifford Page. *Irish Songs.* Philadelphia: Oliver Ditson, 1935.

E. A. Palmer   *Edgar A. Palmer. *G. I. Songs.* New York: Sheridan House, 1944.

R. Palmer 1971   *Roy Palmer. *Room for Company.* Cambridge University Press, 1971.

R. Palmer 1972   *Roy Palmer. *Songs of the Midlands.* Yorkshire: Ep Publishing Co., 1972.

R. Palmer 1973a   *Roy Palmer. *The Valiant Sailor.* Cambridge University Press, 1973.

R. Palmer 1973b   *Roy Palmer. *The Painful Plough.* Cambridge University Press, 1973.

R. Palmer 1974a   *Roy Palmer. *A Touch on the Times:* songs of social change, 1770-1914. Penguin Books, 1974.

R. Palmer 1974b   *Roy Palmer. *Poverty Knock.* Cambridge University Press, 1974.

*Pammelia *Pammelia: Musick's Miscellanie or Mixed Varietie.* London: William Barley, 1609. [Copy at Music Division, New York Public Library, Drexel 4211].

Parker   *Priscilla Post Parker. *California Song Book.* Lancaster, California, 1950.

*Parlor Companion *The Parlor Companion; or, Boston Musical Library.* Boston: Oliver Ditson, 1859.

E. Parry   *Enid Parry. *Wyth Gân Werin [Eight Folk Songs].* Cardiff: Hughes A'i Fab, 1949.

J. Parry i - vi   *Joseph Parry; David Rowlands. *Cambrian Minstrelsie (Alawon Gwalia);* a national collection of Welsh songs. 6 Vols., T. C. & E. C. Jack, 1893.

Patridge   *W. W. Partridge. *School and Home:* a new singing book. Cleveland: S. Brainard's Sons, 1869.

Paskman   *Dailey Paskman; Sigmund Spaeth. *"Gentlemen, Be Seated!"* Garden City, New York, 1928.

Pat Malloy The Pat Malloy Songster. New York: Robert M. De Witt, 1866.

Pat Reilley Pat Reilley's McGrogan the Cop Songster. New York: Popular Publishing Co., 188-.

Pat Rooney 1882a *Pat Rooney's Clarabel Magie Songster.* New York: A. J. Fisher, 1882.

Pat Rooney 1882b *Pat Rooney's Is that Mr. Reilly Songster.* New York: Popular Publishing Co., #205, 1882.

Pat Rooney 188- *Pat Rooney's When I Take the President's Chair Songster.* New York: Popular Publishing Co., 188-.

P. Patterson *Patt Patterson; Lois Dexter. *Songs of the Roundup Rangers.* New York: George T. Worth, 1932.

R. Patterson *Robert Patterson. *Patterson's Church Music.* Cincinnati: Looker & Wallace, 1815.

Pauline Markham *The Pauline Markham Songster.* New York: Robert M. De Witt, #82, 1869.

Peacock *Kenneth Peacock. *Songs of the Newfoundland Outports.* 3 Vols. [with continuous pagination]. Ottawa: National Museum of Canada, 1965.

Pearl Songster *The Pearl Songster.* New York: C. P. Huestis, 1849.

Peat *Frank E. Peat; Lee Orean Smith. *Legion Airs.* New York: Leo Feist, 1932.

Peloubet *F. N. Peloubet. *Select Songs for the Singing Service.* New York: Bigelow & Main, 1885.

Penny Melodist i - vi *The Penny Melodist.* 6 issues. London: Penny Melodist Office, 1870-75.

[*Penny Songs Books*] *Penny Song Books*, #1 - #9. [See: Eaton].

[Percy] Thomas Percy. *Reliques of Ancient English Poetry.* [See: Wheatley].

[*Perfect Cure*] *The Perfect Cure.* [See: *Great Comic Volume* i].

H. S. Perkins *H. S. Perkins. *The Song Echo.* New York: J. L. Peters, 1871.

P. Perkins *Polly Perkins. *Songs for the Liberated Woman.* London: Kahn & Averill, 1973.

R. Perkins i - iii *Raymond Perkins. *Playtime Melody Library.* 3 Vols., New York: Hearst's International Library Co., 1914.

Peter J. Downey *Peter J. Downey's A Workingman's Thoughts Songster.* New York: Popular Publishing Co., 1879?

Peterson Index Harold Daniel Peterson. "A syllabus of the ballad collection of Edwin Ford Piper." M. A. Thesis (English), University of Iowa, 1934.

J. W. Peterson 1963 *John W. Peterson. *Youth Favorites.* Grand Rapids, Michigan: Zondervan Publishing House, 1963.

J. W. Peterson 1966 *John W. Peterson. *Sing-ing Youth.* Grand Rapids, Michigan: Zondervan Publishing House, 1966.

Petrie 1855 *George Petrie. *Ancient Music of Ireland.* Reprint, 1969. (1st ed., Dublin, 1855).

Petrie # *[Charles Villiers Stanford]. *The Complete [George] Petrie Collection of Irish Music.* 3 Vols. [with continuous numbering of items]. London: Boosey & Co., 1902-1905.

Phillips i - ii *Philip Phillips. *Hallowed Songs, Newly Revised.* 2 Vols. in 1 [Vol. ii is a separately paginated appendix with notated music but no texts]. New York: Philip Phillips, 1865-71.

Philo 1001 †*The Old Songs* (Margaret MacArthur). Philo Records 1001.

Philo 1022 †*Ted Ashlaw:* Adirondack woods singer. Jacket notes (Robert D. Bethke). Philo Records 1022.

Piano Prize *Piano Prize* [a collection of individual sheet music issues, not numbered or paginated]. Boston: Louis P. Goullard, 1877.

Pilgrim Hymnal *The Pilgrim Hymnal.* 3rd ed., Boston: The Pilgrim Press, 1958. (1st ed., 1931).

[*Pills*] *Wit and Mirth, or Pills to Purge Melancholy.* [See: D'Urfey].

Piper *The Edwin Ford Piper Collection [a manuscript collection including some newspaper clippings, not numbered or paginated, at University of Iowa Library, Iowa City, Ms C 40; see also: Peterson Index].

Pittman *J. Pittman; Colin Brown; Charles Mackay. *The Songs of Scotland.* London: Boosey & Co., 1877.

[Playford] *Henry Playford. *The English Dancing Master* (1651). [See: Dean-Smith 1957].

Plumstead *W. H. Plumstead. *The Beauties of Melody.* London: Dean & Munday, 1827.

PMLA Proceedings of the Modern Language Association, 1884-.

Pocket Song Book *Pocket Song Book.* London: Worker's Music Association, 1948.

Polwarth 1966 *Gwen Marchant Polwarth. *Folk Songs of Northumberland.* University of Newcastle Upon Tyne, 1966.

Polwarth 1969 *Gwen [Marchant] Polwarth; Mary Polwarth. *North Country Songs.* Newcastle Upon Tyne: Frank Graham, 1969.

Polwarth 1970 *Gwen [Marchant] Polwarth; Mary Polwarth. *Folk Songs from the North.* Newcastle Upon Tyne: Frank Graham, 1970.

Popular California Songs *Popular California Songs* [a collection of nineteenth century broadsides published in San Francisco, at the Bancroft Library, University of California at Berkeley, F855.3.P7.x].

Posselt *Eric Posselt. *Give Out! Songs.* New York: Arrowhead Press, 1943.

Poston 1956 *Elizabeth Poston. *Songs of the Women of Britain.* London: Boosey & Co., 1956.

Poston 1961 *Elizabeth Poston. *The Children's Song Book.* London: the Bodley Head, 1961.

Poston 1965 *Elizabeth Poston. *The Penguin Book of Christmas Carols.* Harmondsworth: Penguin Books, 1965.

Poston 1968 *Elizabeth Poston. *A New Garland of English Folk Songs.* London: Ascherberg, Hopwood & Crew, 1968.

Pound 1916 Louise Pound. *Folk Songs of Nebraska and the Central West.* Nebraska Academy of Sciences Publications, Vol. 9, 1916.

Pound 1922 Louise Pound. *American Ballads and Songs.* Reprint, New York, 1972. (1st ed., 1922).

*Powder River *Powder River Jack & Kitty Lee's Cowboy Song Book.* Butte, Montan-: McKee Printing Co., 1934.

Powell *John Powell. *Five Virginia Folk Songs.* New York: J. Fischer & Bro., 1938.

Presley *I. H. Presley. *Gospel Melodies.* Franklin Springs, Georgia: Publishing House of the Pentecostal Holiness Church, 1939.

Prest i - ii T. Prest. *The Singer's Penny Magazine and Reciter's Album.* 2 Vols., London: G. Drake, 1835.

Price *M. Katherine Price. *The Source Book of Play Party Games.* Minneapolis: Burgess Publishing Co., 1949.

Prize Song Book The Prize Song Book. Boston: Elias Howe, 187-.

*PSB *People's Songs Bulletin,* 1947-49.

*PTFLS *Publications of the Texas Folk Lore Society,* 1926-.

Punch Punch's Comic Songster. New York: Nafis & Cornish, [after 1843].

Purcell *Henry Purcell. *Orpheus Brittanicus.* London, 1698. (Facsimile reprint, New York: Broude Bros., 1965).

Purslow 1965 *Frank Purslow. *Marrow Bones* [from the Hammond-Gardiner Mss.]. London: English Folk Dance & Song Society, 1965.

Purslow 1968 *Frank Purslow. *The Wanton Seed* [from the Hammond-Gardiner Mss.]. London: English Folk Dance & Song Society, 1968.

Purslow 1972 *Frank Purslow. *The Constant Lovers* [from the Hammond-Gardiner Mss.]. London: English Folk Dance & Song Society, 1972.

Purslow 1974 *Frank Purslow. *The Foggy Dew* [from the Hammond-Gardiner Mss.]. London: English Folk Dance & Song Society, 1974.

Putney *Cornelia F. Putney; Jessie L. Flood. *Square Dance U.S.A.* Dubuque, Iowa: Wm. C. Brown, 1955.

[*Put's Golden Songster*] *Put's Golden Songster.* [See: *Pacific Song Book* iii].

[*Put's Original*] *Put's Original California Songster* (1854). [See: *Pacific Song Book* ii].

QC 903 †*Songs of an Ontario Family* (LaRena Clark). Jacket notes (Edith Fowke). QC 903.

Quaver 1844 The Quaver; or The Songster's Pocket Companion. Halifax, England: William Milner, 1844.

Quaver 1858 The Quaver, or the Songster's Pocket Companion: a choice collection of national songs. London: The Booksellers, 1858.

Quiller-Couch Arthur Quiller-Couch. *The Oxford Book of Ballads.* Oxford: Clarendon Press, 1932. (1st ed., 1910).

Quizzical Songster The Quizzical Songster, or Cabinet of Momus. London: J. Walton, 1812?

Rabson *Carolyn Rabson. *Songbook of the American Revolution.* Peak's Island, Maine, 1974.

[Radcliffe-Whitehead] [See: Whitehead].

Raine *James Watt Raine; Cecil J. Sharp. *Mountain Ballads for Social Singing.* Berea [Kentucky] College Press, 1923.

Rainey *Leo Rainey. *Songs of the Ozark Folk.* Branson, Missouri: The Ozarks Mountaineer, 1972.

A. Ramsay i - ii Allan Ramsay. *The Tea-Table Miscellany.* 14th ed., 6 Vols. in 2, Glasgow: John Crum, 1871. (1st ed., 1724-29).

J. T. Ramsay i - ii *J. T. Ramsay. *Comic Songs.* 2 Parts, London: Duncombe & Moon, 183-.

Randolph i - iv *Vance RAndolph. *Ozark Folksongs.* 4 Vols., The State Historical Society of Missouri, 1946-50.

Randolph 1955 Vance Randolph. *The Devil's Pretty Daughter.* Columbia University Press, 1955.

Ranson *Joseph Ranson. *Songs of the Wexford Coast.* Enniscorthy, Ireland: Redmond

Brothers, 1948.

Raph *Theodore Raph. *The Songs We Sang*. New York, 1964.

Ratcliff *T. P. Ratcliff. *The News Chronicle Song Book*. London: Novello & Co., n. d.

J. Raven 1971 *John Raven. *Kate of Coalbrookdale* [songs from broadsheets of the eighteenth and nineteenth centuries]. London: Robbins Music Corp., 1971.

J. Raven 1972 *Jon Raven. *Songs of a Changing World*. London: Ginn & Co., 1972.

K. Raven 1974 *Kate Raven; Jon Raven. *Canal Song*. London: Broadside Records, 1974.

M. Raven i - iii *Michael Raven. *Folk Lore and Songs of the Black Country and West Midlands*. 3 Vols., Wolverhampton Folk Song Club, 1965-67.

Reddal *Henry Frederic Reddall; Dudley Buck. *Songs that Never Die*. Chicago: Monarch Book Co., 1892.

Reed James Reed. *The Border Ballads*. London: The Athlone Press, 1973.

Reeves 1958 James Reeves. *The Idiom of the People*. London, 1958.

Reeves 1960 James Reeves. *The Everlasting Circle* [texts from the Gould, Hammond and Gardiner Mss.]. New York: Macmillan, 1960.

Renfro Valley *Renfro Valley [Kentucky] Hymn Book*. Powell, Missouri: Albert E. Brumley & Sons, 19--.

Rentz-Santley *Rentz-Santley Novelty Co. Songster*. New York: Popular Publishing Co., 1880.

Revival Echoes *Revival Echoes for Uldine Utley:* standard songs of evangelism. Chicago: Tabernacle Publishing Co., 1926.

Rexford *George C. Rexford. *Beadle's Dime School Melodist*. New York: Beadle & Co., 1860.

Reynardson *Herbert Frederick Birch Reynardson. *Sussex Songs* [collected by Lucy E. Broadwood]. London: Leonard & Co., 1890.

H. Reynolds Harry Reynolds. *Minstrel Memories:* the story of burnt cork minstrelsy in Great Britain from 1836 to 1927. London: Alston Rivers, 1928.

W. J. Reynolds *William Jensen Reynolds. *Hymns of Our Faith*. Nashville, Tennessee: Broadman Press, 1964.

RG 150 †*Sweet England* (Shirley Collins). Argo Records RG 150.

Rhinehart *William R. Rhinehart. *The American, or Union Harmonist*. Chambersburg, Pennsylvania: Henry Ruby, 1831.

Rice Edward Le Roy Rice. *Monarchs of Minstrelsy*. New York: Kenny Publishing Co., 1911.

[*Richard Dyer-Bennet*] [see: Dyer-Bennet].

B. Richards *Brinley Richards; Ceiriog Hughes. *Caneuon Cymru [The Songs of Wales]*. 4th ed., London: Boosey & Co., 1884. (1st ed., 1873).

C. H. Richards 1881 *Charles H. Richards. *Songs of Christian Praise*. New York: Taintor Brothers, 1881.

C. H. Richards 1883 *Charles H. Richards. *Songs of Praise and Prayer*. New York: Taintor Brothers, 1883.

Richardson *Ethel Park Richardson; Sigmund Spaeth. *American Mountain Song*. New York, 1927.

Richman *Gloria Richman. *Ivy League Song Book*. Greenville, Delaware: Rolor Publishing Co., 1958.

Richmond *W. Edson Richmond. *Studies in Folklore*. Indiana University Press, 1957.

Rickaby *Franz Rickaby. *Ballads and Songs of the Shanty-Boy*. Harvard University Press, 1926.

Riley i - ii *Edward Riley. *Riley's Flute Melodies*. 2 Vols. in 1, reprint, New York, 1973. (1st ed., New York, 1816, 1820).

Rimbault 1850 *Edward F. Rimbault. *Musical Illustrations of Bishop Percy's Reliques of Ancient English Poetry*. London: Cramer, Beale & Co., 1850.

Rimbault 1851 Edward Francis Rimbault. *A Little Book of Songs and Ballads*. London: John Russell Smith, 1851.

Rimbault i - vi *Edward F[rancis] Rimbault. *The Christy-Minstrel Song-Book*. 6 Folios [separately paginated] in 2 Vols., London: Chappell & So., 1861?

Ring Ms. *Constance Varney Ring; Martha Beckwith. *Mid-Hudson Popular Songs and Verse* [a manuscript on microfilm at Vassar College Library, Poughkeepsie, New York].

L. Ring *Lyle R. Ring. *New England Folk-Songs*. Boston: E. C. Schirmer Music Co., 1937.

Rising of the Moon *The Rising of the Moon Songster*. New York: Robert M. De Witt, #87, 1869.

Ritchie 1953 *Jean Ritchie. *A Garland of Mountain Songs*. New York, 1953.

Ritchie 1963 *Jean Ritchie. *Singing Family of the Cumberlands*. New York, 1963.

Ritchie 1964 *Jean Ritchie. *Swapping Song Book*. New York, 1964.

Ritchie 1965a *Jean Ritchie. *Folk Songs of the Southern Appalachians*. New York,

1965.

Ritchie 1965b *Jean Ritchie; Alfred d'Auberge. *The Newport Festival Songbook*. New York: Alfred Music Co., 1965.

Ritchie 1966 *Jean Ritchie. *From Fair to Fair*. New York: Henry Z. Walck, 1966.

Ritchie 1971 *Jean Ritchie. *Celebration of Life*. New York: Geordie Music Publishing Co., 1971.

Ritson 1794 i - ii *Joseph Ritson. *Scottish Songs*. 2 Vols., London: J. Johnson, 1794.

Ritson 1813 i - iii *Joseph Ritson. *A Select Collection of English Songs*. 2nd ed., 3 Vols., London: F. C. & J. Rivington, 1813. (1st ed., 1783).

Ritson Collection Joseph A. Ritson. *A Collection of Thirty-Seven Popular Songbooks*, ca. 1800. Yale University Library, I b57 t800.

RLP 12-602 †*Songs of an Irish Tinker Lady* (Margaret Barry). Riverside RLP 12-602.

RLP 12-603 †*Merry Ditties* (Milt Okun). Jacket notes (Norman Cazden). Riverside RLP 12-603.

RLP 12-618 †*English Drinking Songs* (A. L. Lloyd). Jacket notes. Riverside RLP 12-618.

RLP 12-621 - 12-628 †*The English and Scottish Popular Ballads* (Ewan MacColl and A. L. Lloyd). Booklets (Ken Goldstein). 4 Vols. in 8 Discs, Riverside RLP 12-621 - 12-628.

RLP 12-631 †*The Old Chisholm Trail* (Merrick Jarrett). Riverside RLP 12-631.

RLP 12-634 †*Traditional American Love Songs* (Milt Okun, Ellen Stekert). Jacket notes (Stekert). Riverside RLP 12-634.

RLP 12-643 †*Gambling Songs* (Logan English). Jacket notes (Goldstein). Riverside RLP 12-643.

RLP 12-648 †*Timber-r-: Folksongs and Ballads of the Lumberjack* (Paul Clayton). Riverside RLP 12-648.

RLP 12-654 †*Gold Rush Songs* (Pat Foster). Jacket notes (Goldstein). Riverside RLP 12-654.

RLP 12-656 †*English and Scottish Love Songs* (Ewan MacColl, Isla Cameron). Jacket notes (A. L. Lloyd). Riverside RLP 12-656.

RLP 12-814 †*English Folk Songs* (John Runge). Riverside RLP 12-814.

RLP 12-820 †*Songs of the Irish Republican Army* (Dominic Behan). Jacket notes. Riverside RLP 12-820.

RLP 199-34 †*Folk Songs* (Richard Dyer-Bennet). Remington RLP 199-34.

I. Roberts *Ifor Roberts; Donald C. Gibbard; John S. Murray. *British Columbia Sings*.

British Columbia Centennial Committee, 1958.

J. Roberts John S. Roberts. *The Legendary Ballads of England and Scotland*. London: Frederick Warne, 1868.

L. Roberts *Leonard Roberts; C. Buell Agay. *Sang Branch Settlers*. Memoirs of the American Folklore Society #60, 1974.

Robertson *James Stewart Robertson. *The Athole Collection of the Dance Music of Scotland*. Facsimile reprint, Edinburgh: Oliver & Boyd, 1961. (1st ed., 1884).

[Robin] *The Robin*. [See: *Orpheus* 1749 iii].

C. S. Robinson *Charles S. Robinson. *Songs of Christian Praise*. New York: A. S. Barnes & Co., 1868.

E. Robinson *Earl Robinson. *Young Folk Song Book*. New York, 1963.

G. C. Robinson *George C. Robinson. *Hymns and Tunes* for prayer and social meetings. Cincinnati: Poe & Hitchcock, 1860.

Roche i - ii *F. Roche. *Collection of Irish Airs, Marches and Dance Tunes*. 2 Vols., Dublin: Pigott & Co., 1911.

Rocky Road *The Rocky Road to Dublin Songster*. New-York: Robert M. De Witt, #9, 1868.

Rodeheaver 191- *Homer A. Rodeheaver; Charles H. Gabriel. *Awakening Songs*. Chicago: The Rodeheaver Co., 191-.

Rodeheaver 1916 *Homer A. Rodeheaver; Cha[rle]s H. Gabriel. *Songs for Servcice*. Chicago: Rodeheaver Gospel Music Co., 1916.

Rodeheaver 1925 *Homer A. Rodeheaver; Charles H. Gabriel. *Victorious Service Songs* [containing photographs of John W. Peterson, Homer A. Rodeheaver, Billy Sunday and others]. Chicago: The Rodeheaver Co., 1925.

Rodeheaver 1928 *Homer A. Rodeheaver. *Sociability Songs*. Chicago: The Rodeheaver Co., 1928.

Rodeheaver 1939 *Homer A. Rodeheaver, et al. *Christian Service Songs*. Winona Lake, Indiana: The Rodeheaver Co., 1939.

Rodeheaver 1945 *Homer Alvan Rodeheaver; George N. Sanville. *112 Familiar Hymns and Gospel Songs*. Winona Lake, Indiana: The Rodeheaver Hall-Mack Co., 1945.

Rodeheaver 1956 *Homer A. Rodeheaver; George [N.] Sanville; B. D. Ackley. *Hymns for Praise and Service*. Winona Lake, Indiana: The Rodeheaver Co., 1956.

Rohrbough 1931a *Lynn Rohrbough. *Play Party Games*. Delaware, Ohio: Coöperative

Recreation Service, 1931.

Rohrbough 1931b *Lynn Rohrbough. *Quadrilles*. Delaware, Ohio: Coöperative Recreation Service, 1931.

Rohrbough 1941 *Lynn Rohrbough. *Quadrilles*. Delaware, Ohio: Coöperative Recreation Service, 1941.

Rohrbough 1946 *Lynn Rohrbough. *Country Life Songs*. Delaware, Ohio: Coöperative Recreation Service, 1946.

Rollins Hyder E. Rollins. *An Analytical Index to the Ballad Entries (1557-1709) in the Register of the Company of Stationers of London*. University of North Carolina Press, 1924.

Rollinson *T. H. Rollinson. *Favorite Reels, Jigs and Hornpipes*. Boston: Oliver Ditson, 1907.

Rooney 1905 *Hubert E. Rooney. *The Well-Known Songs of Ireland*. Dublin: James Duffy & Co., 1905.

Rooney 1918 *Hubert E. Rooney. *An Smólac* [Irish Songs]. Dublin: Maunsel & Co., 1918.

Rooney 1922 *Hubert E. Rooney. *The Popular Album of Irish Songs*. Dublin: Maunsel & Roberts, 1922.

Root *George F. Root. *The Triumph*. Chicago: Root & Cady, 1868.

Rosalie, or The Prairie Flower Melodist. Boston: Russell & Tolman, 1859.

Rosenberg Index Bruce A. Rosenberg. *The Folksongs of Virginia:* a checklist of library holdings. University Press of Virginia, 1969.

Rosenberg T82 - T91 †Bruce A. Rosenberg [collection of tape recordings of songs and dance tunes from the W. P. A. Federal Music Project, Virginia]. Alderman Library, University of Virginia, Item 1547 tapes T82 - T91.

Rosenfeld *Monroe H. Rosenfeld. *Dana's College Songs and Glees*. Boston: Dana Music Co., 1899.

Rough & Ready The Rough and Ready Songster. New York: Nafis & Cornish, 1848?

Rounder 0017 †*Ballads and Hymns from the Ozarks* (Almeda Riddle). Booklet. Rounder Records 0017.

Roxburghe i - viii [William Chappell; J. W. Ebsworth]. *The Roxburghe Ballads*. 8 Vols., London: The Ballad Society, 1868-95.

Rozwenc Edwin C. Rozwenc; Edward C. Martin; Martin W. Sandler. *The Restless Americans*. Lexington, Massachusetts: Ginn & Co., 1972.

*RPSB *Reprints from People's Songs Bulletin*. New York, 1961.

*RSO # *Reprints from Sing Out*, 1951-.

Rubin *Ruth Rubin. A *Treasury of Jewish Folksongs*. New York: Schocken Books, 1950.

*Ruff-Stuff *Ruff-Stuff*. Boston: C. C. Birchard, 1921.

Russell Russell's Friendly Neighbors Songster. New York: Popular Publishing Co., 188-.

[H. Russell] †Henry Russell. *100 Popular Songs and Scenas*. [See: *D'Alcorn's Musical Miracles* ii].

Ruth *Viola Ruth. *Pioneer Western Folk Tunes*. Phoenix, Arizona, 1948.

Ryan 1926 zGrace L. Ryan. *Dances of Our Pioneers: Music*. New York: A. S. Barnes, 1926.

Ryan 1939 *Grace L. Ryan; Robert T. Benford. *Dances of Our Pioneers*. 2nd ed., New York: A. S. Barnes, 1939.

[Rymour Club] *Miscellanea* of the Rymour Club [Edinburgh]. [See; *Miscellanea*].

S 2053 *The Best of Oscar Brand*. Tradition S 2053.

Sackett 1961 *S. J. Sackett; William E. Koch. *Kansas Folklore*. University of Nebraska Press, 1961.

Sackett 1967 *S. J. Sackett. *Cowboys and the Songs They Sang*. New York, 1967.

[Sacred Harp] *The Sacred Harp*. [See: Cooper; Denson; B. F. White].

Sailor's Medley The Sailor's Medley. Philadelphia: Matthew Carey, 1800.

Salisbury Square The Salisbury Square Song Book. London: Jennings, 1820.

[Sam Cowell] *Sam Cowell's Comic Songster*. [See: *Great Comic Volume* ii].

Sam Devere Sam Devere's Jumbo Songster. New York: Popular Publishing Co., 188-.

Sam Eskin i - iv *Sam Eskin Collection* [a manuscript collection including some material from New York State sources; some items are in paginated volumes]. Fenimore House Library Archives, New York State Historical Society, Cooperstown.

*Sam Henry # *Sam Henry. *Songs of the People* contributed to *The Northern Constitution* (Coleraine, Ireland), 1924-38 [facsimiles of printed newspaper copies, with tunes in Tonic-Sol-Fa notation only; the copies in the B. B. C. Collection, housed at the Vaughan Williams Memorial Library, Cecil Sharp House, London, and at the Library of Congress, Washington, lack #247 - #465, which were not collected by Sam Henry].

175

Sam Henry Index #   The Sam Henry Ms. Collection, Songs of the People: a working checklist of songs and ballads, Coleraine, Ireland, 1939 [a typescript with annotations by Gale Huntington]. [Copy at Northeast Folklore Archives, University of Maine at Orono].

Sam Sharpley   Sam Sharpley's Iron Clad Songster. New York: Dick & Fitzgerald, 1864.

Sampson   *John Sampson. The Seven Seas Shanty Book.* London: Boosey & Co., 1927.

[*San Francisco Songster*]   *A San Francisco Songster.* [See: Lengyel ii].

C. Sandburg 1927   *Carl Sandburg. The American Songbag.* New York, 1927.

C. Sandburg 1950   *Carl Sandburg. New American Songbag.* New York: Broadcast Music Inc., 1950.

H. Sandburg   *Helga Sandburg; Richard Harrison. Sweet Music:* a book of family reminiscence and song. New York: The Dial Press, 1963.

Sankey 1894   *Ira D. Sankey; James McGranahan; George C. Stebbins. Gospel Hymns, Nos. 1 to 6.* Cincinnati: The John Church Co., 1894. (Reprint, New York, 1972).

Sankey 1911   *Ira Allen Sankey. Hallowed Hymns.* Chicago: The Bigelow & Main Co., 1911.

Sayles   *Harold F. Sayles; Elisha A. Hoffman. Best Hymns No. 3.* Chicago: Evangelical Publishing Co., 1903.

Scammell   *A[rthur] R. Scammell. My Newfoundland.* Montreal: Harvest House, 1966.

Scarborough 1925   *Dorothy Scarborough. On the Trail of Negro Folk-Songs.* Harvard University Press, 1925.

Scarborough 1937   *Dorothy Scarborough. A Song Catcher in the Southern Mountains.* Reprint, New York, 1966. (1st ed., 1937).

Schinhan iv - v   *Jan Philip Schinhan. North Carolina Folklore: The Frank C. Brown Collection,*
   iv. *The Music of the Ballads.*
   v. *The Music of the Folk Songs.*
Duke University Press, 1957, 1962.

*Schools National   *Schools National Music Festival* [a sheet music issue of the song *Mo Slan Le Dutract D'Eirinn (My Affectionate Farewell to Ireland)*]. The Irish League, n. d.

C. K. Scott   *Charles Kennedy Scott. The Chelsea Song Book.* London: The Cresset Press, 1927.

H. Scott   *Harold Scott. English Song Book.*

New York: Robert W. McBride, 1926.

W. Scott i - iv   Walter Scott. *Minstrelsy of the Scottish Border.* 4 Vols., Edinburgh: Oliver and Boyd, 1932. (1st ed., 1801).

*Scottish Songs   *Scottish Songs.* London: Bayley & Ferguson 1935.

*Scottish Students   *The Scottish Student's Song Book.* London: Bayley & Ferguson, 1891.

Scudder   *M. L. Scudder. The Wesleyan Psalmist, or Songs of Canaan.* Re-issue, New-York: Lane & Scott, 1849. (1st ed., Boston, 1842).

Sedley   *Stephen Sedley. The Seeds of Love.* London: Essex Music, 1967.

Charles Seeger   *Charles Seeger. Studies in Musicology, 1935-1975.* University of California Press, 1977.

Peggy Seeger 1960   *Peggy Seeger; Ewan MacColl. The Singing Island.* London: Mills Music, 1960.

Peggy Seeger 1960a   *Peggy Seeger. The Five-String Banjo American Folk Style.* New York: Hargail Music Press, 1960.

Peggy Seeger 1964   *Peggy Seeger. Folk Songs of Peggy Seeger.* New York: Oak Publications, 1964.

Peggy Seeger 1970   *Peggy Seeger; Ewan MacColl. The Singing Island.* 2nd Melody Edition, New York: Belwin Mills, 1970.

Pete Seeger 1961   *Pete Seeger. American Favorite Ballads.* New York, 1961.

Pete Seeger 1964   *Pete Seeger. The Bells of Rhymney.* New York: Oak Publications, 1964.

Pete Seeger 1965   *Pete Seeger. Bits and Pieces.* New York: Ludlow Music Co., 1965.

Pete Seeger 1972   *Pete Seeger; Jo Metcalf Schwartz. The Incompleat Folksinger.* New York: Simon & Schuster, 1972.

Pete Seeger 1973   *Pete Seeger. Henscratches and Flyspecks.* New York, 1973.

Ruth Seeger 1948   *Ruth Crawford Seeger. American Folk Songs for Children.* Garden City, New York: Doubleday & Co., 1948.

Ruth Seeger 1950   *Ruth Crawford Seeger. Animal Folksongs for Children.* Garden City, New York: Doubleday & Co., 1950.

*Select Gems   *Select Gems.* Philadelphia: American Baptist Publication Society, 1889.

[*Sentimental & Patriotic*]   *Sentimental and Patriotic Songs.* [See: *Songs of Our Land* ii].

Sentimental Songs   Sentimental Songs for the Lady's Songster. Philadelphia: Fisher & Bro., 184-.

Serposs   *Emile H. Serposs; Ira C. Singleton.*

Music in Our Heritage. Morristown, New Jersey: Silver Burdett, 1969.

Seventy-Nine Seventy-Nine Black-Letter Ballads and Broadsides (1559-1597). London: Joseph Lilly, 1867. (Reprint, Detroit, 1968).

Sewanee Sewanee Review, 1893-.

Seward *Theodore F. Seward; George L. White. *Jubilee Songs*. Enlarged ed., New York: Bigelow & Main, 1884. (1st ed., 1872).

SFQ Southern Folklore Quarterly, 1937-.

[*Shamrock*] *The Shamrock, or Songs of Old Ireland*. [See: *Universal Book of Songs* iv].

Shamrock Four The Shamrock Four's Smart Little Bit of a Man Songster. New York: Popular Publishing Co., #273, 1882.

Shamrock Shore The Shamrock Shore Songster. Lowell, Massachusetts: James Perkinson 1872.

Shapiro *Elliott Shapiro. *Grand Old Songs*. New York: Shapiro, Bernstein & Co., 1928.

C. J. Sharp 1902 *Cecil J. Sharp. *A Book of British Song*. London: John Murray, 1902.

C. J. Sharp 1908 *Cecil J. Sharp. *English Folk Songs* [a series of choral arrangements issued as individual sheet mucis copies]. London: Schott & Co., 1908.

[C. J. Sharp *FSE*] *Cecil J. Sharp. *Folk Songs of England* for schools. 9 Vols., London: Novello & Co., 1908-12. [See: *Novello* i - ix].

C. J. Sharp *FSS* *Cecil J. Sharp. *Folk Songs from Somerset*. 5 Vols., London: Novello & Co., 1908-10.

C. J. Sharp *Selection* i - ii *Cecil J. Sharp; Ralph Vaughan Williams. *A Selection of Collected Folk-Songs*. 2 Vols., London: Novello & Co., 1908.

[C. J. Sharp 1912] *Cecil J. Sharp. *Folk Songs from Various Counties*. London: Novello & Co., 1912. [See: C. J. Sharp 1961 iv].

[C. J. Sharp 1913] *Cecil J. Sharp. *Folk-Song Carols*. London: Novello & Co., 1913. [See: *Novello* #245].

C. J. Sharp 1914 *Cecil J. Sharp. *English Folk Chanteys*. London: Simkin Marshall, 1914.

[C. J. Sharp #261] *Cecil J. Sharp. *Ballads*. London: Novello & Co., n. d. [See: *Novello* #261].

[C. J. Sharp #262] *Cecil J. Sharp. *Pulling Chanteys*. London: Novello & Co., n. d. [See: *Novello* #262].

[C. J. Sharp #263] *Cecil J. Sharp. *Capstan Chanteys*. London: Novello & Co., n. d. [See: *Novello* #263].

C. J. Sharp 1916 *Cecil J. Sharp. *One Hundred English Folk-Songs*. Boston: Oliver Ditson, 1916. (Reprint, New York: Dover Books, 1976).

C. J. Sharp 1920 i - ii *Cecil J. Sharp. *English Folk Songs, Selected Edition*. 2 Vols., London: Novello & Co., 1920. (Re-issued in 1 Vol. as *Centenary Edition*, 1959).

C. J. Sharp 1932 i - ii *Cecil J. Sharp; Olive Dame Campbell; Maud Karpeles. *English Folk-Songs from the Southern Appalachians*. Reprint, 2 Vols. in 1, Oxford University Press, 1960. (1st ed., 1932).

C. J. Sharp 1961 i - v *Cecil J. Sharp. *English County Songs* [a reprint in one volume, with continuous pagination, of five volumes originally published by Novello & Co., 1908-12, and comprising:

   i. H. E. D. Hammond; Cecil J. Sharp. *Folk Songs from Dorset* (1908).

   ii. Ralph Vaughan Williams. *Folk Songs from the Eastern Counties* (1908).

   iii. George B. Gardiner; Gustav Holst. *Folk Songs from Hampshire* (1909).

   iv. Cecil J. Sharp. *Folk Songs from Various Counties* (1912).

   v. W. Percy Merrick; Ralph Vaughan Williams. *Folk Songs from Sussex* (1912)].

London: Novello & Co., 1961.

C. J. Sharp 1965 *Cecil J. Sharp. *English Folk-Song: Some Conclusions*. 4th revised ed., edited by Maud Karpeles (1965), reprint by Ep Publishing Co., 1972 (1st ed., 1907).

[C. J. Sharp 1974] *Cecil Sharp's Collection of English Folk Songs*. [See: *Karpeles 1974*].

J. W. Sharp i - ii John W. Sharp. *The Vauxhall Comic Song-Book*. 2 Vols., London: Thomas Allman, 1847.

Shaw *William F. Shaw [publisher]. *Popular Songs & Ballads No. 1* [not paginated]. W. F. Shaw, 1882.

Shay 1924 Frank Shay. *Iron Men and Wooden Ships*. Garden City, New York, 1924.

Shay 1929 *Frank Shay. *Drawn from the Wood*. New York, 1929.

Shay 1961 *Frank Shay. *My Pious Friends and Drunken Companions* (1927), and *More Pious Friends and Drunken Companions* (1928). Reprint in 1 Vol., New York, 1961.

Shealy *Alexander Shealy. *Second Omnibus of Folk Songs*. New York: Hansen Publications, 1972.

Shearin Hubert G. Shearin; Josiah H. Combs. *A Syllabus of Kentucky Folk-Songs*. Lexington, Kentucky, 1911.

Shekerjian *Haig Shekerjian; Regina Shekerjian; Robert De Cormier. *A Book of Ballads, Songs and Snatches*. New York: Harper & Row, 1966.

Shellans *Herbert Shellans. *Folk Songs of the

Blue Ridge Mountains. New York: Oak Publications, 1968.

Shelton   *Robert Shelton; Walter Raim. *The Josh White Song Book*. Chicago: Quadrangle Book, 1963.

Sherwin 1932   *Sterling Sherwin; Louis Katzman. *Songs of the Gold Miners*. New York, 1932.

Sherwin 1933   *Sterling Sherwin; Henry A. Powell. *Bad Man Songs of the Wild and Woolly West*. New York: Sam Fox, 1933. (2nd ed., Cleveland, 1938).

Sherwin 1943   *Sterling Sherwin; Harry K. McClintock. *Railroad Songs of Yesterday*. New York: Shapiro, Bernstein & Co., 1943.

Sherwin 1944   *Sterling Sherwin. *Singin' in the Saddle*. Boston: Boston Music Co., 1944.

Shilling Song Book i - ii   *The Shilling Song Book*. 2 Vols., Boston: Oliver Ditson, 1860, 1862.

Shimer & West [N. B.] *Shimer and [Frank B.] West's Songster*. 187-.

Shoemaker   *Henry Wharton Shoemaker. *Mountain Minstrelsy of Pennsylvania*. 3rd ed., Philadelphia: Henry F. McGirr, 1931. (1st ed., 1919).

Showalter   *Noah D. Showalter. *Joseph Funk's New Harmonia Sacra: a Compilation of Genuine Church Music*. 20th ed., Dayton, Virginia: Ruebush-Kieffer Co., 1942. (1st ed. of *Harmonia Sacra*, 1832; see also: Funk).

Shower of Pearls *The Shower of Pearls*. Boston: Oliver Ditson, 1862.

Siegmeister 1944a   *Elie Siegmeister. *Songs of Early America*. New York, 1944.

Siegmeister 1944b   *Elie Siegmeister. *Work & Sing*. New York: William R. Scott, 1944.

SIF 1001   †*Peter Bellamy*. Green Linnet Records SIF 1001.

Silber 1963   *Irwin Silber; Jerry Silverman. *Hootenanny Song Book* [reprints from *Sing Out*]. New York: Consolidated Music Publishers, 1963.

Silber 1964   *Irwin Silber; Jerry Silverman. *Soldier Songs and Home-Front Ballads*. New York: Oak Publications, 1964.

Silber 1965   *Irwin Silber; Happy Traum. *The Great Atlantic and Pacific Song Book*. New York: Amsco Music Publishers, 1965.

Silber 1967   *Irwin Silber; Earl Robinson. *Songs of the Great American West*. New York: Macmillan, 1967.

Silber 1973a   *Irwin Silber. *Songs of Independence*. Harrisburg, Pennsylvania: Stackpole Books, 1973.

Silber 1973b   Irwin Silber; Fred Silber. *Folksinger's Wordbook*. New York: Oak Publications, 1973.

Silver Chord *The Silver Chord*. Boston: Oliver Ditson, 1862.

Silverman 1966   *Jerry Silverman. *The Panic Is On*. New York: Oak Publications, 1966.

Silverman 1975 i - ii   *Jerry Silverman. *Folk Song Encyclopedia*. 2 Vols., New York: Chappell Music Co., 1975.

Simms   William Gilmore Simms. *War Poetry of the South*. New York: Richardson & Co., 1867.

Simon   *William L. Simon; Dan Fox; Clair N. Van Ausdall. *Reader's Digest Family Songbook of Faith and Joy*. Pleasantville, New York: The Reader's Digest Association, 1975.

Simpson   *Claude M. Simpson. *The British Broadside Ballad and Its Music*. Princeton University Press, 1966.

Sing *Sing* [a periodical, London], 1954-.

Sing Care Away i - iv *Sing Care Away*. 4 Vols., London: Novello & Co., 1951.

[*Sing Out*] *Sing Out* [a periodical]. [See: *SO*].

Sing Together *Sing Together: a Girl Scout songbook*. New York: Girl Scouts of the U.S.A., 1949.

Singabout *Singabout* [a periodical, Sydney: Bush Music Club], 1956-.

Singabout Songster *Singabout Songster No. 1*. Sydney: Bush Music Club, 1968.

Singer's Companion *The Singer's Companion*. New York: Stringer & Townsend, 1854.

Singer's Gem *The Singer's Gem*. Philadelphia: Fisher & Bro., 18--.

Singer's Journal # *Singer's Journal* [a periodical, probably issued fortnightly, ca. 1869; #1 - #138 on microfilm *ZB 138 at Music Division, New York Public Library; among variant titles are *De Marsan's Singer's Journal* and *New Comic and Sentimental Singer's Journal;* see also: Henderson].

[*Singer's Own Book*] *The Singer's Own Book*. [See: *American Singer*].

[*Singer's Penny Magazine*] *The Singer's Penny Magazine*. [See: Prest].

Sires   *Ina Sires. *Songs of the Open Range*. Boston: C. C. Birchard, 1928.

Siringo   Charles A. Siringo. *The Song Companion of a Lone Star Cowboy*. Reprint, Norwood Editions, 1975. (1st ed., 1919).

Sixty Variety Songs *Sixty Old Time Variety Songs*. London: Francis, Day & Hunter, 19-.

Sky-Lark *The Sky-Lark:* a choice selection of the most admired popular songs. London: Thomas Tegg, 1825.

SL 206 †*English Folk Songs* (edited by Peter Kennedy and Alan Lomax. Booklet. (Columbia World Library of Folk and Primitive Music, Vol. 3). Columbia SL 206.

SLF *Sounds Like Folk* [a series of booklets issued at irregular intervals]. London: English Folk Dance & Song Society, 1972-.

SLP 9 †*Folksay, Vol. 3.* Stinson Records SLP 9.

SLP 49 †*Ozark Mountain Folk Songs, Vol. 1* (Ellen Stekert). Jacket notes (Kenneth S. Goldstein). Stinson Records SLP 49.

SLP 57 †*A Pete Seeger Concert.* Stinson Records SLP 57.

SLP 65 †*Jack Was Every Inch a Sailor* (Milt Okun). Stinson Records SLP 65.

SLP 68 †*Ballads and Folksongs* (Robert and Louise De Cormier. Jacket notes. Stinson Records SLP 68.

SLP 71 †*I Sing of Canada!* (Milt Okun). Jacket notes. Stinson Records SLP 71.

SLP 72 †*Catskill Mountain Folksongs* from the Camp Woodland Collection (Robert and Louise De Cormier). Jacket notes (Norman Cazden). Stinson Records SLP 72.

SLP 73 †*Texas Folk Songs* (Hally Wood). Stinson Records SLP 73.

SLP 74 †*More Southern Mountain Folk Songs* (Harry & Jeanie West). Stinson Records SLP 74.

SLP 80 †*Haul on the Bowlin'* (A. L. Lloyd, Ewan MacColl). Stinon Records SLP 80.

SLP 81 †*Off to Sea Once More* (A. L. Lloyd, Ewan MacColl). Stinson Records SLP 81.

SLP 82 †*Adirondack Folk Songs and Ballads* from the Marjorie L. Porter Collection of North Country Lore (Milt Okun). Jacket notes (Porter, Goldstein). Stinson Records SLP 82.

A. B. Smith *Alfred B. Smith. Inspiring Hymns.* Grand Rapids, Michigan: Singspiration, 1951.

C. F. Smith *C. Fox Smith. A Book of Shanties.* Boston: Houghton Mifflin, 1927.

F. H. Smith 1939 *Frank H. Smith. Square Dances of the Great Smoky Mountains.* Delaware, Ohio: Coöperative Recreation Service, 1939.

F. H. Smith 1955 *Frank H. Smith. The Appalachian Square Dance.* Berea, Kentucky: Berea College, 1955.

J. T. Smith *James T. Smith. Fifty Gems of Scottish Song.* London, 190-.

L. A. Smith *Laura Alexander Smith. The Music of the Waters.* London: Kegan Paul, 1888.

L. O. Smith *Lee Orlean Smith; Theodore Morse. Good Old Timers* [folio]. New York: Leo Feist, 1922.

P. S. Smith Paul S. Smith; David A. Spalding; Frank Sutton. *Cum All Yo Cutlin Heroes.* Sheffield City Museum, 1967.

R. Smith 1925 *Reed Smith. The Traditional Ballad and Its South Carolina Survivals.* University of South Carolina Extension Division, 1925.

R. Smith 1928 Reed Smith. *South Carolina Ballads.* Harvard University Press, 1928.

R. Smith 1937 *Reed Smith. American Anthology of Old World Ballads.* New York, 1937.

R. A. Smith i - vi *Robert A[rchibald] Smith. The Scottish Minstrel.* 4th ed., 6 Vols., Edinburgh: J. Purdie, 1820-24.

R. A. Smith 1828a *Robert A[rchibald] Smith. The Irish Minstrel.* Edinburgh: Robt. Purdie, 1828.

R. A. Smith 1828b *Robert A[rchibald] Smith. Select Melodies.* Edinburgh: Robt. Purdie, 1828.

R. B. Smith R. Brian Smith. *Bangor Scout and Guide Club* [Songs]. University College of North Wales, 1970.

W. J. Smith *[William J.] Smith's Collection of Mountain Ballads and Cowboy Songs.* New York: William J. Smith, 1932.

SMP i - vi *The Songster's Multum in Parvo,* 1808-11 [6 volumes issued].

SO *Sing Out* [a periodical, New York], 1950.

Sociability Songs *Sociability Songs.* Toronto: Gordon V. Thompson, 1937.

[*Social Harp*] *The Social Harp.* [See: McCurry].

Society of Brothers *Society of Brothers; Marlys Swinger. Sing through the Day.* Rifton, New York: Plough Publishing House, 1968.

Sol Smith Russell 1869 *Sol Smith Russell's American Humorist and Character Vocalist.* New York: Dick & Fitzgerald, #99, 1869.

Sol Smith Russell 1876 *Sol Smith Russell's Jeremy Jolly Boy Comic Songster.* New York: Robert M. De Witt, 1876.

Soldiers & Sailors *Soldiers' and Sailors' Patriotic Songs.* New York: The Loyal Publication Society, May 1864.

Solomon *Maynard Solomon. British Ballads and Folk Songs from the Joan Baez Songbook.* New York: Ryerson Music Publishers, 1964.

Song Ballads *Song Ballads* and other songs of
the Pine Mountain [Kentucky] Settlement
School, 1923.
Song Jewels *Song Jewels*. Lynn, Mas-
sachusetts: W. N. Swett & Co., 1891.
Song Purpose *Songs for Every Purpose and
Occasion*. Minneapolis: Schmitt, Hall &
McCreary, 1938.
[Songs for Canadian Boys] *Songs for Cana-
dian Boys*. [See: *Canadian Boys*].
Songs for Harvard *Songs for Harvard, Yale
and Princeton Students*. Boston: White-
Smith, 1885.
Songs Forever *Songs That Will Live
Forever*. Racine, Wisconsin: Whitman Pub-
lishing Co., n. d.
[Songs of All Time] *Songs of All Time*. [See:
All Time].
Songs of Columbia *Songs of Columbia*. New
York: Taintor Brothers, 1876.
Songs of Faith *Songs of Faith*. Nashville,
Tennessee: The Broadman Press, 1933.
[Songs of Many Nations] *Songs of Many
Nations*. [See: *Many Nations*].
Songs of Our Land i - iii *Songs of Our Land* [a
compilation of three songsters with separate
pagination:
　i. *[Irish] Sentimental and Patriotic Songs*
　　(185-).
　ii. *The Irish Comic Songster* (185-).
　iii. *Irish Melodies by Thomas Moore*
　　(1852)].
　Boston: Patrick Donahoe, 185-.
[Songs of Scotland] *The Songs of Scotland*.
[See; :M. B. Foster, Pittman].
[Songs of the Florences] *Songs of the Flor-
ences*. [See: *Florences*].
[Songs of the Gardens] *Songs of the Gardens*.
[See: *Gardens*].
[Songs of the North] *Songs of the North*.
[See: Boulton, MacLeod].
Songs of Zion *Songs of Zion*. New York:
American Tract Society, 1851.
[Songs That Never Grow Old] *Songs that
Never Grow Old*. [See: *Never Grow Old*].
Songs to Keep. *Songs to Keep*. Delaware,
Ohio: Coöperative Recreation Service, 1962.
Songs & Recitations *Songs and Recitations
of Ireland*. Cork, 1960.
Songster #1 *Songster, Miscellaneous #1* [at
Library of Congress, M1628.S68 No. 1].
Songster's Favourite Companion *The Song-
ster's Favourite Companion*. Glasgow: A.
MacGoun, 1803.
Songster's Repository *The Songster's Re-
pository*. New York: Nathaniel Dearborn,
1811.

Sonneck Oscar George Theodore Sonneck;
William Treat Upton. *A Bibliography of
Early Secular American Music*. The Library
of Congress Music Division, 1945.
Southern Ethiopian *The Southern Ethiopian
Operatic Songster*. Philadelphia: Fisher &
Bro., 18--.
Souvenir Minstrel *The Souvenir Minstrel, or
Singer's Remember Me*. Philadelphia: J. B.
Berry, 1842.
Spaeth 1926 *Sigmund Speath. *Read 'Em and
Weep*. Garden City, New York, 1926.
Spaeth 1927 *Sigmund Spaeth. *Weep Some
More, My Lady*. Garden City, New York,
1927.
Spaeth 1948 Sigmund Spaeth. *A History of
Popular Music in America*. New York: Ran-
dom House, 1948.
Spicker *Max Spicker. *Songs of the British
Isles*. New York: G. Schirmer, 1909.
Spirit *The Spirit of the Nation: Ballads and
Songs*. Dublin: James Duffy, 1845. (Reprint,
Dublin, 1934).
Sport's Own *The Sport's Own Songster*. [Not
paginated]. New York: Geo. Blackie & Co.,
1874.
SRIE *Selected Reports, Institute of Eth-
nomusicology* [University of California at
Los Angeles], 1972-.
SRL 7624 †*Folksong & Minstrelsy*. Vanguard
Records SRL 7624.
SS *Scottish Studies* [a periodical], 1956-.
Stamphill *Ira Stamphill; John T. Benson.
Heart Warming Songs. West Palm Beach,
Florida: Hymntime Publishers, 1956.
Stamps *Virgil O. Stamps. *Favorite Radio
Songs Number Two*. Dallas, Texas: Stamps-
Baxter Music & Printing Co., 1939.
Standford 1895 *Charles Villiers Stanford.
The Irish Melodies of Thomas Moore. Lon-
don: Boosey & Co., 1895.
Stanford 1906 *Charles Villiers Stanford. *The
National Song Book*. London: Boosey &
Co., 1906.
[Stanford 1909] *Charles Villiers Stanford.
*The Complete Petrie Collection of Irish
Music*. [See: Petrie #1].
Stanford 1958 *Charles Villiers Stanford;
Martin Shaw; Herbert Wiseman; Sydney
Northcote. *The New National Song Book*.
New edition, London: Boosey & Hawkes,
1958. (1st ed., 1906).
Stavis *Barry Stavis; Frank Harmon
[pseudonym for Fred Hellerman]. *The Songs
of Joe Hill*. New York, 1955.
St. Cecilia *St. Cecilia, or The British Song-
ster*. Edinburgh: Campbell Donovan, 1782.

180

Steeleye Span *Steeleye Span*. London: Libra Music, 1972.

Stekert 1961 Ellen Stekert. *"The Farmer's Curst Wife,* a modified historical-geographical study." M. A. Thesis, Indiana University, 1961.

Stekert 1969 Ellen Stekert. "Two voices of tradition" [including Listing B, 261-68, the repertory of an informant from the lumber-camp tradition of the New York-Pennsylvania border; Listing N, 269-74, the repertory of an informant from eastern Kentucky-southern Indiana]. Dissertation, University of Pennsylvania, 1965 (University Microfilms, 1969).

Stenhouse *William Stenhouse. *The Scots Musical Museum, Volume Two,* containing illustrations of the lyric poetry and music of Scotland [Bound with: David Laing, *Additional Illustrations. . .,* see: Laing]. Reprint, Folklore Associates, 1962. (1st ed., 1853).

Stern *Dick Stern. *Those Wonderful Years.* New York: Big Three Music Corp., 1972.

Stephens Stephens' Fenian Songster. New York: Wm. H. Murphy, 1866.

C. W. Stevens *Charles Wistar Stevens. *College Song Book, Enlarged Edition.* New York: S. T. Gordon & Son, 1888. (1st ed., 1871).

G. A. Stevens George Alexander Stevens. *The Choice Spirit's Chaplet; or, A Poesy from Parnassus.* London: John Dunn, 1771.

Stevenson 1859 *John A[ndrew] Stevenson; J. W. Glover. [*Thomas*] *Moore's Irish Melodies.* Dublin: James Duffy, 1859.

Stevenson 1891 *John [Andrew] Stevenson; Henry Bishop. [*Thomas*] *Moore's Irish Melodies,* with symphonies and accompaniments. Dublin, 1891.

C. Stewart *Charles Stewart. *The Killin Collection of Gaelic Songs.* Edinburgh, 1884.

D. Stewart Douglas Stewart; Nancy Keesing. *Old Bush Songs.* Sydney, 1957.

Stokoe *John Stokoe; Samuel Reay. *Songs and Ballads of Northern England.* Newcastle-on-Tyne: Walter Scott, 1899.

C. Stone Christopher Stone. *Sea Songs and Ballads.* Oxford: Clarendon Press, 1906.

[J. A. Stone] [John A. Stone]. *Put's Original California Songster.* [See: *Pacific Song Book* ii].

[J. A. Stone] [John A. Stone]. *Put's Golden Songster.* [See: *Pacific Song Book* iii].

R. M. Stone Roy Maxwell Stone. *Our Hymns and Gospel Songs.* New York: Carlton Press, 1972.

Stonewall Stonewall Song Book. Richmond, Virginia: West & Johnson, 1864.

Stout Earl J. Stout. *Folklore from Iowa.* Memoirs of the American Folklore Society, #29, 1936.

Street Literature An Album of Street Literature [a bound collection of broadsides, ca. 1800-1850, at the Bancroft Library, University of California at Berkeley, PR 1181.A52].

Street & Smith Street & Smith's Wild West Weekly, 1928-.

A. Stuart *Alexander Stuart. *Musick for Allan Ramsay's Collection of Scots Songs.* 6 Vols. in 1, Edinburgh: Allan Ramsay [ca. 1726].

F. Stuart *F. Stuart *Forbes Stuart; Geoffrey Winters; Janet Archer. *Stories of Britain in Song.* London: Longman, 1972.

Stubbs *Ken Stubbs. *The Life of a Man.* London: English Folk Dance & Song Society, 1970.

Studer i - xiv Norman Studer. *The Story of Camp Woodland* [in fourteen chapters] Ms. Catskill Folklife Archive, Olive Free Library, W. Shokan, N.Y.

Sturgis *Edith B. Sturgis; Robert B. Hughes. *Songs from the Hills of Vermont.* New York: G. Schirmer, 1919.

Sumner *Heywood Sumner. *The Besom Maker & Other Country Folk Songs.* London: Longmans, Green & Co., 1888. (Reprint, Norwood Editions, 1973).

Surette *Thomas Whitney Surette; Archibald T. Davison. *The Home & Community Song Book.* Boston: E. C. Schirmer, 1931.

C. L. Swan Clara LeGrand Swan. "A collection of ballads and songs from Morning Sun, Iowa." M. A. Thesis (English), University of Iowa, 1929.

M. L. Swan *M. L. Swan. *The New Harp of Columbia.* Nashville, Tennessee: Smith & Lamaro, 1921. (1st ed., 1867).

Sweeney & Ryland Sweeney & Ryland's Twinkling Songster. New York: Popular Publishing Co., 1882.

*Sweet Freedom *Sweet Freedom's Song,* issued for the 150th anniversary of the State of Ohio. Delaware, Ohio: Coöperative Recreation Service, 1953.

Sweney 1881 *John R. Sweney; William J. Kirkpatrick. *The Wells of Salvation.* Philadelphia: John Hood, 1881.

Sweney 1882 i - iii *Jno. R. Sweney; William J. Kirkpatrick. *The Trio* [3 Vols. in 1, comprising:

   i. *The Garner* (1878).

   ii. *The Quiver* (1880).

   iii. *The Ark of Praise* (1882)].

Philadelphia: John J. Hood, 1882.

Sweney 1882 *Jno. R. Sweney; T. C. O'Kane; C. C. McCabe; W[illiam] J. Kirkpatrick. *Songs of Redeeming Love.* Philadelphia: John J. Hood, 1882.

Sweney 1886 i - iii *John R. Sweney; William J. Kirkpatrick. *The Temple Trio* [3 Vols. in 1, comprising:
  i. *On Joyful Wing* (1886).
  ii. *Melodious Sonnets* (1885).
  iii. *Precious Hymns* (1885)].
Philadelphia: John J. Hood, 1886.

Sweney 1888 *John R. Sweney; William J. Kirkpatrick. *Showers of Blessing.* Philadelphia; John J. Hood, 1888.

Tabernacle iii - vi *Tabernacle Hymns* No. 3, No. 4. Chicago: Tabernacle Publishing Co., 1934, 1941.

Taggert & Witt Taggert and Witt's Masterpiece of Song The Moth and the Flame Songster. New York: W[illiam H.] Delaney, 1897.

Talley *Thomas W. Talley. *Negro Folk Rhymes.* New York: Macmillan, 1922.

*Taverners *The Taverners Songbook.* London, 1973.

*Ten More *Ten More Folk-Songs and Ballads.* Boston: E. C. Schirmer Music Co., 1932.

*Tent & Trail *Tent and Trail Songs.* Delaware, Ohio: Coöperative Recreation Service, 1962.

Terry 1919 i - ii *Richard Runciman Terry. *Sailor Shanties.* 2 Vols., London: Curwen & Sons, 1919.

Terry 1921 i - ii *Richard Runciman Terry. *The Shanty Book.* 2 Vols., London: Curwen & Sons, 1921.

Terry 1931 *Richard Runciman Terry. *Salt Sea Ballads.* London: J. Curwen & Sons, 1931.

TFB Tennessee Folklore Bulletin, 1934-.

That's the Style That's the Style for Me Songster. New York: Robert M. De Witt, #74, 1869.

Thede *Marion Thede. *The Fiddle Book.* New York, 1967.

*Thirty-Three *Thirty-Three Prison and Mountain Songs.* New York: Shapiro, Bernstein, 1932.

*This & That *This and That.* Delaware, Ohio: Coöperative Recreation Service, 194-.

Thomas 1931 *Jean Thomas. *Devil's Ditties.* Chicago, 1931.

Thomas 1939 *Jean Thomas. *The Singin'*

Gatherin'. New York, 1939.

Thomas 1964 *Jean Thomas. *Ballad Makin- in the Mountains of Kentucky.* Reprint, New York: Oak Publications, 1964. (1st ed., 1939).

D. Thompson Dave Thompson; Kathleen Thompson. *Songs that Mother Used to Sing.* Chicago: A. C. McClurg & Co., 1931.

H. Thompson 1940 Harold W. Thompson. *Body, Boots and Britches.* Reprint, New York, 1962. (1st ed., 1940).

H. Thompson 1958 Harold W. Thompson. *A Pioneer Songster*: texts from the Stevens-Douglass manuscript of western New York, 1841-56. Cornell University Press, 1958.

[Harold Thompson Archives] *Harold Thompson Archives. [See: HTA].

W. Thompson i - ii *William Thompson. *Orpheus Caledonius.* 2 Vols. in 1, Reprint: Folklore Associates, 1962. (1st ed., 1725).

Thomson *John Thomson; W. S. Roddie. *Lays of the Heather*: a collection of highland and lowland songs. Inverness: Logan & Co., 19--.

Thorp i - ii *N. Howard ("Jack") Thorp. *Songs of the Cowboys* (1908) [ii], with variants, commentary, notes and lexicon by Austin E. and Alts S. Fife, and music edited by Naunie Gardner [i]. 2 Vols. in 1, separately paginated, New York: Clarkson N. Potter, 1966.

Thurman *John Thurman; Rex Hazlewood; A. Mackintosh. *The Gilwell Camp Fire Book.* London: C. Arthur Pearson, 1957. [See also: Hazlewood].

*Tip Top 1935 *Tip Top Songs of the Roaming Ranger.* New York, 1935.

*Tip Top 1936 *Tip Top Album of Carson J. Robison Songs.* New York, 1936.

TLP 1015 †*Classic Scots Ballads* (Ewan MacColl). Tradition Records TLP 1015.

TLP 1029 †*Texas Folksongs* (Alan Lomax). Jacket notes. Tradition Records TLP 1029.

TLP 1047 †*Heather and Glen.* Jacket notes (Alan Lomax). Tradition records TLP 1047.

Tobitt *Janet E. Tobitt. *The Ditty Bag.* New York: Janet E. Tobitt, 1946.

*Tocher *Tocher* [a periodical], 1971-.

Tomlins *W. L. Tomlins. *The Laurel Song Book.* Boston: C. C. Birchard, 1901.

Tomlyn *Alfred W. Tomlyn. *The Gem Selection of Scottish Songs.* Edinburgh: Anderson, 19--.

Tommy Armstrong Tommy Armstrong Sings. Newcastle Upon Tyne: Frank Graham, 1971.

Tony Oakes Tony Oakes' Songster. San Francisco: Wm. P. Harrison, 1878.

Tony Pastor i - x *Tony Pastor's Book of Six Hundred Comic Songs* [an expansion of a compilation of songsters first issued in 1864; each of the ten divisions issued and paginated separately:

    i. *Tony Pastor's Waterfall Songster* (1867).
    ii. *Tony Pastor's Opera House Songster* (1864).
    iii. *Tony Pastor's Carte de Visite Album Songster* (186-).
    iv. *Tony Pastor's 444 Combination Songster* (1864).
    v. *Tony Pastor's New Irish Comic Songster* (1864).
    vi. *Will Carleton's Dandy Pat Songster* (1866).
    vii. *Tony Pastor's Great Sensation Songster* (1864).
    viii. *Tony Pastor's Own Comic Vocalist* (1863).
    ix. *Tony Pastor's Comic Songster* (1864).
    x. *Tony Pastor's Union Songster* (1864).
New York: Dick & Fitzgerald, 1867.

Tony Pastor 1862 Tony Pastor's Comic and Eccentric Songster. New York: Dick & Fitzgerald, 1862.

Tony Pastor 1867 Tony Pastor's 201 Bowery Songster. New York: Dick & Fitzgerald, 1867.

Tony Pastor 1872 Tony Pastor's Irish American Comic Song Book. Glasgow: Cameron & Ferguson, ca. 1872.

Tony Pastor 1873 The Songs of Tony Pastor's Opera House. New York: Robert M. De Witt, 1873.

Tony Pastor 1881 Tony Pastor's The Metropolitan Favorites Songster. New York: Popular Publishing Co., #136, 1881.

Topic 12T123 †*Her Mantle So Green* (Margaret Barry). Jacket notes (A. L. Lloyd). Topic Records 12T123.

Topic 12T140 †*Canadian Garland* (LaRena Clark). Topic Records 12T140.

Topic 12T147 †*The Manchester Angel* (Ewan MacColl). Jacket notes. Topic Records 12T147.

Topic 12T157 †*Songs of Courtship* (The Folk Songs of Britain, Vol. 1). Booklet (A. L. Lloyd). Topic Records 12T157.

Topic 12T158 †*Songs of Seduction* (The Folk Songs of Britain, Vol. 2). Booklet (A. L. Lloyd). Topic Records 12T158.

Topic 12T159 †*Jack of All Trades* (The Folk Songs of Britain, Vol. 3). Booklet (A. L. Lloyd). Topic Records 12T159.

Topic 12T160 †*The Child Ballads 1* (The Folk Songs of Britain, Vol. 4). Booklet (A. L. Lloyd). Topic Records 12T160.

Topic 12T161 †*The Child Ballads 2* (The Folk Songs of Britain, Vol. 5). Booklet (A. L. Lloyd). Topic Records 12T161.

Topic 12T198 †*Songs of Animals and Other Marvels* (The Folk Songs of Britain, Vol. 10). Booklet (A. L. Lloyd). Topic Records 12T198.

Touch the Elbow Touch the Elbow Songster. New York: Dick & Fitzgerald, 1862.

*Tourjée *Eben Tourjée. *The Tribute of Praise*. Pittsburgh: Board of Publication of the Methodist Protestant Church, 1884.

*Travelin' On *Travelin' On with the Weavers*. New York: Harper & Row, 1966.

*Treasure Chest 1935 *Treasure Chest of Cowboy Songs*. New York, 1935.

*Treasure Chest 1936 *Treasure Chest of Darn Fool Ditties*. New York, 1936.

*Treasure Chest 1943 *Treasure Chest of Irish Songs, Jigs and Reels*. New York, 1943.

*Trevine *Owen Trevine. *Deep Sea Chanties*. London: J. B. Cramer & Co., 1921.

*Trident *The Trident Society. *The Book of Navy Songs*. Garden City, New York: Doubleday, Page & Co., 1926.

*Trifet 1886 *F. Trifet. *The Acme*: a collection of the best of American songs by American composers. Augusta, Maine: P. O. Vickery, 1886.

*Trifet 1890 *Trifet's Multum in Parvo Songster* [largely a re-issue of Howe 1874]. Boston: F. Trifet, 1890.

*Trifet 1892 *Trifet's Monthly Budget of Music #93*: 600 English, Irish, Scotch and American songs [also containing the *Multum in Parvo Songster* of 1890]. Boston: F. Trifet, 1892.

*True Blue *The True Blue Song Book*. Omaha School Supply Co., 1926.

*Tunes Dad Whistled *The Tunes Dad Whistled*. Cincinnati: Baldwin Piano Co., 1921.

J. W. Turner *Joseph W. Turner; E. T. Bates. *One Hundred Comic Songs*. Boston: Oliver Ditson, 1858.

M. R. Turner *Michael R. Turner; Anthony Miall. *The Parlour Song Book*. New York: Viking Press, 1973.

[Twain] Mark Twain. [See: Clemens].

*24 Mountain Songs *Twenty-Four Mountain Songs*. Chicago: Belmont Music Co., 1937.

UFL   *Ulster Folk Life*, 1955-.

Uncle True   *Uncle True Songster*. Philadelphia: Fisher & Bro., 1850.

United States   *The United States Songster*. Cincinnati: U. P. James, 1836.

Universal Book   *Universal Book of Songs and Singer's Companion* [a compilation of five songsters, also issued and paginated separately:
  i. *Moore's Irish Melodies* [texts] (1864).
  ii. *Frank Brower's Black Diamond Songster* (1863).
  iii. *Camp Fire Songster* (1863?).
  iv. *The Shamrock, or Songs of Ireland* (1862).
  v. *The Convivial Songster* (1864?)].
New York: Dick & Fitzgerald, 1864.

Universal Irish   *The Universal Irish Song Book*. New York: P. J. Kenedy, 1898.

Universal Songster i - iii   *The Universal Songster or Museum of Mirth*. 3 Vols., London: 1825, 1826, 1827. (Also re-issued, 1832, 1834, 1837).

Universal Songster 1832   *The Universal Songster*. New York: J. H. Turney, 1832.

University Songbook   *The University Songbook*. London: Grant Richards, 1901.

University of Toronto   *The University of Toronto Song Book*. Toronto: I. Suckling & Sons, 1887.

Unsworth 1859   *[James] Unsworth's Burnt Cork Lyrics*. New York: Robert M. De Witt, #44, 1859.

Unsworth 1861   *[James] Unsworth's Comic Songs: The Charcoal Man* and *Comic Banjo Song* [word sheets only]. London, 1861 [copies at British Museum Library, 11621.h.1 (161) and (164)].

Urbani i - ii   *Pietro Urbani. A Select Collection of Original Scocttish Airs*. 2 vols., Edinburgh: Urbani & Liston, 1804, 1816.

Varian   Ralph Varian. *The Harp of Erin*. Dublin: M'Glashan & Gill, 1869.

Vauxhall i - ii   *Vauxhall Comic Song Books*, series 1 and 2. London: T. Allman, 1847.

Veal   *Arthur Veal. *The Singing Cowboy*. London: Boosey & Hawkes, 1964.

Veitch i - ii   John Veitch. *The History and Poetry of the Scottish Border*. 2 Vols., Edinburgh and London: Blackwood & Sons, 1893. (1st ed., 1890).

Vernon   *Grenville Vernon. *Yankee Doodle-Doo:* a collection of songs of the early American stage. New York: Payson & Clarke, 1927.

Victor 20502   †*Casey Jones* (Vernon Dalhart). Victor 20502.

Victorian Tear Jerkers   *Victorian Tear Jerkers*. English Folk Dance & Song Society, 1974.

Vinson   *Lee Vinson. *The Early American Songster*. Englewood Cliffs, New Jersey: Prentice-Hall, 1974.

Violin Complete   *The Violin Complete*. Boston: Oliver Ditson, 1850.

Violin Made Easy   *The Violin Made Easy*. Boston: Oliver Ditson, 1851.

Virginia Writers Project   *Virginia Writers Project. *Folk Songs to Sing*. Virginia State Board of Education, 1942.

Vocal Companion   *The Vocal Companion; or The Singer's Own Book*. London: Thomas Tegg & Son, 1838.

Vocal Library   *The Vocal Library*. London: Richard Phillips & Co., 1822.

Vocal Lyre   *The Vocal Lyre:* a collection of popular songs. New-York: W. Borredaile, 1825.

Vocal Magazine   *The Vocal Magazine; or, Compleat British Songster*. London: Harrison & Co., 1781.

Vocal Medley   *The Vocal Medley*. Alexandria, Virginia: Cotton & Stewart, 1801.

Vocal Miscellany i - ii   *The Vocal Miscellany*. 2 Vols., London: Joseph Hazard, 1734. [Copies at Music Division, New York Public Library, Drexel 2589, 2590].

Vornholt   *Dan C. Vornholt. *The Folk Singer*. Madison: University of Wisconsin College of Agriculture, 1943.

Vox 632   †*Minstrel Songs of the U. S. A.* (Richard Dyer-Bennet). Vox Album 632.

VRS 479   †*The Three Ravens* (Alfred Deller). Jacket notes. Vanguard VRS 479.

VRS 1001   †*The Wraggle-Taggle Gipsies* (Alfred Deller). Jacket notes. Vanguard VRS 1001.

VRS 1031   †*Western Wind* (Alfred Deller). Jacket notes. Vanguard VRS 1031.

VRS 9010   †*The Weavers at Carnegie Hall*. Vanguard VRS 9010.

VRS 9013   †*The Weavers on Tour*. Vanguard VRS 9013.

VRS 9078   †*Joan Baez*. Vanguard VRS 9078.

VRS 9094   †*Joan Baez, Vol. 2*. Vanguard VRS 9094.

VRS 9107   †*I Ain't Got No Home* (Cisco Houston). Vanguard VRS 9107.

VSD 57, 58   †*The Essential Paul Robeson*. 2 Discs, Vanguard VSD 57, 58.

Wade *J[oseph] A[ugustus] Wade. *Christy's Minstrels' One Hundred and Forty-Five New Songs and Choruses.* 3 Vols. in 1, London: C. Sheard, 18--.

Waite 1868 *Henry R. Waite. *Camina Collegensia.* Boston: Oliver Ditson, 1868.

Waite i - ii *Henry R. Waite. *University Songs* [2 Parts, separately paginated, in 1 volume; contents are the same as in the 1876 edition of *Carmina Collegensia*]. Boston: Oliver Ditson, 1877.

Waite 1890 *Henry R. Waite. *College Songs.* Boston: Oliver Ditson, 1890.

[Waiting for a Broadway Stage] Waiting for a Broadway Stage Songster. [See: *Broadway Stage*].

Wakefield *LeRoy James Wakefield. *Ballads and Songs from Ohio* [collected by Mary O. Eddy]. 3 Vols., Cleveland: Works Projects Administration District 4, 1939.

Wales *Tony Wales. *The Yetties Song Book.* London: English Folk Dance & Song Society, 1971.

Walker *William Walker. *Southern Harmony.* Facsimile reprint, New York, 1939. (1st ed., New Haven, 1835.).

[Walker 1866] *William Walker. *The Christian Harmony* (1866). [See: *Deason*].

Walking Down Broadway The Walking Down Broadway Songster. New York: Robert M. De Witt, 1869.

[Walsh] *Patrick A. Walsh. [See: Padraig Breathnach].

Walton 132 [Martin A.] Walton's 132 Best Irish Songs and Ballads. Dublin: Walton's Musical Instrument Galleries, n. d.

Walton Treasury [Martin A.] Walton's Treasury of Irish Songs and Ballads. Dublin: Walton's Musical Instrument Galleries, n. d.

Walton i - ii [Martin A.] Walton's New Treasury of Irish Songs and Ballads. 2 Vols., Dublin: Walton's Musical Instrument Galleries, 1966, 1968.

J. J. Ward *John J. Ward. *John Ward's Collection of Irish Comic Songs.* Oak Park, Illinois: Ward Music Publishing Co., 1947.

R. Ward *Russell Ward. *Three Street Ballads* (The Black Bull Chapbooks, #5). Ferntree Gully: The Rams Skull Press, 1959.

Ward & Lynch Ward & Lynch's Invitation Songster. New York: Popular Publishing Co., 188-.

D. Warner *Dorothy Warner; Theodor Warner. *Englische Volkslieder und Kanons.* Frankfurt a. M.: Verlag Moritz Diesterweg, 1937.

F. M. Warner Frank M. Warner. *Folk Songs and Ballads of the Eastern Seabord.* Macon, Georgia: Southern Press, 1963.

J. Warner *James Warner. *Songs That Made America.* New York: Grossman Publishers, 1972.

L. Warner *Lorraine d'Oremieulx Warner. *A Kindergarten Book of Folk-Song* (Concord Series No. 9). Boston: E. C. Schirmer, 1923.

W. C. Coup W. C. Coup's Monster Clown Songster. New York: Popular Publishing Co., 1882.

Wearing of the Green The Wearing of the Green Songster. New York: Robert M. De Witt, #4, 1866.

Weatherly *Denis Weatherly. *Songs of Northumbria.* Newcastle Upon Tyne: Frank Graham, 1972.

*[Weavers] *The Weavers. [See: *Travelin' on*].

*Weavers Song Book *The Weavers Song Book.* New York: Harper & Row, 1960.

Weckerlin *Jean-Baptiste Weckerlin. *Échos d'Angleterre.* Paris: Durand et Schoenwerke, 1929.

Wehman # Henry J. Wehman. *Broadside Sheets* [individual issues]. New York, 1886-.

Wehman i - iv Wehman Brothers [publishers]. *Good Old-Time Songs.* 4 Vols., New York: Wehman Brothers, 1910-16.

*Wehman's Collection # Henry J. Wehman [publisher]. *Wehman's Collection of Songs,* #1 (1886)-.

*Wehman's Irish i - iv Henry J. Wehman [publisher]. *Wehman's Irish Song Books.* 4 Vols., New York, 1887-93.

Wehman 617 Wehman Brothers [publishers]. *Six Hundred and Seventeen Irish Songs and Ballads.* New York, 190-.

Wehman's Universal # Wehman's Universal Songster, #1 - #21. New York: Henry J. Wehman 1881-83.

Wehman 1916 *Henry J. Wehman [publisher]. *The New York Musical Album* [not paginated]. New York, 1916.

Well Known Songs Well Known Songs of Ireland. New York: Irish Industries Depot, 1924.

Wellman *Manly Wade Wellman; Frances Wellman. *The Rebel Songster.* Charlotte, North Carolina: Heritage House, 1959.

C. Wells 1902 Carolyn Wells. *A Nonsense Anthology.* New York, 1902.

C. Wells 1936 Carolyn Wells. *The Book of Humorous Verse.* 2nd ed., Garden City, New York: Garden City Publishing Co., 1936. (1st ed., 1920).

E. K. Wells *Evelyn Kendrick Wells. *The Ballad Tree.* New York, 1950.

Welsch *Roger L. Welsch. *A Treasury of Nebraska Pioneer Folklore*. University of Nebraska Press, 1966.

[*Wesleyan Psalmist*] *The Wesleyan Psalmist, or Songs of Canaan*. [See: Scudder].

[*Wesleyan Sacred Harp*] *The Wesleyan Sacred Harp*. [See: W. McDonald].

Wessels *Katharine Tyler Wessels. *The Golden Song Book*. New York: Simon & Schuster, 1945.

WF *Western Folklore*, 1947-.

Whall *W. B. Whall. *Sea Songs and Shanties*. 6th ed., Glasgow, 1927. (Reprint, 1963; 1st ed., 1910).

W. H. Arnold W. H. Arnold's Billy's Request Songster. New York: Popular Publishing Co., 1880.

Wheatley i - iii Henry B. Wheatley. [*Thomas Percy's*] *Reliques of Ancient English Poetry*. New ed., 3 Vols., London: Frederick Warne, 1876-77. (Reprint, New York, 1955; 1st ed., London, 1765).

Wheatley & Traynor Wheatley and Traynor's Dublin Boys Songster. New York: Popular Publishing Co., #263, 1883.

Wheeler *Mary Wheeler; Clara Gregory Bridge. *Kentucky Mountain Folk-Songs*. Boston: Boston Music Co., 1937.

B. F. White *B. F. White; E. J. King. *The Sacred Harp* [facsimile of the 3rd ed. of 1859]. Nashville, Tennessee: The Broadman Press, 1968. (1st ed., 1844).

E. L. White *E. L. White. *The Boston Melodeon, Vol. 1*. Boston: Oliver Ditson, 1852. (5th ed., 1846).

J. White 1929 *John White. *Lonesome Cowboy Songs*. New York: George T. Worth, 1929.

J. White 1934 *John White. *Cowboy Songs of Death Valley Days*. New York: Pacific Coast Borax Co., 1934.

J. I. White *John I. White. *Git along, Little Dogies*. University of Illinois Press, 1975.

[*Josh White*] *The Josh White Song Book*. [See: Shelton].

N. I. White Newman I. White. *American Negro Folk-Songs*. Harvard University Press, 1928. (Reprint, Folklore Associates, 1965).

White's Serenaders *White's Serenader's Song Book* [of which a re-issue was announced for inclusion also in the compilation *Christy and White's Ethiopian Melodies*, 1854]. Philadelphia: T. B. Peterson & Brothers, 1851.

Whitehead *Jane Byrd Radcliffe Whitehead. *Folk-Songs and Other Songs for Children*. Boston: Oliver Ditson, 1903.

W. G. Whittaker i - vi *W. G. Whittaker; Herbert Wiseman; John Wishart. *The Clarendon Song Book*. 6 Vols., Oxford University Press, 1929-30.

W. J. Whittaker *William J. Whittaker. *North Countrie Ballads, Songs & Pipe Tunes*. London: J. Curwen & Sons, 1921.

Whittier Perkins *Whittier Perkins Book* (1790) [a manuscript collection of dancing tunes, marches and song tunes, at Columbia University Library, Special Collections X780.973.C68].

Wier 1915 *Albert E. Wier. *Songs the Whole World Sings*. New York: D. Appleton & Co., 1915.

Wier 1918a *Albert E. Wier. *The Book of a Thousand Songs*. New York: World Syndicate Co., 1918.

Wier 1918b *Albert E. Wier. *The Child's Own Music Book*. New York: World Syndicate Co., 1918.

Wier 1924 *Albert E. Wier. *Sentimental Songs* (The Ideal Home Music Library, Vol. 9). New York: Charles Scribner's Sons, 1924. (1st ed., 1913).

Wier 1929 *Albert E. Wier. *Songs of the Sunny South*. New York: D. Appleton & Co., 1929.

Wier 1931 *Albert E. Wier. *Favorite Songs of Every Character* (Scribner's Radio Music Library, Vol. 8). New York: Charles Scribner's Sons, 1931.

Wilk *Max Wilk. *Memory Lane:* the golden age of American popular music. New York: Ballantine Books, 1973.

Wilkinson i - ii *Winston Wilkinson. *Collection of Traditional Music of Virginia, 1932-41*, chiefly from Albemarle County. [Numbered separately are: i., *Songs;* ii., *Dance Tunes*]. Ms. 4824 at Alderman Library, University of Virginia, Microfilms M 666, 667.

Wilkinson 128 *Wilton Wilkinson. *Notated Songs and Dance Tunes* from the W. P. A. Federal Music Project, Virginia [partially paginated]. Ms. 128 at Alderman Library, University of Virginia.

Wilkinson 510 *Wilton Wilkinson. *Traditional Songs of Virginia Gentlefolk: The Purcel Book*. Mx. 510 at Alderman Library, University of Virginia, Microfilm M 1507.

[*Will Carleton*] *Will Carleton's Dandy Pat Songster* (1866). [See: *Tony Pastor* vi].

Willan i - ii *Healey Willan. *Songs of the British Isles*. 2 Vols., London: Frederick Harris Co., 1928.

William Litten *William Litten's Fiddle Tunes, 1800-1802* [edited by Gale Huntington]. Vineyard Haven, Massachusetts: Hines Point Publishers, 1977.

A. Williams Alfred Williams. *Folk Songs of the Upper Thames*. London: Novello & Co., 1923.

A. M. Williams Alfred M. Williams. *Studies in Folk-Songs and Popular Poetry*. London: Elliot Stock, 1895.

H. Williams *Harry Williams; Aaron Hoffman; Egbert Van Alstyne. *Fol de Rol Dol*, from the musical *Tom, Dick and Harry*. New York: Jerome H. Remick & Co., 1905.

I. Williams *Iola A. Williams. *English Folk-Songs and Dance*. London: Longmans, Green & Co., 1935.

J. Ll. Williams *J. Lloyd Williams; Arthur Somervell. *Welsh Melodies*. London: Boosey & Co., 1907.

[R. V. Williams 1908] *Ralph Vaughan Williams; Cecil J. Sharp. *Folk Songs from the Eastern Counties*. [See: C. J. Sharp 1961 iii]. London: Novello & Co., 1908.

[R. V. Williams 1912] *Ralph Vaughan Williams. *Folk Songs for Schools*. [See: *Novello* vi #232].

R. V. Williams 1959 *Ralph Vaughan Wiliams; A[lbert] L. Lloyd. *The Penguin Book of English Folk Songs*. Harmondsworth: Penguin Books, 1959.

W. S. G. Williams *W. S. Gwynn Williams. *Welsh National Music and Dance*. London: J. Curwen & Sons, n. d.

H. R. Wilson *Harry Robert Wilson. *Songs of the Hills and Plains*. Chicago: Hall & McCreary Co., 1943.

J. R. Wilson *James Reginald Wilson. "Ballad tunes of the Miramichi." Master's Thesis, New York University, 1961.

Joe Wilson Joe Wilson. *Tyneside Songs & Drolleries*. Reprint, London, 1970. (1st ed., 186-).

Winn 1974 *Marie Winn; Allan Miller. *The Fireside Book of Fun And Games Songs*. New York: Simon & Schuster, 1974.

J. E. Winner 189- *Joseph E. Winner. *The Song Folio*. San Francisco: John J. Newbegin, 189-.

J. E. Winner 1894 *Joseph E. Winner. *Winner's Gems of Music*. San Francisco: John J. Newbegin, 1894.

S. Winner 1866 *Septimus Winner. *Winner's Music of the Dance*. Boston: Oliver Ditson, 1866.

S. Winner 1885 *Septimus Winner. *Winner's World of Song*. New York and St. Louis:

N. D. Thompson Publishing Co., 1885.

Winsett 1908 *R. E. Winsett. *Songs of Pentecostal Power Complete*. Dayton, Tennessee: R. E. Winsett Music Co., 1908.

Winsett 1920 *R. E. Winsett. *Songs of Revival Power and Glory*. East Chattanogga, Tennessee, 1920.

Winsett 1942 *R. E. Winsett. *Joys Supernal*. Dayton, Tennessee: R. E. Winsett Music Co., 1942.

Winsett 1948 *R. E. Winsett. *Red Foley's Sacred Album Number 1*. Nashville, Tennessee: Home Folks Music Shop, 1948.

Winslow Ola Elizzbeth Winslow. *American Broadside Verse*. Yale University Press, 1930. (Reprint, New York, 1974).

Wise *Herbert Wise. *Folk Song Sing Along*. New York: Amsco Music Publishing Co., 1962.

[Wit & Mirth] *Wit and Mirth, or Pills to Purge Melancholy*. [See: D'Urfey].

Wittke Carl Wittke. *Tambo and Bones:* a history of the American minstrel stage. Duke University Press, 1930.

WLP 724 †*Whaling Ballads* (Ewan MacColl, A. L. Lloyd). Washington WLP 724.

WLP 731 †*Songs from the Hills of Donegal* (Margaret Barry). Jacket notes (Goldstein). Washington WLP 731.

Wm. J. Scanlan Wm. J. Scanlan's Peggy O'Moore Songster. New York: J. A. Leider, 1885?

Wolf Index Edwin Wolf 2nd. *American Song Sheets, Slip Ballads and Poetical Broadsides, 1850-1870*. Philadelphia: The Library Company, 1963.

Wolford *Leah Jackson Wolford. *The Play Party in Indiana*. Indiana Historical Commission, 1916.

L. C. Wood 1934 Leslie C. Wood. *Rafting on the Delaware River*. Livingston Manor, New York: Livingston Manor Times, 1934. [Copy at New York Public Library Annex, VQY].

L. C. Wood 1950 Leslie C. Wood. *Holt! t'Other Way!* Middletown, New York: Leslie C. Wood, 1950.

T. Wood *Thomas Wood. *The Oxford Song Book, Vol. 2*. London, 1928.

Woodbury 1853a *I[saac] B[aker] Woodbury; H. Mattison. *The Lute of Zion*. New York: Carlton & Phillips, 1853.

Woodbury 1853b *I[saac] B[aker] Woodbury. *The Violin*. Boston: Oliver Ditson, 1853.

Woodbury 1856 *I[saac] B[aker] Woodbury. *The New Lute of Zion*. New York: Carlton & Porter. 1856.

Woodgate 1951 *Leslie Woodgate. *The Pen-

guin Song Book. Harmondsworth: Penguin
Books, 1951.

Woodgate 1956 *Leslie Woodgate. *The Puffin
Song Book*. Harmondsworth: Penguin
Books, 1956.

Work *John W. Work. *American Negro
Songs*. Philadelphia: Theodore Presser Co.,
1948.

World's Best *The World's Best Home Songs*.
New York: University Society, 1966.

Woychuk *N. A. Woychuk. *Making Melody*.
St. Louis, Missouri: Bible Memory Association, 1969. (1st ed., 1949).

Wright *Robert L. Wright. *Irish Emigrant
Ballads and Songs* [containing texts and
tunes in facsimile]. Bowling Green University Popular Press, 1975.

Wrubel *Elias Paul Wrubel. *Salty Tunes*.
New York: Crawford Music Co., 1932.

Wyeth *Wyeth's Repository of Sacred Music*.
Facsimile reprint, New York, 1974, from 5th
ed. of 1824. (1st ed., 1813).

Wyld *Lionel D. Wyld. *Low Bridge!* Folklore
of the Erie Canal. Syracuse University
Press, 1962.

Wyman 1916 *Loraine Wyman: Howard
Brockway. *Lonesome Tunes*. New York,
1916.

Wyman 1920 *Loraine Wyman: Howard
Brockway. *Twenty Kentucky Mountain
Songs*. Boston, 1920.

XTV 62202/3 †*Folksingers 'Round Harvard
Square*. Veritas Records XTV 62202/3.

Yankee Robinson *Yankee [Fayette
Lodawick] Robinson's Beautiful Amazon
Songster*. New York: Robert M. De Witt,
#89, 1870.

Yetties *The Yetties. *Out in the Green Fields*.
London: Wise Publications, 1974.

YIFMC *Yearbook of the International Folk
Music Council*, 1969-.

Yolen *Jane Yolen; Barbara Green. *The
Fireside Book of Birds and Beasts*. New
York: Simon & Schuster, 1972.

Yorkshire Musical Miscellany *The Yorkshire
Musical Miscellany*. Halifax, England: C.
Jacobs, 1800.

Young Canada *Young Canada Sings*. Ottawa: Department of the Secretary of State,
1968.

Young Lady The Young Lady's Songster.
Philadelphia: Fisher & Bro., 183-.

Zanzig 1940 *Augustus D. Zanzig. *Singing
America*. Boston: C. C. Birchard & Co.,
1940.

Zanzig 1962 *Augustus D. Zanzig. *Songs to
Keep*. Delaware, Ohio: Coöperative Recreation Service, 1962.

ZDA 66 - 75 †*The Long Harvest:* some tradi-
tional ballads in their English, Scots and
North American variants (Ewan MacColl,
Peggy Seeger). Booklets. 10 Discs, Argo
Records ZDA 66 - 75.

Zielonko June Zielonko. "Some American
variants of Child Ballads." Master's Thesis,
Columbia University, 1945.

Zimmerman *Georges-Denis Zimmerman.
"Irish political street ballads and rebel
songs, 1780-1900." Thesis, Université de
Génève, 1966.